WHAT RESEARCH HAS TO SAY ABOUT

EDITORS **S. JAY SAMUELS** AND
ALAN E. FARSTRUP

READING

INSTRUCTION

FOURTH EDITION

INTERNATIONAL
Reading Association
800 BARKSDALE ROAD, PO BOX 8139
NEWARK, DE 19714-8139, USA
www.reading.org

The International Reading Association attempts, through its publications, to provide a
forum for a wide spectrum of opinions on reading. This policy permits divergent
viewpoints without implying the endorsement of the Association.

Executive Editor, Publications   Shannon Fortner
Managing Editor   Christina M. Terranova
Editorial Associate   Wendy Logan
Design and Composition Manager   Anette Schuetz
Design and Composition Associate   Lisa Kochel

Cover Design   Adam Bohannon

The publisher would appreciate notification where errors occur so that they may be
corrected in subsequent printings and/or editions.

Library of Congress Cataloging-in-Publication Data
What research has to say about reading instruction / S. Jay Samuels & Alan E.
Farstrup, editors. -- 4th ed.
      p. cm.
  Includes bibliographical references and index.
  ISBN 978-0-87207-829-1
  1. English language--Grammar--Study and teaching (Elementary) 2. English
language--Grammar--Study and teaching (Secondary) I. Samuels, S. Jay. II. Farstrup,
Alan E.
  LB1631.W376 2011
  428.4--dc22

                                    2011003662

Suggested APA Reference
Samuels, S.J., & Farstrup, A.E. (2011). *What research has to say about reading
instruction* (4th ed.). Newark, DE: International Reading Association.

This book is dedicated to teachers and teacher educators,
wherever they may be, who work so hard to develop the abilities
necessary for students to love reading and to excel in life.

Contents

About the Editors vii

Contributors ix

Acknowledgments xi

Introduction
The Critical Importance of Teacher Quality 1
Alan E. Farstrup and S. Jay Samuels

Chapter 1
The Relation Between Alphabetic Basics, Word Recognition, and Reading 4
Marilyn Jager Adams

Chapter 2
Eye Movements and Reading: What Teachers Need to Know 25
S. Jay Samuels, Timothy V. Rasinski, and Elfrieda H. Hiebert

Chapter 3
Essential Elements of Fostering and Teaching Reading Comprehension 51
Nell K. Duke, P. David Pearson, Stephanie L. Strachan, and Alison K. Billman

Chapter 4
Reading Fluency: What It Is and What It Is Not 94
Timothy V. Rasinski and S. Jay Samuels

Chapter 5
Reading Engagement Among African American and European American Students 115
John T. Guthrie and Angela McRae

Chapter 6
The Importance of Independent Reading 143
Linda B. Gambrell, Barbara A. Marinak, Heather R. Brooker, and Heather J. McCrea-Andrews

Chapter 7
Integrating Reading Strategies and Knowledge Building in Adolescent Literacy Instruction 159
Julie E. Learned, Darin Stockdill, and Elizabeth Birr Moje

Chapter 8
Developmental Changes in Reading Comprehension: Implications for Assessment and Instruction 186
Suzanne M. Adlof, Charles A. Perfetti, and Hugh W. Catts

Chapter 9
Are Current Reading Research Findings Applicable to Students With Intellectual Disabilities? 215
Terri Fautsch-Patridge, Kristen L. McMaster, and Susan C. Hupp

Chapter 10
Research on Reading/Learning Disability Interventions 236
Richard L. Allington

Chapter 11
Implementing a Response to Intervention Model to Improve Reading Outcomes for All Students 266
Elizabeth Swanson and Sharon Vaughn

Chapter 12
Technologies, Digital Media, and Reading Instruction 286
Jay S. Blanchard and Alan E. Farstrup

Chapter 13
Teaching Reading in English as a Foreign Language to Young Learners: A Global Reflection 315
Annie Hughes

Chapter 14
What the Research Says About Intentional Instruction 359
Douglas Fisher, Nancy Frey, and Diane Lapp

Chapter 15
Using Assessment to Improve Teaching and Learning 379
Sheila W. Valencia

Chapter 16
Parents and Reading: What Teachers Should Know About Ways to Support Productive Home–School Environments 406
Jeanne R. Paratore

Chapter 17
Diversity and Literacy 425
Alfred W. Tatum

Chapter 18
How Reading Research and Federal Policy on Reading Instruction Have Interrelated Over the Past 35 Years 448
Richard M. Long and Ramsay Selden

Author Index 463

Subject Index 479

About the Editors

S. Jay Samuels

S. Jay Samuels started teaching elementary school shortly after the end of World War II. At that time, the schools were crowded and teachers were in short supply. Los Angeles needed teachers, so recruiters came to the New York area. Jay took a job offered by a recruiter because he knew that Muscle Beach, the Mecca for bodybuilding, would be conveniently located to where he would be teaching. He entered the University of California, Los Angeles, doctoral program, where he received a doctorate in educational psychology.

Jay later joined the Educational Psychology Department at the University of Minnesota and has been there for over 40 years. Through Psychology Professor David LaBerge, Jay developed an interest in reading fluency. At the university, Jay received a Distinguished Teaching Award for his large teacher training lecture class on learning, cognition, and assessment. The National Reading Conference and the International Reading Association also have recognized Jay with research awards for reading. Jay was inducted into the Reading Hall of Fame in 1990. Jay is also a member of the National Reading Panel.

Jay met Alan Farstrup when Alan was a doctoral student at the University of Minnesota. Over the years Alan and Jay have worked together to produce books that they trust will provide teachers with the latest in research and pedagogy from the leaders in the reading field.

Alan E. Farstrup

Alan E. Farstrup is former Executive Director of the International Reading Association (IRA), having retired in 2009. He remains active in the reading research and instruction profession. He attended Grand View College in Des Moines, Iowa, then completed his Bachelor of Arts degree at the University of Iowa, earned his teaching credential at the University of California at Berkeley, and received his PhD in Reading Curriculum and Instruction from the University of Minnesota in 1977.

Alan has been a middle school reading and English teacher and a member of reading education faculties of the University of Texas at San Antonio and the University of Rhode Island. He has served as a reading curriculum specialist and consultant on literacy and technology applications in schools and continues to provide expert advice in these areas. He directed the Institute of Human Science and Services at the University of Rhode Island. He also served as a U.S. Peace Corps rural development volunteer in Afghanistan in 1965 and 1966.

Alan was IRA's director of research before assuming the post of Executive Director in 1992. Throughout his career, he has provided administrative leadership, insight on evidence-based literacy instruction, expert testimony to governmental and international agencies and organizations, and has worked with a wide range of nongovernmental and nonprofit professional organizations worldwide. He has been a member of the United Nations Educational, Scientific, and Cultural Organization's International Literacy Prize Jury. Alan has extensive experience in the development of educational policy, standards, and assessments.

Alan is coeditor with S. Jay Samuels of *What Research Has to Say About Reading Instruction* (Second and Third Editions), *What Research Has to Say About Fluency Instruction*, and *What Research Has to Say About Vocabulary Instruction*.

Contributors

Marilyn Jager Adams
Visiting Professor
Department of Cognitive, Linguistic,
    and Psychological Sciences
Brown University
Providence, Rhode Island, USA

Suzanne M. Adlof
Postdoctoral Research Fellow
Learning Research and Development Center
University of Pittsburgh
Pittsburgh, Pennsylvania, USA

Richard L. Allington
Professor of Literacy Studies
University of Tennessee
Knoxville, Tennessee, USA

Alison K. Billman
Literacy Research Specialist
University of California, Berkeley
Berkeley, California, USA

Jay S. Blanchard
Professor
Teachers College
Arizona State University
Tempe, Arizona, USA

Heather R. Brooker
Doctoral Student
Clemson University
Clemson, South Carolina, USA

Hugh W. Catts
Professor and Chair
Speech-Language-Hearing: Sciences
    & Disorders
University of Kansas
Lawrence, Kansas, USA

Nell K. Duke
Professor
Michigan State University
East Lansing, Michigan, USA

Alan E. Farstrup
Former Executive Director
International Reading Association
Former Associate Professor of Education
University of Rhode Island
Kingston, Rhode Island, USA

Terri Fautsch-Patridge
Teaching Specialist
University of Minnesota
Minneapolis, Minnesota, USA

Douglas Fisher
Professor of Language
    & Literacy Education
San Diego State University
San Diego, California, USA

Nancy Frey
Professor of Literacy
San Diego State University
San Diego, California, USA

Linda B. Gambrell
Distinguished Professor of Education
Eugene T. Moore School of Education
Clemson University
Clemson, South Carolina, USA

John T. Guthrie
Professor Emeritus
University of Maryland, College Park
College Park, Maryland, USA

Elfrieda H. Hiebert
Researcher
TextProject
Santa Cruz, California, USA

Annie Hughes
Senior Teaching Fellow
Department of Education
University of York
York, UK

Susan C. Hupp
Professor
Department of Educational Psychology
University of Minnesota
Minneapolis, Minnesota, USA

Diane Lapp
Distinguished Professor of Education
San Diego State University
San Diego, California, USA

Julie E. Learned
Doctoral Student
School of Education
University of Michigan
Ann Arbor, Michigan, USA

Richard M. Long
Director, Government Relations
International Reading Association
Washington, DC, USA

Barbara A. Marinak
Assistant Professor and Graduate Program
    Coordinator for Literacy Education
Penn State University at Harrisburg
Middletown, Pennsylvania, USA

Heather J. McCrea-Andrews
High School English Teacher
West Oak High School
Doctoral Student
Clemson University
Clemson, South Carolina, USA

Kristen L. McMaster
Associate Professor of Special Education
University of Minnesota
Minneapolis, Minnesota, USA

Angela McRae
Doctoral Student
College of Education, Department of Human
    Development
University of Maryland, College Park
College Park, Maryland, USA

Elizabeth Birr Moje
Associate Dean for Research and Arthur F.
    Thurnau Professor of Literacy, Language,
    and Culture
School of Education
University of Michigan
Ann Arbor, Michigan, USA

Jeanne R. Paratore
Professor
Boston University
Boston, Massachusetts, USA

P. David Pearson
Professor, Language, Literacy & Culture
University of California, Berkeley
Berkeley, California, USA

Charles A. Perfetti
Distinguished University Professor
    of Psychology
Director, Learning Research
    and Development Center
University of Pittsburgh
Pittsburgh, Pennsylvania, USA

Timothy V. Rasinski
Professor of Literacy Education
Kent State University
Kent, Ohio, USA

S. Jay Samuels
Professor of Educational Psychology
    and Curriculum Instruction
University of Minnesota
Minneapolis, Minnesota, USA

Ramsay Selden
Project Director (Retired)
Council of Chief State School Officers
Washington, DC, USA

Darin Stockdill
Doctoral Student
School of Education
University of Michigan
Ann Arbor, Michigan, USA

Stephanie L. Strachan
Doctoral Student
Teacher Education Department
Michigan State University
East Lansing, Michigan, USA

Elizabeth Swanson
Research Assistant Professor
The Meadows Center for Preventing
    Educational Risk
The University of Texas at Austin
Austin, Texas, USA

Alfred W. Tatum
Associate Professor and Director,
    UIC Reading Clinic
University of Illinois at Chicago
Chicago, Illinois, USA

Sheila W. Valencia
Professor, Language, Literacy, and Culture
University of Washington
Seattle, Washington, USA

Sharon Vaughn
Executive Director
The Meadows Center for Preventing
    Educational Risk
The University of Texas at Austin
Austin, Texas, USA

Acknowledgments

We want to acknowledge and thank the outstanding, hard-working publications staff at the International Reading Association for their efforts and advice in preparing this book for publication. We want to especially thank Corinne Mooney for her guidance of the editorial and production processes. In addition, this book would not have been possible without the editorial skills and hard work of Erin Cushing, Shannon Fortner, Anne Fullerton, and Anette Schuetz.

—AEF, SJS

Introduction

The Critical Importance of Teacher Quality

Alan E. Farstrup and S. Jay Samuels

Welcome to the fourth edition of *What Research Has to Say About Reading Instruction*. Even a relaxed journey through the table of contents of all four editions of these edited books on reading instruction reveals some interesting information about our profession. We may note that as teachers strive to achieve their goal of success for all students, there is a constant influx of new understandings, ideas, and methods. These changes are reflected as new topics are addressed across all four editions. For example, a partial list of new topics encountered includes fluency, vocabulary, whole language, eye movements, text structure, home influences, technology and electronic media, Response to Intervention, and phonemic awareness. Of course, there are also the core, stable elements of reading instruction, such as skill development in word recognition and comprehension, and these stable, nonchanging elements are found and updated in each of our volumes.

There is yet another stable, unchanging characteristic that one may find in all four editions, which relates to the philosophy that underlies these books. We firmly believe that teachers appreciate knowing the scientific theories and research that support the instructional recommendations found between the covers of these four editions. Thus, as in previous editions, this new volume strives to maintain a balance between theories, supporting research, and instruction. In pursuit of these goals, some of the leading researchers and practitioners in the field of reading have shared their work in these pages.

The original idea that theory, research, and application should be melded was an outgrowth of an idea strongly expressed by former International Reading Association President Constance McCullough. Prior to her term as president, she noted that many of the papers given at the Association's Annual Convention were either overly prescriptive or overly theoretical and that a balance was needed. Consequently, while organizing the 1975 convention, she focused on papers that brought together theory and applications. These papers, along with several others, became the basis of the first edition. The same philosophy has guided us in all later editions.

In our current edition, we would like to emphasize an important fact that emerged from the massive first-grade studies that were done nearly a half-century ago (Bond & Dykstra, 1967). The purpose of the first-grade investigation was to find out if any particular method of teaching beginning reading was more effective than the others. One of the important understandings to emerge from these studies was that good teachers who provided quality instruction could be successful with almost any approach. It is not our intent to argue here that all reading methods are equally effective, but rather the contrary. The final report of the National Reading Panel (2000) emphasized that some instructional reading practices appear to be more effective in helping students learn to read.

We argue here that if the goal of education is to give all of our children an equal opportunity to have happy, successful lives, then quality of instruction is of the utmost importance. Specifically, one of the goals of the 2001 No Child Left Behind legislation is "to ensure that all children have a fair, equal, and significant opportunity to obtain a high-quality education and reach, at a minimum, proficiency on challenging State academic achievement standards and state academic assessments" (Elementary and Secondary Education Act, sec. 1001). The emphasis on excellence and effective instruction is seen in education policy and related reform and improvement efforts worldwide. Unfortunately, not all of our children are receiving uniformly good instruction, because in some situations, family income can be an indicator of the quality of instruction students receive. The federal lawmakers in the United States who wrote the No Child Left Behind Act were aware of the importance of teacher quality and required states to ensure the presence of high-quality teachers for all students by the year 2006. Two prerequisites of quality instruction are to guarantee that all teachers hold at least a bachelor's degree from an accredited institution and that they be trained in the area in which they are assigned to teach. Whereas state data forwarded to the U.S. Department of Education suggested that the states are making good progress in this direction

> for 2007–2008, with 95 percent of secondary-level core academic classes having good teachers. But the staffing data that teachers themselves reported during [the] same period told a different story.

The survey reported an actual out-of-field rate three times as high as the state-reported rates. According to those actually doing the teaching, about 15 percent of secondary core academic classes are taught by educators with neither certification nor an academic major in that subject area. In high-poverty secondary schools, students were still almost twice as likely to be taught by a first-year or out-of-field teacher as were their more-affluent peers. ("Editorial," 2010, paras. 5–6)

It is our position that improving and maintaining teacher quality is an essential component if we are to achieve the goal of universal proficiency in reading. There are several routes to this goal, and one of them is to ensure that all instruction is done by teachers who are well prepared in the specialization in which they deliver instruction. Given that the field of reading instruction is ever changing as new understandings and approaches are revealed through research, the second imperative is that preservice and inservice education needs to keep up with new discoveries and train teachers to effectively use the new ideas. We are aware that the challenges are great, but the importance of the goal of excellent teaching for all children makes it worth the effort.

This fourth edition of *What Research Has to Say About Reading Instruction* provides a powerful professional resource and tool for teachers, for those who prepare them, and for those who provide them with ongoing professional development.

REFERENCES

Bond, G.L., & Dykstra, R. (1967). The Cooperative Research Program in First-Grade Reading Instruction. *Reading Research Quarterly, 32*(4), 348–427.

Editorial: Get serious about improving teaching. (2010, November 30). *Star Tribune*, p. 8.

Elementary and Secondary Education Act of 1965, 20 U.S.C. § 6301 *et seq.* (U.S. Department of Education, 2004).

The final report of the National Reading Panel: Hearings before the Senate Appropriations Committee, Subcommittee on Labor, Health and Human Services, and Education (April 13, 2000) (testimony of Duane Alexander, M.D., Director, National Institute of Child Health and Human Development).

Chapter 1

The Relation Between Alphabetic Basics, Word Recognition, and Reading

Marilyn Jager Adams

One day at the end of a regional inservice, I was approached by some teachers for advice about an 8-year-old boy. The boy had come to their school from Haiti nearly two years earlier. At the time, he knew virtually no English and none of his letters. Since then, the teachers had been working hard to give him one-on-one support with English language development and reading.

For his English language development, their core approach had been centered on reading books aloud to him, actively engaging him throughout. For his reading, they had set out a systematic plan, beginning with the basics. His English was coming nicely, but his reading was not. Even though he had mastered letter recognition, primary letter–sound knowledge, and initial letter segmentation, learning to decode was proving very difficult. In the effort to get him going, the teachers had been staying after school with him four days a week to work on decoding the nonsense words from the Dynamic Indicators of Basic Early Literacy Skills (DIBELS; see dibels.uoregon.edu) materials. And still he was making little progress.

The question addressed in this chapter is whether the teachers' approach toward developing the student's decoding skills was well founded, and why or why not.

From reading the research, the teachers were convinced that the ability to decode was critical for learning to read. They believed that strong decoding would be particularly important for this child as it would enable him to sound out and, through that, to learn new English words through his reading. Research and experience had also taught them that decoding is easier with short, orthographically simple words than with words that are longer or involve more complex spelling conventions. Yet so many of the shortest words in English are irregular.

What Research Has to Say About Reading Instruction (4th ed.) edited by S. Jay Samuels and Alan E. Farstrup.
© 2011 by the International Reading Association.

There are more than 20 different DIBELS nonsense word forms, most containing 50 two- and three-letter items. Within each list, every letter unambiguously corresponds to its most frequently occurring sound, and all primary letter–sound pairs are represented (Camine, Silbert, Kame'enui, & Tarver, 2004). With these thoughts in mind, the DIBELS nonsense word sets seemed to the teachers an opportune resource for developing and practicing the child's decoding abilities.

These basic premises are right on. Reading with fluency and productive comprehension depends integrally on having acquired deep and ready working knowledge of spelling–sound correspondences (Adams, 1990; Adams, Treiman, & Pressley, 1998). In addition, it is well documented that the decoding of younger and weaker readers is more accurate when they are given short words with simple, regular letter–sound correspondences. Accuracy dwindles with consonant clusters, and still more with complex or inconsistent vowel spellings; with polysyllabic words, all such difficulties are compounded even as issues of syllable division and stress placement are added (Duncan & Seymour, 2003; Laxon, Gallagher, & Masterson, 2002; Rack, Snowling, & Olson, 1992).

In fact, the nonsense word sets in the DIBELS battery were not intended for use in instructing children to decode. Rather, they were intended for use in assessing that ability. Subtests measuring children's ability to sound out regularly spelled, pronounceable nonwords (also called "nonsense words" or "pseudowords") are quite common in batteries designed for assessing the needs and progress of developing readers. As examples, lists of decodable nonwords are included in the Word Attack subtest of the Woodcock-Johnson (Woodcock, McGrew, & Mather, 2001), in the nonword section of the Test of Word Reading Efficiency (Torgesen, Wagner, & Rashotte, 1999), in Roswell, Chall, Curtis, and Kearns's (2005) Diagnostic Assessments of Reading, in the Gray diagnostic battery (Bryant, Wiederholt, & Bryant, 2004), and in Wechsler's (2005) Individual Achievement Test.

The motive for including such probes is precisely that nonsense words, because they are not words, will be unfamiliar to readers. After all, if the children have never seen the "words" before, then what are their options? They cannot visually recognize the word as a whole as they have never seen it before; they cannot correct their pronunciation of it based on familiarity or vocabulary matching as they have never heard it before. A nonsense word's spelling–sound correspondences offer the only basis on which readers can figure out how to pronounce it or check the pronunciation they produce. The rationale, in other words, is that lists of nonsense words offer "clean" tests of readers' working knowledge of spelling–sound correspondences and their ability to blend.

Another argument often offered for using lists of nonsense words in tests is that the ability to read them has been shown to correlate strongly with overall reading ability (Bell & Perfetti, 1994; Shankweiler et al., 1999; Swanson, Trainin, Necoechea, & Hammill, 2003). As a matter of fact, mature readers can read aloud pseudowords very nearly as quickly as they can read aloud familiar, real words. The difference is measurable in, at most, a few hundredths of a second.

Clearly not even the most skilled reader can possibly sound and blend the separate graphemes of a novel string of letters in so little time. Instead, by every measure and comparison, skilled readers behave as if they *recognize* such well-spelled nonwords. But again, nonwords are not words. They are used in such experiments precisely because no reader is likely to have seen them before. How in the world might people "recognize" a string of letters they've never seen? That's where things begin to get interestingly complicated.

Since the 1970s, researchers have published hundreds upon hundreds of studies directed toward understanding this paradox and its implications with respect to the knowledge and processes underlying reading. The earliest studies exploited the then-new capacity for millisecond timing, using it not only to control durations and sequencing of the materials presented but also to measure the speed of people's responses depending on their abilities or what they were shown. As examples, differences in response times allow researchers to study the order in which events are processed by the mind, to evaluate the effortfulness or automaticity of processing, and to look for signs of facilitation (faster recognition) or interference (slower recognition) so as to identify how different kinds of information are organized during processing. Over the years, the millisecond timer has been complemented by eye-movement technologies (see Rayner, 1997; Rayner & Pollatsek, 1989), computer simulations (e.g., Seidenberg & McClelland, 1989), and today, an ever-growing array of brain-imaging techniques that enable researchers to locate and trace the flow and interaction of processes involved in word recognition across different areas of the brain. (For a readable and informative overview of the latter, see Dehaene, 2009.)

A conclusion from all this work is that, as it turns out, well-spelled nonsense words truly *are* recognized by skilled readers. This happens in a region of the brain called the *visual word form area* located near the back and bottom of the lower left side (McCandliss, Cohen, & Dehaene,

2003). As its name implies, this little area of the brain is devoted to the visual perception of individual words. It responds to the sight of printed words but, in itself, is indifferent to their sounds or pronunciations, their meanings, their contexts, and even to whether they are actually words. Also as implied by its name, the responsiveness of this area is specific to the *form* or structure of printed words. However, it is not the word's physical form that matters. The visual word form area is indifferent to the size or location or even the fonts or cases of letter strings; for example, it treats *TABLE*, *table*, *TaBle*, and *tAbLe* as identical (Dehaene et al., 2004). Rather, the responsiveness of the visual word form area is determined by the familiarity of the orthographic structure or spelling of the word in focus. It barely registers scrambled or unpronounceable strings of letters, but it is highly responsive to words and also to well-spelled, pronounceable nonwords (Binder, Medler, Westbury, Liebenthal, & Buchanan, 2006; Bruno, Zumberge, Manis, Lu, & Goldman, 2008; Kronbichler et al., 2007).

For skilled readers, it takes about 150 milliseconds for the letters of a word to get from the eye, through the visual cortex, to their registration in the backmost sector of the visual word form area. Again, at this point, the letters have ceded their shapes to their identities—that is, an **A** is an *A* is an ɑ. The visual word form area then progressively reconstructs the spelling of the letter string by combining the visual information it receives with its own knowledge, accrued through past experience, about frequent and allowable pairs or sequences of letters, about the behaviors of vowels versus consonants, about the spellings of syllables that are common to many different words, and even about the spellings of whole words that are extremely familiar to the reader, especially those that are short and irregular. The activity within the visual word form area rolls from back, where the letters gain entry, to front as it works with increasingly large and more complex orthographic constraints (Dehaene, 2009; Maurer, Brem, Bucher, & Brandeis, 2005).

As the reconstructed string of letters approaches the front of the visual word form area, there arises an explosion of activity, spread broadly throughout the linguistic and conceptual areas of the brain. It is through this activity that the word is recognized and interpreted. It is also through the dynamic of this activity that reading becomes productive and fluent. Let us consider this dynamic more closely.

Spelling–Sound Knowledge Connects Print to Language

The recognition of spellings that happens within the visual word form area seems to be the only component of the reading process that belongs exclusively to the domain of print as distinct from the domains of language and thought more generally. In its basic operation, the visual word form area sends the orthography or perceived spelling of each word upward to the phonological processor through the associations that have been established between the letters of the word and its phonemes. As the spelling thus selects the word's pronunciation, the phonological processor in turn relays activation to the many areas of the brain that are involved in generating the word's meanings and in working out its usage and specific significance within the context in which it has been encountered. Thus, the mappings from orthography to phonology—that is, from spelling to pronunciation—are the nexus between seeing and understanding the print on a page (Adams, 1990; Dehaene, 2009; Seidenberg & McClelland, 1989).

Once the printed word has been translated to language, the job is to give it meaning. In this quest, the connectivity of the brain is extensive, serving to relay activity among all experientially related aspects of the reader's knowledge. For example, reading a word such as *stagger, limp,* or *tiptoe* activates the motor areas in the brain that are involved in controlling the legs and feet, whereas reading a word such as *chop* or *carve* activates those controlling the hands (Kemmerer, Castillo, Talavage, Patterson, & Wiley, 2008). Whereas understanding a sentence about *eating* activates the areas related to gustatory sensations, understanding a visual description activates areas of the visual cortex (Olivetti Belardinelli et al., 2009; Palmiero et al., 2009). In turn, each of these areas is itself diffusely connected to other related knowledge that is distributed about the brain (Martin, 2007). As Martin and Chao (2001) summarize, "The same regions are active, at least in part, when objects from a category are recognized, named, imagined, and when reading and answering questions about them" (p. 199). One must imagine that this broad, modality-free connectivity is of enormous advantage for young readers and English learners in that much of the understanding required for reading need not be learned *through* language. Even so, when reading, none of this knowledge can be accessed, much less modified or added to, except by means of the words and wordings of a text.

In complement to such connections that recruit all potentially relevant knowledge, there are a number of others devoted to winnowing it down to what matters here and now. As one example, researchers have identified a specific area of the brain that specializes in deciding when the meanings of two words are related (e.g., *couch* and *sofa*, *hunt* and *hunter*, but not *corn* and *corner*) (Devlin, Jamison, Matthews, & Gonnerman, 2004). Another area has been identified as responsible for figuring out the combined meaning of the words comprising sentences (Vandenberghe, Nobre, & Price, 2002). Still another seems devoted to picking out the specific meanings of a word as appropriate to its context (Rodd, Davis, & Johnsrude, 2005). Indeed, it seems that the more scientists look (and devise clever experiments to see), the more the number of specialized areas of the brain they find, all richly interconnected so as to support the process of reading and language comprehension in their interaction.

Again, each of these meaning-construction and disambiguation capabilities resides in the parts of the brain that are devoted to language and thought in general. That is, once developed, they are available for speaking, listening, and writing as well as reading. As educators, however, it is ✗ worth bearing in mind that these meaning-construction and disambiguation processes are principally the product of learning that is primarily afforded through experience with written language (Olson, 1994, 2009).

Bidirectionality and Feedback Circuits

The second key to this dynamic is that connections in the brain are bidirectional. That is, when one area activates a second, the second reciprocally sends activation back to the first: The better the match, the stronger the feedback. Getting strong feedback causes the sending node to issue still more activation to an answering node which, in turn, directs more activation back to the sending node. In this way, a feedback loop is created that quickly sets apart the best matches from any others that might initially have attracted activation. Meanwhile, of course, as each receiving node is also sending activation outward and upward to other nodes with which it is connected, the same thing happens at the next level and the next, and so on. In result, the separate, pair-wise activation loops quickly become bound together into an extended and coherent, resonant whole (see Goldinger & Azuma, 2003; Hebb, 1949).

For the skilled reader, the consequence of these self-defining neural circuits is that once the spelling of a familiar word establishes activation in the visual word form area, its sight, sound, and meaning seem to pop to mind at once. Moreover, the extensiveness of this dynamic ensures that the more familiar and knowledgeable readers are about the words, language, and topic of a text, the richer and more effortless will be their interpretation.

In fact, feedback patterns between any two nodes need not match perfectly to generate resonance. It's just that the resonance they support may be too weak or too diffuse to efficiently single out a winner. Perhaps the child has correctly read most but not all of the letters of the word (see Frith, 1980), perhaps the mapping from spelling to sound is not specific or unique (e.g., "bead" activates both /bĕd/ and /bēd/), or perhaps the child's knowledge of the meaning of the word is confused or too sparse to offer key semantic or grammatical links. These sorts of weaknesses in what Perfetti (2007; Perfetti & Hart, 2001, 2002) calls "lexical quality" are characteristic of poorer readers and, as his research demonstrates, they are costly, resulting in sluggish comprehension that may be minimally successful at best.

At the extreme, where the match is critically incomplete, information may diffuse so broadly that it is wholly unhelpful. Further, large mismatches or gaps prohibit resonance altogether. In these cases, when no chain is able to resolve itself, understanding is out of reach. Minimally, the reader will balk, as young readers often do. Where the readers find themselves unable to repair or gloss the problem, they are stuck.

Our teachers' student is stuck. And that brings us to the third key dynamic of the system: It learns.

Learning

The classic Hebbian explanation of learning, named in honor of Donald Hebb's (1949) seminal work, is that when one set of neurons reliably fires with another, the strength of the connection between the two sets grows. In other words, once a reliable, consistent connection is set up, learning will result through repeated encounter. But this raises two questions: First, if the link between A and B is incomplete and, therefore, unreliable or inconsistent, how does it get cleaned up? Second, how does the link get set up in the first place?

Refining the Connections

The role of attention in disambiguating, strengthening, or "cleaning up" learning is axiomatic within the field of cognition and learning, and examples equally abound in the domain of word recognition. In particular, as the process of decoding words couples the spellings of words with their pronunciations, it pressures alignment between the word's graphemes and its phonemes. Thus, for example, as children learn to decode words that are in their oral vocabularies, the phonemic significance of the words' letters serves to refine their diction (e.g., "one, two, free" becomes "one, two, three"; "bisgetti' becomes "spaghetti").

This sort of phonological restructuring, along with the increases in phonological sensitivity that it brings about, are among the strongest outcomes of learning to read an alphabetic language (Morais, 2003). Because this sort of tightening of a word's identity also sharpens or reduces diffusion of the activation flow, it improves children's ability to access and refine their understanding of the word's meaning.

In keeping with this, Rosenthal and Ehri (2008; see also Ehri & Wilce, 1979) have shown that seeing the spelling of a new word increases children's memory for both its pronunciation and its meaning. In this study, children in second and fifth grades were asked to learn two sets of low-frequency, picturable words. For the second graders, all of the to-be-learned words had consonant-vowel-consonant (CVC) spellings (e.g., *keg, sod, nib*); for the fifth graders, all were two- or three-syllable words (e.g., *mullock, frenulum*). Following research on best practices (Sadoski, 2005), the vocabulary instruction for children in both grades provided pictures and definitions of the words as well as a number of sentences for further supporting their meanings and illustrating their usage. In addition, the children were individually and actively engaged, with feedback, in producing and recalling the words and their meanings throughout the study sessions. The difference of interest was that, for one of the sets of to-be-learned words, the words themselves were printed at the bottom of their picture cards during training and corrective feedback. Importantly, because the words were pronounced by the teacher whenever the cards were shown, the children really had no need to read them; nor were the children asked to read the words or even to look at them. The words were just there. Even so, the results showed that the opportunity to see the printed words while attending to their pronunciations and meanings was of great benefit to all of the children at both ages, resulting in their learning the words' pronunciations and meanings significantly faster and retaining them significantly better. The older children were additionally posttested on their ability to use the words in new cloze sentences. Those who had seen the words fared far better, correctly transferring them to new sentences nearly half again as often.

More recently, Rosenthal and Ehri (2010) have demonstrated that, in reverse, causing children to attend to the pronunciations of printed words that they see also enhances learning. In this study, fifth graders were given brief passages and asked to read them silently. Each passage was about the meaning of a specific word, such as *kerfuffle*; that is, the meaning of the word was the topic of the passage. Within each passage, the target word occurred three times, always underlined. Half of the children were asked to stop and pronounce the underlined word aloud wherever it arose; the other half were asked to place a checkmark next to each occurrence of the underlined word, indicating whether it had appeared earlier in the passage. Through oral retelling of the passages, Rosenthal and Ehri affirmed that the children's comprehension of the passages—and, therefore, of the meanings of the target words—was comparable whether or not they had been required to read the words aloud. However, the children's retention of the words themselves differed markedly, whether measured by spelling, by recall of the word in response to a definition, or by choosing the words' definition in a multiple-choice test. Among the better readers, those in the say-aloud condition showed themselves significantly more able to recall the word in response to the definitional queries; those who had not been required to say the words aloud were slightly less likely to recall the words and, when they did, were much more likely to produce approximate rather than correct pronunciations of them. Among poorer readers, fewer than 40% were able to recall even an approximately acceptable pronunciation of even one of the target words; in contrast, 90% of those who had been required to stop and read the target words aloud succeeded in doing so.

Cleaning up the linkage between orthography and phonology is not just about improving pronunciation. It is about conferring a more distinct identity to the word and, as a result, enabling it to more powerfully, efficiently, and unambiguously direct energy exactly and only to its meaning. This in turn affords resources and focus for strengthening and refining the word's meaning.

Also consistent with the mind's dependence on "good matches" is the fact that meanings and spellings of words with ambiguous or confusing spelling–sound correspondences, such as *imminent, eminent,* and *immanent,* are harder to learn (Katz & Frost, 2001). Sometimes phonologically ambiguous spelling–sound correspondences are constrained morphologically. Among older school children, for example, even though *fatter* rhymes with *ladder,* the prominence of *fat* in *fatter* ensures that it will be "heard" and spelled with medial /t/ rather than /d/ (Ehri & Wilce,

1986). Sometimes phonologically ambiguous spelling–sound correspondences can be instructionally corrected. For example, leading children to pronounce schwas as they are spelled (e.g., cho-co-late rather than cho-kə-lət, har-mo-ny rather than har-mə-ny, cor-res-pond rather than cor-rəs-pond, or man-a-tee rather than man-ə-tee) is shown to promote the words' correct spelling (Drake & Ehri, 1984). (And, after all, the schwa is not really a phoneme, but only a phonotactic consequence of reduced stress.)

On the other hand, English spelling–sound correspondences are notoriously complex and inconsistent. Beyond schwas, there are long and short vowels (both unreliably signaled), digraphs, unruly letter doubling (*pepper* vs. *paper, common* vs. *comic, demon* vs. *lemon*), silent letters (*comb, knit, gauge*), and irregular words (*colonel, island*). The same letter or spelling may map to several different phonemes (e.g., *cow, low; get, gem; read, read*) and, worst of all, the same phoneme can be spelled in many, many different ways. For example, Edward Rondthaler, longtime spelling reformer and chairman of the American Literacy Council, lists 18 different spellings for the long /oo/ phoneme: oo (*moon*), ou (*group*), ui (*fruit*), ue (*glue*), ew (*drew*), wo (*two*), u (*flu*), oe (*canoe*), ough (*through*), u...e (*rule*), ieu (*lieu*), oo...e (*loose*), o...e (*lose*), oup (*coup*), ui...e (*bruise*), eu...e (*deuce*), eu (*sleuth*), ous (*rendezvous*), and ou...e (*mousse*) (See American Literacy Council, 2008). Further, whereas the permissible syllables of most languages are limited to CV, CVC, and VC structures, English syllables can (and often do) sport multiple consonant sounds on either side of the vowels (e.g., *sprints*) with the result that, relative to other languages, the permissible syllables in English are far greater in number and phonologically far more complex.

Moreover, just as there is a cost to learning spelling–sound mappings poorly, there is a big cost to the fact that English spelling–sound mappings are so hard to learn. In English-speaking countries, the inci-★ dence of dyslexia is far higher and the acquisition of basic literacy skills takes far longer than in countries with more regular or orderly alphabetic systems. (For a review, see Ziegler & Goswami, 2005.) In European countries with highly regular orthographies, such as Germany, Greece, and Finland, nearly all children can read simple one- and two-syllable pseudowords and nearly any real word in their speaking vocabulary by the end of first grade (Seymour, Aro, & Erskine, 2003). In English-speaking countries, it is at least the middle grades before most children reach this level.

Creating the Connections

In short, where the challenge is learning to read English, the amount of attention, time, care, and study required is considerable. But then, all of the difficulties and fixes just discussed are far in the future for our teachers' young student, who is still struggling with the basics. Which takes us back to the question, How does the system get set up in the first place?

"Aha!" astute readers might say to themselves. "The grapheme–phoneme connections are established through the visual word form area!"

Yes, that is essentially what must happen. However, the visual word form area doesn't even exist in prereaders; it develops only gradually through reading growth and experience. Whether our teachers knew it or not, by drilling their young student on phonics, it is the visual word form area that they are seeking to develop. Research tells us that the prerequisites for learning to decode are letter recognition, letter–sound knowledge, and phonemic awareness. Since this child has learned to recognize and sound the individual letters, let us focus on phonemic awareness.

Phonemes are the smallest units of spoken language that make a difference to meaning. For example, the spoken word "rope" comprises three phonemes, /r/ /ō/ /p/, and differs by only one phoneme from such words as *dope, road, rip,* and *roach*. In principle, phonemes are the sounds that are represented by the letters of an alphabetic language. Again, the mapping between graphemes and phonemes is messy in English, partly because there are fewer letters (26) than there are phonemes (38 to 47, depending on who is counting) and partly because some phonemes (especially the vowels) are variously represented through a number of different letters and combinations of letters. Nevertheless, the principle still holds.

What, then, is phonemic awareness? This is the critical question for our teachers. The National Reading Panel defines phonemic awareness as "the ability to focus on and manipulate phonemes in spoken words" (National Institute of Child Health and Human Development, 2000, p. 2-1), and continues with a list of tasks through which it is commonly practiced or assessed:

- Phoneme isolation—e.g., "Tell me the first sound in *paste*." (/p/)
- Phoneme identity—e.g., "Tell me the sound that is the same in *bike, boy,* and *bell*." (/b/)
- Phoneme categorization—e.g., "Which word does not belong? *bus, bun, rug*" (*rug*)
- Phoneme blending—e.g., "What word is /s/ /t/ /o/ /p/?" (*stop*)

- Phoneme segmentation—e.g., "How many phonemes are there in *ship*?" (three: /sh/ /i/ /p/)
- Phoneme deletion—e.g., "What is *smile* without the /s/?" (*mile*)

Many educators have adopted this definition of phonemic awareness. Since the National Reading Panel's charge was to identify scientifically based instructional practices, this is understandable.

But hold it: The National Reading Panel's task, more specifically, was to determine which instructional practices yielded statistical gains that were robust across soundly designed, peer-reviewed, experimental studies. Given this, it was essential that the panel define phonemic awareness in terms of its quantitative measurement. Yet assessing phonemic awareness is not the same as teaching it. Where the primary task is one of helping children to acquire phonemic awareness, knowing how to test it is not good enough: It is vital to understand what it is at a conceptual level, as well as how it develops.

So, first: How is phonemic awareness defined at that conceptual level? Phonemic awareness is the insight that every spoken word can be conceived as a sequence of phonemes (Adams, Treiman, & Pressley, 1998; Snow, Burns, & Griffin, 1998). Because phonemes are the units of sound represented by the letters of an alphabet, an awareness of phonemes is key to understanding the logic of the alphabetic principle and thus to learning phonics and spelling.

Second, how does phonemic awareness develop? As described earlier, learning is the result of creating new links between established representations in the mind. In decoding, the links are between the spellings of words and the phonological representations of the words. Toward building these links, what are the representations that are available within the mind? On one side are the taught sounds that the letters represent. But what is it on the other side?

Based on a wealth of evidence of many different kinds and sources, science concurs, over and over again, that the representations on the other side are *individual words* (e.g., Adams, 1990; Byrne & Fielding-Barnsley, 1990; Ehri, 1992; Lewkowicz, 1980; Morais, 2003, Murray; 1998; Perfetti, 1992; Seidenberg & McClelland, 1989; Share, 1995; Skjelfjord, 1976; Treiman, 1993).

Children approach the challenge of learning to read with a fairly extensive listening and speaking vocabulary. Necessarily, as part of that vocabulary knowledge, the elementary phonetic and articulatory structure of individual words and the differences between them must be represented at some level. However, these representations are not conscious but instead are embodied in a precognitive, biologically specialized subsystem that operates automatically (Liberman & Liberman, 1992; Liberman & Mattingly, 1989). This is the gift of human language. In speaking and listening, we do not need to think or expend attention in analyzing or piecing words together, phoneme by phoneme. Instead, a word such as *bag* is heard and pronounced on call as a single, seamless unit.

It is because these processes are automatic and preconscious that we can so swiftly and effortlessly produce and understand spoken language. On the other hand, a basic premise of phonics is that, to learn to read, children need only link the letters to the phonemes. If the phonemes are unavailable to consciousness, then how is this possible?

The answer is that emergent readers must work with the phonological information to which they *can* gain awareness and restructure it to fit the writing system. Whether studied historically across the evolution of literacy or developmentally across its acquisition, evidence attests that people's conscious sensitivity to the phonological structure of their language progresses only gradually to the level of phonemes. That is, people (historically) and children (developmentally) gain awareness of words before syllables, syllables before onsets or rimes, and onsets and rimes before phonemes (Anthony & Lonigan, 2004; Olson, 1994; Treiman, 1993).

Furthermore, sensitivity to phonemes arises only as the consequence of learning an alphabetic writing system. As Murray (1998) expressed it, "To identify a phoneme is to perceive it as the same vocal gesture repeated across different words (i.e., a familiar and recognizable entity)" (p. 462). That is, if the child can recognize that the spoken word "man" begins with the phoneme /m/, he or she can build a new connection, pairing the initial letter of the written word *man* with the initial sound of its pronunciation.

It is through the mappings from the spellings of words to their pronunciations that print becomes bound to the language centers of the brain. For beginning readers, the very process of decoding leaves a trace in memory that connects the letters of a word's spelling with the matching components of its pronunciation. Phonemic sensitivity grows as the same letter maps to and clarifies the "same" sound in many words while, reciprocally, the pronunciation of each word will come to be represented in terms of its phonemes as defined by its spelling. Just as it is easier to hear the initial phoneme of a word, the children's spelling–sound knowledge tends to begin with initial consonants, progressing to final consonants, medial vowels, and blends (Duncan, Seymour, & Hill, Treiman, 1993).

Provided that a word is read and understood in context, the activation from the word's spelling will extend through its pronunciation to its meanings and usage. Each time the word is seen, this link will automatically be recalled, thus strengthening and refining the connections that hold it together. Through this process, as the connections between spelling, sound, and meaning become completely and reliably represented and bound together, the word will become readable at a glance; it will become a "sight word." Further, as multiple words reach for the same substrings of letters, the child's knowledge of orthography will progressively expand from single letters to larger spelling patterns.

The most obvious benefit of phonics is that it enables readers to sound out the occasional unknown word they encounter in print. Beyond the beginning stages, however, its most important benefit may be that it leads to decoding automaticity. Decoding automaticity is rooted in the reader's cumulative knowledge of spelling–sound correspondences. Over time, as the product of their cumulative decoding experience, readers progressively refine their phonological sensitivity even as common pronunciations of word parts become tied to common spellings. As this knowledge grows in breadth and depth, it provides a support structure by which nearly every new word is partly learned already, enabling readers to read and spell new words with ease and to retain them distinctly. A side-effect of such knowledge is that it enables them to "recognize" pseudowords.

The Development of the Visual Word Form Area

For mature readers, regardless of the language they speak or the type of writing system they have learned, the location of the visual word form area is the same. It is centered in a region of the cortex that generally specializes in recognizing visual stimuli such as faces and tools that demand foveal viewing and are distinguished by subtle detail. Unlike neighboring areas, however, the visual word form area develops only in the left hemisphere of the brain, rather than bilaterally in both right and left hemispheres. The specific area in which the visual word form area is centered is adjacent to the phonological centers in the brain, which are left-lateralized from birth.

Developmentally, the first sign of specialized activity in the region that will become the visual word form area is a relatively rapid response to letters that arises as children become expert in letter recognition (Maurer et al., 2005). At this early stage, however, the region is still very immature. Its responsiveness to letters is no stronger in the left hemisphere than in its symmetrically matched region in the right hemisphere. It is only gradually, after nearly two years of reading instruction (and in degree correlated with children's reading growth), that the area begins to show a clear preference for real letters as compared with other letter-like symbols (Maurer et al., 2006). Among on-pace children, it is not until fourth grade that the visual word form area begins to produce adult-like responses to high-frequency words, though even then it shows little generalization to well-spelled pseudowords (McCandliss et al., 2003). In keeping with this, behavioral evidence shows that children's perception of print, including their facility in reading pseudowords, is strongly determined by the specific words with which they are familiar (Booth, Perfetti, & MacWhinney, 1999; Laxon, Masterson, Gallagher, & Pay, 2002; Van den Broeck, Geudens, & van den Bos, 2010). Not until children are about 16 years old does the area's responsiveness to different kinds of tasks and letter strings become mature, though even then it is slower than is normal for adults (Schlaggar & McCandliss, 2007).

Over the primary grades, as the left hemisphere comes to dominate the right hemisphere in visual word perception, accompanying changes are seen in the visual word form area's connections and communications with the language centers of the brain. In the beginning, activity is characterized by slow and effortful letter-to-sound processing. Gradually, as the responsiveness of the visual word form area grows from back to front, both the speed of the system's responses and the complexity of the spelling patterns that gain direct connection to the language centers increase—though again, it is not until adolescence that the full system works in adult-like ways (Sandak, Mencl, Frost, & Pugh, 2004). However, even among mature readers—those who have developed swift responses to frequent spelling patterns whether in words or pseudowords—the responsiveness of the system appears to be firmly anchored on their experience and familiarity with real words that they have learned to read (Bruno et al., 2008).

As described, the changes in the visual word form area's responsiveness and their timing are for children who are developing on pace. Research shows the actual timing of these changes at each stage is correlated, not with age, but with children's reading ability (Maurer et al., 2006; Sandak et al., 2004; Shaywitz et al., 2002). Moreover, the responsiveness of the visual word form area is weak or aberrant in developmental dyslexics and illiterates (Schlaggar & McCandliss, 2007), but has been shown to develop through a similar progression in response to instruction in decoding, writing, and reading (Brem et al., 2010; James, 2010; Shaywitz et al., 2004; Temple et al., 2003).

Conclusion

Back to our teachers. They were very correct to be reading and discussing literature with the child, for both word recognition and reading comprehension depend on language development. They were also correct that many of the shortest and most frequent words in English tend to be irregularly spelled. (In view of this and as noted in Adams, 2009, teachers are urged to teach the basic function words—for example, *the*, *of, do*—early, helping children to grasp their usage and to recognize them visually before moving into reading proper.). The teachers were also correct in their belief that helping this child learn to decode accurately and confidently is extremely important toward furthering his language and literacy development.

Where they went awry was in using a test to teach. In this case, the specific problem happened to be that the items in the test were nonwords rather than real, meaningful, knowable words. But think of the many other instances where teachers have endeavored to use assessment methods and materials to teach. In urging teachers to use the findings and products of research, it is critically important that researchers, policymakers, and teacher educators do a better job of clarifying when and how such findings and products are useful.

Finally and for the sake of clarification, the issue here is not whether words should be taught in context or isolation. Engaging children in reading and writing words in isolation serves to hasten learning of the words' spelling and their recognition. Leading children to read words in meaningful contexts hastens their command of the words' usage and meaning. Both are important to young readers, and equally so. But whatever the teaching or learning activity, it is important to make sure that children see and say the word and understand and think about its meaning in course. The brain does not grow block by block from bottom up. It grows through its own efforts to communicate and find coherence within itself.

Questions for Reflection

1. Research has shown that games and activities for developing children's phonemic sensitivity and awareness have greater impact

when the phoneme is represented by its letter than by, for example, blocks or bingo markers. Based on what you learned from this chapter, why does this make sense?

2. The automaticity of recognizing a word or word part depends on securing strong connections not just between its spelling and pronunciation but also between its spelling/pronunciation and its meaning and usage. For each of the following sets of suffixes, create a set of exercises to help children master the spellings, pronunciations, meanings, and usages of suffixes and real words. (Do not neglect associated spelling issues such as final consonant doubling, dropping final *e*, and changing *y* to *i*.)

    - -ing, -ed
    - -er, -est
    - -ness, -less, -ful

3. Once they have some knowledge of the letters and a basic understanding of the alphabetic principle, encouraging kindergartners and first graders to write using inventive (phonetic) spelling is among the most powerful practices for promoting their reading growth. Thinking about what you learned from this chapter, explain why this is so.

4. It has been shown that word-recognition growth is hastened when the words in children's earliest texts (levels equivalent to the traditional preprimers and primers) are coordinated with their phonics lessons. In what ways may this help young readers both to appreciate and to internalize their phonics lessons? Why?

5. Many basic function words in English pose problems for young readers in two ways. First, these words are poorly distinguished orally ("I want a glass uh milk"). Second, many sport spelling–sound correspondences that are irregular, or at least sophisticated relative to entry-level phonics standards. Because these words arise so frequently (and take on new importance) in written text, it is wise to help students master their spellings and usages before decodable texts are introduced. Following is a list of very frequently occurring words. Invent activities (e.g., language activities, writing activities, rebus texts) through which you could engage kindergartners in using and learning their spellings and usages.

- the, a, an
- of, to, in, for, on, with, at, from, by
- and, or, but, not
- am, is, are, was, were, will, have, has, had, do, does, did
- I, we, you, he, she, they, it
- me, us, you, him, her, them
- my, our, your, her, his, their, its

REFERENCES

Adams, M.J. (1990). *Beginning to read: Thinking and learning about print.* Cambridge, MA: MIT Press.

Adams, M.J. (2009). Decodable text: When, why, and how? In E.H. Hiebert & M. Sailors (Eds.), *Finding the right texts: What works for beginning and struggling readers* (pp. 23–46). New York: Guilford.

Adams, M.J., Treiman, R., & Pressley, M. (1998). Reading, writing, and literacy. In W. Damon (Series Ed.), I.E. Sigel, & K.A. Renninger (Vol. Eds.), *Handbook of child psychology. Vol. 4: Child psychology in practice* (5th ed., pp. 275–355). New York: Wiley.

American Literacy Council. (2008). Soundspel. Boulder, CO: Author. Retrieved November 18, 2010, from www.americanliteracy.com/soundspel.html

Anthony, J.L., & Lonigan, C.J. (2004). The nature of phonological awareness: Converging evidence from four studies of preschool and early grade school children. *Journal of Educational Psychology, 96*(1), 43–55. doi:10.1037/0022-0663.96.1.43

Bell, L.C., & Perfetti, C.A. (1994). Reading skill: Some adult comparisons. *Journal of Educational Psychology, 86*(2), 244–255. doi:10.1037/0022-0663.86.2.244

Binder, J.R., Medler, D.A., Westbury, C.F., Liebenthal, E., & Buchanan, L. (2006). Tuning of the human left fusiform gyrus to sublexical orthographic structure. *NeuroImage, 33*(2), 739–748. doi:10.1016/j.neuroimage.2006.06.053

Booth, J.R., Perfetti, C.A., & MacWhinney, B. (1999). Quick, automatic, and general activation of orthographic and phonological representations in young readers. *Developmental Psychology, 35*(1), 3–19. doi:10.1037/0012-1649.35.1.3

Brem, S., Bach, S., Kucian, K., Guttorm, T.K., Martin, E., Lyytinen, H., et al. (2010). Brain sensitivity to print emerges when children learn letter–speech sound correspondences. *Proceedings of the National Academy of Sciences, 107*(17), 7939–7944. doi:10.1073/pnas.0904402107

Bruno, J.L., Zumberge, A., Manis, F.R., Lu, Z., & Goldman, J.G. (2008). Sensitivity to orthographic familiarity in the occipito-temporal region. *NeuroImage, 39*(4), 1988–2001. doi:10.1016/j.neuroimage.2007.10.044

Bryant, B.R., Wiederholt, J.L., & Bryant, D.P. (2004). *Gray diagnostic reading tests* (2nd ed.). Austin, TX: PRO-ED.

Byrne, B., & Fielding-Barnsley, R. (1990). Acquiring the alphabetic principle: A case for teaching recognition of phoneme identity. *Journal of Educational Psychology, 82*(4), 805–812. doi:10.1037/0022-0663.82.4.805

Camine, D.W., Silbert, J., Kame'enui, E.J., & Tarver, S.G. (2004). *Direct instruction reading* (4th ed.). Upper Saddle River, NJ: Pearson.

Dehaene, S. (2009). *Reading in the brain: The science and evolution of a human invention.* New York: Viking.

Dehaene, S., Jobert, A., Naccache, L., Ciuciu, P., Poline, J.-B., Le Bihan, D., et al. (2004). Letter binding and invariant recognition of masked words: Behavioral and neuroimaging evidence. *Psychological Science, 15*(5), 307–313. doi:10.1111/j.0956-7976.2004.00674.x

Devlin, J.T., Jamison, H.L., Matthews, P.M., & Gonnerman, L.M. (2004). Morphology and the internal structure of words. *Proceedings of the National Academy of Sciences, 101*(41), 14984–14988. doi:10.1073/pnas.0403766101

Drake, D.A., & Ehri, L.E. (1984). Spelling acquisition: Effects of pronouncing words on memory for their spellings. *Cognition and Instruction, 1*(3), 297–320. doi:10.1207/ s1532690xci0103_2

Duncan, L.G., & Seymour, P.H.K. (2003). How do children read multisyllabic words? Some preliminary observations. *Journal of Research in Reading, 26*(2), 101–120. doi: 10.1111/1467-9817.00190

Duncan, L.G., Seymour, P.H.K., & Hill, S. (1997). How important are rhyme and analogy in beginning reading? *Cognition, 63*(2), 171–208. doi:10.1016/S0010-0277(97)00001-2

Ehri, L.C. (1992). Reconceptualizing the development of sight word reading and its relationship to recoding. In P.B. Gough, L.C. Ehri, & R. Treiman (Eds.), *Reading acquisition* (pp. 107–144). Hillsdale, NJ: Erlbaum.

Ehri, L.C., & Wilce, L.S. (1979). The mnemonic value of orthography among beginning readers. *Journal of Educational Psychology, 71*(1), 26–40. doi:10.1037/0022-0663.71.1.26

Ehri, L.C., & Wilce, L.S. (1986). The influence of spellings on speech: Are alveolar flaps /d/ or /t/? In D.B. Yaden & S. Templeton (Eds.), *Metalinguistic awareness and beginning literacy: Conceptualizing what it means to read and write* (pp. 101–114). Portsmouth, NH: Heinemann.

Frith, U. (1980). Unexpected spelling problems. In U. Frith (Ed.), *Cognitive processes in spelling* (pp. 495–516). New York: Academic Press.

Goldinger, S.D., & Azuma, T. (2003). Puzzle-solving science: The quixotic quest for units in speech perception. *Journal of Phonetics, 31*(3/4), 305–320. doi:10.1016/S0095-4470(03) 00030-5

Hebb, D.O. (1949). *The organization of behavior: A neuropsychological theory.* New York: John Wiley & Sons.

James, K.H. (2010). Sensori-motor experience leads to changes in visual processing in the developing brain. *Developmental Science, 13*(2), 279–288. doi:10.1111/j.1467-7687.2009 .00883.x

Katz, L., & Frost, S.J. (2001). Phonology constrains the internal orthographic representation. *Reading and Writing: An Interdisciplinary Journal, 14*(3/4), 297–332. doi:10.1023/A:1011165407770

Kemmerer, D., Castillo, J.G., Talavage, T., Patterson, S., & Wiley, C. (2008). Neuroanatomical distribution of five semantic components of verbs: Evidence from fMRI. *Brain and Language, 107*(1), 16–43. doi:10.1016/j.bandl.2007.09.003

Kronbichler, M., Bergmann, J., Hutzler, F., Staffen, W., Mair, A., Ladurner, G., et al.

(2007). Taxi vs. taksi: On orthographic word recognition in the left ventral occipitotemporal cortex. *Journal of Cognitive Neuroscience, 19*(10), 1584–1594. doi:10.1162/ jocn.2007.19.10.1584

Laxon, V., Gallagher, A., & Masterson, J. (2002). The effects of familiarity, orthographic neighbourhood density, letter-length and graphemic complexity on children's reading accuracy. *British Journal of Psychology, 93*(2), 269–287. doi:10.1348/000712602162580

Laxon, V., Masterson, J., Gallagher, A., & Pay, J. (2002). Children's reading of words, pseudohomophones, and other nonwords. *The Quarterly Journal of Experimental Psychology Section A, 55*(2), 543–565. doi:10.1080/02724980143000479

Lewkowicz, N.K. (1980). Phonemic awareness training: What to teach and how to teach it. *Journal of Educational Psychology, 72*(5), 686–700. doi:10.1037/0022-0663.72.5.686

Liberman, A.M., & Mattingly, I.G. (1989). A specialization for speech perception. *Science, 243*(4890), 489–494. doi:10.1126/ science.2643163

Liberman, I.Y., & Liberman, A.M. (1992). Whole language versus code emphasis: Underlying assumptions and their implications for reading instruction. In P.B. Gough, L.C. Ehri, & R. Treiman (Eds.), *Reading acquisition* (pp. 343–365). Hillsdale, NJ: Erlbaum.

Martin, A. (2007). The representation of object concepts in the brain. *Annual Review of Psychology, 58*, 25–45. doi:10.1146/annurev .psych.57.102904.190143

Martin, A., & Chao, L.L. (2001). Semantic memory and the brain: Structure and processes. *Current Opinion in Neurobiology, 11*(2), 194–201. doi:10.1016/S0959-4388(00)00196-3

Maurer, U., Brem, S., Bucher, K., & Brandeis, D. (2005). Emerging neurophysiological specialization for letter strings. *Journal of Cognitive Neuroscience, 17*(10), 1532–1552. doi:10.1162/089892905774597218

Maurer, U., Brem, S., Kranz, F., Bucher, K., Benz, R., Halder, P., et al. (2006). Coarse neural tuning for print peaks when children learn to read. *NeuroImage, 33*(2), 749–758 . doi:10.1016/j.neuroimage.2006.06.025

McCandliss, B.D., Cohen, L., & Dehaene, S. (2003). The visual word form area: Expertise for reading in the fusiform gyrus. *Trends in Cognitive Sciences, 7*(7), 293–299. doi:10.1016/ S1364-6613(03)00134-7

Morais, J. (2003). Levels of phonological representation in skilled reading and in learning to read. *Reading and Writing, 16*(1/2), 123–151. doi:10.1023/A:1021702307703

Murray, B.A. (1998). Gaining alphabetic insight: Is phoneme manipulation skill or identity knowledge causal? *Journal of Educational Psychology, 90*(3), 461–475. doi:10.1037/0022-0663.90.3.461

National Institute of Child Health and Human Development. (2000). *Report of the National Reading Panel. Teaching children to read: An evidence-based assessment of the scientific research literature on reading and its implications for reading instruction: Reports of the subgroups* (NIH Publication No. 00-4754). Washington, DC: U.S. Government Printing Office.

Olivetti Belardinelli, M., Palmiero, M., Sestieri, C., Nardo, D., Di Matteo, R., Londei, A., et al. (2009). An fMRI investigation on image generation in different sensory modalities: The influence of vividness. *Acta Psychologica, 132*(2), 190–200. doi:10.1016/j.actpsy.2009.06.009

Olson, D.R. (1994). *The world on paper: The conceptual and cognitive implications of writing and reading.* New York: Cambridge University Press.

Olson, D.R. (2009). A theory of reading/writing: From literacy to literature. *Writing Systems Research, 1*(1), 51–64. doi:10.1093/wsr/wsp005

Palmiero, M., Olivetti Belardinelli, M., Nardo, D., Sestieri, C., Di Matteo, R., D'Ausilio, A., & Romani, G.L. (2009). Mental imagery generation in different modalities activates sensory-motor areas. *Cognitive Processing, 10*(Suppl. 2), 268–271. doi:10.1007/s10339-009-0324-5

Perfetti, C.A. (1992). The representation problem in reading acquisition. In P.B. Gough, L.C. Ehri, & R. Treiman (Eds.), *Reading acquisition* (pp. 145–174). Hillsdale, NJ: Erlbaum.

Perfetti, C.A. (2007). Reading ability: Lexical quality to comprehension. *Scientific Studies of Reading, 11*(4), 357–383.

Perfetti, C.A., & Hart, L. (2001). The lexical basis of comprehension skill. In D.S. Gorfein (Ed.), *On the consequences of meaning selection: Perspectives on resolving lexical ambiguity* (pp. 67–86). Washington, DC: American Psychological Association.

Perfetti, C.A., & Hart, L. (2002). The lexical quality hypothesis. In L. Verhoeven, C. Elbro, & P. Reitsma (Eds.), *Precursors of functional literacy* (pp. 189–213). Philadelphia: John Benjamins.

Rack, J.P., Snowling, M.J., & Olson, R.K. (1992). The nonword reading deficit in developmental dyslexia: A review. *Reading Research Quarterly, 27*(1), 28–53. doi:10.2307/747832

Rayner, K. (1997). Understanding eye movements in reading. *Scientific Studies of Reading, 1*(4), 317–339. doi:10.1207/s1532799xssr0104_2

Rayner, K., & Pollatsek, A. (1989). *The psychology of reading.* Hillsdale, NJ: Erlbaum.

Rodd, J.M., Davis, M.H., & Johnsrude, I.S. (2005). The neural mechanisms of speech comprehension: fMRI studies of semantic ambiguity. *Cerebral Cortex, 15*(8), 1261–1269. doi:10.1093/cercor/bhi009

Rosenthal, J., & Ehri, L.C. (2008). The mnemonic value of orthography for vocabulary learning. *Journal of Educational Psychology, 100*(1), 175–191. doi:10.1037/0022-0663.100.1.175

Rosenthal, J., & Ehri, L.C. (2010). Pronouncing new words aloud during the silent reading of text enhances fifth graders' memory for vocabulary words and their spellings. *Reading and Writing.* doi:10.1007/s11145-010-9239-x

Roswell, F.G., Chall, J.S., Curtis, M.E., & Kearns, G. (2005). *Diagnostic assessments of reading* (2nd ed.). Rolling Meadows, IL: Riverside.

Sadoski, M. (2005). A dual coding view of vocabulary learning. *Reading & Writing Quarterly, 21*(3), 221–238. doi:10.1080/10573560590949359

Sandak, R., Mencl, W.E., Frost, S.J., & Pugh, K.R. (2004). The neurobiological basis of skilled and impaired reading: Recent findings and new directions. *Scientific Studies of Reading, 8*(3), 273–292. doi:10.1207/s1532799xssr0803_6

Schlaggar, B.L., & McCandliss, B.D. (2007). Development of neural systems for reading. *Annual Review of Neuroscience, 30*, 475–503. doi:10.1146/annurev.neuro.28.061604.135645

Seidenberg, M.S., & McClelland, J.L. (1989). A distributed, developmental model of word recognition and naming. *Psychological Review, 96*(4), 523–568. doi:10.1037/0033-295X.96.4.523

Seymour, P.H.K., Aro, M., & Erskine, J.M. (2003). Foundation literacy acquisition in European orthographies. *British Journal of Psychology, 94*(2), 143–174. doi:10.1348/000712603321661859

Shankweiler, D., Lundquist, E., Katz, L., Stuebing, K.K., Fletcher, J.M., Brady, S., et al. (1999). Comprehension and decoding: Patterns of association in children with reading difficulties. *Scientific Studies of Reading, 3*(1), 69–94. doi:10.1207/s1532799xssr0301_4

Share, D.L. (1995). Phonological recoding and self-teaching: *Sine qua non* of reading acquisition. *Cognition, 55*(2), 151–218. doi:10.1016/0010-0277(94)00645-2

Shaywitz, B.A., Shaywitz, S.E., Blachman, B.A., Pugh, K.R., Fulbright, R.K., Skudlarski, P., et al. (2004). Development of left occipitotemporal systems for skilled reading in children after a phonologically-based intervention. *Biological Psychiatry, 55*(9), 926–933. doi:10.1016/j.biopsych.2003.12.019

Shaywitz, B.A., Shaywitz, S.E., Pugh, K.R., Mencl, W.E., Fulbright, R.K., Skudlarski, P., et al. (2002). Disruption of posterior brain systems for reading in children with developmental dyslexia. *Biological Psychiatry, 52*(2), 101–110. doi:10.1016/S0006-3223(02)01365-3

Skjelfjord, V.J. (1976). Teaching children to segment spoken words as an aid in learning to read. *Journal of Learning Disabilities, 9*(5), 297–306. doi:10.1177/002221947600900507

Snow, C.E., Burns, M.S., & Griffin, P. (Eds.). (1998). *Preventing reading difficulties in young children*. Washington, DC: National Academy Press.

Swanson, H.L., Trainin, G., Necoechea, D.M., & Hammill, D.D. (2003). Rapid naming, phonological awareness, and reading: A meta-analysis of the correlation evidence. *Review of Educational Research, 73*(4), 407–440. doi:10.3102/00346543073004407

Temple, E., Deutsch, G.K., Poldrack, R.A., Miller, S.L., Tallal, P., Merzenich, M.M., et al. (2003). Neural deficits in children with dyslexia ameliorated by behavioral remediation: Evidence from functional MRI. *Proceedings of the National Academy of Sciences, 100*(5), 2860–2865. doi:10.1073/pnas.0030098100

Torgesen, J.K., Wagner, R.K., & Rashotte, C.A. (1999). *TOWRE: Test of word reading efficiency*. Austin, TX: PRO-ED.

Treiman, R. (1993). *Beginning to spell: A study of first-grade children*. New York: Oxford University Press.

Vandenberghe, R., Nobre, A.C., & Price, C.J. (2002). The response of the left temporal cortex to sentences. *Journal of Cognitive Neuroscience, 14*(4), 550–560. doi:10.1162/08989290260045800

Van den Broeck, W., Geudens, A., & van den Bos, K.P. (2010). The nonword-reading deficit of disabled readers: A developmental interpretation. *Developmental Psychology, 46*(3), 717–734. doi:10.1037/a0019038

Wechsler, D. (2005). *Wechsler individual achievement test* (2nd ed.). San Antonio, TX: Psychological Corporation.

Woodcock, R.W., McGrew, K.S., & Mather, N. (2001). *Woodcock-Johnson III tests of cognitive ability*. Itasca, IL: Riverside.

Ziegler, J.C., & Goswami, U. (2005). Reading acquisition, developmental dyslexia, and skilled reading across languages: A psycholinguistic grain size theory. *Psychological Bulletin, 131*(1), 3–29. doi:10.1037/0033-2909.131.1.3

Chapter 2

Eye Movements and Reading:
What Teachers Need to Know

S. Jay Samuels, Timothy V. Rasinski, and Elfrieda H. Hiebert

From time to time, students in teacher training programs express curiosity about the coursework they are required to take in preparation for being credentialed as teachers. Why, for example, as some students would like to know, are they being asked to take courses in child development or the psychology of reading? Why not simply take methods courses that focus directly on erasing the achievement gap in reading? In truth, this is an important question that the students are asking, because the answer to this question relates directly to how one prepares professionals in disciplines such as medicine, law, and education. Our best colleges of education are in the business of developing professionals. This being the case, what are the most important characteristics of a profession? The answer to this question is that to be considered a professional, it is assumed that the practitioner possesses a body of theoretical knowledge that can be used to assist in solving the problems encountered in pursuit of that profession. For example, if some students are unmotivated to learn in a classroom setting, is there a body of knowledge that the teacher can use to enhance student engagement with the learning process? Or, if despite the use of efficient reading methods, a student still has continued difficulty learning how to read, does the teacher have the theoretical knowledge necessary to diagnose the problem and resolve it? Highly educated teaching professionals understand the multifaceted nature of motivation and the complex nature of learning disability such that they can help students who are experiencing problems in learning.

Of equal importance to theoretical knowledge, it is assumed that the professionally trained teacher has mastered the applied skills required to help students achieve the instructional goals of the classroom. In today's educational marketplace, the demands placed on teachers have increased enormously, and it is becoming increasingly common to expect that every teacher will be able to move students along a skill trajectory that leads to

What Research Has to Say About Reading Instruction (4th ed.) edited by S. Jay Samuels and Alan E. Farstrup. © 2011 by the International Reading Association.

reading proficiency. To meet the increasing demands of the marketplace, teachers need to know more than which methods seem to work. They also need theoretical background knowledge that may prove to be useful as they work with students who are experiencing difficulty learning. For example, they should know how to motivate reluctant readers, and they need to know about the work of the eye in reading In addition, if there is a problem that relates to the eyes or faulty eye movements, teachers should be aware of the symptoms so that the problem can be identified and corrected. In essence, coursework that students take is designed to help them pursue their work with competency. Consequently, this chapter will explain the role of eye movements in reading and also explain what teachers can do to help students who are experiencing difficulties with the eye movements that are essential to the reading process.

Discovery of Eye Movements and Eye Physiology

We are all aware that over the course of history, humans have held many misconceptions that science has attempted to correct. For example, in the early 1600s, it was commonly thought that the earth was the center of the solar system. When Galileo, the famous physicist and astronomer, tried to correct this error by stating that it was actually the sun that was the center of the solar system, he was tried by the Inquisition, found vehemently guilty of heresy, forced to recant his views, and spent the rest of his life under house arrest. However, that event took place about four centuries ago. One need not go back that far in time to find more recent errors that needed correction. A little more than one hundred years ago, it was apparent to all observers that the human eyes glanced here, there, and everywhere, and it was thought that as the eyes moved across a scene, they were constantly taking in information and feeding this information to the brain.

This same line of reasoning was used in attempting to understand the reading process. It was thought that as the eyes moved across the line of print, they were constantly taking in information from the page and providing that information to the brain, which then analyzed the information for meaning. However, in 1879, Javal, a French scientist, made an important discovery. He found out that the commonly held belief about how the moving eye took in information was incorrect. Contrary to common belief, he noted that when reading a text or viewing a scene outdoors, the eyes did not continuously take in information as they moved across the visual field of the page or the outdoor scene. Instead, he observed that the eyes seemed to jump from spot to spot and paused at each spot where they jumped. He concluded correctly that the eyes took in information only when they paused and not when they were moving. He called these oculomotor eye movements *saccades.*

Almost 20 years later, Dodge (1900) supported Javal's conclusions by indicating that when the eye movements were unbroken the observer was unable to tell what had been exposed. In fact, before an eye movement occurs, vision is suppressed to prevent the reader from seeing the blur that occurs during a saccade (Latour, 1962). These oculomotor eye movements that take place while reading fall into three categories:

1. *Fixations*—These occur when the eye pauses momentarily on a line of print. During this pause, the information contained in the eye fixation is taken up and fed to the brain for analysis and meaning. However, it is also possible that during a fixation pause, information from several fixation pauses are interpreted for their meaning.

2. *Forward saccades*—Because English is written from left to right, the eyes jump from left to right on a line of print when reading English script. When coming to the end of a line of print, however, the eye movement drops down to the next line. It is important to note that the direction of eye movements when reading depends on what language the text is printed. When reading Hebrew or Arabic script, which is written from right to left, the eye movements are in the opposite direction compared with English.

3. *Backward saccades*—Backward eye motions may occur for different reasons. It would be unrealistic to think that the reading process would occur perfectly with excellent comprehension at each point in time. In reality, there are times when comprehension is difficult and rereading of the text is needed. In rereading English texts, these eye movements move backward and go from the right to the left. Rereadings typically go backward across several words and are primarily for the purpose of improving comprehension and sometimes for correcting faulty eye movements. Since all eye movements are muscular motions, they are subject to errors. Backward eye movements, termed *regressions,* occur to correct faulty eye movements that put the focal point in the wrong place, which impairs word recognition. Generally, regression goes backward about one word or less. Conversely, rereading allows the eye to reexamine a previously fixated portion of the text. In rereading, a student moves several words back to a prior section of a line and then proceeds to reread from that point forward as a comprehension check.

Instructional Implications of Eye Movements

Eye motions are a natural part of what humans do to observe a scene outdoors or read a text. A relatively recent discovery of how the eye processes the information on a printed page indicates that the information is taken in for processing only when the eye pauses during an eye fixation. To process all the information on a page, the eye must move rapidly from point to point to cover the page, and it is only when the eye pauses during an eye fixation that there is an uptake of information that is subsequently fed to the brain, where it is analyzed for meaning. Because the reading process does not always proceed smoothly, there are errors that must be corrected, which are of two types. One type of error takes place when the reader becomes aware of a comprehension difficulty, in which case there is a backward eye motion called *rereading*. Rereadings usually go backward several words. The other type of backward eye motion is termed *regression*. Regressions are used to correct faulty eye motions that place the point of focus in the wrong location, thus impairing word recognition, and the distance the eye moves in a backward direction is usually one word or less. Faulty eye movements that impair word recognition may occur with experienced as well as beginning readers, but regressions are far more common with beginning readers. Teachers should be aware of the fact that some beginning readers may be experiencing problems learning to read because of faulty eye motions.

As seen in Figure 2.1, the eye is remarkably similar to a camera. Reduced to its utmost simplicity, the eye's pupil consists of a hole through

Figure 2.1. The Human Eye

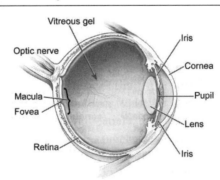

Note. From National Eye Institute, National Institutes of Health. (The figure and note are reprinted from "Eye Movements Make Reading Possible," by S.J. Samuels, E.H. Hiebert, & T.V. Rasinski, 2010, in E.H. Hiebert & D.R. Reutzel [Eds.], *Revisiting Silent Reading: New Directions for Teachers and Researchers* [p. 27], Newark, DE: International Reading Association.)

which light images from the page of print move. Behind the opening of the pupil is the lens, which focuses the images from the page toward the back of the eye onto the retina. Using the camera analogy, the retina contains the light-sensitive film, from which the visual information is transported along the optic nerve to the brain.

The major parts of the human eye consists of three parts: the cornea, the retina, and the optic nerve. The cornea, situated in the front of the eye, acts like a glass window and allows visual images from the printed page to pass through to settle on the retina. The retina contains cells, some of which are sensitive to letter and word shapes. Because the cells in the retina have different purposes, only some of them are capable of identifying letters and words. To make matters even more difficult with regard to recognition, the cells that are used for letter and word recognition are found in only a small part of the retina. The problems this poses will be discussed shortly. The optic nerve, which is a collection of communication wires, carry information from the retina to the brain.

The cornea of the eye contains a hole called the pupil through which visual information from the page passes through on its way to the retina. Surrounding the pupil is the iris, which is the colored portion that gives eyes their brown, black, blue, or green color. The iris also contains muscles that alter the size of the opening of the pupil so that under dim light, the opening of the pupil is larger to admit more light, and under bright light, the opening is smaller to admit less light. Located directly behind the pupil is the lens, whose purpose is to focus the visual images from the page as sharply as possible on the retina. The retinal cells function like the film in a camera. They collect the images and pass them on to the optic nerve, which then sends the visual information to different parts of the brain. Some specialized parts of the brain, in turn, control the oculomotor eye motions that we will discuss shortly.

Different Kinds of Retinal Cells

A key idea in this article is that the human eye is not ideally designed for reading, but one of the strategies used for overcoming its shortcomings is through eye motions. The major shortcoming of the eye with regard to reading is that in any eye fixation, only a small part of what is printed on the page is in focus on the retina. Imagine, for a moment, that you are trying to identify the person who is standing in front of you. As you look at this person, all that is in sharp focus is the person's nose and eyes. The rest is fuzzy, but you can detect shape. To identify the person, you rapidly shift your points of focus to other parts so that in time, the various parts of the individual's face and body are in sharp focus. The difficulty in determining the identity of this person is somewhat similar to the problem of recognizing words when reading a text.

The problem with the eye when reading is that at any given moment, only a tiny amount of printed material from a page is in sharp enough focus to enable easy reading. Consequently, rapid eye motions are required to bring different parts of a text onto that tiny area on the retina that can see the letters and words clearly. The area of the retina where the visual image is in sharp focus is known as the fovea. The retina contains two kinds of cells: rods and cones. Both kinds are important and have different reading functions. Cone cells provide the visual acuity that enables readers to see letters and words clearly.

A major design flaw of the eye for reading is that the cone cells, which enable the reader to see letters most clearly, are unevenly distributed across the retina and are concentrated in the fovea of each eye. There are about 10 million cone cells packed into the tiny fovea area, where vision is most acute. It is only in this small area of the fovea where the cone cells are packed together that the reader can identify words with the least effort. It is the quality of resolution of the letters that are the first consideration for word identification.

The rod cells of the retina also contribute to word recognition. These cells are situated outside of the fovea and serve a double function. They are sensitive to word shape and word length. Words that are printed in lowercase letters have characteristic shapes, or skylines, and skilled readers automatically use shape as one of the cues for word recognition. In addition to word shape, the other task performed by the rod cells is planning the distance to jump with each left-to-right forward eye saccade. In planning how far to move, the brain uses word length, which is determined by the white space that surrounds each word. At this point, we can ask, What is a word? So far as the brain is concerned for the purpose of calibrating what is a word to plan how far to jump, word meaning is not a relevant dimension. All the brain needs to know is that a word is a letter or group of letters surrounded by space.

Because of the importance of knowing how many letters that fall on the fovea are in sharp focus, we contacted two leaders in the field of eye movement research. Dr. Keith Rayner (personal communication, May 10, 2009) stated,

> The number of letters falling in the fovea depends on letter size and viewing angle. In general, 3–4 letters usually occupy 1 degree of visual

angle. Since the fovea is about 2 degrees, it would be 6–8 letters in the fovea.

The second expert, Dr. George McConkie (personal communication, May 10, 2009), stated,

> The foveal region is the area where we think visibility of letters drops off pretty fast as they move outward from the center of vision. Thus, the problem in answering this question is setting a "clarity" criterion. I suppose that a criterion might be: even the most similar letters can be distinguished at this distance.... What Keith and I were after in our original studies was to determine the region within which letter distinctions make a difference. We found this to be about 4 letters to the left and 8 to the right of the directly fixated letter. The greater distance on the right is probably (there is some supportive evidence) an attentional factor rather than retinal resolution differences to left and right.

Legge et al.'s (2007) research suggests that only six or seven letters surrounding the fixation point on the fovea can be identified with 80% accuracy, and as one moves farther away from the fixation point, accuracy of identification drops. For example, within four letter spaces to the left of the fixation point, or eight letter spaces to the right of the fixation point, accuracy of identification drops to about 60%. In summary, the evidence from the experts is that the size of the window from which letters can be seen with accuracy and clarity falls in a range of 6–8 letters. It also appears that the shape of the window is asymmetrical with fewer letters in focus to the left of fixation and more letters in focus to the right of fixation. It is also commonly acknowledged that there is a rapid drop-off of acuity from the point of visual focus that makes word recognition difficult (Feinberg, 1949).

The experts make a good point that there is no hard and fast rule about the number of letters that are in clear focus on the fovea, because it is a function of the letters' size and the distance at which they are being viewed. However, there is agreement that the number of letters in focus is not large. McConkie (personal communication, May 10, 2009) notes there is useful information that skilled readers can use that extends beyond the fovea, and that information source comes from the parafoveal region where the rod cells that can detect word shape and length are found. Rayner and Sereno (1994) agree that the parafoveal region surrounding the fovea can provide information that is useful for word recognition and planning the distance to be moved for the saccadic jumps as the eye moves from point to point. The fovea contains a concentration of cone cells that enables the eye to identify letters with clarity, while the parafoveal region contains the rod cells that are sensitive to word shape and word length information. Information received in the periphery of the eye helps guide the eye to its next eye fixation destination. In essence, the rod cells are part of the eye's guidance system. For skilled readers, word shape provides an additional cue to word recognition. The white spaces surrounding words are important clues as to word boundaries and length. Word length is established by the white space surrounding a word, and this information is used by peripheral vision to plan the distance the eye should jump with each saccade.

Instructional Implications

Unfortunately, the human eye is not ideally suited for the task of reading. Because the cone cells of the eye that allow sharp focus of letters and words are packed into such a tiny portion of the retina, the problem of how to make sense of what we look at extends to virtually everything we see, not just reading. Therefore, the strategy of using eye movements to allow an understanding of what one is viewing is used in all that we look at. According to the experts, the number of letters in sharp focus with each eye fixation is approximately 6–8 letters. It is clear to anyone who takes the time to count how many letters are in common English words we encounter when we read that the range of 6–8 letters in sharp focus would encompass most of the words printed on the page. Regrettably, however, there are also many words that we encounter when we read that are longer than this. Therefore, readers resort to an eye movement strategy that places all the letters in words in focus.

There are a number of clues that readers use in identifying a word. First, there is spelling information from each of the letters used in the word. For example, *going* is correctly spelled, whereas *gonig* is not. Second, there is information that comes from word shape when the words are printed in lowercase. This knowledge about word shape comes primarily from reading. The adage of "read more, read better" holds true in this case. In order for the eye to jump the proper distance, the student must know that a word is simply a letter or group of letters surrounded by space. Consequently, the white space surrounding words becomes an important cue that is used by the eye in calibrating how far to jump with each saccade.

There are several important questions about the work of the eyes in reading that have not yet been addressed, but they will be discussed shortly. One question pertains to the speed at which the eye fixations occur, and another relates to how much visual information from each word is processed with each fixation. As we shall see, the number of letters that are processed with each eye fixation is a product of how skilled the reader is and the frequency at which the word is encountered in reading.

The Fixation Pause

Before we embark on a more detailed description of the different eye movements used in reading, we shall describe a robust finding that sheds light on the word recognition process. What is interesting about this finding is that although the study was originally designed to test two competing explanations of how word identification takes place, in time the study led to a new way to conceptualize and measure reading fluency. Although most teachers would agree that fluency is one of the holy grails of reading instruction, unfortunately fluency has fallen on hard times because of the difficulties reading scholars have had in agreeing on a definition of *fluency* and the methods used in assessing it.

The controversy over how words are recognized actually began with Cattell (1885–1886/1947), who presented letters and words to graduate students in Wilhelm Wundt's lab in Leipzig, Germany. The purpose of the study was to find out what size visual unit was used in word recognition. Was it the single letters in words or the entire word? Cattell concluded from his studies that it was the entire word. His findings were used in the United States to resolve the instructional controversy of the day, the spelling method, in which students spelled a word before pronouncing it, or the look–say method, in which the students simply said the word without first spelling it. Cattell's report in favor of the whole word resolved the conflict for a while, and the look–say method became the method of choice. Years later, Gough (1972) stated in his classic description of the reading process, "One Second of Reading," that the size of the visual unit used in word recognition was the letter, and that each additional letter in a word added about 50 milliseconds of processing time to the recognition.

To test the competing explanations of word recognition, we designed a study in which students looked at a computer screen and, if the word they saw was an animal word, they had to press a button as quickly as possible. The computer then measured response accuracy and how much time it took to recognize the word as an animal word. The words the students saw varied in length from three to five letters. All the 3–5-letter animal words were controlled for word frequency. The logic for the study was simple: If Gough was correct, and the unit of word recognition was the letter, then longer words should take longer to recognize, and the shorter words should take less time. However, if Cattell was correct, and the visual unit used in word recognition was the word, then there should be no difference in processing time based on word length, since the unit size was the entire word, and a chunk is a chunk.

For this study, we used students from different grade levels: second, fourth, sixth, and college. All of the students received the same corpus of words. To our surprise, we found that both Cattell and Gough were correct, but only for a different group of students. The size of the visual unit used in word recognition by the college students and by the sixth graders was the entire word, so for these groups, Cattell was correct. For sixth graders and college students, long and short words were recognized in the same amount of time. However, for the second and fourth graders, the letter was the unit, and the longer words took longer to recognize. Looking at the word recognition process across grade levels, one might conclude that for beginning readers, the size of the visual unit used in word recognition was the letter or some unit smaller than the entire word. Yet, as reading skill developed over time and practice, the size of the visual unit increased so that by sixth grade and college, the unit of recognition was the entire word.

Over several years, modifications and improvements were made in the design of the study that tested what size visual unit is used in word recognition. The shortcoming of the original study was that the body of animal words used to test the size of the unit of recognition was very small. We wanted to test not only animal words but also other words in English. To achieve this goal, we changed the task and the instructions to the following: "If the word you see on the computer screen is a real word, press the button as quickly as you can." We used real words that varied in length from three to five letters, and all the words were of the same frequency. Even after changing the task, we got the same results. Less skilled readers used letter units smaller than the whole word as the unit of recognition, whereas the sixth graders and college students used the entire word as the unit.

This type of study was replicated in Taiwan with students who were reading Chinese words (Su, 2000). It is true that the Chinese orthography does not use alphabet letters, but their words vary in the number of strokes used to write each word. The researchers found that beginning readers in Chinese read stroke by stroke. The more strokes in a word, the longer it took to recognize it. However, the highly skilled readers were chunking the word as an entire visual unit, so the time to recognize a word was not related to the number of strokes or letters in the word, as they were in the United States.

One might wonder what the difference is in the process used to recognize words while reading between the second grader and the college student. With some justification, one might argue that the college student is a fluent reader, whereas the second grader is not. What exactly can a fluent reader do that the nonfluent reader cannot? Automaticity theory states that one is automatic at a skill such as reading if two complex things can be done at the same time. If two skills can be done at the same time, then at least one of them is automatic. The two complex skills that the fluent reader can do at the same time with a single eye fixation is decode (i.e., word recognition) and comprehend, whereas the nonfluent reader must do each task separately. The beginning reader uses all the cognitive capacity in word recognition and then must switch attention to comprehension, which is a two-step process that may require a second eye fixation, whereas the fluent reader can do both tasks at once.

Herein lies a dilemma: How can decoding and comprehension take place at the same time? Surely, decoding must precede comprehension. The dilemma is resolved when one considers the time sequence of what happens during an eye fixation. During a typical eye fixation for a fluent reader that lasts about 330 milliseconds, about one third of a second, two things get done in the time span of the fixation: decoding and comprehension, as seen in Figure 2.2. However, for the nonfluent

Figure 2.2. Activities That Take Place During an Eye Fixation by a Fluent Reader

---

|←0.10 sec: stabilize and focus, word recognition, and decoding→|

|←0.23 sec: comprehension and planning next saccade→|

|←   330 msec (about one third of a second): a single eye fixation   →|

---

reader, during that same 330 milliseconds time span, only one thing gets done: the decoding or word recognition. Then, the nonfluent reader must fixate the word again to comprehend it, completing the two-step process.

As just noted, the typical eye fixation pause lasts for about 330 milliseconds. This pause, however, can be separated into components representing the different processing tasks that must be performed to read with understanding (Abrams & Zuber, 1972).

Essentially, five tasks are performed with each fixation pause by a fluent reader. The typical pause comes at the end of an eye movement when the eye has just completed a rapid motion from one spot on a text to the next one, somewhat like an automobile that comes to an abrupt stop at a stop sign. In the case of the automobile, there is still residual motion that must be halted and stabilized, and in the case of the eye, it must be stabilized so that it can focus on the print.

1. *Stabilize*—The first task following a saccade is to stabilize the eye.

2. *Focus*—Once the eye is stabilized sufficiently, the next requirement is to focus the visual images from the page on the retina of the eye where the fovea is located.

3. *Decode*—Next, convert the word into its sound representation. With the visual image from the page focused on the retina, engage in word recognition, also known as the decoding process. If the reader is highly skilled and automatic at word recognition, the task is done quickly and accurately and requires minimal amounts of the cognitive resources and attention. While the typical duration of an eye fixation is approximately 0.33 second, if a person is a skilled reader, the amount of time required for the word recognition process may only require 0.10 second, leaving 0.23 second for comprehension.

4. *Word meaning and comprehension*—The defining characteristic of fluency is the ability to decode and comprehend in the same eye fixation. For skilled fluent readers, the decoding task is done quickly and requires so little of the cognitive resources that comprehension can take place at the same time (LaBerge & Samuels, 1974).

5. *Plan next saccade*—The final task for the reader is to plan where the next eye movement will be (Abrams & Jonides, 1988; Abrams & Zuber, 1972). Since this is a fluent reader, the usual unit of word

recognition is the word, which is surrounded by space. Space is a critical cue used by the rod cells in planning the trajectory for the next leap, which will probably be the next word.

If, however, the reader is not at the automatic stage of word recognition, there are some important differences in what happens during an eye fixation. First, for nonfluent readers, the word recognition process is usually slower, less accurate, and may use up all of the cognitive resources available at the moment. Thus, during that one eye fixation, the single major accomplishment for the nonfluent reader is word recognition. To add to the complexity of word recognition for the less than fluent reader, the unit of word recognition is smaller than the entire word, leaving the student in the position of having to piece together the letter clusters that make up the word. Since only 6–8 letters on the fovea are in sharp focus, along with some additional letters that spill off to the right that are not so distinct, the student may resort to selective attention to process the letter cluster. However, once the student has the word, the student's next task is to switch attention to the comprehension process. This constant switching of attention back and forth from decoding to comprehension places a heavy load on short-term memory and makes learning to read much harder for the less skilled reader than for the accomplished reader.

Figure 2.2 is an important visual, because it strikes at the heart of the debate on what is reading fluency. This figure shows that skilled readers can decode and comprehend what is in the text within an eye fixation. Unfortunately, beginning readers cannot do both tasks at the same time. Nonfluent readers first decode the text and then switch attention and try to comprehend what they have decoded. The products of the dual process are stored briefly in short-term memory, but the decoding–comprehension process must be completed within the 10-second duration of that short-term memory system, or what was briefly stored will be lost. If the beginning reader loses what was stored, the student simply repeats the process. On the second attempt, the process is faster, having worked through the text previously.

There is supporting evidence from another source showing that for the nonfluent reader, the size of the unit used in word recognition is smaller than the entire word, whereas for the fluent reader, the unit used is the word. Taylor (1971) had students from grades 1–12 read 100-word passages silently for meaning. While the students read, eye cameras recorded the number of eye fixations for the passage. First graders had 224 eye fixations, which meant that with each fixation, they processed only 0.45 word. The 12th graders, however, needed only 96 fixations. Thus, each fixation for these fluent readers encompassed more than a single word.

Instructional Implications

One way to define *reading fluency* is to state that the fluent reader can decode and comprehend during the time span of a single eye fixation. In order for the cognitive resources of the student to be able to do the two tasks during the eye fixation, the decoding task must be automatic. This automaticity of decoding comes about only after a long period of reading practice. Therefore, the student must be motivated to be a reader. Again, read more, read better holds true.

By now, it should be clear that eye movements are essential to overcome the problems created by the fact that the cone cells that can see letters and words clearly are located in only a tiny portion of the retina. To see all the words on the page clearly, the eye must dart about the page in a systematic fashion. Different kinds of cells on the retina have different functions. The rod cells are sensitive to word shape and word length. Word length is determined by the white space surrounding each word. In the history of writing, words as we know them today did not exist. It was not until medieval times that spaces were used to demark words, and the space information is used by the eye to plan how far to move the eye with each movement. Thus, with regard to how eye physiology influences reading instruction, it is essential that students know that, so far as planning the trajectory of how far the eye should move for a saccade, a word is defined simply as a letter or group of letters surrounded by space.

Eye fixations in reading are critical, because it is during the fixation pause that the eye takes in information from the printed page and begins to process it for meaning. The duration of the typical fixation pause is about 300 milliseconds, but pauses can be as short as 100 milliseconds or as long as 500 milliseconds. It is assumed that during these longer fixation pauses, considerable cognitive processing is going on, such as attempting to grasp the meaning of a sentence or integrating information across several sentences. Although the term *fixation pause* implies that the eye is motionless, this is not actually the case. There is a slight eye tremor, the purpose of which is to activate the neurons in the retina, so they will continue firing (Gilbert, 1959). Even taking into account the rather brief amount of time it takes to make a forward saccade, in which the eye moves from one fixation pause to the next, in the space of a single second, the eye can make approximately three fixations. When viewing a scene or a page of printed material, the typical person seems to be unaware that the information being processed by the brain has been coming in at a rate of three bursts a second, and each information burst must be processed rapidly, because the visual image coming with each burst survives for less than a second and is then lost. If, however, the processing is too slow, and the visual image disappears from the retina, all is not lost, because the reader can refixate the original image. This tendency to refixate an image that is lost has led to new scientific terminology. The term *eye fixation pause* represents the time spent on a single fixation, whereas the term *gaze duration* suggests the total amount of time the reader spends on a word across several eye fixations.

Because of the rapid loss of the visual image from a fixated word or word part, the reader must transform the visual image into its sound representation. For example, when the reader encounters the printed word *cat*, it is transformed into its phonological form /c a t/ and then placed in short-term memory. The advantage gained by transferring visual into phonological information and placing the phonological information in short-term memory is that the shelf life of the acoustical information in short-term memory is about 10 seconds, which is considerably longer than the duration of visual information, which is about 1 second (Peterson & Peterson, 1959). For the acoustical information that is in short-term memory, 10 seconds is usually sufficient time in most cases for skilled readers to complete tasks such as decoding the text, integrating sentence meaning, and moving the information that was temporarily stored in short-term memory into long-term semantic memory. This need to transform the visual form of words into their phonological representations has led linguists such as Fries (1962) to define *reading* as a mapping problem, in which the reader must learn to map the printed word onto its oral-phonological-auditory representation. According to Fries, once the visual word is transferred into its spoken representation, understanding text is akin to listening to speech in one's head.

Since eye physiology is such that the eye takes in different kinds of information from three different areas, foveal, parafoveal, or peripheral, the total span of information is rather large. Beginning readers have a span of apprehension that is 12 letters to the right, and skilled readers have a span of 15 spaces. However, one should not assume that words can be recognized that far out, although word length and shape information is obtained (Ikeda & Saida, 1978; Rayner, 1998). Foveal information enables one to identify words, while the parafoveal area provides information on shape and length (Rayner, Well, & Pollatsek, 1986). McConkie and Rayner (1976) have shown that as skill increases, the span of recognition increases, but not beyond one or two words.

To the person reading a text or viewing a scene outdoors, the entire operation appears to be seamless, and it is the seamless nature of the operation that led to the mistaken belief before Javal's time that the eye continuously took in information as it swept across a page of print. In terms of transfer of training, it seems as if several of the eye motion mechanisms used in viewing a scene outdoors are also used in reading a text. For example, regardless of whether one is viewing an outdoor scene or reading a text, virtually no information is taken in during the saccade while the eye is in motion, and it is only during the fixation pause that the brain gathers information for processing. The number of fixation pauses per second for viewing a scene outdoors is about the same as for reading a text (Taylor & Robinson, 1963), about three fixations per second. Since beginning readers may not be able to recognize a word or parts of a word that they are focusing on during a single fixation, they may have to refixate the target word more than once to recognize it.

With each eye fixation when reading, the number of letters that fall on the fovea that can be seen clearly comes to about four or five letters (Feinberg, 1949), which easily encompasses the number of letters in a high-frequency word. If the reader is skilled, and the unit of word recognition is the word, in the space of one second, a good reader should be able to process 3 words per second, and in one minute, the reader should be able to read at a rate of about 180 words a minute with comprehension, which is a little on the shy side of the figure that Germane and Germane (1922) reported as the silent reading rate for good readers in eighth grade.

An important question that eye movement researchers have addressed is whether the eye fixates on each word in a text or skips certain words.

It appears that the eye will skip certain words, and the words that tend to be skipped are determined, in part, by word length. Short words such as *the, a,* and *of,* for example, tend to be skipped most often, because they are not critical to understanding (Brysbaert & Vitu, 1998). Additionally, high-frequency words and words that can be predicted from context may be skipped (Paulson & Goodman, 1999).

Gilbert (1940, 1959) noted that oral reading is slower than silent reading. This simple fact poses a problem in many classrooms where round-robin reading is practiced. With the round-robin reading system, one student reads orally from a text while the others follow along, reading silently from the same text. However, when a poor reader reads orally, with typical slow reading rate and lack of expression, it forces the better readers who are reading silently into twice as many eye fixations and regressions. Gilbert's concern was that the round-robin reading practice was training poor oculomotor habits in students. He cautioned teachers that this common practice should be discontinued, which left them in a quandary. Of course, teachers had no desire to train students in poor eye movement habits, but they monitored students' progress by having them read orally. If one follows Gilbert's admonition and discontinues using round-robin reading, how can a teacher do progress monitoring without training poor eye movement habits in children?

Deno's (1986) brilliant solution to progress monitoring was to have students read orally for one minute and to count the number of correct words read in that brief period. By keeping a running record on each student's reading rate over a period of time, teachers could determine if there was consistent improvement in rate up to some asymptote. As good as Deno's method is, there is the problem that comprehension is not measured, only rated. Despite warnings that meaning should not be sacrificed for the sake of reading rate, some teachers continue this practice. Because of the problems associated with just using reading rate as the yardstick for measuring progress, the time has come for researchers to develop a testing method that will focus attention on comprehension as well as reading speed.

During an eye fixation, exactly what part of the word the eye is focused on is important if the reader wants to infer the word using only partial information. Different parts of a word vary in the amount of information they provide the reader. Broerse and Zwaan (1966) found, for example, that not all parts of a word are equally informative for purposes of word recognition. If a word is separated into its beginning, middle, and end, they found that it is the beginning part that carries the most information for purposes of word recognition. For example, if the reader has identified the context in "Father was cutting the green," and the letter string on the fovea for the next eye fixation begins with "gr," then it is an easy task to infer that the next word is "grass." Paulson and Goodman (1999) believe that under certain conditions, the reader may skip words in a text and, if context is strong enough, may use partial information to infer the word. However, as Taylor (1971) states, "Though the average span for a given reader is calculated to be a fraction of a word or one or two words... it is not probable that a reader attempts to apprehend words in fractional parts." However, as Paulson and Goodman report, there are times when words are inferred and recognized through their parts. In planning an eye movement, the preferred location for a fixation is halfway between the beginning and middle of a word (McConkie, Kerr, Reddex, & Zola, 1988), because given the span of apprehension and the typical length of common words, the highly informative beginning of a word would be on the fovea.

An important question about the role of eye fixations in reading is to consider how much information is taken in and processed with each fixation pause. The answer is that the eye provides the brain with information from three areas: the fovea, the parafoveal region, and the peripheral region. Although all three regions are important, the foveal information is most important, because it is here that the letters that fall across the fovea are in sharp focus. The foveal area extends two degrees of visual angle for a maximum of eight letter spaces asymmetrically distributed about the point of focus, with fewer letters in focus to the left of fixation and more to the right (McConkie & Rayner, 1976). Yet, as Feinberg (1949) noted, beyond 4–5 letter spaces from the fixation point, there is a sharp drop-off of clarity. However, for skilled readers, the amount of information that is available in a single eye fixation is usually sufficient to permit rapid identification of the word.

Although the parafoveal and peripheral regions do not provide sharp, detailed information, they nevertheless provide important information in a number of ways. There is word length information (e.g., short words may be skipped), which is provided by the white space boundaries that skilled readers use in the decoding process. There is also word shape information. Words printed in lowercase have a characteristic shape, or skyline, that aids word recognition. In addition, the white space surrounding words is used in planning the trajectory for the next saccade.

The division of printed words by spaces is a relatively recent invention that turns out to be a useful cue to readers. Gaur (1992) has stated that the division of words and sentences developed only gradually, and these changes occurred between 600 and 800 AD. The scribes who wrote the texts were so well versed that they did not need any aids as to word boundaries. It was not until about the year 1200 that monks preparing medieval manuscripts began to include spaces, so readers who were less skilled could determine where the word boundaries were, and it is this very word boundary information that is used today when the brain plans the next saccade. If the saccadic movement is incorrect, and the eye overshoots the target, the flow of meaningful information can be interrupted, and the reader may have to self-correct by means of regressive eye movements. To illustrate how difficult reading becomes when word shape and length information are eliminated, try reading the following text:

ONLYRECENTLYHAVEEYEMOVEMENTSANDEYE
FIXATIONSBEENRECOGNIZEDFORWHATTHEYREALLY
ARETHEYAREUSEDINTHEWORDRECOGNITIONPROCESS

Just as the duration of eye fixations varies as a function of reader skill, with skilled readers requiring less time per fixation, so too does the number of eye fixations reflect reader skill. From Taylor's (1971) research, we learned that to read a 100-word text, first graders needed 224 eye fixations, and 12th graders needed only 94 fixations. There are yet other factors that should influence eye fixations. For example, how do the goals of the reader influence eye movements? At times, the goals may be to study a text carefully to pass an exam, while at other times, the reader only desires a casual, surface-level overview of a text. Surely, we might wonder how these differences in goals for reading will influence visual factors such as duration of eye fixations, span of apprehension, the distribution of attention over the text, the length of a saccade, and regressions.

Regressions and Rereading

To advance through an English text from beginning to end, the direction of eye fixation motion moves from the left to the right. However, there are eye fixations when reading English texts that move in the opposite direction, from the right to the left. Fixations following right-to-left eye movements, excluding return sweeps from one line of print to the next, may be considered regressions. Some scholars differentiate between regressions and rereading (Taylor, 1971). Taylor believes that some unnecessary regressions that serve no purpose may reflect poor habits formed during the learning-to-read stage, and these inefficient habits may persist for long periods of time. Other regressions, however, may be purposeful and indicate that the reader has encountered an unanticipated word and is going back to do a comprehension check.

Regression may occur for any number of reasons. For example, in the earliest stages of learning to read, the student must learn how to adjust the accuracy of each eye movement, and at times, the trajectory of the forward eye fixation is faulty, requiring a regression to overcome the error. Regressions may also simply reflect poor reading habits that were formed during round-robin reading, when better readers try to follow the oral reading of a less fluent student. Large numbers of regressions may also reflect the decoding problems of readers who need to return to previous portions of a text to ensure the accuracy of what they have decoded. Or, in the case of skilled readers reading a difficult text, the regressions may reflect what good readers do when they attempt to ensure that they understand the passage they are reading: They return to a previously read portion of the text to do a comprehension check.

Taylor's (1971) research uncovered sizable differences in the number of regressive eye fixations made as a function of reading skill. For example, Taylor found that for every 100 words read, the first-grade students made 52 regressions, whereas the 12th grade students had only 17 regressive eye movements. How does one account for this large difference in backward eye movements between the unskilled and the skilled readers? The research literature on eye movements suggests two possible reasons for regressions. First, poor habits are acquired in the early grades and are then overcome to some extent with increased skill in the later grades. The second reason for regressions acknowledges the need for comprehension checks which may require regressions. Still another reason to regress may occur when the eye misses its mark during a saccade, and the reader tries to adjust by a regressive eye correction.

In addition to these reasons for a regression, we suggest another possibility. When beginning readers attempt to construct meaning from the text, they engage in a two-step process; first, they decode the words, and then they attempt to get the words' meanings. During this two-step process, the decoded words or word parts are moved to short-term memory, where they are held for 10 seconds before they are lost. Once lost, the reader must start the process over again. Speed is of the essence in this process. We have all noticed during oral reading how beginning readers will laboriously work their way through a sentence, stop, and then regress back to an earlier section of text and start over again. What has happened is the student took too long, got timed out, and what was temporarily stored in short-term memory was lost Therefore, the student had to regress and start over.

By the time students reach college, the number of eye regressions is only 17% per 100 words read, but for first graders, it is 52%. Not only do less skilled readers make more backward regressive eye movements, but also the duration of each eye fixation is longer, which accounts in part for the slower reading speeds of the less skilled readers. Text difficulty also influences eye movements in several ways. Increases in text difficulty are usually accompanied by increases in the duration of the fixation pause, the unfamiliar low-frequency words in the text are fixated longer, the distance the eye moves with each saccade decreases, and more regressions occur as more comprehension checks are needed.

Forward Saccades

When reading English, forward saccades are characterized by eye movement jumps that move from left to right. During an eye movement, vision is suppressed, because the movement is so fast that the brain cannot process the information. The amount of time required to move the eye from fixation to fixation requires only 0.20 second. The distance the eye moves in each forward saccade ranges between 1 and 20 letter spaces, with the average being 4–5 characters, or the length of a shorter word. It would appear, then, that for skilled readers, for whom the unit of word recognition is the word, the eye jumps from word to word. For skilled readers, what controls the distance the eye jumps with each saccade are the rod cells that are sensitive to the white spaces that mark word boundaries. Ideally, the saccade would place the image of the word so that the letters are spread across the fovea of the eye where letters are in sharpest focus. As we move away from the focal point, clarity of the letters decreases, and in less than 10 letter spaces out from the point of fixation, visual acuity has dropped by 45%, and ease of word recognition becomes more of a problem (Feinberg, 1949; Legge et al., 2007). Consequently, as Rayner (1983) states, the planning of how far to move the eye with a forward saccade is critically important.

It is by means of the forward eye movements that the reader is able to advance through a text from its beginning to its end, but as important as the forward eye movements are, they exact a heavy price. They slow down reading speed and impair comprehension. It has been shown, for example, that when readers look at a point on a computer screen, and all the words from a text are presented one at a time to that point, very high rates of reading accompanied by modest comprehension can be obtained, with rates that range between 700 to 1,000 words per minute. However, this procedure, which requires no eye movements, embodies a serious problem. It prevents the reader from making regressions that are essential for comprehension checks (Rayner & Pollatsek, 1989).

Rayner and Pollatsek (1989) make an important point that advances our understanding of reading fluency. They state that each forward eye movement ends with an eye fixation. During the eye fixation, one of the primary goals is to decode the words that are on the fovea of the retina. Yet, the researchers also raise the possibility that during that single eye fixation, more is taking place than only decoding. They raise the possibility that parallel process is taking place, such that in addition to word recognition during the eye fixation pause, the reader is also processing meaning. Nonfluent readers cannot decode and process meaning at the same time, because a significant amount of their cognitive resources are used simply to get the decoding task done (LaBerge & Samuels, 1974).

In summary of this section on eye movements, by means of several kinds of eye movements (i.e., forward saccades, regressions, fixations), readers are able to overcome the limitations presented by the fact that in any given instant, the eye can only see with clarity about one short word, or eight letter spaces, at a time. In the next section, we will examine some of the problems that readers experience with eye motions.

Indicators of Eye Problems in Reading

We take the position that oculomotor deficiencies can contribute to reading problems for inexperienced as well as more experienced readers. Certainly, lack of visual acuity for distance viewing can be picked up through Snellen eye charts and corrected through properly fitted glasses, but the charts are not useful for detecting problems in close-up viewing, which is required in reading. One of the more persistent sources of difficulty in reading is the tracking problem, in which readers have difficulty maintaining the focus of the eye on a line of print that is being processed. Some readers with a tracking problem may actually skip entire lines. This problem is not limited to the beginning reader, as many experienced readers share this problem. Although loss of place on a line can occur at any location, it is most commonly encountered at the end of a line when the line of print extends across an entire page. The longer the line, the more difficult it is to keep one's place. In fact, the tendency to lose one's place because of long stretches of text across the page led many newspapers across the country in the 1950s to adopt the practice of using rather narrow columns of text as a way to reduce tracking problems (Tinker, 1958). A simple way to help beginning readers maintain proper focus on the line of print is to slide a blank index card under the line that is being read.

Binocular coordination is essential for efficiency in reading. However, with some individuals, each eye may not always fixate on the same letter during reading. Ideally, each eye should coordinate with the other, and both eyes should work as a team. When both eyes are working properly, we have binocular coordination. With some individuals, however, the eyes fail to coordinate, and the reader must expend considerable effort while reading. Lack of coordination can become so disruptive that the individual closes one eye and reads only from the preferred eye. When there is a lack of binocular coordination, the effort it takes to read may become so great that the individual avoids reading whenever possible. Teachers should look for indicators of lack of binocular coordination, as in students who seem to be reading from one eye or avoid reading altogether. Lack of binocular coordination may show up as double images of the words on the page, and the visual disturbance leads to increases in the number of eye fixations combined with increases in the duration of the fixation pauses. An excessive number of eye fixations can only be identified with the use of eye motion devices such as the visagraph. Adults who have faulty binocular coordination also report that when driving, they may see two cars, one to the left and one to the right, when in fact there is only one automobile. Therefore, they have to figure out which of the car images is the real one.

A somewhat related eye problem is known as convergence insufficiency, which occurs when the ability of the eyes to converge and focus properly is compromised. When reading, it is necessary for the eyes to turn inward toward each other as well as focus on the letters of the words being read., If convergence insufficiency occurs, the student may report blurred or double vision, headaches when trying to read, burning of the eyes, and excessive tearing.

Before leaving this topic of visual problems that may impede reading progress, we want to identify indicators that educators can use to identify readers with possible underlying oculomotor problems that may require professional intervention outside of school, especially if in addition to the following symptoms, the individual is having difficulty with reading (Taylor & Solan, 1959):

- Reports visual discomfort

- Is willing to read only for short periods of time

- Eyes burn or fill with tears when reading

- Has headaches when reading

- Frequently loses place in a line of text

- Words seem blurred or fuzzy

- Has difficulty concentrating when reading or desires escape from reading

- Reports seeing double

- Uses finger to keep track in a line of text

- Frequently omits words when reading orally

- Has one eye that drifts or points in a different direction from the other eye

- Squints or closes one eye or covers one eye with hand while reading

A Brief Summary

Eye movements are characteristic components of all vision and are an essential component of the reading process. In fact, without eye movements, visual reading could not take place. The physiology of the eye that makes eye movements essential to reading is that the cells of the eye that are sensitive to letter and word identification are located in only a tiny portion of the retina. Thus, the focus of the eye must be moved about to different parts of the page to bring all the words of interest into sharp focus. There are three kinds of oculomotor reading behaviors: eye fixations, forward movements, and backward movements. The speed at which these movements occur is so fast that these movements may be easily overlooked. The visual units used in word recognition depend in large measure on the skill of the reader. The units and cues used in word recognition consist of individual letters, digraphs, whole words, word shape, and word length. Some beginning reading problems may be linked to faulty eye movements, and this article identifies many of their indicators. Like all aspects of skill development, practice is essential, and reading must be practiced to get good at it.

Questions for Reflection

1. Why are eye movements an essential component of reading from a text?

2. There is reliable evidence that the size of the visual unit used in word recognition increases as reading skill improves. What are the instructional implications of this finding?

3. What are the indicators that teachers should be aware of that students may be experiencing difficulty with their eyes or eye movement, and what can teachers do to help students overcome these problems?

REFERENCES

Abrams, R.A., & Jonides, J. (1988). Programming saccadic eye movements. *Journal of Experimental Psychology: Human Perception and Performance, 14*(3), 428–443.

Abrams, S.G., & Zuber, B.L. (1972). Some temporal characteristics of information processing during reading. *Reading Research Quarterly, 8*(1), 40–51.

Broerse, A.C., & Zwaan, E.J. (1966). The information value of initial letters in the identification of words. *Journal of Verbal Learning and Verbal Behavior, 5*(5), 441–446. doi:10.1016/S0022-5371(66)80058-0

Brysbaert, M., & Vitu, F. (1998). Word skipping: Implications for theories of eye movement control in reading. In G. Underwood (Ed.), *Eye guidance in reading and scene perception* (pp. 125–147). New York: Elsevier. doi:10.1016/B978-008043361-5/50007-9

Cattell, J.M. (1947). On the time required for recognizing and naming letters and words, pictures, and colors. In A.T. Poffenberger (Ed.), *James McKeen Cattell, 1860–1944: Man of science. Vol. 1: Psychological research* (pp. 13–25). Lancaster, PA: Science Press. (Original work published 1885–1886)

Deno, S.L. (1986). Formative evaluation of individual student programs: A new role for school psychologists. *School Psychology Review, 15*(3), 358–374.

Dodge, R. (1900). Visual perception during eye movement. *Psychological Review, 7*(5), 454–465. doi:10.1037/h0067215

Feinberg, R. (1949). A study of some aspects of peripheral visual acuity: Part I. *American Journal of Optometry and Archives of American Academy of Optometry, 26*(2), 49–56.

Fries, C.C. (1962). *Linguistics and reading.* New York: Holt, Rinehart and Winston.

Gaur, A. (1992). *A history of writing* (Rev. ed.). New York: Cross River Press.

Germane, C.E., & Germane, E.G. (1922). *Silent reading: A handbook for teachers.* Chicago: Row, Peterson & Co.

Gilbert, L.C. (1940). Effect on silent reading of attempting to follow oral reading. *The Elementary School Journal, 40*(8), 614–621. doi:10.1086/457813

Gilbert, L.C. (1959). Saccadic movements as a factor in visual perception in reading. *Journal of Educational Psychology, 50*(1), 15–19. doi:10.1037/h0040752

Gough, P.B. (1972). One second of reading. In J.F. Kavanaugh & I.A. Mattingly (Eds.), *Language by ear and by eye: The relationships between speech and reading* (pp. 331–358). Cambridge, MA: MIT Press.

Ikeda, M., & Saida, S. (1978). Span of recognition in reading. *Vision Research, 18*(1), 83–88. doi:10.1016/0042-6989(78)90080-9

Javal, L.E. (1879). *Essai sur la physiologie de la lecture* [Essay on the physiology of reading]. *Annales d'Oculistique, 82*, 242–253.

LaBerge, D., & Samuels, S.J. (1974). Toward a theory of automatic information processing in reading. *Cognitive Psychology, 6*(2), 293–323. doi:10.1016/0010-0285(74)90015-2

Latour, P.L. (1962). Visual threshold during eye movements. *Vision Research, 2*(7/8), 261–262. doi:10.1016/0042-6989(62)90031-7

Legge, G.E., Cheung, S., Yu, D., Chung, S.T.L., Lee, H., & Owens, D.P. (2007). The case for the visual span as a sensory bottleneck in reading. *Journal of Vision, 7*(2), 1–15. doi:10.1167/7.2.9

McConkie, G.W., Kerr, P.W., Reddix, M.D., & Zola, D. (1988). Eye movement control during reading: I. The location of initial eye fixations on words. *Vision Research, 28*(10), 1107–1118. doi:10.1016/0042-6989(88)90137-X

McConkie, G.W., & Rayner, K. (1976). Asymmetry of the perceptual span in reading. *Bulletin of the Psychometric Society, 8*(5), 365–368.

Paulson, E., & Goodman, K. (1999). Eye movements and miscue analysis: What do the eyes do when a reader makes a miscue? *Southern Arizona Review, 1*, 55–62.

Peterson, L., & Peterson, M.J. (1959). Short-term retention of individual verbal items. *Journal of Experimental Psychology, 58*(3), 193–198. doi:10.1037/h0049234

Rayner, K. (1983). *Eye movements in reading: Perceptual and language processes.* New York: Academic Press.

Rayner, K. (1998). Eye movements in reading and information processing: 20 years of research. *Psychological Bulletin, 124*(3), 372–422. doi:10.1037/0033-2909.124.3.372

Rayner, K., & Pollatsek, A. (1989). *The psychology of reading.* Hillsdale, NJ: Erlbaum.

Rayner, K., & Sereno, S.C. (1994). Eye movements in reading: Psycholinguistic studies. In M.A. Gernsbacher (Ed.), *Handbook of psycholinguistics* (pp. 57–81). San Diego, CA: Academic Press.

Rayner, K., Well, A.D., & Pollatsek, A. (1986). Asymmetry of the effective visual field in reading. *Perception & Psychophysics, 27*(6), 537–544.

Su, Y.F. (2000). Units of Chinese character recognition: The development of automaticity in character recognition. Tapei, National Science Council, (NSC. Publication NSC 89-2413-H-003-F18)

Taylor, S.E. (1971). *The dynamic activity of reading: A model of the process* (Research and Information Bulletin No. 9). Huntington, NY: Educational Developmental Laboratories.

Taylor, S.E., & Robinson, A.H. (1963, February). *The relationship of the oculo-motor efficiency of the beginning reader to his success in learning to read.* Paper presented at the annual meeting of the American Educational Research Association.

Taylor, E., & Solan, H. (1959). *Functional Readiness Questionnaire for School and College Students.* New York: Reading and Study Skills Center.

Tinker, M.A. (1958). Recent studies of eye movements in reading. *Psychological Bulletin, 55*(4), 215–231. doi:10.1037/h0041228

Chapter 3

Essential Elements of Fostering and Teaching Reading Comprehension

Nell K. Duke, P. David Pearson, Stephanie L. Strachan, and Alison K. Billman

If learning to read effectively is a journey toward ever-increasing ability to comprehend texts, then teachers are the tour guides, ensuring that students stay on course, pausing to make sure they appreciate the landscape of understanding, and encouraging the occasional diversion down an inviting and interesting cul-de-sac or byway. The evidence for this role is impressive. In one study, some teachers of first-grade students in a high-poverty school district got 80% of their students to grade level in reading comprehension by the end of the year, while others in the same school district got only 20% of their students to grade level (Tivnan & Hemphill, 2005). In another study, Taylor, Pearson, Peterson, and Rodriguez (2003) found that second through fifth graders showed dramatically different rates of growth in reading comprehension over the course of the school year, depending on their teacher and the specific practices in which he or she engaged. Teachers can even overcome disadvantages in reading comprehension that students bring to school. For example, Snow, Barnes, Chandler, Goodman, and Hemphill (1991) found that students whose home environments were poor with respect to promoting reading comprehension development nonetheless made adequate progress in reading comprehension if they had strong teachers of reading comprehension for two consecutive years. If otherwise similar students had a strong comprehension teacher for only one year, only 25% made adequate progress, and none of the students who experienced two years of poor comprehension instruction overcame the effects of poor support for reading comprehension development at home. In sum, teachers matter, especially for complex cognitive tasks like reading for understanding.

What Research Has to Say About Reading Instruction (4th ed.) edited by S. Jay Samuels and Alan E. Farstrup. © 2011 by the International Reading Association.

So, what makes successful teachers of reading comprehension successful? What goes into reading comprehension instruction that works for a broad range of students? In this chapter, we focus on 10 essential elements of effective reading comprehension instruction that research suggests every teacher should engage in to foster and teach reading comprehension:

1. Build disciplinary and world knowledge.

2. Provide exposure to a volume and range of texts.

3. Provide motivating texts and contexts for reading.

4. Teach strategies for comprehending.

5. Teach text structures.

6. Engage students in discussion.

7. Build vocabulary and language knowledge.

8. Integrate reading and writing.

9. Observe and assess.

10. Differentiate instruction.

These practices should be implemented within a gradual release of responsibility model, incrementally turning over responsibility for meaning-making practices from teacher to student, then cycling back through this release with increasingly complex texts, while simultaneously employing instructional approaches that include several essential elements of effective comprehension instruction. To understand why these 10 elements are essential to fostering and teaching reading comprehension, we must understand the nature of reading comprehension itself. We must understand how skilled comprehenders construct meaning, so we can help students learn to construct meaning in the same way. Thus, the first section of this chapter discusses theory and research about the nature of reading comprehension. Next, we address each of the 10 essential elements, providing specific examples of how each can be enacted in classrooms and identifying the research base that supports those enactments. Finally, we end with future directions for research and development in reading comprehension and a tool for evaluating your own fostering and teaching of reading comprehension.

How Skilled Comprehenders Construct Meaning

Over the past 20 years, cognitive psychologists have reached broad consensus on the nature of comprehension. Of all the current models of comprehension, Kintsch's (1998, 2004) Construction–Integration model is recognized as the most complete and fully developed. His model shares a lot in common with the older but more popular schema theory model (see R.C. Anderson & Pearson, 1984), in that both models carve out a central role for readers' prior knowledge in the comprehension process. In both schema theory and the Construction–Integration model, a virtuous (the opposite of a vicious) cycle drives the process: We bring knowledge to the comprehension process, and that knowledge shapes our comprehension. When we comprehend, we gain new information that changes our knowledge, which is then available for later comprehension. So, in that positive, virtuous cycle, knowledge begets comprehension, which begets knowledge, and so on. In a very real sense, we literally read and learn our way into greater knowledge about the world and greater comprehension capacity.

The two terms in the name of Kintsch's (1998) model, *construction* and *integration*, are both crucial in the comprehension process. When we read, we use our knowledge along with our perceptions of what we think the text says to literally build, or construct, mental representations of what the text means. Once those representations are constructed, we can merge, or integrate, the information in those models with the knowledge stored in our minds. When we achieve that integration, we call it learning; we literally know more than we did before the reading.

In Kintsch's (1998) model, two levels of representation are critical: the text base and the situation model. For Kintsch, the text base involves an accurate reading of the text for the purpose of getting the key ideas from the text into working memory. Yet, knowledge plays a key role even in building that accurate representation of the text. We use our knowledge of the world, along with our knowledge of how language and text work, to make all the local inferences required to connect the sentences to one another—to build, if you will, a coherent representation of what the text says. Connecting pronouns to their antecedents is one kind of linking inference, for example, figuring out that the "he" in sentence 2 refers to "Roberto" in sentence 1:

1. Roberto desperately wanted to buy a new bicycle.

2. He took an after-school job sweeping out the bodega around the corner from his family's apartment.

Another kind of local inference is making logical connections among ideas or events in the text. In the example sentences, this means that a local inference is involved in figuring out that wanting the new bicycle was a key motive in prompting Roberto to take the job at the bodega. The kind of reading involved in constructing a text base is what the recently issued Common Core State Standards (Council of Chief State School Officers & National Governors Association [CCSSO& NGA], 2010) for reading refer to when the demand is made to "read closely to determine what the text says explicitly" (p. 10).

The second level of representation, the situation model, is the coherent mental representation of the events, actions, and conditions in the text that represent the integration of the text base with relevant prior knowledge from readers' store of knowledge in long-term memory. To develop a satisfactory situation model, readers must meet two standards: (1) The model has to be consistent with the text base encountered to that point in the reading, and (2) the model must correspond with their relevant prior knowledge of how the world works. In short, readers must integrate information from the text base (i.e., words, sentences, paragraphs) with available and relevant prior knowledge retrieved from long-term memory and fold it all into an emerging situation model of the meaning of the text at that point in the process. If the text base is an account of what the text says, then the situation model can be thought of as an account of what the text means.

When readers build a situation model, they rely even more heavily on background knowledge and inferential processes than when building a text base. In our scenario with Roberto and the bodega, for example, readers might infer, even on the basis of minimal information from the text base, that Roberto is a self-motivated, independent person who understands that he has to work for what he wants in life. They might also have to connect the term *bodega* with their schema for neighborhood grocery store and infer that the neighborhood in which Roberto lives has a sizable Latino population. At a simpler level, a first grader who reads that George Washington chopped down a cherry tree will infer that he used a hatchet or an ax to perform the act. Writers of narratives often omit the motives that drive characters to particular actions in a story on precisely the grounds that they expect readers to use their knowledge of stories, life experiences, and human nature to infer those motives.

Constructing a situation model is central to reading comprehension and is the mechanism that allows readers to integrate what they already know with what they read in the service of building new knowledge structures. These new constructs will modify or replace those currently in long-term memory. Just as knowledge drives comprehension, so does comprehension provide the reader with new knowledge to modify the existing knowledge structures in long-term memory. This is the kind of reading that is emphasized in standards 7–9 in the Common Core State Standards (CCSSO & NGA, 2010) for reading:

7. Integrate and evaluate content presented in diverse media and formats, including visually and quantitatively, as well as in words.

8. Delineate and evaluate the argument and specific claims in a text, including the validity of the reasoning as well as the relevance and sufficiency of the evidence.

9. Analyze how two or more texts address similar themes or topics in order to build knowledge or to compare the approaches the authors take. (p. 10)

To be intentionally redundant, knowledge begets comprehension begets knowledge in just the sort of virtuous cycle we would like students to experience. This cycle has a down side, in that some readers do not come to the task with a knowledge base, inferential capacities, motivations, or dispositions sufficient to enable comprehension.

Skilled readers have several advantages over less skilled readers when it comes to model building. They have greater facility with text processing—everything from recognizing words and reading them fluently to applying skills and strategies to construct meaning, including those identified in Table 3.1. Skilled readers also possess greater stores of knowledge, including language knowledge (e.g., vocabulary, of complex syntax or grammar), textual knowledge (e.g., of text structures and textual devices), and world knowledge (e.g., disciplinary, interpersonal). Thus, skilled readers are more readily able to integrate broader arrays of relevant elements from the text base and bring wider and deeper knowledge to the task of constructing a situation model. Skilled readers are also more motivated and engaged readers, reading more actively and more voluminously, thus further developing their knowledge and skill (Guthrie, 2004).

Fortunately, all of these characteristics of good readers are amenable to teacher intervention. The 10 instructional practices featured in the remainder of this chapter are precisely the practices that teachers should employ to help all readers acquire these understandings, strategies, and dispositions.

Table 3.1. What Good Readers Do When They Read

- Good readers are *active* readers.
- From the outset, they have clear *goals* in mind for their reading. They constantly *evaluate* whether the text, and their reading of it, is meeting their goals.
- Good readers typically *look over* the text before they read, noting such things as the *structure* of the text and text sections that might be most relevant to their reading goals.
- As they read, good readers frequently *make predictions* about what is to come.
- They read *selectively*, continually making decisions about their reading—what to read carefully, what to read quickly, what not to read, what to reread, and so forth.
- Good readers *construct, revise, and question* the meanings they make as they read.
- Good readers try to determine the meanings of *unfamiliar words and concepts* in the text, and they deal with inconsistencies or gaps as needed.
- Good readers draw from, compare, and *integrate their prior knowledge* with material in the text.
- They think about the *authors* of the text, their style, beliefs, intentions, historical milieu, and so forth.
- Good readers *monitor their understanding* of the text, making adjustments in their reading as necessary.
- Good readers *evaluate the text's quality and value* and react to the text in a range of ways, both intellectually and emotionally.
- Good readers *read different kinds of text differently*.
- When reading narrative, good readers attend closely to the setting and characters.
- When reading expository text, good readers frequently construct and revise summaries of what they have read.
- For good readers, text processing occurs not only during "reading," as we have traditionally defined it, but also during short breaks taken during reading…[and] even after the reading has ceased.
- Comprehension is a consuming, continuous, and complex activity, but one that, for good readers, is both *satisfying and productive*.

Note. Modified from "Effective Practices for Developing Reading Comprehension," by N.K. Duke & P.D. Pearson, 2002, in A.E. Farstrup & S.J. Samuels (Eds.), *What Research Has to Say About Reading Instruction* (3rd ed., pp. 205–206), Newark, DE: International Reading Association.

The 10 Essential Elements of Fostering and Teaching Reading Comprehension

Build Disciplinary and World Knowledge

Our first principle follows inevitably from the account of the reading comprehension process in Kintsch's (1998, 2004) Construction–Integration model. The amount of related domain or world knowledge that a reader brings to a text significantly affects that reader's comprehension of that text; this is a fact that has been established over the course of many years (e.g., R.C. Anderson & Pearson, 1984; Bos & Anders, 1990; Kendeou & van den Broek, 2007; McNamara, Floyd, Best, & Louwerse, 2004; McNamara & Kintsch, 1996; Paul, 1990), as discussed previously. This basic finding was confirmed, but with an interesting twist, once again in a recent study designed to understand the importance of world knowledge and decoding skills as related to young readers' comprehension. McNamara and colleagues (2004) engaged third-grade students in reading two texts, one narrative and one expository. The researchers found that comprehension of the expository text, in contrast to the narrative text, was significantly related to the student's amount of world knowledge. Again, this evidence suggests that efforts to provide readers with opportunities to build domain and world knowledge support their subsequent reading comprehension.

Although it stands to reason that wide reading of a variety of texts results in more world knowledge, many approaches take on the goal of building knowledge directly by situating knowledge-building goals alongside reading comprehension or literacy goals (Cervetti, Pearson, Bravo, & Barber, 2006; Cunningham & Stanovich, 2001; Guthrie, Anderson, Alao, & Rinehart, 1999; Palincsar & Magnusson, 2001; Romance & Vitale, 2001). For example, the IDEAS (in-depth expanded applications of science) model replaces literacy instruction with a two-hour block of integrated science–literacy instruction. Students receiving this instruction have consistently outpaced students receiving regular language arts and science programs on national norm-referenced assessments (Romance & Vitale, 2001).

Featured Approach: Seeds of Science/Roots of Reading. Two of us, Billman and Pearson, have worked for several years on a program known as Seeds of Science/Roots of Reading (Cervetti et al., 2006), which was designed to promote science and literacy integration. The program's fundamental premise is that reading, writing, and language (e.g., vocabulary, discourse) are best developed when they are put to work as tools to help students acquire knowledge and inquiry skill in a specific domain, such as science. Somewhat ironically, the evidence gathered thus far (Goldschmidt, 2010; Wang & Herman, 2005) indicates that the effects for the development of deep science knowledge are the strongest, followed in order by durable but decreasingly strong effects, in writing, vocabulary, and reading comprehension development. Vis-à-vis comprehension instruction, two particularly notable features of the Seeds of Science/Roots of Reading curriculum are worth elaborating. First, the approach takes advantage of a fundamental isomorphism, or at least a strong similarity, between reading comprehension strategy instruction (e.g., predicting outcomes on the basis of textual evidence and world knowledge) and science inquiry strategies (e.g., making predictions based on hands-on evidence and topical knowledge of the domain being taught). This means that the inquiry component of science and the strategy component of reading are mutually reinforcing and synergistic, in that what one learns in the one improves the other. Second, concept development in science (e.g., learning the stages of the water cycle) is viewed as tightly linked to reading vocabulary development. So, students are not only learning words but also learning new ideas and acquiring new labels to name those ideas. Words are not the point of words; ideas are. In Seeds of Science/Roots of Reading as well as in IDEAS, Concept-Oriented Reading Instruction (CORI; an approach discussed later in this chapter under the topic of motivation), or any number of other integrated approaches to instruction (see Pearson, Moje, & Greenleaf, 2010), the emphasis is on the idea that when we link knowledge development to reading for comprehension, both knowledge and comprehension are the beneficiaries.

This tight link raises a fundamental dilemma for reform initiatives, of which No Child Left Behind is the most obvious example, that advocate an even greater piece of the curricular pie for reading and, to a slightly lesser extent, mathematics at the elementary level. Such efforts almost inevitably will and already have eclipsed curricular space for social studies and science, as the data suggest (Dorph et al., 2007; McMurrer, 2008). The irony, of course, is that the knowledge that students would gain in more vigorous social studies and science instruction would, as Kintsch's (1998, 2004) Construction–Integration model dictates, fuel comprehension development directly and powerfully. The possibility exists that by emphasizing generic reading instruction at the expense of disciplinary learning, we may be, as the saying goes, cutting off our noses to spite our faces.

Provide Exposure to a Volume and Range of Texts

It is widely accepted that effective and engaged comprehenders tend to read more than their struggling counterparts (e.g., Guthrie, 2004). Particularly, the volume of experiences students have interacting with texts both in and out of the classroom significantly correlates with their overall reading success (e.g., Donahue, Finnegan, Lutkus, Allen, & Campbell, 2001; Taylor, Pearson, Clark, & Walpole, 2000), which suggests that effective comprehension instruction should provide students with ample opportunities to engage with texts. For example, experimental studies of voluntary summer reading have found that increasing the volume of texts to which students have access over the summer significantly improves their overall reading achievement (e.g., Allington et al., 2010; Kim & White, 2008). Similarly, Neuman (1999) found that increasing the volume of texts in child-care centers led to increased engagement with texts and improvements in children's early literacy measures. This may be due in part to the influence that reading can have in developing students' verbal skills and domain knowledge, both of which positively influence one's reading success (Cunningham & Stanovich, 2001). In addition to volume as an influencing factor, the quality and range of books to which students are exposed (e.g., electronic texts, leveled books, student/teacher published work) has a strong relationship with students' reading comprehension (e.g., Hoffman, Sailors, Duffy, & Beretvas, 2004).

In providing exposure to a range of texts, one important dimension to consider is the genre of the text, particularly its communicative purpose. Because reading success does not necessarily transfer between different genres (Duke & Roberts, 2010), students should be exposed, in volume, to the full range of genres we want them to be able to comprehend. Our curricula should include narrative genres, whose purpose is to share and make meaning of experience, as with fairy tales, realistic fiction, and many true stories (Duke, Caughlan, Juzwik, & Martin, in press). Equally as important are informational genres, whose primary purpose is to convey information about the natural or social world (Duke, 2000), as in websites, books, or articles that describe plants, animals, or places or explain natural or social processes or phenomena. Then, there are the hybrid or in-between genres, both print and digital, that are not easily classified as narrative or informational: biographical and autobiographical texts, whose purpose is "to convey information and to communicate a perspective on a person's life" (Duke et al., in press); texts whose purpose is to tell us how to do something (i.e., procedural, how-to); texts intended to persuade or convince us of something (i.e., persuasive); poetry; drama; and so forth. Including so-called functional genres, such as signs, labels, coupons, lists, and letters, may also help students recognize important purposes for comprehension.

The texts we include in classrooms should vary in other respects as well. For example, we want to include texts that are very well written and facilitative of comprehension, as well as those that may cause students some difficulty, thus catalyzing the use and instruction of comprehension strategies and helping students think about how they, as writers, can make text easier or more difficult to understand. Texts should represent a range of complexity, as emphasized in the Common Core State Standards (CCSSO & NGA, 2010). We certainly want readers to have opportunities to read texts that are not difficult for them, but we also want readers to have access to texts that challenge them. Although it has long been recommended that we prevent readers from reading frustration-level texts, it is becoming clear that challenging texts, at least as determined by word-reading accuracy, may not in fact be frustrating to students (Halladay, 2008). In some cases, these challenging texts may have other equally, if not more, important attributes, such as promoting high engagement, providing material for students' content area investigations or writing, or providing inducement to apply fix-up and other coping strategies. When such texts are used, teachers will have to employ a variety of instructional strategies, such as partner reading and collaborative strategy use, to provide the extra measure of scaffolding needed to support students' comprehension of more challenging text (Billman, Hilden, & Halladay, 2009).

Provide Motivating Texts and Contexts for Reading

Motivation is highly correlated with learning in general and reading comprehension in particular (e.g., Brophy, 2004; Guthrie, 2004; Guthrie et al., 2006; Naceur & Schiefele, 2005). Motivated reading behavior is characterized by students valuing and engaging in the act of reading with expectations of success and with greater persistence and stamina when encountering difficulty; as such, motivation is directly tied to personal interest and self-efficacy as well as achievement (Ainley, 2006; Fink, 1995; Guthrie, 2004). Reading motivation is fostered by complex interactions of text topics and text characteristics, classroom social norms, and instructional practices (e.g., Guthrie et al., 2006; Nolen, 2001, 2007; Pressley et al., 2003; Pressley, Wharton-McDonald, Allington, Block, & Morrow, 1998; Schraw, Flowerday, & Lehman, 2001; Turner & Paris, 1995). Importantly, texts or materials that trigger or capitalize on a student's interests contribute to motivation (e.g., Jiménez & Duke, 2011). Students' motivation to read is also enhanced by providing contexts, materials, or tasks that catch students' spontaneous attention or situational interest. Instruction that includes hands-on activities, opportunities to engage in reading for authentic purposes, and texts with a clear structure and vivid, concrete examples is associated with motivated engagement and, subsequently, better recall and learning (Guthrie et al., 2006; Purcell-Gates, Duke, & Martineau, 2007; Sadoski, Goetz, & Rodriguez, 2000; Schraw et al., 2001).

This and other research lead us to think that we must be concerned with the will and thrill, not just the skill, of comprehension. One critical element of will and thrill is motivating texts for reading. Some texts seem inherently interesting to many students. For example, it is a rare day when a book about shark attacks or one by Steven Jenkins does not garner great interest in many students. However, other texts can be quite interesting to some students while decidedly uninteresting to others, with important consequences for the reader and the teacher. A study by Jiménez and Duke (2011) illustrates this well. Fourth-grade students were surveyed about expository text topics of which they like to read. From the responses, a group of students with inverse reading interests was identified; half were interested in reading about working animals but not about robotics, and half were interested in reading about robotics but not about working animals. All students in the group were asked to read six texts, three on working animals and three on robotics, thinking aloud as they did so and providing an oral recall after each set of three. When students read on the topic of reported interest to them, whether working animals or robotics, they employed a greater number and range of comprehension processes. This tells us that if our goal is to stretch students' comprehension muscles, we should provide them with texts of interest. Some teachers use interest surveys or other tools to learn about students' interests and then stock individualized book crates with texts likely to be of interest. Some teachers give individual students keywords they can use when consulting a librarian or conducting searches in the library that may yield texts of interest to them. Notably, although it makes sense to be concerned with helping students find texts that are a good fit for their reading level as well as their interests, we can be somewhat flexible in this regard. In the Jiménez and Duke study, even after controlling for prior knowledge, students' actual comprehension, as measured by recall, was much higher when students were reading on a topic of interest. Too often we think of a student in regards to a predetermined reading level (e.g., M, magenta, 16), when in reality, as this and other studies have shown, a student's reading level varies depending on his or her interest in the text, as well as other factors, including background knowledge, as discussed earlier in this chapter. Think of interest as a compensatory factor, one that can get the job done when the text is extra challenging or the student's skill level is not quite up to the task.

Of course, interesting texts are not the only way to generate interest in reading. A study of highly effective teachers of literacy found that they kept students engaged 90% or more of the time (Pressley et al., 1998);

they didn't do this using interesting texts alone. Turner and Paris (1995) have written about six Cs of motivating contexts for literacy learning: choice, challenge, control, collaboration, constructing meaning, and consequences. Most important, in our view, are compelling reasons to comprehend, not simply to fulfill the requirements of an assignment or to earn a grade but for reasons deeper than that, such as to learn material to teach a group of younger students, to learn how to make something to give to a friend, or to be absorbed by a good tale. One study found that second and third graders whose teachers engaged them in reading and writing texts more like those you would find outside of school, for reasons similar to those for which people read and write outside of school, showed higher growth in reading comprehension; students whose teachers employed more school-like texts and tasks, such as reading a chapter of the textbook and answering the questions at the end, showed lower rates of comprehension growth (Purcell-Gates et al., 2007).

Featured Approach: Concept-Oriented Reading Instruction. An approach that is highly effective at developing reading comprehension, and places motivation front and center, is CORI (Guthrie, Wigfield, & Perencevich, 2004). In this approach, which has been tested with third and fifth graders, teachers focus 60–90 minutes of the literacy block on a conceptual theme in science, such as animal survival, over a series of weeks. Students collaborate, make choices, and set goals for learning and sharing learning, all related to the conceptual theme. For example, one group's goal might be to learn about, develop, and present a poster about animal locomotion to another group. To accomplish this goal, students are engaged in reading and writing daily, all in the service of learning about the conceptual theme (see Table 3.2 for a CORI lesson structure; for more information, visit www.cori.umd.edu). CORI is notable in addressing many, if not all, of the 10 essential elements of fostering and teaching reading comprehension. There are the motivating contexts for reading, of course, but there is also a heavy focus on building disciplinary and world knowledge, exposure to a volume and range of texts (class or team sets of 24 different informational books, 23 novels, 3 storybooks, and 1 poetry book, as well as additional texts for struggling readers), teaching strategies for comprehending, integrating reading and writing, and so forth. This discussion reinforces a crucial point in our approach, that the essential elements of fostering and teaching reading comprehension that we present in this chapter can be addressed simultaneously, and perhaps even work synergistically, to develop reading comprehension.

Table 3.2. Structure of a Concept-Oriented Reading Instruction Lesson

- *10 minutes*—Students practice their oral-reading fluency with poetry or informational books (three days per week), or hands-on science activity and/or study of science concepts.
- *10 minutes*—The teacher provides a comprehension minilesson on self-monitoring, inferencing, or fix-up strategies, including rereading, chunking, discussing, questioning, visualizing, connecting, looking up, reading ahead, reading aloud, and using knowledge.
- *15 minutes*—One of three teacher-led guided reading group uses texts related to the conceptual theme, during which the teacher models, scaffolds, and provides guided practice in the application of reading comprehension strategies to serve learning related to the conceptual theme.
- *15 minutes*—While the teacher is with the second guided reading group, students write about information and concepts learned from the guided reading text or about their responses to a theme-related novel they are reading.
- *15 minutes*—While the teacher is with the third guided reading group, students engage in independent reading of novels for which they have book clubs.

Note. Some teachers added up to 5 minutes to each activity for a total of 90 minutes of Concept-Oriented Reading Instruction. Adapted from "Contributions of Concept-Oriented Reading Instruction to Knowledge About Interventions for Motivations in Reading," by J.T. Guthrie, A. McRae, & S.L. Klauda, 2007, *Educational Psychologist*, 42(4), 237–250.

Teach Strategies for Comprehending

Effective teachers of reading comprehension help their students develop into strategic, active readers, in part, by teaching them why, how, and when to apply certain strategies shown to be used by effective readers (e.g., Duke & Pearson, 2002). Although many teachers teach comprehension strategies one at a time, spending several weeks focused on each strategy, a study that was conducted with second graders reading informational text has suggested that this may not be the best way to organize strategy instruction (Reutzel, Smith, & Fawson, 2005). In that study, teachers were assigned at random to introduce a set of strategies briefly and then quickly move students to applying or juggling multiple strategies simultaneously, which resulted in students with stronger performance on some measures. Studies and reviews of various integrated approaches to strategy instruction, such as reciprocal teaching (e.g., Palincsar & Brown, 1984), have suggested that teaching students comprehension routines that include developing facility with a repertoire of strategies from which to draw during independent reading tasks can lead to increased understanding (e.g., Brown, 2008; Guthrie, Wigfield, Barbosa, et al., 2004; Spörer, Brunstein, & Kieschke, 2009). In addition, teaching students to read strategically has been shown to significantly increase students' comprehension of texts in various content area domains, such as science and social studies (e.g., Klingner, Vaughn, Arguelles, Hughes, & Leftwich, 2004; Lederer, 2000; Romance & Vitale, 2001). In an interesting twist on strategy instruction, Block, Parris, and Whiteley (2008) observed that the integration of kinesthetic learning aids into transactional strategy lessons (e.g., moving one's arm across the body to signal an inference) for a period of 12 weeks led to significant improvement on measures of explicit and implicit comprehension, with the largest effects seen in students in grades K–2.

The list of strategies that research indicates are worth teaching—that is, if taught, they improve reading comprehension—varies from one research review to another (Duke & Pearson, 2002; National Institute of Child Health and Human Development [NICHD], 2000) but often includes the following:

- Setting purposes for reading
- Previewing and predicting
- Activating prior knowledge
- Monitoring, clarifying, and fixing
- Visualizing and creating visual representations
- Drawing inferences
- Self-questioning and thinking aloud
- Summarizing and retelling

In addition to these, there are strategies worth teaching for only some genres, such as attending to story elements for narrative text (e.g., Baumann & Bergeron, 1993; Idol, 1987) and searching and skimming with informational text (e.g., Symons, MacLatchy-Gaudet, Stone, & Reynolds, 2001).

The model we recommend for teaching any comprehension strategy is the gradual release of responsibility (Pearson & Gallagher, 1983). In this model (see Figure 3.1), responsibility for the use of a strategy gradually transfers from the teacher to the student through five stages (Duke & Pearson, 2002, pp. 208–210):

1. *An explicit description of the strategy and when and how it should be used.* "Predicting is making guesses about what will come next in the text you are reading. You should make predictions a lot when

Figure 3.1. An Adapted Version of the Gradual Release of Responsibility Model

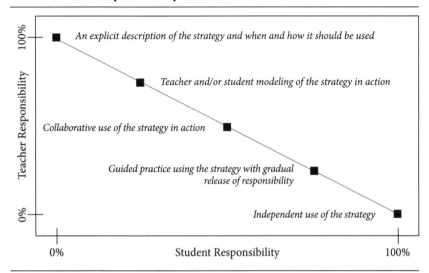

Note. Adapted from "The Instruction of Reading Comprehension," by P.D. Pearson & M.C. Gallagher, 1983, *Contemporary Educational Psychology, 8*(3), 317–344.

you read. For now, you should stop every two pages that you read and make some predictions."

2. *Teacher and/or student modeling of the strategy in action.* "I am going to make predictions while I read this book. I will start with just the cover here. Hmm...I see a picture of an owl. It looks like he—I think it is a he—is wearing pajamas, and he is carrying a candle. I *predict* that this is going to be a make-believe story because owls do not really wear pajamas and carry candles. I predict it is going to be about this owl, and it is going to take place at nighttime...."

3. *Collaborative use of the strategy in action.* "I have made some good predictions so far in the book. From this part on I want you to make predictions with me. Each of us should stop and think about what might happen next.... Okay, now let's hear what you think and why...."

4. *Guided practice using the strategy with gradual release of responsibility.* Early on...

"I have called the three of you together to work on making predictions while you read this and other books. After every few pages

I will ask each of you to stop and make a prediction. We will talk about your predictions and then read on to see if they come true."

Later on...

"Each of you has a chart that lists different pages in your book. When you finish reading a page on the list, stop and make a prediction. Write the prediction in the column that says 'Prediction.' When you get to the next page on the list, check off whether your prediction 'Happened,' 'Will not happen,' or 'Still might happen.' Then make another prediction and write it down."... (This example is based on the reading Forecaster Technique from Mason and Au described and cited in Lipson and Wixson [1991]. Note that this technique should not be used daily but rather periodically with students who are working to internalize the practice of predicting.)

5. *Independent use of the strategy.* "It is time for silent reading. As you read today, remember what we have been working on—making predictions while we read. Be sure to make predictions every two or three pages. Ask yourself why you made the prediction you did—what made you think that. Check as you read to see whether your prediction came true. Jamal is passing out Predictions! bookmarks to remind you."

It is important to emphasize how critical that middle portion of the release, collaborative and guided practice, is to effective instruction. We have noticed a number of teachers who provide explicit teaching but expect students to independently apply strategies too soon. A key finding of research on highly effective teachers serving high-poverty students is that they spend a good deal more time coaching (i.e., providing guided practice for) students—that is, being the "guide on the side" as students try out their developing facility to apply strategies in actual reading and writing tasks (Taylor et al., 2000). Similarly, these researchers found that coaching during real-time reading was effective for word identification strategies as well as comprehension strategies. The secret seems to be in helping students use strategies for solving problems, whether word recognition or comprehension, while they are reading.

We cannot leave this discussion of the gradual release of responsibility without noting two complexities of its use. First, it is inherently recursive in the sense that once students reach independent use of the strategy, as in the lower right-hand corner of Figure 3.1, they will inevitably end up back in the middle or even sometimes in the upper left-hand corner of the figure's release continuum. Each time readers encounter a new topic or a text that is more complex, such as with complex language or excessively obscure words, they will need a little scaffolding to "get their sea legs" in those new textual waters. Also, students sometimes forget a lesson overnight or over a weekend, at least temporarily, so when they return to school, they may not remember how to independently enact the strategy they were using effortlessly the previous school day. The point for teachers is to get used to sliding up and down that release continuum as circumstances demand. Second, once students develop enough facility with a strategy that it becomes part of their ongoing repertoire of strategies, they do not really need to use it every day for the rest of their lives. We have seen a disturbing tendency in recent years for certain strategies to become overused to the point of diminishing returns (e.g., predicting outcomes). The time students spend predicting what will happen next on the basis of the pictures should not swamp the time spent reading and comprehending the text. Periodic review of each strategy is certainly called for, but repeated practice for days on end is unnecessary. Most often, and for most encounters with text, the primary focus should actually be reading, for compelling purposes, with teachers guiding and helping students select strategies as needed for students to meet their comprehension goals while working through the tough parts of the texts they encounter.

Strategy instruction has recently experienced harsh professional critique, not so much of thoughtfully designed and executed strategy instruction, but of poor or rigidly implemented instruction (e.g., McKeown, Beck, & Blake, 2009; Wilkinson & Son, 2011). We believe strategy instruction is most vulnerable to critique when implemented in a heavily scripted fashion. Driven by the need to describe instruction in advance and universally, programs have lessons that are independent of and unresponsive to a specific context or a particular group of students. The dynamic, adaptive, and responsive character of strategy instruction found in research studies demonstrating its efficacy can be compromised in this setting, and the instruction can become rigid and inflexible. Even worse, if strategy instruction becomes the object of assessment, as is likely in our current hyperaccountability context, it is more apt to become set in stone. There is nothing new in this danger. Indeed, in the second edition of this book, Pearson, Roehler, Dole, and Duffy (1992) cautioned that (a) good reading strategies are as adaptable as they are intentional, and (b) good strategy instruction is as adaptable as it is intentional, and both are at risk in an environment that requires strict adherence to accountability demands.

Rigid, highly routinized strategy instruction may not be as effective as conventional discussions focused on knowledge acquisition (McKeown et al., 2009; Wilkinson & Son, 2011). Moreover, it may breed an excessive reliance on abstract, content-free, metacognitive introspection about strategy use (Pearson & Fielding, 1991). When too generic and abstract, too isolated from the goal of acquiring knowledge and insight, strategy instruction is in danger of becoming an end unto itself, an introspective nightmare that is more complicated than the ideas the strategies are supposed to help the students acquire (Pearson & Fielding, 1991).

In a sense, strategies suffer from the same problem as phonics rules. Ideally, either is only a means to an end. When phonics rules or strategies become their own goals, the system runs amok. Either breeds a mock compliance when put into a special, school talk box hauled out only for the lesson. The only way to block this sort of mock compliance is to provide real apprenticeships in strategy use—the kind of reading internship that helps students learn two key lessons about strategies: (1) when, why, and how to apply strategies, and (2) that by being able to pull out just the right tool to get over a hurdle at just the right moment, students become smarter, more effective, and more strategic readers.

Teach Text Structures

Just as discipline and world knowledge are known to influence comprehension, the role that knowledge of text structure plays in recalling and comprehending text has been well established (e.g., Armbruster, Anderson, & Ostertag, 1987; Meyer, Brandt, & Bluth, 1980; Richgels, McGee, Lomax, & Sheard, 1987; Robinson & Kiewra, 1995; Slater, Graves, & Piché, 1985). Although exposure to a variety of genres contributes to building familiarity with various text structures, as discussed earlier in this chapter, direct instruction around the structures commonly found in different genres also benefits students, especially those students who may struggle with reading (Gersten, Fuchs, Williams, & Baker, 2001). Text structure instruction can take different forms, including explicit instruction of various structures as well as instructional supports such as graphic organizers (Goldman & Rakestraw, 2000). Most early text structure research focused on the impact of this instruction on the comprehension and learning of upper elementary and older students (Goldman & Rakestraw, 2000). More recent studies have shown that explicit text structure instruction also improves primary-grade students' comprehension (e.g., Hall, Sabey, & McClellan, 2005; Stevens, Van Meter, & Warcholak, 2010; Williams et al., 2007; Williams, Stafford, Lauer, Hall, & Pollini, 2009). In a six-week intervention embedded in guiding reading instruction, children were taught a compare/contrast text structure while reading expository texts. The instruction included the use of graphic organizers, explicit instruction emphasizing clue words, and practice analyzing exemplar texts. Students in the treatment condition had a better conceptual understanding of the compare/contrast structure and produced more structured summaries of expository paragraphs postintervention. This evidence suggests that including text structure instruction from early on is not only beneficial but also accessible for our youngest readers.

Key to effectively implementing text structure instruction is understanding how texts are structured. Table 3.3 identifies and illustrates common elements of many narratives, and Table 3.4 identifies and illustrates common structures found in informational texts. In our view, it is unlikely to make sense to teach all of these elements and structures within a given year. Rather, teachers might work together across grades, guided by standards and curricular documents, to determine which elements and structures might be taught when. The stakes in these decisions about sequencing instruction may not be as high as you think. We believe that the most important thing about text structure instruction is not so much

Table 3.3. Elements of Structure in a Narrative Text[a]

Element	Description	Example
Characters	Who the story was about	A girl named Little Red Riding Hood, her grandmother, and the wolf
Setting	Where and when the story happened	The forest and Grandmother's cabin, during the day
Goal	What the main character was trying to do	Little Red Riding Hood set out to deliver a basket of food to her sick grandmother.
Problem	Why the main character took certain actions	Little Red Riding Hood was not aware that the wolf had eaten Grandmother.
Plot or action	What happened to the main character or what she or he did to try to solve a problem	She met the wolf on her way to Grandmother's, and the wolf pretended to be Grandmother.
Resolution	How the problem was solved and how the story ended	A nearby hunter rescued Little Red Riding Hood and her grandmother from the wolf.
Theme(s)	General lessons or ideas	You shouldn't talk to strangers.

Source: The list of elements is drawn from Baumann and Bergeron (1993), Morrow (1996), and Pressley et al. (1990).
[a] Not all stories contain examples of conflict. The panel provides the *Little Red Riding Hood* example to illustrate one option for describing these elements to students. Some students from various cultural backgrounds may not be familiar with certain folktales like this one. Teachers should construct lessons around texts that are best suited to their students.
(*Note.* The table and notes are reprinted and cited from *Improving Reading Comprehension in Kindergarten Through 3rd Grade* [NCEE 2010-4038; p. 19], by T. Shanahan, K. Callison, C. Carriere, N.K. Duke, P.D. Pearson, C. Schatschneider, et al., 2010, Washington, DC: National Center for Education Evaluation and Regional Assistance, Institute of Education Sciences, U.S. Department of Education.)

Table 3.4. Structures of Informational Text

Structure	Description	Example	Common clue words	Sample activities
Description	What something looks, feels, smells, sounds, tastes like, or is composed of	Characteristics of a hurricane		Have students use the details in a descriptive paragraph to construct an illustration or three-dimensional display.
Sequence	When or in what order things happen	A storm becomes a hurricane	first, then, next, after, later, finally	Assign each student to represent one event in a sequence. Ask the class to line up in order and, starting at the front of the line, to explain or enact their respective events in turn.
Problem and solution	What went wrong and how it was or could be fixed	Hurricane Katrina destroyed homes and stores, so groups like the Red Cross had to bring food and medicine from other parts of the US	because, in order to, so that, trouble, if, problem	Provide opportunities for students to act out key phases of a passage.
Cause and effect	How one event leads to another	What happened to the people who lived in Louisiana after Hurricane Katrina	because, therefore, cause, effect, so	Have students match up pictures representing "causes" and "effects" in a game-like activity.
Compare and contrast	How things are alike and different	How hurricanes are the same as or different from tornadoes	both, alike, unalike, but, however, than	Set out overlapping hula hoops, one to represent each side of the comparison, and have students sort visual representations of each characteristic into the shared and different areas of each hoop.

Source: The list of structures was derived from Williams et al. (2007) and Duke (2000). The panel developed the definitions and examples for illustrative purposes.
(Note. The table and notes are reprinted and cited from *Improving Reading Comprehension in Kindergarten Through 3rd Grade* [NCEE 2010-4038; p. 20], by T. Shanahan, K. Callison, C. Carriere, N.K. Duke, P.D. Pearson, C. Schatschneider, et al., 2010, Washington, DC: National Center for Education Evaluation and Regional Assistance, Institute of Education Sciences, U.S. Department of Education.)

which structures are taught when, but (a) that students learn that text is structured and (b) that they develop the ability to take advantage of any particular text's structure in learning and remembering its key information. This disposition will serve students especially well when they come across texts that employ multiple text structures or use unconventional approaches to organize information or convey an experience.

Many of the essential elements discussed elsewhere in this chapter can facilitate text structure instruction, such as having a range of well-structured texts at hand and having compelling reasons for understanding the structure of a text (e.g., identify the setting and characters of a narrative to perform it as a play, identify causes and effects of a particular phenomenon for use in creating public-service announcements for the local community). The gradual release of responsibility model presented earlier can also facilitate text structure instruction. As with comprehension strategies, we want to explicitly describe text structures, model their use in reading (and writing), identify and use the structures of text collaboratively with students, guide students as they take increasing responsibility for attending to text structure on their own, and provide students with independent opportunities to engage with the structure of texts.

Another important tool to support text structure instruction is the use of graphic organizers, such as story maps, Venn diagrams for compare/contrast, and flowcharts for problem/solution. These and other visual representations can be powerful tools for comprehending, learning, and remembering material from, in, and with text. As we explained in the previous edition of this volume,

> The point about visual representations is that they are *re*-presentations; literally, they allow us to present information *again*. It is through that active, transformative process that knowledge, comprehension, and memory form a synergistic relationship—whatever improves one of these elements also improves the others. (Duke & Pearson, 2002, p. 219)

Engage Students in Discussion

Recognizing that comprehension is an active and often collaborative process of making meaning, effective teachers of reading comprehension tend to employ classroom discussion to help readers work together to make meaning from the texts they encounter (e.g., Langer, 2001). As might be expected, certain approaches to discussion may be more effective than others in increasing students' literal and inferential understanding of texts (Murphy, Wilkinson, Soter, Hennessey, & Alexander, 2009).

One consistent finding from the research is that classroom teachers who employ higher order questioning during discussions promote greater rates of active participation among their students (Murphy, et al., 2009); a less consistent, although generally robust, finding is that discussion also promotes higher levels of reading comprehension (e.g., Applebee, Langer, Nystrand, & Gamoran, 2003; Bitter, O'Day, Gubbins, & Socias, 2009; McKeown et al., 2009; Taylor et al., 2003). Discussion in which students show a good understanding of and critical thinking about the text often includes listening and linking to others' ideas, providing evidence from the text to support one's thinking, and regular student participation (Wolf, Crosson, & Resnick, 2004). In their study of fourth-grade classrooms, Chinn, Anderson, and Waggoner (2001) found that text-based discussion emphasizing collaborative reasoning increased higher level thinking and overall reading engagement more than recitation styles of interaction (i.e., Initiate-Respond-Evaluate). Dong, Anderson, Kim, and Li (2008) have also found that collaborative reasoning has deep and lasting effects on the quality of arguments that students make when writing in response to texts they have read and discussed in their quasi-debate approach to querying the text. Similarly, Van den Branden (2000) revealed that primary-grade students who engaged in conversation around texts had higher comprehension than those who did not collaboratively negotiate meaning. She hypothesized that higher comprehension may have resulted from the challenges of explaining oneself to others or the collaborative effort to repair breakdowns in comprehension.

Featured Approach: Questioning the Author. Beginning in the early 1990s, Beck and McKeown, along with a group of colleagues at the University of Pittsburgh and in the surrounding schools, began work on a comprehension routine called Questioning the Author (QtA). Quite literally inspired by their own insights (see Beck, McKeown, Sandora, Kucan, & Worthy, 1996) from revising text to make it more considerate (Beck, McKeown, & Gromoll, 1989), Beck and her colleagues bootstrapped this approach to engaging students with text. The idea was that if they, as knowledgeable adult readers, found the process of trying to figure out what authors had in mind in writing a text in a certain way, might not students benefit similarly from querying the author in a similar spirit? Hence, they developed a set of generic questions that could be asked as a teacher and group of students made their way through a text. The essential approach is to query a text collaboratively, section by section, with questions like those listed in Table 3.5.

Table 3.5. Questions to Guide the Discussion in Questioning the Author

Goal	Candidate questions
Initiate the discussion.	• What is the author trying to say? • What is the author's message? • What is the author talking about?
Help students focus on the author's message.	• That is what the author says, but what does it mean?
Help students link information.	• How does that connect with what the author already told us? • What information has the author added here that connects to or fits in with…?
Identify difficulties with the way the author has presented information or ideas.	• Does that make sense? • Is that said in a clear way? • Did the author explain that clearly? Why or why not? What's missing? What do we need to figure out or find out?
Encourage students to refer to the text either because they've misinterpreted a text statement or to help them recognize that they've made an inference.	• Did the author tell us that? • Did the author give us the answer to that?

Note. From "Questioning the Author: A Yearlong Classroom Implementation to Engage Students With Text," by I.L. Beck, M.G. McKeown, C. Sandora, L. Kucan, & J. Worthy, 1996, *The Elementary School Journal, 96*(4), p. 389.

The expectation is that students who experience this sort of instructional approach to text inquiry will develop improved understanding of the texts to which the routine is applied, improved understanding of texts they meet on their own at a later time, and most important, a critical disposition toward texts in general. Ideally, this approach will help students entertain the possibility that a comprehension failure may have as much to do with the author's failure to provide a considerate message as it does with the failure of the reader to bring appropriate cognitive and affective resources to bear in trying to understand it.

The data on the efficacy of QtA (see Beck et al., 1996; McKeown et al., 2009) are quite encouraging. First, with the support of a professional community, teachers can learn to transform their text discussions from traditional recitations to these more student-centered, interpretive, and decidedly critical discussions. Second, when the routine is implemented, students assume a greater role in the overall text discussions, nearly doubling their piece of the discussion pie compared with traditional discussions, and initiate many more interactions. Third, and most important, students become much more successful at higher level comprehension and monitoring their comprehension as a result of participating in QtA. It is equally empowering to teachers and students. Perhaps the most stringent test of QtA occurred in the 2009 study (McKeown et al., 2009), which produced superior results to either a no-treatment control group or a strategy instruction group (albeit, in our collective view, a highly scripted version of strategy instruction). Those who wish to implement QtA should consult the works that Beck and her colleagues have written for classroom teachers (particularly Beck & McKeown, 2006; Beck, McKeown, Hamilton, & Kucan, 1997).

Build Vocabulary and Language Knowledge

The relationship of language and vocabulary to reading comprehension is well established, and as such, defining the nature and characteristics of best practices for vocabulary instruction has been the focus of much research (see Baumann, 2009, for a review; NICHD, 2000). In reviewing research in this area, the National Reading Panel (NICHD, 2000) drew several broad conclusions:

- Vocabulary impacts comprehension.
- It is learned incidentally while reading and listening to books.
- Repeated exposure, especially in different contexts, is the key to learning word meanings.
- Prereading instruction of keywords can be helpful.
- Computerized programs seem to increase vocabulary knowledge.

We would add that vocabulary instruction should relate new words to known words, embed instruction in relevant contexts, and include experiences surrounded with meaningful talk (e.g., Baumann, 2009; Hiebert & Kamil, 2005; Stahl & Nagy, 2006).

Reading aloud, a common instructional strategy, is one widely researched context that is rich with opportunities for teaching vocabulary. Read-aloud experiences that include direct explanations of words along with dialogic interactions that foster deep understanding result in significant gains in vocabulary and reading comprehension (e.g., Apthorp,

2006; Biemiller & Boote, 2006; Brabham & Lynch-Brown, 2002; Coyne, McCoach, & Kapp, 2007; Silverman & Hines, 2009; Spycher, 2009). In a study examining adults' read-aloud styles with first and third graders, Brabham and Lynch-Brown found that an interactional read-aloud style resulted in greater gains in amount of vocabulary and reading comprehension across both grade levels. Others have shown that instruction that fosters metalinguistic awareness and understanding of multiple meanings of words also impacts students' general vocabulary knowledge and reading comprehension (Burns, Dean, & Foley, 2004; Nagy, Berninger, & Abbott, 2006; Nelson & Stage, 2007; Zipke, Ehri, & Cairns, 2009). In one study, an intervention focused on multiple-meaning words that introduced the varied meanings on day 1 followed by contextually based instruction and practice on day 2 resulted in vocabulary acquisition and reading comprehension gains for third and fifth graders who entered the study with low achievement in both areas (Nelson & Stage, 2007). Even morphological instruction has entered the portfolio of effective vocabulary interventions (Carlisle, 1995).

Featured Approach: Semantic Ambiguity Instruction. Zipke and colleagues (2009) have documented the efficacy of a novel and engaging approach to teaching students how to deal with the multiple meanings of words, particularly homophones. Taking their cue from Amelia Bedelia, the notorious heroine in the children's books by Herman Parish, they encourage students to engage with semantic ambiguity, how to resolve it, and how to manipulate it to create word puzzles, puns, and other jokes (e.g., a chocolate mousse depicted as a moose made of chocolate). Building on research by Yuill (1998), Zipke et al. designed four 45-minute lessons to create this sort of metalinguistic awareness among third-grade students. Delivered individually, the lessons focused, in order, on (a) multiple meanings of words, (b) multiple meanings of sentences (e.g., the dog chased the man on a bike), (c) analyzing and creating riddles, and (d) reading, interpreting, and enjoying Amelia Bedelia books. Robust transfer effects were found on one of two standardized reading comprehension assessments when compared with a control condition that, to control for a Hawthorne effect, emphasized rich literature discussions. What is especially encouraging about this particular approach is its emphasis on engaging language play as compared with the heavy-handed tone of much comprehension instruction.

Integrate Reading and Writing

Current understanding in the field of literacy dictates that reading and writing mutually reinforce one another and rely on some of the same cognitive processes (e.g., Fitzgerald & Shanahan, 2000; Shanahan, 2006; Tierney & Shanahan, 1996). This insight suggests that instruction may be more effective when teachers integrate reading and writing experiences in the classroom. Research confirms that exemplary teachers who produce high-achieving readers and writers tend to integrate the two domains regularly and thoroughly in the classroom (e.g., Knapp, 1995; Morrow, Tracey, Woo, & Pressley, 1999; Pressley, Yokoi, Rankin, Wharton-McDonald, & Mistretta, 1997; Thomas & Barksdale-Ladd, 1995; Wharton-McDonald, Pressley, & Hampston, 1998). Further, as evidence of a seemingly bidirectional relationship between reading and writing (Berninger, Abbott, Abbott, Graham, & Richards, 2002; Shanahan & Lomax, 1986), children's writing abilities have been shown to predict later reading comprehension (e.g., Parodi, 2007; Shatil, Share, & Levin, 2000), and reading comprehension has been shown to predict students' composition skills (e.g., Abbott, Berninger, & Fayol, 2010). Although fewer experiments have looked at the effects of reading and writing integration, results suggest that combining instruction in writing and reading may promote increased literacy levels in students (e.g., Craig, 2006; Graham & Hebert, 2010; Konopak, Martin, & Martin, 1990; Raphael, Englert, & Kirschner, 1989; Raphael, Kirschner, & Englert, 1988).

Perhaps the strongest examples of reading and writing integration come from approaches previously discussed: Seeds of Science/Roots of Reading, IDEAS, CORI. Although all of the developers of these approaches would claim that they are more about integration across curricular boundaries than across the bridge between reading and writing, the programs inevitably promote reading–writing relationships in systematic ways and, in what may be an equally important effort, link both reading and writing to oral-language development. So, for example, in Seeds of Science/Roots of Reading (Cervetti et al., 2006), when students encounter a new word in a science text, they are encouraged, and almost required, to use it in their oral discourse when working together in a hands-on investigation and later when writing to explain the results of that investigation. Similar cross-modal (i.e., where modes are reading, writing, talking, and doing, as in hands-on science) connections are made for discourse and argument structures as well as words. Thus, through their hands-on investigation in a unit on designing mixtures, students learn about ingredients that make for a good glue and about the nature of the evidence that distinguishes strong glues from weak ones. Later, the students are asked to design a new mixture that will serve some other everyday use, such as hair gel. Following a similar cross-modal process, students read about the properties of various ingredients, carry out a series of experiments designed to test the effectiveness of their product, and at each step, write explanations and arguments that use the same criteria for strength of evidence that they have encountered in their reading and hands-on activities. They might even read a narrative account about another class of students conducting a similar experiment and be asked to evaluate the validity of the arguments made by the students in the narrative. Thus, oral and written language continually reinforce one another, as do reading and writing.

De La Paz (2005) has been working on similar integration strategies in social studies. Working with eighth-grade students, she evaluated an integrated social studies and language arts unit designed to promote historical understanding and argumentative writing skills. English teachers taught students a strategy for planning and composing argumentative essays. In parallel, the social studies teachers promoted historical reasoning instantiated as reading and reconciling primary and secondary documents to understand complex historical events in the texts they encountered. The experimental students, when compared with a business-as-usual control condition, were able to produce significantly better essays, in which quality was indexed by historical accuracy, persuasiveness, length, and the nature and density of their arguments.

Featured Approach: Writing Intensive Reading Comprehension (WIRC). Collins and colleagues (Collins, Lee, Fox, & Madigan, 2011) have developed, implemented, and evaluated an approach to improving fourth and fifth graders' reading comprehension that focuses directly and systematically on linking writing to reading comprehension. Theoretically driven by Kintsch's (1998, 2004) Construction–Integration model of reading and Bereiter and Scardamalia's (1987) problem space model of writing, WIRC requires students to complete a variety of visual representations of key ideas prompted by a target text. (Collins et al. term these visual representations *think sheets* and insist that they are not worksheets.) Situated within a district-mandated basal reading program, in which students would normally engage in a variety of discussion and worksheet activities surrounding the text of the week, WIRC substitutes the think sheets for many of the normal comprehension activities that are suggested in the teacher manual. The think sheets are designed to ensure that students develop a rich text base and situation model for the text of the week as they prepare to write a culminating response to the text at week's end. Figure 3.2 is a graphic depiction of these important relationships. The key point is that through talk and writing, students are able to build a richer representation of the content of the texts they read (i.e., the content knowledge box in the figure) and deal with the question that vexes every writer: How can I find a way to say that so others will understand (i.e., the rhetorical knowledge box in the figure).

Collins and colleagues (2011) have conducted a rigorous evaluation of WIRC, finding that it produces robust effects on transfer tests of reading comprehension (modeled after the National Assessment of Educational Progress–influenced state standards tests in the state of New York) in comparison to the basal-driven, business-as-usual control group. The researchers also found that the longer the implementation and the more faithful the implementation to the intervention design, the stronger the effects on comprehension. This is powerful evidence of the value of using writing, and the systematic use of talk, to support reading comprehension.

Figure 3.2. Structure of the Sociocognitive Problem-Solving Space

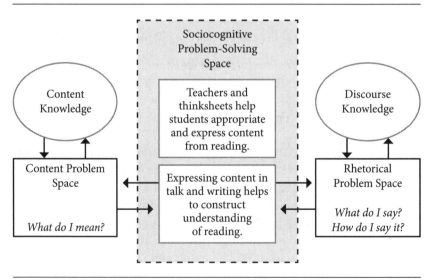

Note. Adapted from *Bringing Together Reading and Writing: An Experimental Study of Writing Intensive Reading Comprehension (WIRC) in Low-Performing Urban Elementary Schools*, by J.L. Collins, J. Lee, & J. Fox, 2011, manuscript submitted for publication.

Taking a step back to look at all of these salutary findings that occur when reading and writing—and in most cases, talk—are employed in the name of improved comprehension, it may well be that revisiting and re-representing important ideas in many modes is what matters most. When we read, we represent the ideas we encounter semantically, but it is verbal representation in the case of talk, and orthographic in the case of writing. These multiple and varying representations may be responsible for the observed improvement in understanding and memory for key ideas encountered in the text. If they are only encountered in reading, without benefit of the verbal recoding prompted by conversation or the orthographic recoding required when students set pen to paper (or finger energy used to view images in our technological world), the bonds students are able to make between new information from text and existing knowledge in memory are weaker and less likely to endure long enough to reshape that knowledge. In other words, it may be that talk and writing are really aids to learning (i.e., changing what is in our store of knowledge in memory).

Observe and Assess

There are many different ways to comprehend a text (e.g., Wade, 1990; Wade, Trathen, & Schraw, 1990), and readers bring different strengths and weaknesses to the process. For example, one reader might have strong prior knowledge related to a text that compensates for relatively poor clarifying and fix-up strategies, whereas another reader might have weak prior knowledge related to a text but make up for it by using a variety of strategies that help build meaning in such circumstances. Similarly, there are many different reasons a reader may struggle with comprehension (e.g., Duke, Pressley, & Hilden, 2004). Unfortunately, scores on most comprehension assessments do not tell us why a reader is struggling. For example, a study by Buly and Valencia (2002) found that students who scored below proficient on their state's fourth-grade high-stakes comprehension assessment were struggling for very different reasons. Some appeared to struggle primarily because of word reading and fluency difficulties; their vocabulary and meaning construction processes were actually a relative strength. Others, referred to as word callers, had strong word reading and fluency but relatively poor vocabulary and meaning construction processes (see Cartwright, 2010, for further discussion of and interventions for such readers).

As we argue in the next section, we assume that teachers' responses to and instruction for students should differ depending in part on their assessment of students' comprehension strengths and weaknesses. If so, then careful observation and assessment is needed to ascertain students' comprehension strengths and weaknesses. For this task, a mere comprehension score or level will be insufficient. Assessments required for this task must provide more details and diagnostics by examining several aspects of and/or contributors to comprehension.

A growing repertoire of assessments aims to address this need. For example, the Qualitative Reading Inventory developed by Leslie and Caldwell provides information about the student's background knowledge related to a passage, the nature of the student's miscues (e.g., does he or she reflect concern with what makes sense?), the student's approach to retelling a passage, and the student's literal and inferential comprehension. The Benchmark Assessment System created by Fountas and Pinnell provides information on the nature of students' miscues; students' key understandings of material within, beyond, and about the text; and the students' ability to write about what they have read. The Concepts of Comprehension Assessment developed by Billman and colleages and the Informational Strategic Cloze Assessments designed by Hilden and colleagues assess students' comprehension of graphics within a text, vocabulary knowledge and strategies, knowledge of informational text features, and use of comprehension strategies. The Diagnostic Assessment of Reading Comprehension (see Francis et al., 2006) assesses students' inferencing, text memory, recall of knowledge, and the ability to integrate prior knowledge with information in the text.

Unfortunately, virtually no research has as yet tested the impact of comprehension assessment, let alone different forms of comprehension assessment, on either the nature or quality of teacher instruction and/or student learning. One exception is a study by Bolt, Duke, Billman, and Betts (2011), in which they randomly assigned grades 1 and 2 teachers to administer an informational comprehension assessment (i.e., the Concepts of Comprehension Assessment) three times per year to a subset of students in their classes; and the teachers also received scores from the researchers for another subset. Results showed that students in classrooms in which teachers administered the assessment showed greater growth as measured by the comprehension assessment as well as by an assessment of informational writing; this transfer effect is important because it suggests that what students learned was not driven by narrowly teaching to the test. However, much more research is needed, including studies of the impact of different comprehension assessments on both teachers' comprehension instruction and students' comprehension growth.

Differentiate Instruction

As explained in the previous section, students have different strengths and weaknesses with respect to comprehension, suggesting the need for different foci for and kinds of instruction. Unfortunately, we have found that much comprehension instruction is provided in a whole-class format. For example, the entire class is provided with explicit instruction and modeling of the predicting strategy. If the bulk of the class is not predicting or not predicting well, then this makes sense. However, if some of the students are already making well-founded predictions regularly, they do not need this instruction. Additionally, if some students are still not monitoring their reading for meaning, instruction in that may be a higher priority for them. It is possible that instruction may lead to excessive reliance on a single strategy at the expense of developing a broader and more balanced portfolio of strategies (Hilden, 2009).

For these reasons, we suggest that much comprehension instruction be conducted in small groups or individually based on students' needs (e.g., Connor et al., 2009; Taberski, 2000). The idea of needs-based grouping is not at all new; it has been recommended by experts as an alternative to ability grouping for as long as we have worried about individual differences in schooling (see R.H. Anderson, 1962), but it isn't implemented as regularly as it should be, either for comprehension instruction or basic decoding skills. To illustrate how it might be employed, a group of students whose retellings reflect a lack of attention to the structure of the text might constitute a small group for instruction, a second group of students who would especially benefit from the opportunity to discuss texts with others in a structured format might form another group, and so forth. Notably, students with the same needs may not necessarily be reading at the same level in terms of word recognition. In these cases, it may make sense to select a text that is relatively easy from a word recognition perspective but difficult from a comprehension one (e.g., an easy-to-read text with relatively unfamiliar science content). In other cases, it may work just fine to teach and coach students in a group without all of them reading the same text. In the CORI approach discussed earlier, small groups of students form "idea circles," in which students meet to discuss the same idea (e.g., a particular adaptation for animal survival) as explored through different texts, each at the appropriate reading level of only one member or a subset of members of the group (Guthrie & McCann, 1996). Much more research and development is needed around needs-based grouping for comprehension instruction, but at this point, we believe that the complexity of comprehension processes and variation in comprehenders means that differentiation should be a priority.

Directions for Reading Comprehension Research and Development

As we hope this chapter has indicated, we know a great deal about how to foster and teach reading comprehension well (see Figure 3.3 for a useful tool for evaluating your own fostering and teaching of reading comprehension). However, we know far less about how to help teachers learn to orchestrate this panoply of practices. Despite decades of research identifying effective practices for improving reading comprehension, comprehension instruction remains rare (e.g., Connor, Morrison, & Petrella, 2004) and poorly done (e.g., Dewitz, Jones, & Leahy, 2009). We need to understand far better how great teachers of comprehension became great and how to help many more teachers become so. We need case studies of teachers learning to teach reading comprehension (e.g., Hilden & Pressley, 2007), research that examines the knowledge teachers need to engage in specific practices supportive of comprehension (e.g., Kucan, Hapgood, & Palincsar, in press), development of innovative approaches to preservice and inservice teacher education around reading comprehension (e.g., Kucan & Palincsar, 2008–2011), and studies of the impact of specific professional development models on students' reading comprehension growth (e.g., García et al., 2006; García, Pearson, Taylor, Bauer, & Stahl, in press; Pearson, Taylor, & Tam, 2005; Taylor, Pearson, Peterson, & Rodriguez, 2005).

In our chapter on effective practices for developing reading comprehension in this volume's last edition, we asked, "Will our definition and fundamental understanding of comprehension keep pace with the changing nature of text?" (Duke & Pearson, 2002, p. 232). As pressing as that question seemed in 2002, it is all the more pressing now. Forms of text widely read today (e.g., Twitter feed, blogs) did not even exist less than a decade ago. If research on different genres of text to date is any indication, readers will use somewhat different processes and strategies, and apply somewhat different structural and featural knowledge to understand these different forms of text (Coiro & Dobler, 2007; Duke & Roberts, 2010; Leu et al., 2005). We have been learning to modify our comprehension instruction for different genres of text, on- and offline (Duke et al., in press), but we need to make rapid progress in this area if we are to prepare readers to be versatile enough to comprehend the historically unprecedented range of text available to them.

Figure 3.3. A Tool for Evaluating Your Fostering and Teaching of Reading Comprehension

☐ Is much of the day devoted to building disciplinary or world knowledge?
    ☐ Is a combination of hands-on experience and text employed?
    ☐ Is emphasis placed on the discourse and practices of the discipline, as well as content?
    ☐ Are reading, writing, speaking, and listening presented as tools to help students acquire knowledge and inquiry skill?
☐ Are students provided with exposure to a volume and wide range of texts?
    ☐ Does instruction include texts that meet the following criteria?
        ☐ Of a wide range of genres
        ☐ On a wide range of topics
        ☐ Of a wide range of reading levels
        ☐ In both digital and print formats
    ☐ Is instruction tailored to specific genres and contexts during the literacy block and content area instruction?
    ☐ Do students have access to a wide range and large volume of texts for take-home and summer reading?
☐ Are students offered motivating texts and contexts for reading?
    ☐ Are students provided with texts of individual interest to them?
    ☐ Are classroom activities designed to involve choice, challenge, student control, collaboration, emphasis on constructing meaning, and consequences for students' effort?
    ☐ Are students reading (and writing) texts similar to those that occur outside of school for purposes similar to those for which people read and write outside of school?
☐ Are students taught to become strategic readers?
    ☐ Does instruction help students coordinate and use multiple strategies while reading?
    ☐ Does instruction focus on the following strategies that research indicates are worth teaching?
        ☐ Setting purposes for reading
        ☐ Previewing and predicting
        ☐ Activating prior knowledge
        ☐ Monitoring, clarifying, and fixing up
        ☐ Visualizing and creating visual representations
        ☐ Drawing inferences
        ☐ Self-questioning and thinking aloud
        ☐ Summarizing and retelling
    ☐ Does strategy instruction follow a gradual release of responsibility framework with an explicit description of when and how to use the strategy, modeling and collaborative use of the strategy in action, and guided and independent practice?
☐ Are students taught about text structures?
    ☐ Is instruction of text structures organized in a meaningful way across grade levels to enable students to do the following?
        ☐ Understand that text is structured
        ☐ Take advantage of this knowledge in learning and recalling key information in texts

(continued)

Essential Elements of Fostering and Teaching Reading Comprehension   83

Figure 3.3. A Tool for Evaluating Your Fostering and Teaching of Reading Comprehension *(continued)*

- □ Are students taught visual representations of common text structures through the use of graphic organizers (e.g., story maps, Venn diagrams, flowcharts)?
- □ Does instruction employ a gradual release of responsibility by explicitly describing text structures, modeling their use in reading and writing, using the structures of text collaboratively with students, and guiding them as they take increasing responsibility for attending to text structure?

- □ Is there an emphasis on engaging students in discussion around texts?
  - □ Do discussions place emphasis on the following?
    - □ Higher order questioning
    - □ Listening and linking to others' ideas
    - □ Providing evidence from the text to support one's thinking
    - □ Regular student participation

- □ Is a good portion of the day spent building students' vocabulary and language knowledge?
  - □ Does instruction provide students with multiple experiences with a wide variety of words (e.g., multiple-meaning words, related words, content area vocabulary)?
  - □ Is vocabulary and language knowledge instruction embedded in relevant contexts?
  - □ Do read-aloud experiences promote language learning through direct explanations of words along with meaningful discussion to foster deeper understanding?

- □ Are reading and writing connections emphasized?
  - □ Does instruction integrate reading and writing in a meaningful manner, such as through content area instruction or response to literature?
  - □ Is there an emphasis on helping students build a rich representation of the content from their readings through writing and oral discussion?
  - □ Do students have ample opportunities to revisit and re-represent important ideas in reading, writing, speaking, and listening?

- □ Is careful observation and assessment utilized regularly to ascertain students' comprehension weaknesses and strengths?
  - □ Are a range of assessment and observation tools used to understand different aspects of students' comprehension, such as their background knowledge, literal and inferential comprehension, and understanding of graphics?
  - □ Does information gathered via observation and assessment inform comprehension instruction in the classroom?

- □ Is instruction thoughtfully differentiated in the classroom?
  - □ Are lessons taught to the whole class only when most of the students in the room would benefit from that particular instruction at that particular time?
  - □ Does comprehension instruction include regular use of small groups based on students' particular comprehension strengths and needs?

Another key task facing research and development in reading comprehension is to understand how reading comprehension instruction is best coordinated across entire schools and districts. The relative scarcity of effective reading comprehension instruction in the past has meant the practices we have described in this chapter were sparsely implemented in schools (e.g., maybe 1 or 2 teachers in a staff of 15–20 might actually use them). What might happen when this kind of instruction is a focus every year in every classroom at every grade level? Do we, for example, teach the same comprehension strategies and text structures at each grade level, or does there come a point at which dividing and conquering these strategies and structures by year is more productive? What can we expect of students who have had years of high-quality comprehension instruction? How can we continue to challenge these students? Although these questions are complex and difficult to research, they also represent a welcome development. Having to deal with the aftermath of years of high-quality, comprehensive reading comprehension instruction would be a good problem to have.

Questions for Reflection

1. Find a text that is difficult for you to comprehend, such as a text in biochemical engineering, and note the processes you use to try to comprehend the text. How do these compare with the description of how skilled comprehenders construct meaning presented at the outset of this chapter?

2. While reading comprehension strategy instruction has taken hold in many classrooms, although not always in the manner we would like, many other essential elements of fostering and teaching comprehension identified in this chapter have not. Based on your experience in schools and classrooms, which of these elements are most neglected, and what factors do you think contribute to their neglect?

3. The essential elements we have presented apply well beyond the core reading program or the reading/language arts or literacy block. How can you imagine each of the essential elements mapping on the different parts of the school day and materials?

4. Arrange to observe comprehension instruction in a local school and classroom. Which essential elements do you see enacted in this classroom and how? Which elements deserve greater attention in the classroom, and how might that be accomplished?

REFERENCES

Abbott, R.D., Berninger, V.W., & Fayol, M. (2010). Longitudinal relationships of levels of language in writing and between writing and reading in grades 1 to 7. *Journal of Educational Psychology, 102*(2), 281–298. doi:10.1037/a0019318

Ainley, M. (2006). Connecting with learning: Motivation, affect and cognition in interest processes. *Educational Psychology Review, 18*(4), 391–405.

Allington, R.L., McGill-Franzen, A., Camilli, G., Williams, L., Graff, J., Zeig, J., et al. (2010). Addressing summer reading setback among economically disadvantaged elementary students. *Reading Psychology, 31*(5), 411–427. doi:10.1080/02702711.2010.505165

Anderson, R.C., & Pearson, P.D. (1984). A schema-theoretic view of basic processes in reading comprehension. In P.D. Pearson, R. Barr, M.L. Kamil, & P. Mosenthal (Eds.), *Handbook of reading research* (Vol. 1, pp. 255–291). New York: Longman.

Anderson, R.H. (1962). Organizing groups for instruction. In N.B. Henry & F.T. Tyler (Eds.), *Individualizing instruction* (pp. 239–264). Chicago: National Society for the Study of Education.

Applebee, A.N., Langer, J.A., Nystrand, M., & Gamoran, A. (2003). Discussion-based approaches to developing understanding: Classroom instruction and student performance in middle and high school English. *American Educational Research Journal, 40*(3), 685–730. doi:10.3102/00028312040003685

Apthorp, H.S. (2006). Effects of a supplemental vocabulary program in third-grade reading/language arts. *Journal Educational Research, 100,* 67–79.

Armbruster, B.B., Anderson, T.H., & Ostertag, J. (1987). Does text structure/summarization instruction facilitate learning from expository text? *Reading Research Quarterly, 22*(3), 331–346.

Baumann, J.F. (2009). Vocabulary and reading comprehension: The nexus of meaning. In S.E. Israel & G.G. Duffy (Eds.), *Handbook of research on reading comprehension* (pp. 323–346). New York: Routledge.

Baumann, J.F., & Bergeron, B.S. (1993). Story map instruction using children's literature: Effects on first graders' comprehension of central narrative elements. *Journal of Literacy Research, 25*(4), 407–437. doi:10.1080/10862969309547828

Beck, I.L., & McKeown, M.G. (2006). *Improving comprehension with questioning the author: A fresh and expanded view of a powerful approach.* New York: Scholastic.

Beck, I.L., McKeown, M.G., & Gromoll, E.W. (1989). Learning from social studies texts. *Cognition and Instruction, 6*(2), 99–158. doi:10.1207/s1532690xci0602_1

Beck, I.L., McKeown, M.G., Hamilton, R.L., & Kucan, L. (1997). *Questioning the author: An approach for enhancing student engagement with text.* Newark, DE: International Reading Association.

Beck, I.L., McKeown, M.G., Sandora, C., Kucan, L., & Worthy, J. (1996). Questioning the author: A yearlong classroom implementation to engage students with text. *The Elementary School Journal, 96*(4), 385–414. doi:10.1086/461835

Bereiter, C., & Scardamalia, M. (1987). *The psychology of written composition.* Hillsdale, NJ: Erlbaum.

Berninger, V.W., Abbott, R.D., Abbott, S.P., Graham, S., & Richards, T. (2002). Writing and reading: Connections between language by hand and language by eye. *Journal of Learning Disabilities, 35*(1), 39–56. doi:10.1177/002221940203500104

Biemiller, A., & Boote, C. (2006). An effective method for building vocabulary in primary grades. *Journal of Educational Psychology, 98,* 44–62.

Billman, A.K., Hilden, K., & Halladay, J.L. (2009). When the "right texts" are difficult for struggling readers. In E.H. Hiebert & M. Sailors (Eds.), *Finding the right texts: What works for beginning and struggling readers* (pp. 203–226). New York: Guilford.

Bitter, C., O'Day, J., Gubbins, P., & Socias, M. (2009). What works to improve student literacy achievement? An examination of instructional practices in a balanced literacy approach. *Journal of Education for Students Placed at Risk, 14*(1), 17–44. doi:10.1080/10824660802715403

Block, C.C., Parris, S.R., & Whiteley, C.S. (2008). CPMs: A kinesthetic comprehension strategy. *The Reading Teacher, 61*(6), 460–470. doi:10.1598/RT.61.6.3

Bolt, S., Duke, N.K., Billman, A.K., & Betts, J. (2011). *Facilitating early comprehension of informational text: Consequential validity of the Concepts of Comprehension Assessment*

(COCA). East Lansing: Michigan State University.

Bos, C.S., & Anders, P.L. (1990). Effects of interactive vocabulary instruction on the vocabulary learning and reading comprehension of junior-high learning disabled students. *Learning Disability Quarterly, 13*(1), 31–42.

Brabham, E.G., & Lynch-Brown, C. (2002). Effects of teachers' reading-aloud styles on vocabulary acquisition and comprehension of students in the early elementary grades. *Journal of Educational Psychology, 94*(3), 465–473.

Brophy, J. (2004). *Motivating students to learn* (2nd ed.). Mahwah, NJ: Erlbaum.

Brown, R. (2008). The road not yet taken: A transactional strategies approach to comprehension instruction. *The Reading Teacher, 61*(7), 538–547. doi:10.1598/RT.61.7.3

Buly, M.R., & Valencia, S.W. (2002). Below the bar: Profiles of students who fail state reading assessments. *Educational Evaluation and Policy Analysis, 24*(3), 219–239. doi:10.3102/01623737024003219

Burns, M.K., Dean, V.J., & Foley, S. (2004). Preteaching unknown key words with incremental rehearsal to improve reading fluency and comprehension with children identified as reading disabled. *Journal of School Psychology, 42*(4), 303–314.

Carlisle, J.F. (1995). Morphological awareness and early reading achievement. In L.B. Feldman (Ed.), *Morphological aspects of language processing* (pp. 189–209). Hillsdale, NJ: Erlbaum.

Cartwright, K.B. (2010). *Word callers: Small-group and one-to-one interventions for children who "read" but don't comprehend.* Portsmouth, NH: Heinemann.

Cervetti, G.N., Pearson, P.D., Bravo, M.A., & Barber, J. (2006). Reading and writing in the service of inquiry-based science. In R. Douglas, M.P. Klentschy, & K. Worth (Eds.), *Linking science and literacy in the K–8 classroom* (pp. 221–244). Arlington, VA: National Science Teachers Association Press.

Chinn, C.A., Anderson, R.C., & Waggoner, M.A. (2001). Patterns of discourse in two kinds of literature discussion. *Reading Research Quarterly, 36*(4), 378–411. doi:10.1598/RRQ.36.4.3

Coiro, J., & Dobler, E. (2007). Exploring the online reading comprehension strategies used by sixth-grade skilled readers to search for and locate information on the Internet.

Reading Research Quarterly, 42(2), 214–257. doi:10.1598/RRQ.42.2.2

Collins, J.L., Lee, J., Fox, J., & Madigan, T. (2011). *Bringing together reading and writing: An experimental study of Writing Intensive Reading Comprehension (WIRC) in low-performing urban elementary schools.* Manuscript submitted for publication.

Collins, J.L., & Madigan, T.P. (2010). Using writing to develop struggling learners' higher level reading comprehension. In J.L. Collins & T.G. Gunning (Eds.), *Building struggling students' higher level literacy: Practical ideas, powerful solutions* (pp. 103–124). Newark, DE: International Reading Association.

Connor, C.M., Morrison, F.J., & Petrella, J.N. (2004). Effective reading comprehension instruction: Examining child x instruction interactions. *Journal of Educational Psychology, 96*(4), 682–698. doi:10.1037/0022-0663.96.4.682

Connor, C.M., Piasta, S.B., Fishman, B., Glasney, S., Schatschneider, C., Crowe, E., et al. (2009). Individualizing student instruction precisely: Effects of child x instruction interactions on first graders' literacy development. *Child Development, 80*(1), 77–100.

Council of Chief State School Officers & National Governors Association. (2010). *Common core state standards for English language arts and literacy in history/social studies, science, and technical subjects.* Retrieved November 2, 2010, from www.corestandards.org/assets/CCSSI_ELA%20Standards.pdf

Coyne, M.D., McCoach, D.B., & Kapp, S. (2007). Vocabulary intervention for kindergarten students: Comparing extended instruction to embedded instruction and incidental exposure. *Learning Disability Quarterly, 30*(2), 74–88.

Craig, S.A. (2006). The effects of an adapted interactive writing intervention on kindergarten children's phonological awareness, spelling, and early reading development: A contextualized approach to instruction. *Journal of Educational Psychology, 98*(4), 714–731. doi:10.1037/0022-0663.98.4.714

Cunningham, A.E., & Stanovich, K.E. (2001). What reading does for the mind. *Journal of Direct Instruction, 1*(2), 137–149.

De La Paz, S. (2005). Effects of historical reasoning instruction and writing strategy mastery in culturally and academically diverse middle school classrooms. *Journal of Educational Psychology, 97*(2), 139–156. doi:10.1037/0022-0663.97.2.139

Dewitz, P., Jones, J., & Leahy, S. (2009). Comprehension strategy instruction in core reading programs. *Reading Research Quarterly, 44*(2), 102–126. doi:10.1598/RRQ.44.2.1

Donahue, P.L., Finnegan, R.J., Lutkus, A.D., Allen, N.L., & Campbell, J.R. (2001). *The nation's report card: Fourth-grade reading 2000* (NCES 2001-499). Washington, DC: National Center for Education Statistics, U.S. Department of Education.

Dong, T., Anderson, R.C., Kim, I., & Li, Y. (2008). Collaborative reasoning in China and Korea. *Reading Research Quarterly, 43*(4), 400–424. doi:10.1598/RRQ.43.4.5

Dorph, R., Goldstein, D., Lee, S., Lepori, K., Schneider, S., & Venkatesan, S. (2007). *The status of science education in the Bay Area.* Unpublished manuscript, University of California, Berkeley.

Duke, N.K. (2000). For the rich it's richer: Print experiences and environments offered to children in very low- and very high-socioeconomic status first-grade classrooms. *American Educational Research Journal, 37*(2), 441–478.

Duke, N.K., Caughlan, S., Juzwik, M.M., & Martin, N. (in press). *Doing genre with purpose in the K–8 classroom.* Portsmouth, NH: Heinemann.

Duke, N.K., & Pearson, P.D. (2002). Effective practices for developing reading comprehension. In A.E. Farstrup & S.J. Samuels (Eds.), *What research has to say about reading instruction* (3rd ed., pp. 205–242). Newark, DE: International Reading Association.

Duke, N.K., Pressley, M., & Hilden, K. (2004). Difficulties with reading comprehension. In C.A. Stone, E.R. Silliman, B.J. Ehren, & K. Apel (Eds.), *Handbook of language and literacy: Development and disorders* (pp. 501–520). New York: Guilford.

Duke, N.K., & Roberts, K.L. (2010). The genre-specific nature of reading comprehension. In D. Wyse, R. Andrews, & J. Hoffman (Eds.), *The Routledge international handbook of English, language and literacy teaching* (pp. 74–86). New York: Routledge.

Fink, R.P. (1995). Successful dyslexics: A constructivist study of passionate interest reading. *Journal of Adolescent & Adult Literacy, 39*(4), 268–280.

Fitzgerald, J., & Shanahan, T. (2000). Reading and writing relations and their development. *Educational Psychologist, 35*(1), 39–50. doi:10.1207/S15326985EP3501_5

Francis, D.J., Snow, C.E., August, D., Carlson, C.D., Miller, J., & Iglesias, A. (2006). Measures of reading comprehension: A latent variable analysis of the Diagnostic Assessment of Reading Comprehension. *Scientific Studies of Reading, 10*(3), 301–322. doi:10.1207/s1532799xssr1003_6

García, G.E., Bray, T.M., Mora, R.A., Ricklefs, M.A., Primeaux, J., Engel, L.C., et al. (2006). Working with teachers to change the literacy instruction of Latino students in urban schools. In J.V. Hoffman, D.L. Schallert, C.M. Fairbanks, J. Worthy, & B. Maloch (Eds.), *55th yearbook of the National Reading Conference* (pp. 155–170). Oak Creek, WI: National Reading Conference.

García, G.E., Pearson, P.D., Taylor, B.M., Bauer, E.B., & Stahl, K.A.D. (in press). Socio-constructivist and political views on teachers' implementation of two types of reading comprehension approaches in low-income schools. *Theory Into Practice.*

Gersten, R., Fuchs, L.S., Williams, J.P., & Baker, S. (2001). Teaching reading comprehension strategies to students with learning disabilities: A review of research. *Review of Educational Research, 71*(2), 279–320. doi:10.3102/00346543071002279

Goldman, S.R., & Rakestraw, J.A., Jr. (2000). Structural aspects of constructing meaning from text. In M.L. Kamil, P.B. Mosenthal, P.D. Pearson, & R. Barr (Eds.), *Handbook of reading research* (Vol. 3, pp. 545–561). Mahwah, NJ: Erlbaum.

Goldschmidt, P. (2010). *Evaluation of Seeds of Science/Roots of Reading: Effective tools for developing literacy through science in the early grades.* Los Angeles: University of California Press. Retrieved December 15, 2010, from www.scienceandliteracy.org/sites/scienceand literacy.org/files/bibio/seeds_eval_in_cresst _deliv_fm_060210_pdf_97520.pdf

Graham, S., & Hebert, M. (2010). *Writing to read: Evidence for how writing can improve reading: A report from Carnegie Corporation of New York.* Washington, DC: Alliance for Excellent Education.

Guthrie, J.T. (2004). Teaching for literacy engagement. *Journal of Literacy Research, 36*(1), 1–29. doi:10.1207/s15548430jlr3601_2

Guthrie, J.T., Anderson, E., Alao, S., & Rinehart, J. (1999). Influences of Concept-Oriented Reading Instruction on strategy use and conceptual learning from text. *The Elementary School Journal, 99*(4), 343–366. doi:10.1086/461929

Guthrie, J.T., & McCann, A.D. (1996). Idea circles: Peer collaborations for conceptual learning. In L.B. Gambrell & J.F. Almasi (Eds.), *Lively discussions! Fostering engaged reading* (pp. 87–105). Newark, DE: International Reading Association.

Guthrie, J.T., McRae, A., & Klauda, S.L. (2007). Contributions of Concept-Oriented Reading Instruction to knowledge about interventions for motivations in reading. *Educational Psychologist, 42*(4), 237–250.

Guthrie, J.T., Wigfield, A., Barbosa, P., Perencevich, K.C., Taboada, A., Davis, M.H., et al. (2004). Increasing reading comprehension and engagement through Concept-Oriented Reading Instruction. *Journal of Educational Psychology, 96*(3), 403–423. doi:10.1037/0022-0663.96.3.403

Guthrie, J.T., Wigfield, A., Humenick, N.M., Perencevich, K.C., Taboada, A., & Barbosa, P. (2006). Influences of stimulating tasks on reading motivation and comprehension. *Journal of Educational Research, 99*(4), 232–246. doi:10.3200/JOER.99.4.232-246

Guthrie, J.T., Wigfield, A., & Perencevich, K.C. (Eds.). (2004). *Motivating reading comprehension: Concept-Oriented Reading Instruction.* Mahwah, NJ: Erlbaum.

Hall, K.M., Sabey, B.L., & McClellan, M. (2005). Expository text comprehension: Helping primary-grade teachers use expository texts to full advantage. *Reading Psychology, 26*(3), 211–234. doi:10.1080/02702710590962550

Halladay, J.L. (2008). *Difficult texts and the students who choose them: The role of text difficulty in second graders' text choices and independent reading experiences.* Unpublished doctoral dissertation, Michigan State University, East Lansing.

Hiebert, E.H., & Kamil, M.L. (Eds.). (2005). *Teaching and learning vocabulary: Bringing research to practice.* Mahwah, NJ: Erlbaum.

Hilden, K.R. (2009, December). *Profiles for informational text comprehension in second grade.* Paper presented at the 59th annual meeting of the National Reading Conference, Albuquerque, NM.

Hilden, K.R., & Pressley, M. (2007). Self-regulation through transactional strategies instruction. *Reading & Writing Quarterly, 23*(1), 51–75. doi:10.1080/10573560600837651

Hoffman, J.V., Sailors, M., Duffy, G.R., & Beretvas, S.N. (2004). The effective elementary classroom literacy environment: Examining the validity of the TEX-IN3 observation system. *Journal of Literacy Research, 36*(3), 303–334. doi:10.1207/s15548430jlr3603_3

Idol, L. (1987). Group story mapping: A comprehension strategy for both skilled and unskilled readers. *Journal of Learning Disabilities, 20*(4), 196–205. doi:10.1177/002221948702000401

Jiménez, L., & Duke, N.K. (2011). *Interest matters: Fourth-graders reading multiple high- and low-interest texts.* Manuscript submitted for publication.

Kendeou, P., & van den Broek, P. (2007). The effects of prior knowledge and text structure on comprehension processes during reading of scientific texts. *Memory & Cognition, 35*(7), 1567–1577.

Kim, J.S., & White, T.G. (2008). Scaffolding voluntary summer reading for children in grades 3 to 5: An experimental study. *Scientific Studies of Reading, 12*(1), 1–23. doi:10.1080/10888430701746849

Kintsch, W. (1998). *Comprehension: A paradigm for cognition.* New York: Cambridge University Press.

Kintsch, W. (2004). The Construction-Integration model of text comprehension and its implications for instruction. In R.B. Ruddell & N.J. Unrau (Eds.), *Theoretical models and processes of reading* (5th ed., pp. 1270–1328). Newark, DE: International Reading Association.

Klingner, J.K., Vaughn, S., Arguelles, M.E., Hughes, M.T., & Leftwich, S.A. (2004). Collaborative strategic reading: "Real-world" lessons from classroom teachers. *Remedial and Special Education, 25*(5), 291–302. doi:10.1177/07419325040250050301

Knapp, M.S. (with Adelman, N.E., Marder, C., Mc-Collum, H., Needels, M.C., Padilla, C., et al.). (1995). *Teaching for meaning in high-poverty classrooms.* New York: Teachers College Press.

Konopak, B.C., Martin, S.H., & Martin, M.A. (1990). Using a writing strategy to enhance sixth-grade students' comprehension of content material. *Journal of Literacy Research, 22*(1), 19–37. doi:10.1080/10862969009547692

Kucan, L., Hapgood, S., & Palincsar, A.S. (in press). Teachers' specialized knowledge for supporting student comprehension in text-based discussions. *The Elementary School Journal.*

Kucan, L., & Palincsar, A. (2008–2011). *The iterative design of modules to support reading comprehension instruction.* Grant R305A080005 from the National Center for

Education Statistics, Institute of Education Sciences, U.S. Department of Education.

Langer, J.A. (2001). Beating the odds: Teaching middle and high school students to read and write well. *American Educational Research Journal*, *38*(4), 837–880. doi:10.3102/00028312038004837

Lederer, J.M. (2000). Reciprocal teaching of social studies in inclusive elementary classrooms. *Journal of Learning Disabilities*, *33*(1), 91–106. doi:10.1177/002221940003300112

Leu, D.J., Castek, J., Hartman, D.K., Coiro, J., Henry, L.A., Kulikowich, J.M., et al. (2005). *Evaluating the development of scientific knowledge and new forms of reading comprehension during online learning: Final report.* Naperville, IL: North Central Regional Educational Laboratory, Learning Point Associates.

Lipson, M.Y., & Wixson, K.K. (1991). *Assessment and instruction of reading disability: An interactive approach.* New York: HarperCollins.

McKeown, M.G., Beck, I.L., & Blake, R.G.K. (2009). Rethinking reading comprehension instruction: A comparison of instruction for strategies and content approaches. *Reading Research Quarterly*, *44*(3), 218–253. doi:10.1598/RRQ.44.3.1

McMurrer, J. (2008). *Instructional time in elementary schools: A closer look at changes for specific subjects.* Washington, DC: Center on Education Policy. Retrieved November 9, 2010, from www.cep-dc.org/index.cfm?fuseaction=document.showDocumentByID&nodeI%0D%0AD=1&DocumentID=234

McNamara, D.S., Floyd, R.G., Best, R., & Louwerse, M. (2004). *World knowledge driving young readers' comprehension difficulties.* Paper presented at the sixth biennial meeting of the International Society of the Learning Sciences, Santa Monica, CA.

McNamara, D.S., & Kintsch, W. (1996). Learning from texts: Effects of prior knowledge and text coherence. *Discourse Processes*, *22*(3), 247–288. doi:10.1080/01638539609544975

Meyer, B.J.F., Brandt, D.M., & Bluth, G.J. (1980). Use of top-level structure in text: Key for reading comprehension of ninth-grade students. *Reading Research Quarterly*, *16*(1), 72–103.

Morrow, L.M., Tracey, D.H., Woo, D.G., & Pressley, M. (1999). Characteristics of exemplary first-grade literacy instruction. *The Reading Teacher*, *52*(5), 462–476.

Murphy, P.K., Wilkinson, I.A.G., Soter, A.O., Hennessey, M.N., & Alexander, J.F. (2009). Examining the effects of classroom discussion on students' comprehension of text: A meta-analysis. *Journal of Educational Psychology*, *101*(3), 740–764. doi:10.1037/a0015576

Naceur, A., & Schiefele, U. (2005). Motivation and learning–the role of interest in construction of representation of text and long-term retention: Inter- and intraindividual analyses. *European Journal of Psychology of Education*, *20*(2), 155–170. doi:10.1007/BF03173505

Nagy, W.E., Berninger, V.W., & Abbott, R.D. (2006). Contributions of morphology beyond phonology to literacy outcomes of upper elementary and middle-school students. *Journal of Educational Psychology*, *98*(1), 134–147.

National Institute of Child Health and Human Development. (2000). *Report of the National Reading Panel. Teaching children to read: An evidence-based assessment of the scientific research literature on reading and its implications for reading instruction* (NIH Publication No. 00-4769). Washington, DC: U.S. Government Printing Office.

Nelson, J.R., & Stage, S.A. (2007). Fostering the development of vocabulary knowledge and reading comprehension though contextually-based multiple meaning vocabulary instruction. *Education and Treatment of Children*, *30*(1), 1–22.

Neuman, S.B. (1999). Books make a difference: A study of access to literacy. *Reading Research Quarterly*, *34*(3), 286–311. doi:10.1598/RRQ.34.3.3

Nolen, S.B. (2001). Constructing literacy in the kindergarten: Task structure, collaboration, and motivation. *Cognition and Instruction*, *19*(1), 95–142. doi:10.1207/S1532690XCI1901_3

Nolen, S.B. (2007). Young children's motivation to read and write: Development in social contexts. *Cognition and Instruction*, *25*(2/3), 219–270.

Palincsar, A.S., & Brown, A.L. (1984). Reciprocal teaching of comprehension-fostering and comprehension-monitoring activities. *Cognition and Instruction*, *1*(2), 117–175. doi:10.1207/s1532690xci0102_1

Palincsar, A.S., & Magnusson, S.J. (2001). The interplay of first-hand and second-hand investigations to model and support the development of scientific knowledge and reasoning. In S.M. Carver & D. Klahr (Eds.), *Cognition and instruction: Twenty-five years* of progress (pp. 151–193). Mahwah, NJ: Erlbaum.

Parodi, G. (2007). Reading–writing connections: Discourse-oriented research. *Reading and Writing, 20*(3), 225–250. doi:10.1007/s11145-006-9029-7

Paul, R. (1990). Comprehension strategies: Interactions between world knowledge and the development of sentence comprehension. *Topics in Language Disorders, 10*(3), 63–75.

Pearson, P.D., & Fielding, L. (1991). Comprehension instruction. In R. Barr, M.L. Kamil, P. Mosenthal, & P.D. Pearson (Eds.), *Handbook of reading research* (Vol. 2, pp. 815–860). New York: Longman.

Pearson, P.D., & Gallagher, M.C. (1983). The instruction of reading comprehension. *Contemporary Educational Psychology, 8*(3), 317–344.

Pearson, P.D., Moje, E.B., & Greenleaf, C. (2010). Literacy and science: Each in the service of the other. *Science, 328*(5977), 459–463. doi:10.1126/science.1182595

Pearson, P.D., Roehler, L.R., Dole, J.A., & Duffy, G.G. (1992). Developing expertise in reading comprehension. In S.J. Samuels & A.E. Farstrup (Eds.), *What research has to say about reading instruction* (2nd ed., pp. 145–199). Newark, DE: International Reading Association.

Pearson, P.D., Taylor, B.M., & Tam, A. (2005). Epilogue: Effective professional development for improving literacy instruction. In R. Indrisano & J.R. Paratore (Eds.), *Learning to write, writing to learn: Theory and research in practice* (pp. 221–234). Newark, DE: International Reading Association.

Pressley, M., Dolezal, S.E., Raphael, L.M., Mohan, L., Roehrig, A.D., & Bogner, K. (2003). *Motivating primary-grade students.* New York: Guilford.

Pressley, M., Wharton-McDonald, R., Allington, R.L., Block, C.C., & Morrow, L.M. (1998). *The nature of effective first-grade literacy instruction* (CELA Research Report No. 11007). Albany: National Research Center on English Learning & Achievement, State University of New York.

Pressley, M., Yokoi, L., Rankin, J., Wharton-McDonald, R., & Mistretta, J. (1997). A survey of the instructional practices of grade 5 teachers nominated as effective in promoting literacy. *Scientific Studies of Reading, 1*(2), 145–160. doi:10.1207/s1532799xssr0102_3

Purcell-Gates, V., Duke, N.K., & Martineau, J.A. (2007). Learning to read and write

genre-specific text: Roles of authentic experience and explicit teaching. *Reading Research Quarterly, 42*(1), 8–45. doi:10.1598/RRQ.42.1.1

Raphael, T.E., Englert, C.S., & Kirschner, B.W. (1989). Students' metacognitive knowledge about writing. *Research in the Teaching of English, 23*(4), 343–379.

Raphael, T.E., Kirschner, B.W., & Englert, C.S. (1988). Expository writing program: Making connections between reading and writing. *The Reading Teacher, 41*(8), 790–795.

Reutzel, D.R., Smith, J.A., & Fawson, P.C. (2005). An evaluation of two approaches for teaching reading comprehension strategies in the primary years using science information texts. *Early Childhood Research Quarterly, 20*(3), 276–305. doi:10.1016/j.ecresq.2005.07.002

Richgels, D.J., McGee, L.M., Lomax, R.G., & Sheard, C. (1987). Awareness of four text structures: Effects on recall of expository text. *Reading Research Quarterly, 22*(2), 177–196.

Robinson, D.H., & Kiewra, K.A. (1995). Visual argument: Graphic organizers are superior to outlines in improving learning from text. *Journal of Educational Psychology, 87*(3), 455–467. doi:10.1037/0022-0663.87.3.455

Romance, N.R., & Vitale, M.R. (2001). Implementing an in-depth expanded science model in elementary schools: Multiyear findings, research issues, and policy implications. *International Journal of Science Education, 23*(4), 373–404.

Sadoski, M., Goetz, E.T., & Rodriguez, M. (2000). Engaging texts: Effects of concreteness on comprehensibility, interest, and recall in four text types. *Journal of Educational Psychology, 92*(1), 85–95. doi:10.1037/0022-0663.92.1.85

Schraw, G., Flowerday, T., & Lehman, S. (2001). Increasing situational interest in the classroom. *Educational Psychology Review, 13*(3), 211–224. doi:10.1023/A:1016619705184

Shanahan, T. (2006). Relations among oral language, reading, and writing development. In C.A. MacArthur, S. Graham, & J. Fitzgerald (Eds.), *Handbook of writing research* (pp. 171–183). New York: Guilford.

Shanahan, T., Callison, K., Carriere, C., Duke, N.K., Pearson, P.D., Schatschneider, C., et al. (2010). *Improving reading comprehension in kindergarten through 3rd grade* (NCEE 2010-4038). Washington, DC: National Center for Education Evaluation and Regional Assistance, Institute of Education Sciences, U.S. Department of Education.

Shanahan, T., & Lomax, R.G. (1986). An analysis and comparison of theoretical models of the reading–writing relationship. *Journal of Educational Psychology, 78*(2), 116–123. doi:10.1037/0022-0663.78.2.116

Shatil, E., Share, D.L., & Levin, I. (2000). On the contribution of kindergarten writing to grade 1 literacy: A longitudinal study in Hebrew. *Applied Psycholinguistics, 21*(1), 1–21. doi:10.1017/S0142716400001016

Silverman, R., & Hines, S. (2009). The effects of multimedia-enhanced instruction on the vocabulary of English-language learners and non-English-language learners in prekindergarten through second grade. *Journal of Educational Psychology, 101*(2), 305–314. doi:10.1037/a0014217

Slater, W.H., Graves, M.F., & Piché, G.L. (1985). Effects of structural organizers on ninth-grade students' comprehension and recall of four patterns of expository text. *Reading Research Quarterly, 20*(2), 189–202.

Snow, C.E., Barnes, W.S., Chandler, J., Goodman, I.F., & Hemphill, L. (1991). *Unfulfilled expectations: Home and school influences on literacy.* Cambridge, MA: Harvard University Press.

Spörer, N., Brunstein, J.C., & Kieschke, U. (2009). Improving students' reading comprehension skills: Effects of strategy instruction and reciprocal teaching. *Learning and Instruction, 19*(3), 272–286. doi:10.1016/j.learninstruc.2008.05.003

Spycher, P. (2009). Learning academic language through science in two linguistically diverse kindergarten classes. *The Elementary School Journal, 109*(4), 359–379. doi:10.1086/593938

Stahl, S.A., & Nagy, W.E. (2006). *Teaching word meanings.* Mahwah, NJ, Erlbaum.

Stevens, R.J., Van Meter, P., & Warcholak, N.D. (2010). The effects of explicitly teaching story structure to primary grade children. *Journal of Literacy Research, 42*(2), 159–198. doi:10.1080/10862961003796173

Symons, S., MacLatchy-Gaudet, H., Stone, T.D., & Reynolds, P.L. (2001). Strategy instruction for elementary students searching informational text. *Scientific Studies of Reading, 5*(1), 1–33. doi:10.1207/S1532799XSSR0501_1

Taberski, S. (2000). *On solid ground: Strategies for teaching reading K–3.* Portsmouth, NH: Heinemann.

Taylor, B.M., Pearson, P.D., Clark, K., & Walpole, S. (2000). Effective schools and accomplished teachers: Lessons about primary-grade reading instruction in low-income schools. *The Elementary School Journal, 101*(2), 121–165. doi:10.1086/499662

Taylor, B.M., Pearson, P.D., Peterson, D.S., & Rodriguez, M.C. (2003). Reading growth in high-poverty classrooms: The influence of teacher practices that encourage cognitive engagement in literacy learning. *The Elementary School Journal, 104*(1), 3–28. doi:10.1086/499740

Taylor, B.M., Pearson, P.D., Peterson, D.S., & Rodriguez, M.C. (2005). The CIERA school change framework: An evidence-based approach to professional development and school reading improvement. *Reading Research Quarterly, 40*(1), 40–69. doi:10.1598/RRQ.40.1.3

Thomas, K.F., & Barksdale-Ladd, M.A. (1995). Effective literacy classrooms: Teachers and students exploring literacy together. In K.A. Hinchman, D.J. Leu, & C.K. Kinzer (Eds.), *Perspectives on literacy research and practice: The 44th yearbook of the National Reading Conference* (pp. 169–179). Chicago: National Reading Conference.

Tierney, R.J., & Shanahan, T. (1996). Research on the reading–writing relationship: Interactions, transactions, and outcomes. In R. Barr, M.L. Kamil, P.B. Mosenthal, & P.D. Pearson (Eds.), *Handbook of reading research* (Vol. 2, pp. 246–280). Mahwah, NJ: Erlbaum.

Tivnan, T., & Hemphill, L. (2005). Comparing four literacy reform models in high-poverty schools: Patterns of first-grade achievement. *The Elementary School Journal, 105*(5), 419–441. doi:10.1086/431885

Turner, J., & Paris, S.G. (1995). How literacy tasks influence children's motivation for literacy. *The Reading Teacher, 48*(8), 662–673.

Van den Branden, K. (2000). Does negotiation of meaning promote reading comprehension? A study of multilingual primary school classes. *Reading Research Quarterly, 35*(3), 426–443. doi:10.1598/RRQ.35.3.6

Wade, S.E. (1990). Using think alouds to assess comprehension. *The Reading Teacher, 43*(7), 442–451.

Wade, S.E., Trathen, W., & Schraw, G. (1990). An analysis of spontaneous study strategies. *Reading Research Quarterly, 25*(2), 147–166.

Wang, J., & Herman, J. (2005). *Evaluation of Seeds of Science/Roots of Reading project: Shoreline Science and Terrarium Investigations.* Los Angeles: National Center for Research on Evaluation, Standards, and Student Testing, University of California. Retrieved December 15, 2010, from www

.scienceandliteracy.org/sites/scienceand
literacy.org/files/biblio/wang_herman_2005
_cresst_pdf_21395.pdf

Wharton-McDonald, R., Pressley, M., & Hampston, J.M. (1998). Literacy instruction in nine first-grade classrooms: Teacher characteristics and student achievement. *The Elementary School Journal, 99*(2), 101–128. doi:10.1086/461918

Wilkinson, I.A.G., & Son, E.H. (2011). A dialogical turn in research on learning and teaching to comprehend. In M.L. Kamil, P.D. Pearson, E.B. Moje, & P.P. Afflerbach (Eds.), *Handbook of reading research* (Vol. 4, pp. 359–387). New York: Routledge.

Williams, J.P., Nubla-Kung, A.M., Pollini, S., Stafford, K.B., Garcia, A., & Snyder, A.E. (2007). Teaching cause–effect text structure through social studies content to at-risk second graders. *Journal of Learning Disabilities, 40*(2), 111–120. doi:10.1177/00222194070400 020201

Williams, J.P., Stafford, K.B., Lauer, K.D., Hall, K.M., & Pollini, S. (2009). Embedding reading comprehension training in content-area instruction. *Journal of Educational Psychology, 101*(1), 1–20. doi:10.1037/a0013152

Wolf, M.K., Crosson, A.C., & Resnick, L.B. (2004). Classroom talk for rigorous reading comprehension instruction. *Reading Psychology, 26*(1), 27–53. doi:10.1080/027027 10490897518

Yuill, N. (1998). Reading and riddling: The role of riddle appreciation in understanding and improving poor text comprehension in children. *Current Psychology of Cognition, 17*(2), 313–342.

Zipke, M., Ehri, L.C., & Cairns, H.S. (2009). Using semantic ambiguity instruction to improve third graders' metalinguistic awareness and reading comprehension: An experimental study. *Reading Research Quarterly, 44*(3), 300–321. doi:10.1598/RRQ.44.3.4

Chapter 4

Reading Fluency:
What It Is and What It Is Not

Timothy V. Rasinski and S. Jay Samuels

After years of neglect (Allington, 1983), the report of the National Reading Panel (National Institute of Child Health and Human Development [NICHD], 2000) finally returned the concept of reading fluency to the forefront of critical elements in effective reading instruction. Along with phonemic awareness, phonics or word decoding, vocabulary, and reading comprehension, the panel determined that there was sufficient and compelling research evidence to support identifying reading fluency as an essential component of reading instruction that was most likely to be effective in leading children to acquire literacy.

Despite the promising reemergence of fluency into the reading curriculum, the first decade of the 21st century saw controversy over what actually constitutes fluency, how it is best measured in students, at what grade levels fluency should be presented in the reading curriculum, how it is best taught in classrooms, to what extent fluency is associated only with oral reading, and what constitutes the characteristics of texts that are most appropriate for teaching fluency. In this chapter, we respond to these central questions. Although definitive answers may not be available at present, our hope is that we might frame future research into reading fluency and provide practitioners with some reasonable guidance for making informed instructional and curricular decisions regarding the teaching of fluency to students at all grade and achievement levels.

Defining Reading Fluency

Although most teachers of reading can distinguish between oral reading that is considered fluent and oral reading that is considered disfluent, the specific nature of reading fluency is not fully agreed upon by all reading scholars. Fluency has been described as the bridge from phonics to comprehension (Pikulski & Chard, 2005). Most recent reviews of

What Research Has to Say About Reading Instruction (4th ed.) edited by S. Jay Samuels and Alan E. Farstrup.
© 2011 by the International Reading Association.

the research (e.g., Kuhn, Schwanenflugel, & Meisinger, 2010; Rasinski, Reutzel, Chard, & Linan-Thompson, 2011) suggest that reading fluency has two major components that are associated with adequate levels of reading comprehension: automaticity in word recognition (LaBerge & Samuels, 1974) and prosody or expressiveness in oral reading (Schreiber, 1980, 1987, 1991; Schreiber & Read, 1980). Both of these components deal with the surface or observable level of text processing.

Automaticity is that part of the fluency bridge that connects to phonics or word recognition (see Figure 4.1). It refers to the ability of readers to decode words not just accurately but effortlessly or automatically. When readers are automatic in their word recognition, they are able to devote their finite cognitive resources to the more important task in reading—that is, comprehension. When readers are automatic in their word recognition their available cognitive resources are sufficiently large that they can at the same time process meaning.

Logan's (1997) instance theory provides an explanation for how automaticity is developed. Every encounter with reading a word creates a trace representation in memory of the word. Initial encounters require thinking or cognitive processing in order for the word to be processed. As the number of encounters increases, knowledge of the word becomes more extensive. Processing then becomes based on quick, automatic retrieval of memory traces from previous encounters rather than the slower, more cumbersome, attention-filled cognitive reasoning process.

Disfluent readers are not automatic in word recognition and have to devote significant portions of their finite cognitive resources to that task. As a result, these readers tend to read at a slower rate than would normally be expected at their age or grade level. Further, although they may be able to decode the words in text accurately, because so much of their cognitive energy is devoted to word recognition, they have less to devote to comprehension.

When we think of someone who is a fluent speaker or reader, we generally think of someone who speaks or reads orally in an expressive voice

Figure 4.1. Fluency: The Bridge From Phonics to Comprehension

Phonics ⟵⟶ Automaticity---Prosody ⟵⟶ Comprehension

(Word Recognition)   (Fluency)

that reflects the meaning of the passage. Prosody, the melodic features of oral language, is that part of fluency that completes the metaphorical bridge; it connects fluency to comprehension (see Figure 4.1). To read with prosody, readers must monitor the meaning of the text. They must have a sense of the meaning of a passage to know when to pause within sentences, to raise or lower their voice, to insert dramatic pauses, to emphasize particular words or parts of words.

Whether prosodic reading precedes or is a result of comprehension has not been determined. Nevertheless, it is reasonable to expect that when a reader is provided instruction in reading with appropriate expression, the focus must be on the making of meaning with one's voice. Research has shown that readers who read with good oral prosody and text phrasing tend to have better comprehension in silent reading than readers who are less proficient in the use of prosody (Daane, Campbell, Grigg, Goodman, & Oranje, 2005; Pinnell, Pikulski, Wixson, Campbell, Gough, & Beatty, 1995; Rasinski, Rikli, & Johnston, 2009).

Thus, when considering fluency, it is important that teachers keep in mind that to be comprehensive, fluency instruction needs to address both the automaticity component and the prosody component. In many schools, the focus of fluency instruction has been biased toward automaticity through instructional programs aimed at improving reading rate. Without commensurate attention to prosody and comprehension, reading fluency is an empty vessel. A view of fluency as referring to reading speed may be likened to driving a car in neutral gear. The driver can have the engine spinning at thousands of revolutions a minute, but until the gears are engaged, the car will not move. The rapidly revolving car engine is like the student who has been taught to decode words rapidly, but because the emphasis is on how fast she can read, the student never makes an attempt to engage comprehension. Some students have poor comprehension but adequate decoding skills because, like the driver who does not engage the gears, they have not made the connection between decoding and the need to engage in the comprehension process.

Because of this ill-conceived and illogical notion of reading fluency, many reading experts no longer view it as an important or worthy component of effective reading instruction (Cassidy & Cassidy, 2009). To gain a more precise and appropriate view of fluency, we now explore just what fluency is and what it is not.

Fluency Is Not Fast Reading

As we mentioned earlier, automaticity in reading fluency can be inferred or measured by the speed at which a reader reads. Readers who read at rates that are at or above grade-level norms give evidence that their word recognition is at an appropriately automatic level. And because these readers are able then to use less of their finite cognitive energy for word recognition and more for constructing meaning, reading comprehension tends to be strongly correlated with reading rate.

The correlation between reading rate and reading comprehension, as well as the ease and quickness with which reading rate can be determined, has led to the development of fluency instruction programs that focus primarily on increasing reading speed, with minimal attention given to prosody or comprehension. This overemphasis on reading rate has led students to think of proficient reading as fast reading. The increase in reading rate norms over the past decade for both proficient and less proficient readers, with little accompanying increase in reading comprehension or overall reading proficiency, is evidence of this singular emphasis (Rasinski & Hamman, 2010). But although reading rate can be an indicator or measure of one aspect of reading fluency, fast reading is decidedly not fluent reading (Rasinski, 2006; Samuels, 2007). A reader can actually be disfluent by reading too fast, at a speed that does not reflect comprehension or that gives evidence that the reader is not attending to the meaning of the text. As a measure of automaticity, reading rate may be highly correlated with reading comprehension, but correlation does not imply causation.

We feel that increased reading rates are an outcome of the development of automaticity in word recognition. Comprehension also is an outcome of automaticity—as readers become more automatic in word recognition, they are able to attend more to the making of meaning—and, thus, reading rate and reading comprehension are highly correlated. But one is not the cause of the other. Both are caused by the fluency factor—that is, automaticity in word recognition.

Rather than teach reading by focusing on reading rate, fluency is most appropriately taught by focusing on the development of word-recognition automaticity within the larger process of comprehension. This is done through approaches such as assisted reading, wide reading, and repeated readings. As automaticity improves, reading rate, reading comprehension, and overall reading proficiency will also improve.

Fluency Is Not Just for the Primary Grades

In her model of reading, Chall (1996) identified fluency as a developmental milestone achieved in the stages of reading development that generally occur in the primary grades. The model suggests that once it is achieved, higher-level reading processes (vocabulary, reading comprehension, etc.) take the main stage and fluency no longer is or should be an issue for instruction.

We feel that students deal with fluency at all stages of reading development. The oral reading studies included as part of the U.S. National Assessment of Educational Progress (NAEP) found that nearly half of all fourth-grade students had not achieved levels of fluency expected for their grade levels and that these students also demonstrated lower levels of overall reading achievement (Daane et al., 2005; Pinnell et al., 1995). Given Chall's (1996) model and its emphasis on fluency only in the primary grades, it is not unreasonable to expect that if students have not achieved adequate levels of fluency in the early years of schooling, it is unlikely that they will do so in subsequent grades. If fluency is an issue for the primary grades, teachers of intermediate and higher grades will not view fluency as a major concern, will not have training in teaching fluency, and likely are using instructional programs in reading that do not include fluency as a major strand.

Further, although a student may be fluent in reading primary-level material, he may not be fluent with all texts. As students move into the intermediate, middle, and secondary grades, the texts they are expected to read become more challenging, not only in terms of content, but also in terms of word difficulty.

In recent studies by Rasinski, Padak, McKeon, Wilfong, Friedauer, and Heim (2005) and Rasinski et al (2009), a substantial relationship was found between fluency (whether defined and measured as automaticity or prosody), reading comprehension, and overall reading achievement for upper elementary, middle school, and secondary school students. Moreover, in both studies a significant number of students at all levels demonstrated inadequate levels of fluency in their reading. Thus, research is suggesting that reading fluency is an important issue beyond the primary grades for a significant number of students and that it needs to be taught in the intermediate, middle, and secondary years.

Fluency Is Not Simply Oral Reading

Most models of reading posit that fluency is a proficiency that manifests itself in oral reading. Indeed, in many models, the term *fluency* is often preceded by the modifier *oral*—oral reading fluency. This may make sense, as we often associate oral reading fluency with fluency in speaking, and prosody can be demonstrated through oral reading. Yet beyond the primary grades, most reading is silent. If fluency is found only in oral reading and oral reading diminishes substantially after the primary grades, then reading fluency's later relevance in the reading curriculum is tenuous at best.

We feel that fluency is a proficiency manifest in *both* oral and silent reading. Conceptually, it is clear that the same processes that occur during oral reading also happen during silent reading. When reading silently, readers must decode words; automatic word decoding in silent reading allows them to focus on meaning. The correlation between silent reading and oral reading rates is strong. Many readers report hearing an internal voice while reading silently. This suggests that prosody, most prominent in oral reading, is also a component of silent reading. Schreiber (1980, 1987, 1991) argues that one of the main functions of oral reading prosody is to assist readers in parsing text into meaningful phrasal units. The process of phrasing a text is also present during silent reading.

Indeed, it is highly reasonable to expect that the way one reads orally will be reflected in the way one reads silently. We feel that the processes of word-recognition automaticity and prosodic reading found in oral reading are also manifested in silent reading and can affect, positively or negatively, silent reading performance. A significant body of research has shown strong correlations between measures of oral reading fluency and silent reading comprehension or overall reading achievement as measured by a silent reading assessment (Deno, 1985; Deno, Mirkin, & Chiang, 1982; Rasinski, 1985). The large-scale NAEP oral reading studies found strong correlations between oral reading fluency and silent reading comprehension for fourth-grade students (Daane et al., 2005; Pinnell et al., 1995). Similarly, Rasinski et al. (2005) and Rasinski et al. (2009) found significant and substantial correlations between oral reading fluency measures and silent reading comprehension for students in third, fifth, eighth, and ninth grades.

With the relationship between oral and silent reading in mind, Hiebert (2006) noted the need for fluency interventions that "provide opportunities for students to transfer their skills to silent reading" (p. 208). Responding to this need, Reutzel and colleagues (Reutzel, Fawson, & Smith, 2008; Reutzel, Jones, Fawson, & Smith, 2008) developed a silent reading fluency protocol entitled Scaffolded Silent Reading. This modified approach to Sustained Silent Reading allows for greater teacher input and makes students more accountable for time spent reading silently. Reutzel and his colleagues report gains in fluency similar to those found in guided repeated reading, a more traditional oral reading fluency protocol.

The bottom line to this growing body of research is that oral reading and silent reading are similar processes, and both manifest aspects of fluency. Instruction in reading fluency, whether oral or silent, needs to be mindful that the effects of such instruction will also be found in both forms of reading.

If Not to Increase Speed, How Is Fluency Best Taught?

We have argued that fluency instruction aimed only at increasing reading speed is not appropriate or sufficiently comprehensive. Keep in mind that automaticity is only one component of fluency. Teaching students to read quickly does not begin to deal with prosody, the other component of fluency. What we need are instructional methods that aim to improve students' word-recognition automaticity and, at the same time, their prosody—in both oral and silent reading.

We suggest an acronym, MAPPS, as a guide for working on fluency with students. In the following sections we describe what we mean with each letter of the acronym.

M—Modeling Fluent Reading for Students

For students to become fluent readers, they need to have an idea of what is meant by fluency. Through many current instructional programs that focus on increasing reading rate, many developing readers may come to think that fluency is nothing more than reading as fast as possible. But, as discussed throughout this chapter, fluency is the ability to decode words in text accurately and automatically *and* to read with prosody— thus indicating that comprehension is simultaneously occurring. For students to develop this internal definition of fluency, they need to experience such fluent reading. The best way for students to experience such fluency is to hear it produced by another, more fluent reader. In practice, this means that teachers need to read aloud to students meaningfully and expressively.

Reading to students is already recommended for a number of reasons: Students who are read to regularly are more motivated to read, have larger vocabularies, and are more proficient in reading comprehension. Now we have another reason to read to students—namely, to model for them what is meant by fluency.

From time to time after reading to your students, discuss with them how you used your voice to reflect and add to the meaning of the passage. It is important to indicate that when the ideas and information in a text are difficult, a reader should slow down to understand—that reading too fast can be detrimental to comprehension. Direct students' attention to the fact that you read at a fairly quick pace overall, but that you slowed down in certain parts of the reading and sped up at others, that you changed your voice when you became different characters, that you raised and lowered the tone and volume of your reading at different points, that you marked punctuation by pausing, and that you used dramatic and extended pauses to add meaning that went beyond the actual text itself; in sum, that through your oral rendering of the text you were reflecting the meaning of the passage, and that you were adding meaning by creating inferences with your voice. Your read-aloud can help students see that meaning is embedded not just in the words of the passage, but also in the way that the words are read. And, of course, the message to students is that they should try to read in this way when reading orally (and silently).

Students can often learn from a negative example as well. Sometimes (but not often), read to them in ways that are clearly disfluent. Use a monotone, without regard to punctuation, in a word-by-word manner that is very slow or extremely fast. You won't get far before students protest. At that point, you should discuss what caused the problems for students in listening to and attempting to make sense of your reading. You might point out that you were reading the words correctly. Again, this will lead students to discover meaning depends not just on reading the words correctly, but also on the manner in which the words are read.

Of course, you might also want to talk with your students about how you achieved fluency—most notably from repeated practice or rehearsal aimed not at speed, but at developing an expressive and meaningful reading of the passage. The human brain needs time to think and digest what it is reading. Read a difficult text to students at a fast rate and ask them if they can understand it. Next, slow down and ask if they understand better. When driving a car at high speed, the scenery passes by too fast to be noticed or appreciated. To enjoy the scenery, one needs sometimes ⟵ to slow down.

A—Assisted Reading for Support

Assisted reading is a fluency approach that we liken to learning to ride a bicycle by attaching training wheels or having mom or dad run alongside, making sure the new rider stays up. After some time riding successfully with support, the child can ride independently without it—and can also ride another bike with little difficulty. What she learned by riding one bike transfers to other bikes.

This is a nice analogy, because in some ways reading is the same. A text that a student is unable to read successfully on her own can often be read with the assistance of a more fluent reader who, like the training wheels or an assisting parent, reads alongside. With sufficient practice, the student will learn to read the text without assistance. Moreover, the fluency gained through the assistance given on one passage transfers to other passages the student has not yet experienced: She is able to read other texts on her own with a higher degree of fluency (and comprehension).

Assisted reading can take a variety of forms. Perhaps the most common is choral or group reading (Rasinski, 2010), which takes place in many elementary classrooms. When reading with a group, the less-than-fluent reader is supported by listening to other, more fluent members of the group who are simultaneously reading the same text. Eventually, the practiced text can be read independently and the reading of other texts will improve as well.

When done with a single more fluent partner, choral reading is known as paired reading (Rasinski, 2010; Topping, 1987a, 1987b). The protocol for paired reading is a bit more complex than for choral reading. In a paired reading lesson, a student and tutor (parent, teacher, classroom volunteer or aide, older student, or peer) sit side by side with one text, normally chosen by the student. They read the text aloud together, with the tutor adjusting the pace of his voice to allow the student to read along. The student should use his finger to track the text visually as the tutor leads him through. Paired reading is designed to give the student some control over the process. If the student feels confident to read a section of the text alone, he signals the tutor (a slight nudge with an elbow usually suffices) to be quiet. The student continues reading, with the tutor either following along silently or shadowing the student's reading in a soft voice. Should the student come to an area of difficulty, the tutor jumps back into the lead. This process continues for 10 to 15 minutes. The tutor may wish to take note of any words that the student had difficulty with and provide a very brief minilesson on those words at the end of the reading.

Topping (1987a, 1987b) found that paired reading done by parents with their children on a regular basis resulted in significant improvements in both fluency and reading comprehension. This is not unexpected. If fluency is the bridge between phonics and comprehension, we should expect to find improvements in comprehension as a result of fluency instruction.

Another approach to assisted reading employs technology by having students listen to a text on audiotape or disk or as a podcast. This audio-assisted reading results in much the same experience as paired reading. Of course, with audio-assisted reading, the student may not actually have a copy of the text and be tracking it visually, and the recorded version does not allow for the personal modifications and adjustments that a parent or teacher can make to provide additional assistance to the student during the reading. Nevertheless, research into using various forms of audio-assisted reading on a regular basis (15 to 25 minutes daily) has demonstrated powerful results for fluency, comprehension, and overall reading achievement, especially for struggling readers (Carbo, 1978a, 1978b; Chomsky, 1976; Pluck, 1995).

A passive form of assisted reading can be found in something most students do every day—watch television. Turning on the television's captioning function turns it into an assisted-reading device. Readers see text while simultaneously, or nearly simultaneously, hearing the words uttered. Some preliminary research has shown positive effects for students watching captioned television (Koskinen, Bowen, Gambrell, Jensema, & Kane, 1996), and although more research is certainly needed, captioned television provides some interesting possibilities for turning a daily activity into a passive form of fluency instruction.

Every time a student sees a word (whether on a printed page, a computer monitor, or a television screen) and hears the word read, both the sight and sound of the word will form a trace in the student's memory. Done repeatedly, the sight and sound of the word will eventually become embedded in memory to the point where the student can access the pronunciation of the word instantly from seeing its visual display. The word becomes a sight word, recognized instantly. This is the foundation for automaticity.

P—Practice Reading, Wide and Deep

Whether one is learning to drive, becoming a chef or a surgeon, making a jump shot in basketball, or reading, we would all agree that practice is necessary. Engaging in an activity regularly helps a learner master it. Practice makes perfect.

In reading, we most often think of practice in the form of wide reading, the kind of reading that most readers do. Wide reading refers to maximizing the sheer volume of what a person reads. When we finish reading a book, we usually move on to the next book—and the next and the next. This is wide reading, and it dominates traditional reading instruction. When students finish reading a story in their basal reader or a trade book or a chapter in a content area textbook, after a bit of instruction aimed at deepening their understanding of the text, they are usually assigned to read the next story, the next book, or the next chapter. Clearly, wide reading forms the basis for reading and reading instruction from childhood to adulthood. A large and wide amount of reading is necessary for students to become fluent and proficient readers.

However, we suggest that another form of practice also needs to be made part of the instructional milieu for developing readers— namely, deep or repeated reading. Sometimes readers need to read a text more than once to master it and set the stage for the next reading. University students, for example, routinely do deep, repeated reading of the same text to master its contents.

Consider the following. A student reads a text for the first time and does not read it well—not an uncommon experience in most classrooms. But, in a need to finish the textbook, the teacher moves on to the next chapter, which the student also reads in at best a mediocre manner. This is followed by another and another and another new reading, all done less than fluently. Isn't the result simply that the student has practiced mediocre reading? Should we be surprised if we end up with mediocre results for the student?

In addition to engaging in wide reading (one passage after another), we feel that students, especially our younger and less fluent readers, need to read certain texts or portions of texts repeatedly until they can read the passage fluently before moving on to the next passage. This form of reading practice is called repeated or deep reading.

Samuels' (1979) classic study of repeated reading showed us the benefits that come from having students read a text more than once. Samuels had struggling primary grade children read a short text several times until they could read it with a degree of fluency. As expected, he found that every time the students read the same text, their word recognition, fluency, and comprehension all improved. It was when he moved the students on to new passages, passages never previously read before, in the same text that Samuels demonstrated the power of repeated readings. The initial reading of the new passage was done with greater fluency and comprehension than the initial reading of the previous passage. Since the passages were from the same text, some of the words from the preceding passage appeared in the new passage. By practicing one passage, students learned something that transferred to subsequent passages that had not been seen previously. Real learning was taking place! Since that original study, a strong body of research has developed that has shown that repeated reading is a powerful tool for developing fluency in struggling and developing readers (Rasinski et al., 2011).

If you are working with readers who are making minimal progress through wide reading, we hope you will consider complementing it with a daily repeated reading routine. During one session, have students read 50- to 250-word passages at their individual instructional levels repeatedly until they attain some degree of fluency. (This normally takes about four readings.) On the following day, have the students go through the same routine with a new passage that is as challenging or slightly more challenging than the one before. The bootstrapping effect that comes from practicing with successively more challenging texts will lead to improvements in fluency, comprehension, and overall reading achievement.

Making Repeated Readings Valid, Authentic, and Effective. As a result of this powerful research, several commercial fluency instruction programs have been developed that incorporate repeated readings as a core element. In these programs, the main method for measuring progress and determining when a student should move from repeated reading of one passage to the next is reading rate or speed—that is, once students achieve a certain reading rate through repeated practice, they move on to the next text.

We feel that this instructional approach to repeated readings lacks authenticity and validity. As mentioned earlier, one aspect of fluency, automaticity, can be assessed through reading rate. But improvements in reading rate are a consequence, not the cause, of improved fluency. In these instructional programs, reading rate is viewed as the cause of fluency—that is, they assume that if rate can be improved, then fluency itself will also improve. As a result of this emphasis on repeated reading for rate, students define good reading as "reading fast" and believe that improvements in reading are made by learning to read ever more quickly.

We can think of very few, if any, instances in real life where one is asked to read something repeatedly for the purpose of increasing how fast it is read. But where in real life do people engage in repeated readings for real purposes? Our answer is in performance. Whether in dance, music, theater, or sports, performers practice or rehearse their performance repeatedly until it achieves a level of automaticity.

Language-based performing arts include theater, poetry, song, oratory, and others. And when performers rehearse their texts, the goal is not simply to develop automaticity, but to present with appropriate prosody or expression so that a listening audience will be able to take full meaning from the performance. Thus, repeated reading of texts meant to be performed is not only an authentic approach to fluency instruction, it is also comprehensive because it aims to develop both automaticity and prosody.

A growing body of classroom-based research on this approach to repeated reading instruction has demonstrated its validity and potential. Whether the repeated reading protocol is manifested in regular instructional routines built around Readers Theatre (Martinez, Roser, & Strecker, 1999; Young & Rasinski, 2009), poetry and rhymes (Rasinski & Stevenson, 2005), song (Biggs, Homan, Dedrick, Minick, & Rasinski, 2008), or some combination of performances (Griffith & Rasinski, 2004), fluency and other aspects of reading proficiency improve. In one classroom study using various authentic texts for repeated readings (Griffith & Rasinski, 2004), fourth-grade teacher Lorraine reported that her struggling students made, on average, 2.9 years' growth in overall reading proficiency in one year in her classroom. Moreover, although rate was never an instructional priority for the repeated readings (one does not repeatedly practice a poem or song in order to read it fast), improvements in reading rate were, nevertheless, remarkable: The struggling fourth graders made average gains of close to 60 words per minute over the year. Rate is an outcome of good fluency instruction; it is not the aim of such instruction.

P—Phrasing of Words in Meaningful Groups

Arguably, the hallmark of disfluent reading is staccato word-by-word reading that does not attend to phrase and sentence boundaries and does not sound at all like real language. Fluent reading, on the other hand, is marked by reading in which groups of words (phrases) are chunked together and read with prosody reflecting the phrasing.

Rasinski (2010) suggests that the natural unit of reading may not be the word at all but the phrase, clause, or other grouping of words that reflects meaning as it is expressed in a sentence. Prepositions such as *in*, *if*, and *on*, noun markers such as *a*, *an*, and *the*, and conjunctions such as *and*, *or*, and *but* have little meaning by themselves. They have to be embedded into a phrase, clause, or sentence to express their meaning.

Given the importance of phrases and the fact that disfluent readers tend not to attend to phrases when reading, it seems logical that instruction on phrasing text while reading can have a beneficial impact on readers' fluency and overall reading proficiency. In reviews of research on phrasing, Rasinski (1990, 1994) found compelling evidence that such instruction can positively affect students' proficiency in reading.

Phrasing instruction can take a variety of forms, and here we suggest two. // First, / brief texts / for students to read / can be formatted / or marked / in advance / to demonstrate graphically / the location of phrase and sentence boundaries / when reading. // That is, students are given specific, visual cues as to how to parse a text into meaningful units, as shown in the preceding sentence. Students can practice the text (repeated reading) until they can read so that they honor phrases and phrase boundaries. Additional repeated readings can be added to the protocol by asking students then to practice the same passage with the marked phrased boundaries deleted. In this way, students transfer the knowledge gained from practicing a phrase-cued text to texts that are written in a more conventional manner.

A second approach is simply to have students practice reading short phrases or sentences. Fry and Rasinski (2007) developed an approach in which the phrases that students are given to practice are made up of high-frequency words:

- my little sister
- your big brother
- in the house
- by the water
- this and that
- Give it to me.

Through repeated practice over several days, students learn to recognize high-frequency words as they appear in chunks in meaningful phrases and short sentences.

S—Synergy to Make the Whole Greater Than the Sum of Its Parts

The first four letters in our MAPPS acronym outline the elements of effective fluency instruction. Each by itself will help students develop fluency and clarify their understanding of what is meant by fluent reading. We hope that each of these elements—modeling, assisted reading, practice, and phrasing—finds a place in your classroom or intervention reading program. However, as important as each of these elements is by itself, combining various elements into more complex instructional protocols will create synergy—and the total impact of instruction will become more than simply the sum of each of the elements implemented individually.

The development of a synergistic instructional routine involves both science and art. First, with respect to science, a good body of research supports modeling fluent reading, assisted reading, wide and repeated reading, and phrasing instruction, as noted in the studies cited throughout this chapter. How these elements are combined to create the fluency routine is where the art of teaching comes in. Teachers, aware of their own students' strengths and weaknesses, their own style of teaching, their own time and setting constraints, and the materials available to them, need to artistically weave the elements of fluency instruction into a seamless whole that can be delivered on a regular and sustained basis. Two such fluency routines are the Fluency Development Lesson and Fast Start.

The Fluency Development Lesson. The Fluency Development Lesson (FDL; Rasinski, Padak, Linek, & Sturtevant, 1994) was developed in response to some schools' expressed need for instruction for primary students who had developed some proficiency in phonics, but had yet to break out of word-by-word reading of connected written discourse to more fluent reading that reflected the meaning of the text. The FDL was designed as a daily 10- to 15-minute lesson in which students work with one short text, usually an age-appropriate poem or an excerpt from the basal reading program used in the classroom. The teacher prepares two copies of the text for each student along with a large display version (overhead transparency or chart). The daily routine includes the following steps:

1. The teacher introduces the text and reads it from the display version two or three times, asking students to follow along silently. The teacher changes her or his voice in order to alter the delivery of the oral text.

2. The teacher leads the students in a brief discussion of the meaning of the passage and also of her or his oral rendering of the piece.

3. The teacher passes out two copies of the text to each student. Teacher and students together chorally read the text two or three more times from either the display copy or students' individual

copies, using various choral forms (group choral, antiphonal choral, echo reading, cumulative choral, etc.).

4. The children form pairs. One student in each pair reads the text to his or her partner two or three times while the partner follows along, provides assistance, and gives positive feedback. Roles are then reversed.

5. The teacher arranges for students to perform their reading for various audiences (small groups of classmates, a visiting parent, other classrooms, the school principal and other school staff, etc.) in various forms (individual, pairs, trios, quartets, etc.). As students become more adept at performing, they orchestrate their own form of performance.

6. A five-minute word study ensues in which words are chosen from the text for a short period of word work (e.g., display on the word wall and further reading, identifying and expanding on word families, word sorting, word games).

7. Students place one copy of their text into their "poetry folder" for further reading and weekly poetry parties.

8. The second text copy goes home with students, who are instructed to read the poem to family members as many times as possible with expression and meaning. Family members who listen (some as many as five or six times) provide positive feedback. In some classrooms, the teacher has listeners sign the back of the text copy and include a positive comment about the reading. Many students are highly motivated to come to school the next morning with the reverse side of their text filled with signatures (and even paw prints from pets who had listened).

9. Subsequent days' texts are introduced using the same routine. However, before a new lesson, the teacher reviews texts from previous days with students.

We hope you notice that embedded in the FDL are modeling of fluent reading, assisted reading, and repeated reading. And because a new text is used daily, wide reading also is a feature of the lesson.

A growing body of evidence has demonstrated the effectiveness of the FDL in improving fluency and overall reading achievement for students at a variety of reading levels, but in particular readers who struggle (Kulich, 2009; Rasinski et al., 1994). The FDL has been a core instructional element of the Kent State University Reading Clinic for the past decade. Students in the clinic, all struggling readers, make remarkable progress in all facets of reading as a result of daily employment of the FDL.

Fast Start. Fast Start (FS; Padak & Rasinski, 2004, 2005; Rasinski, 1995) is a variant of the FDL that recognizes the limits of the school day, the benefits of parent involvement, and the relative simplicity of the FDL. Essentially, FS employs a daily text, usually supplied by a teacher (again, a short rhyme works very well), that parents can use to work with their children for 10 to 15 minutes per day in the following routine:

1. The parent (or other caregiver) reads the text to the child two or three times while the child follows along silently.
2. Parent and child together chorally read the text two or three times.
3. The child reads the text to the parent two or three times, with the parent providing assistance as necessary.
4. The parent and child engage in word study (e.g., identifying the -eep word family in Little Bo Peep and expanding on it to create other -eep words such as *sleep, keep, beep, jeep*).

The simplicity and ease of the lesson makes it something that parents can feel confident in doing and will do regularly and with fidelity.

Again, the research supporting FS with young readers is strong. In a three-month implementation, Rasinski and Stevenson (2005) found that the most at-risk first-grade students in an urban school made close to twice the progress in word recognition and fluency using FS at home than did at-risk students who received the same instruction in school and took home a daily poem, but did not do the FS routine with their parents. Moreover, parents who used FS with their children were enthusiastic about it and felt that they were making a substantive contribution to their children's literacy development.

Such results should not be a surprise. When informed teachers combine scientifically sound instructional elements into artistically engaging instructional routines, students will respond enthusiastically and with academic gains, as has been demonstrated through research.

Conclusion

Although the National Reading Panel identified fluency as a critical element of effective reading instruction (NICHD, 2000), it has yet to measure up to its potential in actual classroom instruction. Hence, reading fluency is "not hot" (Cassidy & Cassidy, 2009) and again risks becoming the neglected goal of the reading curriculum. In this chapter we have explored the reasons for fluency's cool reception: It is viewed as something only for the primary grades, as only an oral reading competency, and as nothing more than teaching students to read fast. These are all partially or wholly incorrect ideas about fluency.

There is much that we still need to learn about reading fluency. In addition to the issues that emerge from the concerns raised in the previous paragraph, other questions are worthy of scientific inquiry. Among these are the following:

- Is there a particular type of text that is best suited for fluency instruction?
- Is there a particular level of text difficulty that maximizes student progress in reading?
- Is there a certain number of repeated readings that maximizes progress?
- Should repeated readings be massed (in one day) or spaced (over several days)?
- How much time per day should be devoted to fluency instruction in the classroom?

Although fluency has lost some of its luster in the eyes of reading educators over the past few years, the research suggests that it has remarkable potential for improving students' reading proficiency and that many students have not achieved adequate levels of fluency in their reading. Fluency must not be abandoned. We feel that when fluency is viewed as that critical link from phonics to comprehension, when it is defined as simultaneous automaticity, prosody, and comprehension in reading, and when it is taught in ways that reflect authentic, real-life reading and use scientifically based methods, fluency will indeed become the "hot topic" that it should be.

Questions for Reflection

1. Think about those students in your class who struggle in reading and comprehension. To what extent do those students struggle with reading fluency? To what extent do you think these students' difficulties in reading comprehension are due to fluency concerns?

2. How does fluency instruction fit into your classroom? Is there an equal emphasis on comprehension, prosody, and automaticity in your instruction? If not, what can you do to make fluency instruction more balanced?

3. How do your students respond to fluency instruction? Do they find it authentic and enjoyable? Would they tend to define reading fluency as "reading fast"? If so, what might you do to move your students away from this concept?

4. What kinds of texts do you use to teach fluency? Have you tried Readers Theatre scripts, poetry, songs, and some alternative genres for fluency, for which students need to rehearse before performing for an audience? How have they responded to these texts?

5. How do you think you might alter fluency instruction in your classroom as a result of reading this chapter?

REFERENCES

Allington, R.L. (1983). Fluency: The neglected reading goal. *The Reading Teacher, 36*(6), 556–561.

Biggs, M., Homan, S., Dedrick, R., Minick, V., & Rasinski, T. (2008). Using an interactive singing software program: A comparative study of struggling middle school readers. *Reading Psychology, 29*(3), 195–213.

Carbo, M. (1978a). A word imprinting technique for children with severe memory disorders. *Teaching Exceptional Children, 11*(1), 3–5.

Carbo, M. (1978b). Teaching reading with talking books. *The Reading Teacher, 32*(3), 267–273.

Cassidy, J., & Cassidy, D. (2009). What's hot for 2009. *Reading Today, 26*(4), 1, 8–9.

Chall, J.S. (1996). *Stages of reading development* (2nd ed.). Fort Worth, TX: Harcourt Brace.

Chomsky, C. (1976). After decoding: What? *Language Arts, 53*(3), 288–296.

Daane, M.C., Campbell, J.R., Grigg, W.S., Goodman, M.J., & Oranje, A. (2005). *Fourth-grade students reading aloud: NAEP 2002 special study of oral reading* (NCES 2006-469). Washington, DC: National Center for Education Statistics, Institute of Education Sciences, U.S. Department of Education.

Deno, S.L. (1985). Curriculum-based measurement: The emerging alternative. *Exceptional Children, 52*(3), 219–232.

Deno, S.L., Mirkin, P.K., & Chiang, B. (1982). Identifying valid measures of reading. *Exceptional Children, 49*(1), 36–45.

Fry, E., & Rasinski, T. (2007). *Increasing fluency with high frequency word phrases* (Grades 1–5). Huntington Beach, CA: Shell Education.

Griffith, L.W., & Rasinski, T.V. (2004). A focus on fluency: How one teacher incorporated fluency with her reading curriculum. *The Reading Teacher, 58*(2), 126–137. doi:10.1598/RT.58.2.1

Hiebert, E.H. (2006). Becoming fluent: Repeated reading with scaffolded texts. In S.J. Samuels & A.E. Farstrup (Eds.), *What research has to say about fluency instruction* (pp. 204–226). Newark, DE: International Reading Association.

Koskinen, P.S., Bowen, C.T., Gambrell, L.B., Jensema, C.J., & Kane, K.W. (1996, April). *Captioned television and literacy development: Effects of home viewing on learning disabled students.* Paper presented at the annual meeting of the American Educational Research Association, New York.

Kuhn, M.R., Schwanenflugel, P.J., & Meisinger, E.B. (2010). Review of research. Aligning theory and assessment of reading fluency: Automaticity, prosody, and definitions of fluency. *Reading Research Quarterly, 45*(2), 230–251. doi:10.1598/RRQ.45.2.4

Kulich, L.S. (2009). *The English reading development of Karen children using the fluency development lesson in an intensive English language program: Three descriptive case studies.* Unpublished doctoral dissertation, University of Akron, OH.

LaBerge, D., & Samuels, S.J. (1974). Toward a theory of automatic information processing in reading. *Cognitive Psychology, 6*(2), 293–323. doi:10.1016/0010-0285(74)90015-2

Logan, G.D. (1997). Automaticity and reading: Perspectives from the instance theory of automatization. *Reading & Writing Quarterly, 13*(2), 123–146. doi:10.1080/1057356970130203

Martinez, M., Roser, N., & Strecker, S. (1998). "I never thought I could be a star": A Readers Theatre ticket to fluency. *The Reading Teacher, 52*(4), 326–334.

National Institute of Child Health and Human Development. (2000). *Report of the National Reading Panel. Teaching children to read: An evidence-based assessment of the scientific research literature on reading and its implications for reading instruction* (NIH Publication No. 00-4769). Washington, DC: U.S. Government Printing Office.

Padak, N., & Rasinski, T.V. (2004). Fast Start: A promising practice for family literacy programs. *Family Literacy Forum, 3*(2), 3–9.

Padak, N., & Rasinski, T. (2005). *Fast Start for early readers.* New York: Scholastic.

Pikulski, J.J., & Chard, D.J. (2005). Fluency: Bridge between decoding and reading comprehension. *The Reading Teacher, 58*(6), 510–519. doi:10.1598/RT.58.6.2

Pinnell, G.S., Pikulski, J.J., Wixson, K.K., Campbell, J.R., Gough, P.B., & Beatty, A.S. (1995). *Listening to children read aloud: Data from NAEP's integrated reading performance record (IRPR) at grade 4.* Washington, DC: National Center for Education Statistics, Office of Educational Research and Improvement, U.S. Department of Education.

Pluck, M. (1995). Rainbow Reading Programme: Using taped stories: The Nelson Project. *Reading Forum, 1*, 25–29.

Rasinski, T.V. (1985). *A study of factors involved in reader–text interactions that contribute to fluency in reading.* Unpublished doctoral dissertation, Ohio State University, Columbus.

Rasinski, T.V. (1990). *The effects of cued phrase boundaries on reading performance: A review.* Kent, OH: Kent State University. (ERIC Document Reproduction Service No. ED313689)

Rasinski, T.V. (1994). Developing syntactic sensitivity in reading through phrase-cued texts. *Intervention in School and Clinic, 29*(3), 165–168. doi:10.1177/105345129402900307

Rasinski, T.V. (1995). Fast Start: A parental involvement reading program for primary grade students. In W.M. Linek & E.G. Sturtevant (Eds.), *Generations of literacy: The seventeenth yearbook of the College Reading Association* (pp. 301–312). Harrisonburg, VA: College Reading Association.

Rasinski, T. (2006). Reading fluency instruction: Moving beyond accuracy, automaticity, and prosody. *The Reading Teacher, 59*(7), 704–706. doi:10.1598/RT.59.7.10

Rasinski, T.V. (2010). *The fluent reader: Oral and silent reading strategies for building fluency, word recognition and comprehension* (2nd ed.). New York: Scholastic.

Rasinski, T.V., & Hamman, P. (2010). Reading fluency: Why it is "not hot." *Reading Today, 28*(1), 26.

Rasinski, T.V., Padak, N., Linek, W., & Sturtevant, E. (1994). Effects of fluency development on urban second-grade readers. *The Journal of Educational Research, 87*(3), 158–165. doi:10.1080/00220671.1994.9941237

Rasinski, T.V., Padak, N.D., McKeon, C.A., Wilfong, L.G., Friedauer, J.A., & Heim, P. (2005). Is reading fluency a key for successful high school reading? *Journal of Adolescent & Adult Literacy, 49*(1), 22–27. doi:10.1598/JAAL.49.1.3

Rasinski, T.V., Reutzel, R., Chard, D., & Linan-Thompson, S. (2011). Reading fluency. In M.L. Kamil, P.D. Pearson, E.B. Moje, & P.P. Afflerbach (Eds.), *Handbook of reading research* (Vol. 4, pp. 286–319). Mahwah, NJ: Erlbaum.

Rasinski, T., Rikli, A., & Johnston, S. (2009). Reading fluency: More than automaticity? More than a concern for the primary grades? *Literacy Research and Instruction, 48*(4), 350–361. doi:10.1080/19388070802468715

Rasinski, T., & Stevenson, B. (2005). The effects of Fast Start reading: A fluency-based home involvement reading program, on the reading achievement of beginning readers. *Reading Psychology, 26*(2), 109–125. doi:10.1080/02702710590930483

Reutzel, D.R., Fawson, P.C., & Smith, J.A. (2008). Reconsidering silent sustained reading: An exploratory study of scaffolded silent reading. *The Journal of Educational Research, 102*(1), 37–50. doi:10.3200/JOER.102.1.37-50

Reutzel, D.R., Jones, C.D., Fawson, P.C., & Smith, J.A. (2008). Scaffolded silent reading: A complement to guided repeated oral reading that works! *The Reading Teacher, 62*(3), 194–207. doi:10.1598/RT.62.3.2

Samuels, S.J. (1979). The method of repeated readings. *The Reading Teacher, 32*(4), 403–408.

Samuels, S.J. (2007). The DIBELS tests: Is speed of barking at print what we mean by reading fluency? *Reading Research Quarterly, 42*(4), 563–566.

Schreiber, P.A. (1980). On the acquisition of reading fluency. *Journal of Reading Behavior, 12*(3), 177–186.

Schreiber, P.A. (1987). Prosody and structure in children's syntactic processing. In R. Horowitz & S.J. Samuels (Eds.), *Comprehending oral and written language* (pp. 243–270). New York: Academic.

Schreiber, P.A. (1991). Understanding prosody's role in reading acquisition. *Theory Into Practice, 30*(3), 158–164. doi:10.1080/00405849109543496

Schreiber, P., & Read, C. (1980). Children's use of phonetic cues in spelling, parsing, and—maybe—reading. *Bulletin of the Orton Society, 30*, 209–224. doi:10.1007/BF02653719

Topping, K. (1987a). Paired reading: A powerful technique for parent use. *The Reading Teacher, 40*(7), 608–614.

Topping, K. (1987b). Peer tutored paired reading: Outcome data from ten projects. *Educational Psychology, 7*(2), 133–145. doi:10.1080/0144341870070206

Young, C., & Rasinski, T. (2009). Implementing Readers Theatre as an approach to classroom fluency instruction. *The Reading Teacher, 63*(1), 4–13. doi:10.1598/RT.63.1.1

Chapter 5

Reading Engagement Among African American and European American Students

John T. Guthrie and Angela McRae

Introduction

Perspectives on African American Motivation

This chapter addresses the motivational characteristics of African American students. The prevailing analyses of achievement in reading, and education in general, address the attainments and dilemmas of African American students, with an emphasis on structural and cultural forces. An outstanding synthesis of these viewpoints, entitled *More Than Just Race: Being Black and Poor in the Inner City,* was recently published by William Julius Wilson (2009), a respected Harvard sociology professor. In discussing structural forces, he refers to the traditional domain of sociology, which includes such social acts as discrimination in hiring, admission to educational institutions, and job promotions or the lack thereof. Aligned with social acts are social processes, which refer to joblessness, declining wages, and technological changes in the workplace that challenge those with lower educational opportunities. For example, African Americans are disproportionately represented in low-skilled jobs such as the textile industry. The sociological variables of low wages, joblessness, and low skills that characterize a large proportion of African American families are associated with low educational attainment and low reading achievement specifically. The inclination of sociologists has been to attribute low achievement of students in schools to the structural barriers faced by low-income families. However, it is much more likely that the variables are reciprocal with high structural barriers producing low achievement, and low reading achievement producing high barriers at the same time. Irrespective of the direction of causality, educators cannot utilize sociological information constructively to benefit students. It

What Research Has to Say About Reading Instruction (4th ed.) edited by S. Jay Samuels and Alan E. Farstrup.
© 2011 by the International Reading Association.

is not within our power to increase jobs or decrease poverty. Educators must look beyond sociological analyses for guidance.

Wilson (2009) continues to portray the cultural forces impacting African Americans, including traditions, belief systems, values, preferences, and linguistic patterns. He claims that central to any cultural understanding is the recognition that African Americans are subject to an ideology of racial domination in which beliefs that one race is inferior "lead to prescriptions about how that race should be treated in society" (p. 15). Concurring with this view, Ogbu (2003) argues that as African American students experience these cultural beliefs, they take an oppositional stance toward schooling. He claims that students act out against injustice by rejecting the regimen of hard work and dedication demanded in schools. His interviews with middle school adolescents reveal well-entrenched resistance among African American students to the activities and commitments needed for school success. A limitation of this perspective is that it does not allow for processes of resiliency within the self system of the individual to overcome the barriers presented by societal beliefs and enable the individual to become a self-determining, dedicated, successful reader.

An alternative perspective to the structural and cultural studies of African American families and students has been expressed by Hudley (2009) and others. Within a 36-chapter volume entitled *Handbook of African American Psychology*, Hudley asserts in his chapter that to understand African American students, we must investigate who they are as individuals. Joined by Courtland Lee (1984) and others, Hudley emphasizes the qualities of the motivations of students that enable them to be self-determining. In contrast to the view that achievement is structurally determined by sociological variables or culturally enforced through societal beliefs, her claim is that the individual has a role to play in determining who he or she is. These self-views of individuals are traditionally termed motivations, encompassing the goals, beliefs, dispositions, and behaviors that direct and energize students' lives. As Hudley states, "I explore the extent to which motivationally relevant variables, including self-beliefs and perceptions of barriers to success, account for individual differences in African American student achievement" (p. 188).

In this chapter, we take the self-oriented perspective in attempting to characterize the reading engagement of African American students. In this endeavor, we emphasize the range of beliefs, competencies, and attainments within the population of African American students. We are not attending primarily to the differences between African American and

European American students in their motivations, but rather the ways in which high-achieving African Americans can be contrasted to lower achieving African American peers. To the extent that there are powerful forces operating within the African American student population to impact achievement, the argument that achievement is attributable to structural or cultural forces is weakened, if not entirely nullified. Thus, we seek pathways to achievement in reading through motivation and engagement where the destination is established by the higher achieving and academically more successful African American students in various populations. This leads us to seek qualities of African American students, or research variables, that correlate to achievement within this population. We are not attempting to report variables that represent differences in level between African Americans and European Americans, but rather variables that represent empowerments toward achievement within the minority population.

Behavioral Engagement in Reading

Evidence-Based Model. In an inclusive review that encompassed both African American and European American students, we constructed an evidence-based model of engagement and achievement in reading (Guthrie, Wigfield, & You, in press). In this model, we documented with more than 40 studies that the following linkage system holds quite strongly across a range of ages in schooling. The first link is represented by classroom practices that support motivation and engagement, such as nurturing student interest and assuring opportunity for learning from authentic tasks. The second link is student motivation that consists of intrinsic motivation (i.e., enjoyment in reading) or valuing (i.e., believing that reading is important). The third link consists of behavioral engagement, which is the time, effort, and persistence in reading activities that are productive for success in school. Last in the chain is school achievement, referring to test scores or grades. The evidence from a variety of paradigms points to the causal impact of classroom practices on motivations, the impact of motivations on behavioral engagement, and the impact of behavioral engagement on reading achievement. Although African American students were not included in the large majority of studies on which the previous model was constructed, we report in this chapter the results of investigations that used African American students.

As an example of the findings from the inclusive review, Voelkl (1995) reported that a national sample of 13,000 eighth-grade students in the

United States revealed reading comprehension test scores to be positively associated with classroom and academic participation. Participating in reading during school is considered behavioral engagement, as it includes

- *Attendance*—The number of times missing school or arriving late
- *Activity*—Teachers' reports of the student completion of homework and attention in class
- *Preparation*—Students' reports of the times they prepared for class and completed homework
- *Behavior*—Students' reports of the disruptive behaviors in classroom

In other words, when the background variables of gender, income, region, and ethnicity were held constant, behavioral engagement in reading was highly predictive of reading comprehension achievement. Our goal is to determine whether this pattern appears for African American students.

Multiple Motivations. For African Americans, investigations have often reported several motivation and engagement qualities at the same time. For example, Long, Monoi, Harper, Knoblauch, and Murphy (2007) reported the extent that African American students possessed learning goals (i.e., wanting to understand the material), performance goals (i.e., wanting to gain the best grades), work avoidance (i.e., seeking to minimize effort and time in reading), self-efficacy (i.e., confidence in their reading level), and interest in school subject matters, along with students' academic achievement. Other investigators have reported other clusters of motivational qualities, such as desire for choice, orientation to social interaction in classrooms, and belief in one's capacity (Connell, Spencer, & Aber, 1994). In these and other similar studies, all of these motivational qualities are correlated with each other at a moderate level. It is reasonable that students' self-efficacy (i.e., self-confidence in reading) should be associated with their perceived autonomy (i.e., enjoyment in making choices about their own reading). Furthermore, in studies that examine many qualities at the same time, several usually have a simple correlation with achievement.

There are one or two exceptions to this pattern of clustered factors influencing achievement. The exceptions are intrinsic motivation for reading and global self-esteem. Several investigations, such as Long et al. (2007) and Guthrie, Coddington, and Wigfield (2009), reported that intrinsic motivation, which refers to enjoyment of reading, was not highly correlated with achievement for African American students. This finding contradicts the widely observed result with European American students that intrinsic motivation correlates positively with achievement. Although no definitive explanation has been documented empirically, it appears that African American students, while they have strong interests and favorite activities, tend not to link their reading to these personally significant interests. Regarding self-esteem (i.e., global belief in one's well-being), several investigators, especially Mickelson (1990) and Osborne (1997), have shown that it is not correlated with reading achievement among African American students. In other words, while European Americans who achieve highly have a high general sense of well-being and satisfaction, and lower achieving European American students have a decreased sense of well-being, this association is simply not present for African American students. One explanation frequently offered is that this is a protective mechanism that African American students use to maintain their sense of self-worth in the face of low achievement or threats to their school success.

Behavioral Engagement and Achievement

There are a number of factors that are highly correlated with achievement within African American groups. A variable that stands out, consisting of effort, time, and persistence in reading, is behavioral engagement. Consistent with the definitions of scholars in motivation theory (Fredricks, Blumenfeld, & Paris, 2004; Skinner, Kindermann, & Furrer, 2009), behavioral engagement refers to the activities students participate in that enable them to gain cognitive skills, perform well on assessments, and attain relatively high grades. In one study that has defined *behavioral engagement* in the literature, Finn and Rock (1997) identified resilient students who were behaviorally engaged in the sense that they stayed in school, attained average to high scores on reading tests in grades 8 and 10, and were attentive. In other words, these students showed participation and involvement in school activities. The qualities of these behaviorally engaged students as reported by the teachers were that they worked hard trying to do well in school, were participatory and cooperative in the classroom, and attended class regularly. In addition, the students were rarely absent or late to class. From the student perspective, these behaviorally engaged students had high attendance, were well prepared, and did not initiate trouble in classrooms. In one qualitative study (Howard, 2002), students articulated that teachers who emphasized behavioral engagement were "strict about having work done, emphasized how you study and write down notes and stuff for tests" (p. 437). These descriptions of behavioral engagement resonate with the term *dedication*, so we use these terms interchangeably within this chapter.

It is evident that behavioral engagement may apply equally to students of all ages and levels from grade 1 through grade 12. In a three-year longitudinal study of students' from grades 1–3, Hughes, Luo, Kwok, and Loyd (2008) showed the power of these qualities operating reciprocally with each other. They found that students' levels of behavioral engagement (i.e., effort, attention, persistence, cooperative participation) in learning to read predicted their grade 2 reading level, even when their grade 1 reading achievement was controlled, which is a way of investigating growth. In other words, behavioral engagement in grade 1 predicted growth of skills from grades 1 to 2. In addition, grade 2 reading level led to growth of engagement from grades 2 to 3. Simultaneously, grade 2 reading behavioral engagement produced high growth in reading from grades 2 to 3. In other words, in grades 1–3 across time, behavioral engagement and reading achievement were mutually reinforcing. This finding appeared for an academically at-risk population with a large Hispanic and African American membership.

With an exclusively African American population of students from grades 7–12, Sirin and Rogers-Sirin (2005) reported that school grades in language arts and test scores of vocabulary are uniquely predicted by two qualities of behavioral engagement. The first quality consists of school participation (i.e., paying attention in class) and getting along well with teachers. The second quality is school expectations, which refers to students' level of expectation that they will continue their education beyond high school. African American students who were highly participatory with solid expectations for their future education were substantially higher achievers than students with less participation and lower expectations. These factors were so powerful that they appeared after many other aspects of their lives which may influence achievement were controlled. These behavioral engagement variables were connected to achievement for both boys and girls, at all six of the grade levels, irrespective of their academic aptitude in the form of vocabulary scores and their mothers' education. In other words, behavioral engagement outdistanced all demographic variables (i.e., gender, socioeconomic status) and cognitive aptitude factors of spoken and reading vocabulary in generating academic performance for African American adolescents.

Working with three different samples of African American students in three locations in the United States, Connell et al. (1994) investigated how context, self, and action contributed to positive and negative outcomes. In this alignment of factors that impact outcomes in the form of grades and test scores, the overwhelming quality of students' individual characteristics was behavioral engagement, which was termed *action*. Action referred to high rates of participation, enthusiastic effort, and high rates of attention. Positive forms of these behavioral engagements generated positive outcomes of grades and relatively high test scores, whereas low levels of these behavioral engagements generated negative outcomes of truancy, low achievement, and dropping out of school. Although students' motivations played a contributing role to outcomes, the role was indirect. Motivations in the form of self-confidence and intrinsic motivation for reading in school did not directly produce positive results but enabled positive outcomes indirectly by increasing levels of behavioral engagement. In other words, behavioral engagement mediated the effect of motivations on positive outcomes for these African American adolescents.

Confirmation of these findings with many statistical controls can be found in other, simpler investigations of African American adolescents. For example, Mau and Lynn (1999) reported that reading achievement and the amount of time spent daily on homework correlated significantly for African American students in 10th and 12th grades (0.23 and 0.13, respectively), as well as for European American students (0.28 and 0.23, respectively) and Hispanic students (0.31 and 0.11, respectively). Thus, the simple behavioral indicator of homework completed predicts achievement for national samples of students from several ethnic groups.

In a quantitative study using path analysis, Cokley (2003) reported that for African American college students, grade point average was significantly decreased by motivation. The construct of amotivation pertains to students who do not perceive their behaviors as linked to any outcomes. In other words, they believe they are driven by external forces out of their control and feel helpless as students or readers. At the same time, this study confirmed the widespread findings that intrinsic motivation is not connected to grade point average in college for these African American students, and extrinsic motivation (i.e., working in school to attain a good job after college or avoid the threat of punishment) is unrelated to students' academic achievement.

Finally, Hall, Merkel, Howe, and Lederman (1986) reported that active learning was associated with reading achievement in the form of test scores, even though attitudes toward school and peers were independent of test scores. These investigators characterized active learning as experimenting (i.e., trying new ways to achieve), observing (i.e., watching other students closely), preparing (i.e., gathering materials), and discussing (i.e., talking with students actively about texts and answers to questions).

Summary

It is apparent from these studies that for African American students, behavioral engagement is a quality of the individual that highly impacts reading achievement. Behavioral engagement empowers achievement across all the demographic variables examined, including gender, socioeconomic status, mother's education, and at-risk characteristics. Furthermore, behavioral engagement has been shown to interrelate with achievement in grades 1–3, through middle and high school, and into college levels. This implies that irrespective of the structural variables associated with achievement appearing in sociological analyses, or the cultural factors that impact students' beliefs, the behaviorally engaged African American student is likely to increase in reading success as indicated by test scores, grades, and school completion. This illustrates that in the domain of reading achievement, many African American students are self-determined. High achievers among the African American student body are showing that they are in charge of their own educational success and destiny. In comparison to their peers who are behaviorally passive or avoidant of texts and reading activities, behaviorally engaged African American students are in a cycle of participation and accomplishment.

Can Dedication Close the Achievement Gap?

The Achievement Gap Nationally and Locally

In any discussion of the reading characteristics of African American and European American students, it is impossible to ignore the achievement gap. Since researchers for the National Assessment of Educational Progress began collecting data in 1970, they have repeatedly documented the finding that European Americans score higher than African Americans at grades 4, 8, and 12 in reading, with only minor fluctuations in the difference appearing over the years. Likewise, local studies of selective populations in different portions of the United States document this achievement gap in grade 1 (Rabiner, Murray, Schmid, & Malone, 2004), grade 5 (Lee & Bowen, 2006), and the secondary grades (Carpenter & Ramirez, 2008). Beyond achievement levels on assessments, some investigators point to a gap in the dropout rate, showing that African Americans are more at risk for dropping out of school than European

Americans, which is usually a consequence of low achievement in reading and other subject matters (Carpenter & Ramirez, 2008).

We have been investigating the differences between African American and European American students in all middle schools in a district for a five-year period. Within this mid-Atlantic, middle income school district, the achievement gap is evident. This district shows demographic associations with achievement that are extremely similar to national samples and other local investigations. Within this district, seventh-grade European Americans had a mean grade equivalent on a standardized comprehension test of 7.5 at the beginning of the year, whereas African Americans on the same test had a mean of 5.6, which is nearly a two-year gap. Likewise, other gaps appeared as one might expect, including the finding that females read at the 7.2 grade level, whereas males had a mean of 6.0. Consistent with other national studies, income played a substantial role in achievement, with the lowest income group two years behind, reading at a grade level of 5.5, whereas the middle and upper income groups were reading at the 7.6 grade level. Similar to trends reported by Jencks and Phillips (1998) in our local sample, African American females were similar in level to both male and female European American students, whereas African American males were significantly lower, reading at two grade levels or more behind the other three demographic groups. Ultimately, the result that African American males scored especially low in reading was not found for the lowest income group; in this case, the African American females were nearly as low as the African American males.

Having seen that the reading achievement gap is marked in our local circumstance, we next attempted to identify whether it was associated with dedication or behavioral engagement in reading. Our indicator of dedication was students' effort, time, and persistence in reading for school. In a questionnaire measuring motivation, we gave students the following statements for their reactions:

- I read books for school as often as possible.
- I read challenging books in school, so I will learn.
- I put in as much effort as necessary in reading books for school.
- I never attempt to avoid reading for school.

(In actual practice these items were presented in their negative form in the context of many other items and were then recoded for reasons presented elsewhere [Wigfield, Cambria, & Ho, in press].) The most dedicated students who were in the top 25% of the total distribution were responding with strong agreement to each of these statements. Among African American students, nearly 30% of the population was highly dedicated according to this indicator. At the same time, for African American students, approximately 25% were the opposite of dedicated, which we designated as avoidant. That is, they rarely attempted to put forth maximum effort or spend time to complete the expected readings for school. In the middle were two other groups who were moderately dedicated with medium levels of commitment to spending the time and energy necessary to succeed at school reading.

Dedication yielded remarkable benefits for the African American students in our local sample. The most highly dedicated African American students were reading more than two grade levels higher than the least dedicated students. Upon entry into seventh grade, the less dedicated students were reading at the fifth grade level or below, and the highly dedicated students were reading above grade level at the beginning of the school year. Although this is not a simple cause–effect relationship, the amount and level of dedication to reading for African American students was remarkably associated with their reading comprehension, according to standardized test scores.

For European American students, approximately 31% were highly dedicated to reading, and about 25% were in the avoidant group. These proportions were quite similar for the African American and European American students. However, for the European American students, dedication, although it benefited students' reading proficiency, did not have as marked an effect as it did for African American students. The most highly dedicated European American students were at the 9.5 grade equivalent, and the more avoidant European American students were at an 8.0 grade equivalent, which shows that dedication yielded a benefit of 1.5 grade-equivalent units for European American students. Although the achievement gap is obvious in the sense that the mean reading levels were higher for European American students than African American, the dedication benefit is also obvious, because the advantages of high dedication among African Americans actually exceeded the benefits of dedication for European Americans.

Link of Dedication to Achievement for African American and European American Students

We have seen that a sizable proportion of African American students are highly dedicated to reading in school. These students put forth effort in their assignments and spend time in completing required work. They persevere whether they find the text interesting or not; their goal is to complete the job successfully rather than pursue their interests. As we described previously, studies show that intrinsic motivation for reading in school is not associated with achievement for African Americans. It appears then that high-achieving African American students are motivated more consistently by their dedication to successful academic performance than to pursuing their interests.

Our next question was whether this dedication is powerful enough to reduce or even close the achievement gap for African American students. For this purpose, we placed African American and European American students on the same framework, with varying dedication and achievement levels, as shown in Figure 5.1. In other words, we asked, Is dedication having an effect on achievement for African American students, and is this benefit similar to the benefit experienced by European American students? As seen in the figure, the scores for standardized reading comprehension tests range from 5.0 to 8.0 grade-equivalent levels, and dedication ranges from very low (1), which reflects avoidance of school reading, to very high (4), which reflects undiminished dedication. The

Figure 5.1. Dedication and Reading Achievement for African American and European American Students

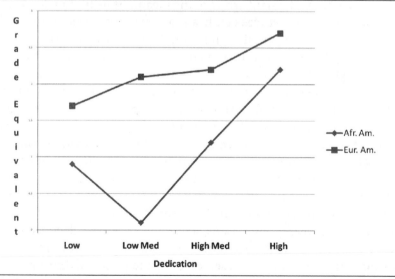

Note. The grade-equivalent scores on the *y*-axis are for standardized reading comprehension tests.

figure shows that European American students were reading relatively higher and surpassed the African American students, which confirms the achievement gap we described previously.

It is also evident that dedication conferred benefits to achievement for European American students. The most avoidant European American students were reading below grade level at about a 6.8 grade equivalent, and the most highly dedicated European American students were reading at about a 7.8 grade equivalent. For African American students, the avoidant students at levels 1 and 2 were below grade level, reading at approximately levels 5.3–5.7. What is most remarkable is that for African American students from dedication level 2, which has a grade level of 5.3, to dedication level 4, there is a marked increase in reading achievement. The benefit African Americans derive from dedication is greater, as shown by the steeper line, representing the contribution that their commitment to reading and their dedication make to their measured achievement in reading has a higher incline than the line representing the benefit for European Americans. This suggests that dedication, as it increases for African American students, closes the gap between them and the European Americans in reading achievement.

Statistical analysis confirms the interpretation that we can make by visual inspection of this figure. The difference between African Americans and European Americans at level 1 of dedication, that is, for the most avoidant readers, was statistically significant (i.e., the mean difference was more than three standard errors of the mean). At dedication level 2, the achievement differences are significant, and at achievement level 3, the differences are also statistically significant, showing that for the lowest three levels of dedication, the achievement gap continues to appear. However, at the highest level of dedication for African American and European American students, the gap in achievement is not statistically significant. Although there is a small advantage for European American students, it is highly overlapping with the distribution for African Americans. This shows that as African Americans increase their dedication to reading in school, their achievement accelerates more rapidly than does the achievement of European Americans. Likewise, as African Americans decline in dedication to time and effort in reading, their achievement drops more precipitously than for European American students.

In making these comparisons, we should emphasize that income was controlled throughout. In addition, we controlled for three motivation factors—intrinsic motivation, self-efficacy, and perceived difficulty—that contribute to achievement for both ethnic groups, which are explained more fully by Wigfield et al. (in press). In the context of these variables, gender did not contribute significantly to the explained variance and was consequently deleted from the analyses. The conclusion is that when controlling for income and gender, as well as three motivational attributes of students, dedication contributes more strongly to achievement for African American students than European American. The strength of this advantage is sufficient to reduce the achievement gap between African American and European American students to a trivial, statistically insignificant disparity.

Interpreting the Link Between Dedication and Achievement for African American Students

Some critics may claim that the benefits of dedication are trivial, because it has already been observed that some African Americans can achieve highly. For instance, Ben Carson is an African American who became a surgeon at Johns Hopkins Hospital despite his background of poverty and inconsistent parenting. Additionally, Barack Obama is the first African American president of the United States and graduated with honors from Harvard. Furthermore, Karla Holloway has written a magnificent book on the reading tastes and commitments of African American writers such as Richard Wright. She documents how deeply two dozen nationally known African American writers read voraciously to feed their intellectual desires, which shaped the contours of their writing styles. However, we propose that these illustrative examples of excellence are often regarded as charismatic figures who represent exceptions to the rule of lower African American attainments. Consequently, these accomplishments are not used as realistic aspirations for African American students in elementary or middle school.

Our evidence reveals that dedication for reading works across the spectrum for African Americans in a typical, moderately achieving school district. When African American students in an average seventh grade choose to commit themselves to school reading consistently over time, they become highly achieving. This powerful quality of dedication is not a gift bestowed on a few, but rather a choice that can be made by many. Any student can decide to complete his homework today, tomorrow, and the next day. This commitment is a form of self-determination, and where it appears frequently, it generates high yields in school performance. Our findings show that these qualities of dedication and commitment are not limited to any one group. They can occur for boys as well as girls, for students from lower income families as well as higher income, and for students who experience minority cultural beliefs as well as those who hold mainstream cultural beliefs. In other words, dedication is equitable and accessible to all individuals. It does not depend on a demographic characteristic or an intellectual attribute. It is a decision made by the individual in a particular time and circumstance. With the self-discipline to make repeated decisions to commit to an act of school reading, students will grow in achievement, as these data document. Such growth is likely to feed forward into higher levels of commitment. Although we do not have evidence at present, it is likely that dedication and achievement are reciprocally determined. In other words, as dedication grows and generates achievement, achievement increases dedication simultaneously. As shown in previous studies by Hughes et al. (2008) for first to third graders and Skinner et al. (2009) for college students, dedication and behavioral engagement are codetermining with achievement.

One might ask why such an innocent-looking quality as dedication to time, effort, and persistence in reading should close the achievement gap in reading comprehension when other, apparently more prominent, variables such as income, gender, and cultural beliefs have not been shown to close it. Our proposal is that the qualities of dedication to reading are qualities of an individual's self-determination. They are decisions made by the individual irrespective of other ecologically valid parameters that impinge on our lives. Yet, these self-oriented attributes are intimately tied to reading achievement. The tie is intimate, because to score well on a reading test, an individual must interact with text, using cognitive competencies. At the same time, the decision to complete a reading assignment in school also demands that the individual interact with text using cognitive competencies. The same event that enables a student to fulfill a school expectation, when it is repeatedly performed, enables the individual to be a high achiever in reading. In other words, the reading act generated by dedication is proximal to reading achievement.

Dedication, while it occurs with the same texts across time and situations, is the same event that occurs when an individual is showing his or her achievement on a test or a final project in a curriculum. In contrast, a variable such as income is remote from the reading task, reading test, and reading grade. Income operates only indirectly on reading achievement through the opportunities of the individual, information accessible to the individual, or resources that enable the individual to participate in reading activities. However, the resource of income may be present while the decision to be dedicated is absent. Conversely, despite a low income, it is physically possible to be dedicated to reading a text supplied publicly by the school system and become a more proficient reader. In the next section, we search for the sources and forces that enable students to become dedicated readers.

Classroom Contexts for Reading Dedication

The main message in this chapter up to this point is that reading dedication is a student quality that is capable of closing the achievement gap between African American and European American students. At the same time that dedication is a high-impact variable, all motivations of individual students energize and direct their dedication. Highlighted among the motivations are valuing, which predominates as the single strongest contributor to dedication, and self-efficacy, which is a natural enabler of effortful time spent reading. The advantage of the constructs of motivation and dedication is that classroom contexts can make a difference in them.

We are proposing student characteristics that can be impacted in the short and long terms through explicit classroom actions by the teacher. There are specific practices that teachers can undertake to reliably foster students' reading dedication and the motivations that fuel them. A vast majority of educators are eager to see approaches that may improve the achievement of African American students, and some educators are so committed that they become zealous for their favorite innovation. Although it is well intentioned, this zeal may sometimes lead to misconceptions.

To avoid promising, but ineffective, approaches to improving achievement, the first quality to look for in teaching practices is whether they explicitly include extended behavioral engagement or dedication. In other words, Does the practice involve the students in high amounts of time and effort in reading activity? For the "high amounts of time," we are referring to weeks and months, not minutes and hours. To measurably improve reading comprehension requires hundreds of hours of deep reading for which the students are held accountable. We are all aware that expert pianists, chess players, ballet dancers, wrestlers, chefs, architects, and novelists gain their expertise through hours of daily devotion. Expertise in reading is no different. It demands to be part of one's lifestyle, not a passing moment in a fugitive event. To accept extended behavioral engagement as a crucial aspect of an effective practice for raising achievement, we exclude such approaches as a one-day event in school in which everyone celebrates reading. Although it is desirable to celebrate reading, and in fact may be fun and even inspiring, this day will not fiercely improve achievement. Many teachers and media specialists applaud the excitement of finding the one perfect book for a reader.

Certainly, this is a fine accomplishment, but it cannot be expected to change achievement, because it is insufficient to meet the criterion of extended behavioral engagement in reading activities. Thus, the quality we are referring to endures over time in the life of the student; it is not situated to a moment in time, a place, or a single text.

Another quality of an effective practice for improving students' dedication in reading is that it should facilitate a student experience well correlated with dedication or achievement. Although activities that introduce reading with an interest-piquing activity are valuable, they must be followed by high volumes of reading time. For example, a sports event in which students play baseball for two hours and then discuss books on baseball for five minutes is unlikely to impact achievement, because playing sports is not directly correlated with reading dedication. Another example that attempts to build students' sense of belonging to a school may be thought of as a community-building activity, which targets dedication for reading. However, the literature is clear that a sense of school belonging does not correlate with dedication or achievement for African American students (Long et al., 2007; Strambler & Weinstein, 2010). Although a sense of belonging may be valuable in itself, one should not suppose that it will generate reading dedication for African American students.

Principles of Effective Practice for Reading Dedication

In our five-year partnership with a school district in Maryland, we have implemented Concept-Oriented Reading Instruction (CORI) for all students in grade 7 in the district. Taught by teachers in reading/language arts classrooms, CORI is provided 90 minutes per day for six weeks in the spring. In this version of CORI, the theme of biodiversity is taught, with the reliance on videos for multimedia presentations of the interactions of plants and animals in a diverse array of biomes. Books are linked to these videos, and students pursue their questions and curiosities by reading more than 25 trade books in this unit. In a weekly record, students record their experiences in the classroom, including the extent to which they perceived the following instructional practices to be taking place: relevance of books to their background experience, choices of books, collaboration with other students for comprehension, awareness of the importance of books for building knowledge, success in performing complex tasks of inferencing, summarizing, concept mapping challenging texts, and perceiving the thematic unit as a support for success in reading.

Within the CORI unit, some teachers emphasized various practices more than other teachers. Consequently, the student experiences of differing intensities of these supports for motivation and engagement serve as a basis for comparing the effectiveness of instructional practices for dedication. We compared the students' perceptions of instructional practices with their growth in dedication to reading information books from April to June. A questionnaire administered to students in mid-April and again in mid-June revealed not only growth for all individuals but also differing levels of growth depending on the shifts of emphasis on practices across teachers. Consequently, we could map the students' experiences of instructional emphasis and their growth in dedication for reading.

Contributions of Classroom Practices to Dedication Growth

For students who were in the bottom 40% in reading, which was below the 7.4 grade equivalent in April of the grade 7 year, all five instructional practices we investigated made a significant contribution to students' growth in dedication. These practices included relevance, collaboration, choice, emphasis on importance, and thematic units. For each practice, we compared whether it provided a bigger advantage in dedication for African American or European American students. For individuals in the bottom 40% of the district on achievement test scores, the teaching practice of relevance increased dedication significantly more for African American students than European American.

In the CORI program, the teaching practice of relevance referred to providing students with videos of many aspects of biodiversity, such as predation in the Serengeti Plain, locomotion as a form of defense from predators in freshwater lakes, and parasitism of tapeworms in the intestine of a mammal. After viewing the videos, students wrote observations, composed questions, and read texts to answer the question of the day, which was continually posted. Watching the videos, which were derived from the Discovery Channel archives, gave students a sense that they had seen, heard, and been present in environments where plant and animal interactions were taking place. The vivid experiences seemed to have happened to them personally. When they read trade books with photos similar to the audiovisual presentation and text on precisely the topic they had viewed within the past 15–30 minutes, students found the books to be relevant to their experience. A typical student reaction to the texts after seeing the videos was that "this material connects to my immediate experience." One student said, "I know what this book is talking about, because I just saw a video on it."

The intriguing finding was that the impact of perceived relevance on dedication was higher for African American students than European American. African American students who perceived the instruction to provide high amounts of relevance spent more time, effort, and persistence in reading than African Americans who did not experience the relevance as highly. Although this same trend appeared for European American students, it was weaker for them. Likewise, the absence of a video or the limited experience of the video in some classrooms for some African American students led them to exhibit less growth and dedication during the unit of instruction than the growth observed for students perceiving high amounts of relevance in this instructional unit. In some lower achieving students in the district, relevance as an instructional practice increased dedication more markedly for African American students than European American, although it was beneficial for both groups.

For students reading in the top 40% of all individuals in the school district, which was higher than the grade equivalent of 10.0 in April of the grade 7 year, multiple instructional practices were valuable for African American students. For this relatively high-achieving group, the instructional practices of providing collaboration, giving choices, emphasizing the importance of books, and providing linkages to assure a thematic unit increased the dedication of African American students more significantly than for European American students. Collaboration was provided in the classrooms by arranging partners to interpret texts, and teams to build lists of inferences and create culminating posters. Choices were provided daily for particular texts that were used, for whether students worked as individuals or pairs, and for the number of inferences or summaries the students elected to make for various texts. Emphasis on importance was provided by the teacher in the form of discussion with students about what they learned from different media, including videos, group discussions, and reading and writing activities. In these discussions on the importance of reading, books invariably surfaced as the major source of information and conceptual knowledge in the science learning activities.

The thematic unit was provided as a support for dedication by linking books to each other through a "question of the week" and a "question of the day." Topics of biodiversity were linked conceptually across the six weeks, and the question of the day enabled students to track the relationships between animal and plant interactions, and between defense and survival mechanisms across biomes for diverse species. The thematic unit increased dedication, because it enabled students to read productively and learn coherently across the concepts within the thematic unit. For all students, including African American and European American individuals, these four practices significantly fostered dedication growth during the unit. However, the benefit was substantially, and statistically significantly, higher for African American students than European American. The benefit of relevance was the same for both ethnic groups.

For on-grade students in the range of grade-equivalent 7.4–10.0, the four practices of providing collaboration, assuring choices, emphasizing importance, and providing the thematic unit increased dedication for African American and European American students equally. Relevance did not have a statistically significant effect on dedication for this level of students in either ethnic group. These patterns are shown in Table 5.1.

Summary

It is evident that classroom contexts designed to foster reading dedication can be especially beneficial for African American students. It is especially significant that certain teaching approaches are actually more beneficial for increasing dedication among African American and European American students. Among lower achieving students in the bottom 40% of the distribution of achievement, which includes struggling readers and students with Individualized Education Plans, the teaching practice of assuring the relevance of texts is especially

Table 5.1. Contributions of Classroom Practices to African American and European American Students' Dedication Growth

Classroom practices	Student groups		
	Below grade level (GE < 7.5; 40%)	On grade level (GE = 7.5–10; 20%)	Above grade level (GE > 10; 40%)
Relevance	AA	Not significant	AA = EA
Collaboration	AA = EA	AA = EA	AA
Choice	AA = EA	AA = EA	AA
Importance	AA = EA	AA = EA	AA
Thematic unit	AA = EA	AA = EA	AA

Note. In the cells labeled "AA," the classroom practice enabled African American students to make higher gains in dedication than European Americans. In the cells labeled "AA = EA," the classroom practice benefited both groups equally in increasing dedication. AA = African American. EA = European American. GE = grade equivalent.

powerful. It was this practice that provided the more dramatic advantages for African American students. Beyond the advantages of relevance, the teaching practices of collaboration, choice, emphasizing importance, and providing thematic units increased dedication for both groups equally and significantly. For higher achieving students who scored in the top 40% of the district, it is noteworthy that four instructional practices were more effective for African American learners than European American: collaboration, choice, emphasizing importance, and providing thematic units. These practices accelerated dedication of the African American students to a greater extent than the European American students. This shows that not only is there a student quality that is especially beneficial for African American students consisting of dedication or behavioral engagement in reading, but also there are instructional practices that are particularly advantageous for accelerating the dedication of African American students. Thus, progress down the pathway toward achievement consisting of enhanced dedication in reading can be actively promoted by teachers with high expectations of success for African American students.

Illustrations of Classroom Practices Promoting Motivation and Dedication

Each of the classroom practices we discussed previously can be presented by any teacher in any classroom in a variety of ways (Guthrie, 2008; Kelley & Clausen-Grace, 2009). The practices are not limited to high-achieving, low-achieving, mainstream, or minority students. However, because we know that the practice of assuring relevance is especially valuable for African American students who are below grade level in reading comprehension, we present several examples of instruction that highlight relevance of reading. When we say the practice underscores relevance, we mean that it enables the students to connect the book to themselves, see how events in the book relate to happenings in their lives, find the text familiar, and be able to extend their own lived experiences through their literacy experience.

Real-World Materials. When it is possible to bring media based in the real world into classroom instruction, the text becomes relevant. For example, in a social studies class studying civil rights, the teacher found a poignant newspaper article. It described an elderly female protester who was on a picket line objecting to racist policies. Although she was a civil rights activist, she behaved hypocritically by owning a segregated grocery store. The article captivated students' attention, and through their critical analysis of the text and the historical situation, they developed keen insights about the economic and moral pressures surrounding racism (Johnson & Cowles, 2009).

Relevant texts are commonplace in vocational schools and courses. One vocational school's students worked in shops that were run like real job sites. Students were presented many opportunities to participate in work-related scenarios. As well as providing services to the community, such as changing car oil or repairing brakes, they read texts on auto mechanics, construction, electricity, plumbing, graphic design, and computer technology. The school did not have to stretch to provide students with authentic tasks or reading materials. Because of their relevance, the students valued these reading tasks. Most students dedicated themselves to mastering these texts despite their complexity (Darvin, 2006). Whether they are newspapers, job-related texts, or part of the popular culture, texts from the real world are relevant in themselves.

Poignant Topics. A powerful source of relevant texts for young adolescents is novels or biographies on the theme of freedom. As Bean and Harper (2006) showed, young adolescents are captivated by *The Breadwinner,* a novel by Deborah Ellis about Parvana, a 12-year old girl living in Afghanistan under Taliban rule. In an act of survival, Parvana poses as a boy selling goods to earn money for her family. She achieves some freedom by making her femininity invisible, but she loses some of her ethnic identity. While reading this book, students become immersed in her loss of religious identity as she gained economic freedoms. Many students discover that they have paid a price for freedoms as well. Relevance of this text to their lives generates dedicated reading.

The quickest way to locate topics relevant to students' interests is to enable them to select a topic for project-based activities. In one example, students in an upper elementary school class selected topics on social justice, which was new to them. In the school's media center and on the Internet, they found books and articles on injustices in housing, employment, and access to health care. Reading these multiple self-selected texts, students composed five-panel comic strips using computer software to explain their particular topics. They read deeply and wrote sharply to portray and explain the injustices they unearthed.

In a study at the elementary school level, students volunteered that their personal interests were the main factor that made them want to read a narrative text. The following are some of the answers received from students when asked why they chose certain books:

- I like dolphins. I think they are cool because they live in the ocean and I like oceans.
- It was important because I like different cultures.
- Because it was about an Indian and I am interested in Indians.

Identifying students' topical interests through a conversation or questionnaire can enable teachers to heighten the relevance of books and entice students into dedicated reading.

Events

Teacher Creations of Relevance. It is often impossible to locate real-world materials or enable students to choose topics. On many occasions, the teacher needs to create relevance by designing events that enable students to see connections between text and themselves. For example, a middle school class was reading *Night* by Elie Wiesel, an account of the author's experiences during the Holocaust. Taking place on another continent in an earlier generation, students did not take much interest in the scene in which Jewish individuals were herded like cattle into a railroad car. To render the scene more personal, the teacher made a large rectangle of red tape on the classroom floor. He asked the class to crowd into this limited space. After students' giggling and complaining subsided, the teacher explained that this is how Jews would have to stand for days at a time on a moving train. Following this weak simulation, students began to ask about the people and their circumstances, and the students' reading was reignited.

A teacher-guided event that generates relevance consists of enabling students to create their own questions about text. In one social studies class, students were expected to learn about the five basic freedoms embodied in the Constitution and write their questions about the freedoms of religion, speech, assembly, petition, and the press. Students read for definitions, historical origins, and limits of all these freedoms and prepared a 6–8-minute oral report. Each report centered on a single person, event, battle, or place of the Civil War that is connected to one of these freedoms. By enabling students to be guided by their own questions as well as the curricular framework, students bring their knowledge, interests, and idiosyncrasies into their reading activities. As a consequence, their willingness to spend time and effort grows, and their products display the benefits of dedicated reading.

For students at many ages, including elementary, the teacher may set up situations involving a discrepant event, a reality that conflicts with what the students might expect to see. For example, as Duke, Purcell-Gates, Hall, and Tower (2006) reported in a study on light, one teacher set up a prism on the overhead projector while her class was out of the room. When the students returned, there were many oohs and aahs for the rainbows on the ceiling, and a rush of questions about how they occurred. The teacher led students to find and read informational text on light to help them answer their questions. Such discrepant events may be created for literature and fiction as well. If the students are asked to predict the outcome of a chapter or what a character will do in a scene, the teacher can create a discrepancy between the students' expectations and the events in the book. Exploring and explaining the discrepancies between students' predictions and the actual events can lead to teachable moments that deepen students' comprehension and enhance their reading dedication.

Relationships of teachers and students in elementary school can often be built around the process of finding the right books for students. If teachers use an interest inventory to determine topics that students enjoy, they can often find great books based on this information. Highlighting these books in book talks, book commercials, or other means helps build students' faith in teachers' ability to find relevant materials for them. In teacher–student conferences during independent reading, teachers can help students find and stick with a good book. As students gain trust in the teacher as an ally in finding and enjoying books, students' all-important time spent in reading grows.

How Relevance Works. Students connect a book to themselves by linking it to their individual opinions, values, geographic location, cultural experiences, or family characteristics. In one investigation, students were asked how their own characteristics affected the way they read a particular webpage and whether Taiwan had taken a correct political position. A few students replied with the following:

- I favor the status quo over reunification and do not think that reunification is the best solution.

- Maybe my view would be different if I lived in China, but that's a different story.
- The propaganda in the social studies classes affects my reading on this issue.
- I do live in Taiwan, but I have no opinion on the government parties here.

In this case, the students built relevance to their reading of this Web-based article by linking it to their opinions, cultural experiences, friends, perspectives, or their own political viewpoints. Whenever these qualities of knowledge, experience, and personal values are well tapped, a text emerges as relevant and thus evokes dedicated literacy.

For African American students in elementary school, relevance of books is often based on characters. In a study of factors that influenced African American students' reading, authors concluded that "connecting to the character was the most important criterion used by students to select books" (Gray, 2009, p. 477). In commenting on a favorite book, *Gettin' Through Thursday* by Melrose Cooper, one student wrote the following:

> I like *Getting' Through Thursday* better because they go through almost the same thing we go through. That's why I chose this story instead of the other one. It's a good book to me because they had to pretend they were having a party because the mom didn't have any money.... I've been through some of those things. Me and my family do and I know yours do, tell me the truth, don't they?

Although many students identify with characters with everyday experiences like their own, some see connections with figures in historical fiction. Students reported finding connections not constrained by demographic qualities such as gender, or limited to certain cultural backgrounds or historical trends affecting their minority subgroup, but rather they chose books based on idiosyncratic experiences, such as having trouble swimming or enjoying an adventure in a desert, which are features of their individual personalities and past experiences.

Relevance of Reading to the Teacher–Student Relationship. As past International Reading Association President Carol Santa (2006) wrote,

Students tend to work harder for teachers they like and put little effort into classes where they feel disconnected and misunderstood.... Students put more effort into learning when they have a relationship with their teachers; they don't want to let their teachers down. (p. 472)

Text can have another form of relevance, serving as a bridge between the teacher and the students. In many high-accountability schools with structured curricula, certain texts become required work for teacher and student alike. Students must read them, because teachers must teach them. In such cases, teachers can give students the gift of empowerment by teaching them a fruitful strategy and, in turn, may legitimately expect to see students show dedication to the text. When students believe that the teacher is acting on their behalf by working hard to teach effectively, they respond with effort in reading and writing to return the favor and fulfill the social contract with their teacher (Murdock & Miller, 2003). Thus, students' dedication to reading is often a form of commitment to a teacher who has enabled them to succeed or enjoy or persevere with a literacy activity.

Closing

There are two predominant trends in the professional literature on African American student achievement. First, the quantitative research that provides objective findings replicable across particular individuals or specific settings are frequently conducted from the perspective of sociology or historical-cultural processes. The sociological analyses focus on such societal structures as income, housing, and demographics, which are not subject to education policy or practice. Cultural analyses focus on historical events that impact ensuing beliefs, which incline toward enumerating the barriers to achievement. In contrast, the self-determination perspective focuses on the empowerments within African American individuals. It identifies personal strengths that enable some African American students to read proficiently and succeed in school. This self-perspective features a trait that dominates successful African American students: dedication to reading. High-achieving African Americans from all regions of the nation share the virtue of being behaviorally engaged. They read, write, listen, and focus attentively in school. Propelling this engagement is the belief that reading is important because it informs you about interesting matters, enables you to attain long-term goals, and helps you become self-generating.

Conversely, African Americans who avoid text, retreat from academic literacy tasks, and devalue reading are more prone to school failure than European American students. Most important, behavioral engagement buoys the fortunes of African American students irrespective of income, gender, and location. For education, this is good news, because teachers are adept at fostering dedication if they prioritize it daily using practices portrayed in this chapter.

Questions for Reflection

1. How do behaviorally disengaged students look in your classroom?

2. What does it mean to say that dedication closes the achievement gap between African American and European American students?

3. How are African American and European American students similar and different in their motivations for reading?

4. In your classroom, how have you used one of the teaching practices outlined in this chapter that support dedication?

5. What are five motivation approaches that you can use with African American students?

REFERENCES

Bean, T.W., & Harper, H.J. (2006). Exploring notions of freedom in and through young adult literature. *Journal of Adolescent & Adult Literacy, 50*(2), 96–104. doi:10.1598/JAAL.50.2.2

Carpenter, D.M., II, & Ramirez, A. (2008). More than one gap: Dropout rate gaps between and among black, Hispanic, and white students. *Journal of Advanced Academics, 19*(1), 32–64.

Cokley, K.O. (2003). What do we know about the motivation of African American students? Challenging the "anti-intellectual" myth. *Harvard Educational Review, 73*(4), 524–558.

Connell, J.P., Spencer, M.B., & Aber, J.L. (1994). Educational risk and resilience in African-American youth: Context, self, action, and outcomes in school. *Child Development, 65*(2), 493–506.

Darvin, J. (2006). "Real-world cognition doesn't end when the bell rings": Literacy instruction strategies derived from situated cognition research. *Journal of Adolescent & Adult Literacy, 49*(5), 398–409.

Duke, N.K., Purcell-Gates, V., Hall, L.A., & Tower, C. (2006). Authentic literacy activities for developing comprehension and writing. *The Reading Teacher, 60*(4), 344–355. doi:10.1598/RT.60.4.4

Finn, J.D., & Rock, D.A. (1997). Academic success among students at risk for school failure. *Journal of Applied Psychology, 82*(2), 221–234. doi:10.1037/0021-9010.82.2.221

Fredricks, J.A., Blumenfeld, P.C., & Paris, A.H. (2004). School engagement: Potential of the concept, state of the evidence. *Review of Educational Research, 74*(1), 59–109. doi:10.3102/00346543074001059

Gray, E.S. (2009). The importance of visibility: Students' and teachers' criteria for selecting African American literature. *The Reading Teacher, 62*(6), 472–481.

Guthrie, J.T. (Ed.). (2008). *Engaging adolescents in reading.* Thousand Oaks, CA: Corwin.

Guthrie, J.T., Coddington, C.S., & Wigfield, A. (2009). Profiles of reading motivation among African American and Caucasian students.

Journal of Literacy Research, 41(3), 317–353. doi:10.1080/10862960903129196

Guthrie, J.T., Wigfield, A., & You, W. (in press). Instructional contexts for engagement and achievement in reading. In S. Christensen, C. Wylie, & A. Reschly (Eds.), *Handbook of research on student engagement*. New York: Springer.

Hall, V.C., Merkel, S., Howe, A., & Lederman, N. (1986). Behavior, motivation, and achievement in desegregated junior high school science classes. *Journal of Educational Psychology, 78*(2), 108–115. doi:10.1037/0022-0663.78.2.108

Howard, T.C. (2002). Hearing footsteps in the dark: African American students' descriptions of effective teachers. *Journal of Education for Students Placed at Risk, 7*(4), 425–444. doi:10.1207/S15327671ESPR0704_4

Hudley, C. (2009). Academic motivation and achievement of African American youth. In H.A. Neville, B.M. Tynes, & S.O. Utsey (Eds.), *Handbook of African American psychology* (pp. 187–197). Thousand Oaks, CA: Sage.

Hughes, J.N., Luo, W., Kwok, O., & Loyd, L.K. (2008). Teacher–student support, effortful engagement, and achievement: A 3-year longitudinal study. *Journal of Educational Psychology, 100*(1), 1–14. doi:10.1037/0022-0663.100.1.1

Jencks, C., & Phillips, M. (Eds.). (1998). *The black–white test score gap*. Washington, DC: Brookings Institution.

Johnson, A.S., & Cowles, L. (2009). Orlonia's "literacy-in-persons": Expanding notions of literacy through biography and history. *Journal of Adolescent & Adult Literacy, 52*(5), 410–420. doi:10.1598/JAAL.52.5.5

Kelley, M.J., & Clausen-Grace, N. (2009). Facilitating engagement by differentiating independent reading. *The Reading Teacher, 63*(4), 313–318. doi:10.1598/RT.63.4.6

Lee, C.C. (1984). An investigation of psychosocial variables related to academic success for rural black adolescents. *The Journal of Negro Education, 53*(4), 424–434.

Lee, J., & Bowen, N.K. (2006). Parent involvement, cultural capital, and the achievement gap among elementary school children. *American Educational Research Journal, 43*(2), 193–218. doi:10.3102/00028312043002193

Long, J.F., Monoi, S., Harper, B., Knoblauch, D., & Murphy, P.K. (2007). Academic motivation and achievement among urban adolescents. *Urban Education, 42*(3), 196–222. doi:10.1177/0042085907300447

Mau, W., & Lynn, R. (1999). Racial and ethnic differences in motivation for educational achievement in the United States. *Personality and Individual Differences, 27*(6), 1091–1096. doi:10.1016/S0191-8869(99)00051-3

Mickelson, R.A. (1990). The attitude-achievement paradox among black adolescents. *Sociology of Education, 63*(1), 44–61.

Murdock, T.B., & Miller, A. (2003). Teachers as sources of middle school students' motivational identity: Variable-centered and person-centered analytic approaches. *The Elementary School Journal, 103*(4), 383–399. doi:10.1086/499732

Ogbu, J.U. (with Davis, A.). (2003). *Black American students in an affluent suburb: A study of academic disengagement*. Mahwah, NJ: Erlbaum.

Osborne, J.W. (1997). Race and academic disidentification. *Journal of Educational Psychology, 89*(4), 728–735. doi:10.1037/0022-0663.89.4.728

Rabiner, D.L., Murray, D.W., Schmid, L., & Malone, P.S. (2004). An exploration of the relationship between ethnicity, attention problems, and academic achievement. *School Psychology Review, 33*(4), 498–509.

Santa, C.M. (2006). A vision for adolescent literacy: Ours or theirs? *Journal of Adolescent & Adult Literacy, 49*(6), 466–476. doi:10.1598/JAAL.49.6.2

Sirin, S.R., & Rogers-Sirin, L. (2005). Components of school engagement among African American adolescents. *Applied Developmental Science, 9*(1), 5–13. doi:10.1207/s1532480xads0901_2

Skinner, E.A., Kindermann, T.A., & Furrer, C.J. (2009). A motivational perspective on engagement and disaffection: Conceptualization and assessment of children's behavioral and emotional participation in academic activities in the classroom. *Educational and Psychological Measurement, 69*(3), 493–525. doi:10.1177/0013164408323233

Strambler, M.J., & Weinstein, R.S. (2010). Psychological disengagement in elementary school among ethnic minority students. *Journal of Applied Developmental Psychology, 31*(2), 155–165. doi:10.1016/j.appdev.2009.11.006

Voelkl, K.E. (1995). School warmth, student participation, and achievement. *Journal of Experimental Education, 63*(2), 127–138. doi:10.1080/00220973.1995.9943817

Wigfield, A., Cambria, J., & Ho, A. (in press). Motivation for reading information texts. In J.T. Guthrie, S. Klauda, & D. Morrison (Eds.), *Adolescents' engagement in academic literacy*. Oak Park, IL: Bentham Science.

Wilson, W.J. (2009). *More than just race: Being black and poor in the inner city*. New York: W.W. Norton.

Chapter 6

The Importance
of Independent Reading

Linda B. Gambrell, Barbara A. Marinak, Heather R. Brooker,
and Heather J. McCrea-Andrews

We want our students to become proficient and independent readers who choose to read for both pleasure and information. The
ability to read well can provide the foundation for a life of security and
fulfillment, while the lack of reading ability may lead to a life of vulner-
ability and apprehension. According to Kasten and Wilfong (2005), "As
literacy educators, we have *two* goals. The first is to teach our students to
read. The second is to teach our students to *want to read*. The latter is the
more challenging" (p. 656). Kasten and Wilfong go on to make the case
for both the time and opportunity for students to engage in independent
silent reading in order to meet both of these important goals.

Independent reading can be defined as the time spent silently reading self-selected texts. Two commonly cited goals of independent reading in the classroom are to promote positive attitudes toward reading
(Heathington, 1979; Manning, Lewis, & Lewis, 2010; Midgley, 1993;
Mizelle, 1997) and to provide students with the reading practice they need
to become proficient (Allington, 1977, 2009; Gambrell, 2009). Teachers
promote "lasting literacy behaviors" when they model good habits of
reading and provide time for students to enjoy reading (Manning et al.,
2010, p. 113).

A number of terms have been used in the literature to describe the
period of time devoted to silent independent reading. Perhaps the first
was Hunt's (1970) Uninterrupted Sustained Silent Reading (USSR),
which later became Sustained Silent Reading (SSR). Other terms include
voluntary reading, free reading, leisure reading, recreational reading,
self-selected reading, and wide reading. Regardless of the term used to
describe it, the consistent notion is that students are provided with both
time and opportunity to engage in the independent silent reading of self-
selected texts. In addition, it is commonly understood that independent

What Research Has to Say About Reading Instruction (4th ed.) edited by S. Jay Samuels and Alan E. Farstrup.
© 2011 by the International Reading Association.

reading time is an addition to and not a substitution for reading instruction (Schaudt, 1983).

The Relationship Between Time Spent Reading and Reading Achievement

Anderson, Wilson, and Fielding (1988) investigated the relationship between time spent reading outside of school and the reading achievement of fifth-grade students. They found that the amount of time spent reading books was the best predictor of gains in reading achievement between second and fifth grade. Students who scored in the 90th percentile in reading achievement spent nearly 5 times as many minutes per day reading books as those who scored in the 50th percentile and over 200 times more than students who scored in the 10th percentile. Anderson et al. (1988) concluded, "Among all the ways children spent their time, reading books was the best predictor of several measures of reading achievement" (p. 285), including reading comprehension, vocabulary, and reading speed.

Another insight from Anderson et al.'s (1988) study is the finding that teachers had an important influence on the amount of time children spent reading books outside of school. The authors attribute teachers' influence on student motivation to their engaging in activities such as reading aloud and providing independent reading time during school hours. This finding supports the positive effects of independent reading time on students' reading achievement.

In a classic and often-cited study, Cunningham and Stanovich (1991) investigated the effect of exposure to print, or wide reading, for fourth, fifth, and sixth graders on vocabulary, general knowledge, and spelling. Findings revealed that print exposure showed significant positive correlations with vocabulary, verbal fluency, word knowledge, spelling, and general knowledge when both general ability and phonological coding ability were controlled. Cunningham and Stanovich (1998) asserted that reading has cognitive benefits that extend beyond simply getting meaning from the page. Their research supports the notion that the very act of reading can help students compensate for modest levels of cognitive ability by increasing both their vocabulary and general knowledge. Perhaps the most significant finding from this line of research is that ability is not the only variable that counts in the development of intelligence. Students who read a lot will enhance their verbal intelligence, regardless of their ability level. Cunningham and Stanovich's work revealed that everyone benefited from time spent reading, but struggling readers benefited most.

It is well-accepted within the research and academic community that the acquisition of basic reading skills such as phonemic awareness and phonics and the development of higher-level reading skills such as vocabulary, fluency, and comprehension are necessary components in learning to become a skilled reader. It is also well accepted that many of these skills need to be modeled and scaffolded through explicit instruction. However, there are many studies that show that these skills can be strengthened and further developed by providing students with time to read high-quality, developmentally appropriate, self-selected materials independently.

Research Support for Independent Reading

An impressive number of research studies have been conducted to investigate the effects of independent reading on reading attitudes and achievement. While many have been correlational, a considerable number of studies have used experimental and quasi-experimental research designs. Scholars have also conducted a number of reviews and meta-analyses of the research literature on topics related to independent reading during the past four decades, with most focusing on SSR, the most prevalent form of independent reading used in classrooms (Manning et al., 2010).

Reviews of Sustained Silent Reading

The term *sustained silent reading* began to appear in the early 1970s as a result of Hunt's (1970) work. By 1985 three reviews of the literature on self-selected reading had been published in peer-reviewed journals (Moore, Jones, & Miller, 1980; Sadoski, 1980; Wiesendanger & Birlem, 1984). These reviews were consistent in their conclusion that, overall, SSR has a consistent and positive effect on reading attitudes, specifically when the activity is conducted in concert with an instructional reading program; however, evidence also indicated that SSR is neither more nor less effective than other approaches to reading. In addition, the three reviews of the literature concluded that when compared to other approaches, the findings for benefits to higher-level reading skills for SSR were inconclusive. They also noted that studies that did not yield significant differences in support of SSR were of short duration.

Yoon (2002) conducted a meta-analytic investigation based on three decades of research on SSR to determine its overall effect on attitude toward reading. From a sample of 350 studies identified from the ERIC (Education Resources Information Center) and UMI (University

Microfilms) databases, including unpublished doctoral dissertations, unpublished articles, and peer-reviewed publications, only 7 met the following criteria for inclusion in the analysis: (a) an SSR group compared to a control group, (b) reports of effect size, and (c) outcome measures for reading attitude. The findings of this review support earlier claims that providing SSR time for students to read texts of their own choosing, either for pleasure or information, facilitated development of positive attitudes toward reading.

One Decade, Two Major Reports

In the first decade of this century, two major and somewhat opposing reports were released that raised important issues related to the role of independent reading in the literacy curriculum. The first was *Teaching Children to Read*, the report of the U.S. National Reading Panel (NRP) (National Institute of Child Health and Human Development [NICHD], 2000); the second was the report of the National Endowment for the Arts (NEA; 2007), *To Read or Not to Read*.

A major paradigm shift regarding the role of independent reading in reading development occurred as a result of the publication of the NRP report (NICHD, 2000; see also Cunningham, 2001; Garan & DeVoogd, 2008; Krashen, 2002; Samuels & Wu, 2003). The NRP set off shrills of controversy in the education world when it reported the lack of research support for independent reading, thereby challenging the practice of providing classroom time for SSR and related activities. The NRP concluded that there were insufficient numbers of scientifically based research studies conducted on independent reading that met its methodological guidelines, which included a requirement for quantitative methods, an experimental or quasi-experimental design, and random assignment of subjects to treatment groups. In the NRP review of the research, only 10 SSR studies were identified that met their criteria. In five of the studies, there were no statistically significant effects for SSR on reading achievement, and in the five remaining studies, the effect sizes were small. While the NRP could not report sufficient scientifically based research to support independent reading, it did acknowledge that there are literally hundreds of correlational studies that find that good readers read the most and poor readers read the least. The panel also noted that these studies suggest that the more children read, the better their fluency, vocabulary, and comprehension.

Some researchers contend that many of the misconceptions about SSR, or independent reading generally, stem from the NRP report (see, e.g., Allington, 2009; Garan & DeVoogd, 2008; Krashen, 2002). What is clear in the current literature is that even though the NRP report was published over a decade ago, it continues to influence research, policy, and practice.

Seven years after the release of the NRP report, the National Endowment for the Arts addressed the role of pleasure reading in the United States (NEA, 2007). In its report, the NEA sought to gather the best current national data available to provide a comprehensive view of American reading habits. The data sources consisted of large, national studies by U.S. federal agencies, as well as surveys conducted by scholars and academic institutions, foundations, and businesses. These data sources yielded the unsettling conclusions that Americans are spending less time reading and, consequently, their reading comprehension skills are declining.

While this report focused on the role of pleasure reading, it also raised a number of issues related to the importance of independent reading. And while the authors caution that none of the data presented should be regarded as drawing a causal relationship between independent reading, reading skills, and other variables, the consistent associations between independent reading and advanced reading skills and other benefits are compelling. One of the report's major conclusions is that pleasure reading correlates strongly with academic achievement. The NEA report concluded that individuals who engage in reading for pleasure are better readers and writers than are nonreaders. In addition, the study reported that children and teenagers who read for pleasure on a daily or weekly basis scored better on reading tests than did infrequent readers.

One of the most unsettling statistics in the NEA report was that nearly half of all Americans ages 18 to 24 reported reading no books for pleasure. From 1984 to 2004, the percentage of 13-year-olds who reported that they "read for fun" on a daily basis declined from 35% to 30%, and for 17-year-olds the decline was from 31% to 22%. Teens and young adults reported reading less often and for shorter amounts of time when compared with other age groups and with Americans of the past (NEA, 2007, p. 29)

The NEA report also concluded that as individuals read less, they read less well, resulting in a decline in reading skills and lower levels of academic achievement. The report also noted that average reading scores among male students declined more than for females, and the reading gap between males and females widened for both adolescents and adults. The NEA report concluded that proficient readers with strong comprehension skills accrue personal, professional, and social advantages, while less proficient readers run higher risks of failure in all three of these areas.

Shortcomings of the NEA report have been noted, including the difficulties involved in defining "pleasure reading," especially in this digital age, given the report's emphasis on books and literary texts (Bauerlein et al., 2008; Kirschenbaum, 2007). Further, the report has been criticized for its reliance on largely correlational data. But in spite of the possible limitations of the NEA report, it relied on a number of large-scale data sources to tell a consistent and disturbing story about changes in American reading habits. Of considerable concern is the finding that both the reading ability and the habit of regular reading have greatly declined among college graduates. Whether or not people read, and how much and how often they read, affects their lives in crucial ways. In light of the two goals of reading instruction—developing students who can read and who choose to read—the reports of the NRP and the NEA have caused reading educators to more seriously consider the role of independent reading in the literacy curriculum.

Recent Studies

The most recent update and meta-analysis of the research on sustained silent reading was conducted by Manning et al. (2010). These researchers cast a wide net for their review, identifying studies published in journals, unpublished doctoral dissertations, and other documents identified through the ERIC database. They included experimental, quasi-experimental, and correlational studies. Criteria for inclusion in the review were as follows: SSR was measured in time spent reading, SSR had to be independent of the core reading program, and subject samples were limited to students from kindergarten to grade 12. They identified 29 studies that met these criteria, 17 conducted with quantitative methodologies and 12 with qualitative. Manning et al. concluded from their analysis of the research that SSR is a valuable intervention that makes a worthwhile difference in developing students' vocabulary and reading comprehension. They noted that none of the studies reported that students who participated in SSR scored significantly lower on any reading achievement measure than did students who had regular reading instruction with no additional reading time. With respect to improving attitudes toward reading, Manning et al. reported that the research was mixed and inconclusive.

However, as Manning et al. (2010) noted, there has been a decline in studies on independent silent reading since the publication of the

NRP report (NICHD, 2000), though that report itself called for more scientifically based research to determine the efficacy of providing time for independent reading in the classroom. For a discussion of some of the practicalities and problems on conducting research on independent reading, see Garan and DeVoogd (2008).

Research studies using more robust experimental and quasi-experimental designs are now slowly beginning to emerge. Samuels and Wu (2003) investigated whether differences in the amount of time devoted to independent reading, when provided in addition to a balanced reading program, affected reading outcomes in third- and fifth-grade classrooms. They reported that additional reading practice was beneficial to all students; however, the amount of time spent in independent reading should match the students' reading ability and capacity to maintain attention.

Reutzel, Fawson, and Smith (2008) compared the effects of scaffolded silent reading (ScSR) with guided repeated oral reading (GROR), a strategy recommended by the NRP (NICHD, 2000) as established and scientifically supported, on students' fluency and comprehension. In ScSR the teacher makes use of silent, wide reading of independent-level texts selected from varied genres, monitors and interacts with individual students, and holds students accountable through the completion of book-response assignments. Quantitative results revealed no significant differences between ScSR and GROR. Qualitative results revealed an interesting insight about both ScSR and GROR—namely, teachers and students indicated that over time, when used exclusively, both practices tended toward tedium and decreased enjoyment of reading.

Kuhn and Schwanenflugel (2009) compared wide reading to fluency-oriented reading instruction (FORI; Stahl & Heubach, 2005), an NRP-endorsed research-based instructional strategy for increasing both fluency and general reading ability (NICHD, 2000). While this investigation compared approaches that involved oral rather than silent reading and the texts were not self-selected, it does address the role of wide reading and has implications for independent reading. In the FORI treatment condition, students read and reread a single text each week, while in the wide reading treatment condition, students read and reread three different texts. Equivalent time was spent on reading across the two groups. At the end of year 1, the students in the wide reading condition demonstrated greater text reading fluency than did those in the FORI condition. In addition, in self-assessments, students in the wide reading group rated themselves as having more positive self-concepts as readers. The findings of this study suggest that "it is increased reading practice that perhaps matters more than which technique is used to foster expanded reading activity" (Allington, 2009, p. 33).

Software programs designed to increase and manage the amount of reading students undertake have been the focus of several investigations. These programs typically make use of computerized formative assessments of children's reading performance to indicate the difficulty level of books each student is allowed to select. The two most popular programs today are Accelerated Reader and Reading Counts! Both assess students' initial reading level and then allow students to choose and read books at that level. After completing a book, the student takes a computerized comprehension quiz. A recent study by Hansen, Collins, and Warschauer (2009) investigated the use of such software for implementing and assessing the effects of independent reading on students' reading achievement and attitudes toward reading. They concluded that "schools that use reading management programs tend to have more books in their libraries, allow more time for sustained silent reading in class, and have students who read more books, than schools that do not use these programs" (p. 70). The researchers caution, however, that more substantial empirical evidence is needed to support the effects of reading management programs on reading achievement. They also point out the importance of a strong commitment to professional development that focuses on teacher training and teacher motivation to use class time for voluntary reading programs.

Topping, Samuels, and Paul (2007) conducted a study on students in grades 1 through 12 who used the Accelerated Reader program. They explored whether it was purely reading volume that affected reading achievement, or if reading quality (measured as successful comprehension) and the teacher were also integral factors. Findings suggested that reading quality and classroom teacher were as important as quantity or volume of reading for student gains in reading achievement across all grade levels. From these findings, the authors concluded that time spent reading without guidance has only a modest influence on reading achievement.

This recent line of research on independent reading suggests that there are student learning differences that require teacher monitoring in order for independent reading to increase reading achievement. Teacher guidance and support appear to be critical components of successful reading practice for developing readers. How the teacher guides and implements independent reading time influences reading achievement.

"Thus, practice does not make perfect—but attuned, successful practice makes perfect…. Appropriate, effective implementation involves not only the monitoring of reading practice, but also implies action to guide the student towards successful comprehension" (Topping et al., 2007, p. 262).

Research-Informed Visions of Independent Reading in the Classroom

Allington (2009) concluded from his review of the research on reading volume and independent reading that "almost everyone with a stake in the issue…indicates that the research currently available includes experimental evidence for a causal role for reading volume in fostering improved reading proficiency" (p. 33). A number of characteristics of successful implementation of independent reading have been identified, including the need for teacher scaffolding, determining what constitutes effective practice, the amount of time that should be devoted to independent reading, the need for students to read appropriate-level texts, and inclusion of social interaction (see, e.g., Allington, 2009; Hiebert & Reutzel, 2010; Kelley & Clausen-Grace, 2006; Reutzel et al., 2008; Samuels & Wu, 2003). These are discussed in the next sections.

Teacher Scaffolding for Successful Reading Practice

Current research is providing insights about how we can more effectively support attuned reading practice in the classroom. According to Hiebert and Reutzel (2010), "We are beginning to get a sense that the stamina of readers can be supported by effective independent, silent reading practice conditions put into place by well-informed and vigilant classroom teachers" (p. 296). Reutzel et al. (2008) discuss several scaffolds to increase the perseverance of students' silent reading during allocated independent reading time, including teaching students to select appropriate-level texts, holding individual conferences with students during which students read aloud from their books, teacher–student discussion of the book, and setting reasonable goals for completing the book.

Kelley and Clausen-Grace (2010) describe R^5, an independent reading approach with three phases: Read and Relax, Reflect and Respond, and Rap. The key elements of R^5 include

- The teacher assists with book selection.
- Students keep track of their reading.
- Students complete a response activity about their reading.

- Teacher and students engage in discussion.
- During independent reading, the teacher provides support for students and engages in record keeping.

In R^5, teachers monitor the degree to which students sustain their engagement with books during independent reading and provide support when needed. Kelley and Clausen-Grace (2010) note that many struggling readers benefit from some sense of accountability for their reading.

Brenner and Hiebert (2010) describe a series of professional development modules designed to provide teachers with specific techniques to help students keep their eyes on the page during silent reading. Even with access to these modules and on-site coaching from peers, the teachers required a great deal of guidance to make even small changes to support effective independent reading practices in their classrooms.

Effective Practice and Engaged Reading

The research shows some evidence that not all children may be engaged in real reading during the time allotted in the classroom for independent reading. This is true particularly of struggling readers. Guthrie (2004) uses the term *engaged reading* to describe the nature of extended practice during which students actively use cognitive processes and strategies while reading (see also Guthrie & Humenick, 2004). Simply providing independent reading time does not ensure that students are actually on task or engaged in the reading process. Students may not be engaged in reading because they have selected books that are too easy or too difficult, which inhibits rather than fostering engaged independent reading.

Topping et al. (2007) have made the argument that the quality of the time spent reading makes a difference. Thus, it is successful practice, or what they call "attuned practice," that makes a difference. Not all practice is equally effective for all students. The literature suggests a number of ways that teachers can support students in having successful reading practice. They can take steps to ensure that students are spending independent reading time with books that are at an appropriate level, while at the same time providing for student choice. Teachers can construct opportunities for social interaction about books by providing time for students to talk with peers about the books they are reading and by conducting individual teacher–student conferences on a consistent basis. There is emerging research that suggests that rather than the amount of time devoted to independent reading, it is the quality of the experience that is influential in reading development.

Time Devoted to Independent Reading in School

While an impressive number of studies have documented a positive relationship between the amount of time spent reading and reading achievement, studies also indicate that the volume of reading students do during the school day "has remained at a relatively low constant over the past 30 years" (Brenner, Hiebert, & Tompkins, 2009, p. 125).

Research has not provided clear insights about the amount of time that should be devoted to independent reading. However, some researchers have recommended specific guidelines for the duration of independent reading. For example, Allington (1983, 1984, 2006) suggests that students should engage in 90 minutes of independent reading during each school day. Fisher and Ivey (2006) recommend that the amount of time spent in reading and writing should be greater than the amount devoted to instruction.

Appropriate Levels of Text for Independent Reading

If successful practice makes a difference in the development of reading proficiency, then attention must be given to the difficulty level of the texts that students read during independent reading time. While giving students choice in what they read is a key feature of independent reading, some students are more capable than others of selecting appropriate text.

There is some evidence that reading easy texts (that are read with higher levels of accuracy) promotes reading engagement and achievement to a greater extent than does reading more difficult texts (Fisher & Berliner, 1985; Gambrell, Wilson, & Gantt, 1981; Jorgenson, Klein, & Kumar, 1977). Evidence suggests that for independent reading, struggling readers in particular may need a steady diet of "high-success" reading experiences with books they can read with at least 99% accuracy (Allington, 2009; Torgesen & Hudson, 2006). Teacher guidance may be needed in order to ensure that struggling readers are choosing appropriate-level text for independent reading.

Social Interactions Around Books During Independent Reading

Studies have documented that social interaction promotes achievement, higher-level cognition, and intrinsic desire to read (Almasi, 1995; Guthrie, Schafer, Wang, & Afflerbach, 1995). A classroom environment

that fosters social interaction is more likely to foster intrinsic motivation in students than are more individualized, solitary learning environments (Ames, 1984; Deci & Ryan, 1991; Guthrie et al., 1995). Guthrie et
al. (1998) found that students who had opportunities to interact socially
with peers during literacy activities were more intrinsically motivated
to read, and they read more widely and more frequently than students
who had less social interaction. In a report on trends revealed from the
National Assessment of Educational Progress, Perie, Moran, and Lutkus
(2005) noted that students who engaged in frequent discussions about
reading with friends and family were more motivated to read and had
higher reading achievement scores than students who did not have such
interactions.

More specifically, Manning and Manning (1984) compared fourth
graders in three classrooms over the course of a school year. Three
models of reading practice were implemented across the classrooms. In
one classroom traditional SSR was implemented, the second classroom
implemented SSR with peer interaction through book discussion, and
the third classroom implemented SSR with student–teacher conferences
on self-selected books. Students in all three classrooms received traditional reading instruction. The SSR with peer interaction model was
most effective in increasing both reading achievement and attitudes.
Clearly, research supports the potential benefits of including some form
of social interaction as a component of independent reading.

Conclusion

It is clear that practicing on particular reading skills and subskills does
not translate into the development of the reading habit (Allington, 2009).
It is equally clear that opportunities to engage in independent reading
enhance both reading achievement and intrinsic motivation to read
(McRae & Guthrie, 2009).

Independent reading time is of great importance since we know that
many students do not spend sufficient time reading (Allington, 2009;
Gambrell, 2007; Hiebert & Reutzel, 2010). According to Hiebert (2009),
one source of students' disinterest in reading can be traced to an insufficient amount of time spent reading in the classroom. She notes that
even at a time when national policies mandate increasing the amount of
time devoted to reading in the classroom, the time that students spend
engaged in independent reading has not increased substantially from
earlier eras.

In summary, the research base supports the notion that the reading curriculum should incorporate time and opportunities for students to engage in independent reading. It is clear that the amount of time spent reading is a critical consideration in reading development. We have long known that students who spend more time reading are better readers (Allington & McGill-Franzen, 2003; Anderson et al., 1988; Cunningham & Stanovich, 1998) and that students who have more experience with reading are better prepared for reading success than their counterparts with less experience (Allington, 1991; Neuman & Celano, 2001).

The most basic goal of any reading curriculum is the development of independent readers who *can* read and who *choose* to read. According to Hiebert and Reutzel (2010),

> There is a need and desire among educators to increase students' opportunities to engage with books and reading not only for the love of reading but also for the expectation that time spent in silent reading practice will lead to increased student achievement, fluency, and motivation to read. (p. xiii)

It may be that reading achievement is less about ability than it is about the opportunity to read. Only with the practice and expertise that comes from sufficient opportunities to engage in independent silent reading will students reach their full literacy potential.

Questions for Reflection

1. Think about your pleasure reading across the years. Make a list of books that have been most significant in your life. Why are those books meaningful? Share your "reading history" with your students, and then ask your students to make a list of their "Most Important Books and Why." Have them share this information in small groups and with you. This may provide you with valuable information about student reading preferences and interests.

2. With your colleagues, share memories about pleasure reading experiences. What did your teachers do to motivate you to read? Did you read at home? What were your reading rituals, routines, and habits? Consider how this information might inform the creation of a classroom context that fosters engaged, independent reading for your students.

3. Ask your colleagues to explain how they implement independent reading time in their classrooms. Discuss what makes independent reading time most productive for students. Discuss and describe the critical features of effective independent reading time.

4. Along with other teachers, contact the curriculum coordinator of your school or district. Suggest working together to create a cross-curricular document to describe and support effective independent reading in a variety of classroom settings. Distribute a draft document to your students for their comments, suggestions, and reactions.

REFERENCES

Allington, R.L. (1977). If they don't read much, how they ever gonna get good? *Journal of Reading, 21*(1), 57–61. doi:10.1598/JAAL.21.1.10

Allington, R.L. (1983). The reading instruction provided readers of differing reading abilities. *The Elementary School Journal, 83*(5), 548–559. doi:10.1086/461333

Allington, R.L. (1984). Content coverage and contextual reading in reading groups. *Journal of Reading Behavior, 16*(1), 85–96.

Allington, R.L. (1991). The legacy of "slow it down and make it more concrete." In J. Zutell & S. McCormick (Eds.), *Learner factors/teacher factors: Issues in literacy research and instruction* (40th yearbook of the National Reading Conference, pp. 19–30). Chicago: National Reading Conference.

Allington, R.L. (2006). *What really matters for struggling readers: Designing research-based programs* (2nd ed.). Boston: Allyn & Bacon.

Allington, R.L. (2009). If they don't read much... 30 years later. In E.H. Hiebert (Ed.), *Reading more, reading better* (pp. 30–54). New York: Guilford.

Allington, R.L., & McGill-Franzen, A. (2003). The impact of summer setback on the reading achievement gap. *Phi Delta Kappan, 85*(1), 68–75.

Almasi, J.F. (1995). The nature of fourth graders' sociocognitive conflicts in peer-led and teacher-led discussions of literature. *Reading Research Quarterly, 30*(3), 314–351.

Ames, C. (1984). Achievement attributions and self-instructions under competitive and individualistic goal structures. *Journal of Educational Psychology, 76*(3), 478–487. doi:10.1037/0022-0663.76.3.478

Anderson, R.C., Wilson, P.T., & Fielding, L.G. (1988). Growth in reading and how children spend their time outside of school. *Reading Research Quarterly, 23*(3), 285–303. doi:10.1598/RRQ.23.3.2

Bauerlein, M., Munson L., Prehoda, L., Stotsky, S., Greene, J.P., & O'Connor, E. (2008). To read or not to read: Responses to the new NEA study. *Academic Questions, 21*(2), 195–220.

Brenner, D., & Hiebert, E.H. (2010). The impact of professional development on students' opportunity to read. In E.H. Hiebert & D.R. Reutzel (Eds.), *Revisiting silent reading: New directions for teachers and researchers* (pp. 198–217). Newark, DE: International Reading Association.

Brenner, D., Hiebert, E.H., & Tompkins, R. (2009). How much and what are third graders reading? Reading in core programs. In E.H. Hiebert (Ed.), *Reading more, reading better* (pp. 118–140). New York: Guilford.

Cunningham, A.E., & Stanovich, K.E. (1991). Tracking the unique effects of print exposure in children: Associations with vocabulary, general knowledge, and spelling. *Journal of Educational Psychology, 83*(2), 264–274. doi:10.1037/0022-0663.83.2.264

Cunningham, A.E., & Stanovich, K.E. (1998). What reading does for the mind. *American Educator, 22*(1/2), 8–15.

Cunningham, J.W. (2001). The National Reading Panel report. *Reading Research Quarterly, 36*(3), 326–335. doi:10.1598/RRQ.36.3.5

Deci, E.L., & Ryan, R.M. (1991). A motivational approach to self: Integration in personality. In R.A. Dienstbier (Ed.), *Perspectives on motivation: Nebraska symposium on motivation, 1990* (Vol. 38, pp. 237–288). Lincoln: University of Nebraska Press.

Fisher, C.W., & Berliner, D.C. (1985). *Perspectives on instructional time.* New York: Longman.

Fisher, D., & Ivey, G. (2006). Evaluating the interventions for struggling adolescent readers. *Journal of Adolescent & Adult Literacy, 50*(3), 180–189. doi: 10.1598/JAAL.50.3.2

Gambrell, L.B. (2007). Reading: Does practice make perfect? *Reading Today, 24*(6), 16.

Gambrell, L.B. (2009). Creating opportunities to read more so that students read better. In E.H. Hiebert (Ed.), *Reading more, reading better* (pp. 251–266). New York: Guilford.

Gambrell, L.B., Wilson, R.M., & Gantt, W.N. (1981). Classroom observations of task-attending behaviors of good and poor readers. *Journal of Educational Research, 74*(6), 400–404.

Garan, E.M., & DeVoogd, G. (2008). The benefits of sustained silent reading: Scientific research and common sense converge. *The Reading Teacher, 62*(4), 336–344. doi:10.1598 /RT.62.4.6

Guthrie, J.T. (2004). Teaching for literacy engagement. *Journal of Literacy Research, 36*(1), 1–29. doi:10.1207/s15548430jlr3601_2

Guthrie, J.T., Cox, K.E., Anderson, E., Harris, K., Mazzoni, S., & Rach, L. (1998). Principles of integrated instruction for engagement in reading. *Educational Psychology Review, 10*(2), 177–199. doi:10.1023/A:1022189603904

Guthrie, J.T., & Humenick, N.M. (2004). Motivating students to read: Evidence for classroom practices that increase reading motivation and achievement. In P. McCardle & V. Chhabra (Eds.), *The voice of evidence in reading research* (pp. 329–354). Baltimore: Paul H. Brookes.

Guthrie, J.T., Schafer, W., Wang, Y.Y., & Afflerbach, P. (1995). Relationships of instruction to amount of reading: An exploration of social, cognitive, and instructional connections. *Reading Research Quarterly, 30*(1), 8–25.

Hansen, L.E., Collins, P., & Warschauer, M. (2009). Reading management programs: A review of the research. *Journal of Literacy and Technology, 10*(3), 55–80.

Heathington, B.S. (1979). What to do about reading motivation in the middle school. *Journal of Reading, 22*(8), 709–713.

Hiebert, E.H. (Ed.). (2009). *Read more, read better.* New York: Guilford.

Hiebert, E.H., & Reutzel, D.R. (Eds.). (2010). *Revisiting silent reading: New directions for teachers and researchers.* Newark, DE: International Reading Association.

Hunt, L.C., Jr. (1970). The effect of self-selection, interest, and motivation upon independent, instructional, and frustrational levels. *The Reading Teacher, 24*(2), 146–151.

Jorgenson, G.W., Klein, N., & Kumar, V.K. (1977). Achievement and behavior correlates of matched levels of student ability and material difficulty. *Journal of Educational Research, 71*(2), 100–103.

Kasten, W.C., & Wilfong, L.G. (2005). Encouraging independent reading with ambience: The Book Bistro in middle and secondary school classes. *Journal of Adolescent & Adult Literacy, 48*(8), 656–664. doi:10.1598/JAAL.48.8.3

Kelley, M., & Clausen-Grace, N. (2006). R[5]: The sustained silent reading makeover that transformed readers. *The Reading Teacher, 60*(2), 148–156. doi:10.1598/RT.60.2.5

Kelley, M.J., & Clausen-Grace, N. (2010). R[5]: A sustained silent reading makeover that works. In E.H. Hiebert & D.R. Reutzel (Eds.), *Revisiting silent reading: New directions for teachers and researchers* (pp. 168–180). Newark, DE: International Reading Association.

Kirschenbaum, M. (2007). How reading is being reimagined. *Chronical of Higher Education, 54*(15), p. B20

Krashen, S.D. (2002). More smoke and mirrors: A critique of the National Reading Panel report on fluency. In R.L. Allington (Ed.), *Big brother and the national reading curriculum: How ideology trumped evidence* (pp. 112–124). Portsmouth, NH: Heinemann.

Kuhn, M.R., & Schwanenflugel, P.J. (2009). Time, engagement, and support: Lessons from a 4-year fluency intervention. In E.H. Hiebert (Ed.), *Reading more, reading better* (pp. 141–160). New York: Guilford.

Manning, G.L., & Manning, M. (1984). What models of recreational reading make a difference? *Reading World, 23*(4), 375–380.

Manning, M., Lewis, M., & Lewis, M. (2010). Sustained silent reading: An update of the research. In E.H. Hiebert & D.R. Reutzel (Eds.), *Revisiting silent reading: New directions for teachers and researchers* (pp. 112–128). Newark, DE: International Reading Association.

McRae, A., & Guthrie, J.T. (2009). Promoting reasons for reading: Teacher practices that impact motivation. In E.H. Hiebert (Ed.),

Reading more, reading better (pp. 55–76). New York: Guilford.

Midgley, C. (1993). Motivation and middle level schools. In P.R. Pintrich & M.L. Maehr (Eds.), *Advances in motivation and achievement. Vol. 8: Motivation in the adolescent years* (pp. 219–276). Greenwich, CT: JAI Press.

Mizelle, N.B. (1997). Enhancing young adolescents' motivation for literacy learning. *Middle School Journal, 28*(3), 16–25.

Moore, J.C., Jones, C.J., & Miller, D.C. (1980). What we know after a decade of sustained silent reading. *The Reading Teacher, 33*(4), 445–450.

National Endowment for the Arts. (2007). *To read or not to read: A question of national consequence* (Research Report No. 47). Washington, DC: Author. Retrieved November 24, 2010, from www.nea.gov/research/toread.pdf

National Institute of Child Health and Human Development. (2000). *Report of the National Reading Panel. Teaching children to read: An evidence-based assessment of the scientific research literature on reading and its implications for reading instruction* (NIH Publication No. 00-4769). Washington, DC: U.S. Government Printing Office.

Neuman, S.B., & Celano, D. (2001). Access to print in low-income and middle-income communities: An ecological study of four neighborhoods. *Reading Research Quarterly, 36*(1), 8–26. doi:10.1598/RRQ.36.1.1

Perie, M., Moran, R., & Lutkus, A.D. (2005). *NAEP 2004 trends in academic progress: Three decades of student performance in reading and mathematics* (NCES 2005-464). Washington, D.C.: National Center for Education Statistics, Institute of Education Sciences, U.S. Department of Education.

Reutzel, D.R., Fawson, P.C., & Smith, J.A. (2008). Reconsidering silent sustained reading: An exploratory study of scaffolded silent reading. *The Journal of Educational Research, 102*(1), 37–50. doi:10.3200/JOER.102.1.37-50

Sadoski, M.C. (1980). Ten years of uninterrupted sustained silent reading. *Reading Improvement, 17*(2), 153–156.

Samuels, S.J., & Wu, Y. (2003). *How the amount of time spent on independent reading affects reading achievement: A response to the National Reading Panel*. Minneapolis: University of Minnesota.

Schaudt, B.A. (1983). Another look at sustained silent reading. *The Reading Teacher, 36*(9), 934–936.

Stahl, S.A., Heubach, K.M., & Holcomb, A. (2005). Fluency-oriented reading instruction. *Journal of Literacy Research, 37*(1), 25–60. doi:10.1207/s15548430jlr3701_2

Topping, K.J., Samuels, J., & Paul, T. (2007). Does practice make perfect? Independent reading quantity, quality and student achievement. *Learning and Instruction, 17*(3), 253–264. doi:10.1016/j.learninstruc.2007.02.002

Torgesen, J.K., & Hudson, R.F. (2006). Reading fluency: Critical issues for struggling readers. In S.J. Samuels & A.E. Farstrup (Eds.), *What research has to say about fluency instruction* (pp. 130–158). Newark, DE: International Reading Association.

Wiesendanger, K.D., & Birlem, E.D. (1984). The effectiveness of SSR: An overview of the research. *Reading Horizons, 24*(3), 197–201.

Yoon, J. (2002). Three decades of sustained silent reading: A meta-analytic review of the effects of SSR on attitude toward reading. *Reading Improvement, 39*(4), 186–195.

Chapter 7

Integrating Reading Strategies and Knowledge Building in Adolescent Literacy Instruction

Julie E. Learned, Darin Stockdill, and Elizabeth Birr Moje

How to effectively teach literacy knowledge and skills to adolescent students as they learn content concepts and practices is a topic of much discussion and debate among teachers, researchers, and policymakers. In regard to reading, there is debate about whether it is better for students to attend to text content or the ways in which they build knowledge with text while reading. The latter approach, focusing students' attention on the processes they use to learn from text, typically takes the shape of reading strategy instruction. A process-oriented approach to reading instruction is often positioned as antithetical to a content-oriented approach in contemporary scholarship, as if one approach precludes the other. Therein lies the crux of the content-process debate. Do we learn more from text and subsequently build richer knowledge by attending to what we read or to how we understand what we read?

In this chapter, we hope to problematize what we view as an increasingly dichotomous rendering of content learning and strategy use in adolescent literacy instruction and suggest, instead, that reading strategies can and should work in the service of disciplinary knowledge building. To effectively apply a reading (or writing) strategy, students depend heavily on word, world, and domain knowledge; thus, strategy instruction should be as much about knowledge development as it is about teaching kids to use strategies independently.

In a recent review of the research on reading instruction, Palincsar and Schutz (in press) take on this same question of balancing strategy use and instruction with content learning and knowledge building. The authors state that the "goal of strategy instruction is to equip learners with the means to undertake complex problem solving in more efficient ways; with practice the strategies lead to skills that learners use

What Research Has to Say About Reading Instruction (4th ed.) edited by S. Jay Samuels and Alan E. Farstrup.
© 2011 by the International Reading Association.

automatically" (p. 3). They claim that dualistic thinking about strategies and knowledge building is problematic, as they should work in tandem, and argue that some of the presentations of strategy instruction today, which view it apart from knowledge building, represent a separation from the theoretical roots of strategy instruction.

Serving as an exemplar of how contemporary research conceptualizes strategy instruction, McKeown, Beck, and Blake (2009) conducted a study comparing reading gains between students receiving content-focused reading instruction and students receiving strategies-focused reading instruction. In the content group, instruction maintained students' attention on content through open, meaning-based questions about the texts, a method based on questioning the author (QtA; Beck & McKeown, 2006; Beck, McKeown, Sandora, Kucan, & Worthy, 1996). The strategy group focused instruction on summarizing, predicting, drawing inferences, question generation, and comprehension monitoring. In the end, the researchers found that students in the content group performed similarly to and in some instances slightly better than students in the strategies group on several measures of reading ability. These findings led the researchers to conclude that if content-focused approaches are equally effective and allow "students to consider text meaning directly rather than indirectly through strategies," then the productivity of strategy instruction should be questioned (McKeown et al., 2009, p. 245).

Notable for our purposes is the way that this study's design, findings, and implications cast strategy instruction and knowledge building as competing constructs. This is a bit surprising given that original research on strategy instruction tended to conceptualize strategies and content learning as more intertwined; that is, original research considered how strategies facilitated learning or knowledge development while reading. However, when reviewing the current landscape of strategy research and practice, we more often see the promotion of strategies without discussion of the important role of knowledge in making meaning from text. Indeed, it seems that many scholars and teachers increasingly discuss, research, and employ reading strategies as if they were a means unto themselves. For example, a reading lesson involving questioning might focus solely on how well students formulate questions instead of on how questioning helps students seek answers in the text, monitor comprehension, and subsequently build knowledge (Scott, 2009). Given the present-day manifestation of strategy instruction, we understand why McKeown et al. (2009) framed strategy and content-focused instruction dichotomously. Ironically, however, we believe that the researchers' content instruction based on QtA represents an ideal marriage of strategy use and knowledge building. Although McKeown et al. do not consider QtA a strategy, we suggest that it exemplifies a set of strategies that are appropriately and inextricably linked to knowledge development.

What seems at issue, then, is in part how we define *reading strategy*, *content*, and *knowledge*. In addition to clarifying definitions, our main goal in this chapter is to recast strategy instruction in its historical context and then attempt to move it forward, which requires abandoning a strategy versus content perspective. To that end, we foreground the learning of subject matter concepts and disciplinary practices as the primary objective of subject matter reading instruction. We suggest that considering how reading strategies, indeed how disciplinary literacy practices, work in service of disciplinary knowledge building is a more productive stance for improving adolescent literacy learning.

To begin, we describe the content- or knowledge-based perspective as well as the process-based perspective on reading, and then proceed to review exemplars of historical research to understand the original intentions of and trends in reading strategy instruction as they related to knowledge development. Next, we discuss several works from the past 10 years of adolescent literacy research and theoretical writing related to both content and process models of reading to highlight the important contributions each perspective has made to an understanding of reading and reading instruction. Finally, we argue that content and process models should be integrated and viewed as interactive and interdependent, and we review exemplar studies which we feel demonstrate this integration.

Knowledge and Process-Oriented Perspectives on Reading

Historically, a knowledge-oriented approach to reading places a premium on content or knowledge to be gleaned from a text (Mandel, 1980; Peters & Wixson, 2003). Hirsch (1987, 2006) has argued that students need to learn a core set of cultural knowledge and that, in fact, the achievement gap stems from denying children from nondominant backgrounds access to this core knowledge (cf. Ravitch & Finn, 1987). Reading comprehension, according to Hirsch (2003), requires knowledge of both "words and the world" (p. 10). Hirsch (2003) wrote, "Prior knowledge about the topic speeds up basic comprehension and leaves working memory free to make connections between the new material and previously learned information" (p. 13). He suggests that content immersion and coherent language experiences build vocabulary and domain knowledge. Conversely, Hirsch (2003) cautioned against spending too much time "teaching formal comprehension skills," such as "predicting, classifying, and looking for the main idea" (p. 22). He stated that "in the classroom, reading comprehension and vocabulary are best served by spending extended time on reading and listening to texts on the same topic and discussing the facts and ideas in them" (p. 28). From his perspective, reading is best supported by focusing on content and knowledge building instead of strategy instruction, which is thought to detract from learning new information.

Critics of Hirsch and the core knowledge model point out that it does not directly discuss how to build knowledge except through content immersion, a rather vague instructional notion. In addition, critics assert that it is at best unfeasible and at worst elitist to believe that teachers can identify and teach all "core knowledge." The overarching criticism made of the knowledge model, be it directed at knowledge-focused teaching generally or the core knowledge camp specifically, is that it does not attend to how readers make meaning with text, that is, how readers construct knowledge.

However, a process model focuses on the ways a reader makes meaning with text, countering the notion that content lies on a page (or a website, T-shirt, or billboard) waiting to be picked up "as is" by a reader. The concept of reading process signals a host of literacy concepts including, but not limited to, the role of prior knowledge and experience in a reader's sense-making, the features of text and text structure, the purpose for which one reads, the importance of a reader's awareness of the process (i.e., metacognition), and perhaps most central, the dynamic interrelationship of the text, reader, activity, and context of the reading activity (Biancarosa & Snow, 2004; Peters & Wixson, 2003).

Studies have identified several comprehension strategies that effective readers use to make meaning with text, including comprehension monitoring, predicting, questioning, visualizing, summarizing, and inferring (Biancarosa & Snow, 2004; National Institute of Child Health and Human Development [NICHD], 2000). Studies have shown that explicit instruction which helps students become metacognitive about strategy use (i.e., aware of how they understand while they read) can benefit comprehension (Palincsar & Brown, 1984). Research on teacher and student think-alouds has shown that students can develop this type of metacognitive awareness through social interaction and structured dialogue

(Biancarosa & Snow, 2004; Kucan & Beck, 1997). Critics of strategy instruction counter that such approaches needlessly draw readers' attention away from text content and meaning, thus positioning process and content in opposition to each other. As already suggested, we argue that these approaches are not mutually exclusive and can indeed happen in tandem, and in the latter part of this chapter, we discuss studies which demonstrate this relationship.

A Historical Perspective on Strategy and Knowledge in Reading Research

Before moving on to examine exemplars of strategy research to explore if or how they frame knowledge, it is helpful to situate the work within the history of reading research generally. Research on reading in the first half of the 20th century grew out of the work of scholars such as Watson and Thorndike and focused on scientific measurement of observable skills. Beginning in the late 1940s and continuing into the 1950s, however, a small group of scholars began to discuss the need for research that looked deeper into the human mind. Thus, in the early 1960s, influenced by scholars in various academic disciplines such as Piaget, Kohler, Lashley, and Chomsky, the field of cognitive psychology began to emerge (Lagemann, 2000).

By the 1980s, cognitive psychology was the dominant paradigm in educational research, as cognitive researchers sought to explain the nature of problem solving, memory, perception, learning, and other mental functions. Both the strategic processes of reading and the use and development of knowledge were studied in this framework, as scientists began to look into the ways in which the human mind interacts with, organizes, and applies new information (Shuell, 1986). Reading, as a means of learning, was (and continues to be) an area of interest for cognitive researchers, because it involves a complex integration of many cognitive functions from perception to memory to comprehension of meaning (Shuell, 1986). Prior to this cognitive shift, reading on the secondary level was often assumed to be a fully developed skill, and much of the research on secondary reading and its instruction centered on remediation of struggling readers. The cognitive perspective, however, sought to understand how reading happens and what must take place in order for readers to comprehend text.

The study of secondary reading and writing as areas of continuing learning emerged more clearly with Herber (1978), who coined the phrase *content area reading*. He argued that middle and high school students need literacy instruction within content areas and suggested that a content teacher had two major responsibilities: teaching the content knowledge of the subject and teaching the processes through which this content is produced and learned (Herber & Sanders, 1969). Herber thus reinforced the content-process framework, but he described an integrated approach in which process is not taught for its own sake but rather to promote learning content from text.

Cognitively oriented research into secondary reading was also rooted in the idea that adolescents thought and learned differently from younger children. This was a relatively novel hypothesis in American education in the mid-1900s and grew primarily out of the work done by Piaget in the 1950s and 1960s. Ausubel and Ausubel (1966) wrote about the transition into adolescence, adapting the Piagetian perspective that children pass from a stage Piaget called concrete operations into another he termed formal operations as they approach high school age. According to Ausubel and Ausubel, the high school student then became "an abstract verbal learner," and high school teachers could engage in "a new type of verbal expository teaching that uses concrete-empirical experience primarily for illustrative purposes, i.e., to clarify or dramatize truly abstract meanings rather than to generate intuitive meanings" (pp. 409–410). In this framework, high school readers had to connect experience to ideas; thus, prior knowledge and experience took on new importance.

Huhn (1980), referring back to other work by Ausubel, described cognition as having a binary nature "consisting of cognitive structure and cognitive functions" (p. 30). In this framework, cognitive structure was made up of hierarchically ordered ideas obtained through prior experience and schooling, whereas cognitive functions consisted of problem-solving capacities. The application of this conceptualization to teaching reading lies in the idea that teachers must be sure their students have both the prior knowledge and skills necessary to succeed in a learning task. If the students are not ready for a particular type of learning, then the teacher needs to provide instruction to prepare them in whichever area (i.e., structure and/or function) requires development.

One of the outgrowths of the recognition of the importance of function was an interest in the differences between how skilled and less skilled readers approached text. A series of studies in the 1970s looked at people identified as good and poor readers and compared their reading processes. This work in part led to the development of strategy instruction, as researchers made recommendations to teachers based on their findings with respect to what good readers did and did not do while reading (Palincsar & Schutz, in press). To characterize the different strategies that skilled and less skilled readers employed, Golinkoff (1975) compared the "reading comprehension processes in good and poor comprehenders" (p. 623) in a research review of comprehension studies. She concluded that skilled readers were better able to employ text organization processes (i.e., obtain meaning from longer stretches of text), whereas poor readers approached reading with a word-by-word process. Whether prior knowledge was necessary or helpful to the skilled readers was not directly examined.

In a later study, Paris and Myers (1981) studied the comprehension skills of two groups of fourth graders identified as good and poor readers to explore the differences in text processing across the two groups. The researchers focused in particular on comprehension monitoring among the children and found that the better readers consistently showed more evidence of awareness of their own comprehension and reading process. These studies of good and poor readers signaled the beginning of a focus on process and strategy and again did not directly discuss the possibility that topic or content knowledge served as additional differentiating factors between good and poor readers.

Reviewing the research literature on instructional routines during the same time period, Brown, Campione, and Day (1981) discussed how best to help students learn to learn. The researchers set up strategy use as distinct from knowledge building and noted that "training studies aimed at improving students' academic performance can succeed by adding substantially to the students' knowledge; or they can succeed by instructing students in ways to enhance their own knowledge" (p. 14). They went on to argue that the "latter outcome...is most desirable" (p. 14). The authors thus seemed to perceive a choice between focusing on knowledge and focusing on the processes of building knowledge, as opposed to doing both in a more synergistic paradigm.

Nevertheless, strategy use and knowledge building were still recognized as connected components of reading comprehension in the research. Paris, Wixson, and Palincsar (1986) described several studies that looked at "cognitive prompts for elaborating text" (p. 101). These prompts took the form of "instructional aids such as directions, questions, organizers, and supplementary material/activities that are provided to readers" (p. 101). With another reference to the work of Ausubel, they discussed advance organizers, which seemed to help students scaffold new ideas as they organize them into their prior knowledge and experience base. Thus, there was a clear recognition that strategies like organizers could serve to build and organize new knowledge.

Working within this framework, Graves, Cooke, and LaBerge (1983) considered knowledge building as part of strategic instruction in their study of the effect of preview guides as reading aids on the comprehension of short stories by secondary students with lower abilities in reading. For the purposes of the study, the authors defined previews as "introductory material presented to students before they read specific selections. Text previews provide students with a framework within which they can understand a selection and give them specific information about the contents of the material itself" (p. 264). This investigation involved over 70 junior high and high school students, all reading significantly below level. Students participating in the study read short stories both with and without previews over periods of 2–4 weeks. Knowledge building, in this approach, served as an instructional strategy to help prepare students for reading. After reading the stories with and without previews, the students were given multiple-choice tests comprised of factual and inferential questions. Statistical analysis of comprehension and recall measures showed that students answered more questions correctly and recalled more details about the stories when instructors previewed the material. Moreover, students who experienced the previews showed greater gains on the inferential question scores than on factual questions.

Expanding on such strategy instruction research, Palincsar and Brown (1984) conducted two studies that focused directly on strategies people use while reading text. They investigated the impact of comprehension-fostering and comprehension-monitoring activities on seventh-grade students with poor reading comprehension. The authors developed and implemented what they referred to as reciprocal teaching, in which a tutor and a student take turns leading a conversation about text employing four activities or strategies: summarizing, questioning, clarifying, and predicting. In reciprocal teaching, the adult models good strategy use and gradually transfers responsibility for employing these strategies to the student. Palincsar and Brown (1984) documented sizable gains in the experimental group on "criterion tests of comprehension, reliable maintenance over time, generalization to classroom comprehension tests, transfer to novel tasks that tapped the trained skills of summarizing, questioning, and clarifying, and improvement in standardized comprehension scores" (p. 117). Despite its focus on strategy instruction, the overarching goal of reciprocal teaching, according to Palincsar and Brown, was that children would build knowledge and learn from text through the use of reading strategies. In a review of strategy instruction literature, Palincsar and Schutz (in press) argued that because the second iteration of reciprocal teaching (Palincsar & Brown, 1988) used texts on science concepts related to animal survival, it therefore represented a better example of strategy use in the service of knowledge development.

As a result of research like the studies above, the role of prior knowledge and schemata in learning, as well as the use of previewing and structural organizers, remained important throughout the 1980s and into the 1990s, as researchers sought to improve students' abilities to comprehend text (Paris, Wixson, & Palincsar, 1986). Some researchers, however, recognizing the important role of knowledge in text comprehension, focused their attention on texts themselves, seeking not to change the learner's strategy use but to enhance access to information in texts. Beck, McKeown, Sinatra, and Loxterman (1991) examined the role of the text in reading comprehension in a study in which they revised social studies text to improve comprehension.

Beck et al.'s (1991) analysis of the text in question showed that this particular history text demanded certain prior knowledge of student readers, information that was not available in the text but was necessary for understanding its target concepts. For example, in a section on the French and Indian War, students needed to know that many colonists were still loyal to Britain in the 1760s to understand the tensions that ensued during the war, and they also needed to know that Britain and France were contesting territory at that time and that the Indians were resistant to British colonization to understand why the Indians would take up arms for the French. Indeed, even the name for this war is potentially confusing to a reader who possesses little knowledge of the British–French tensions in Europe at the time period; many adolescent readers might reasonably assume that the French fought the Indians in this war. The French and Indian War is a particularly good example of the critical role of knowledge in text comprehension. The conflict was actually a European one, and the French and Indian War was merely the North American theater of that European war. The conflict was so dubbed by the British, whose enemies in the battle were the French and the native people, the Indians, of North America. Without this prior knowledge, which was not explained in the target text, students could struggle with comprehension of the main ideas of the text.

In their revision of the text, Beck et al. (1991) added sentences to provide the necessary background information to readers who might not have it. The researchers built a short chronological narrative that included information about preconditions for the conflict between France and Britain. Presenting original and revised texts to two groups within a sample of 85 fourth and fifth graders, the researchers found that students in the treatment group (i.e., those who read revised text) showed greater comprehension and retention of important information on recall and question-answering assessments, despite having the same prior knowledge as readers in the control group (i.e., those who read the standard text). Beyond a focus on reading strategy then, this study looked at text development and the knowledge demands of text. Texts can be written to build necessary knowledge for the reader, although for a host of reasons, classroom textbooks routinely lack the structure and knowledge development to support the inference-making necessary for proficient comprehension (Chambliss & Calfee, 1998).

Along with interest in the text, researchers also began looking more closely at the social nature of learning in classrooms and how the building of knowledge through reading was also a social, not just individual, process. Anderson and Roit (1993) developed an approach called collaborative strategy instruction, in which students worked to learn content concepts and develop comprehension skills through teacher-led discussions and thinking aloud. As students worked with texts, they asked themselves and each other different types of questions to elicit information not only about the types of strategies they were using while reading but also about their prior knowledge on the topic. In their study, Anderson and Roit compared a control group to a collaborative strategy instruction group and found that more students in the intervention group demonstrated gains on comprehension tests. Although not focusing directly on the need to build knowledge while reading, collaborative strategy instruction acknowledged the importance of building knowledge through questioning and dialogue.

Continuing this line of inquiry, Kucan and Beck (1997) reviewed research on reading comprehension and thinking aloud, which grew out of the increased interest in the social nature of knowledge building. In their framework, thinking aloud served as a form of instruction, a medium of social interaction for learning, and a means of inquiry. They reviewed research in which collaborative discussions were used to help students build meaning from texts. They mentioned the importance of prior knowledge to reading comprehension but did not focus directly on knowledge or knowledge building, even in their discussion of strategy instruction research. In the framework of reading they presented, a reader's existing knowledge helped the reader create a model of understanding from text, which the reader adapted as he or she encountered more text.

Kucan and Beck (1997) did, however, discuss a constructivist shift in reading instruction research in the 1980s and 1990s, in which

> developments in teaching mathematics and science began to draw edu-cators' attention to the importance of taking into account the construc-tive nature of learning by helping students to evaluate and use what they already knew and to engage in extending or revising that understanding through collaborative problem solving. (p. 285)

In this context, Kucan and Beck discussed the importance of helping students acquire new knowledge and also learning how they build knowledge and develop an awareness of their own epistemologies through social interaction and thinking aloud.

Finally, the work of Alexander, Jetton, and Kulikowich (1995) took up questions similar to those of the good and poor reader studies by looking at the characteristics of readers in relationship to reading proficiency, but also sought to complicate and elaborate on both the questions and their answers. They examined the role of knowledge in reading, particularly how knowledge enables strategic reading, and developed profiles of readers across different sets of the characteristics they identified. Alexander and her colleagues carried out a study on knowledge, interest, and recall among undergraduate and graduate students, looking to see how their domain knowledge interacted with topic interest and their ability to recall information from text. Analyzing student scores across measures for knowledge, interest, and recall with a cluster analysis, they found clusters of higher and lower performing students. When compared with higher students, the lower students tended to know less and have less interest, and they remembered less on the recall measure. The authors also identified smaller clusters of mixed-profile students, including those who knew a fair amount but seemed unwilling or unable to use strategic reading processes, and those who seemed more willing or able to strate-gically engage with text but had less knowledge of the topic. Overall, the researchers concluded that knowledge and interest were interactive and mutually beneficial in recall tasks. Higher performing students had both more knowledge and more ability to read strategically, which resulted in better knowledge recall.

In a follow-up study, Alexander and Murphy (1998) explored simi-lar questions in a study of 329 undergraduate students in an educational psychology class. The researchers used pre- and posttest measures of domain knowledge, interest, and reading strategies; the pretest was framed as a tool to help shape the course in which the students were enrolled, and the posttest as a final exam. They analyzed patterns in student responses across these measures, leading to the development of four profiles in which students were clustered: learning-oriented, strong knowledge, effortful processor, and nonstrategic reader. The authors found that knowledge, interest, and strategic ability all interacted across the profiles; not one of these factors alone was sufficient for reading comprehension and performance on the assessment. Domain knowledge, however, did seem to contribute to better performance, but it diminished in importance over time if students did not also have interest and the ability to strategically engage with text. In other words, Alexander and her colleagues found that knowledge was necessary for achievement, but knowledge combined with interest and the ability to strategically process text led to the highest levels of performance.

Research in the 1980s and 1990s thus recognized that reading strategically was a way to build knowledge, but also that a certain amount of knowledge was necessary to use strategic processes. Researchers working on reading instruction at that time recommended a variety of approaches, including advance organizers, questioning and predicting, collaborative discussion, and think-alouds, to help students engage strategically with text and build knowledge at the same time. Although some of the work done in this time period focused on either knowledge or process, the general trend was to recognize that knowledge and processes were linked in the act of comprehension.

Recognizing and Maintaining the Integration of Knowledge and Strategy

Whereas knowledge development and strategy instruction were not necessarily seen as oppositional in past research, there appears to be a trend in the last 10 years that positions them as independent of one another at best and as antithetical at worst. Nonetheless, more recent research, which focuses primarily on strategy instruction without explicit attention to knowledge development, has contributed greatly to our understanding of the use of strategic processes in instruction. In this section, we begin by discussing the developing body of research on strategy instruction by examining current research that highlights the application of reading strategies. Next, we consider the role of knowledge in strategy use by looking at strategy-focused studies that take up knowledge, often knowledge of language (e.g., word knowledge, genre knowledge, text structure knowledge). Finally, we explore the important connection between knowledge building—what teachers do or could do when students do not have the necessary knowledge to bear on a text—and strategy use by showcasing research that addresses strategies and knowledge development in tandem. Ultimately, we suggest that conceiving of strategy use in the service of knowledge development is a productive instructional stance that greatly benefits secondary readers.

Contemporary Research and Policy Related to Strategy Instruction

One of the most influential policy documents in adolescent literacy from the past 10 years is *Reading Next—A Vision for Action and Research in Middle and High School Literacy* (Biancarosa & Snow, 2004), a Carnegie Corporation report borne out of an adolescent literacy panel convened by the National Institutes of Health in 2002. With the publication of *Reading Next*, adolescent literacy received widespread, national attention for the first time. Previously, federal policymakers and federal literacy programs had focused exclusively on early literacy development, the most recent iteration being the Reading First program in No Child Left Behind. *Reading Next* garnered momentum for adolescent literacy in general and secondary-level reading strategy instruction in particular.

Drawing on a wide range of adolescent literacy studies, the *Reading Next* report made 15 recommendations for effective adolescent literacy programs, one of which is explicit strategy instruction. These 15 recommendations have been repeated in other policy documents and been taken up, often apart from the rest of the report, by school districts seeking to reform their adolescent literacy instruction. Although *Reading Next* recognizes that reading strategies are important to the development of content area knowledge, the report does not explicitly discuss knowledge building within the 15 recommended practices. Specifically, the recommendations do not include any mention of the role of knowledge in comprehension of complex texts, nor do the recommendations draw teachers' or literacy specialists' attention to the teacher's role in eliciting or developing adolescent students' knowledge.

Although the policy does not explicitly discuss content or disciplinary knowledge development, it notably calls for literacy instruction embedded in the content areas. Recommending that subject matter teachers provide literacy instruction specific to their subject areas is not a radically new idea in research and practice, but *Reading Next* is the first time the idea received a highly publicized endorsement. In acknowledging that reading and writing skills are domain-specific, the authors of *Reading Next* renewed a call made several decades earlier by Herber (1978), that every teacher should be a teacher of reading.

The idea that all secondary teachers would teach domain-specific literacy skills, although embraced by policy setters such as the Council of Chief State School Officers (2010; see their Adolescent Literacy Toolkit), it is not clear that secondary school teachers have taken up these 15 recommendations to the extent imagined by those who study adolescent literacy (Carnegie Council on Advancing Adolescent Literacy, 2010). Rather, *Reading Next* brought adolescent literacy into national attention and made a strong case for reading strategy instruction as an important, but not exclusive, component of content area learning.

Indeed, ample evidence exists to support the claim that strategy instruction helps adolescents read more productively. For example, Schorzman and Cheek (2004) conducted a study in which they reviewed three strategies popular among middle school teachers: directed reading–thinking activity (Stauffer, 1969), the prereading plan (Langer & Nicolich, 1981), and graphic organizers (Barron, 1969). The study employed short stories from an adolescent literature anthology and thus potentially tapped multiple knowledge bases depending on the particulars of each story. The researchers found significant differences between the experimental and control groups on informal measures of reading ability; the students exposed to reading strategy instruction performed better than their peers who had not learned strategies. Similarly, Stevens (2003) investigated middle school literacy instruction by implementing and evaluating a program called Student Team Reading and Writing. A key element of the literacy program was explicit reading comprehension strategy instruction, along with cooperative learning, high-interest materials, integrated reading and writing instruction, and a writing process approach. Stevens found students in schools implementing Student Team Reading and Writing had significantly higher achievement in reading vocabulary, reading comprehension, and language expression than students in the study's comparison schools.

Strategies have also been found to be helpful when students engage in digital literacy (e.g., reading websites, e-mails, blogs). Dalton and Proctor (2007) examined strategy instruction in a universally designed digital literacy environment. Grounding their work in the National Reading Panel report (NICHD, 2000), reciprocal teaching (Palincsar & Brown,

1984), multimedia learning (Mayer, 2001), and research on hypertext comprehension and digitally supported literacy environments (Dalton & Strangman, 2006), the authors show that strategy instruction benefits students' reading comprehension of digital texts.

The three studies examined here demonstrate the efficacy of strategy use in secondary reading situations. Students' reading comprehension can be bolstered when they attend to how they make sense of the text. We suggest that this kind of successful strategy deployment likely hinges on students having relevant background knowledge, which is not directly explored in these studies. We wonder, then, how strategy use is influenced when students do not have necessary knowledge to bear on a text. In addition, what role can teachers play in the development of necessary or disciplinary knowledge before and during reading? The following studies begin to help us consider these questions.

Some studies of strategic reading consider the role of knowledge, and it is often knowledge of language (e.g., language structure, function, meaning) rather than knowledge about deep disciplinary concepts or practices. We do not mean to downplay the benefits adolescents gain by becoming more aware of how language works in general and within particular disciplines, which certainly bolsters strategic reading and comprehension, nor do we mean to falsely tease apart language and knowledge, because we acknowledge that language in many respects creates knowledge. That is, the words we use to define a concept and how we talk about an idea indeed make up the concept. However, by highlighting these next two studies, we hope to showcase how knowledge is conceptualized in some adolescent literacy research and how that conceptualization can help advance even greater development of necessary content knowledge.

For instance, Greenleaf, Schoenbach, Cziko, and Mueller (2001) conducted a study of reading apprenticeship, a secondary literacy program designed to help students become more metacognitive while reading and better able to implement strategies purposefully. Reading apprenticeship has four dimensions: social, personal, cognitive, and knowledge building. Knowledge building, in this instance, involves supporting students' understanding of "word construction, vocabulary, text structure, genre, and language" (Greenleaf et al., 2001, p. 91). High school students in the study, who were academically underperforming, participated in an academic literacy class based on reading apprenticeship and gained two years of reading growth within one academic year, as measured by a standardized test of reading comprehension. In a similar vein, Schleppegrell, Achugar, and Oteíza (2004) investigated the role of language knowledge in reading. In a case study with secondary English language learners, the researchers showed that improving students' and teachers' understanding of grammatical relations through functional linguistic analysis can support students' understanding of historical relationships in history texts.

In both studies, the researchers and curriculum developers emphasized the importance of understanding how knowledge of language works in the subject area and is an important aspect of strategy use. Yet, the knowledge component of both, at least as discussed in these pieces, appeared to focus predominantly on language structures. Little was said about the domain and world knowledge necessary for making sense of new content concepts to be learned, as illustrated in the Beck et al. (1991) study cited previously about a text reading on the French and Indian War. What ideas did young people have to already know to comprehend the new knowledge they were expected to learn from the text? Alexander and colleagues (1995) refer to this as bridging knowledge, and Moje (2011) as necessary knowledge, of which linguistic and text knowledge are but two components. Whatever the term, the important point is that the knowledge needed to make sense of new ideas is multidimensional.

Another arm of contemporary strategy research investigates disciplinary reading practices and strategies. Shanahan and Shanahan (2008) studied how disciplinary experts (i.e., scholars and professionals with years of experience in their respective fields) approach texts, employ strategies, and make meaning when reading. Shanahan and Shanahan found meaningful differences in how experts from different fields read and use strategies, but they did not address how disciplinary knowledge accumulated through years of study is brought to bear on reading.

Mastropieri, Scruggs, and Graetz (2003) also investigated disciplinary strategies, but instead of working with experts, they studied students with learning challenges in secondary science and social studies classes. Attending more to the role of knowledge, they suggested that "deliberate intensive interaction with the text content appears to make the information more familiar and more memorable for students" (p. 114), but they made no explicit link between knowledge and reading comprehension and, perhaps more important, did not describe teaching practices that would facilitate "deliberate intensive interaction" with content.

From *Reading Next* to a recent meta-analysis of reading intervention studies for struggling, older readers (Edmonds et al., 2009), wide support is found for reading comprehension strategies. Strategies have been found to boost reading comprehension in both print and digital environments, but we are concerned that strategies may be increasingly taken up without attention to knowledge building, which undermines their effectiveness (McKeown et al., 2009). Attending to knowledge of language, particularly to disciplinary-specific language features, has also been found to aid strategic reading. In addition to knowledge of language, attention to how disciplinary knowledge gets cultivated while reading is also necessary, especially when students have limited topic knowledge before reading.

Research on how strategy use changes across different disciplinary texts and contexts is important for secondary students who engage in content area reading and learning. Still, practicing content teachers who are expected to integrate literacy instruction into their content teaching require more research-based information about how disciplinary knowledge enables strategy use, how reading strategies serve to build knowledge, and what they can do instructionally when adolescents lack sufficient knowledge to approach a text.

The Integration of Knowledge and Strategy

Although much adolescent literacy research may be tending away from deep, topic knowledge development, here we make the case for the integration of knowledge and strategy by highlighting research from McKeown et al. (2009), Wigfield, Guthrie, Tonks, and Perencevich (2004), Moje and Speyer (2008), and Bulgren, Deshler, and Lenz (2007). These studies help us imagine how strategies and knowledge development work in concert to support adolescent reading.

We look again to the work of McKeown et al. (2009), which is discussed in the introductory text of this chapter. Although they did not present their study in this frame, as stated earlier, we think their study showed the importance of connecting strategy use to building knowledge. In the two-year study, they compared the effectiveness of two experimental comprehension instructional approaches (i.e., content, strategies) and a control approach. Students were all fifth graders from a low-performing urban district. Students in the strategies group were taught summarizing, predicting, drawing inferences, and monitoring for misunderstanding, and their attention was maintained on the process of strategy use. Students in the content group received instruction based on QtA (Beck et al., 1996), an approach that matches students' attention closely to author intention and text content through targeted questioning, and as discussed earlier, we believe QtA exemplifies good strategy instruction, although the authors do not refer to QtA as a strategy.

Students in the control group received their district's basal instruction. The researchers found that students receiving QtA instruction outperformed on narrative recall and expository learning probes the students receiving strategy instruction absent attention to content and knowledge building. Students in the basal group occasionally also outperformed students in the strategies group on the same measures.

More explicitly tying strategy use and knowledge development together, Wigfield et al. (2004) developed and studied an approach they called concept-oriented reading instruction. In this approach, teachers provide explicit instruction in reading strategies based on the processes of reading comprehension, including "activating background knowledge, questioning, searching for information, summarizing, organizing graphically, and learning story structure" (p. 302). Student reading, as supported by this strategy instruction, is then used to pursue specific knowledge goals that are clearly connected to an array of interactive activities undertaken in the classroom. For example, students on a nature walk might see a particular bug, find it interesting, and then with support from the teacher, generate some questions about the bug. Upon return to the classroom, they would then read to answer these questions using the reading strategies they have been taught. In this context, students have some choice of topics and texts, are expected to talk about and share their work with others to develop their self-expression, and engage in active practice of strategic reading with clear knowledge-building goals.

In the study described by the authors, concept-oriented reading instruction was put into place in two schools across eight third-grade classrooms with 150 students and compared with a model only using strategy instruction with 200 third graders for the same time period. Teachers provided 12 weeks of instruction using this model for 90–120 minutes a day. Students were given pre- and posttest assessments that consisted of reading comprehension and motivation measures. Analysis of the pre and post data show that students in concept-oriented reading instruction classrooms showed greater growth in their intrinsic motivation to read as well as in their reading self-efficacy in comparison to the strategy instruction model.

Moje and Speyer (2008) also explored the relationship between knowledge building and strategy use. In a study of the reading and writing required in an immigration unit, they analyzed the types of knowledge students were asked to bring to bear on classroom texts during their lessons. The researchers found that students needed at least six different kinds of knowledge to effectively engage with only one passage of text that was six lines long:

1. Semantics (i.e., knowledge of word meanings)

2. Mathematical knowledge to calculate quotes

3. Historical knowledge of prior immigration patterns, cultural values toward various groups, nationalist tensions, dominant religious groups, and so forth

4. Geographical knowledge, including knowledge of physical geography (e.g., where various countries of origin were in the world) as well as knowledge of cultural geography, which provided insight into why certain immigrant groups were looked upon with disdain or fear

5. Discursive knowledge of why the text—an excerpt of U.S. immigration law—would be written using particular linguistic devices and with a certain text structure

6. Pragmatic knowledge, which provided the readers with a sense of the purpose for which they were reading the passage

To fully grasp this text on immigration quotas, students needed to bring each of these types of understanding to bear and, at the deepest levels of comprehension, be able to integrate these dimensions of knowledge. For example, knowing something about the cultural values and political tensions of the time (historical knowledge) would support the knowledge that the text might be written in a discourse of equity (discursive knowledge), when in fact, the consequence of law was highly inequitable for certain groups deemed undesirable at the time. This kind of critical comprehension is highly dependent on access to information. No amount of strategy use could reveal the deep-level implications of the law as written in the official text.

Yet, as Moje and Speyer (2008) presented texts to students during their unit, they discovered that students often lacked components of the necessary knowledge required by texts. To help build this knowledge, the researchers presented related texts, such as tables with immigration statistics of various countries by year so that students could analyze trends, and provided minilessons and discussions targeted at both providing overviews of helpful information and discussing and unpacking concepts. Moje and Speyer also read texts aloud with students, discussed the texts, guided the students through looking up difficult words, and then helped them discuss different interpretations of word meanings.

The researchers modeled questioning strategies aimed at connecting to prior knowledge and also problem solving while reading. For example, the word *quota* was important to understanding a particular text, so they read different definitions as a group and then constructed the most relevant definition given the text and the historical context.

Moje and Speyer (2008) also recognized the important connection between knowledge and purpose for reading, arguing that "expert readers either ask for, articulate, or have in their minds an explicit purpose when approaching a text" (p. 193). The awareness of this purpose comes from knowledge of the discipline and its discourse, and many adolescent readers have yet to develop this understanding. In this context, they sought to model historical questioning and problem framing to guide students' reading and provide a clear activity with a strong purpose. Reading strategies in this framework were not an ends but a means to build knowledge and understanding.

Sharing many elements with Moje and Speyer's (2008) approach, content enhancement routines (CERs; Bulgren et al., 2007) situate reading as a learning activity in the process of disciplinary inquiry and attend to both strategic reading and knowledge building. CERs help teachers prepare and deliver effective instruction to a range of students, including students with learning disabilities, in the history classroom. According to the researchers, an important component of CERs is that "they assure that the adequate prior knowledge needed in the content area is already present, or they provide the scaffolds to acquire the critical facts, concepts, vocabulary, principles, procedures, and propositions that represent foundational knowledge" (Bulgren et al., 2007, p. 123). Thus, in this model, knowledge is recognized as key to the comprehension of and learning from text. For example, during a planning step in CERs, teachers analyzed texts to assess knowledge demands and then considered whether students have the requisite knowledge. Instruction in this model "can deliver domain-specific content knowledge, support various levels of higher-order thinking associated with expanded literacy requirements, and provide strategic cognitive and metacognitive supports for learning that can be generalized within and across domains" (Bulgren et al., 2007, p. 126).

To accomplish these goals, Bulgren et al. (2007) recommended the use of general strategies as well as disciplinary strategies for learning and reading, including but not limited to questioning, summarizing, and identification of key ideas. They also advocated the use of graphic organizers as scaffolds to help with comparison, concept development, and the understanding of cause-and-effect relationships by students. In sum, they presented a model of disciplinary instruction in which necessary knowledge for reading and learning is assessed and built through scaffolded instruction. Students engage with text for content learning through the use of different comprehension strategies and graphic organizers, and they build knowledge in this process. Using one particular lesson developed and delivered through the use of CERs with a sample of 150 seventh graders, Bulgren, Deshler, and Schumaker (1998) found that the experimental group who received CER-based instruction was able to study and explain cause-and-effect relationships more effectively after reading a new text on a new topic when compared with the control group who received standard instruction. Bulgren and her colleagues represent an encouraging direction for adolescent literacy research and practice, one that accounts for necessary knowledge development before students read and then capitalizes on strategy use to foster further knowledge building.

Research-based evidence supports a call for the integration of knowledge building and strategies in literacy instruction. To focus on strategies as only generic processes is to move away from the original theoretical base that grounds strategy use. Equally important to consider is what knowledge must be present for students to employ strategies. The relationship between knowledge building and strategy use, therefore, is complex, and instruction that aims to foreground that relationship is likely productive for secondary readers.

Conclusion

How content area reading instruction is conceptualized in policy, operationalized in research, and enacted in practice has shifted in important ways over the past 50 years. Although content-reading instructional theory began by emphasizing the teaching of reading strategies as integrated with the development of content knowledge, the field has witnessed a shift in the last 10 years to an argument for either strategy instruction or knowledge instruction. This dichotomous discourse about content area reading threatens to undermine the valuable attention garnered in recent years for adolescent literacy development. However, when we return our focus to how young people comprehend, use, and compose the complex texts of content areas, we see that both strategy and knowledge instruction play important roles in achieving that goal.

As they engage in content area learning, students need to call on a variety of knowledge types, including word knowledge, genre knowledge, and topic knowledge. How the knowledge is used in comprehending a given text also varies, especially across the content areas. A good reader might easily understand the meaning of the words in a math word problem, but without the requisite background knowledge in math, such as knowing why one might try to solve a particular problem, the passage may hold little mathematical meaning. In science, a student might understand on some level how plants grow and produce energy, but a lack of vocabulary knowledge might prohibit him or her from reading a science passage about these processes. Classroom discourse will also shift across the content areas, and the purpose and structure of reading activity will vary as well. During one day of school, young people will be asked to negotiate the demands of these varying texts and tasks and move from one discourse community to another.

The strategies recommended in much of the reading comprehension literature, including prediction, questioning, self-monitoring, and summarization, are also important in content area literacy and learning. However, these practices also do not happen in the same way across the content areas and are guided by the different epistemological approaches of each academic domain. The act of questioning while reading, for example, is similar across these areas in some ways, but it may also vary in dramatic ways. Questioning is different in science and history, in part because of the purposes and goals of each discipline, so strategies need to be adapted to disciplinary needs and ways of building knowledge. The reasons for reading and writing in history, for example, are different from those in mathematics (Moje, Stockdill, Kim, & Kim, 2011). Nevertheless, despite these differences, reading and writing are generally used to help students learn new information.

Strategy instruction, which has the potential to help students gather and organize this information, is not a problem in and of itself and is an important area for both research and practice. Because literacy is both dependent on and generative of knowing something about the world (and "the word," to quote Freire & Macedo, 1987), it is crucial to recognize that "strategies—absent some level of knowledge, a purpose for engaging in the literate practice, and an identification with the domain or the purpose for reading—will not take readers or writers very far" (Moje, 2011, p. 52). Therefore, the building of knowledge has to be central to the use of reading in school, and by knowledge, we mean to reference a broad range of knowledge types including, but not limited to, knowledge of topic, content, domain, discourse, and language. Indeed, students come to school with a broad range of experiences and knowledge. They are most definitely not the blank slates of the old tabula rasa model, and they use their existing knowledge to interpret the texts they encounter.

Moll and various colleagues have explored the notion of funds of knowledge and posit that learners bring a broad base of knowledge and knowledge resources to literate practice (Moll, Amanti, Neff, & Gonzalez, 1992). Mosborg (2002) found that two different groups of high school students interpreted the same text in different ways based on differences in their life experiences, histories of schooling, worldviews, and cultural backgrounds. Each group of students brought different types of knowledge to bear on the text and topic of study and thus generated different sorts of conclusions. Likewise, Epstein (2000) found that students' family, cultural, and racial backgrounds played a role in how they interpreted new information. In the best cases, this knowledge can be helpful, but it can also be loaded with misconceptions or inappropriately applied (Lee, 2005). Strategies that activate prior knowledge without exploring it run the risk of reinforcing misunderstandings or misconceptions.

There seems to be assumption in policy documents that teachers will only provide students texts for which they already have sufficient background knowledge for comprehension. Prior knowledge needs to be activated so that students can build connections between what they already know and what they are learning. Yet, what happens when teachers inadvertently give students texts which demand knowledge that students do not yet have? Are there times when teachers may want to purposefully give students texts for which they do not yet have the knowledge base? How do teachers know whether their students have the necessary knowledge for comprehending a text, and what do teachers do about it when students do not?

Instruction in and with reading strategies can be used to build this knowledge. Thus, educators must analyze the texts they use and assess the knowledge demands of the text. They must also assess their students. When students do not have the knowledge necessary to comprehend a particular text, such knowledge needs to be built; one cannot activate what is not there, and one cannot strategize about things one does not know. Yet, it is also important that teachers do not simply give over information. They need to preview the materials and concepts of instruction and establish what students need to know to enable comprehension of the given texts of a lesson. Teachers then need to assess students' existing knowledge and build what is missing or not fully developed through a host of teaching practices that engage students in knowledge construction coupled with text reading and writing (see, e.g., Moje, 2011; Moje &

Speyer, 2008). Finally, teachers can use strategies to model the application of new and prior knowledge to the interpretation of text.

In the end, we contend that we do not have to choose between teaching strategies and building knowledge. As many educators already know, teachers and researchers can integrate these goals and help students strategically read to learn new information, which is necessary to read and learn even more. The false binary of content instruction versus strategy instruction is not a helpful paradigm, and as we move into the future of reading research and instruction, we need to acknowledge that good reading comprehension requires both knowledge and strategic approaches, and good instruction can accomplish these goals simultaneously.

Questions for Reflection

1. Why is knowledge important to reading comprehension? Some might say knowledge develops as a result of reading, but what is the role of knowledge during reading?

2. What aspects of classroom life or what challenges of instruction might explain why strategy instruction often gets separated from knowledge development in teaching and research?

3. How can teachers know whether their students have the necessary knowledge for comprehending a text? If students have not developed the necessary knowledge, what can teachers do about it? How can teachers facilitate knowledge development without just lecturing or telling?

4. How can reading strategies work in the service of disciplinary knowledge development across different disciplines (e.g., mathematics, science, history)?

5. What might the challenges be in implementing adolescent literacy instruction that marries content- and process-based approaches to reading? How might teachers, schools, and school districts manage those challenges?

6. Looking back over the chapter, what were some examples of literacy instruction that integrated knowledge development and strategy use? What was effective about these instructional programs or approaches?

REFERENCES

Alexander, P.A., Jetton, T.L., & Kulikowich, J.M. (1995). Interrelationship of knowledge, interest, and recall: Assessing a model of domain learning. *Journal of Educational Psychology, 87*(4), 559–575. doi:10.1037/0022-0663.87.4.559

Alexander, P.A., & Murphy, P.K. (1998). Profiling the differences in students' knowledge, interest, and strategic processing. *Journal of Educational Psychology, 90*(3), 435–447. doi:10.1037/0022-0663.90.3.435

Anderson, V., & Roit, M. (1993). Planning and implementing collaborative strategy instruction for delayed readers in grades 6–10. The Elementary School Journal, 94(2), 121–137.

Ausubel, D.P., & Ausubel, P. (1966). Cognitive development in adolescence. *Review of Educational Research, 36*(4), 403–413.

Barron, R.F. (1969). The use of vocabulary as an advance organizer. In H.L. Herber & P.L. Sanders (Eds.), *Research in reading in the content areas: First year report* (pp. 29–39). Syracuse, NY: Reading and Language Arts Center, Syracuse University.

Beck, I.L., & McKeown, M.G. (2006). *Improving comprehension with questioning the author: A fresh and expanded view of a powerful approach.* New York: Scholastic.

Beck, I.L., McKeown, M.G., Sandora, C., Kucan, L., & Worthy, J. (1996). Questioning the author: A yearlong classroom implementation to engage students with text. *The Elementary School Journal, 96*(4), 385–414. doi:10.1086/461835

Beck, I.L., McKeown, M.G., Sinatra, G.M., & Loxterman, J.A. (1991). Revising social studies texts from a text-processing perspective: Evidence of improved comprehensibility. *Reading Research Quarterly, 26*(3), 251–276.

Biancarosa, G., & Snow, C.E. (2004). *Reading next—A vision for action and research in middle and high school literacy: A report to Carnegie Corporation of New York.* Washington, DC: Alliance for Excellent Education.

Brown, A.L., Campione, J.C., & Day, J.D. (1981). Learning to learn: On training students to learn from texts. *Educational Researcher, 10*(2), 14–21.

Bulgren, J., Deshler, D.D., & Lenz, B.K. (2007). Engaging adolescents with LD in higher order thinking about history concepts using integrated content enhancement rou-

tines. *Journal of Learning Disabilities, 40*(2), 121–133. doi:10.1177/00222194070400020301

Bulgren, J.A., Deshler, D.D., & Schumaker, J.B. (1998). *Reasoning strategies and teaching routines for use in mainstream content classrooms: Final research report.* Washington, DC: Special Education Services, U.S. Department of Education.

Carnegie Council on Advancing Adolescent Literacy. (2010). *Time to act: An agenda for advancing adolescent literacy for college and career success.* New York: Carnegie Corporation of New York.

Chambliss, M.J., & Calfee, R.C. (1998). *Textbooks for learning: Nurturing children's minds.* Malden, MA: Blackwell.

Council of the Chief State School Officers (2010). *Adolescent Literacy Toolkit.* Retrieved February 21, 2011 from http://programs.ccsso .org/projects/adolescent_literacy_toolkit/

Dalton, B., & Proctor, C.P. (2007). Reading as thinking: Integrating strategy instruction in a universally designed digital literacy environment. In D.S. McNamara (Ed.), *Reading comprehension strategies: Theories, interventions, and technologies* (pp. 421–440). Mahwah, NJ: Erlbaum.

Dalton, B., & Strangman, N. (2006). Improving struggling readers' comprehension through scaffolded hypertexts and other computer-based literacy programs. In M.C. McKenna, L.D. Labbo, R.D. Keiffer, & D. Reinking (Eds.), *International handbook of literacy and technology* (Vol. 2, pp. 75–92). Mahwah, NJ: Erlbaum.

Edmonds, M.S., Vaughn, S., Wexler, J., Reutebuch, C., Cable, A., Tackett, K.K., et al. (2009). A synthesis of reading interventions and effects on reading comprehension outcomes for older struggling readers. *Review of Educational Research, 79*(1), 262–300. doi:10.3102/0034654308325998

Epstein, T. (2000). Adolescents' perspectives on racial diversity in U.S. history: Case studies from an urban classroom. *American Educational Research Journal, 37*(1), 185–214.

Freire, P., & Macedo, D. (1987). *Literacy: Reading the word and the world.* Westport, CT: Bergin & Garvey.

Golinkoff, R.M. (1975). A comparison of reading comprehension processes in good and poor comprehenders. *Reading Research Quarterly, 11*(4), 623–659.

Graves, M.F., Cooke, C.L., & LaBerge, M.J. (1983). Effects of previewing difficult short stories on low ability junior high school students' comprehension, recall, and attitudes. *Reading Research Quarterly, 18*(3), 262–276.

Greenleaf, C.L., Schoenbach, R., Cziko, C., & Mueller, F.L. (2001). Apprenticing adolescent readers to academic literacy. *Harvard Educational Review, 71*(1), 79–129.

Herber, H.L. (1978). *Teaching reading in content areas* (2nd ed.). Englewood Cliffs, NJ: Prentice Hall.

Herber, H.L., & Sanders, P.L. (1969). *Research in reading in the content areas: First year report.* Syracuse, NY: Reading and Language Arts Center, Syracuse University. (ERIC Document Reproduction Service No. ED037305)

Hirsch, E.D., Jr. (1987). *Cultural literacy: What every American needs to know.* Boston: Houghton Mifflin.

Hirsch, E.D., Jr. (2003). Reading comprehension requires knowledge—of words and the world: Scientific insights into the fourth-grade slump and the nation's stagnant comprehension scores. *American Educator, 27*(1), 10, 12–13, 16–22, 28–29, 48.

Hirsch, E.D., Jr. (2006). Building knowledge: The case for bringing content into the language arts block and for a knowledge-rich curriculum core for all children. *American Educator, 30*(1), 8–29.

Huhn, R.H. (1980). Readiness as a variable influencing comprehension in content-area reading at the secondary level: A cognitive view. *Learning Disability Quarterly, 3*(4), 29–33.

Kucan, L., & Beck, I.L. (1997). Thinking aloud and reading comprehension research: Inquiry, instruction, and social interaction. *Review of Educational Research, 67*(3), 271–299.

Lagemann, E.C. (2000). *An elusive science: The troubling history of education research.* Chicago: University of Chicago Press.

Langer, J.A., & Nicolich, M. (1981). Prior knowledge and its effect on comprehension. *Journal of Reading Behavior, 13*(4), 373–379.

Lee, P.J. (2005). Putting principles into practice: Understanding history. In M.S. Donovan & J.D. Bransford (Eds.), *How students learn: History in the classroom* (pp. 31–77). Washington, DC: National Academies Press.

Mandel, B.J. (Ed.). (1980). *Three language-arts curriculum models: Pre-kindergarten through college.* Urbana, IL: National Council of Teachers of English.

Mastropieri, M.A., Scruggs, T.E., & Graetz, J.E. (2003). Reading comprehension instruction for secondary students: Challenges for struggling students and teachers. *Learning Disability Quarterly, 26*(2), 103–116.

Mayer, R.E. (2001). *Multimedia learning.* New York: Cambridge University Press.

McKeown, M.G., Beck, I.L., & Blake, R.G.K. (2009). Rethinking reading comprehension instruction: A comparison of instruction for strategies and content approaches. *Reading Research Quarterly, 44*(3), 218–253. doi:10.1598/RRQ.44.3.1

Moje, E.B. (2011). Developing disciplinary discourses, literacies, and identities: What's knowledge got to do with it? In M.G.L. Bonilla & K. Englander (Eds.), *Discourses and identities in contexts of educational change: Contributions from the United States and Mexico* (pp. 49–74). New York: Peter Lang.

Moje, E.B., & Speyer, J. (2008). The reality of challenging texts in high school science and social studies: How teachers can mediate comprehension. In K.A. Hinchman & H.K. Sheridan-Thomas (Eds.), *Best practices in adolescent literacy instruction* (pp. 185–211). New York: Guilford.

Moje, E.B., Stockdill, D., Kim, K., & Kim, H. (2011). The role of text in disciplinary learning. In M.L. Kamil, P.D. Pearson, E.B. Moje, & P.P. Afflerbach (Eds.), *Handbook of reading research* (Vol. 4, pp. 453–486). New York: Routledge.

Moll, L.C., Amanti, C., Neff, D., & Gonzalez, N. (1992). Funds of knowledge for teaching: Using a qualitative approach to connect homes and classrooms. *Theory Into Practice, 31*(2), 132–141.

Mosborg, S. (2002). Speaking of history: How adolescents use their knowledge of history in reading the daily news. *Cognition and Instruction, 20*(3), 323–358.

National Institute of Child Health and Human Development. (2000). *Report of the National Reading Panel. Teaching children to read: An evidence-based assessment of the scientific research literature on reading and its implications for reading instruction* (NIH Publication No. 00-4769). Washington, DC: U.S. Government Printing Office.

Palincsar, A.S., & Brown, A.L. (1984). Reciprocal teaching of comprehension-fostering and comprehension-monitoring activities. *Cognition and Instruction, 1*(2), 117–175. doi:10.1207/s1532690xci0102_1

Palincsar, A.S., & Brown, A.L. (1988). Teaching and practicing thinking skills to promote comprehension in the context of group problem solving. *Remedial and Special Education, 9*(1), 53–59.

Palincsar, A.S., & Schutz, K.M. (in press). Reconnecting strategy instruction with its theoretical roots. *Theory Into Practice.*

Paris, S.G., & Myers, M. (1981). Comprehension monitoring, memory, and study strategies of good and poor readers. *Journal of Literacy Research, 13*(1), 5–22.

Paris, S.G., Wixson, K.K., & Palincsar, A.S. (1986). Instructional approaches to reading comprehension. *Review of Research in Education, 13*, 91–128.

Peters, C.W., & Wixson, K.K. (2003). Unifying the domain of K–12 English language arts curriculum. In J. Flood, D. Lapp, J.R. Squire, & J.M. Jensen (Eds.), *Handbook of research on teaching the English language arts* (2nd ed., pp. 573–589). Mahwah, NJ: Erlbaum.

Ravitch, D., & Finn, C.E. (1987). *What do our 17-year-olds know? A report on the first national assessment of history and literature.* New York: Harper & Row.

Schleppegrell, M.J., Achugar, M., & Oteíza, T. (2004). The grammar of history: Enhancing content-based instruction through a functional focus on language. *TESOL Quarterly, 38*(1), 67–93.

Schorzman, E.M., & Cheek, E.H. (2004). Structured strategy instruction: Investigating an intervention for improving sixth-graders' reading comprehension. *Reading Psychology, 25*(1), 37–60. doi:10.1080/02702710490271828

Scott, S.E. (2009). *Knowledge for teaching reading comprehension: Mapping the terrain.* Unpublished doctoral dissertation, University of Michigan, Ann Arbor.

Shanahan, T., & Shanahan, C. (2008). Teaching disciplinary literacy to adolescents: Rethinking content-area literacy. *Harvard Educational Review, 78*(1), 40–59.

Shuell, T.J. (1986). Cognitive conceptions of learning. *Review of Educational Research, 56*(4), 411–436.

Stauffer, R.G. (1969). *Directing reading maturity as a cognitive process.* New York: Harper & Row.

Stevens, R.J. (2003). Student team reading and writing: A cooperative learning approach to middle school literacy instruction. *Educational Research and Evaluation, 9*(2), 137–160. doi:10.1076/edre.9.2.137.14212

Wigfield, A., Guthrie, J.T., Tonks, S., & Perencevich, K.C. (2004). Children's motivation for reading: Domain specificity and instructional influences. *The Journal of Educational Research, 97*(6), 299–310. doi:10.3200/JOER.97.6.299-310

Chapter 8

Developmental Changes in Reading Comprehension: Implications for Assessment and Instruction

Suzanne M. Adlof, Charles A. Perfetti, and Hugh W. Catts

Concerted efforts have been made in recent years to understand the development of reading comprehension skills, but translating knowledge gained from this research into improved instructional practices can be difficult. Reading comprehension is complex; it involves numerous cognitive processes and is influenced by many task-related factors. Models that illustrate how different knowledge sources and cognitive processes might interact to transform linguistic units into meaning in the mind can be helpful for researchers who wish to delineate the potential types of knowledge and skills involved in reading (see, e.g., Perfetti, 1999). However, their complexity can be overwhelming for practitioners. The goal for classroom teachers, special educators, paraprofessionals, administrators, parents, and others is to teach children to read with understanding. To accomplish this, practitioners need to assess children's current literacy skills, identify those who are at risk for reading difficulties, and determine which types of instruction will be most effective for which types of students.

Simplifying Comprehension

In the "simple view of reading" (Gough & Tunmer, 1986; Hoover & Gough, 1990), reading comprehension is modeled as the product of word reading and language comprehension. Word reading involves decoding or translating the letters on a page or screen into pronounceable words. Language comprehension involves making sense of the decoded words. Language comprehension is sometimes measured by asking individuals to listen to a text and answer questions about it. Other times, it is measured with assessments of separate language domains, such as oral vocabulary or syntax (grammar). However, the basic idea is that understanding language is similar whether it is communicated by ear or by eye.

What Research Has to Say About Reading Instruction (4th ed.) edited by S. Jay Samuels and Alan E. Farstrup. © 2011 by the International Reading Association.

The multiplicative relationship between word reading and language comprehension underscores two important theoretical points of the simple view. First, both components are necessary, but neither is sufficient for successful reading comprehension. Second, although the two factors are usually highly correlated, they are also dissociable: It is possible to have high ability in one component but low ability in the other.

Imagine yourself reading in an unfamiliar language. If it uses the Latin alphabetic script and you have good decoding skills, you can likely "sound out" the words fairly well. However, if you have no idea what those words mean, your language comprehension is zero—and your reading comprehension will also be zero (because the product of zero and any number is zero). Likewise, it is possible to have strong oral language skills but little decoding ability. For example, imagine trying to read Braille without being taught; similarly, one could learn to speak and understand conversational Chinese without learning to recognize its print characters. In both cases, although oral language knowledge might be very good, reading comprehension will still be zero because decoding is zero.

Numerous studies have shown that measurements of word reading and language comprehension do an excellent job of accounting for individual differences in reading comprehension in populations ranging from primary school through adulthood (Adlof, Catts, & Little, 2006; Braze, Tabor, Shankweiler, & Mencl, 2007; Catts, Hogan, & Adlof, 2005; Chen & Vellutino, 1997; Dreyer & Katz, 1992; Gough, Hoover, & Peterson, 1996; Hoover & Gough, 1990; Kendeou, van den Broek, White, & Lynch, 2009; Landi, 2010; Malatesha Joshi & Aaron, 2000). Studies have also found that modeling an additive relationship between word reading and language comprehension provides nearly as good (or sometimes a better) a fit to the data as does the multiplicative relationship (Chen & Vellutino, 1997; Dreyer & Katz, 1992; Hoover & Gough, 1990; Malatesha Joshi & Aaron, 2000). This finding is likely explained by the fact that the two factors involved in the simple view are correlated, and true zeroes in either are extremely rare.

Longitudinal studies also have shown that measurements of early word reading and language comprehension can be used to predict later performance in reading comprehension (Adlof et al., 2006; Muter, Hulme, Snowling, & Stevenson, 2004; Storch & Whitehurst, 2002). Furthermore, measurement of skills considered precursors of word reading and language comprehension can be used to predict a child's risk for reading comprehension difficulties later on (Adlof, Catts, & Lee, 2010; Catts, Fey, Tomblin, & Zhang, 2002; Scarborough, 1990; Wood, Hill, Meyer, & Flowers, 2005). Thus, the simple view of reading provides a useful model for professionals interested in the assessment and instruction of both typically developing children and children with reading difficulties.

Changes in Reading Comprehension Over Time

To assess reading comprehension skills in a meaningful way, it is important to understand how the task of reading comprehension changes over time. In the early grades, word reading is the primary factor associated with reading comprehension. As students move into the upper elementary grades and beyond, language comprehension becomes the most important factor. This shift was highlighted in a set of longitudinal studies in which 604 children from the U.S. state of Iowa were followed from kindergarten through eighth grade, with assessments of word reading, language comprehension, and reading comprehension occurring at second, fourth, and eighth grades (Adlof et al., 2006; Catts et al., 2005).

Adlof et al. (2006) used latent regression models to assess both the unique and the shared contributions of word reading and language comprehension to reading comprehension concurrently within each grade and predictively from second to fourth grades and from fourth to eighth grades. Three important findings are displayed in Figures 8.1 (concurrent

Figure 8.1. Variance in Reading Comprehension Explained by Concurrent Word Reading and Language Comprehension Skills

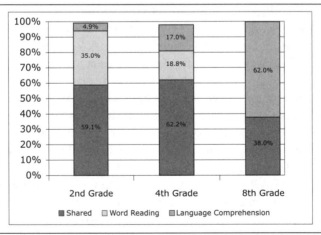

Note. Reported in "Should the Simple View of Reading Include a Fluency Component?" by S.M. Adlof, H.W. Catts, and T.D. Little, 2006, *Reading and Writing: An Interdisciplinary Journal, 19*(9), pp. 944–946.

models) and 8.2 (predictive models). First, nearly all the individual differences in reading comprehension could be explained by the word reading and language comprehension factors in each grade (98–100% in the concurrent models, and 90–97% in the predictive models). Second, a large amount of the explained variance in reading comprehension was shared between word reading and language comprehension, underscoring the fact that, for most individuals, the two are highly related. Third, there was a striking difference in the importance of each component between second and eighth grades. In the concurrent models, word reading by itself accounted for 94% of the variance in reading comprehension in second grade, whereas it accounted for only 38% of the variance in eighth grade, and all of that was shared with language comprehension. Because language comprehension and reading comprehension shared all of their reliable variance in eighth grade, they formed a unitary construct. Thus, language comprehension accounted for 100% of the variance in reading comprehension in eighth grade compared with 64% in second grade.

When comparing these results to those of other studies, it is important to note that the contribution of each component—word reading and language comprehension—to reading comprehension is influenced

Figure 8.2. Variance in Fourth- and Eighth-Grade Reading Comprehension Explained by Second- and Fourth-Grade Component Skills

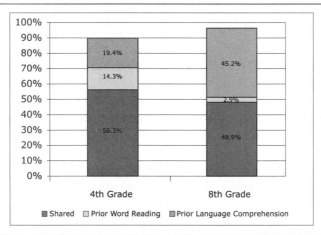

Note. Reported in Reported in "Should the Simple View of Reading Include a Fluency Component?" by S.M. Adlof, H.W. Catts, and T.D. Little, 2006, *Reading and Writing: An Interdisciplinary Journal, 19*(9), pp. 946–947.

by the type of test used. Some tests, especially those that employ very short passages, are more highly correlated with word reading skills, while others show a stronger reliance on language comprehension (Cutting & Scarborough, 2006; Francis, Fletcher, Catts, & Tomblin, 2005; Keenan, Betjemann, & Olson, 2008; Nation & Snowling, 1997). However, the general pattern of association remains the same: Regardless of the tests employed, the correlation between word reading and reading comprehension decreases with progression through the grades, whereas that between language comprehension and reading comprehension increases (Francis et al., 2005; Gough et al., 1996; Keenan et al., 2008).

Why does this shift occur? For starters, word reading always sets a ceiling for comprehension, as demonstrated in our example of reading Braille. In the early grades, children are just beginning to learn how to decode print, and their spoken language knowledge far exceeds their decoding abilities; thus, in early grades, word reading skills best explain individual differences in reading comprehension. However, by the later grades, word reading accounts for less variance because most people know how to read most words.

Another possible reason for the shift is that the nature of the materials to be comprehended changes across grades. Consider the reading materials presented to second-grade students versus eighth-grade students. Second graders typically encounter far more narrative than expository text, which tends to follow a predictable structure that most children are familiar with. Even when expository texts are presented to children of this age, they generally use simple sentence structures and a restricted, familiar, and sometimes repetitive vocabulary. They are often about familiar topics for which children have a good amount of background knowledge. Overall, the language in texts for second graders is not that different from the language that might be used to talk to second graders about the same topics.

Take as an example this excerpt from *Penguins* by Bobbie Kalman (1995), an expository text recommended for skilled second-grade readers:

> Penguins may not look like other birds, but they are birds. Like all birds, penguins are covered with feathers. They are **warm-blooded,** which means their body stays the same temperature no matter how warm or cold their surroundings are. All birds, including penguins, hatch from eggs.
>
> Penguins have different shapes and colors. Some penguins have only black and white feathers. Others, such as the emperor penguin on the left, have brightly colored patches of feathers. Special head markings

help penguins recognize other members of their species. (pp. 5–6; emphasis in original)

The average sentence length in this brief passage is 10.4 words. Although the word *penguin* might be difficult initially for children to decode, it is repeated seven times. The average frequency of the content words (i.e., words that carry meaning, as opposed to function words that convey grammatical relationships) in texts appropriate for school-age children is high: 448 per million words, according to the *Educator's Word Frequency Guide* database (Zeno, Ivens, Millard, & Dubburi, 1995).

Comprehension questions for this type of text might ask, What kind of animal is a penguin? What does it mean to be warm-blooded? How are baby penguins born? How do penguins recognize other members of the species? Most children who have read the text should be able to answer these questions correctly (and some—especially those who have seen any of the films about penguins that have been released in recent years—could probably answer at least a few without reading). Comprehension assessments used with children in the early grades tend to stress word reading; if the children are able to read the words in the text, they can generally answer the comprehension questions.

In contrast, by the eighth grade, children encounter more expository texts than narrative, and they usually have less background knowledge about the topics. In second grade, children are learning to read; by eighth grade, they are expected to be reading to learn (Chall, 1983). Students at this age are building background knowledge about academic subjects through assigned readings. Word reading should be occurring automatically, but comprehension requires more cognitive effort.

Compared with texts for younger children, the sentence structures in texts in the later grades are more complex, and they contain more advanced, topic-specific, and abstract vocabulary. The language used in these texts is usually more complex than the language used in conversations—or even in classroom instruction. Here is an excerpt from *The Field Guide to Geology*, a trade book by David Lambert and The Diagram Group (2007) written at an early high school reading level:

Earth is a rocky spinning ball—one of nine planets and many lesser bodies (moons, asteroids, and comets) orbiting a star (the Sun). All of these together constitute our solar system.

Earth is tiny compared to the four largest planets. But our solar system's largest and most influential body is the Sun, a glowing ball of gases a million times the volume of Earth and far bigger than all the other objects orbiting the Sun. The Sun's immense gravitational force prevents the entities around it from flying outward into space. And its electromagnetic radiations produce the heat and light that help make life possible on Earth—the third nearest planet to the Sun. Most planets closer in or farther out appear too hot or cold for life.

Earth's behavior and that of its Moon determine time on Earth. Like all planets, Earth spins on a central axis with imaginary ends at the poles. Each rotation of about 24 hours produces day and night. (p. 14)

The sentences in this passage average 16.6 words, longer than those in the second-grade text, and they are more complex. The vocabulary is also more difficult. Although there are few rare words in this passage, the average frequency of the content words, at 295 per million, is lower than in the second-grade passage.

To understand this passage, you need to have at least some familiarity with words and concepts such as *planet, solar system, gravitational,* and *orbiting.* You need to understand that *bodies* in this paragraph does not refer to human or animal forms. You need to understand the use of parentheses. Several simple fact-based questions could be asked about this text, such as What is the biggest body in the solar system? or What keeps planets from flying into space? But more advanced comprehension questions for this text might ask, Why does Earth orbit the Sun? How is gravity related to the existence life on earth? It is unlikely that a student without considerable background knowledge could answer these questions without sufficient skills in language comprehension.

Reading Dimensions and Reading Subgroups

As we have explained, skilled readers usually show strengths in word reading and language comprehension, while less skilled readers generally show weaknesses in both areas. However, the correlation is not perfect, and studies employing factor analysis and latent modeling procedures have demonstrated that the constructs of word reading and language comprehension are separable (Aaron, Joshi, & Williams, 1999; Adlof et al., 2006; Kendeou, Savage, & van den Broek, 2009; Landi, 2010).

Because readers can vary along dimensions of word reading and language comprehension, four basic profiles of readers are predicted, as displayed in Figure 8.3. (It is important to remember that these subgroups are not distinct, but rather indicate profiles of relative strength and weakness.) Individuals in the top right quadrant have relatively good skills

Figure 8.3. Basic Profiles of Readers

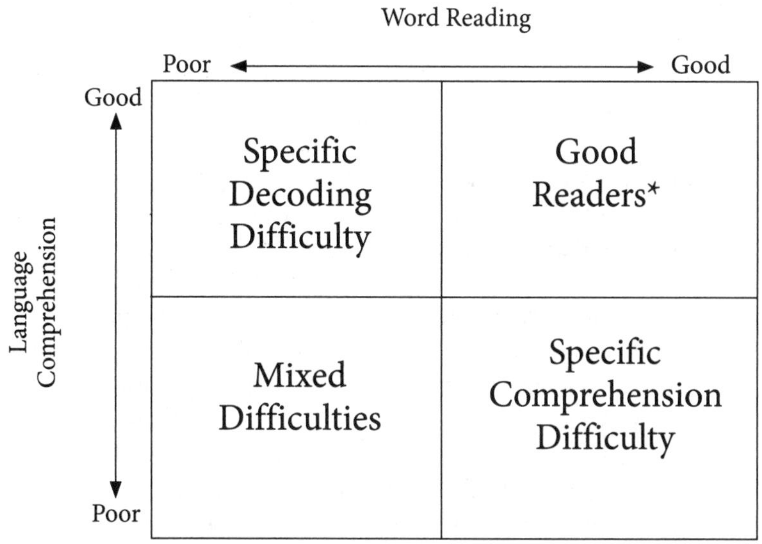

Word Reading

	Poor ←————————————→ Good
Good ↑	Specific Decoding Difficulty / Good Readers*
Language Comprehension	Mixed Difficulties / Specific Comprehension Difficulty
Poor ↓	

*Some children who are predicted to be good readers using this model still experience difficulties. In Catts and colleagues' studies, poor readers who fall in this quadrant are said to have "non-specified" reading difficulties (Catts et al., 2003; Catts et al., 2005).

in both word reading and language comprehension and are expected to be good readers, whereas individuals in the other three quadrants are expected to have reading difficulties. Those with low skills in both word reading and language comprehension fall in the lower left quadrant. This "mixed-difficulties" group displays the most common profile of reading difficulty, and individuals fitting it could be described as "garden-variety poor readers" (Gough et al., 1996; Stanovich, 1988). The top-left quadrant includes children with specific decoding deficits in spite of relatively good language skills. These children might also be described as having dyslexia (Catts & Kamhi, in press). In the lower right quadrant are children with specific comprehension deficits, whose language comprehension is low relative to their word reading abilities.

With the Iowa longitudinal data set described earlier, Catts and colleagues (Catts et al., 2005; Catts, Hogan, & Fey, 2003) used this model to examine developmental changes in the proportion of poor readers in each subgroup in second, fourth, and eighth grades. A "poor reader" was defined as any child who scored at least one standard deviation below the mean (i.e., below the 16th percentile) on the composite measure of reading comprehension. The same cutoff was used as the delineation between "good" and "poor" word reading and language comprehension skills. Table 8.1 lists the percentage of poor readers who fit the criteria for each of the subgroups at each grade. Across all grades, the poor readers who fell in the mixed-difficulties quadrant formed the largest subgroup; approximately one-third of poor readers in each grade showed difficulties with both word reading and language comprehension. However, there was an interesting shift in the proportion of poor readers in each of the specific-deficit subgroups. In the decoding-deficit subgroup, the proportion of poor readers decreased from 32% in second grade to 22% in fourth grade to 13% in eighth grade. In contrast, the proportion of poor readers in the comprehension-deficit subgroup increased from 16% in second grade to approximately 30% in fourth and eighth grades.

The shift in size of the different poor-reader subgroups across grades was not caused by children from one subgroup moving into a different subgroup. Rather, most children who were identified as having decoding deficits in second grade continued to show the same profile in fourth and eighth grades: Their word reading performance remained low relative to their measured language comprehension. Likewise, children with specific comprehension deficits in eighth grade tended to show low comprehension skills relative to word reading skills in second and fourth grades. What changed was whether the child was considered to be a poor reader, based on his or her score on the reading comprehension composite. Children with specific decoding deficits were more likely to score low in reading comprehension in earlier grades, whereas children with specific comprehension deficits were more likely to score low in reading

Table 8.1. Percentage of Poor Readers in Each Simple View Subgroup by Grade

	Specific decoding difficulties	Mixed difficulties	Specific comprehension difficulties	Nonspecified difficulties
Grade 2	32.3%	36.3%	16.3%	15.0%
Grade 4	22.3%	32.9%	31.0%	13.8%
Grade 8	13.3%	33.0%	30.1%	23.6%

Note. Reported in "Developmental Changes in Reading and Reading Disabilities" (pp. 29–31) by H.W. Catts, T.P. Hogan, and S.M. Adlof, 2005, *The Connections Between Language and Reading Disabilities* edited by H.W. Catts & A.G. Kamhi, Mahwah, NJ: Erlbaum. Rows all do not sum to 100% due to rounding.

comprehension in later grades. Thus, the shift in the profiles of children identified as poor readers corresponded to the shift in skills most related to reading comprehension as children progress through the grades.

A fourth subgroup of poor readers scored above the cutoffs for word reading and language comprehension, but still scored below the cutoff on the reading comprehension measure. In Catts and colleagues' studies (Catts et al., 2003; Catts et al., 2005), these children were said to have "nonspecified" reading difficulties. As in the comprehension-deficit subgroup, the number of children meeting the criteria for this subgroup also increased over time, from 15% in second grade to 24% in eighth grade. Note that most were just slightly above the cutoffs for inclusion in the other subgroups, and nearly all showed below average language comprehension. Thus, it appeared that relatively mild oral language weaknesses were associated with more severe reading comprehension difficulties.

Late-Emerging Poor Readers

Recently, there has been increasing interest in children who appear to be good readers in the early grades but show reading difficulties around fourth grade and beyond (e.g., Badian, 1999; Catts & Hogan, 2002; Compton, Fuchs, Fuchs, Elleman, & Gilbert, 2008; Leach, Scarborough, & Rescorla, 2003; Lipka, Lesaux, & Siegel, 2006). The simple view model helps explain why children with specific comprehension deficits appear to have late-emerging reading difficulties. Because early assessments of reading comprehension are explained primarily by word reading skills, these children initially appear to be good readers. When comprehension demands on reading assessments increase after second or third grade, children's reading comprehension difficulties may emerge as a surprise to parents and teachers.

There is evidence that some specific decoding deficits can be late to emerge (Leach et al., 2003; Lipka et al., 2006). The mechanisms behind such deficits are not clear, but it is possible that very subtle early word-reading difficulties could become more severe in later grades, when phonologically and morphologically complex words become more prevalent. However, the evidence also suggests that children with specific comprehension deficits are most at risk for late identification. For example, Leach et al. (2003) identified 18 children with specific decoding deficits, 12 with specific reading comprehension deficits, and 26 with mixed deficits in grades 1 through 5. Just over a third of the children with specific decoding deficits (39%) and mixed deficits (38%) were late identified, whereas 83% of the children with specific reading comprehension deficits were late identified. Similarly, Catts, Adlof, and Ellis Weismer (2006) found that eighth graders with specific reading comprehension deficits had an average reading comprehension standard score of 95 in second grade. (Note that children with specific reading comprehension deficits, also known as "poor comprehenders," have good word reading skills but poor reading comprehension, which is slightly different from the subgroup previously described with language comprehension deficits. In the Iowa longitudinal data, there is a very significant overlap between children identified using each method in later grades but slightly less overlap in early grades, when, as noted previously, reading comprehension measures are more reliant on word reading skills.) Likewise, Nation, Clarke, Marshall, and Durand (2004) have referred to the language deficits of children with specific reading comprehension difficulties as "hidden deficits," because parents and teachers rarely report any concerns about reading or language achievement before a formal assessment has been conducted.

The characterization of "late-emerging" poor readers is based solely on reading measures. However, as we will explain, measures of oral language skills can be used to identify children who are at risk for reading difficulties prior to the onset of reading instruction. Following a simple-view model, one might expect that predictors of word reading difficulties might differ from those of comprehension difficulties. Likewise, prediction of risk for "early-emerging" reading difficulties (which generally involve word reading problems) might involve different measures than prediction of risk for later reading problems (which typically involve comprehension). Before turning to this discussion, however, we first consider whether factors should be added to the simple-view model.

What's Missing? Considering Additions to the Simple View

Although word reading and language comprehension generally account for substantial amounts of variance in reading comprehension, studies employing regression analyses often report a large amount of variance not explained by these factors. Estimation of variance is always limited by the precision of the measures employed, so many of the effect-size differences across studies are likely related to differences in measurement. Other differences may be related to sampling.

Still, the simple view of reading comprehension is *simple*, and many have considered whether other predictors should be added to the model. In Perfetti's (1977) conception, for example, reading comprehension was modeled as the sum of word reading, language comprehension, and X, with X being open to an "everything else" interpretation. Here we consider four potential additions: fluency, vocabulary, background knowledge, and nonverbal cognitive abilities.

Fluency

According to verbal-efficiency theory, when word reading is fluent, or automatic, cognitive resources that would otherwise be allocated to decoding can instead be devoted to comprehension (LaBerge & Samuels, 1974; Perfetti, 1985). Based on this theory, as well as recent emphasis on fluency in the field (e.g., National Institute of Child Health and Human Development [NICHD], 2000), some have considered whether speed of word reading might influence comprehension above and beyond accuracy, and if so, whether measures of reading speed should be added to the simple view (e.g., Aaron et al., 1999; Adlof et al., 2006; Tilstra, McMaster, van den Broek, Kendeou, & Rapp, 2009).

Overall, there is little evidence to support such an addition. Although studies employing regression analyses found that fluency (accuracy + speed) accounted for small amounts of unique variance in reading comprehension after controlling for word reading and language comprehension (e.g., Aaron et al., 1999; Tilstra et al., 2009), a study drawing on the Iowa longitudinal database—employing a larger sample, latent factors composed of norm-referenced assessments, and three time points (second, fourth, and eighth grades)—found that speed did not ever account for unique variance (Adlof et al., 2006). Rather, the speed construct was always very highly correlated with accuracy and moderately to highly correlated with language comprehension. Follow-up analyses were conducted among individual participants in the Iowa study to determine whether speed might be independently related to reading comprehension difficulties for any children in any grade. In the full sample of more than 500 children, no child could be found whose reading comprehension problems could be attributed to speed alone. That is, children who were accurate but slow readers *always* had good reading comprehension if their language comprehension was also good. Those who had poor reading comprehension also showed language comprehension problems. These findings suggest that fluency develops as an outcome of good word reading and language skills. Fluency is important, but speed itself does not appear to be an independent source of comprehension difficulty.

In the Iowa second-grade data, the best fit was achieved by modeling accuracy and fluency as a unitary construct. This indicates that the same information was provided by the measures of accuracy as by the measures of fluency. Children who were able to read more difficult words in the accuracy assessments (the word attack and word identification subtests of the Woodcock Reading Mastery Test—Revised [Woodcock, 1998] and the accuracy score from the GORT-3 [Wiederholt & Bryant, 1994]) were also able to read more total words, and more difficult words, in the fluency assessments (the sight words and decoding subtests of the Test of Word Reading Efficiency [Torgesen, Wagner, & Rashotte, 1999] and the fluency score from the GORT-3).

Some definitions of fluency also include reading with appropriate prosody or intonation (e.g., Miller & Schwanenflugel, 2008; NICHD, 2000; Rasinski, Rikli, & Johnston, 2009). When defined this way, fluency is best characterized as an outcome of efficient word reading and comprehension, rather than as a predictor of comprehension. In other words, oral reading with appropriate prosody can be construed as a marker that sentence-level comprehension is occurring, but prosody is most likely not a causal factor for comprehension. Fluency defined as accuracy + speed + prosody *should* be affected when comprehension is difficult.

These findings have implications for how we approach fluency in practice. Measures of reading speed can be especially useful for measuring children's progress with word reading skills. They can be faster to administer than accuracy measures, and they may also identify children with more subtle word reading difficulties or those who may be in a period of "illusory recovery," with deficits that appear to have been remediated but will resurface later (e.g., Compton et al., 2008; Scarborough & Dobrich, 1990). These children, as well as those who have benefited from intensive interventions (e.g., Torgesen et al., 2001), may be able to decode grade-level words accurately but not at the level of automaticity. They might benefit from additional practice in word reading, but they do not have a specific "fluency" deficit.

Passage-level fluency measures may also be useful to assess progress in overall reading skills, including both word reading and comprehension (e.g., Good & Kaminski, 2002a), but users of these tests must realize that slow reading can be caused by a variety of factors. Likewise, we do not want to encourage children to become speed-readers, but rather to read for comprehension (e.g., Samuels, 2007). We should also be cautious about assuming that a child comprehends a text fully just because her oral reading sounds fluent; the level of comprehension needed for appropriate prosody is likely lower than the level needed to build a situation model. Interventions to improve fluency in reading connected text, such as wide reading and repeated readings, are sometimes effective for improving reading comprehension (e.g., Edmonds et al., 2009; Meyer & Felton, 1999; O'Connor, White, & Swanson, 2007; Schwanenflugel et al., 2009; cf. Wexler, Vaughn, Roberts, & Denton, 2010), likely because they improve both word reading and language comprehension skills. One benefit of the wide reading approach is that it exposes students to a variety of complex texts, which include more vocabulary and more content. Finally, these approaches are likely to be most effective when used in combination with other activities aimed at improving language and reading comprehension skills.

Vocabulary

Typically, vocabulary is conceptualized as a part of language comprehension; obviously, knowledge of word meanings is crucial for understanding text. This does not mean that vocabulary knowledge is not important for word reading. Although one can decode words without knowing their meanings, there is substantial evidence that vocabulary knowledge does influence word reading for both skilled and unskilled readers (see Nation, 2008, for a review). At the most basic level, it is easier to recognize a word if one already knows that it exists in the world. Evidence suggests that even shallow knowledge of word meanings is associated with better word reading, especially for words with irregular or inconsistent letter–sound mappings (Nation & Cocksey, 2009; Ouellette, 2006; Perfetti, 2007; Perfetti & Hart, 2001).

Vocabulary size may also indirectly influence the development of word reading abilities through phonological awareness in young children. In the lexical restructuring model, Metsala, Walley, and colleagues (Metsala & Walley, 1998; Walley, Metsala, & Garlock, 2003) hypothesize that children begin with coarse-grained phonological representations of words, but as their vocabularies grow, their word representations become increasingly fine-grained due to the need to distinguish similar sounding words in the mental lexicon. In line with this hypothesis, Metsala (1999) reported positive associations between individual differences in vocabulary size and phonological awareness; Lonigan (2007) more recently reviewed converging evidence from longitudinal studies. Metsala (1999) also found that children performed better at phonological awareness tasks for real-word items as opposed to nonwords, for familiar words as opposed to unfamiliar, and for words with many similar-sounding neighbors in the child's mental lexicon. Recent results reported by Hogan (2010) and De Cara and Goswami (2003) provide supporting evidence but suggest that a child's vocabulary must be of sufficient size before lexical restructuring can occur.

At least three additional studies—Braze et al. (2007), Ouellette and Beers (2010), and Verhoeven and van Leeuwe (2008)—have shown that vocabulary knowledge accounts for unique variance in reading comprehension over and above that explained by word recognition and listening comprehension measures. Our point, however, is not necessarily to propose that vocabulary needs to be added to the simple-view model, but rather to highlight the pivotal role of vocabulary knowledge as the link between word reading and comprehension (e.g., Perfetti, 2010). Because of its fundamental importance to reading overall, assessment of vocabulary knowledge is informative both for explaining current reading skills and for predicting future reading achievement. Furthermore, as vocabulary interventions have been shown to increase reading comprehension skills (e.g., Elleman, Lindo, Morphy, & Compton, 2009), vocabulary instruction should be considered an essential component of any reading curriculum.

Background Knowledge

It is commonly reported that to comprehend a text, a reader must know most of the words it contains (e.g., Nagy & Scott, 2000). The role of background knowledge in reading comprehension is similar: The more one knows about a topic, the easier it is to comprehend a text about it (Adams, Bell, & Perfetti, 1995; Spilich, Vesonder, Chiesi, & Voss, 1979). (Logically, there should also be a relationship between background knowledge and vocabulary: The more one knows about a topic, the more likely one is to be familiar with vocabulary specific to that topic.) An individual with significant background knowledge about a topic needs only to update her preexisting situation model with the new information provided in the text; an individual with no previous background knowledge must construct a new model (e.g., Kintsch, 1988). Individual differences in reading experience are significantly correlated with adult knowledge across a variety of domains (Stanovich & Cunningham, 1993). Thus, the relationship between knowledge and reading comprehension is logically reciprocal. The more one knows, the more one can comprehend—and the more one learns.

Background knowledge affects language comprehension just as it affects reading comprehension. Thus, for general reading comprehension, no additional background knowledge component is needed.

Standardized reading and listening comprehension assessments often attempt to limit the influence of background knowledge on performance by using multiple texts on a variety of topics or texts for which the knowledge required for understanding is assumed to be very general. Unfortunately, there is frequently a large gap in even very general world knowledge between children from economically advantaged versus disadvantaged backgrounds (Burkam & Lee, 2002; Chall, Jacobs, & Baldwin, 1990). Thus, low background knowledge can be a source of generally poor reading comprehension performance for some children. Without appropriate instructional support, this gap is expected to grow over time. High-quality, content-rich instruction has the potential to level the playing field and reduce the knowledge gap (Hirsch, 2001, 2003; Neuman, 2006).

As children move into the upper grades, comprehension of texts in different academic disciplines requires attention to different aspects of the text. Experts in different disciplines read differently. For example, Shanahan and Shanahan (2008) discovered that historians pay considerable attention to the author's perspective when reading a historical text. They are not merely looking for a timeline of events and characters; rather, they are looking for the connections between the events and explanations of why things happened. These explanations can differ depending on perspective; "truth" in history is in the eye of the beholder. In contrast, because knowledge in chemistry is generated through experimentation and objective data, chemists might place less emphasis on the source of information but more on understanding the process behind the experiment that produced the finding. Therefore, chemists tend to pay more attention to figures, graphs, and formulas, relating those with the information presented in the prose. They try to visualize the process of the experiment and predict the conditions in which it can or cannot be replicated. Thus, knowing what information should be attended to is another source of background knowledge needed for advanced comprehension.

Nonverbal Cognitive Abilities

Some evidence suggests that cognitive skills that go beyond language processing may be involved in reading comprehension. For example, Cutting, Materek, Cole, Levine, and Mahone (2009) found that 9- to 14-year-old children with specific reading comprehension deficits (i.e., good word reading but poor reading comprehension) showed significantly worse performance on tasks involving nonverbal executive function that require planning, organization, and self-monitoring (such as mazes) than good readers of the same age. Similarly, using data from the Iowa database, Catts and Compton (in preparation) found that late-emerging poor readers are as likely to have had deficits in nonverbal IQ as in oral language skills. In a related analysis, Adlof et al. (2010) found that kindergarten measures of nonverbal IQ were better predictors of eighth-grade reading difficulties than of second-grade reading difficulties. These findings are interesting in light of the fact that nonverbal cognitive skills are not predictive of response to early reading instruction (see, e.g., Stuebing, Barth, Molfese, Weiss, & Fletcher, 2009). Furthermore, they suggest that the higher level cognitive skills needed for reading comprehension in later grades may not be restricted to language.

Implications for Assessment and Instruction: What Matters and When?

Developmental changes in the relative influence of word reading and language comprehension on reading comprehension have important implications for how reading assessment and instruction should be carried out. First, it is important to understand that poor reading performance is affected by different underlying skills in early versus later grades. Therefore, different types of assessments are needed to explain or predict reading outcomes in early versus later grades. Second, it is important to foster the development of language skills that will facilitate comprehension throughout schooling, especially for children with oral language weaknesses that place them at risk for reading comprehension problems.

Rather than recommend that specific tests or interventions be used, our goal in this section is to provide basic guidelines with reference to the developmental timeline. (We cite some commonly used assessments merely as examples.)

Assessment

There are many different reasons for assessing reading skills, and often they vary according to the developmental period. In the preschool and kindergarten years, the goal of assessment is typically to determine a child's risk for having reading difficulties later on. In the elementary grades, after reading instruction has begun, assessments can be used to evaluate current reading skills, to measure progress in the reading curriculum, and to identify risk for future problems. At each point along the developmental continuum, it is important to be mindful of the relative roles of word reading and language comprehension in reading comprehension when planning assessments.

Preschool and Kindergarten. Typically, studies aimed at the early identification of risk for reading difficulties (e.g., in preschool or kindergarten) focus on reading outcomes in the primary grades (e.g., Elbro, Borstrøm, & Petersen, 1998; Gallagher, Frith, & Snowling, 2000; Lonigan, Burgess, & Anthony, 2000). Thus, they tend to emphasize measures that are predictive of skills in word reading, such as phonological awareness, alphabet knowledge, and rapid automatic naming (RAN). See the report of the National Early Literacy Panel (National Center for Family Literacy, 2008) for a review.

These measures, as well as demographic risk factors such as a family history of reading difficulties (Elbro et al., 1998; Scarborough, 1989), are very useful for predicting early reading outcomes. Generally, accuracy of prediction is greatest when a combination of these measures is used. It is important to keep in mind that measures related to word reading may be somewhat less useful for identifying children with mild oral language weaknesses that might lead to reading comprehension problems later on. Therefore, the addition of broader, nonphonological language assessments, such as those that consider vocabulary, grammar, and discourse skills, may also be useful.

In a recent study using the Iowa longitudinal database, Adlof and colleagues (2010) confirmed that the kindergarten measures needed to best predict a child's likelihood of having reading problems in second grade were different from those needed to predict problems in eighth grade. The kindergarten battery included assessments of cognition, alphabet knowledge, and a variety of oral language skills, as well as mother's education level. In both second and eighth grades, children were classified as poor readers if they scored more than one standard deviation below the mean on a composite measure of reading comprehension (i.e., the same criteria used in the subgrouping study described previously). All children who scored above this cutoff were considered good readers. Notably, just under half of the children who were classified as "poor" readers in second grade were considered "good" readers in eighth grade, and vice versa.

The analyses examined all possible combinations of variables to find the best models in terms of prediction accuracy, parsimony, and statistical goodness of fit. Across multiple models, several variables were found to be highly predictive of outcome status in both second and eighth grades. These included measures of sentence imitation, phoneme deletion, RAN, and mother's level of education. However, kindergarten alphabet knowledge was highly predictive of reading outcome status in second grade, but not in eighth grade. Likewise, measures of grammatical knowledge and nonverbal intelligence were predictive of eighth-grade outcome status, but not second-grade.

Eighth-grade outcomes were predicted with nearly as high accuracy as second-grade (90% concordance rate in second grade vs. 86% in eighth grade). The slight difference in accuracy of prediction resulted in a higher false-positive rate for eighth grade. In other words, to make sure that all eighth graders with reading problems were correctly identified as "at risk," the model overidentified students who were not at risk. Further, more research is needed to develop more sensitive and specific early predictors of later reading outcomes.

Numerous screening batteries are available for assessing children's risk for reading difficulties in the primary grades (e.g., Bridges & Catts, 2010; Catts, Fey, Zhang, & Tomblin, 2001; Good & Kaminski, 2002b; Invernizzi, Swank, & Juel, 2007; Wood et al., 2005). Until preschool and kindergarten batteries that can predict later reading outcomes are available, practitioners may wish to supplement with screens of vocabulary, grammar, and narrative or discourse skills, such as those used by speech-language pathologists (e.g., Dunn & Dunn, 2007; Justice et al., 2006; Rice & Wexler, 2001; Semel, Wiig, & Secord, 2004; Williams, 2007; Zimmerman, Steiner, & Pond, 2002). However, it is important to note that the language difficulties of children likely to have specific reading comprehension deficits in later grades may not be severe enough to be flagged by these measures (Catts et al., 2006; Nation et al., 2004; Nation, Cocksey, Taylor, & Bishop, 2010). Most important, the emergent literacy skills of students who are already receiving speech-language services should be monitored closely, as they are most at risk for later comprehension problems.

Early School Years. Assessments during the primary grades, when formal reading instruction has begun, can be used to monitor progress in reading, as well as to identify risk for later difficulties. At this stage, it is important to ensure that children are acquiring good word reading skills. A thorough assessment will include measurements of children's decoding skills (e.g., their ability to "sound out" nonsense words) and their ability to recognize both regularly and irregularly spelled real words (e.g., Torgesen et al., 1999; Woodcock, 1998). Children who have difficulty with word reading may need more intensive instruction to develop phonological awareness and knowledge of letter–sound correspondence, and they may need extra practice to ensure that word recognition becomes automatic, especially for irregularly spelled words.

As noted previously, reading comprehension measures in the early grades are reliant on assessment of word reading abilities, and these alone may not be sufficient to identify children who will have comprehension difficulties later on. Thus, supplemental assessments of language comprehension skills can be useful for obtaining a clearer picture. Several of the commercially available reading assessment batteries for school-age children include listening comprehension and vocabulary assessments for this purpose (e.g., MacGinitie, MacGinitie, Maria, Dreyer, & Hughes, 2006; Stanford Achievement Test Series, 2003; Williams, Cassidy, & Samuels, 2001). Note that children with word reading difficulties may need to complete oral, rather than written, vocabulary assessments. Children who show mild difficulties with language comprehension may benefit from supplemental comprehension-focused instruction. Those with more severe difficulties may need to be referred to a speech-language pathologist for in-depth testing and possible language intervention.

Middle Grades and Beyond. By around fifth grade, children should have a solid foundation in both word reading and language comprehension. At this point, it is probably not as important to assess for "risk" of future reading problems as it is to identify children with current problems.

For most children, performance in the classroom is an adequate indicator of reading progress. Some children may show difficulty with reading in a particular content area, and they may demonstrate better comprehension once they have been provided with background information to familiarize them with the topic. Other children may show difficulty with comprehension across several subject areas. For them, a standardized assessment of reading comprehension will confirm whether general reading skills are progressing normally. For children who earn low scores, follow-up assessments of word reading (decoding and sight words) and language comprehension (vocabulary, grammar, discourse) are needed to determine the source of difficulty. It is also useful to assess children's knowledge and use of general reading strategies, such as self-monitoring of comprehension. Although lack of reading strategies is not likely a primary cause of reading difficulties, evidence suggests that children with reading difficulties are less aware of inconsistencies in text and do not make attempts to repair comprehension breakdowns (e.g., Oakhill, Hartt, & Samols, 2005; van der Schoot, Vasbinder, Horsley, Reijntjes, & van Lieshout, 2009).

Once areas of weakness are identified, plans for addressing them may include supplemental instruction or referral to a reading or speech-language specialist for further assessment or intervention.

Informed Instruction

If the goal of reading instruction is to teach children to read with understanding, then instruction must include a focus on the code-based skills needed for word recognition, as well as the broad language skills needed for comprehension. Embedding instruction of these skills in a content-rich curriculum will facilitate the development of world knowledge, which in turn supports comprehension.

Over the past 30 years, a great deal of research on beginning word reading and dyslexia has provided us with valuable guidelines for word reading instruction. We know that high-quality instruction in word reading explicitly and systematically teaches phonological awareness, the alphabetic principle, and letter–sound correspondence, and it employs plenty of practice to facilitate automatic word recognition (e.g., NICHD, 2000; Snow, Burns, & Griffin, 1998). Furthermore, we know that most children with word reading difficulties do not need qualitatively different instruction to make gains in reading, but they do need longer, more explicit, and more intensive instruction to increase their skills (Torgesen et al., 2001; Vellutino et al., 1996).

Partly because of the push for evidence-based practice in teaching reading—and of the growth in studies of word reading—there can be a tendency in the primary grades to focus nearly exclusively on decoding and code-based skills, especially in special education classrooms and in high-poverty schools where the knowledge gap is widest (e.g., Duke, 2000; Klingner, Urbach, Golos, Brownell, & Menon, 2010; Neuman, 2006). Even when comprehension instruction is included, it is often very shallow (Klingner et al., 2010). While it is true that code-based skills have the largest influence on reading performance in the early grades, the evidence we have reviewed highlights the importance of focusing also on language comprehension, even in the early years. The influence of language skills on reading comprehension is observable throughout all grades, and language skills are the strongest predictor of comprehension in the later grades. Most children who turn out to be poor readers in later grades show difficulties with language comprehension in early grades. Language skills develop along a slower trajectory than code-based skills, and early gaps in language skills and world knowledge can be difficult to close. By explicitly focusing on language comprehension skills early (in addition to code-based instruction), we should be able to reduce the number of children who experience comprehension difficulties later on.

Facilitating the growth of these skills involves building children's vocabulary knowledge, ensuring that they understand complex syntactic structures, teaching them to draw inferences, and supporting their understanding of abstract language. None of this requires actual reading, so it can begin as early as preschool. The same is true for building children's world knowledge and knowledge in the academic disciplines, and even for comprehension strategies such as self-monitoring. Teaching these during oral activities—during teacher read-alouds, for example—can be useful in the early grades, when children can understand much more complex topics and language than appear in their grade-level reading materials. Recent studies investigating the efficacy of comprehension-oriented instruction for preschoolers have found that it does improve oral language skills, with gains maintained for several months after training ended (Bianco et al., 2010; Bowyer-Crane et al., 2008). These studies also show that gains in comprehension following oral language instruction do not generalize to code-based skills, nor do gains in code-based skills following instruction in them generalize to language comprehension. Thus, both types of instruction are necessary for optimal development.

The benefit of the assessment approach we have proposed is that it guides practitioners to provide individualized instruction according to each student's profile of strengths and weaknesses in word reading and language comprehension. Children enter school with varying levels of skills in each area, and a one-size-fits-all approach is not likely to optimize reading achievement for every student. Work by Connor and colleagues (Connor, Morrison, Fishman, Schatschneider, & Underwood, 2007; Connor et al., 2009) has shown that precise individualization of first-grade reading instruction based on each child's word reading and vocabulary knowledge leads to stronger growth in both word reading and reading comprehension skills. In these studies, a computer algorithm was used to prescribe the appropriate amounts of code-focused and meaning-focused instruction that each child should receive, as well as the amont of time that each type of instruction should be teacher managed or child managed. Future research to incorporate information from additional language skills and from older children may provide more guidance in ways to increase reading comprehension levels for all students across the school grades.

Conclusion

The relative importance of skills influencing reading comprehension changes over time, with word reading abilities having a greater influence on early reading comprehension and language skills having a greater influence on later reading comprehension. Facilitating the development of advanced comprehension requires attention to both word reading and language comprehension skills from an early age.

Risk for difficulty with word reading and comprehension can be identified at least as early as kindergarten, using assessments of precursor skills. As children begin formal reading instruction, progress in word reading can be measured using assessments designed for this purpose, while progress in comprehension can be measured using assessments of listening comprehension and oral language. In the middle grades, word reading abilities should be well established, but oral language assessments may be useful for evaluating the source of problems among individuals with reading difficulties.

By attending to children's individual profiles of relative strength and weakness in word reading and broader language skills, teachers can provide individualized instruction for optimal reading achievement across the school grades.

Questions for Reflection

1. Interview an elementary school teacher or principal and ask how reading skills and reading progress are assessed in different grades. Are both word reading and comprehension skills assessed? How does assessment inform instruction?

2. Observe a language arts period in an elementary school classroom. What kinds of texts are being used? How are word reading and comprehension skills addressed? What positive aspects of instruction did you observe? Were there any things you would do differently?

3. A parent comes to you for help in determining why his daughter is having trouble in reading. Sarah is in fifth grade, and she recently scored below average on a large-scale reading assessment. Her former teachers always described her as a good reader. Sarah's father is concerned that she is just not motivated or that she may not be paying attention in class. How will you respond to his concerns?

REFERENCES

Aaron, P.G., Joshi, M., & Williams, K.A. (1999). Not all reading disabilities are alike. *Journal of Learning Disabilities, 32*(2), 120–137. doi:10.1177/002221949903200203

Adams, B.C., Bell, L.C., & Perfetti, C.A. (1995). A trading relationship between reading skill and domain knowledge in children's text comprehension. *Discourse Processes, 20*(3), 307–323. doi:10.1080/01638539509544943

Adlof, S.M., & Catts, H.W. (2007, November). *Classification of children with poor reading comprehension.* Paper presented at the annual convention of the American Speech-Language-Hearing Association, Boston, Massachusetts.

Adlof, S.M., Catts, H.W., & Lee, J. (2010). Kindergarten predictors of second versus eighth grade reading comprehension impairments. *Journal of Learning Disabilities, 43*(6), 332–345. doi:10.1177/0022219410369067

Adlof, S.M., Catts, H.W., & Little, T.D. (2006). Should the simple view of reading include a fluency component? *Reading and Writing: An Interdisciplinary Journal, 19*(9), 933–958. doi:10.1007/s11145-006-9024-z

Badian, N.A. (1999). Reading disability defined as a discrepancy between listening and reading comprehension: A longitudinal study of stability, gender differences, and prevalence. *Journal of Learning Disabilities, 32*(2), 138–148. doi:10.1177/002221949903200204

Bianco, M., Bressoux, P., Doyen, A.-L., Lambert, E., Lima, L., Pellenq, C., et al. (2010). Early training in oral comprehension and phonological skills: Results of a three-year longitudinal study. *Scientific Studies of Reading, 14*(3), 211–246. doi:10.1080/10888430903117518

Bowyer-Crane, C., Snowling, M.J., Duff, F.J., Fieldsend, E., Carroll, J.M., Miles, J., et al. (2008). Improving early language and literacy skills: Differential effects of an oral language versus a phonology with reading intervention. *Journal of Child Psychology and Psychiatry, 49*(4), 422–432. doi:10.1111/j.1469-7610.2007.01849.x

Braze, D., Tabor, W., Shankweiler, D.P., & Mencl, W.E. (2007). Speaking up for vocabulary: Reading skill differences in young adults. *Journal of Learning Disabilities, 40*(3), 226–243. doi:10.1177/00222194070400030401

Bridges, M.S., & Catts, H.W. (2010). *Dynamic screening for phonological awareness (DSPA).* East Moline, IL: LinguiSystems.

Burkam, D.T., & Lee, V.E. (2002). *Inequality at the starting gate: Social background differences in achievement as children begin school.* Washington, DC: Economic Policy Institute.

Catts, H.W., Adlof, S.M., & Ellis Weismer, S. (2006). Language deficits in poor comprehenders: A case for the simple view of reading. *Journal of Speech, Language, and Hearing Research, 49*(2), 278–293. doi:10.1044/1092-4388(2006/023)

Catts, H.W., Fey, M.E., Tomblin, J.B., & Zhang, X. (2002). A longitudinal investigation of reading outcomes in children with language impairments. *Journal of Speech, Language, and Hearing Research, 45*(6), 1142–1157. doi:10.1044/1092-4388(2002/093)

Catts, H.W., Fey, M.E., Zhang, X., & Tomblin, J.B. (2001). Estimating the risk of future reading difficulties in kindergarten children: A research-based model and its clinical implementation. *Language, Speech, and Hearing Services in Schools, 32*(1), 38–50. doi:10.1044/0161-1461(2001/004)

Catts, H.W., & Hogan, T.P. (2002, June). *The fourth grade slump: Late emerging poor readers.* Paper presented at the ninth annual meeting of the Society for the Scientific Study of Reading, Chicago, IL.

Catts, H.W., Hogan, T.P., & Adlof, S.M. (2005). Developmental changes in reading and reading disabilities. In H.W. Catts & A.G. Kamhi (Eds.), *The connections between language and reading disabilities* (pp. 23–36). Mahwah, NJ: Erlbaum.

Catts, H.W., Hogan, T.P., & Fey, M.E. (2003). Subgrouping poor readers on the basis of individual differences in reading-related abilities. *Journal of Learning Disabilities, 36*(2), 151–164. doi:10.1177/002221940303600208

Catts, H.W., & Kamhi, A. (in press). *Language and reading disabilities* (3rd ed.). Boston: Pearson.

Chall, J.S. (1983). *Stages of reading development.* New York: McGraw-Hill.

Chall, J.S., Jacobs, V.A., & Baldwin, L.E. (1990). *The reading crisis: Why poor children fall behind.* Cambridge, MA: Harvard University Press.

Chen, R.S., & Vellutino, F.R. (1997). Prediction of reading ability: A cross-validation study of the simple view of reading. *Journal of Literacy Research, 29*(1), 1–24. doi:10.1080/10862969709547947

Compton, D.L., Fuchs, D., Fuchs, L.S., Elleman, A.M., & Gilbert, J.K. (2008). Tracking children who fly below the radar: Latent transition modeling of students with late-emerging reading disability. *Learning and Individual Differences, 18*(3), 329–337. doi:10.1016/j.lindif.2008.04.003

Connor, C.M., Morrison, F.J., Fishman, B.J., Schatschneider, C., & Underwood, P. (2007). The early years: Algorithm-guided individualized reading instruction. *Science, 315*(5811), 464–465. doi:10.1126/science.1134513

Connor, C.M., Piasta, S.B., Fishman, B., Glasney, S., Schatschneider, C., Crowe, E., Underwood, P., & Morrison, F.J. (2009). Individualizing student instruction precisely: Effects of child x instruction interactions on first graders' literacy development. *Child Development, 80*(1), 77–100. doi:10.1111/j.1467-8624.2008.01247.x

Cutting, L.E., Materek, A., Cole, C.A.S., Levine, T.M., & Mahone, E.M. (2009). Effects of fluency, oral language, and executive function on reading comprehension performance. *Annals of Dyslexia, 59*(1), 34–54. doi:10.1007/s11881-009-0022-0

Cutting, L.E., & Scarborough, H.S. (2006). Prediction of reading comprehension: Relative contributions of word recognition, language proficiency, and other cognitive skills can depend on how comprehension is measured. *Scientific Studies of Reading, 10*(3), 277–299. doi:10.1207/s1532799xssr1003_5

De Cara, B., & Goswami, U. (2003). Phonological neighbourhood density: Effects in a rhyme awareness task in 5-year-old children. *Journal of Child Language, 30*(3), 695–710. doi:10.1017/S0305000903005725

Dreyer, L.G., & Katz, L. (1992). An examination of "the simple view of reading." In C.K. Kinzer & D.J. Leu (Eds.), *Literacy research, theory, and practice: Views from many perspectives* (41st yearbook of the National Reading Conference, pp. 169–175). Chicago, IL: National Reading Conference.

Duke, N.K. (2000). For the rich it's richer: Print experiences and environments offered to children in very low– and very high–socioeconomic status first-grade classrooms. *American Educational Research Journal, 37*(2), 441–478. doi:10.3102/00028312037002441

Dunn, L.M., & Dunn, D.M. (2007). *Peabody picture vocabulary test* (4th ed.). Minneapolis, MN: Pearson.

Edmonds, M.S., Vaughn, S., Wexler, J., Reutebuch, C., Cable, A., Tackett, K.K., et al. (2009). A synthesis of reading interventions and effects on reading comprehension outcomes for older struggling readers. *Review of Educational Research, 79*(1), 262–300. doi:10.3102/0034654308325998

Elbro, C., Borstrøm, I., & Petersen, D.K. (1998). Predicting dyslexia from kindergarten: The importance of phonological representations of lexical items. *Reading Research Quarterly, 33*(1), 36–60. doi:10.1598/RRQ.33.1.3

Elleman, A.M., Lindo, E.J., Morphy, P., & Compton, D.L. (2009). The impact of vocabulary instruction on passage-level comprehension of school-age children: A meta-analysis. *Journal of Research on Educational Effectiveness, 2*(1), 1–44. doi:10.1080/19345740802539200

Francis, D.J., Fletcher, J.M., Catts, H.W., & Tomblin, J.B. (2005). Dimensions affecting the assessment of reading comprehension. In S.G. Paris & S.A. Stahl (Eds.), *Children's reading comprehension and assessment* (pp. 369–394). Mahwah, NJ: Erlbaum.

Gallagher, A., Frith, U., & Snowling, M.J. (2000). Precursors of literacy delay among children at genetic risk of dyslexia. *Journal of Child Psychology and Psychiatry, and Allied Disciplines, 41*(2), 203–213. doi:10.1111/1469-7610.00601

Good, R.H., & Kaminski, R.A. (2002a). *DIBELS oral reading fluency passages for first through third grades* (Technical Report No. 10). Eugene, OR: University of Oregon.

Good, R.H., & Kaminski, R.A. (Eds.). (2002b). *Dynamic indicators of basic early literacy skills* (6th ed.). Eugene, OR: Institute for the Development of Educational Achievement. Retrieved November 12, 2010, from oregonreadingfirst.uoregon.edu/downloads/assessment/admin_and_scoring_6th_ed.pdf

Gough, P.B., Hoover, W.A., & Peterson, C.L. (1996). Some observations on a simple view of reading. In C. Cornoldi & J. Oakhill (Eds.), *Reading comprehension difficulties: Processes and intervention* (pp. 1–13). Mahwah, NJ: Erlbaum.

Gough, P.B., & Tunmer, W.E. (1986). Decoding, reading, and reading disability. *Remedial and Special Education, 7*(1), 6–10. doi:10.1177/074193258600700104

Hirsch, E.D. (2001). Overcoming the language gap: Make better use of the literacy time block. *American Educator, 25*(2), 4–7. Retrieved January 5, 2011, from www.aft.org/newspubs/periodicals/ae/summer2001/index.cfm

Hirsch, E.D. (2003). Reading comprehension requires knowledge—of words and the world. *American Educator*, *27*(1), 10–13, 16–22, 28–29, 48.

Hogan, T.P. (2010). A short report: Word-level phonological and lexical characteristics interact to influence phoneme awareness. *Journal of Learning Disabilities*, *43*(4), 346–356. doi:10.1177/0022219410369083

Hoover, W.A., & Gough, P.B. (1990). The simple view of reading. *Reading and Writing: An Interdisciplinary Journal*, *2*(2), 127–160. doi:10.1007/BF00401799

Invernizzi, M., Swank, L., & Juel, C. (2007). *Phonological awareness literacy screening—Kindergarten* (6th ed.). Charlottesville, VA: University of Virginia.

Justice, L.M., Bowles, R.P., Kaderavek, J.N., Ukrainetz, T.A., Eisenberg, S.L., & Gillam, R.B. (2006). The index of narrative microstructure: A clinical tool for analyzing school-age children's narrative performances. *American Journal of Speech-Language Pathology*, *15*(2), 177–191. doi:10.1044/1058-0360(2006/017)

Keenan, J.M., Betjemann, R.S., & Olson, R.K. (2008). Reading comprehension tests vary in the skills they assess: Differential dependence on decoding and oral comprehension. *Scientific Studies of Reading*, *12*(3), 281–300. doi:10.1080/10888430802132279

Kendeou, P., Savage, R., & van den Broek, P. (2009). Revisiting the simple view of reading. *The British Journal of Educational Psychology*, *79*(2), 353–370. doi:10.1348/978185408X369020

Kendeou, P., van den Broek, P., White, M.J., & Lynch, J.S. (2009). Predicting reading comprehension in early elementary school: The independent contributions of oral language and decoding skills. *Journal of Educational Psychology*, *101*(4), 765–778. doi:10.1037/a0015956

Kintsch, W. (1988). The role of knowledge in discourse comprehension: A construction-integration model. *Psychological Review*, *95*(2), 163–182. doi:10.1037/0033-295X.95.2.163

Klingner, J.K., Urbach, J., Golos, D., Brownell, M., & Menon, S. (2010). Teaching reading in the 21st century: A glimpse at how special education teachers promote reading comprehension. *Learning Disability Quarterly*, *33*(2), 59–74.

LaBerge, D., & Samuels, S.J. (1974). Toward a theory of automatic information processing in reading. *Cognitive Psychology*, *6*(2), 293–323. doi:10.1016/0010-0285(74)90015-2

Landi, N. (2010). An examination of the relationship between reading comprehension, higher-level and lower-level reading subskills in adults. *Reading and Writing: An Interdisciplinary Journal*, *23*(6), 701–717. doi:10.1007/s11145-009-9180-z

Leach, J.M., Scarborough, H.S., & Rescorla, L. (2003). Late-emerging reading disabilities. *Journal of Educational Psychology*, *95*(2), 211–224. doi:10.1037/0022-0663.95.2.211

Lipka, O., Lesaux, N.K., & Siegel, L.S. (2006). Retrospective analyses of the reading development of grade 4 students with reading disabilities: Risk status and profiles over 5 years. *Journal of Learning Disabilities*, *39*(4), 364–378. doi:10.1177/00222194060390040901

Lonigan, C.J. (2007). Vocabulary development and the development of phonological awareness skills in preschool children. In R.K. Wagner, A.E. Muse, & K.R. Tannenbaum (Eds.), *Vocabulary acquisition: Implications for reading comprehension* (pp. 15–31). New York: Guilford.

Lonigan, C.J., Burgess, S.R., & Anthony, J.L. (2000). Development of emergent literacy and early reading skills in preschool children: Evidence from a latent-variable longitudinal study. *Developmental Psychology*, *36*(5), 596–613. doi:10.1037/0012-1649.36.5.596

MacGinitie, W.H., MacGinitie, R.K., Maria, K., Dreyer, L.G., & Hughes, K.E. (2006). *Gates-MacGinitie reading tests* (4th ed.). Chicago: Riverside.

Malatesha Joshi, R., & Aaron, P.G. (2000). The component model of reading: Simple view of reading made a little more complex. *Reading Psychology*, *21*(2), 85–97. doi:10.1080/02702710050084428

Metsala, J.L. (1999). Young children's phonological awareness and nonword repetition as a function of vocabulary development. *Journal of Educational Psychology*, *91*(1), 3–19. doi:10.1037/0022-0663.91.1.3

Metsala, J.L., & Walley, A.C. (1998). Spoken vocabulary growth and the segmental restructuring of lexical representations: Precursors to phonemic awareness and early reading ability. In J.L. Metsala & L.C. Ehri (Eds.), *Word recognition in beginning literacy* (pp. 83–111). Mahwah, NJ: Erlbaum.

Meyer, M.S., & Felton, R.H. (1999). Repeated reading to enhance fluency: Old approaches and new directions. *Annals of Dyslexia*, *49*(1), 283–306. doi:10.1007/s11881-999-0027-8

Miller, J., & Schwanenflugel, P.J. (2008). A longitudinal study of the development of reading prosody as a dimension of oral reading fluency in early elementary school children. *Reading Research Quarterly, 43*(4), 336–354. doi:10.1598/RRQ.43.4.2

Muter, V., Hulme, C., Snowling, M.J., & Stevenson, J. (2004). Phonemes, rimes, vocabulary, and grammatical skills as foundations of early reading development: Evidence from a longitudinal study. *Developmental Psychology, 40*(5), 665–681. doi:10.1037/0012-1649.40.5.665

Nagy, W.E., & Scott, J.A. (2000). Vocabulary processes. In M.L. Kamil, P.B. Mosenthal, P.D. Pearson, & R. Barr (Eds.), *Handbook of reading research* (Vol. 3, pp. 269–284). Mahwah, NJ: Erlbaum.

Nation, K. (2008). Learning to read words. *The Quarterly Journal of Experimental Psychology, 61*(8), 1121–1133. doi:10.1080/17470210802034603

Nation, K., Clarke, P., Marshall, C.M., & Durand, M. (2004). Hidden language impairments in children: Parallels between poor reading comprehension and specific language impairment? *Journal of Speech, Language, and Hearing Research, 47*(1), 199–211. doi:10.1044/1092-4388(2004/017)

Nation, K., & Cocksey, J. (2009). The relationship between knowing a word and reading it aloud in children's word reading development. *Journal of Experimental Child Psychology, 103*(3), 296–308. doi:10.1016/j.jecp.2009.03.004

Nation, K., Cocksey, J., Taylor, J.S.H., & Bishop, D.V.M. (2010). A longitudinal investigation of early reading and language skills in children with poor reading comprehension. *Journal of Child Psychology and Psychiatry, 51*(9), 1031–1039. doi:10.1111/j.1469-7610.2010.02254.x

Nation, K., & Snowling, M. (1997). Assessing reading difficulties: The validity and utility of current measures of reading skill. *The British Journal of Educational Psychology, 67*(3), 359–370.

National Center for Family Literacy. (2008). *Developing early literacy: Report of the National Early Literacy Panel*. Washington, DC: National Institute for Literacy.

National Institute of Child Health and Human Development. (2000). *Report of the National Reading Panel. Teaching children to read: An evidence-based assessment of the scientific research literature on reading and its implications for reading instruction. Reports of the subgroups* (NIH Publication No. 00-4754). Washington, DC: U.S. Government Printing Office.

Neuman, S.B. (2006). The knowledge gap: Implications for early education. In D.K. Dickinson & S.B. Neuman (Eds.), *Handbook of early literacy research* (Vol. 2, pp. 29–40). New York: Guilford.

O'Connor, R.E., White, A., & Swanson, H.L. (2007). Repeated reading versus continuous reading: Influences on reading fluency and comprehension. *Exceptional Children, 74*(1), 31–46.

Oakhill, J., Hartt, J., & Samols, D. (2005). Levels of comprehension monitoring and working memory in good and poor comprehenders. *Reading and Writing: An Interdisciplinary Journal, 18*(7–9), 657–686. doi:10.1007/s11145-005-3355-z

Ouellette, G., & Beers, A. (2010). A not-so-simple view of reading: How oral vocabulary and visual-word recognition complicate the story. *Reading and Writing: An Interdisciplinary Journal, 23*(2), 189–208. doi:10.1007/s11145-008-9159-1

Ouellette, G.P. (2006). What's meaning got to do with it: The role of vocabulary in word reading and reading comprehension. *Journal of Educational Psychology, 98*(3), 554–566. doi:10.1037/0022-0663.98.3.554

Perfetti, C.A. (1977). Language comprehension and fast decoding: Some psycholinguistic prerequisites for skilled reading comprehension. In J.T. Guthrie (Ed.), *Cognition, curriculum, and comprehension* (pp. 20–41). Newark, DE: International Reading Association.

Perfetti, C.A. (1985). *Reading ability*. New York: Oxford University Press.

Perfetti, C.A. (1999). Comprehending written language: A blueprint of the reader. In C.M. Brown & P. Hagoort (Eds.), *The neurocognition of language* (pp. 167–208). New York: Oxford University Press.

Perfetti, C. (2007). Reading ability: Lexical quality to comprehension. *Scientific Studies of Reading, 11*(4), 357–383. doi:10.1080/10888430701530730

Perfetti, C. (2010). Decoding, vocabulary, and comprehension: The golden triangle of reading skill. In M.G. McKeown & L. Kucan (Eds.), *Bringing reading research to life* (pp. 291–303). New York: Guilford.

Perfetti, C.A., & Hart, L. (2001). The lexical bases of comprehension skill. In D.S. Gorfein (Ed.), *On the consequences of meaning selec-*

tion (pp. 67–86). Washington, DC: American Psychological Association.

Rasinski, T., Rikli, A., & Johnston, S. (2009). Reading fluency: More than automaticity? More than a concern for the primary grades? *Literacy Research and Instruction, 48*(4), 350–361. doi:10.1080/19388070802468715

Rice, M.L., & Wexler, K. (2001). *Rice/Wexler test of early grammatical impairment.* San Antonio, TX: Pearson.

Samuels, S.J. (2007). The DIBELS tests: Is speed of barking at print what we mean by reading fluency? *Reading Research Quarterly, 42*(4), 563–567.

Scarborough, H.S. (1989). Prediction of reading disability from familial and individual differences. *Journal of Educational Psychology, 81*(1), 101–108. doi:10.1037/0022-0663.81.1.101

Scarborough, H.S. (1990). Very early language deficits in dyslexic children. *Child Development, 61*(6), 1728–1743. doi:10.2307/1130834

Scarborough, H.S., & Dobrich, W. (1990). Development of children with early language delay. *Journal of Speech and Hearing Research, 33*(1), 70–83.

Schwanenflugel, P.J., Kuhn, M.R., Morris, R.D., Morrow, L.M., Meisinger, E.B., Woo, D.G., Quirk, M., & Sevcik, R. (2009). Insights into fluency instruction: Short- and long-term effects of two reading programs. *Literacy Research and Instruction, 48*(4), 318–336. doi:10.1080/19388070802422415

Semel, E., Wiig, E.H., & Secord, W.A. (2004). *CELF-4 screening test.* San Antonio, TX: Pearson.

Shanahan, T., & Shanahan, C. (2008). Teaching disciplinary literacy to adolescents: Rethinking content-area literacy. *Harvard Educational Review, 78*(1), 40–59.

Snow, C.E., Burns, M.S., & Griffin, P. (Eds.). (1998). *Preventing reading difficulties in young children.* Washington, DC: National Academy Press.

Spilich, G.J., Vesonder, G.T., Chiesi, H.L., & Voss, J.F. (1979). Text processing of domain-related information for individuals with high and low domain knowledge. *Journal of Verbal Learning and Verbal Behavior, 18*(3), 275–290. doi:10.1016/S0022-5371(79)90155-5

Stanford Achievement Test Series (10th ed.). (2003). San Antonio, TX: Pearson.

Stanovich, K.E. (1988). Explaining the differences between the dyslexic and the garden-variety poor reader: The phonological-core

variable-difference model. *Journal of Learning Disabilities, 21*(10), 590–604. doi:10.1177/002221948802101003

Stanovich, K.E., & Cunningham, A.E. (1993). Where does knowledge come from? Specific associations between print exposure and information acquisition. *Journal of Educational Psychology, 85*(2), 211–229. doi:10.1037/0022-0663.85.2.211

Storch, S.A., & Whitehurst, G.J. (2002). Oral language and code-related precursors to reading: Evidence from a longitudinal structural model. *Developmental Psychology, 38*(6), 934–947. doi:10.1037/0012-1649.38.6.934

Stuebing, K.K., Barth, A.E., Molfese, P.J., Weiss, B., & Fletcher, J.M. (2009). IQ is not strongly related to response to reading instruction: A meta-analytic interpretation. *Exceptional Children, 76*(1), 31–51.

Tilstra, J., McMaster, K., van den Broek, P., Kendeou, P., & Rapp, D. (2009). Simple but complex: Components of the simple view of reading across grade levels. *Journal of Research in Reading, 32*(4), 383–401. doi:10.1111/j.1467-9817.2009.01401.x

Torgesen, J.K., Alexander, A.W., Wagner, R.K., Rashotte, C.A., Voeller, K.K., & Conway, T. (2001). Intensive remedial instruction for children with severe reading disabilities: Immediate and long-term outcomes from two instructional approaches. *Journal of Learning Disabilities, 34*(1), 33–58. doi:10.1177/002221940103400104

Torgesen, J.K., Wagner, R.K., & Rashotte, C.A. (1999). *TOWRE: Test of word reading efficiency.* Austin, TX: PRO-ED.

van der Schoot, M., Vasbinder, A.L., Horsley, T.M., Reijntjes, A., & van Lieshout, E.C.D.M. (2009). Lexical ambiguity resolution in good and poor comprehenders: An eye fixation and self-paced reading study in primary school children. *Journal of Educational Psychology, 101*(1), 21–36. doi:10.1037/a0013382

Vellutino, F.R., Scanlon, D.M., Sipay, E.R., Small, S.G., Pratt, A., Chen, R., et al. (1996). Cognitive profiles of difficult-to-remediate and readily remediated poor readers: Early intervention as a vehicle for distinguishing between cognitive and experiential deficits as basic causes of specific reading disabilities. *Journal of Educational Psychology, 88*(4), 601–638. doi:10.1037/0022-0663.88.4.601

Verhoeven, L., & van Leeuwe, J. (2008). Prediction of the development of reading comprehension: A longitudinal study.

Applied Cognitive Psychology, 22(3), 407–423. doi:10.1002/acp.1414

Walley, A.C., Metsala, J.L., & Garlock, V.M. (2003). Spoken vocabulary growth: Its role in the development of phoneme awareness and early reading ability. *Reading and Writing, 16*(1–2), 5–20. doi:10.1023/A:1021789804977

Wexler, J., Vaughn, S., Roberts, G., & Denton, C.A. (2010). The efficacy of repeated reading and wide reading practice for high school students with severe reading disabilities. *Learning Disabilities Research & Practice, 25*(1), 2–10. doi:10.1111/j.1540-5826.2009.00296.x

Wiederholt, J.L., & Bryant, B.R. (1994). *GORT-3: Gray oral reading tests* (3rd ed.). Austin, TX: PRO-ED.

Williams, K.T. (2007). *Expressive vocabulary test (EVT)* (2nd ed.). Minneapolis, MN: Pearson.

Williams, K.T., Cassidy, J., & Samuels, S.J. (2001). *GRADE: Group reading assessment and diagnostic evaluation.* Circle Pines, MN: American Guidance Service.

Wood, F.B., Hill, D.F., Meyer, M.S., & Flowers, D.L. (2005). Predictive assessment of reading. *Annals of Dyslexia, 55*(2), 193–216. doi:10.1007/s11881-005-0011-x

Woodcock, R.W. (1998). *Woodcock reading mastery tests-Revised normative update.* San Antonio, TX: Pearson.

Zeno, S.M., Ivens, S.H., Millard, R.T., & Dubburi, R. (1995). *The educator's word frequency guide.* Brewster, NY: Touchstone Applied Science Associates.

Zimmerman, I.L., Steiner, V.G., & Pond, R.E. (2002). *Preschool language scale-4 screening test.* Minneapolis, MN: Pearson Assessment.

LITERATURE CITED

Kalman, B. (1995). *Penguins.* New York: Crabtree.

Lambert, D., & The Diagram Group. (2007). *The field guide to geology* (New ed.). New York: Facts on File.

Chapter 9

Are Current Reading Research Findings Applicable to Students With Intellectual Disabilities?

Terri Fautsch-Patridge, Kristen L. McMaster, and Susan C. Hupp

Until recently, evidenced-based practice in reading for students with intellectual disabilities (IDs) has focused on decontextualized sight-word training rather than a balanced approach to reading instruction. In this chapter, we highlight recent research conducted for students with IDs that focuses on the five skill components identified by the National Reading Panel (NRP): phonemic awareness, phonics, fluency, vocabulary, and comprehension strategies (National Institute of Child Health and Human Development [NICHD], 2000). We explore questions regarding which aspects of students' cognitive abilities most significantly influence their reading achievement, and describe research-based instructional approaches that capitalize on students' strengths and adapt to their specific needs. We conclude that despite global intellectual challenges, many students with IDs are capable of learning to read with appropriate instructional support.

For students with IDs, reading is a critical skill to attain a level of independence and an improved quality of life. The importance of reading cannot be overestimated in the daily life of any individual. From a task as simple as reading labels on consumer products, to engaging in current communication technologies such as texting and e-mail, to experiencing the joys of leisure reading, being literate means being included in the everyday life of our society. Yet, for many individuals with IDs, reading has been an elusive goal. Although these individuals experience many learning challenges, their lack of reading achievement may often be the result of ineffective instruction, or lack of instruction, and not always a problem that results from their disability. This situation has improved with a new focus of reading research directed toward this population, and a new commitment for all students to reach their potential in learning to read.

What Research Has to Say About Reading Instruction (4th ed.) edited by S. Jay Samuels and Alan E. Farstrup. © 2011 by the International Reading Association.

In this chapter, we first define IDs to clarify the research base that targets this group. Then, we briefly describe historical approaches to teaching students with IDs to read and how these approaches have changed with shifts in federal legislation. Next, we highlight the five components of reading defined by the NRP (NICHD, 2000) and, within each area, discuss relevant cognitive factors and their implications for intervention for students with IDs. Throughout, we emphasize the importance of focusing on individual strengths and needs in developing instructional programs to improve reading outcomes for students with IDs.

Defining IDs

There is often confusion about what constitutes an ID. Students with specific learning disabilities, for example, are not included in the ID category. IDs are conceptualized as affecting individuals in more global ways, both intellectually and in day-to-day functioning. Individuals who score 70 or below on a standardized, individualized measure of intellectual functioning and also score significantly below average on a standardized measure of adaptive behavior (e.g., communication, social skills, self-care skills) are defined as having IDs if these disabilities occur before the age of 18. This definition is based on clinical guidelines, such as the *Diagnostic and Statistical Manual of Mental Disorders* (American Psychiatric Association, 2000), as well as special education law (i.e., Individuals with Disabilities Education Act [IDEA] of 2004) and describes what was formerly known as mental retardation.

While an average score of 100 indicates a person has "normal" intelligence, scores between 70 and 85 indicate a person has a "low" or borderline IQ (intelligence quotient). It is only when IQ scores are at 70 or below that individuals are considered to have global intellectual impairments that will cause them to learn more slowly than typically developing peers. In our discussion of the current research, we primarily focus on individuals within two ranges of functioning: mild ID (IQs between 50 and 70) and moderate ID (IQs between 35 and 50). These categories may overlap in some studies, because much of this research has been done with individuals with specific diagnoses (e.g., Down syndrome), which typically have very large or overlapping ranges of intellectual functioning.

It should be emphasized that defining IDs solely in the context of IQ is considered a dated notion in this field. Current emphasis by the American Association on Intellectual and Developmental Disabilities

(2010) focuses not only on IQ and adaptive skills but also on delivering appropriate levels of support that are specifically designed to ensure that all persons are able to reach their highest level of functioning. This position recognizes an individual's deficits or needs and focuses on an individual's strengths by providing the supports needed to be a lifelong learner. We next describe historical approaches to teaching students with IDs to read, and describe why these approaches may be insufficient to support such lifelong learning.

A Brief History of Teaching Students With IDs to Read

Historically, students with IDs were often separated from their typically developing peers in classroom placements and, as a consequence, were often separated from the general education curriculum (Wehmeyer, 2006). Approaches to reading instruction for students with IDs in these settings varied from no instruction (Kliewer, 1998; Kliewer & Biklen, 2001; Kliewer, Biklen, & Kasa-Hendrickson, 2006) to decontextualized preparatory subskill-based training (i.e., prerequisite skills); skills taught in these contexts were rarely mastered and rarely led to meaningful reading. Later, many educators believed that the specialized learning needs of this group of students were better served by focusing their reading instruction on functional or survival words using whole-word or sight-based instruction (Browder, Wakeman, Spooner, Ahlgrim-Delzell, & Algozzine, 2006; Katims, 2000). Although sight-based instruction can be effective for teaching specific words, this approach has typically not helped students learn "untrained" words.

Most recently, federal legislation (i.e., No Child Left Behind Act of 2001, IDEA of 2004) has required that all students participate in some form of assessment and that instructional goals reference core instructional standards. This legislation has led to examining all students' achievement in the area of reading or reading-related skills, including the achievement of students with IDs. The funding of recent research studies (e.g., Allor, Mathes, Jones, Champlin, & Cheatham, 2010; Browder, Ahlgrim-Delzell, Courtade, Gibbs, & Flowers, 2008) that focus on the literacy development of children with IDs underscores the importance of improving outcomes for this group. We discuss the results of some of these efforts in this chapter.

Five Components of Reading Instruction Defined by the NRP

Along with federal mandates to improve the learning of all students, the last decade has seen an increased national focus on reading. The NRP was assembled at the request of the U.S. Congress in 1997 and published its report in 2000. This report was intended to review strategies or methods of reading instruction, determine their effectiveness, and address the current state of what was known about how to teach reading (NICHD, 2000). The NRP report has become a gold standard, informing educators on research concerning the five essential components of reading instruction: phonological/phonemic awareness, phonics, fluency, vocabulary, and comprehension strategies (NICHD, 2000). Each of these components is briefly defined within subsequent sections of this chapter. The NRP report is available online and should be consulted to acquire a more in-depth understanding of these components.

Although each of the five NRP components is addressed in scientifically based reading curricula for typically developing children, the same cannot be said for the reading instruction used for many children with IDs. Rather, as mentioned previously, instruction for these children has often focused solely on whole-word or sight-based approaches. The NRP findings are based on research with typically developing readers, and it is important to understand that instructional strategies that have been successful with typically developing students, or with students with specific learning disabilities, may not necessarily work as well with students who have global IDs. Thus, until research provides conclusive evidence regarding the most effective approaches to teaching reading to children with IDs, educators must consider whether it is best to continue with the sight-word approach or apply state-of-the-art knowledge about how to teach reading as defined by the NRP.

The phrase *least dangerous assumption*, coined by Donnellan (1984), seems appropriate in this context. She contended that when conclusive data are not available, educators should decide on the course of action that, if incorrect, will have the least dangerous effect on the future independence of the student. Continuing to focus only on functional sight words will not result in literacy. This is not the least dangerous assumption, because it limits students to reading only words that have been specifically taught (for a review and further discussion of this point, see Browder et al., 2006). By contrast, a phonics approach is generative, allowing students to use a strategy to decode new words independently.

As such, it allows for self-teaching (Share, 1995) and has a much higher likelihood of progressing to literacy. If students with IDs are to learn to read, we must apply the least dangerous assumption. At the same time, we must conduct research to determine whether the same NRP components of reading will be successful with these students.

Next, we address recent research on each of the five components identified by the NRP as they relate to individuals with IDs. Within each component's section, we explore aspects of students' cognitive abilities that may significantly influence their reading achievement, along with instructional implications. We focus primarily on phonological/phoneme awareness and phonics, because they are areas that are crucial for the acquisition of reading and have been largely ignored for students with IDs (Browder et al., 2006; Joseph & Seery, 2004; Saunders, 2007).

Phonological/Phonemic Awareness

A large body of research on beginning word reading has focused on phonological awareness (PA). PA is the metacognitive ability to manipulate the sounds of speech independent of meaning. PA is evidenced by a child's progressive ability to detect and manipulate rhymes (e.g., create a rhyme for a nonsense word), syllables (e.g., tap out number of syllables), and phonemes (e.g., blend or segment, delete a phoneme in a word and say the remainder; Anthony & Lonigan, 2004). The awareness of and ability to manipulate the smallest meaningful unit of speech, the phoneme, is most highly correlated with the ability to learn to read. In fact, phonemic awareness has been shown to have a causal relationship to learning to read (Wagner & Torgesen, 1987). Because of its high correlation in learning to read, the NRP focuses only on phonemic awareness. Phonemic awareness, which is an auditory skill, is seen as necessary for the reader to understand that printed letters and letter combinations represent sounds. This is known as the alphabetic principle (Adams, 1990). By linking printed letters or letter combinations to their sounds during reading (i.e., sounding out), the reader is able to decode words. Using printed letters to help students learn letter–sound correspondences and decode words is often referred to as phonics. Individuals who have difficulty with phonemic awareness will also have difficulty with phonics and will likely experience difficulty in learning to read.

Most typically developing children seem to develop PA by progressing through stages to reach phonemic awareness in predictable ways (see Anthony & Lonigan, 2004); however, this developmental progression is not true for all children. Much research indicates that individuals with "normal" intellectual functioning who experience reading difficulties, such as dyslexia (see Shaywitz, 2003; Shaywitz, Morris, & Shaywitz, 2008), have problems with PA and phonemic awareness in particular. People who fit within specific categories of IDs, such as Down syndrome, are known to have similar deficits in phonological processing (e.g., Silverman, 2007); however, until very recently, there has been a lack of evidence on strengths or deficits of individuals within the broad classification of IDs. In our next section, we explore fundamental questions about PA in IDs before moving on to issues regarding interventions in this area.

The Nature of PA in Individuals With IDs. If we intend to use the same strategies for reading instruction offered to typically developing children for children with IDs, we first need to determine whether their phonological skills are intact or in need of remediation. In addition, it is necessary to determine whether students with IDs use their phonological skills in ways that are similar to typical readers.

A controversial claim that individuals with Down syndrome, which is the most common genetic cause of IDs, could read without PA (Cossu, Rossini, & Marshall, 1993) resulted in a significant number of research studies designed to investigate this claim. Recent reviews of literature on this topic (Fautsch-Patridge, 2008; Lemons & Fuchs, 2010b) have showed that individuals with Down syndrome can acquire PA, and although its development is delayed, they do, to a lesser degree, develop PA skills and use them while reading. Because these individuals seem capable of using the PA skills they possess, we believe these findings suggest that children with Down syndrome should be exposed to PA training. Saunders (2007) reviewed many of the same studies as the reviews mentioned previously, including those on Down syndrome and a few related to individuals with other etiologies, such as Williams syndrome, which is a genetic syndrome characterized by IDs and strengths in spoken language. Saunders's review illustrates that PA exists in these populations, although to a lesser degree than in typically developing students, and just as with typically developing readers, these skills were correlated with measures of reading. Again, this correlation suggests that individuals in these other populations are using their partial skills to help in the process of decoding the words presented to them.

With the exception of studies on Down syndrome, surprisingly few researchers have sought to discover how attributes of individuals with different types of IDs might be related to PA development. Numerous conditions are associated with IDs, many of them having physical complications in terms of movement and speech production. For example, many students with IDs may have no spoken-language abilities. Is it reasonable to expect that these children can develop PA? Much more research is needed to determine the concomitant effects of certain characteristics that are common among individuals with different types of IDs. One study along these lines showed that children with cerebral palsy who also have IDs are less adept at phonological tasks than children with cerebral palsy who do not have IDs, and are also less adept than their typically developing peers (Peeters, Verhoeven, van Balkom, & de Moor, 2008). More research is clearly needed to better understand the relationships between IDs and PA.

The majority of studies included in the reviews we have discussed thus far were correlational studies designed to discover the nature of PA and its relationship to reading in this population. It seems fairly clear that individuals with various ID etiologies have delayed PA skills or skills below the level of their reading-matched peers, but the skills they do possess are used during reading. The current research suggests that the manner in which these skills are used is similar to students with more typical development. In other words, students with IDs seem to be using the skills they possess in ways that facilitate their reading of words and nonwords. Further, because these students are often using partial skills, it seems that intervening to alleviate deficits by filling the gaps in these partial skills might prove to be cost effective, because these students will likely learn and use new, more complete skills. For example, if a student uses his or her minimal level of PA to discern only initial phonemes in words, interventions may help the student hear final phonemes, medial phonemes, and eventually all phonemes in a given word. This awareness, together with knowledge of letter–sound correspondence, should help in the decoding of words.

Focused Interventions in PA. The age at which intervention in PA should take place for children with IDs needs further research, but it seems reasonable to begin in the preschool years. The recent National Early Literacy Panel report (Lonigan & Shanahan, 2009) has emphasized the importance of developing PA in the preschool and kindergarten years. Intervening during infancy and preschool is not new for the field of IDs, because early intervention services are mandated under the IDEA of 2004. Whereas early intervention services for typically developing children in programs like Head Start focus heavily on early literacy skills such as PA, there is a dearth of studies to indicate that this kind of systematic focus is routinely implemented in early childhood special educational plans for children with known IDs. Researchers have used an emergent literacy approach combining a literacy-rich environment, storytime, and writing centers (e.g., Katims, 1991) for students with IDs, resulting in improvements in print concepts and writing. Other researchers maintain that fundamental prerequisites such as PA instruction be emphasized for preschool children with disabilities as well as typically developing children (Phillips, Clancy-Menchetti, & Lonigan, 2008). It may be that a new emphasis or intensity in PA is needed in early childhood special education programs particularly for children with IDs, based on an understanding that these skills are necessary for these children, like all children, to learn to read.

PA interventions are of particular interest in certain subpopulations of IDs, such as individuals with Down syndrome, given that, as described earlier, we have evidence that many of these children have difficulty with phonological processing (Silverman, 2007). Improvements made in the usually short duration of most PA interventions is particularly impressive for this subgroup. For example, in a study lasting only six weeks that combined PA and letter–sound correspondences, van Bysterveldt, Gillon, and Moran (2006) had parents of 4-year-old children with Down syndrome implement a systematic program of drawing attention to targeted letters and sounds during shared storybook reading at home. Whereas the typically developing control group children scored significantly higher than children with Down syndrome on pre- and postintervention measures, those with Down syndrome were found to make significant gains in awareness of initial phonemes and letter–sound knowledge. Given that most children with IDs receive early childhood special education services, it seems that PA and early literacy experiences could easily be integrated into individual program plans. This study had a small sample and was of limited duration, and additional research is needed to learn about the extent of the impact that PA instruction may have for young children with IDs.

Phonics

The NRP (NICHD, 2000) defined *phonics* as the use of letters and their corresponding sounds to teach students to read and spell words. Phonics is applied in two ways: analogy/analytic and synthetic. Both ways have been found to be more effective for students without diagnosed disabilities than a no-phonics approach and have not differed in terms of their effectiveness (NICHD, 2000). As these data were not based on students with IDs, it would be premature to generalize to this population without further research.

Analytic and synthetic approaches to phonics instruction may have differing results with students with IDs because of cognitive processing requirements. For example, an analytic approach to phonics is thought to require less short-term memory (Cupples & Iacono, 2002). It is assumed that it is easier for the student to use known letter patterns to say larger units of the word when decoding it. This approach is often used with spelling patterns known as onsets and rimes. The onset is the beginning consonant or consonant blend, and the rime consists of the vowels and consonants after the onset. For example, the following words all have different onsets but the same rime: *cat*, *hat*, and *flat*. This approach is often used when students find the use of a synthetic approach (i.e., articulating each phoneme) difficult. It is thought that an analytic approach puts less of a strain on short-term memory, because there are fewer chunks to hold in memory while preparing to blend the sounds together to decode the word.

Difficulties with short-term auditory memory could affect the success of a phonics strategy with some children with IDs, such as those with Down syndrome who are known to have memory problems (Gathercole & Alloway, 2006). Cupples and Iacono's (2002) small study was based on this fact and conducted to determine the effectiveness of an analytic phonics method with seven children with Down syndrome ages 8–12 and presumed to be in the mild to moderate IQ category. The researchers used a whole-word approach with one group and a word analysis approach focused on combining onsets and rimes with the other group. Both groups showed improvement in learning the target words, but only those in the word analysis condition were significantly better at reading generalization words. The word analysis group also showed improvement in blending but not in segmenting. Cupples and Iacono concluded that students with Down syndrome may benefit from an analytic approach to decoding. Because of its small number of participants and some limitations, this single study does not make the case for using analytic phonics for students with IDs, but it does provide some evidence of the effectiveness of analytic phonics for this group. It also illustrates the complicating effects of disabilities (e.g., deficits in short-term memory), and how strategies can be modified to meet individual needs.

Synthetic phonics instruction involves teaching students to use their knowledge of letter–sound correspondences to decode a word phoneme by phoneme and then blend the sounds together. In a much larger study than that of Cupples and Iacono (2002), Conners, Rosenquist, Sligh, Atwell, and Kiser (2006) used a similar age group (ages 7–12) and the same level of intellectual capability (IQs in the mild to moderate range), but these study participants had a variety of ID etiologies, none of which was Down syndrome. Conners et al. matched 40 students on age, IQ, nonword reading, language, phonemic awareness, knowledge of letters/sounds, sight-word reading, verbal working memory, and articulation speed. With the instructional group, the researchers provided 22 lessons of 20 minutes' duration each, which were taught over an 8–11 week period, 2–3 days a week. Students were taught sound blending, sound matching, and sounding out a VC (vowel-consonant) or CVC (consonant -vowel-consonant) word. The control group received no special instruction. The instructional group performed significantly better than did the control group on sounding out words and nonwords. Students who began the study being able to read more words also performed better on sounding out words and nonwords. These findings are promising, given the short duration of this intervention and the number of factors on which the control group and the instructional group were similar. This study provides evidence that individuals with moderate intellectual impairments are able to benefit from interventions in PA and synthetic phonics training.

PA and Phonics Within the Context of Comprehensive Reading Interventions

Recent studies with students with IDs have incorporated PA and phonics into complete curriculum packages in which all five areas of the NRP effective reading practices are included. Although there are definite advantages in conducting studies of this kind, combining treatments across these areas makes it difficult to disentangle the effects of one component on another. For example, blending or segmenting may have been facilitated by introducing these skills and immediately following them with reading these words in connected text. Research that limits interventions to more specific strategies may result in more specific answers about the efficacy of that intervention across a number of contexts. Conversely, children with IDs have known problems with generalizing their learning. For PA and phonics instruction especially, it seems that a more natural context is likely to result in students understanding why they are engaging in these activities, and is more likely to result in sustained motivation and, as a result, better achievement.

Because of their known difficulties in phonological skills, memory, and in generalizing what they have learned, individuals with Down syndrome are likely to benefit from multicomponent studies. Goetz et al. (2008) conducted one in which learning assistants taught a group of 15 children ages 8–14 with Down syndrome via modified, commercial, phonics-based materials to articulate, blend, and segment sounds. In one-to-one sessions lasting 40 minutes each, five days a week for 16 weeks (group 1) or 8 weeks (group 2), an assistant provided a highly structured session that included a letter and sound for the day, book work, practice on segmenting and blending, more sounds, and reading from a list. Students' letter–sound knowledge showed significant improvement after intervention. PA measures included both initial and final phoneme matching (pictorially presented) tasks. Performance on these tasks was measured pre-, mid-, and postintervention and at a follow-up time five months later. Although there were improvements in reading, using word and nonword subtests from the British Ability Scales II, these differences were not statistically significant; however, the gains the children made were maintained when tested five months after the intervention. At first glance, these results might seem discouraging given the apparent intensity of the intervention; however, it should be noted that this was a balanced reading intervention (i.e., containing book reading and other activities), and not all of the 40-minute session was devoted to practicing the phonics skills. Given the short duration of the study, it is encouraging that improvement, although not significant, was shown in nonword reading.

Using a shorter and less intense treatment time as the one by Goetz et al. (2008), a descriptive study by Lemons and Fuchs (2010a) also had multiple components. The researchers used the same format and lesson plan for reading strategies as had been piloted in a descriptive study by Al Otaiba and Hosp (2004). Lemons and Fuchs included 24 children with Down syndrome ages 7–16 who could read at least one word and one letter sound and had intelligible speech. Children received two 30-minute instructional sessions per day, five days a week for six weeks. These one-to-one tutoring sessions, conducted by highly trained tutors, included PA, letter–sound knowledge, and reading of decodable, sight, and nonsense words. In addition to the specific lesson plan, which was administered with high fidelity, the tutors used a positive reinforcement behavior management strategy. This descriptive study did not include a control group, instead focusing on each child's differential growth and the factors that led to or detracted from it. Results showed that students made significant gains in their knowledge of letter sounds, taught sight words, and decodable words. The factor that correlated with better posttreatment performance in decoding was higher pretreatment word identification scores. Similarly, students with more advanced phoneme segmentation skills prior to the study had higher posttreatment scores in ability to decode nonsense words. Because Lemons and Fuchs's study was not a true experimental design, these results must be viewed with some caution, and growth cannot be said to be causally related to treatment. We note, however, that their sophisticated statistical analyses of growth allowed the researchers to be fairly confident in predictors of responsiveness to treatment.

Similar to Lemons and Fuchs's (2010a) study in its attention to individual student growth, Browder et al. (2008) conducted an intervention study lasting one academic year. The study included the use of a researcher-designed reading curriculum for children with significant disabilities, including children with moderate IDs, with 23 children ages 8–11 years who read below a first-grade level. The researchers' curriculum focused on early literacy skills of print awareness and phonemic awareness, phonics, vocabulary, and comprehension for students with IDs who also had difficulty with verbal responses. The dependent measures for phonemic awareness/phonics included the ability to tap out phonemes, identify letter–sound correspondences, identify first and last sounds, blend, and segment. Using a randomized control group design, Browder et al. compared the performance of the 12 students assigned to the reading curriculum against the 11 students assigned to the control group. Results indicated that the students in the treatment condition showed higher performance on their measure of phonemic awareness and phonics.

While Browder et al.'s (2008) study was impressive in terms of the length of the intervention, Allor, Mathes, Roberts, Jones, and Champlin (2010) reported an even longer intervention lasting two years. Their longitudinal study was a comprehensive approach to all five NRP areas of effective reading instruction that used continuous progress monitoring for growth modeling, and offered systematic and scientifically based reading instruction to 16 students in grades 1–4 (mean age = 9 years) who were diagnosed with moderate IDs (scores of 40–55); 12 similar students composed the contrast group and were not offered any special instruction outside of their normal classroom strategies. The majority of these students (*N* = 23) received their education in self-contained special education classrooms, and four were in the general education classroom with pull-out services. Allor et al.'s curriculum consisted of instructional strands that included concepts of print, phonological/phoneme awareness and phonics (i.e., clapping the number of syllables in a word, initial sound isolation, phoneme segmentation and blending, phoneme discrimination), letter knowledge, word recognition, fluency with connected text, comprehension strategies, and vocabulary and language development. Treatment was given in small groups of 1–4 students in daily sessions, five days per week, that lasted approximately 40 minutes per session for two years. Statistically significant differences were found in phonemic awareness, phonics, vocabulary, and comprehension, favoring the treatment group. This impressive study was based on the idea that given sufficient amounts of time and systematic reading instruction, comprehensive and consistent individuals with moderate IDs can and do progress in their reading skills.

Cautions About PA, Phonics, and Students With IDs

As illustrated earlier in this chapter, individuals with IDs are likely more at risk of complicating factors in PA and phonics, because they often have learning characteristics that could interact in unforeseen ways. There are innumerable combinations of characteristics within the population of children with IDs that could either work as strengths or deficits within the context of PA and phonics. Teachers must be cognizant of how these characteristics might impact their interventions with these students. Because much of the research to date has been conducted with individuals with Down syndrome, we use this subgroup as an illustrative case. Despite variability in this group, there are important common characteristics. For example, problems with cognitive processing speed, generalization and transfer (Silverman, 2007), hearing, auditory processing, articulation and speech production (Chapman & Hesketh, 2000; Roberts, Price, & Malkin, 2007; Stoel-Gammon, 1997), language (Abbeduto, Warren, & Conners, 2007), and short-term memory (Gathercole & Alloway, 2006) could directly impact acquisition of phonological skills.

Because children with Down syndrome most frequently differ from typically developing children not only in cognitive characteristics but also in other characteristics that could affect learning (e.g., mastery motivation; Wishart, 2001), it is reasonable to assume that interactions with instructional strategies for PA and phonics could be significant. Beyond the characteristics that can be viewed as "problems," individuals with Down syndrome are known to have relative strengths in the area of visual processing (Silverman, 2007), which could also affect how phonological processing is mitigated in the process of reading. Although reading achievement is quite variable (Rynders et al., 1997; Turner & Alborz, 2003), individuals with Down syndrome seem to achieve a greater ability to read than would be predicted based on their learning characteristics (Abbeduto et al., 2007; Byrne, MacDonald, & Buckley, 2002). Although there are no easy answers to dealing with these issues, they must be kept in mind when designing interventions.

Vocabulary

Because individuals with IDs are known to have particular problems with vocabulary, this is another area of intense need. To read words, and generally decode them, children must have these words in their vocabularies. Teaching functional sight words is, by its nature, a type of vocabulary-building activity for these children; however, it is necessary to go beyond the concrete lists of words that are generally part of this type of instruction. The NRP (NICHD, 2000) recommended that vocabulary should be directly taught through repetition and multiple exposures, as well as incidentally. The panel made a particular reference to the utility of computer-based learning and emphasized the importance of active interaction with the student when introducing vocabulary.

In an article describing research-based techniques for teaching reading to individuals with IDs, Allor, Mathes, Champlin, and Cheatham (2009) discussed the importance of building vocabulary beyond what is encountered in this population's beginning reading vocabulary. The researchers described techniques used in a successful two-year study, discussed previously, and suggested that reading aloud to students is necessary. Allor et al. selected books to target vocabulary words and provide structured opportunities for discussion. They recommended using pictures, videos, and simple but interactive games that provide examples and nonexamples of concepts. These instructional approaches used to increase vocabulary generally are not more different than those used for typically developing children.

Children with IDs who have more complex speech/language needs, such as those with Down syndrome or children with autism who also have IDs, might require more specialized language intervention. Indeed, some children with IDs may have no expressive language (e.g., children with cerebral palsy and IDs) and must rely on electronic augmentative communication devices that produce speech output. These devices must be programmed to contain vocabulary that will allow them to participate in routine classroom activities, such as storytime, to gain the same benefit as children who can speak (Da Fonte, Pufpaff, & Taber-Doughty, 2010).

Other complicating speech/language issues for other subgroups of children with IDs, such as problems with grammar or morphological analysis skills (e.g., not understanding that *-ed* means past tense or an ending *s* means plural) may require further modification of typical vocabulary-building strategies. For children with particular disabilities known to be associated with complex language issues such as Down syndrome, fragile X syndrome (the most common cause of inherited IDs), or Williams syndrome (see Kumin, 2001; Mervis & Becerra, 2003; Mervis & John, 2008; Roberts, Chapman, & Warren, 2008), it seems reasonable for teachers to consult with experts such as speech/language clinicians to understand both strengths and weaknesses to assist in the development of vocabulary interventions for these children.

Reading Fluency

Reading fluency is often defined as the ability to read individual words accurately and rapidly (Samuels, Ediger, & Fautsch-Patridge, 2005). This definition is not consistent with the NRP's (NICHD, 2000) definition, which is tied to connected text comprehension. The NRP's definition includes automatic word recognition and reading with speed and accuracy, but it also includes the use of proper expression, or prosody. For instance, when presented with a question mark at the end of a sentence, the reader's voice should rise. It would be impossible to read with appropriate expression if the reader did not comprehend the connected text; thus, current definitions of *fluency* also include text comprehension. Word recognition must be automatic, but automatic word recognition does not necessarily lead to fluency (Samuels et al., 2005). In other words, fluent reading is more than mindless "barking at print" (Samuels, 2007, p. 563). Samuels's notion of barking at print (i.e., accurately reading the words aloud but not understanding the meaning) is one that is sometimes heard in reference to individuals with IDs.

Word-level fluency or automatic word recognition must be attained before a reader can become truly fluent. The transition from sounding out the word to automatic recognition is difficult for students with IDs (e.g., Allor et al., 2009). One technique to encourage automatic word recognition is to tell students to read words "the fast way" when they know the word well enough to skip sounding out. In addition, Allor et al.'s study had students read decodable text, read in unison, or do repeated readings (for a description of repeated readings, see Samuels, 1997).

Another issue related to reading fluency is that current fluency assessments rely on reading aloud. Given the speech/language disabilities of many students with IDs, it is difficult to determine whether their halting tone is a reflection of a lack of automatic word recognition, or a reflection of their expressive language problems. Thus, using fluency assessments that require reading aloud could be considered a discriminatory assessment practice according to special education law (e.g., IDEA of 2004).

Comprehension

Building reading comprehension is perhaps the biggest challenge in teaching reading to students with IDs. If a student has difficulty understanding the spoken message, it is likely that he or she will also have difficulty with written language. Some students with IDs are likely to have problems with language comprehension (e.g., those with Down syndrome), background knowledge, understanding concepts, understanding simple syntactic relationships (e.g., long sentences with conjunctions), or morphology (e.g., the addition of –ed to a verb indicates past tense). In a small study by Roch and Levorato (2009), individuals with Down syndrome were able to read more words than a nondisabled reading-matched control group but performed lower on measures of reading comprehension. Listening comprehension predicted reading comprehension for both groups, but for children with Down syndrome, the ability to accurately read single words did not correlate with their ability to comprehend what they read. Word reading for the reading-matched controls was related to comprehension. This finding is problematic and needs further investigation, but it illustrates the complexity of issues in investigating comprehension in the Down syndrome population.

Another complicating factor in reading comprehension is assessment. The nature of characteristics associated with IDs sometimes results in difficulty with typical response formats. For example, children who have difficulty with expressive language may not be able to formulate answers to comprehension questions but could demonstrate their understanding by selecting an answer from a multiple-choice format.

The NRP (NICHD, 2000) listed eight strategies that are useful for reading comprehension: comprehension monitoring, cooperative learning, graphic and semantic organizers, story structure, question answering, question generation, summarization, and multiple-strategy teaching, in which the reader uses several of the procedures in interaction with the teacher. Most of these strategies have not been implemented in scientific studies of reading with students with IDs. However, Allor and colleagues (2009) appear to have successfully included all of these strategies over the duration of their two-year study, suggesting that they are feasible to implement with this population.

In discussing the reading comprehension interventions for students with IDs in their study, Allor et al. (2009) explained the gradual inclusion of comprehension strategies into the student's reading experience. Early comprehension development was primarily focused on reading both narrative and expository books to the students. Basic story grammar, sequencing, discussion consisting of question asking and question generation on the part of the students, and simple graphic organizers were used to ensure that students understood the content. As students progressed in their word recognition skills, the focus shifted from reading books aloud to them to having them read books themselves. The comprehension strategies used early were continued as new, more sophisticated ones were added, including most of the remaining suggestions given by the NRP. After two years in the study, Allor et al. found growth in the area of comprehension, but not significantly more than growth made by the equivalent control group receiving typical special education.

Summary

The research discussed in this chapter suggests that individuals with IDs may be capable of making progress in each of the major components of reading of the NRP report: phonological/phoneme awareness, phonics, vocabulary, fluency, and comprehension (NICHD, 2000). We devoted much of our discussion to phonological/phoneme awareness and phonics, because little research has been done in this area for individuals with IDs, probably because of continued focus on using a sight word–based approach. It appears that this most important characteristic of PA and particularly phoneme awareness are areas that are amenable to remediation in this population. Although little intervention research has been conducted, it seems likely that PA and specifically phoneme awareness will be an area that will require considerable time and effort to address in this population. Indeed, each of the NRP's five components of reading are likely to need substantial and systematic attention to show progress toward literacy for individuals with IDs. Our discussion of research relating to these areas demonstrates promising approaches with new lines of research, but much more needs to be done.

Given the least dangerous assumption (Donnellan, 1984), the instructional strategies used for typically developing children in each of the five reading components should probably be used to teach students with IDs to read. At the same time, educators need to be aware of the great variety of needs within this population. Cognitive characteristics, such as impaired short-term auditory memory, speech and language issues, processing time, increased time to learn, deficits in background knowledge, and ability to generalize, are problems that need to be directly addressed at the outset of intervention planning for each reading component. Such factors may also complicate how we obtain reliable and valid assessment information about the reading skills of students with IDs and their responsiveness to intervention. Whatever assessment procedures are used to determine progress for students with IDs, teachers should be aware that these students may possess the requisite skills but be unable to show it because of their cognitive characteristics and the way the questions are being asked (see Bertelson, 1993).

Because of the impact the cognitive characteristics may have on the specific intervention chosen, teachers need to be able to determine the success of various strategies and be open to changing it if it becomes necessary. Each child must be given instruction that is individually determined. Allor et al. (2010), when describing their reading curriculum, note the importance of tailoring the strategies to promote success. They also clearly describe how they use progress monitoring to ensure that adequate progress is being made across the relevant measures of the reading curriculum. Use of graphically presented performance data taken at routine intervals allows for prompt attention to strategies that may not be working for the student. Teachers may then choose to modify a teaching strategy, provide more intensive one-on-one instruction, or provide more time on task.

We began our chapter with the assertion that for students with IDs, reading is a critical skill. Their reading achievement must go beyond decontextualized learning of "survival" words, not only because most of these individuals are capable of doing so, but also because by becoming readers, they will more fully enjoy the quality of life they deserve.

Questions for Reflection

1. For what reasons was a sight-based approach historically used with children with IDs, and why is it a potentially discriminatory practice?

2. Think of students you know with IDs. What are the cognitive characteristics of these children (e.g., significant problems with articulation), and how would these characteristics impact the use of available instruction materials for each of the five areas of reading instruction?

3. What are the reasons why using progress monitoring is particularly important for children with IDs?

REFERENCES

Abbeduto, L., Warren, S.F., & Conners, F.A. (2007). Language development in Down syndrome: From the prelinguistic period to the acquisition of literacy. *Mental Retardation and Developmental Disabilities Research Reviews, 13*(3), 247–261. doi:10.1002/mrdd.20158

Adams, M.J. (1990). *Beginning to read: Thinking and learning about print.* Cambridge, MA: MIT Press.

Allor, J.H., Mathes, P.G., Champlin, T., & Cheatham, J.P. (2009). Research-based techniques for teaching early reading skills to students with intellectual disabilities. *Education and Training in Developmental Disabilities, 44*(3), 356–366.

Allor, J.H., Mathes, P.G., Jones, F.G., Champlin, T.M., & Cheatham, J.P. (2010). Individualized research-based reading instruction for students with intellectual disabilities: Success stories. *Teaching Exceptional Children, 42*(3), 6–12.

Allor, J.H., Mathes, P.G., Roberts, J.K., Jones, F.G., & Champlin, T.M. (2010). Teaching students with moderate intellectual disabilities to read: An experimental examination of a comprehensive reading intervention. *Education and Training in Autism and Developmental Disabilities, 45*(1), 3–22.

Al Otaiba, S., & Hosp, M.K. (2004). Providing effective literacy instruction to students with Down syndrome. *Teaching Exceptional Children, 36*(4), 28–35.

American Association on Intellectual and Developmental Disabilities. (2010). *Definition of intellectual disability.* Retrieved November 19, 2010, from www.aamr.org/content_100.cfm?navID=21

American Psychiatric Association. (2000). *Diagnostic and statistical manual of mental disorders* (4th ed., text rev.). Arlington, VA: Author.

Anthony, J.L., & Lonigan, C.J. (2004). The nature of phonological awareness: Converging evidence from four studies of preschool and early grade school children. *Journal of Educational Psychology, 96*(1), 43–55. doi:10.1037/0022-0663.96.1.43

Bertelson, P. (1993). Reading acquisition and phonemic awareness testing: How conclusive are data from Down's syndrome? (Remarks on Cossu, Rossini, and Marshall, 1993). *Cognition, 48*(3), 281–283. doi:10.1016/0010-0277(93)90043-U

Browder, D.M., Ahlgrim-Delzell, L., Courtade, G., Gibbs, S.L., & Flowers, C. (2008). Evaluation of the effectiveness of an early literacy program for students with significant developmental disabilities. *Exceptional Children, 75*(1), 33–52. doi:10.1177/0741932508315054

Browder, D.M., Wakeman, S.Y., Spooner, F., Ahlgrim-Delzell, L., & Algozzine, B. (2006). Research on reading instruction for individuals with significant cognitive disabilities. *Exceptional Children, 72*(4), 392–408.

Byrne, A., MacDonald, J., & Buckley, S. (2002). Reading, language and memory skills: A comparative longitudinal study of children with Down syndrome and their mainstream peers. *British Journal of Educational Psychology, 72*(4), 513–529. doi:10.1348/0007 0990260377497

Chapman, R.S., & Hesketh, L.J. (2000). Behavioral phenotype of individuals with Down syndrome. *Mental Retardation and Developmental Disabilities Research Reviews, 6*(2), 84–95. doi:10.1002/1098-2779 (2000)6:2<84::AID-MRDD2>3.0.CO;2-P

Conners, F.A., Rosenquist, C.J., Sligh, A.C., Atwell, J.A., & Kiser, T. (2006). Phonological reading skills acquisition by children with mental retardation. *Research in Developmental Disabilities, 27*(2), 121–137. doi:10.1016/j.ridd.2004.11.015

Cossu, G., Rossini, F., & Marshall, J.C. (1993). When reading is acquired but phonemic awareness is not: A study of literacy in Down's syndrome. *Cognition, 46*(2), 129–138. doi:10.1016/0010-0277(93)90016-O

Cupples, L., & Iacono, T. (2002). The efficacy of 'whole word' *versus* 'analytic' reading instruction for children with Down syndrome. *Reading and Writing, 15*(5/6), 549–574. doi:10.1023/A:1016385114848

Da Fonte, M.A., Pufpaff, L.A., & Taber-Doughty, T. (2010). Vocabulary use during storybook reading: Implications for children with augmentative and alternative communication needs. *Psychology in the Schools, 47*(5), 514–524.

Donnellan, A.M. (1984). The criterion of the least dangerous assumption. *Behavioral Disorders, 9*(2), 141–150.

Fautsch-Patridge, T. (2008). *Phonological awareness and initial reading acquisition in individuals with Down syndrome*. Unpublished manuscript, University of Minnesota, Minneapolis.

Gathercole, S.E., & Alloway, T.P. (2006). Practitioner review: Short-term and working memory impairments in neurodevelopmental disorders: Diagnosis and remedial support. *Journal of Child Psychology and Psychiatry, 47*(1), 4–15. doi:10.1111/j.1469-7610.2005.01446.x

Goetz, K., Hulme, C., Brigstocke, S., Carroll, J.M., Nasir, L., & Snowling, M. (2008). Training reading and phoneme awareness skills in children with Down syndrome. *Reading and Writing, 21*(4), 395–412. doi:10.1007/s11145-007-9089-3

Joseph, L.M., & Seery, M.E. (2004). Where is the phonics? A review of the literature on the use of phonetic analysis with students with mental retardation. *Remedial and Special Education, 25*(2), 88–94. doi:10.1177/07419325040250020301

Katims, D.S. (1991). Emergent literacy in early childhood special education: Curriculum and instruction. *Topics in Early Childhood Special Education, 11*(1), 69–84. doi:10.1177/027112149101100108

Katims, D.S. (2000). Literacy instruction for people with mental retardation: Historical highlights and contemporary analysis. *Education and Training in Mental Retardation and Developmental Disabilities, 35*(1), 3–15.

Kliewer, C. (1998). Citizenship in the literate community: An ethnography of children with Down syndrome and the written word. *Exceptional Children, 64*(2), 167–180.

Kliewer, C., & Biklen, D. (2001). "School's not really a place for reading": A research synthesis of the literate lives of students with severe disabilities. *Journal of the Association for Persons With Severe Handicaps, 26*(1), 1–12.

Kliewer, C., Biklen, D., & Kasa-Hendrickson, C. (2006). Who may be literate? Disability and resistance to the cultural denial of competence. *American Educational Research Journal, 43*(2), 163–192. doi: 10.3102/00028312043002163

Kumin, L. (2001). *Classroom language skills for children with Down syndrome: A guide for parents and teachers*. Bethesda, MD: Woodbine House.

Lemons, C.J., & Fuchs, D. (2010a). Modeling response to reading intervention in children with Down syndrome: An examination of predictors of differential growth. *Reading Research Quarterly, 45*(2), 134–168. doi:10.1598/RRQ.45.2.1

Lemons, C.J., & Fuchs, D. (2010b). Phonological awareness of children with Down syndrome: Its role in learning to read and the effectiveness of related interventions. *Research in Developmental Disabilities, 31*(2), 316–330. doi:10.1016/j.ridd.2009.11.002

Lonigan, C.J., & Shanahan, T. (2009). *Executive summary: Developing early literacy: Report of the National Early Literacy Panel*. Washington, DC: National Institute for Literacy.

Mervis, C.B., & Becerra, A.M. (2003). Lexical development and intervention. In J.A. Rondal & S. Buckley (Eds.), *Speech and language intervention in Down syndrome* (pp. 63–85). London: Whurr.

Mervis, C.B., & John, A.E. (2008). Vocabulary abilities of children with Williams syndrome: Strengths, weaknesses, and relation to visuospatial construction ability. *Journal of Speech, Language, and Hearing Research, 51*, 967–982. doi:10.1044/1092-4388(2008/071)

National Institute of Child Health and Human Development. (2000). *Report of the National Reading Panel. Teaching children to read: An evidence-based assessment of the scientific research literature on reading and its implications for reading instruction* (NIH Publication No. 00-4769). Washington, DC: U.S. Government Printing Office.

Peeters, M., Verhoeven, L., van Balkom, H., & de Moor, J. (2008). Foundations of phonological awareness in pre-school children with cerebral palsy: The impact of intellectual disability. *Journal of Intellectual Disability Research, 52*(1), 68–78.

Phillips, B.M., Clancy-Menchetti, J., & Lonigan, C.J. (2008). Successful phonological awareness instruction with preschool children: Lessons from the classroom. *Topics in Early Childhood Special Education, 28*(1), 3–17. doi:10.1177/0271121407313813

Roberts, J.E., Chapman, R.S., & Warren S.F. (Eds.). (2008). *Speech and language development and intervention in Down syndrome and fragile X syndrome*. Baltimore: Paul H. Brookes.

Roberts, J.E., Price, J., & Malkin, C. (2007). Language and communication development in Down syndrome. *Mental Retardation and Developmental Disabilities Research Reviews, 13*(1), 26–35. doi:10.1002/mrdd.20136

Roch, M., & Levorato, M.C. (2009). Simple view of reading in Down's syndrome: The role of listening comprehension and reading skills. *International Journal of Language & Communication Disorders, 44*(2), 206–223. doi:10.1080/13682820802012061

Rynders, J., Abery, B.H., Spiker, D., Olive, M.L., Sheran, C.P., & Zajac, R.J. (1997). Improving educational programming for individuals with Down syndrome: Engaging the fuller competence. *Down Syndrome Quarterly, 2*(1), 1–11.

Samuels, S.J. (1997). The method of repeated readings. *The Reading Teacher, 50*(5), 376–381.

Samuels, S.J. (2007). The DIBELS tests: Is speed of barking at print what we mean by reading fluency? *Reading Research Quarterly, 42*(4), 563–566.

Samuels, S.J., Ediger, K., & Fautsch-Patridge, T. (2005). The importance of fluent reading. *New England Reading Association Journal, 41*(1), 1–8.

Saunders, K.J. (2007). Word-attack skills in individuals with mental retardation. *Mental Retardation and Developmental Disabilities Research Reviews, 13*(1), 78–84. doi:10.1002/mrdd.20137

Share, D.L. (1995). Phonological recoding and self-teaching: *Sine qua non* of reading acquisition. *Cognition, 55*(2), 151–218. doi:10.1016/0010-0277(94)00645-2

Shaywitz, S. (2003). *Overcoming dyslexia: A new and complete science-based program for reading problems at any level*. New York: Alfred A. Knopf.

Shaywitz, S.E., Morris, R., & Shaywitz, B.A. (2008). The education of dyslexic children from childhood to young adulthood. *Annual Review of Psychology, 59*, 451–475. doi:10.1146/annurev.psych.59.103006.093633

Silverman, W. (2007). Down syndrome: Cognitive phenotype. *Mental Retardation and Developmental Disabilities Research Reviews, 13*(3), 228–236. doi:10.1002/mrdd.20156

Stoel-Gammon, C. (1997). Phonological development in Down syndrome. *Mental Retardation and Developmental Disabilities Research Reviews, 3*(4), 300–306. doi:10.1002/(SICI)1098-2779(1997)3:4<300::AID-MRDD4>3.0.CO;2-R

Turner, S., & Alborz, A. (2003). Academic attainments of children with Down's syndrome: A longitudinal study. *British Journal of Educational Psychology, 73*(4), 563–583. doi:10.1348/000709903322591244

U.S. Department of Education, Office of Special Education and Rehabilitative Services. (2004). Overview information; Special education—research and innovation to improve services and results for children with disabilities—reading interventions for students with mental retardation; notice inviting applicants for new awards for fiscal year (FY) 2004. *Federal Register, 69*(133), 42044–42049.

van Bysterveldt, A.K., Gillon, G.T., & Moran, C. (2006). Enhancing phonological awareness and letter knowledge in preschool children with Down syndrome. *International Journal of Disability, Development and Education, 53*(3), 301–329. doi:10.1080/10349120600847706

Wagner, R.K., & Torgesen, J.K. (1987). The nature of phonological processing and its causal role in the acquisition of reading skills. *Psychological Bulletin, 101*(2), 192–212. doi:10.1037/0033-2909.101.2.192

Wehmeyer, M.L. (2006). Beyond access: Ensuring progress in the general education curriculum for students with severe disabilities. *Research and Practice for Persons With Severe Disabilities, 31*(4), 322–326.

Wishart, J. (2001). Motivation and learning styles in young children with Down syndrome. *Down Syndrome Research and Practice, 7*(2), 47–51.

Chapter 10

Research on Reading/Learning Disability Interventions

Richard L. Allington

Recent educational reforms have muddied the waters when it comes to considering the conceptualization of reading and learning difficulties. Observe the political rhetoric in the United States—"all children reading on grade level by grade 4"—and legislative mandates that establish reading achievement standards for promotion to the next grade. Even taking into account the glibness of political rhetoric, such reform goals represent a substantial shift in educational policy. For most of the 20th century it was expected that half of children would, necessarily, read somewhere below "grade level," whereas half would read above. This was, of course, the result of defining *grade level* psychometrically as the average achievement of children in any given grade. When defined this way, "getting everyone on or above grade level" means everyone being average or above—a mathematical impossibility. Nonetheless, legislative calls for all children to read on grade level abound.

Basic to understanding the current confusion about achievement levels is the history of the U.S. National Assessment of Educational Progress (NAEP) and the shift in reporting NAEP achievement from a *relative* standard—how students performed on an administration of the test relative to performance on previous administrations—to an *absolute* standard—how many students achieve a level of performance set a priori as the desired level. Thus, the reports of NAEP performance have moved from generally positive during the early years of the assessment program, when students were said to be reading a bit better than they used to, to largely negative—too few students meet the newly established absolute standard. However, NAEP performances show no absolute decline in reading achievement across the test's 30-year history (National Center for Education Statistics [NCES], 2009). In fact, at grade 4, reading achievement is at an all-time high, with a pattern of small gains in achievement since 1992.

What Research Has to Say About Reading Instruction (4th ed.) edited by S. Jay Samuels and Alan E. Farstrup.
© 2011 by the International Reading Association.

Still, about a third of all fourth-grade students are reported to perform below the "basic" level in reading, with basic being a predetermined absolute level of achievement. This suggests that "basic" approximates what had been grade-level achievement for most of the 20th century. That is, with approximately two-thirds of the students above and a third below the basic level, that level is just a bit below the average achievement that had been the relative standard.

Whether the average achievement of fourth graders on the NAEP is too low or whether the NAEP absolute standard is too high is a political question, not a research issue per se. However, U.S. fourth graders ranked among the better readers in the world in the most recent international assessments of reading proficiency (although the U.S. ranking declines steadily after fourth grade) (NCES, 2002). This performance suggests that, at least compared with the international competition, U.S. elementary schools are producing elementary-aged children who read reasonably well.

Finally, states are now required to set absolute standards for students at each grade level from 3 to 8. These standards vary enormously and almost none is as rigorous as the NAEP standards (Ravitch, 2010). The U.S. Department of Education supports the adoption of common curriculum standards across states, along with common absolute standards. All of this will require states to substantially revise their current reading assessments and current absolute standards.

The Shifting Nature of Reading Difficulties

The preceding seems necessary as an introduction to any chapter on research into reading difficulties because political discourse and the media often suggest that large numbers of U.S. children are failing to learn to read (e.g., Sweet, 1997), despite accumulated evidence that indicates a very different situation, at least when considered in historic, relative terms. At the same time, setting the absolute "proficient" standard on the NAEP at a level currently achieved by roughly one-quarter of U.S. students has created both an impression that students are not achieving at sufficiently high levels and the possibility that more children might be identified as experiencing difficulties in reading development. The use of new and higher standards of adequacy and the practice of attaching high stakes to those standards (e.g., retention in grade for those failing to achieve the standard, mandating summer school programs for such children, limiting local control when many children fall below the standard) will undoubtedly influence how reading difficulties are conceived and, possibly, redefined.

That said, it seems obvious that too many U.S. children do experience difficulty learning to read and that too few schools or school districts have developed instructional plans that reflect what we have learned about teaching all children to read. Studies indicate that virtually all children entering kindergarten in a public school can achieve grade-level reading proficiencies by the end of first grade (Mathes et al., 2005; Phillips & Smith, 1997/2010; Vellutino et al., 1996). All too predictably, it is the children of poverty whose reading achievement is most often deemed unacceptably low (Entwisle, Alexander, & Olson, 1997), and because minority children are overrepresented among the poor (Wagner, 1995), far too many minority children struggle with literacy acquisition. Unfortunately, explanations of reading difficulties have moved away from a focus on economic disadvantage.

Today, traditional reading difficulties have largely been redefined as learning disabilities. McGill-Franzen (1987) made an early identification of this redefining. She noted that dating from the passage of the Education for All Handicapped Children Act in 1975 there was a steady increase in publication of articles on reading difficulties in special education journals (e.g., *Journal of Learning Disabilities*) and a decline in the publication of such articles in reading journals (e.g., *The Reading Teacher*). Likewise, during this period there was a shift of children from remedial reading programs into special education (learning disability) programs and a shift in federal funding for teacher education from reading teacher preparation to the preparation of special education teachers. In McGill-Franzen's view, the decade between 1975 and 1985 initiated a redefinition of the locus of reading difficulties from an emphasis on economic disadvantage to one that positioned reading difficulties as individual disability. The prominence of learning disability and dyslexia research (Lyon & Moats, 1997), especially that funded by the National Institute of Child Health and Human Development (NICHD), in federal and state legislative activity suggests McGill-Franzen was prescient in her observations.

Linked to this reconceptualization were incentives created for redefining reading difficulties as a disability. First, there was the fiscal incentive. As U.S. federal funding for remedial reading programs (e.g., Title I) declined in real dollars, there was an increased allocation for special education. In addition, federal regulations made children eligible for but did not mandate remedial services (nor did they mandate state funding for them). In contrast, identification of children as learning disabled created an entitlement for special educational services and mandated funding (McGill-Franzen & Goatley, 2002).

Second, identifying children experiencing difficulties as learning disabled routinely exempted them from participating in new state educational accountability schemes. Although children in remedial reading programs took state reading tests and had their results included in the reports of school achievement patterns, the performances of children identified as learning disabled typically were not included in such reports. Schools intent on demonstrating improved achievement could (and often did) identify large numbers of lower achieving children as learning disabled and then reported a manufactured improvement that resulted from the exclusion of these children's results (Allington & McGill-Franzen, 1992; McGill-Franzen, 1994). This issue appeared on the U.S. political agenda after reports of improved performance on the NAEP by some states were followed by reports of substantial increases in the number of low-achieving children exempted from that assessment (Hoff, 1999). Thus, in 1998, Congress legislated inclusion of students with disabilities on state and national assessments of reading proficiency (Heubert & Hauser, 1999). The passage of the No Child Left Behind (NCLB) Act of 2001 included pupils with disabilities as a group whose performance contributed to determining "adequate yearly progress." Now, schools were required to demonstrate that pupils with disabilities were making progress toward on-level literacy proficiency.

The result of the redefinition of reading difficulties also can be seen in the professional consensus that most children identified as learning disabled experience difficulty in acquiring reading and writing proficiencies (Allington & McGill-Franzen, 1996; Lyon & Moats, 1997). Although remedial reading programs still exist, the substantial expansion in the number of students identified as learning disabled over the past 30 years—from 120,000 in 1968 to 2.7 million in 2007 (Cortiella, 2009)—indicates that children experiencing difficulties in reading acquisition are now routinely identified as learning disabled and served in special education programs.

Two problems arise from these issues involved in discussing reading/learning disabilities. First, given the new standards, which students should be considered to be experiencing reading difficulties? And which exhibit learning disabilities? Second, because none of the research currently available has benchmarked student performance against the new standards, what research can be useful in considering the design of effective interventions?

Who Is Reading/Learning Disabled?

Historically, reading achievement had to lag substantively behind what was considered a "normal" pace of reading acquisition for a reading difficulty to be identified. Various schemes were proposed and implemented over the years for identifying which children were candidates for intervention (Harris & Sipay, 1990). In the simplest of these, an arbitrary cutoff level of performance was established (e.g., 27th percentile on a norm-referenced achievement test, or more than a year behind peers), or identification was simply a case of teacher referral. There also were more complicated schemes, which involved attempting to estimate whether a discrepancy existed between aptitude and achievement (e.g., using a measured estimate of intelligence to predicate an appropriate level of achievement, and comparing that with actual measured achievement) or whether certain diagnostic symptoms were present (e.g., visual–perceptual difficulties, letter or word reversals). However, many studies identified significant psychometric limitations of such schemes (e.g., Stanovich, 1991; Stanovich & Siegel, 1994).

More recently, the emphasis of intervention has shifted to whole-school models and in-class support services (LeTendre, 1991). In the former, programs are designed to enhance and intensify instruction for all children in the school, rather than to provide instructional support only for targeted children. In the latter, instructional support is provided in the general education classroom in an attempt to better coordinate such services with the core instructional plan and to foster collaboration between classroom and specialist teachers (Sindelar & Kilgore, 1996; Winfield, 1995). This emphasis on coordination seems to stem from the work of Borman and colleagues (Borman, Wong, Hedges, & D'Agostino, 2001), who found that Title I remediation programs that were well coordinated with classroom reading lessons produced higher academic gains.

Nonetheless, the problematic issue remains of deciding when difficulty in learning to read is sufficient to warrant some extraordinary instructional support, including, for example, tutorials, small-group supplemental instruction, or extended instructional time. Consider, for instance, that in a number of states and school districts, any student who fails to attain an absolute standard is retained in grade. Now, imagine that fewer than half of students achieve this standard. Would all those whose achievement falls below the standard be considered to be experiencing difficulties in reading acquisition? Would all qualify for extraordinary instructional support? Would they be considered reading disabled? Learning disabled? Given the high stakes (grade promotion) attached to achieving the standard, what rationale might be developed for not providing extraordinary instructional support for those students failing to meet it? Should 50% of U.S. students qualify for remedial reading services?

The recent political emphasis on all students achieving at a new, higher standard of reading proficiency produces new definitional issues that simply pile on top of the perennial definitional issues that have yet to be resolved. For instance, there has never been a universally accepted definition of *reading disability*. There has been no unified scheme for identifying which children receive remedial support services. Much the same can be said for the identification of children as learning disabled. This issue has plagued the profession since the first learning disability programs were founded. More than 35 years ago, Kirk and Elkins (1975) studied the characteristics of students identified as learning disabled in federally funded child service demonstration centers. Using the federal definition of specific learning disabilities as their benchmark, they noted,

> It would appear from the data that the majority of children in the projects, although underachieving to some degree, would not qualify as specific learning disabled children, since (a) many of the children were retarded equally in reading, spelling, and arithmetic and were therefore not specific but general in academic retardation, and (b) a substantial proportion were minor or moderate in their degree of under achievement. (p. 37)

They also noted that remedial and corrective reading students had the type of difficulty that most states considered to indicate "learning disabilities" (p. 34).

Fifteen years later, Chalfant (1989) noted the annual increases in the number of children inappropriately identified as learning disabled (even at a time when school enrollments were dropping) and pointed to the definitional difficulties as a primary factor: "Decisions for eligibility are often based on a student's need for some kind of special help rather than on whether or not a student meets rigorous eligibility criteria for learning disabilities services" (p. 395). He recommended capping learning disability enrollments at 2% of school enrollment, although he noted such a cap would be vigorously opposed by many interests. Roughly a decade later Congress seemed to follow his advice by mandating that by 2014, 98% of all school children would meet state grade-level proficiency standards as a major component of demonstrating that all children were making adequate yearly academic progress. Schools failing to meet this standard would usually be reconstituted.

Mercer, Jordan, Allsopp, and Mercer (1996) reported little evidence that official definitions of learning disabilities reflected current research. This continuing difficulty of definition was noted in the preface to an edited volume from a NICHD conference on learning disabilities:

> If we are to ultimately understand learning disabilities from a scientific and clinical perspective, the field must undertake a systematic effort to establish a precise definition for the disorder and a theoretically based classification system that is open to empirical scrutiny.... The development of a reliable and valid definition and classification system for learning disabilities is the most pressing scientific goal currently facing the field. (Lyon, Gray, Krasnegor, & Kavanagh, 1993, p. xvii)

Unfortunately, achieving such a goal will be difficult, if not impossible, for several reasons. Consider that both reading and learning disabilities are largely socially constructed (McGill-Franzen, 1987; Mehan, Hertweck, & Meihls, 1986; Sleeter, 1986; Taylor, 1998). That is, both terms exist only in certain societies—literate societies—and definitions of each have historically varied both within the profession and within schools. The concept of reading/learning difficulties only emerges after societies have developed to the point that schooling is nearly universal. When access to schooling is largely restricted, illiteracy is common and even expected. As school attendance becomes more common, expectations about literacy learning and the demands for literacy then increase and schools begin to identify children who are having difficulty in learning to read (Allington, 1994). Once a society provides a number of years of schooling for virtually all students, as is common in economically developed nations, the young adult who cannot read is in the minority. Once illiteracy is deemed abnormal and uncommon, it typically takes on negative connotations, and societies begin to attempt to explain the abnormality away.

This phenomenon operates in U.S. schools. Where there is high relative achievement (above the national norms), usually in schools located in economically advantaged neighborhoods, reading just below grade level can qualify a student for remedial services and for diagnostic testing designed to locate the etiology of the "difficulty." However, in a nearby school in a far less advantaged community, reading well below grade level will not likely lead to remedial services, nor will there be much evidence of concern for the etiology of the reading "problem"—if only because reading below grade level is common in too many schools that enroll mostly children from poor families.

For instance, for all the popularity of the Success for All (SFA) program in urban schools serving children from poor families, most children attending SFA schools exit fifth grade reading substantially below grade level. Venezky (1998) reanalyzed achievement data from five high-poverty SFA schools in Baltimore, Maryland. He noted that although there were substantive effects for SFA on achievement in kindergarten and first grade, students slipped steadily behind expectations after that point: 87.5% of students were reading below grade level at the end of fifth grade, and 30% were three or more years below expected achievement. At the end of fifth grade across the five SFA schools, the average reading achievement was at the 3.5 grade level—roughly 2.5 years behind grade level—according to results from the Iowa Test of Basic Skills.

Consider that using a definition of reading disability that targeted every child reading below grade level for remedial services would mean that, in these SFA schools, seven of every eight fifth-grade students would qualify for remediation. Using the most common achievement-based definitions of learning disabilities (i.e., students below a 2.9 achievement level, or the 50% discrepancy between grade placement and achievement) would mean that roughly one-third of the students would be eligible for that designation.

Are all low achievers actually reading/learning disabled? An enduring definitional difficulty has been the inability to sort children with a learning disability reliably from children who are experiencing difficulties with reading acquisition but have no learning disability (Spear-Swerling & Sternberg, 1996). Today, the situation is such that almost any child experiencing difficulty in reading could be labeled learning disabled (although the earlier quote from Kirk and Elkins [1975] suggests this has been a longstanding problem). After more than a quarter-century there is still no reliable psychometric instrument, battery, or process to identify which children might be learning disabled (Allington & McGill-Franzen, 1996). An abundance of research, however, indicates that reading difficulties can stem from many sources (Harris & Sipay, 1990; Johnston, 1997; Robinson, 1946)—perhaps, although rarely, even a neurologic basis—but that most children experiencing such difficulties can have their reading development accelerated when they have access to sufficient intensive and expert reading instruction (Vellutino & Fletcher, 2005). Unfortunately, identifying children as reading/learning disabled has not reliably increased their access to such instruction. Denton, Vaughn, and Fletcher (2003) note that most students identified as learning disabled never experience accelerated reading development once they receive special education services. Perhaps achievement is so low because the most common interventions have not been designed actually to accelerate literacy achievement. There is an abundance of research reporting that traditional intervention efforts typically do not enhance either the quantity or quality of literacy instruction (Allington & McGill-Franzen, 1989a, 1989b, 1996; Jenkins, Pious, & Peterson, 1988; McGill-Franzen & Allington, 1991; Puma et al., 1997; Thurlow, Ysseldyke, Graden, & Algozzine, 1984; Vaughn, Linan-Thompson, & Hickman, 2003). Baker and Zigmond (1995) offered a similar conclusion after studying inclusionary learning disability program interventions:

> We believe that students with [learning disabilities] in these models of inclusive education were getting a very good *general* education. They were being taught enthusiastically, not grudgingly, by general education teachers.... Whatever "special" instruction or coaching was needed by the student was generally provided by peers or paraprofessionals. And if a student needed more than that, special education pull-out services were "reinvented." (p. 175; emphasis in original)

> We saw very little "specially designed instruction" delivered uniquely to a student with [a learning disability]. We saw almost no specific, directed, individualized, intensive, remedial instruction of students who were clearly deficient academically and struggling with the schoolwork they were being given. (p. 178)

The available research offers little guidance for reliably identifying children experiencing reading/learning disabilities. Further, the large-scale evaluation studies of current programs offer little evidence of (a) any substantial effect on the achievement of reading/learning disability students or (b) any improved access to expert, intensive, personalized instruction for children served in current remedial and special education programs. Although the evaluation studies indicate few benefits of the current programs, they have been appropriately criticized for lumping together all types of interventions (Light & Pillemer, 1984). So, how might effective interventions be identified?

Research on Effective Interventions

The definitional ambiguities create difficulties in interpreting the research on effective reading/learning disability interventions. For instance, with no consensus on reliable identification criteria, the available research is fraught with multiple operational definitions of subjects in intervention research studies. In other words, if we select any 10 intervention studies from the literature, there would be a good chance that 10 different operational definitions of reading/learning disabilities were used in selecting the students for the intervention treatment. Even a quick look at the intervention literature will turn up some studies that used different school definitions to identify students considered reading/learning disabled even though there is substantial evidence that such definitions vary widely. At the same time, other studies using a more restrictive definition (e.g., achievement below the 15th percentile on a standardized assessment) also will be located, while still others use unique operational definitions. Given the variance in identification of students as reading/learning disabled, it is hardly surprising that the published literature on intervention often seems contradictory. The heterogeneity of the populations impedes the generalization of findings and the ability to replicate results (Lyon & Moats, 1997).

In addition, much of the intervention research has considered only basic skill assessments (e.g., pseudoword pronunciation, isolated word reading, oral reading accuracy, low-level multiple-choice assessments of comprehension) with incredibly few studies measuring summarization, response, or analysis of text. Even when they deem an intervention to be successful, few studies have reported significant improvements in comprehension and virtually none has reported outcomes on large-scale assessments or standardized tests based on new standards that focus on higher order literacy proficiencies (Allington & McGill-Franzen, 2009). In other words, we have more interventions that demonstrate improved pseudoword reading and word recognition in isolation than interventions that result in children actually meeting new literacy standards.

With the important limitations of definitional heterogeneity and limited outcome measures in mind, we can search for useful instructional guidelines that might be derived from the research. Here we can consider interventions of three sorts. First, we can design preventive interventions, which reliably reduce the incidence of reading difficulties. Second, we can create acceleration interventions, designed to accelerate learning so that the literacy development of participating children becomes comparable to their peers. Third, we need to consider longer term support interventions, which are designed to maintain on-level literacy development over time (Allington, 2006). This final intervention design has been little considered, resulting in too many children moving in and out of interventions programs—two years in, one year out, two years in, one year out—and never developing strong literacy proficiencies or habits. Schools, school districts, and state and federal education agencies should be working to create a more or less seamless system of instructional support—a system to replace the current fragmented patchwork of programs, initiatives, and personnel.

Preventive Designs

Some preventive interventions focus on creating more powerful early childhood programs as a strategy for reducing reading difficulties later. Others focus on restructuring primary grade instruction to enhance the instructional opportunities for children experiencing difficulty. Still others recommend adding instructional support programs so that, after early identification of difficulties in reading acquisition, extraordinary instruction designed to accelerate literacy development can be provided. In addition, family-focused interventions have become popular as educational and political leaders call for greater parent involvement in children's schooling. A comprehensive program design would include a coherent plan with each of these components (Allington & Cunningham, 2006; Walmsley & Allington, 1995).

Preschool and Kindergarten. High-quality preschool and kindergarten programs are proven preventive programs. For instance, the High Scope studies (Berrueta-Clement, Schweinhart, Barnett, Epstein, & Weikart, 1984) and the Abecedarian Project study (Frank Porter Graham Child Development Center, 1999) offer powerful evidence of the lasting benefits of early education programs on children's literacy development. Dickinson and Smith (1994), Whitehurst and Lonigan (1998), and McGill-Franzen and Lanford (1994), among others, provide substantial evidence of the benefits of story read-aloud experiences while also demonstrating that the sort of texts read and the adult's style of reading aloud are important factors in preschool literacy development.

A longstanding debate about kindergarten curriculum design has centered around a "skills versus meaning" instructional focus (Dahl, Scharer, Lawson, & Grogan, 1999; Knapp, 1995; Purcell-Gates, McIntyre, & Freppon, 1995; Schweinhart & Weikart, 1998). This seems a false dichotomy, however. Stahl and Miller (1989) completed a meta-analysis of the research on early childhood literacy curriculum and reported that the meaning focus seemed to produce greater benefits in kindergarten than did the skills focus. Likewise, Sacks and Mergendoller (1997) report a comparison of kindergarten outcomes in meaning-versus-skills kindergarten classrooms serving primarily low-income children. Again, the meaning-emphasis curriculum produced superior outcomes. The evidence also suggests, however, that (a) many kindergarten classrooms cannot be described as nicely fitting either emphasis and (b) the development of important emergent literacy proficiencies has often been neglected in kindergarten instruction.

Obviously, all early childhood and kindergarten programs are not equally effective, and many (if not most) could be enhanced if their instructional designs were more often research based. For instance, the work of McGill-Franzen and her colleagues (McGill-Franzen, 2006; McGill-Franzen, Allington, Yokoi, & Brooks, 1999; McGill-Franzen, Payne, & Dennis, 2010), Morrow, O'Connor, and Smith (1990), and Neuman (1999) provides evidence of important program design features for enhancing literacy development among kindergartners. A central feature of each of these efforts was dramatically enhancing children's experiences with print. Kindergarten programs that immerse children in books, stories, and opportunities to engage in writing activity of various sorts (both inventive and more structured) significantly fostered growth in literacy development. Given the evidence on the wide variability of preschool experiences with books, stories, and print, it is unsurprising that children from lower income families benefited enormously from these print-rich programs (McGill-Franzen et al., 1999; McGill-Franzen, Lanford, & Adams, 2002).

Scanlon, Vellutino, Small, Fanuele, and Sweeney (2005) compared a phonological skills-emphasis and a text-emphasis intervention with struggling kindergarten and first-grade students. The kindergarten students were provided twice weekly small-group instruction while the first graders received individual tutorial interventions. These researchers found that the kindergarten lessons significantly reduced the number of children who needed the first-grade intervention. The text-emphasis intervention produced the better results, but the phonological skills intervention produced better performance than demonstrated among the control students. The authors concluded, "It is clear that many children who were identified as poor readers at the beginning of first grade responded well to the instruction they received, regardless of the type of instruction provided" (p. 224). As you will soon see, this finding appears regularly in early intervention studies.

Class-Size Reduction. Class-size reduction does seem to be an effective preventive intervention design. Achilles (1999) provides a comprehensive review of the impact of class-size reduction on the reading proficiency of children. He details the Tennessee Student Teacher Achievement Ratio (STAR) study, an experimental study involving thousands of students, and notes that when class sizes were reduced to 13 to 15 students in kindergarten to grade 3, reading proficiency was improved substantially, as were long-term educational outcomes (fewer dropouts, reduced school suspensions, improved high school grades). The classroom observations suggested, not surprisingly, that smaller classes allowed teachers to better focus on the instructional needs of individual children. Additionally, Nye, Hedges, and Konstantopoulos (1999) found that the positive effects of class-size reduction continued five years after the class-size reduction ended.

Phonological Awareness Intervention. Although the relationship seems less than straightforward (Coles, 2000), many researchers do propose that phonological awareness is linked with literacy development (Foorman, Francis, Shaywitz, Shaywitz, & Fletcher, 1997). For instance, Moustafa (1997) argues that instruction in phonemic segmentation is unnecessary except when electing to teach students through a synthetic phonics approach. She offers an onset–rime strategy for developing effective decoding proficiencies, one similar to that popularized by Cunningham (2004). The work of Gaskins (2005) and her colleagues suggests that an onset–rime approach can be particularly effective with children identified as learning disabled or dyslexic, a finding reported by others as well (e.g., Lovett et al., 1994). Although some have argued that a "phonological core deficit" lies at the root of children's reading difficulties, in an extensive review of the research on phonological awareness interventions, Troia (1999) concluded that few of the published studies met commonly accepted criteria for experimental design and cautioned that the research seemed not to justify much of the enthusiasm for particular intervention efforts. Most studies, for instance, were not designed to investigate the development or role of phonological awareness longitudinally. However, Bus and van IJzendoorn (1999) demonstrated that kindergarten phonological awareness accounts for less than 1% of the variance in reading achievement at fourth grade. In other words, there are a number of other factors that are far more influential as children mature (Pressley & Allington, 1999). Simply put, it seems that most children develop adequate phonological awareness as they acquire literacy proficiency (Allington, 1997; International Reading Association, 1998).

The research suggests, however, that perhaps 10 to 15% of children fail to acquire the basic conceptual insight that English is an alphabetic language and that words can be decomposed into individual phonemes (e.g., *cat* can be decomposed into /c/a/t/). Developing this insight is important in learning to read and spell an alphabetic language such as English. The interventions that most successfully foster phonemic segmentation vary in focus, from those that emphasize "sound stretching" as a component of early classroom invented spelling and morning message activities (McGill-Franzen et al., 1999; Scanlon & Vellutino, 1997), to those that focus more on isolated segmenting through activities such as Turtletalk (Gough, 1998) or with sound boxes or manipulatives (Clay & Cazden, 1990), to those that emphasize blending and even cueing articulatory features (Torgesen, Wagner, Rashotte, Alexander, & Conway, 1997). Wise and Olson (1999) note that from their comparative studies "it appears that the exact method of teaching phonological awareness may be less important than once thought" (n.p.). They suggest that schools worry less about the particular intervention methodology and more about providing targeted training to children who need it. Some children seem not to benefit much from whole-class activities but thrive in small-group or tutorial sessions; some benefit from less structured approaches, and others from more structured models. Very few children (1 to 2%) continue to struggle mightily or experience difficulty after intensive intervention (Vellutino et al., 1996).

At this point, it seems clear that the development of phonological awareness in early readers should be monitored (through their attempts at invented spelling, which is perhaps the most appropriate assessment strategy); when development stalls or lags behind, an intervention should be readily available. The intervention will depend largely on children's responses. Currently, there exists no clear evidence of the superiority of one approach over others—although, as mentioned earlier, more intensive interventions, such as tutorials, have produced the best record in fostering the conceptual development needed for phonemic segmentation for those children who experience difficulties with this learning. Nonetheless, a caution is in order. As Vellutino et al. (1996) noted, very few children develop reading proficiency without ever acquiring proficiency in phonemic segmentation, and not all children who acquire phonemic segmentation became proficient readers.

Techniques for fostering phonemic awareness should be familiar to every early childhood educator, since fostering such expertise was a major focus of the U.S. federal Reading First initiative under the NCLB legislation. While Reading First did not produce better reading achievement (and so has been defunded), it did produce children who were better able to pronounce nonwords in first grade (Gamse, Jacob, Horst, Boulay, & Unlu, 2009). This outcome suggests that teachers now can foster phonemic awareness but that there is still much to be done if improving reading achievement is the ultimate goal.

Family Programs. Programs focusing on parental involvement are popular, but there is limited research indicating significant effects on children's achievement resulting from them. Although researchers have demonstrated that more academically successful children more often have parents who are involved both at school and at home, efforts to increase the involvement of parents of low-achieving children as an intervention to enhance achievement have not been particularly successful (although there are notable exceptions; see, e.g., Paratore, Melzi, & Krol-Sinclair, 1999). This is not to suggest that family programs should be avoided, but rather that such programs are unlikely to serve as a sufficient preventive (or remedial) intervention design.

Acceleration Designs
Acceleration designs run the gamut from classroom corrective reading efforts to remedial tutorials, from in-class specialist support to pull-out add-on interventions.

Classroom Corrective Reading. Duffy-Hester (1999) provides a review of popular interventions focused on restructuring classroom reading and language arts lessons: Four Blocks (Cunningham & Allington, 2010; Cunningham & Hall, 1998), Fluency-Oriented Reading Instruction (Stahl, Heubach, & Holcomb, 2005), Concept-Oriented Reading Instruction (Guthrie et al., 1996), Book Club (Goatley, Brock, & Raphael, 1995), the Kamehameha Early Education Program (Au & Carroll, 1997), Success for All (Slavin, Madden, Dolan, & Wasik, 1996; Venezky, 1998),

Early Literacy Intervention (Taylor, Short, Shearer, & Frye, 1995), Accelerated Schools (Knight & Stallings, 1995), and theme-driven instruction (Walp & Walmsley, 1995).

Some principles can be drawn from Duffy-Hester's (1999) review of effective classroom interventions. First, there are several routes to accelerating reading development; the programs reviewed are not "cookie-cutter" similar. Second, explicit instruction in the context of authentic reading and writing is an important component of such interventions. Some students need more explicit demonstrations of skill and strategy use, but integrating such demonstrations into classroom reading and writing is more effective than isolated skills instruction and practice (Duffy, 1993). Third, classroom instruction needs to be tailored to student needs. This requires teachers to routinely evaluate the appropriateness of reading materials and strategy use. Program designs that provide copies of the same texts for all students—everyone reading the same basal story or the same trade book—will fail to develop reading proficiencies in all students. Finally, developing teacher expertise is important (Scanlon, Gelzheiser, Vellutino, Schatscheneider, & Sweeney, 2008/2010). Teachers with greater professional understanding of instruction and the authority to act on that understanding are central to creating classroom interventions that accelerate the development of all children.

Important research has focused on exemplary elementary teachers. There is a substantial reduction in the number of children who experience reading and learning difficulties in classrooms where teachers deliver exemplary instruction (Allington & Johnston, 2002; Bembry, Jordan, Gomez, Anderson, & Mendro, 1998; Pressley, Wharton-McDonald, Ranking, Mistretta, Yokoi, & Ettenberger, 1996; Pressley et al., 2001; Taylor, Pearson, Clark, & Walpole, 2000). This finding is not surprising, but it is important because so little research has studied the impact of the quality of instruction on reading development and reading difficulties. Effective teachers provide more personalized and small-group instruction, more contextualized skills teaching, substantially more reading and writing opportunities, and more interactive lessons than their less effective peers.

Nye, Konstantopoulos, and Hedges (2004) found that teacher effects are larger than school effects. They question why so much state and federal policy has been focused on school improvement and so little on developing the teaching expertise of teachers. Pianta and his colleagues (Pianta, Belsky, Houts, Morrison, & the National Institute of Child Health and Human Development [NICHD] Early Child Care Research

Network, 2007) reported that between kindergarten and fifth grade, only 14% of the students in their national sample had consistently high-quality instruction, while 20% experienced consistently low-quality instruction. The effects of the quality of classroom instruction have simply been ignored for too long in discussions of reading/learning disabilities. In virtually all schools, some teachers supply the majority of struggling readers to remedial and special education programs while others rarely or never find a child they cannot teach to read. As Vellutino, Fletcher, Snowling, and Scanlon (2004) note, the research suggests that it may be time to consider changing the term *learning disability* to *teacher disability*. They conclude simply, "There is strong evidence that most early reading difficulties are caused primarily by experiential and instructional deficits, rather than basic cognitive deficits associated with neuro-developmental anomaly" (p. 28).

Add-On Instructional Programs. Vellutino and his colleagues (1996, 2004), Pinnell, Lyons, Deford, Bryk, and Seltzer (1994), and Hiebert, Colt, Catto, and Gury (1992) offered add-on instructional interventions to young students, and in each case dramatically reduced the incidence of reading difficulties, both mild and severe. In these cases, struggling readers were provided with instruction outside the classroom, often in tutorial or small-group (two or three children) formats. In each case, use of appropriately difficult texts, focused and personalized expert instruction, and substantial opportunities to read and write characterized the intervention designs. These studies suggest that add-on interventions are ineffective only when poorly designed (Allington, 2008).

Many early interventions involve one-to-one tutoring. The most widely implemented is Reading Recovery (Pinnell et al., 1994), which is also, perhaps, the best researched and the one with the strongest evidence of accelerating the development of early reading. Wasik and Slavin (1993) noted that "the effects of Reading Recovery are impressive at the end of the implementation year, and the effects are maintained for at least 2 years" (p. 187). Independent reviews of Reading Recovery are well summarized by Shanahan and Barr (1995), who reported that although reading development was accelerated through the intervention, some of the effect faded over time as children returned to general education. However, the federal What Works Clearinghouse (2007) gave Reading Recovery a "strong evidence" rating on improving reading achievement. Notably, Reading Recovery is the only program (of more than 150 reviewed) that received that rating, the highest awarded.

Although other tutoring programs (e.g., Orton-Gillingham, Slingerlands) have been available for some years, there is little independent research indicating they have any substantial positive effects on reading achievement (Stahl, Duffy-Hester, & Stahl, 1998). In their review of five tutoring programs, Wasik and Slavin (1993) found that the most comprehensive programs produced larger gains than the more narrowly focused tutorials and that the qualifications of the tutors was also important, with certified teachers as tutors producing better results than paraprofessionals.

Other studies of the use of paraprofessionals (e.g., Achilles, 1999; Boyd-Zaharias & Pate-Bain, 1998; Rowan & Guthrie, 1989) and volunteers (Wasik, 1998) have demonstrated mixed results. Interventions that rely on relatively unskilled, although often enthusiastic, paraprofessionals and volunteers should not be expected to produce high-quality, personalized instruction nor substantial growth in reading proficiencies. Such efforts may be useful in providing extended practice with reading and writing, and such supportive practice opportunities may benefit many children. However, many others need more intensive and more personalized expert instruction, and neither paraprofessionals nor volunteers seem good candidates for providing this.

A number of training packages for volunteers and paraprofessionals have appeared on the market (e.g., Herrmann, 1998; Johnston, Invernizzi, & Juel, 1998; Morris, 1999), but there exists only a modest research base demonstrating their impact. Providing training for paraprofessionals and volunteers is essential, but even with training, their instructional roles must be limited.

Another approach, the small-group add-on, is the most traditional remedial and special education intervention design. In these efforts, targeted students are offered group instruction from a specialist teacher or (increasingly) a paraprofessional. The research suggests that the number of children in the group is important. Although many reading and learning disabilities specialists routinely work with groups of five to nine students, evidence indicates that group size needs to shrink considerably (to around three students) for measurable effects to be achieved.

Recently, Swanson and Hoskyn (1998) reviewed more than 900 studies of educational interventions with reading/learning-disabled students. Only 18 were rated high on methodological quality (and only 180 met even the most minimal quality criteria). Swanson and Hoskyn concluded that, with respect to intervention (as with phonological awareness), much weak research has been published. This accounts for the lack of a consistent message about appropriate instructional interventions.

For instance, when Swanson and Hoskyn (1998) examined the studies that demonstrated high methodological quality, they found that they reported smaller effect sizes (reported gains were smaller) than did the lower quality studies. In addition, studies using standardized outcome measures reported lower effect sizes than studies that used experimenter-developed measures. Only three intervention components contributed unique variance to the overall effect-size estimates: control of task difficulty, use of small interactive instructional groups, and directed responses/questioning (such as that found in reciprocal teaching).

The aggregated data from these studies support the use of explicit instructional strategy teaching in small groups of two or three students in highly interactive sessions in which students read books of an appropriate level of complexity. These seem also to be key features of the successful small-group interventions reported by others (Hiebert et al., 1992; Mathes et al., 2005; Phillips & Smith, 1997/2010; Pinnell et al., 1994; Scanlon, 2011; Vellutino et al., 1996). Unfortunately, few remedial or special education programs seem to match these characteristics (Baker & Zigmond, 1995; Pikulski, 1994; Puma et al., 1997; Vaughn et al., 2003).

Designing More Effective Intervention Plans

There is ample guidance available for the redesign of school literacy programs. However, to be successful, such programs will require reconceptualizing literacy learning difficulties.

We simply have too much evidence to continue arguing that some mythical factor is at the base of a child's reading difficulties. Virtually all struggling readers are victims of their schools. What "causes" reading difficulties is the absence of sufficient high-quality reading instruction. When research teams working with multiple schools in different states and nations can all develop reading instruction whereby 98% of entering kindergarteners are reading on level by the end of first grade (see, e.g., Mathes et al., 2005; Phillips & Smith, 1997/2010; Vellutino et al., 1996, 2004), it is time we rethink the source of reading difficulties.

Reconceptualizing Reading/Learning Disabilities

Reading/learning disability is something akin to the interaction of the normal distribution of proclivity for learning to read and differential access to sufficient, appropriate instruction (McGill-Franzen & Allington, 1991; Vellutino et al., 1996, 2004). In other words, some children learn to read with relative ease, and some struggle when offered classroom reading instruction. In some classrooms far fewer children struggle with reading than in other classrooms. This situation should be viewed as normal. If we can reconceptualize learning to read as an acquisition process that varies in difficulty across the range of children we teach, then the difficulties some children have would be seen as normally occurring, not as some exotic disability. Were the research more closely attended to, school instructional programs might more often be designed with the expectation that some children will need access to larger amounts of more expert, more intensive, and more personalized teaching.

What we now identify as reading/learning disability would, instead, be viewed as an instructional problem to be dealt with as part of the regular course of designing school programs, which would then result in every child learning to read alongside his or her peers. Addressing the issue of reading difficulties would require classroom reading programs that were more expert, more comprehensive, and more flexible than most are today. These programs would focus on early intensive intervention but would acknowledge that some children will undoubtedly require long-term extraordinary instructional support—in some few cases, perhaps, across their school career.

This reconceptualization has some support in the longitudinal epidemiological study conducted by Shaywitz et al. (1992). These researchers found no specific subset of children who actually fit the traditional definition of dyslexic. Instead, the long-term reading development of the large group of children they studied indicated that reading achievement reflected a normal curve distribution—a few very good readers, a few very poor readers, and bunches of readers with generally similar patterns of development. Shaywitz and colleagues offered no instructional intervention but simply evaluated reading achievement year after year. Given the current limited availability of sustained, intensive, expert, extraordinary instructional support, their findings do not seem surprising. Without serious rethinking of support for children who find learning to read more difficult, many will continue to lag behind their peers.

Creating schools in which all children achieve a high absolute standard of literacy proficiency is a more difficult task than creating the typical school in which roughly one-quarter of the students achieve this "proficient" level on the NAEP. Creating such schools may require higher levels of funding than are currently available (Odden, 1997), but a good first step would be designing instructional efforts that make better use of the funding that does exist.

Crafting Comprehensive Literacy Instructional Plans

Any comprehensive instructional plan begins with ensuring the availability of preventive programs. This might include a focus, especially in schools serving large numbers of students from low-income families, on the widely acknowledged variability in preschool experiences with print, stories, and literate talk (McGill-Franzen et al., 1999, 2010; Neuman & Celano, 2001). A coordinated effort by the school to ensure that preschool programs—Head Start, Even Start, prekindergarten, and preschool special education—and the kindergarten program offer print- and language-rich environments would be an initial step. Offering family support in the form of access to the school library collections on weekends and during the summer (Allington & McGill-Franzen, 2008), story hours in the evening and on weekends for preschoolers and their families, and perhaps parent training in dialogic reading (Whitehurst & Lonigan, 1998) could be a second aspect of a coordinated preventive plan.

Primary grade classes should be smaller than 20 students, and enriched professional development for teachers and more extensive classroom curriculum resources (e.g., substantial classroom libraries, multilevel book collections) should be provided to enhance the quality of classroom instruction. Smaller classes work better when teachers are more expert (Pressley, 1998; Scanlon et al., 2008/2010), and investing in the development of instructional staff is critical, despite it being time consuming (Darling-Hammond, 1999; Duffy, 1993).

A comprehensive literacy program would also include well-designed acceleration services. Expert specialist teachers should be available to provide assistance in monitoring children's literacy development, mentor new and less expert teachers, and provide tutorial and small-group intensive instructional interventions for children who find learning to read more difficult. At least some of these services would be available in extended-day programs and during the summer. Staffing such components might make far better use of flextime scheduling than is currently practiced. Convergent research evidence would guide the design of classroom and add-on instructional interventions. Thus, instead of futilely searching for the "one best" or "proven" program, schools would create responsive instructional efforts that responded to the needs of children in flexible, comprehensive ways (Allington & Cunningham, 2006).

Finally, schools would develop longer term instructional support plans. Such planning might use a "census-based" approach (Kaleba, 1999). That is, given historical data on the numbers of children in the school who were experiencing difficulties in acquiring reading proficiencies, each school would engage in longer term planning to create effective interventions (including longer term budgeting projections, professional development offerings, program scheduling, etc.). Currently, most schools have no such planning process in place. Each year, then, there are scattered and uncoordinated planning efforts, typically resulting in a number of ill-conceived and largely uncoordinated instructional support efforts. Rarely does school planning for support programs involve teachers and administrators across the span from prekindergarten to 12th grade, rarely are both general and special education staff collaboratively involved, and all too often after-school and summer school programs are not well linked to core curriculum.

Much of the current fragmentation in school intervention plans can be attributed to federal and state program guidelines (Allington, 1994). Schools cannot simply rely on federal and state programs and funding resources, however, in developing a comprehensive plan. Educating all children well is an unlikely outcome of the current piecemeal planning and budgeting process. When districts begin estimating actual budget needs for a comprehensive program, they also should estimate longer term funds available from federal and state sources that might defray some of the costs. However, when planning begins with individual allocations by building from the several federal and state funding streams and when fiscal support relies almost wholly on those funds, the outcome is, not surprisingly, a collection of uncoordinated program efforts that is expensive and largely ineffective in the longer term. Unfortunately, such fragmented planning and implementation is common today, and the outcomes of these expensive efforts are largely disappointing.

It may be that achieving the sort of standards set by policymakers will require additional funding. At the same time the recent federal emphasis on Response to Intervention allows schools to redirect some special education funding (15% of the total special education budget) to support the delivery of the intervention design (Johnston, 2010). Federal policy seems focused on the prevention of reading difficulties in young children and on replacing expensive and long-term special education services with high-quality, shorter term interventions. The intent is a substantial decrease in the numbers of children who struggle while learning to read and, ultimately, substantially smaller numbers of children being identified as having a learning disability (Allington, 2008).

Conclusion

The past century has seen an enormous expansion of literacy proficiency (Rothstein, 1998). To achieve the universally high standards of literacy now called for, schools must reconceptualize literacy teaching and learning and craft school programs that provide a more coherent and comprehensive instructional plan. Until the current incoherent array of well-meaning intervention efforts are replaced by more comprehensive plans drawing on the convergent research, too many children will be ill-served and too much professional effort will be underproductive.

Central to this rethinking is the idea that we should not be surprised that some children find learning to read and write more difficult than do others. Rather than labeling and segregating those who struggle to become literate, we need to restructure our instructional programs and resources to produce more coherent and more powerful intervention designs as well as more expert classroom literacy instruction. Coles (1998), Mathes et al. (2005), and Duffy and Hoffman (1999) have noted the futility of debates about the "one best method" for developing children's literacy proficiencies. However, it is instructional method and curriculum materials that typically are indicted whenever literacy proficiencies are deemed insufficient. Now that three expert panels (reported in Darling-Hammond, 1997; NICHD, 2000; Snow et al., 1998) have weighed the research evidence and concluded that method and materials are neither the locus of the problem many children face in their efforts to acquire literacy proficiency nor the panacea for addressing it, perhaps we can focus political and professional attention on designing and funding educational efforts that just might deliver on the promise of all children being readers and writers.

Questions for Reflection

1. Interview an elementary school principal and inquire about preventive, acceleration, and longer term instructional support plans currently in place. Are clear links between preschool and elementary programs and between elementary and middle school programs well defined? Is development of phonemic awareness monitored? Is expert tutoring available?

2. Interview a high school teacher and ask if there are students who have difficulty reading the assigned textbooks. Ask what types of interventions are available for such students and how these efforts are linked to the classroom curriculum demands.

3. When schools develop effective programs, individual factors such as family wealth are largely minimized when it comes to school success. Find out whether children from low-income families are overrepresented in remedial and special education classes in your school.

4. Examine several individualized education plans (IEPs) and look for individual learning goals linked to state and district grade-level curriculum standards. Is each IEP well coordinated with classroom instruction?

Author Note

Support for the development of this chapter was provided under the Research and Development Centers Program (R305A60005) as administered by the Office of Educational Research and Improvement (OERI). However, the contents do not necessarily represent the positions or policies of the Department of Education, OERI, or the Institute on Student Achievement.

REFERENCES

Achilles, C.M. (1999). *Let's put kids first, finally: Getting class size right.* Thousand Oaks, CA: Corwin.

Allington, R.L. (1994). What's special about special programs for children who find learning to read difficult? *Journal of Reading Behavior, 26*(1), 95–115.

Allington, R.L. (1997). Overselling phonics. *Reading Today, 15*(1), 15–16.

Allington, R.L. (2006). *What really matters for struggling readers: Designing research-based programs* (2nd ed.). Boston: Allyn & Bacon.

Allington, R.L. (2008). *What really matters in Response to Intervention: Research-based designs.* Boston: Allyn & Bacon.

Allington, R.L., & Cunningham, P.M. (2006). *Schools that work: Where all children read and write* (3rd ed.). Boston: Allyn & Bacon.

Allington, R.L., & Johnston, P.H. (Eds.). (2002). *Reading to learn: Lessons from exemplary fourth grade classrooms.* New York: Guilford.

Allington, R.L., & McGill-Franzen, A. (1989a). School response to reading failure: Instruction for Chapter 1 and special education students in grades 2, 4, and 8. *The Elementary School Journal, 89*(5), 529–542. doi:10.1086/461590

Allington, R.L., & McGill-Franzen, A. (1989b). Different programs, indifferent instruction. In A. Gartner & D.K. Lipsky (Eds.), *Beyond separate education: Quality education for all* (pp. 75–98). Baltimore, MD: Paul H. Brookes.

Allington, R.L., & McGill-Franzen, A. (1992). Unintended effects of educational reform in New York. *Educational Policy, 6*(4), 397–414. doi:10.1177/0895904892006004003

Allington, R.L., & McGill-Franzen, A. (1996). Individual planning. In M.C. Wang, M.C. Reynolds, & H.J. Walberg (Eds.), *Handbook of special and remedial education: Research and practice* (2nd ed., pp. 5–35). New York: Pergamon.

Allington, R.L., & McGill-Franzen, A. (2008). Got books? *Educational Leadership, 65*(7), 20–23.

Allington, R.L., & McGill-Franzen, A. (2009). Comprehension difficulties of struggling readers. In S.E. Israel & G.G. Duffy (Eds.),

Handbook of research on reading comprehension (pp. 551–568). New York: Guilford.

Au, K.H., & Carroll, J.H. (1997). Improving literacy achievement through a constructivist approach: The KEEP demonstration classroom project. *The Elementary School Journal, 97*(3), 203–221. doi:10.1086/461862

Baker, J.M., & Zigmond, N. (1995). The meaning and practice of inclusion for students with learning disabilities: Themes and implications from the five cases. *The Journal of Special Education, 29*(2), 163–180. doi:10.1177/002246699502900207

Bembry, K.L., Jordan, H.R., Gomez, E., Anderson, M., & Mendro, R.L. (1998, April). *Policy implications of long-term teacher effects on student achievement.* Paper presented at the annual meeting of the American Educational Research Association, San Diego, CA.

Berrueta-Clement, J.R., Schweinhart, L.J., Barnett, W.S., Epstein, A.S., & Weikart, D.P. (1984). *Changed lives: The effects of the Perry Preschool Program on youths through age 19.* Ypsilanti, MI: HighScope Press.

Borman, G.D., Wong, K.K., Hedges, L.V., & D'Agostino, J.V. (2001). Coordinating categorical and regular programs: Effects on Title I students' educational opportunities and outcomes. In G.D. Borman, S.C. Stringfield, & R.E. Slavin (Eds.), *Title I: Compensatory education at the crossroads* (pp. 81–118). Mahwah, NJ: Erlbaum.

Boyd-Zaharias, J., & Pate-Bain, H. (1998). *Teacher aides and student learning: Lessons from Project STAR.* Arlington, VA: Educational Research Service.

Bus, A.G., & van IJzendoorn, M.H. (1999). Phonological awareness and early reading: A meta-analysis of experimental training studies. *Journal of Educational Psychology, 91*(3), 403–414. doi:10.1037/0022-0663.91.3.403

Chalfant, J.C. (1989). Learning disabilities: Policy issues and promising approaches. *American Psychologist, 44*(2), 392–398. doi:10.1037/0003-066X.44.2.392

Clay, M.M., & Cazden, C.B. (1990). A Vygotskian interpretation of Reading Recovery. In L.C. Moll (Ed.), *Vygotsky and education: Instructional implications and applications of sociohistorical psychology* (pp. 206–222). New York: Cambridge University Press.

Coles, G. (1998). *Reading lessons: The debate over literacy.* New York: Hill and Wang.

Coles, G. (2000). *Misreading reading: The bad science that hurts children.* Portsmouth, NH: Heinemann.

Cortiella, C. (2009). *The state of learning disabilities.* New York: National Center for Learning Disabilities.

Cunningham, P.M. (2004). *Phonics they use: Words for reading and writing* (5th ed.). Boston: Allyn & Bacon.

Cunningham, P.M., & Allington, R.L. (2010). *Classrooms that work: They can all read and write* (5th ed.). Boston: Allyn & Bacon.

Cunningham, P.M., & Hall, D.P. (1998). The Four Blocks: A framework for literacy in primary classrooms. In K.R. Harris, S. Graham, & D. Deshler (Eds.), *Teaching every child every day: Learning in diverse schools and classrooms* (pp. 32–76). Cambridge, MA: Brookline Books.

Dahl, K.L., Scharer, P.L., Lawson, L.L., & Grogan, P.R. (1999). Phonics instruction and student achievement in whole language first-grade classrooms. *Reading Research Quarterly, 34*(3), 312–341. doi:10.1598/RRQ.34.3.4

Darling-Hammond, L. (1997). *Doing what matters most: Investing in quality teaching.* New York: National Commission on Teaching & America's Future.

Darling-Hammond, L. (1999). *Teacher quality and student achievement: A review of state policy evidence.* Seattle, WA: Center for Teaching Policy, University of Washington.

Denton, C.A., Vaughn, S., & Fletcher, J.M. (2003). Bringing research-based practice in reading intervention to scale. *Learning Disabilities Research and Practice, 18*(3), 201–211. doi:10.1111/1540-5826.00075

Dickinson, D.K., & Smith, M.W. (1994). Long-term effects of preschool teachers' book readings on low-income children's vocabulary and story comprehension. *Reading Research Quarterly, 29*(2), 104–122. doi:10.2307/747807

Duffy, G.G. (1993). Rethinking strategy instruction: Four teachers' development and their low achievers' understandings. *The Elementary School Journal, 93*(3), 231–247. doi:10.1086/461724

Duffy, G.G., & Hoffman, J.V. (1999). In pursuit of an illusion: The flawed search for a perfect method. *The Reading Teacher, 53*(1), 10–16.

Duffy-Hester, A.M. (1999). Teaching struggling readers in elementary school classrooms: A review of classroom reading programs and principles for instruction. *The Reading*

Teacher, 52(5), 480–495. doi:10.1598/
RT.52.5.4

Entwisle, D.R., Alexander, K.L., & Olson, L.S. (1997). *Children, schools, & inequality.* Boulder, CO: Westview.

Foorman, B.R., Francis, D.J., Shaywitz, S.E., Shaywitz, B.A., & Fletcher, J.M. (1997). The case for early reading intervention. In B. Blachman (Ed.), *Foundations of reading acquisition and dyslexia: Implications for early intervention* (pp. 243–264). Mahwah, NJ: Erlbaum.

Frank Porter Graham Child Development Center, University of North Carolina at Chapel Hill. (1999). *Early learning, later success: The Abecedarian Study.* Chapel Hill: Author. Downloaded November 18, 2010, from www.fpg.unc.edu/~abc/ells-04.pdf

Gamse, B.C., Jacob, R.T., Horst, M., Boulay, B., & Unlu, F. (2009). Reading First Impact Study: Final report (Report No. NCEE 2009-4038)). Washington, DC: National Center for Education Evaluation and Regional Assistance, Institute of Education Sciences, U.S. Department of Education.

Gaskins, I.W. (2005). *Success with struggling readers: The Benchmark School approach.* New York: Guilford.

Goatley, V.J., Brock, C.H., & Raphael, T.E. (1995). Diverse learners participating in regular education "Book Clubs." *Reading Research Quarterly, 30*(3), 352–380. doi:10.2307/747621

Gough, P.B. (1998, December). *Overselling phonemic awareness?* Paper presented at the 48th annual meeting of the National Reading Conference, Austin, TX.

Guthrie, J.T., Van Meter, P., McCann, A.D., Wigfield, A., Bennett, L., Poundstone, C.C., et al. (1996). Growth of literacy engagement: Changes in motivations and strategies during Concept-Oriented Reading Instruction. *Reading Research Quarterly, 31*(3), 306–322. doi:10.1598/RRQ.31.3.5

Harris, A.J., & Sipay, E.R. (1990). *How to increase reading ability: A guide to developmental & remedial methods.* New York: Longman.

Herrmann, B.A. (Ed.). (1998). *The volunteer tutor's toolbox.* Newark, DE: International Reading Association.

Heubert, J.P., & Hauser, R.M. (1999). *High stakes: Testing for tracking, promotion, and graduation.* Washington, DC: National Academy Press.

Hiebert, E.H., Colt, J.M., Catto, S.L., & Gury, E.C. (1992). Reading and writing of first-grade students in a restructured Chapter 1

program. *American Educational Research Journal, 29*(3), 545–572.

Hoff, D.J. (1999, May 19). Board won't revise state NAEP scores. *Education Week,* 1, 13.

International Reading Association. (1998). *Phonemic awareness and the teaching of reading: A position statement from the Board of Directors of the International Reading Association.* Newark, DE: Author.

Jenkins, J.R., Pious, C.G., & Peterson, D.L. (1988). Categorical programs for remedial and handicapped students: Issues of validity. *Exceptional Children, 55*(2), 147–158.

Johnston, F.R., Invernizzi, M., & Juel, C. (1998). *Book buddies: Guidelines for volunteer tutors of emergent and early readers.* New York: Guilford.

Johnston, P.H. (1997). *Knowing literacy: Constructive literacy assessment.* York, ME: Stenhouse.

Johnston, P.H. (Ed.). (2010). *RTI in literacy—Responsive and comprehensive.* Newark, DE: International Reading Association.

Kaleba, D. (1999, Summer). California adjusts new census-based funding formula. *The CSEF Resource,* pp. 3–5 Downloaded November 18, 2010, from csef.air.org/publications/csef/csef_resource/resourcejune99.pdf

Kirk, S.A., & Elkins, J. (1975). Characteristics of children enrolled in the child service demonstration centers. *Journal of Learning Disabilities, 8*(10), 31–38.

Knapp, M.S. (1995). *Teaching for meaning in high-poverty classrooms.* New York: Teachers College Press.

Knight, S., & Stallings, J. (1995). The implementation of the Accelerated School model in an urban elementary school. In R.L. Allington & S.A. Walmsley (Eds.), *No quick fix: Rethinking literacy programs in America's elementary schools* (pp. 236–251). New York: Teachers College Press; Newark, DE: International Reading Association.

LeTendre, M.J. (1991). The continuing evolution of a federal role in compensatory education. *Educational Evaluation and Policy Analysis, 13*(4), 328–334.

Light, R.J., & Pillemer, D.B. (1984). *Summing up: The science of reviewing research.* Cambridge, MA: Harvard University Press.

Lovett, M.W., Borden, S.L., DeLuca, T., Lacerenza, L., Benson, N.J., & Brackstone, D. (1994). Treating the core deficits of developmental dyslexia: Evidence of transfer of learning after phonologically- and strategy-based reading training programs. *Developmental Psychology, 30*(6), 805–822. doi:10.1037/0012-1649.30.6.805

Lyon, G.R., Gray, D.B., Krasnegor, N.A., & Kavanagh, J.F. (Eds.). (1993). *Better understanding learning disabilities: New views from research and their implications for education and public policies.* Baltimore: Paul H. Brookes.

Lyon, G.R., & Moats, L.C. (1997). Critical conceptual and methodological considerations in reading intervention research. *Journal of Learning Disabilities, 30*(6), 578–588. doi:10.1177/002221949703000601

Mathes, P.G., Denton, C.A., Fletcher, J.M., Anthony, J.L., Francis, D.J., & Schatschneider, C. (2005). The effects of theoretically different instruction and student characteristics on the skills of struggling readers. *Reading Research Quarterly, 40*(2), 148–182. doi:10.1598/RRQ.40.2.2

McGill-Franzen, A. (1987). Failure to learn to read: Formulating a policy problem. *Reading Research Quarterly, 22*(4), 475–490. doi:10.2307/747703

McGill-Franzen, A. (1994). Compensatory and special education: Is there accountability for learning and belief in children's potential? In E.H. Hiebert & B.M. Taylor (Eds.), *Getting reading right from the start: Effective early literacy interventions* (pp. 13–35). Boston: Allyn & Bacon.

McGill-Franzen, A. (2006). *Kindergarten literacy: Matching assessment and instruction in kindergarten.* New York: Scholastic.

McGill-Franzen, A., & Allington, R.L. (1991). The gridlock of low reading achievement: Perspectives on practice and policy. *Remedial and Special Education, 12*(3), 20–30. doi:10.1177/074193259101200304

McGill-Franzen, A., Allington, R.L., Yokoi, L., & Brooks, G. (1999). Putting books in the classroom seems necessary but not sufficient. *The Journal of Educational Research, 93*(2), 67–74. doi:10.1080/00220679909597631

McGill-Franzen, A., & Goatley, V. (2002). Title 1 and special education: Support for children who struggle to learn to read. In S.B. Neuman & D.K. Dickinson (Eds.), *Handbook of early literacy research* (pp. 471–483). New York: Guilford.

McGill-Franzen, A., & Lanford, C. (1994). Exposing the edge of the preschool curriculum: Teachers' talk about text and children's literary understandings. *Language Arts, 71*(4), 264–273.

McGill-Franzen, A., Lanford, C., & Adams, E. (2002). Learning to be literate: A comparison of five urban early childhood programs. *Journal of Educational Psychology, 94*(3), 443–464. doi:10.1037/0022-0663.94.3.443

McGill-Franzen, A., Payne, R.L., & Dennis, D.V. (2010). Responsive intervention: What is the role of appropriate assessment? In P.H. Johnston (Ed.), *RTI in literacy—Responsive and comprehensive* (pp. 115–132). Newark, DE: International Reading Association.

Mehan, H., Hertweck, A., & Meihls, J.L. (1986). *Handicapping the handicapped: Decision making in students' educational careers.* Stanford, CA: Stanford University Press.

Mercer, C.D., Jordan, L., Allsopp, D., & Mercer, A.R. (1996). Learning disabilities definitions and criteria used by state education departments. *Learning Disability Quarterly, 19*(4), 217–232. doi:10.2307/1511208

Morris, D. (1999). *The Howard Street tutoring manual: Teaching at-risk readers in the primary grades.* New York: Guilford.

Morrow, L.M., O'Connor, E.M., & Smith, J.K. (1990). Effects of a story reading program on the literacy development of at-risk kindergarten children. *Journal of Reading Behavior, 22*(3), 255–275.

Moustafa, M. (1997). *Beyond traditional phonics: Research discoveries and reading instruction.* Portsmouth, NH: Heinemann.

National Center for Education Statistics. (2002). *Highlights from the 2000 Program for International Student Assessment (PISA)* (NCES 2002-116). Washington, DC: Institute of Education Sciences, U.S. Department of Education.

National Center for Education Statistics. (2009). *The Nation's Report Card: Reading 2009* (NCES 2010-458). Washington, DC: Institute of Education Sciences, U.S. Department of Education.

National Institute of Child Health and Human Development. (2000). *Report of the National Reading Panel. Teaching children to read: An evidence-based assessment of the scientific research literature on reading and its implications for reading instruction* (NIH Publication No. 00-4769). Washington, DC: U.S. Government Printing Office.

Neuman, S.B. (1999). Books make a difference: A study of access to literacy. *Reading Research Quarterly, 34*(3), 286–311. doi:10.1598/RRQ.34.3.3

Neuman, S.B., & Celano, D. (2001). Access to print in low-income and middle-income communities: An ecological study of four neighborhoods. *Reading Research Quarterly, 36*(1), 8–26. doi:10.1598/RRQ.36.1.1

Nye, B., Hedges, L.V., & Konstantopoulos, S. (1999). The long-term effects of small classes: A five-year follow-up of the Tennessee class size experiment. *Educational Evaluation and Policy Analysis, 21*(2), 127–142.

Nye, B., Konstantopoulos, S., & Hedges, L.V. (2004). How large are teacher effects? *Educational Evaluation and Policy Analysis, 26*(3), 237–257. doi:10.3102/016 23737026003237

Odden, A. (1997). Raising performance levels without increasing funding. *School Business Affairs, 63*(6), 4–12.

Paratore, J.R., Melzi, G., & Krol-Sinclair, B. (1999). *What should we expect of family literacy? Experiences of Latino children whose parents participate in an intergenerational literacy project.* Newark, DE: International Reading Association.

Phillips, G., & Smith, P. (2010). Closing the gaps: Literacy for the hardest-to-teach. In P.H. Johnston (Ed.), *RTI in literacy—Responsive and comprehensive.* (pp. 219–246). Newark, DE: International Reading Association. (Reprinted from *Closing the gaps: Literacy for the hardest-to-teach*, 1997, Wellington, New Zealand: Council for Educational Research)

Pianta, R.C., Belsky, J., Houts, R., Morrison, F., & the National Institute of Child Health and Human Development (NICHD) Early Child Care Research Network. (2007). Opportunities to learn in America's elementary classrooms. *Science, 315*(5820), 1795–1796. doi:10.1126/science.1139719

Pikulski, J.J. (1994). Preventing reading failure: A review of five effective programs. *The Reading Teacher, 48*(1), 30–39.

Pinnell, G.S., Lyons, C.A., Deford, D.E., Bryk, A.S., & Seltzer, M. (1994). Comparing instructional models for the literacy education of high-risk first graders. *Reading Research Quarterly, 29*(1), 8–39. doi:10.2307/747736

Pressley, M. (1998). *Reading instruction that works: The case for balanced teaching.* New York: Guilford.

Pressley, M., & Allington, R.L. (1999). What should educational research be the research of? *Issues in Education: Contributions From Educational Psychology, 5*(1), 1–35.

Pressley, M., Wharton-McDonald, R., Allington, R., Block, C.C., Morrow, L., Tracey, D., et al. (2001). A study of effective first-grade literacy instruction. *Scientific Studies of Reading, 5*(1), 35–58. doi:10.1207/S1532799XSSR0501_2

Pressley, M., Wharton-McDonald, R., Ranking, J., Mistretta, J., Yokoi, L., & Ettenberger, S. (1996). The nature of outstanding primary grade literacy instruction. In E. McIntyre & M. Pressley (Eds.), *Balanced instruction: Strategies and skills in whole language* (pp. 251–276). Norwood, MA: Christopher-Gordon.

Puma, M.J., Karweit, N., Price, C., Ricciuti, A., Thompson, W., & Vaden-Kiernan, M. (1997). *Prospects: Final report on student outcomes.* Cambridge, MA: Abt Associates.

Purcell-Gates, V., McIntyre, E., & Freppon, P.A. (1995). Learning written storybook language in school: A comparison of low-SES children in skills-based and whole language classrooms. *American Educational Research Journal, 32*(3), 659–685.

Ravitch, D. (2010). *The death and life of the great American School system: How testing and choice are undermining education.* New York: Basic Books.

Robinson, H.M. (1946). *Why pupils fail in reading: A study of causes and remedial treatment.* Chicago: University of Chicago Press.

Rothstein, R. (1998). *The way we were? The myths and realities of America's student achievement.* New York: Century Foundation.

Rowan, B., & Guthrie, L.F. (1989). The quality of Chapter 1 instruction: Results from a study of twenty-four schools. In R.E. Slavin, N.L. Karweit, & N.A. Madden (Eds.), *Effective programs for students at risk* (pp. 195–219). Boston: Allyn & Bacon.

Sacks, C.H., & Mergendoller, J.R. (1997). The relationship between teachers' theoretical orientation toward reading and student outcomes in kindergarten children with different initial reading abilities. *American Educational Research Journal, 34*(4), 721–739.

Scanlon, D.M. (2011). Response to intervention as an assessment approach. In A. McGill-Franzen & R.L. Allington (Eds.), *Handbook of reading disability research* (pp. 139–148). New York: Routledge.

Scanlon, D.M., Gelzheiser, L.M., Vellutino, F.R., Schatschneider, C., & Sweeney, J.M. (2010). Reducing the incidence of early reading difficulties: Professional development for classroom teachers versus direct interventions for children. In P.H. Johnston (Ed.), *RTI in Literacy—Responsive and comprehensive* (pp. 257–295). Newark, DE: International Reading

Association. (Reprinted from *Learning and Individual Differences*, 2008, *18*(3), 346–359.)

Scanlon, D.M., & Vellutino, F.R. (1997). A comparison of the instructional backgrounds and cognitive profiles of poor, average, and good readers who were initially identified as at risk for reading failure. *Scientific Studies of Reading, 1*(3), 191–215. doi:10.1207/s1532799xssr0103_2

Scanlon, D.M., Vellutino, F.R., Small, S.G., Fanuele, D.P., & Sweeney, J.M. (2005). Severe reading difficulties—Can they be prevented? A comparison of prevention and intervention approaches. *Exceptionality, 13*(4), 209–227. doi:10.1207/s15327035ex1304_3

Schweinhart, L.J., & Weikart, D.P. (1998). Why curriculum matters in early childhood education. *Educational Leadership, 55*(6), 57–60.

Shanahan, T., & Barr, R. (1995). Reading Recovery: An independent evaluation of the effects of an early instructional intervention for at-risk learners. *Reading Research Quarterly, 30*(4), 958–996. doi:10.2307/748206

Shaywitz, S.E., Escobar, M.D., Shaywitz, B.A., Fletcher, J.M., & Makuch, R. (1992, January 16). Evidence that dyslexia may represent the lower tail of a normal distribution of reading ability. *The New England Journal of Medicine, 326*, 145–150. doi:10.1056/NEJM199201163260301

Sindelar, P.T., & Kilgore, K.L. (1996). Teacher education. In M.C. Wang, M.C. Reynolds, & H.J. Walberg (Eds.), *Handbook of special and remedial education* (2nd ed., pp. 391–432). New York: Pergamon.

Slavin, R.E., Madden, N.A., Dolan, L.J., & Wasik, B.A. (1996). *Every child, every school: Success for all.* Thousand Oaks, CA: Corwin.

Sleeter, C.E. (1986). Learning disabilities: The social construction of a special education category. *Exceptional Children, 53*(1), 46–54.

Snow, C.E., Burns, M.S., & Griffin, P. (Eds.). (1998). *Preventing reading difficulties in young children.* Washington, DC: National Academy Press.

Spear-Swerling, L., & Sternberg, R.J. (1996). *Off track: When poor readers become "learning disabled."* Boulder, CO: Westview.

Stahl, S.A., Duffy-Hester, A.M., & Stahl, K.A.D. (1998). Everything you wanted to know about phonics (but were afraid to ask). *Reading Research Quarterly, 33*(3), 338–355. doi:10.1598/RRQ.33.3.5

Stahl, S.A., Heubach, K.M., & Holcomb, A. (2005). Fluency-oriented reading instruction.

Journal of Literacy Research, 37(1), 25–60. doi:10.1207/s15548430jlr3701_2

Stahl, S.A., & Miller, P.D. (1989). Whole language and language experience approaches for beginning readers: A quantitative research synthesis. *Review of Educational Research, 59*(1), 87–116.

Stanovich, K.E. (1991). Discrepancy definitions of reading disability: Has intelligence led us astray? *Reading Research Quarterly, 26*(1), 7–29. doi:10.2307/747729

Stanovich, K.E., & Siegel, L.S. (1994). Phenotypic performance profile of children with reading disabilities: A regression-based test of the phonological-core variable-difference model. *Journal of Educational Psychology, 86*(1), 24–53. doi:10.1037/0022-0663.86.1.24

Swanson, H.L., & Hoskyn, M. (1998). Experimental intervention research on students with learning disabilities: A meta-analysis of treatment outcomes. *Review of Educational Research, 68*(3), 277–321.

Sweet, R.W., Jr. (1997, May/June). Don't read, don't tell: Clinton's phony war on illiteracy. *Policy Review, 83*, 38–42.

Taylor, B.M., Pearson, P.D., Clark, K., & Walpole, S. (2000). Effective schools and accomplished teachers: Lessons from primary-grade reading instruction in low-income schools. *The Elementary School Journal, 101*(2), 121–165. doi:10.1086/499662

Taylor, B., Short, R., Shearer, B., & Frye, B. (1995). First grade teachers provide early reading intervention in the classroom. In R.L. Allington & S.A. Walmsley (Eds.), *No quick fix: Rethinking literacy programs in America's elementary schools* (pp. 159–176). New York: Teachers College Press; Newark, DE: International Reading Association.

Taylor, D. (1998). *Beginning to read and the spin doctors of science: The political campaign to change America's mind about how children learn to read.* Urbana, IL: National Council of Teachers of English.

Thurlow, M.L., Ysseldyke, J.E., Graden, J., & Algozzine, B. (1984). Opportunity to learn for LD students receiving different levels of special education services. *Learning Disability Quarterly, 7*(1), 55–67. doi:10.2307/1510262

Torgesen, J.K., Wagner, R.K., Rashotte, C.A., Alexander, A.W., & Conway, T. (1997). Preventive and remedial interventions for children with severe reading disabilities. *Learning Disabilities: A Interdisciplinary Journal, 8*(1), 51–61.

Troia, G.A. (1999). Phonological awareness intervention research: A critical review of the experimental methodology. *Reading Research Quarterly, 34*(1), 28–52. doi:10.1598/RRQ.34.1.3

Vaughn, S., & Linan-Thompson, S., & Hickman, P. (2003). Response to instruction as a means to identifying students with reading/learning difficulties. *Exceptional Children, 69*(4), 391–409.

Vellutino, F.R., & Fletcher, J.M. (2005). Developmental dyslexia. In M.J. Snowling & C.J. Hulme (Eds.), *The science of reading: A handbook* (pp. 362–378). Malden, MA: Blackwell.

Vellutino, F.R., Fletcher, J.M., Snowling, M.J., & Scanlon, D.M. (2004). Specific reading disability (dyslexia): What have we learned in the past four decades? *Journal of Child Psychology and Psychiatry, 45*(1), 2–40. doi:10.1046/j.0021-9630.2003.00305.x

Vellutino, F.R., Scanlon, D.M., Sipay, E.R., Small, S.G., Pratt, A., Chen, R., et al. (1996). Cognitive profiles of difficult-to-remediate and readily remediated poor readers: Early intervention as a vehicle for distinguishing between cognitive and experiential deficits as basic causes of specific reading disability. *Journal of Educational Psychology, 88*(4), 601–638. doi:10.1037/0022-0663.88.4.601

Venezky, R.L. (1998). An alternate perspective on Success for All. In K.K. Wong (Ed.), *Advances in educational policy* (pp. 145–165). Greenwich, CT: JAI.

Wagner, M. (1995). *The contribution of poverty and ethnic background to the participation of secondary school students in special education.* Menlo Park, CA: SRI International.

Walmsley, S.A., & Allington, R.L. (1995). Redefining and reforming instructional support programs for at-risk students. In R.L. Allington & S.A. Walmsley (Eds.), *No quick fix: Rethinking literacy programs in America's elementary schools* (pp. 19–41).

New York: Teachers College Press; Newark, DE: International Reading Association.

Walp, T., & Walmsley, S.A. (1995). Scoring well on tests or becoming genuinely literate: Rethinking remediation in a small rural school. In R.L. Allington & S.A. Walmsley (Eds.), *No quick fix: Rethinking literacy programs in America's elementary schools* (pp. 177–196). New York: Teachers College Press; Newark, DE: International Reading Association.

Wasik, B.A. (1998). Volunteer tutoring programs in reading: A review. *Reading Research Quarterly, 33*(3), 266–291. doi:10.1598/RRQ.33.3.2

Wasik, B.A., & Slavin, R.E. (1993). Preventing early reading failure with one-to-one tutoring: A review of five programs. *Reading Research Quarterly, 28*(2), 178–200. doi:10.2307/747888

What Works Clearinghouse, Institute of Education Sciences, U.S. Department of Education. (2007). *WWC intervention report: Reading Recovery.* Washington, DC: Author. Retrieved November 30, 2010, from ies.ed.gov/ncee/wwc/pdf/WWC_Reading_Recovery_031907.pdf

Whitehurst, G.J., & Lonigan, C.J. (1998). Child development and emergent literacy. *Child Development, 69*(3), 848–872.

Winfield, L. (1995). Change in urban schools with high concentrations of low-income children: Chapter 1 schoolwide projects. In R.L. Allington & S.A. Walmsley (Eds.), *No quick fix: Rethinking literacy programs in America's elementary schools* (pp. 214–235). New York: Teachers College Press; Newark, DE: International Reading Association.

Wise, B.W., & Olson, R.K. (1999, Spring). The Colorado remediation studies. *Early Childhood Update.* Retrieved November 23, 2010, from www2.ed.gov/offices/OERI/ECI/newsletters/99spring/early6.html

Chapter 11

Implementing a Response to Intervention Model to Improve Reading Outcomes for All Students

Elizabeth Swanson and Sharon Vaughn

In the context of reading instruction, Response to Intervention (RTI) "emphasizes increasingly differentiated and intensified instruction or intervention in language and literacy" (International Reading Association, 2010, p. 2) to meet the needs of struggling readers. It is a system-level, proactive, preventative approach that relies on data-based decision making to identify students who are at risk for reading difficulty and subsequently provide instruction that matches student needs; secondarily, the RTI approach uses the resulting data as a resource for identifying students with learning disabilities (Barnes & Harlacher, 2008; Fletcher & Vaughn, 2009). In so doing, effective implementation of RTI has the promise to raise the achievement level of all students.

RTI's roots are in the public health model of intervention, in which multiple tiers of increasingly intense interventions are directed at increasingly smaller segments of the population (Glover, 2010; Mellard & Johnson, 2008). Fundamentally, students are identified for intervention based on their low responses to typically effective instructional practices. In this chapter, we present a three-tiered approach. However, the number of tiers is not the most salient feature of RTI, as four- and even five-tiered approaches are used in schools and districts (see Kovaleski & Black, 2010) to provide effective reading instruction.

Figure 11.1 provides an overview of a typical RTI framework. A basic decision-making process is implemented that begins with providing high-quality, research-based instruction, followed by an assessment of whether the instruction was effective in preventing or remediating reading difficulty. For students who do not make adequate progress, more intensive prevention (younger students) or remediation (older students) instruction is provided, along with further assessment of effectiveness.

What Research Has to Say About Reading Instruction (4th ed.) edited by S. Jay Samuels and Alan E. Farstrup.
© 2011 by the International Reading Association.

Figure 11.1. Response to Intervention Decision-Making Process

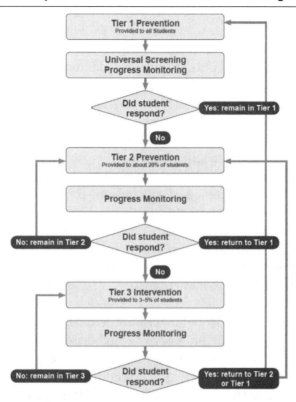

For example, in a three-tiered model, primary prevention occurs in Tier 1, in which all students are provided research-based reading instruction inside the general education classroom. However, no reading curriculum or methodology meets the needs of all students all of the time. Research has shown that typically 80% of students progress adequately with Tier 1 prevention alone. The remaining 20% of students receive more intensive, Tier 2 prevention in the form of supplemental intervention provided by the classroom teacher, a well-supervised instructional assistant, or a specialist, depending on school resources. These short-term prevention programs are usually provided 3–5 days per week in small groups of 3–5 students over approximately 10 weeks, in addition to effective Tier 1 instruction. One of two outcomes results from high-quality Tier 2 prevention instruction. Either students meet grade-level expectations and are no longer provided Tier 2 supplemental intervention, or the students' needs persist. Research has shown that typically 2–3% of students continue to struggle after receiving high-quality Tier 2 intervention. For these students, Tier 3 intervention that is more intensive, individualized, and provided either in addition to or in place of Tier 1 instruction, depending on the severity of student need, is necessary. We would like to note that when students enter Tier 3 intervention varies by school and the needs of students. For example, some students continue in Tier 2 intervention for 20–30 weeks when they make adequate progress.

The thread that ties the three tiers together is a data-based decision-making process that uses universal screening of all students at key points during the school year combined with ongoing progress monitoring for students who struggle with reading. These two data-collection techniques inform decisions within the three-tier model of service delivery, such as (a) whether Tier 1 prevention is effective, (b) when a student needs more intensive prevention (Tier 2) or intervention (Tier 3) instruction, and (c) when a student is ready to move from Tier 2 or Tier 3 back to Tier 1 prevention instruction only.

In this chapter, we describe how data are used during the RTI decision-making process, and then we explore research-based instructional components and data-based decision-making elements of effective Tier 1 and Tier 2 prevention as well as Tier 3 intervention instruction. In addition, we recently recorded teachers' perceptions of RTI through a series of focus groups with 17 elementary school teachers who provide reading intervention within an RTI model. We present their perceptions of RTI's benefits and challenges as a means of setting a context for issues related to the implementation of RTI.

Data-Based Decision Making: Universal Screening and Progress Monitoring

Data-based decision making is an integral component of an RTI model in reading. Universal screening and progress monitoring data are used to do the following (Fuchs & Fuchs, 2008):

- Identify students who require additional or more intensive reading instruction
- Determine whether students respond to Tier 2 prevention or Tier 3 intervention

- Tailor intensive instructional programs for students in need of Tier 3 intervention

Universal Screening

Universal screening procedures are used to assess every student in designated grade levels in a relatively short period of time to determine whether Tier 1 instruction is effective and to identify students who require Tier 2 instruction. A brief measure of reading skill is usually administered in the fall, winter, and spring of each academic year. Curriculum-based measures and other progress-monitoring tools provide a valid and reliable way to collect student performance data to make instructional decisions (for review, see www.progressmonitoring.org). Commonly used progress-monitoring tools include oral-reading fluency measures of words correctly read per minute, word reading lists, maze tasks in which students read connected text and then fill in missing words from three given choices, and tasks such as reading texts with retells. With older students (i.e., grades 4–10), it may be useful to use passages from content area texts that students are required to read.

Student data obtained from these progress-monitoring assessments are summarized and reviewed at each screening point. First, teachers consider grade-level and classroom-level scores to identify students with additional instructional needs and classrooms that require additional instructional support. Published progress-monitoring tools typically provide normative data to allow schools to compare classroom performance and individual student performance against a nationally representative group of typically developing readers. Low-performing classes may indicate that additional professional development, instructional assistance, or coaching would be helpful. Of course, it could also indicate that a disproportionate number of students with reading difficulties are in one class and that additional teacher support is required.

Second, teachers evaluate individual student scores to determine which students are below grade-level expectations or a preestablished cut point (e.g., some districts use cut points for student performance in the fall, winter, and spring of each grade level). A cut point is the level below which students require intervention (Tier 2). A common approach to make these decisions is to use a single cut point to determine risk status. For example, Table 11.1 presents oral-reading fluency scores for a normative sample of second graders (Hasbrouck & Tindal, 2006). Students who score below the 25th percentile are deemed at risk for reading difficulty and are considered for Tier 2 prevention services. However, we have

Table 11.1. Normative Oral-Reading Fluency Scores for Second Graders

	Oral-reading fluency score		
Percentile rank	Fall	Winter	Spring
90	106	125	142
75	79	100	117
50	51	72	89
25	25	52	61
10	11	18	31

Note. Adapted from "Oral Reading Fluency Norms: A Valuable Assessment Tool for Reading Teachers," by J. Hasbrouck & G.A. Tindal, 2006, *The Reading Teacher, 59*(7).

found that schools benefit when considering a multiple-gating procedure that includes teachers' perceptions of students' reading abilities as well as other commonly used measures such as running records.

Progress Monitoring

Once students are identified through universal screening as struggling with reading, teachers monitor their progress more frequently than typical or above-average readers. The rate of gain for students is based on whether their instructional needs are in the basic foundation skills (e.g., letter naming, letter–sound connection, word reading) or more complex reading knowledge (e.g., vocabulary knowledge, background knowledge, comprehension skills and strategies). Rapid gains are much more common with the basic foundation skills than with more complex reading knowledge. Therefore, progress monitoring for the at-risk groups can take place as often as weekly for skills such as letter naming or word reading, and less frequently for more complex strategies related to understanding text. In middle and high schools, student gains are less likely to fluctuate or grow as quickly. In these settings, student progress is typically monitored every 3–4 weeks.

Reading elements (e.g., letter naming, word reading) can be measured using criterion-referenced tests, whereby the tasks on the test align with the elements taught at that grade level. This type of testing is much easier to do in kindergarten, first grade, and second grade, when the foundations of reading instruction align with easily measured areas such as oral text reading, rather than in later grades, which feature difficult-to-measure elements such as vocabulary and comprehension of complex texts.

For the elementary reading task of letter–sound correspondence, for example, a criterion-referenced test is a teacher showing a card for each letter in the alphabet and a student providing each corresponding sound. The score is the number of correct sounds provided. The criterion for mastery is 26 correct letter sounds produced on two consecutive tests (Fuchs & Fuchs, 2008). Criterion-referenced tests can be created for other reading elements, such as sight-word reading and reading consonant-vowel-consonant words. Most core reading programs used in schools today contain criterion-referenced tests that can be used in Tier 1, Tier 2, and Tier 3 for students who struggle with reading.

Student progress can also be measured using a general outcome measure, such as a curriculum-based measure that can be administered repeatedly. In this way, gains over time on similar tasks can be determined. Oral-reading fluency is commonly used as a general measure. Evidence indicates that oral-reading fluency is a marker in younger students (i.e., grades 1–4) of overall reading competence (Fuchs & Fuchs, 1998; Fuchs, Fuchs, Hosp, & Jenkins, 2001) and correlates with reading comprehension (Fuchs & Fuchs, 1998; Fuchs, Fuchs, & Maxwell, 1988; Jenkins, Fuchs, van den Broek, Espin, & Deno, 2003). In addition, oral-reading fluency data are simple to gather and score.

In the most basic form of measuring oral-reading fluency, students read a passage for one minute. The words read correctly within the minute are counted. This total becomes the student's score, which can be graphed over time to determine whether adequate progress is being made in reading. It is also possible to use oral-reading fluency with a more direct measure of reading comprehension. In this case, the student reads a passage orally for one minute, and the words correct per minute are determined. Then, the student is given about three minutes to read the entire passage; afterward, the teacher asks questions to determine the student's understanding of the passage. The teacher then scores the student's reading comprehension; for example, outstanding = 4, good = 3, less than adequate = 2, and poor = 1. These scores are recorded to determine progress in comprehension. Of course, the teacher could extend this scoring system to a seven-point scale, for example, to introduce even greater subtlety in comprehension scoring.

Tier 1 Prevention

"Tier 1 provides the foundation for successful RTI" (Gersten et al., 2009, p. 17).

Instructional Elements of Tier 1 Prevention

Tier 1 prevention provides every student with high-quality, evidence-based, effective reading instruction (Vaughn & Denton, 2008). Tier 1 prevention usually ranges from 90 to 135 minutes per day in the elementary grades, with more time spent on reading in kindergarten through third grade than in fourth and fifth grades (Taylor, Pearson, Clark, & Walpole, 2000; Taylor, Pearson, Peterson, & Rodriguez, 2003). Reading instruction in middle school is often limited to a 50-minute English language arts class, although an increasing number of middle schools are providing reading classes for students with reading difficulties.

Carefully designed Tier 1 instruction can promote student success on a broad scale. For example, Florida implemented a five-year statewide initiative to improve Tier 1 reading instruction (Torgesen, 2002). Initially, 31.8% of Florida first graders performed below the 25th percentile on tests of reading. However, in response to the increase in Tier 1 instructional quality, this number dropped to only 3.7%. Indeed, high-quality Tier 1 instruction meets the needs of most students. Luckily, educators have worked tirelessly over the past decade to identify components of effective reading instruction.

Although the literature is replete with research reports (e.g., Snow, Burns, & Griffin, 1998), syntheses (e.g., Ehri, Nunes, Stahl, & Willows, 2001), and reviews (e.g., Ehri, 2004; Gersten et al., 2009; Taylor, 2008) detailing the essential elements of Tier 1 prevention instruction, these sources converge on several recommendations, including the following:

- Well-distributed instructional time should focus on foundational skills, such as phonological awareness (PA) in preschool through first grade and phonics, as well as deeper processing skills, such as fluency, vocabulary, and comprehension.

- A well-organized, systemic approach to reading that includes screening, ongoing progress monitoring, and explicit instruction is necessary.

- Students need extended opportunities to read and interpret their understanding with peers and teachers across a variety of text genres.

- Differentiated instruction based on student need is effective.

Systematic and Explicit Instruction. Systematic and explicit instruction has been shown to produce greater gains than other forms of instruction, particularly among students who struggle with reading. In one study (Foorman, Francis, Fletcher, Schatschneider, & Mehta, 1998), first and second graders were provided one of three types of reading instruction: (1) direct instruction, in which teachers explicitly taught letter–sound correspondences and practiced using decodable text, (2) embedded instruction, in which spelling patterns were taught less explicitly and embedded in connected text, or (3) implicit instruction, in which no explicit instruction of letter–sound correspondences was provided while reading connected text. Students in the direct instruction group improved in word reading skill at a significantly faster rate than students in the other two groups. In addition, 44% of students who received embedded instruction and 46% of students who received implicit instruction demonstrated no growth on measures of word reading, but only 16% of students who received direct instruction failed to demonstrate growth on the same measures. Other studies have reported similar findings, concluding that approximately 80% of students can benefit from Tier 1 instruction alone when it is effectively implemented (e.g., Olson, Wise, Ring, & Johnson, 1997; Torgesen, 1997).

Explicit instruction is characterized by clear, unambiguous teacher descriptions of concepts and skills plus opportunities for students to practice as a group and then individually while receiving feedback from the teacher about their performance. See Table 11.2 for an example of

Table 11.2. Examples of Explicit Instruction

Phonics/ word study	Teacher:	[writes "ay" on the board] We will learn a new sound today. The sound of these letters [pointing to "ay"] is /a/. What sound?
	Students:	/a/.
	Teacher:	Let's read words that contain our new sound. Examples include *way* and *play*. [The teacher then writes several "ay" words on the board, and students read the words (with teacher assistance, if needed).]
Vocabulary	Teacher:	The first word is *exquisite*. What word?
	Students:	*Exquisite*.
	Teacher:	When something is exquisite, it is beautiful and special. It is a beautiful day outside. That makes the day very special, so I might say, "It is an exquisite day." [The teacher then provides additional examples.] Tell your partner something that you have seen that is exquisite. [After providing time for students to discuss, the teacher calls on one pair of students to share their example with the class.]
	Students:	These flowers are exquisite.
	Teacher:	Yes, those flowers are beautiful and special, so they are exquisite. [The teacher then continues with additional examples.]

explicit phonics/word study and vocabulary instruction. Notice how the teacher explains a skill or concept using clear language, followed by multiple opportunities for students to practice the new skill or concept.

Differentiated Instructional Delivery. Instruction based on students' needs can be effectively delivered during Tier 1 through small, teacher-led groups (Gersten et al., 2009). Teachers make decisions about instructional differentiation using their observations about students' reading and responding, and data they can readily collect, such as program placement or mastery tests, inventories of sight words or letter–sound knowledge, and repeated measures of reading elements. Teachers can use these data to form small groups of students with similar needs that are convened for a few lessons. For example, if assessment data show that in the spring of kindergarten, most students know all letter names and sounds, but four or five students continue to struggle, the teacher could provide a set of lessons to reteach letter names and sounds over a 1–2-week period to this small group of students. Differentiated instruction groups should remain flexible. As the teacher identifies different groups of students with different learning needs, the group composition and instruction change as well.

Data-Based Decision Making in Tier 1

In Tier 1, all students are screened to determine adequate progress in reading, usually three times per year. These screening data accomplish two goals. First, the average rate of gain for a class can be compared with other classes in the school to determine whether student progress is aligned with end-of-year expectations. If one class's average gain is lower than the others, the teacher may need support in delivering effective Tier 1 instruction. Second, teachers monitor closely students who fall below a predetermined cut point (e.g., the bottom 20% of the class, below a norm-referenced cut point) to determine whether Tier 1 instruction alone is adequate to address the students' needs. Typically, if students remain below the cut point for six weeks while continuing to receive high-quality Tier 1 prevention, Tier 2 interventions are considered.

Tier 2 Prevention

"The most important issue to consider is whether the secondary intervention is intensive enough to provide students with a reasonable opportunity to 'catch up' to grade-level expectations" (Vaughn & Denton, 2008, p. 59).

Instructional Elements of Tier 2 Prevention

Tier 2 prevention is a critical point in a struggling reader's schooling. The purpose of Tier 2 instruction is to improve the reading ability of struggling readers so that they begin to read both for pleasure and to learn. Therefore, intervention occurs as early as the reading difficulty is observed and is provided intensively, effectively, and efficiently so that the student is encouraged by progress and spends as little time in intervention as possible (Denton & Vaughn, 2010). Typically, less than 5% of kindergarten and first-grade students remain at risk following effective Tier 2 instruction (Mathes et al., 2005; McMaster, Fuchs, Fuchs, & Compton, 2005). The extent to which students catch up to peers through secondary interventions is related to how far behind they are; thus, struggling readers are significantly more likely to catch up in kindergarten, first grade, and second grade than in later grades (Vaughn et al., 2010).

Wanzek and Vaughn (2007) recently synthesized 18 studies providing long-term interventions (i.e., delivered daily for about 20 weeks for a total of about 100 sessions) to kindergarten through third-grade students at risk for reading difficulty or with a disability. The researchers concluded that such 20-week interventions are feasible for schools and result in positive outcomes for students, particularly when intervention is provided early (i.e., in kindergarten or first grade) or in small groups. No differences in student outcomes were detected between studies implementing highly standardized interventions or interventions with less standardized implementation.

Schools can intensify instruction for struggling readers at the Tier 2 level in several ways, including providing instruction in small groups or even one on one (i.e., one teacher with one student) if feasible and adjusting the focus and duration of instruction.

Small, Homogeneous Intervention Groups. Teachers use data from multiple sources, including screening, progress monitoring, and observations, to identify small groups of students who experience similar difficulties in spite of effective Tier 1 instruction. Although some evidence suggests that one-to-one instruction may be superior to small-group instruction at the Tier 2 level (see Wanzek & Vaughn, 2007), one-on-one instruction may not be feasible for school districts with limited resources (Denton & Vaughn, 2010). In addition, other evidence suggests that small groups are as effective as one-on-one instruction (Elbaum, Vaughn, Hughes, & Moody, 2000).

The homogeneous small-group structure benefits students in several ways. First, because students in such groups have similar needs, teachers may focus on fewer high-priority skills (Gersten et al., 2009). Second, when students are provided Tier 2 intervention within groups of 3–5, they have more opportunities to practice and respond. Students who struggle with reading may require 10 times as many practice opportunities as their peers. When a student is one of four in a group, he or she has five times the opportunity to respond with specific feedback than a student in a group of 20.

Finally, in homogeneous small groups, teachers can more easily provide immediate, explicit feedback to students, making it less likely that errors will become internalized and be repeated (Gersten et al., 2009). Not only are teachers more likely to hear errors, but also teachers can more quickly correct errors, providing additional practice opportunities for students.

Duration of Intervention. Duration may be intensified in two ways: length of each session and the number of sessions provided. Wanzek and Vaughn's (2007) synthesis of extensive interventions reported medium to strong effects for 5–7-month interventions that focused on foundational skills with young children (i.e., kindergarten, first grade). Schneider, Roth, and Ennemoser (2000) provided kindergartners at risk for reading difficulties with a PA intervention or a PA plus letter–sound correspondence intervention over a five-month period. Although all at-risk kindergartners outperformed students not at risk who received typical practice, only students who received the PA plus letter–sound correspondence intervention maintained outcomes equivalent to students not at risk at the end of first and second grade. Indeed, Tier 2 reading instruction that is targeted to match student needs can be effective when implemented for a duration that is feasible within the school setting.

Data-Based Decision Making in Tier 2

Another key feature of Tier 2 instruction is the frequency and nature of progress-monitoring data collection. Figure 11.2 details the process for data-based decision making within Tier 2 intervention.

In Tier 2, teachers usually assess students 1–3 times per week on a measure aligned with students' instructional needs. Using these data, students' progress is assessed after they receive at least 10 weeks of intervention. Options to consider include the following (Vaughn Gross Center for Reading and Language Arts, 2005):

Figure 11.2. Data-Based Decision-Making Process for One Round of Tier 2 Intervention

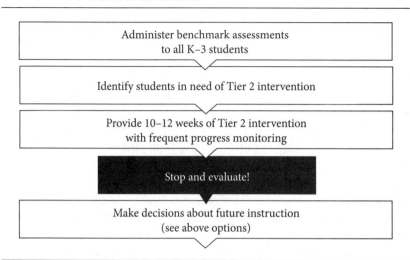

Note. Adapted from *Introduction to the 3-Tier Reading Model: Reducing Reading Difficulties for Kindergarten Through Third Grade Students* (4th ed.), by Vaughn Gross Center for Reading and Language Arts, University of Texas at Austin, 2005, Austin, TX: Author.

- Exiting Tier 2 intervention if the student is able to meet grade-level reading expectations
- Continuing Tier 2 intervention
- Determining that students' needs are more intensive and providing Tier 3 intervention
- Referring for special services (e.g., learning disabilities)

If a student's reading performance is on par with classmates, further intervention may not be needed. However, many students who exit from intervention may require intervention later that year or in subsequent grades (Vaughn et al., 2009; Vaughn, Linan-Thompson, & Hickman, 2003). If a student's scores do not indicate adequate improvement, he or she may receive additional Tier 2 intervention or transition to Tier 3 intervention. To make this decision, teachers determine whether the student is making progress and will eventually meet grade-level expectations; in other words, the Tier 2 intervention is effective, but additional time in intervention is necessary. When students do not make sufficient progress in Tier 2, a more intensive, Tier 3 intervention is required.

Tier 3 Intervention: Instructional Elements

"Tier III provides accelerated instruction that is more explicit, more intensive, and specifically designed to meet [students'] individual needs by 'closing the gap' in their reading performance" (The Meadows Center for Preventing Educational Risk, 2010, para. 6).

If students do not make adequate progress through a combination of high-quality Tier 1 prevention and targeted Tier 2 prevention, Tier 3 intervention may be required. Like Tier 2, Tier 3 intervention is delivered in small, homogeneous groups and consists of carefully designed, intensive, scientifically based reading instruction. However, the intensity of instruction and length of each intervention session increases in Tier 3, and interventions are usually delivered by a reading specialist or special education teacher who is well trained in providing the intervention.

Instructional intensity may be adjusted in several ways within this longer daily intervention session (Good, Kame'enui, Simmons, & Chard, 2002). First, teachers can provide a greater number and range of examples through modeling and explaining. For example, when learning the vocabulary word *explore* in Tier 2, one or two examples may suffice. However, in Tier 3, students may require many different types of examples, including not only discussion of places one may explore but also photos of places commonly explored.

Second, when teachers determine that students do not posses prerequisite knowledge and skills for a particular task, teachers can provide minilessons to address these needs before and during instruction. For example, writing a main idea statement requires several prerequisite skills that could be included in minilessons, such as identifying important information, identifying details, writing a complete sentence, and using capitalization and punctuation.

Third, teachers can extend the number of opportunities students have to respond by using different types of student response techniques. Opportunities range from low intensity (e.g., yes or no responses), to responses that require pointing or stating the answer from several options provided by the teacher, to high intensity (e.g., oral or written responses). Research on Tier 2 interventions is more extensive than research on Tier 3 interventions, just as the efficacy of interventions is better documented with younger students (i.e., kindergarten through third grade) than with older students (i.e., third through fifth grades). Considerably more research on Tier 3 interventions is needed, particularly for minimal responders (Wanzek & Vaughn, 2009).

Perceived Benefits and Difficulties of RTI Implementation

One of the most common questions that reading teachers ask is about the advantages and disadvantages of implementing RTI. In the spring of 2009, we conducted a series of focus groups with elementary school teachers who provided Tier 2 and Tier 3 instruction in a school district that has implemented RTI over the past three years. We also interviewed the director of RTI for the district. We wanted to know about the perceived benefits and difficulties teachers faced in implementing RTI within their schools. After transcribing all focus group meetings using procedures recommended by Brantlinger, Jiménez, Klingner, Pugach, and Richardson (2005), we conducted analyses to determine the most outstanding benefits and difficulties related to RTI implementation.

Benefits of RTI Implementation

Increased Cooperation and Collaboration. The district's RTI director stated, "Our philosophy is to meet 100% of the students' needs 100% of the time." Meeting this lofty goal requires a close working relationship among general educators, special educators, and other instructional resource providers in a school (Vaughn et al., 2008). Teachers frequently identified as a benefit the ability to work with any student experiencing reading difficulty, rather than being restricted to providing support based on funding (e.g., Title I, special education). Simply put, teachers commented that because all professionals could work together and coordinate services for students with reading needs, there were "more people who can help."

Teachers also indicated that they were serving a greater number of students and were better able to meet specific needs. These teachers were pleased that their expertise and specialized training in reading intervention were being used on a broader scale. One teacher reported, "It is nice that [students] can be taught by those of us…with more experience… without being [identified with a disability]." Teachers reported that students no longer "belonged" to one teacher. Said one teacher, "They are not my kids. They are not your kids. They are all of our kids, and we are interventionists for the whole school." These teachers considered RTI as a schoolwide model in which professionals work cooperatively to meet students' needs, contrasting RTI with previous efforts in which teachers and other professionals (e.g., speech language specialists) tended to stay in their "categories" and worked less effectively as a team.

Meeting Student Needs. Teachers praised the focus on the early identification of students who require additional reading support without providing a stigmatizing setting. Teachers valued that all teachers on campus collaborated to meet student needs as early as the needs were expressed, rather than waiting until students were identified with a disability that would entitle them to intervention services. Teachers reported a district-wide focus on identifying the reading needs of and providing services to kindergarten and first-grade students. One teacher said, "The biggest advantage is [teaching] those kids as soon as they show signs of trouble." The teacher went on to characterize the attitude at the school: "This kid is struggling, and I know that based on research and experience, [this] program can help. Let's start it!" Further, teachers said they were able to address student needs successfully, as evidenced by students who had gone through intervention in earlier grades and performed on grade level in subsequent years.

Teachers also cited RTI as meeting the social needs of students who struggle with reading. Prior to RTI implementation, these students often felt ostracized and embarrassed when they left their classrooms to receive additional instruction. Teachers perceived RTI as relieving this stigma, with one teacher stating, "The room is open. The door is open. Kids are coming in and out.... There is safety in numbers."

Proactive Use of Data. Teachers overwhelmingly reported the excitement of seeing improvement in students' reading through review of frequently collected data. One teacher said the following about progress among Tier 2 prevention groups: "We did see improvement. Whether it was miniscule or not, we did see improvement in all of our kids' reading from one administration to the next." Other teachers reported RTI as being a "vehicle" for data collection. Through RTI, they were able to collect data that was "pertinent to the deficit of the child...it's very focused."

Difficulties in RTI Implementation
Although the teachers perceived more advantages to RTI than disadvantages and were generally satisfied, they also identified some challenges. These challenges can be put into two main categories: scheduling and feasibility of collecting and maintaining assessment data.

Scheduling Challenges. Students in public school are scheduled to receive reading, math, science, social studies, special area instruction (e.g., art, music), and physical activities. On top of these scheduling requirements, schools host assemblies and special events. Schools in the early stages of RTI implementation have often not built Tier 2 intervention time into their master schedules, leaving intervention teachers with substantial scheduling challenges. Most teachers expressed concerns about students who are pulled out of the general classroom for Tier 3 instruction. Even if the instruction they receive from an interventionist is of high quality and aligns with the general education curriculum, students still miss some aspects of grade-level instruction by simply being pulled from the classroom. As a result, some intervention teachers provide Tier 3 within the general education classroom for a portion of the reading block, followed by a pull-out session for the remainder of the period.

Several scheduling challenges were identified for Tier 2 instructional delivery. Because Tier 2 instruction is provided in addition to Tier 1, or the core reading time, it is often difficult to find alternative times for instruction. For example, several teachers expressed concerns about students missing social studies or science instruction to receive Tier 2 reading instruction. One teacher commented, "We [can] integrate the social studies into our reading [lessons]…but [students] are in the classroom for science." Other teachers found opportunities, such as during a daily 30-minute block of sustained silent reading, to convene a Tier 2 reading group.

Assessment Feasibility. During universal screening at the beginning, middle, and end of the year, several teachers shared an "all hands on deck" approach to assessing students efficiently. In one school, each intervention teacher was assigned a grade level. Three times per year, her sole task was to assess every student in the grade level. Teachers also spoke of the process several schools used to train the entire faculty on screening measures. For example, one teacher explained,

> The first year we didn't [test] the whole campus…. Last year, the intervention teachers [assessed] the whole school, except the teachers had to take on five kids each so they could practice. This year, intervention teachers [test] only their own students. The regular classroom teachers have to assess their students…. But it's like a growing process…like a stepladder.

Conducting progress-monitoring assessments for many students requires organization of materials, time, and personnel. One teacher shared her struggle with managing assessment materials, saying,

You have to get the probe, the booklet; you have to [copy] the book-lets.... I get so lost in the paperwork. 'I just had it here. Where did it go?' You just have to make sure you have everything you need readily available to you.

Teachers at other schools share the burden of preparing and managing assessment materials and have worked closely with administration to accommodate intensified material-preparation responsibilities.

Other teachers commented on the pressure of continuing intervention in addition to administering assessments, entering data into a computer, analyzing data, and planning lessons accordingly.

With Tier 3, you have to progress monitor [weekly], whereas with Tier 2, it is every two weeks. Well, when you have 12 Tier 3 students total throughout the day [who] you have to progress monitor weekly, it becomes very hard, especially when you have assemblies thrown in... athletics thrown in...or whatever it is. It is very hard to [progress monitor] on a weekly basis.

Conclusion

RTI is a systemwide framework for preventing and remediating learning difficulties that has been most frequently used in reading. The critical elements of a three-tiered RTI framework are universal screening, progress monitoring, Tier 1 (i.e., core reading), Tier 2 (i.e., secondary intervention), and Tier 3 (i.e., intensive intervention). RTI is not a specific curriculum; it is instead a framework that can be modified to meet the instructional needs of the context in which it is used. Essential to the successful implementation of RTI is the early identification and treatment of students with reading difficulties that, without intervention, will likely persist (Francis, Shaywitz, Stuebing, Shaywitz, & Fletcher, 1996; Torgesen & Burgess, 1998). Reading difficulties become more difficult to remediate as students enter upper elementary and middle school grades (Denton & Vaughn, 2010) and present substantial barriers to learning through content area texts, achievement across content areas, and thinking and reasoning using text.

Multitiered reading intervention models provide all students with high-quality, effective reading instruction. Although RTI models require teacher training, support from knowledgeable administrators, and attention to barriers to effective implementation, many educators who have implemented RTI say the outcome for students is worth the effort (e.g.,

Batsche et al., 2005; Griffiths, Parson, Burns, VanDerHeyden, & Tilly, 2007). Through an RTI model, all students in a school can receive high-quality reading instruction that aligns with their needs. Indeed, as the district RTI director said, schools can "meet 100% of the students' needs 100% of the time."

Questions for Reflection

1. Neyla was reported to be an average reader in first grade. However, during the first round of universal screening during second grade, she scored among the bottom 10% of her peers. In a school that implements a three-tiered RTI model, what course of action would you suggest for Neyla?

2. Visit a reading or English language arts classroom and observe instruction for about 30 minutes. What do you notice about the ways in which the teacher uses systematic and explicit instruction and differentiated instruction?

3. During an interview for a teaching position, the principal asks you to describe your understanding of the RTI framework. How would you briefly describe RTI, including the key components of the framework?

4. Angela is a third grader who is gifted in reading and language. How can an RTI framework be used to address her needs within a school setting?

REFERENCES

Barnes, A.C., & Harlacher, J.E. (2008). Clearing the confusion: Response-to-Intervention as a set of principles. *Education & Treatment of Children, 31*(3), 417–431.

Batsche, G., Elliott, J., Graden, J.L., Grimes, J., Kovaleski, J.F., Prasse, D., et al. (2005). *Response to Intervention: Policy considerations and implementation.* Alexandria, VA: National Association of State Directors of Special Education.

Brantlinger, E., Jiménez, R., Klingner, J., Pugach, M., & Richardson, V. (2005). Qualitative studies in special education. *Exceptional Children, 71*(2), 195–207.

Denton, C.A., & Vaughn, S. (2010). Preventing and remediating reading difficulties: Perspectives from research. In T.A. Glover &

S. Vaughn (Eds.), *The promise of Response to Intervention: Evaluating current science and practice* (pp. 78–112). New York: Guilford.

Ehri, L.C. (2004). Teaching phonemic awareness and phonics: An explanation of the National Reading Panel meta-analyses. In P. McCardle & V. Chhabra (Eds.), *The voice of evidence in reading research* (pp. 153–186). Baltimore: Paul H. Brookes.

Ehri, L.C., Nunes, S., Stahl, S.A., & Willows, D.M. (2001). Systematic phonics instruction helps students learn to read: Evidence from the National Reading Panel's meta-analysis. *Review of Educational Research, 71*(3), 393–447. doi:10.3102/00346543071003393

Elbaum, B., Vaughn, S., Hughes, M.T., & Moody, S.W. (2000). How effective are one-to-one tutoring programs in reading for elementary students at risk for reading failure? A meta-analysis of the intervention research. *Journal of Educational Psychology, 92*(4), 605–619. doi:10.1037/0022-0663.92.4.605

Fletcher, J.M., & Vaughn, S. (2009). Response to Intervention: Preventing and remediating academic difficulties. *Child Development Perspectives, 3*(1), 30–37. doi:10.1111/j.1750-8606.2008.00072.x

Foorman, B.R., Francis, D.J., Fletcher, J.M., Schatschneider, C., & Mehta, P. (1998). The role of instruction in learning to read: Preventing reading failure in at-risk children. *Journal of Educational Psychology, 90*(1), 37–55. doi:10.1037/0022-0663.90.1.37

Francis, D.J., Shaywitz, S.E., Stuebing, K.K., Shaywitz, B.A., & Fletcher, J.M. (1996). Developmental lag versus deficit models of reading disability: A longitudinal, individual growth curves analysis. *Journal of Educational Psychology, 88*(1), 3–17. doi:10.1037/0022-0663.88.1.3

Fuchs, L.S., & Fuchs, D. (1998). Treatment validity: A unifying concept for reconceptualizing the identification of learning disabilities. *Learning Disabilities Research & Practice, 13*(4), 204–219.

Fuchs, L.S., & Fuchs, D. (2008). The role of assessment within the RTI framework. In D. Fuchs, L.S. Fuchs, & S. Vaughn (Eds.), *Response to Intervention: A framework for reading educators* (pp. 27–50). Newark, DE: International Reading Association.

Fuchs, L.S., Fuchs, D., Hosp, M.K., & Jenkins, J.R. (2001). Oral reading fluency as an indicator of reading competence: A theoretical, empirical, and historical analysis. *Scientific Studies of Reading, 5*(3), 239–256. doi:10.1207/S1532799XSSR0503_3

Fuchs, L.S., Fuchs, D., & Maxwell, L. (1988). The validity of informal reading comprehension measures. *Remedial and Special Education, 9*(2), 20–28. doi:10.1177/074193258800900206

Gersten, R., Compton, D., Connor, C.M., Dimino, J., Santoro, L., Linan-Thompson, S., et al. (2009). *Assisting students struggling with reading: Response to Intervention (RtI) and multi-tier intervention in the primary grades* (NCEE 2009-4045). Washington, DC: National Center for Education Evaluation and Regional Assistance, Institute of Education Sciences, U.S. Department of Education. Retrieved November 22, 2010, from ies.ed.gov/ncee/wwc/publications/practiceguides

Glover, T.A. (2010). Key RTI service delivery components: Considerations for research-informed practice. In T.A. Glover & S. Vaughn (Eds.), *The promise of Response to Intervention: Evaluating current science and practice* (pp. 7–22). New York: Guilford.

Good, R.H., Kame'enui, E.J., Simmons, D.S., & Chard, D.J. (2002). *Focus and nature of primary, secondary, and tertiary prevention: The CIRCUITS model* (Technical Report No. 1). Eugene: Institute for the Development of Educational Achievement, University of Oregon.

Griffiths, A., Parson, L.B., Burns, M.K., VanDerHeyden, A., & Tilly, W.D. (2007). *Response to Intervention: Research for practice.* Alexandria, VA: National Association of State Directors of Special Education.

Hasbrouck, J., & Tindal, G.A. (2006). Oral reading fluency norms: A valuable assessment tool for reading teachers. *The Reading Teacher, 59*(7), 636–644. doi:10.1598/RT.59.7.3

International Reading Association. (2010). *Response to Intervention: Guiding principles for educators from the International Reading Association.* Newark, DE: Author.

Jenkins, J.R., Fuchs, L.S., van den Broek, P., Espin, C., & Deno, S.L. (2003). Sources of individual differences in reading comprehension and reading fluency. *Journal of Educational Psychology, 95*(4), 719–729. doi:10.1037/0022-0663.95.4.719

Kovaleski, J.F., & Black, L. (2010). Multi-tier service delivery: Current status and future directions. In T.A. Glover & S. Vaughn (Eds.), *The promise of Response to Intervention: Evaluating current science and practice* (pp. 23–56). New York: Guilford.

Mathes, P.G., Denton, C.A., Fletcher, J.M., Anthony, J.L., Francis, D.J., & Schatschneider, C. (2005). The effects of theoretically different instruction and student characteristics on the skills of struggling readers. *Reading Research Quarterly, 40*(2), 148–182. doi:10.1598/RRQ.40.2.2

McMaster, K.L., Fuchs, D., Fuchs, L.S., & Compton, D.L. (2005). Responding to non-responders: An experimental field trial of identification and intervention methods. *Exceptional Children, 71*(4), 445–463.

The Meadows Center for Preventing Educational Risk. (2010). *Implementation examples.* Austin, TX: Author. Retrieved November 22, 2010, from buildingrti.utexas.org/school-examples

Mellard, D.F., & Johnson, E. (2008). *RTI: A practitioner's guide to implementing Response to Intervention*. Thousand Oaks, CA: Corwin.

Olson, R.K., Wise, B., Ring, J., & Johnson, M. (1997). Computer-based remedial training in phoneme awareness and phonological decoding: Effects on the posttraining development of word recognition. *Scientific Studies of Reading, 1*(3), 235–253. doi:10.1207/s1532799xssr0103_4

Schneider, W., Roth, E., & Ennemoser, M. (2000). Training phonological skills and letter knowledge in children at risk for dyslexia: A comparison of three kindergarten intervention programs. *Journal of Educational Psychology, 92*(2), 284–295. doi:10.1037/0022-0663.92.2.284

Snow, C.E., Burns, M.S., & Griffin, P. (Eds.). (1998). *Preventing reading difficulties in young children: Report of the Committee on the Prevention of Reading Difficulties in Young Children*. Washington, DC: National Academy Press.

Taylor, B.M. (2008). Tier 1: Effective classroom reading instruction in the elementary grades. In D. Fuchs, L.S. Fuchs, & S. Vaughn (Eds.), *Response to Intervention: A framework for reading educators* (pp. 5–26). Newark, DE: International Reading Association.

Taylor, B.M., Pearson, P.D., Clark, K., & Walpole, S. (2000). Effective schools and accomplished teachers: Lessons about primary-grade reading instruction in low-income schools. *The Elementary School Journal, 101*(2), 121–165. doi:10.1086/499662

Taylor, B.M., Pearson, P.D., Peterson, D.S., & Rodriguez, M.C. (2003). Reading growth in high-poverty classrooms: The influence of teacher practices that encourage cognitive engagement in literacy learning. *The Elementary School Journal, 104*(1), 3–28. doi:10.1086/499740

Torgesen, J.K. (1997). The prevention and remediation of reading disabilities: Evaluating what we know from research. *Journal of Academic Language Therapy, 1*(Spring/Summer), 11–47.

Torgesen, J.K. (2002). The prevention of reading difficulties. *Journal of School Psychology, 40*(1), 7–26. doi:10.1016/S0022-4405(01)00092-9

Torgesen, J.K., & Burgess, S.R. (1998). Consistency of reading-related phonological processes throughout early childhood: Evidence from longitudinal-correlational and instructional studies. In J.L. Metsala & L.C. Ehri (Eds.), *Word recognition in beginning literacy* (pp. 161–188). Mahwah, NJ: Erlbaum.

Vaughn, S., Cirino, P.T., Wanzek, J., Wexler, J., Fletcher, J.M., Denton, C.D., et al. (2010). Response to Intervention for middle school students with reading difficulties: Effects of a primary and secondary intervention. *School Psychology Review, 39*(1), 3–21.

Vaughn, S., & Denton, C.A. (2008). Tier 2: The role of intervention. In D. Fuchs, L.S. Fuchs, & S. Vaughn (Eds.), *Response to Intervention: A framework for reading educators* (pp. 51–70). Newark, DE: International Reading Association.

Vaughn, S., Fletcher, J.M., Francis, D.J., Denton, C.A., Wanzek, J., Wexler, J., et al. (2008). Response to Intervention with older students with reading difficulties. *Learning and Individual Differences, 18*(3), 338–345. doi:10.1016/j.lindif.2008.05.001

Vaughn, S., Linan-Thompson, S., & Hickman, P. (2003). Response to instruction as a means of identifying students with reading/learning disabilities. *Exceptional Children, 69*(4), 391–409.

Vaughn, S., Wanzek, J., Murray, C.S., Scammacca, N., Linan-Thompson, S., & Woodruff, A.L. (2009). Response to early reading intervention: Examining higher and lower responders. *Exceptional Children, 75*(2), 165–183.

Vaughn Gross Center for Reading and Language Arts, University of Texas at Austin. (2005). *Introduction to the 3-tier reading model: Reducing reading difficulties for kindergarten through third grade students* (4th ed.). Austin, TX: Author.

Wanzek, J., & Vaughn, S. (2007). Research-based implications from extensive early reading interventions. *School Psychology Review, 36*(4), 541–561.

Wanzek, J., & Vaughn, S. (2009). Students demonstrating persistent low response to reading intervention: Three case studies. *Learning Disabilities Research & Practice, 24*(3), 151–163. doi:10.1111/j.1540-5826.2009.00289.x

Chapter 12

Technologies, Digital Media, and Reading Instruction

Jay S. Blanchard and Alan E. Farstrup

Rapid advances in technology and digital media are affecting children, teachers, and reading instruction in dramatic ways. For anyone doubting their potential impact, the following vignette provides insight:

> It is an ordinary school day, as a group of kindergarten students gets off the bus. Suddenly, one of them spots an unusual bird high up in a tree. Running inside, they tell their teachers in excited voices that there is an owl in the tree. Armed with cameras, they run back outside with their teacher, who identifies the bird as a red-tailed hawk as students capture it digitally. Discussing the bird on their way back to the classroom, one student asks, "Can I Google red-tailed hawk?" He does so, sharing his findings with his classmates via large-screen projector. Using multimedia software, each student creates a small piece of illustrated writing about the hawk, some emailing what they have created to their parents. At the students' request, the teacher organizes the class to create a torn-paper collage of the red-tailed hawk, which is framed and displayed prominently in the classroom. (van 't Hooft, Swan, Cook, & Lin, 2007, p. 3)

This simple example of a teacher and young children using multiple technologies and media explains much about the need to better understand what research has to say about technology, digital media, and reading instruction.

Today's children are the most technologically experienced generation ever to walk through the doors of our schools and into our classrooms for reading instruction. Many of these children come to instruction already surfing, blogging, texting, messaging, apping, networking, and gaming. They have been immersed daily in a sea of multimodal technologies whose depth and breadth has been widely documented (e.g., Harrison Group, 2010; Plowman, Stephen, & McPake, 2010; Smith, 2010; Stephen,

What Research Has to Say About Reading Instruction (4th ed.) edited by S. Jay Samuels and Alan E. Farstrup. © 2011 by the International Reading Association.

McPake, Plowman, & Berch-Heyman, 2008). For example, mobile technology used by children and their families has been expanding at a dramatic rate (Druin, 2009; Shuler, 2009). In 2009 it was estimated that 50% of the world's population had access to a cell phone (Open Universiteit Nederland, 2009). As a result of this widespread access and the availability of other new technologies (along with older technologies like television), many of today's students have truly become "children of the screen." Not surprisingly, the Generation M[2] survey (Rideout, Foehr, & Roberts, 2010) found that children spent over six hours a day with technologies and that this time exceeds everything except sleep. (For a review of time-use studies, see Roberts & Foehr, 2008; Vandewater & Lee, 2009; Wallis, 2010.)

Children are also immersed at school. This immersion is so pervasive that Warschauer and Matuchniak (2010), in their recent review of the research on technology, concluded that nearly all U.S. children have access to a computer and the Internet, whether in classrooms or elsewhere (see also Gray & Lewis, 2009). In support of this conclusion, a recent Institute of Education Sciences survey of schools reported that virtually all have computers and Internet access (Gray, Thomas, & Lewis, 2010). However, there is much more to immersion than access to computers and the Internet. In many classrooms, teachers and children have access to multiple technologies for use in reading instruction—interactive whiteboards, DVDs, MP3s, PDAs, iTouches or iPads, apps (applications, usually meaning those used on mobile devices), video games, smart phones (e.g., iPhone, Android), smart toys, podcasts, e-book readers, tablet computers, digital storybooks, electronic learning aids, virtual worlds, and more (Blanchard & Moore, 2010).

There are at least two reasons these technologies have appeared. First, consumer appetites for entertainment and communication technologies, along with business and industry appetites for productivity and efficiency, have increased the speed of development. Second, governments, federal to local, have all invested in technology with the assumption that such investments will convert into societal advantages. As a result, consumers, businesses, and governments have demanded that schools adopt the latest technologies as advantages for teaching and learning. This has left educators struggling to keep pace with the speed of technological development and demand—and to pay for new technologies (Labbo, Kinzer, Leu, & Teale, n.d.; Oakes, 2009). Even though this "buy it because I do" logic seems counterintuitive as justification for educational spending, it has nonetheless led to plenty of spending on technology (Cuban, 2010). For example, in the United States in the fiscal years from 2001 through 2008, a single federal program (the Elementary and Secondary Education Act, Title II, Part D, Educational Technology State Grants) spent more than $3.8 billion on technology in the schools (U.S. Department of Education, 2010a). States and local school districts have also spent significant additional amounts for technology resources.

In an attempt to provide strategic coherence to this spending spree and to respond to the appetite for new technologies, the U.S. government has offered a national educational technology plan (NETP; U.S. Department of Education, Office of Educational Technology, 2010b). In support of the NETP, the Department of Education will fund six Communities of Practice to help teachers and school administrators learn about and understand the best practices, research, and implementation strategies for technology use.

This help and ongoing support is needed. A recent review of the research on technology adoption has suggested that it is an inherently complex, social, and developmental process with teachers constructing new and unique perceptions about technology use despite uncertain effects on student learning (Straub, 2009; Voogt & Knezek, 2008; Wellings & Levine, 2009). Help is also needed because there is a paucity of empirical studies on new technologies and classroom reading instruction (Leu, 2006; Moran, Ferdig, Pearson, Wardrop, & Blomeyer, 2008). Means (2010) recently noted that "we are urging schools and teachers to implement technology with little or no empirically based guidance on how to do so in ways that enhance student learning" (p. 288).

This situation is not exclusive to the United States (see, e.g., Hasebrink, Livingstone, Haddon, & Ólafsson, 2009; Pilkington, 2008). For example, in Germany the classroom use of whiteboards was the subject of a themed issue of the journal *Computer + Unterricht (Computers + Instruction)* (Aufenanger & Bauer, 2010). In Denmark the use of new technology in schools seems widespread and is well established, and teachers are provided with training and other professional development support on a regular basis (M. Jansen, personal communication, August 2010). Danish researcher Jeppe Bundsgaard (2010) has found that Internet searching is an important form of reading among secondary students and is in need of instructional support. Icelandic researcher Gudmundur Kristmundsson (personal communication, August 2010) found that more than 90% of schools and homes have access to a computer, the majority of which are connected to the Internet. He concluded that the immersion of students in a world of digital technology at school and in homes has influenced classroom instruction.

This chapter operationally defines *technology* and *digital media* as, respectively, the tools and the content that infuses life into the tools. This definition reflects the notion that these tools and content are in the reading and literacy lives of children and their teachers every day. It is important to acknowledge at this point, however, that trying to identify and offer strategic, empirically based guidance on the best practices to use with new technologies for reading instruction is complicated by the lack of studies, the growing and changing hodgepodge of tools, and the time needed for new technologies to be introduced, implemented, and studied. While the research syntheses available through the U.S. Department of Education's What Works Clearinghouse (WWC; see ies.ed.gov/ncee/wwc/) are a good start, it is still difficult to get one's head around the issues (Crook & Joiner, 2010).

To bring strategic coherence to consideration of the use of new technologies in reading instruction, it is useful to think of a continuum organized around dimensions of learning *with* technology and learning *from* technology (e.g., Mason, Blanchard, & Daniel, 1983; McKenna, Labbo, & Reinking, 2003; Tondeur, van Braak, & Valcke, 2007). At one end of the continuum, in the widest learning sense, are technologies that can be used as instructional support tools such as whiteboards, word processors, databases, presentation programs, spreadsheets, photo and video production/editing programs, and the like. These technologies enable children to learn with technology. They are generic tools, free of instructional design or subject matter content, and as a result, they allow teachers to maximize their instructional options. Classrooms that feature these types of teaching tools have been referred to as computer-based learning environments, digital teaching platforms, smart classrooms, and e-learning classrooms (Moos & Azevedo, 2009; Walters, Richards, & Dede, 2009; see also Edutopia, at www.edutopia.org, for ongoing discussions).

At the other end of this suggested continuum, and viewed in the narrowest instructional sense, are technologies that purport to teach— that is, they provide reading instruction (e.g., drill and practice). These technologies are often called computer-assisted instruction (CAI), computer-based learning (CBL), computer-assisted learning (CAL), and more recently, Web-based learning (WBL) and application-based learning (ABL, apps).

Somewhere along this continuum are technologies that have more flexibility than CAI programs but do have embedded subject matter content. These technologies can be tailored to specific classroom needs such as learning strategies, instructional practices, curriculum and standards, evaluation, and collaboration. They also can provide technology-based scaffolding of the kind that can be seen and heard in the "help" avatars in applications such as those in the Microsoft Office suite (Yelland & Masters, 2007).

All of the technologies along the continuum apply to within-classroom uses. However, interest in the influences of *outside-classroom* technology on in-school learning is growing (see, e.g., U.S. Department of Education, Office of Educational Technology, 2010b). Obviously, even a disinterested observer would note that the sheer amount of technology available to children outside the classroom far exceeds the quantity available within. While out-of-classroom uses may not always be educationally or developmentally appropriate, they do stand a pretty good chance of influencing child development and, hence, reading instruction (Blanchard & Moore, 2010; Kirkorian, Wartella, & Anderson, 2008; Marsh et al., 2005). Not surprisingly, Means, Toyama, Murphy, Bakia, and Jones (2010) found in survey data that teachers and children are using technology more frequently outside classrooms than in. They also reported that teachers do more learning with technology than learning from it. These findings match the results of several other recent large-scale surveys (e.g., Rideout, Foehr, & Roberts, 2010).

The increasing out-of-school use of new technologies, such as mobile devices with "apps," and of evolving older ones has prompted growing interest among researchers about technology for classroom learning generally (e.g., Alexander, 2010; Calvert & Wilson, 2008; Chlong & Shuler, 2010; Drotner & Livingstone, 2008; Druin, 2009; Glaubke, 2007; Goswami, 2008; Kirkorian et al., 2008; Schmidt & Vandewater, 2008) and in reading and reading instruction specifically (e.g., Bus & Neuman, 2009; Carrington & Robinson, 2009; Coiro, Knobel, Lankshear, & Leu, 2008; Lankshear & Knobel, 2003; Marsh & Singleton, 2009a, 2009b; Willoughby & Wood, 2008). This interest has also highlighted the growing study of digital literacy, which appears to have begun in earnest with the article "A Pedagogy of Multiliteracies: Designing Social Futures" (New London Group, 1996) and continues today through the efforts of researchers including Burke and Hammett (2009), Coiro and colleagues (2008), Jewitt (2009), Leu (2002), Leu, O'Byrne, Zawilinski, McVerry, and Evertt-Cacopardo (2009), and Mills (2010).

As with all literacies, digital literacy begins in the homes and communities of young children as they watch older people use technologies for entertainment and communication—and they begin to use the technologies. For example, McPake, Stephen, and Plowman (2007) reported results from a longitudinal survey conducted in the United Kingdom. The researchers found that young children are surrounded not only by older technologies (television and computers) but also by newer technologies (game consoles, electronic keyboards, DVDs, mobile phones, and smart toys) and were "growing up in an 'e-society', where digital connectivity—use of the internet, mobile phones and other interactive technologies—is essential to daily life" (p. 2).

The impact of new technologies in the daily lives of children clearly supports the view offered more than 30 years ago by Olson and Bruner (1974) that technology-based tools play a central role in thinking and learning and that, "each form of experience, including the various symbolic systems tied to the media, produces a unique pattern of skills for dealing with or thinking about the world" (p. 149; see also Brown, 2002; Papert, 1980). Also supporting this view, Byron (2008) found that "any significant changes in children's early experiences in life, such as a significant change in the amount of technology used during childhood, could potentially have a big impact on how the structure and function of the brain develops [*sic*]" (p. 31). It is not hyperbole to suggest that technology experiences can affect all forms of reading and reading instruction. In earlier times, the research base for a chapter on what research has to say about reading instruction and technology use would have been well established, consisting largely of tightly designed, qualitative or quantitative empirical and ethnographic studies on within-classroom effects. Most of these studies would have come from beginning reading instruction in classroom settings. That research base is important, but so is the emergence of studies on new technologies for use within and outside the classroom. This research suggests that technology, in its many and evolving forms throughout the lives of teachers and children, supports and shapes not only social, cognitive, and language development in general but reading and reading instruction specifically (McHale, Dotterer, & Kim, 2009; Mills, 2010; van den Broek, Kendeou, & White, 2009).

In the pages that follow, this chapter offers a research-based commentary on stages in the history of within-classroom technology use for reading instruction, recent within- and outside-classroom research relative to reading instruction, and elements for implementation of technology from both within- and outside-the-classroom perspectives.

Stages in the History of Within-Classroom Technology Use

The use of technologies in classroom reading instruction has at least a 50-year history (e.g., Blanchard, Mason, & Daniel, 1987; Hisrich & Blanchard, 2009; Kamil & Intrator, 1998; Kamil, Intrator, & Kim, 2000; Kulik & Kulik, 1991; Mason & Blanchard, 1979; Mason et al., 1983; Murphy, Penuel, Means, Korbak, & Whaley, 2001), which can be described in four stages: (1) curiosity, discovery, experimentation; (2) simple adaptation; (3) connectivity (the Internet and the World Wide Web); and (4) integration and coordination. These stages are intended to capture, in general terms, main elements of the evolution from large-scale centralized devices such as mainframe computers to mobile devices including laptops, smart phones, tablet computers, and the like.

Stage 1: Curiosity, Discovery, Experimentation

The first centrally managed mainframe time-share computer systems saw generally isolated use characterized by curiosity and experimentation sparked by a realization of the possibilities they might hold for improvements in reading instruction. Low-cost and often rudimentary personal computers began to appear during this stage of technology development, along with simple tools such as word processing, spreadsheets, and graphic programming. Teachers began to recognize the potential of these technologies but were not sure how best to use them to improve instruction.

This stage was very hardware or "gadget" oriented, and few or no real systems or software examples specifically intended for direct instructional purposes were seen. Very often during this first stage, technology was used for administrative and related record-keeping purposes using rather generic software tools not specifically designed or intended for educational purposes.

Stage 2: Simple Adaptation

Familiar teaching approaches and strategies adapted for use with technology were characteristic of this period. Simple drill-and-practice materials were delivered using computers, computer labs were widely installed, and libraries were reconceived as multimedia facilities. Personal computers begin to appear more commonly in schools, and applications for this new resource became increasingly complex and sophisticated. Mainframe computers linked to classroom terminals were still seen, but their use was beginning to be eclipsed by lower cost personal computers. In the latter part of this stage, children used software such as Oregon Trail, Rocky's Boots, and the like.

The influences of indirect, outside-the-classroom instances of technology, seen increasingly in children's everyday lives, were still not fully recognized or taken advantage of by teachers. Opinion leaders and researchers (e.g., Cuban, 2001) pointed out what they saw as the rather haphazard, trend-driven introduction of technology without any significant evidence of its efficacy for improving student achievement. It was often argued that the appearance of technology had ignited a very expensive cycle of investments without any basis in solid research that it would yield either efficiencies in classroom management or improvements in learning outcomes.

Stage 3: Connectivity—The Internet and the World Wide Web

By this more advanced stage, applications were more directly and specifically designed for instructional or classroom/school management purposes. In reading instruction, uses to promote vocabulary growth, information gathering, problem solving, and critical thinking were increasingly common. Personal computers rapidly became more economical and, simultaneously, more powerful. Connectivity with other systems and the Internet evolved rapidly. The Web and Web browsers appeared and rapidly gained in power and complexity. As they became widely accepted, these resources began to be used with both indirect and direct instruction. They enabled significant and powerful access to information for administrators, teachers, and students. Large numbers of classrooms were "wired" to create school- and districtwide networks and Internet access.

Both lesson materials and research approaches frequently took advantage of the availability of greater computing power and of the Internet. Administrative applications of technology became more prevalent and powerful. Communication with parents and the wider community improved. An increasingly varied range of technological devices beyond personal computers (such as LCD projectors, wireless access systems, smart boards, mobile phones, and the like) became accessible to schools as costs went down. Adoption of these technologies, especially during the early part of this third stage, was still often episodic rather than systematic or well integrated with either other technical systems or with the curriculum for reading instruction. Cuban (2010), Gates (2010), and others underlined the potential of technology for education despite the sometimes haphazard rush to build up its use.

Stage 4: Integration and Coordination

In this final stage, technology systems and devices have become much more integrated and geared more specifically to both curricular and administrative needs. One-to-one systems, in which every student has access to a computer, are common (see, e.g., Warschauer, 2005), and computer labs are used for targeted purposes. Technology is pervasive, and teachers have learned to take advantage of and coordinate both indirect, external technologies and those intended for direct application in the classroom. Teacher- and child-centered systems for instructional support, lesson building, skills practice, support of critical thinking and problem solving, assessment, and provision of real-time information to assist in individualization of instruction are now important tools for teaching and learning. Technology is now not an object of curiosity and experimentation but rather provides indispensable resources used as part of an extensive range of new and traditional instructional tools geared to the needs of children.

With this more complex, sophisticated technology environment comes the need for continuing research on the impact of technology on reading instruction, inside as well as outside the classroom. The widespread use of technologies for instruction as well as for administrative purposes calls out for a better understanding of their effects on instructional efficiency and, most important, learning outcomes. Clearly classroom-based technologies in this final stage are evolving at a rapid pace, with new ones changing and replacing old ones. In a very real sense, these technologies and their uses present a moving target for any consideration of what research has to say about reading instruction.

Within-Classroom Effect Studies

The modern use of technology in reading instruction began in the 1960s with the Stanford Reading Project (Atkinson & Hansen, 1966). (For historical reviews, see Blanchard et al., 1987; Kamil & Intrator, 1998; Kamil et al., 2000; Kulik & Kulik, 1991; Mason & Blanchard, 1979; Mason et al., 1983; Murphy et al., 2001). In general, qualitative or quasi-experimental studies have tended to report positive results on reading achievement with technology use, while empirical studies have reported mixed results often stemming from a host of methodological issues (involving, for example, the specific reading outcomes being assessed, age or grade-level of children, types of computer technologies, types of teachers, classroom or school conditions, design, and so on). Not surprisingly, publications on reading policy and instruction appearing prior to 2000 took a neutral view on the subject of technology and reading instruction, as in this statement from *Preventing Reading Difficulties in Young Children* (Snow, Burns, & Griffin, 1998): "In summary, with the availability of technology, quality software and well-prepared practitioners, there is the potential for students to benefit" (p. 266). Similarly, the executive summary of the report of the U.S. National Reading Panel (NRP; National Institute of Child Health and Human Development [NICHD], 2000) noted, "In sum, the Panel is encouraged by the reported successes in the use of computer technology for reading instruction but relatively few specific instructional applications can be gleaned from the research" (p. 18). It is noteworthy that only 21 studies of technology use met the NRP's requirements for inclusion and formed the basis for its recommendations; of these studies, "very few...directly examined the effects of using computer technology for reading instruction" (p. 6-1).

From the time of the NRP's report (NICHD, 2000) the research focus began to broaden beyond CAI for beginning reading. In 2002, Teale, Leu, Labbo, and Kinzer noted what they considered to be the profound effects of technology on reading and literacy. At about the same time, others noted that technology might be affecting reading and literacy but not classroom instruction. Cuban's 2001 book, *Oversold and Underused: Computers in the Classroom*, offered a strong argument that while millions of dollars had been invested in computer hardware, software tools such as word-processing programs, and network wiring in schools, very little in the way of imaginative or productive classroom instructional use of technology had evolved. Instead, Cuban argued, the use of computers generally focused on simple or "low-end" applications (e.g., word processing) that he saw as doing nothing more than maintaining existing practices of doubtful utility for improving student learning. He offered a useful warning that new technologies were changing our children's habits and abilities *outside* the classroom but perhaps not much *within* the classroom. Cuban continues to sound warnings about the impact of new technologies on teaching (see his blog at larrycuban.wordpress.com). Others have joined him, focusing specifically on reading and reading instruction (e.g., Birkerts, 2010; Carr, 2010; Striphas, 2010).

At about the time of Cuban's (2001) book, the U.S. No Child Left Behind legislation began to focus the federal Department of Education's efforts on critical reviews of educational interventions in a search for scientific evidence of efficacy. As a result, the Department of Education, through its Institute of Education Sciences, created the aforementioned What Works Clearinghouse, which, as of Fall 2010, had reviewed several technology-based and computer-assisted programs related to reading instruction. These reviews are categorized by the WWC under topics of adolescent literacy, beginning reading, early childhood education and emergent literacy, and English language learners. Of course, there are critical reviews in a variety of academic and general education sources beyond the WWC. For example, the effectiveness of Accelerated Reader has been examined in a WWC review as well as by Krashen (2005), Krashen and Neuman (2004), Pipkin, Gadberry, Potter, and Morey (2003), and Rogers (2003).

What follows is a chronological review of major syntheses and meta-analyses of studies published since the NRP report (NICHD, 2000). By focusing on these reviews, we hope to offer an efficient vehicle by which to consider what research has to say about technology and reading instruction rather than attempting to describe all available studies about old and new technologies. However, it should be noted that the reviews are generally long on studies of reading achievement through some form of learning *from* technology (e.g., CAI), short on learning *with* technology, and very short on how technology both inside *and* outside the classroom might be affecting reading achievement and instruction (for a discussion, see Burnett, 2009).

MacArthur, Ferretti, Okolo, and Cavalier (2001) reviewed studies on the use of computer-based technology for children with literacy problems (mild disability or poor reader) published from 1985 to 2000. The studies were grouped into three intervention categories: word identification (14 studies), text comprehension (13 studies), and writing (20 studies). As a whole, the researchers reported mixed results with technology, noting that the most effective interventions related to skills such as phonological awareness and the least effective interventions related to skills in text comprehension. They concluded by cautioning that the effects of technology on efforts to improve literacy instruction "continue to defy a simple synthesis" (p. 298).

Blok, Oostdam, Otter, and Overmaat (2002) examined the effects of multiple CAI methods on a variety of beginning reading skills through a meta-analysis of 42 studies published from 1990 to 2000. They found a small positive effect overall, at least for studies from English-speaking countries.

Burns and Ungerleider (2003) examined primarily Canadian empirical and peer-reviewed studies of computer-based reading and instruction in other content areas published between 1992 and 2002. The researchers concluded that, across all content areas (with the exception of mathematics), "the majority of the research reviewed is contradictory and/or seriously flawed" (p. 45).

Between 2002 and 2005, researchers connected with the Evidence for Policy and Practice Information and Co-ordinating Centre (EPPI-Centre) at the University of London completed a series of comprehensive meta-analytic reviews of information and communication technology (ICT) interventions in literacy learning. There were five categories of reviews in the series, covering children from age 5 to 16:

1. Networked ICT in literacy in English, for which 16 studies found results suggestive but not conclusive of successful intervention (Andrews et al., 2002)

2. ICT in literacy learning in English (Torgerson & Zhu, 2003), with 12 studies reporting no significant conclusions

3. ICT for English language learners (Low & Beverton, 2004), with 8 studies and no significant conclusions

4. ICT literature-related literacies in English (Locke & Andrews, 2004), with 7 studies and no significant conclusions

5. ICT for literacies associated with moving image text (Burn & Leach, 2004), with 9 studies and no significant conclusions

Lankshear and Knobel (2003) examined studies on "computer-based application" technologies in early childhood literacy. In their synthesis of the research from 22 studies (1996–2002) using technologies such as CD-ROM storybooks, computer software, e-mail, and authoring tools, the researchers concluded that only a small body of empirical research existed and it "makes no sense to seek systematic trends at the level of findings" (p. 71).

Cavanaugh, Gillan, Kromrey, Hess, and Blomeyer (2004) examined Web-based CAI instruction across a variety of elementary and secondary subject areas. Using a meta-analysis with 14 studies published from 1999 to 2004, the researchers found effect sizes indicating that children in experimental groups using Web-based programs performed as well as control children in traditional classroom-based programs across all subject areas, including reading among third to eighth graders.

Waller (2006) reviewed selected examples of technology use in early literacy. Studies were categorized into seven groups: play and early literacy, bilingual and multilingual, emergent literacy, print-based literacy, learning to read, collaboration and writing, and scaffolding literacy. The review found that technology use across categories did not reveal "a significant impact on literacy learning in the early years" (p. 49). Waller also concluded that the role of teachers in guiding and assisting young children using technology is critical for success.

As part of the U.S. Ready to Learn Initiative, Pasnik, Strother, Schindel, Penuel, and Llorente (2007) reviewed studies of technology use among young children in the following domains of literacy: concepts of print, comprehension, phonological awareness, vocabulary, and fluency. The researchers considered television and computer studies as well as talking books and multimedia/media synergy (i.e., computers + television + print) published from 1996 to 2007. Focusing here on the last two technologies, the researchers examined nine studies of the use of talking books and found small to large positive effects (range, 0.002–1.056) across all areas, with strongest effect sizes for comprehension. For media synergy, the researchers examined six studies and found small positive effects (0.24) for vocabulary and concepts of print.

Rather than presenting reviews of research, reports from Dynarski and colleagues (2007) and Campuzano, Dynarski, Agodini, and Rall (2009) represent the largest experimental versus control-group trial of technology-based reading programs in the research database. The effort, sponsored by the U.S. federal government, was entitled Effectiveness of Educational Technology Interventions. The two-year, pre–posttest study found little effect on standardized test scores of reading achievement with the use of reading software products at first and fourth grades. In year one of the effort (2004–2005), use of five reading software products in first grade was evaluated with more than 100 teachers and their students; at fourth grade, four software products (core curriculum, resources) were evaluated across roughly the same numbers of schools, teachers, and children (Dynarski et al., 2007). For year two (2005–2006), similar numbers of schools, teachers, and children were evaluated with four of the original reading software products at first grade and two at fourth grade (Campuzano et al., 2009).

Moran et al. (2008) examined the effects of a variety of digital media tools on reading comprehension, primarily in middle school. Using a meta-analysis of 20 studies published from 1988 to 2005 and the What

Works Clearinghouse review evaluation rubric, the researchers found a "robust" (p. 26) overall effect size.

Burnett (2009) examined 38 empirical studies published from 2000 to 2006 and focused on qualitative and quantitative studies of literacy interventions across several technologies, including computers, e-mail, multimedia composition, and Internet searches in elementary classrooms. This research synthesis made an ambitious attempt to separate the studies into those that judged the success of the technology interventions by conventional learning outcomes (i.e., test scores) versus literacy process outcomes (i.e., "holistic insights," p. 28). Burnett concluded that, across methodologies and outcomes, "there is a need to understand more fully what happens when technology is integrated within classroom sites, and the values, processes, interactions and relationships that surround its use" (p. 33).

Outside-Classroom Effect Studies

Determining effects of outside-classroom technology use on in-school instruction presents a difficult research issue. Many technologies are used outside of school, and they can and probably do support classroom reading instruction to varying degrees (Burnett, 2009). For example, educational television might be part of reading instruction in some classrooms—for example, some teachers may do shared reading of titles introduced on the PBS series *Sesame Street* or *Between the Lions* or engage in supplemental activities from the PBS website. In other classrooms, teachers may not use these resources or have much idea of what television programs or websites children engage with outside school. In the case of television, there is a large empirical database that describes outside-the-classroom technology effects on reading (see, e.g., Ennemoser & Schneider, 2007; Gentzkow & Shapiro, 2008; Linebarger & Piotrowski, 2009). Only a small number of empirical studies have examined possible outside-classroom effects on reading instruction of technology other than television (Burnett; Penuel et al., 2009). However, this is not to suggest that researchers are unaware of these effects. For example, Penuel et al. (2002) synthesized 19 studies across subject areas involving four technologies that linked home and school: laptop computers, home desktop computers, software, and voice mail. Concerning reading, this synthesis examined only data for achievement, finding a range of effect sizes with a small overall mean effect size of 0.10. Unfortunately none of the studies provided data on reading instruction. The researchers noted the absence, saying that "another limitation of the currently available research is that the evaluation studies reviewed do not provide evidence for *why* particular results were obtained" (p. 93).

For all technologies except voice mail, the studies examined by Penuel et al. (2002) assumed availability and use of computers at home. Therefore, the small research database on home computer availability and reading achievement should be noted. Here the sometimes contradictory results offer insight into the difficulty of assessing the effects of outside-classroom effects on reading instruction. Clotfelter, Ladd, and Vigdor (2008) found that general computer use and Internet access in the home across a state-wide population did not lead to significantly higher test scores in reading achievement at fifth through eighth grade. In addition, there was little evidence that providing more classroom-directed work related to the technology use offset the observed effects. Fairlie, Beltran, and Das (2010) reported contrary findings. These researchers examined two large U.S. databases (the 2000–2003 Current Population Survey Computer and Internet Use Supplements and the National Longitudinal Survey of Youth, 1997) and concluded that there was a strong positive relationship between home computer use and reading achievement. These contrary results are indicative of the current state of the research database on home-technology effects; see also, for example, Computers for Youth (2010), Fuchs and Woessmann (2004), Malamud and Pop-Eleches (2010), and Schmitt and Wadsworth (2006). This state of affairs suggests that if new technologies used outside of school are expected to affect reading instruction and translate into improved reading achievement, more research needs to be done to guide their implementation.

There is a small but growing number of studies regarding new technologies that are available outside the classroom and that may have effects on in-school reading instruction. While the following have yet to be considered as a whole and do not represent a critical mass of research for analysis, they do offer testimony to possible uses.

- General overviews: Ito and colleagues (2010) and Harrison Group (2010)
- DVDs: Robb, Richert, and Wartella (2009)
- Web-hosted multimedia software: Karemaker, Pitchford, and O'Malley (2010) and Savage, Abrami, Hipps, and Deault (2009)
- Online content: Coiro (2009)
- Virtual worlds: Merchant (2009)

- Blogging: Wallis (2010) and Zawilinski (2009)
- Electronic learning aids: Gray, Bulat, Jaynes, and Cunningham (2009) and Raffle and colleagues (2010)
- Digital storybooks: Verhallen and Bus (2010)
- Media creation tools: Gainer, Valdez-Gainer, and Kinard (2009) and Moylan (2010)
- Collaborative learning: Yuill, Pearce, Kerawalla, Harris, and Luckin (2009)
- Talking books: Wood, Pillinger, and Jackson (2010)
- Video games: Bunce (2010)

It seems clear from this review that technologies used outside of school are finding their way into classrooms, with or without instructional intention, and they stand a good chance of influencing reading and reading instruction.

Implementation of Technology in Reading Instruction

The U.S. national educational technology plan (U.S. Department of Education, Office of Educational Technology, 2010b) calls for the use of new technologies in redesigning and transforming American education. The plan proposes a rich and complex model of technology implementation that

> brings state-of-the-art technology into learning to enable, motivate, and inspire all students, regardless of background, languages, or disabilities, to achieve. It leverages the power of technology to provide personalized learning and to enable continuous and lifelong learning. (p. x)

In a very real sense, this description captures the essence of the argument that effective in-school technology use must be grounded in an effective implementation plan that includes curricular goals (see also Ertmer & Ottenbreit-Leftwich, 2010; Hall, 2010). According to the George Lucas Educational Foundation, "Effective technology integration is achieved when the use of technology is routine and transparent and when technology supports curricular goals" (Edutopia Staff, 2008, ¶2). In other words, the use of technology in classroom reading instruction must be undertaken in the context of the total curriculum, in such a way that students are actively engaged in the reading process and the teacher is able to use a variety of instructional approaches and strategies—including technology—to motivate them to be active and successful learners. This is reinforced in the NETP's call for effective integration of instruction across all curricular areas so that, by gaining deep understanding of each subject and how ideas and concepts are interconnected, children will develop critical and creative thinking abilities. To accomplish this integration, the NETP calls for "connected teaching":

> In a connected teaching model, classroom educators are fully connected to learning data and tools for using the data; to content, resources, and systems that empower them to create, manage, and assess engaging and relevant learning experiences; and directly to their students in support of learning both in and out of school. (p. vii)

The NETP is not alone in suggesting an expanded instructional view of technologies and their effective implementation. The U.S. Common Core State Standards, unveiled in 2010, address technology-based teaching and, we believe, suggest the need for carefully designed classroom implementation. For reading instruction, the standards in many ways combine elements of existing state standards with important elements of standards published by professional organizations including the National Association for the Education of Young Children (NAEYC), the International Reading Association (IRA), and the National Council of Teachers of English (NCTE). For example, Standard 8 of the IRA-NCTE (1996) *Standards for the English Language Arts* states, "Students use a variety of technological and informational resources (e.g., libraries, databases, computer networks, video) to gather and synthesize information and to create and communicate knowledge" (p. 39). IRA (2009) also has a position statement on the importance of new technologies for reading instruction.

New technologies, if successfully implemented, clearly offer a number of promising avenues for innovations in reading instruction and for the improvement of reading achievement. Prerequisite elements for successful implementation, both in and out of school, can be outlined in at least four distinct but closely related areas: infrastructure, professional development, integration, and management and monitoring.

Infrastructure

In order for technology to be integrated successfully with the reading curriculum, the related infrastructure must be fully maintained and up to date. In many countries in the late 1990s and early 2000s, extensive resources were devoted to installation of computer networks and other hardware to permit high-speed access to the Internet. In the United States, this effort was identified as a priority by policymakers, and funding and tax credits were made available to encourage progress. For example, in 1996 the Technology Literacy Challenge Fund was approved and, the next year, it invested $200 million in technology grants. A formative evaluation of the program was conducted that described implementation in five states: Illinois, Massachusetts, Mississippi, Texas, and Washington (Kirshstein, Birman, Quinones, Levin, Stephens, & Loy, 2000). Funds were used in a variety of ways, including for the purchase of hardware, school infrastructure improvements, professional development, and software acquisition. Technical support to maintain the infrastructure was shown to be of great importance.

Professional Development

A strong conclusion emerged from the Kirshstein et al. (2000) evaluation of the Technology Literacy Challenge Fund regarding the importance of and need for high-quality, timely, and ongoing professional development to prepare educators to be effective and innovative users of new technologies:

> Technology alone does not make the difference, but rather how it is used. State-of-the-art technology in the hands of teachers with little or no professional development and little motivation to use it will have less impact on students than older equipment in the classrooms of teachers who have had professional development and want to use it effectively. (p. 19)

Effective and relevant professional development before and during implementation is essential if investments in the technical infrastructure are to bear fruit. For example, an evaluation of North Carolina's 1:1 Learning Initiative Pilot program found that teacher-identified needs included content-specific, hands-on professional development; advice and time to generate lessons that more fully integrated subject matter content and digital technologies; and increased opportunities to collaborate with other teachers in using computers effectively in their classrooms (Corn & Osborne, 2009). A very strong conclusion drawn by these authors was that preparing both teachers and children well in advance of delivering laptops or other hardware to them is critical for implementation of one-to-one technology programs if they are to result in achievement gains. Professional development should include guidance on preparing and testing the technology infrastructure, engaging the support of parents and the community, generating the policies to govern the programs, and making sure that well-qualified technicians and other personnel needed to facilitate trouble-free functioning of systems and software are available to provide support. Building the technical infrastructure and acquiring hardware is the easy part; ensuring these tools are used to provide effective, innovative, well-integrated instruction supported by extensive and ongoing professional development is much more difficult.

Integration

While high-quality, ongoing professional development focused on technology use must be provided, full integration with reading instructional approaches and curriculum is also important. Teachers must not only be competent and confident in their own use of technology to access, read, and critically consider complex information, they must also be able to incorporate these technologies fully into their classroom practices. For example, effective use of the Internet involves far more than using computers and search engines to locate information; it must be considered as an important aspect of literacy itself (Leu et al., 2005, 2009). By treating Internet resources and technology as key aspects of literacy, the professional development process is cast in a much broader context than simple training in the use of technology tools; it expands the purposes of professional development and teaching to support the broader, higher level, and more important aspects of literacy—namely, critical thinking, judgment, problem-solving skills, and development of lifelong reading and thinking habits. In short, technology is not an isolated subject, distinct from the essential content of reading. If it is not perceived and approached as an integrated component, development of a full new vision for literacy can be impeded.

Management and Monitoring

Technology offers powerful tools for teachers to use in managing the classroom and keeping track of both individual and group progress. In a well-integrated system, teachers can readily access important information about performance, enabling them to shape and fit their instruction to the specific needs of their students. A well-designed system can also take advantage of tools such as word processing, spreadsheets, and video presentation applications for communication with children and their families.

Some Recommendations

It is clear that new technologies must be used with care to further reading instruction. At the same time, educators should keep an eye on technologies being used outside the classroom that may affect in-school teaching and learning (Weigel, James, & Gardner, 2009). Teachers who take advantage of new technologies in the classroom while being knowledgeable about out-of-school technology use appear to have the best chance of improving reading instruction. It is also clear that teachers and administrators must capitalize on in- and out-of-school technologies through some form of strategically coherent planning. The following recommendations are intended to support that planning:

1. Technologies in the classroom should not be used to supplant or replace the critical role of the teacher. They should be used in concert with other proven approaches and strategies, based on the needs of individual children and groups.

2. Schools and districts must provide up-to-date technical infrastructure and devices to meet classroom and administrative needs. This infrastructure must be supported and maintained by experienced, well-qualified personnel.

3. Well-integrated, powerful, and flexible hardware and software systems that place lesson-planning capabilities and ongoing monitoring of student results into the hands of the teacher are an essential element. Teachers must be at the heart of the decision-making and instructional-planning process as technologies are introduced and implemented.

4. High-quality, sustainable professional development must be provided to teachers and staff before and during the implementation of all new technologies in schools.

5. All aspects of the reading curriculum should be reviewed for the purpose of identifying aspects where high-quality, productive uses of technology can be incorporated for the benefit of children and their teachers.

6. Technologies of all kinds should be fully integrated into the classroom with the goal of providing teacher- and child-centered learning environments. This integration must be done in light of curricular goals and priorities. Promoting high levels of reading achievement and lifelong reading habits must be the overarching objective.

7. A research component must be included in plans for the implementation and evaluation of technology for instruction. Data on the effects of technology and related instruction on reading achievement should be systematically gathered and continually assessed.

8. While technology use, both inside and outside of school, has great potential for positive effects on reading achievement and learning, there are also negative aspects to be considered. Technology-based activities, including social networking, instant messaging, and texting, can be misused for purposes such as cyberbullying that can harm children, families, and schools (see, e.g., Hoffman, 2010). This complex and troubling issue highlights the importance of parents, teachers, and schools being aware of how children use, and sometimes misuse, new technologies.

In Summary

Research findings from the past several decades are mixed regarding the impact of technologies on reading instruction and achievement. The more recent findings and policy commentaries, however, suggest that new technologies, when implemented in a carefully planned way with effective and ongoing professional development and support, can have a positive effect. This seems obvious. What is not so obvious is the need for reading educators to take into account the effects of rapidly expanding technologies in children's lives outside school and the impact these technologies can have within the classroom (Harrison Group, 2010). They must also consider the growing use of new technologies with younger and younger children and the resulting effects on emergent literacy development (Macaruso & Walker, 2008; Pinkley, 2010; Waller, 2006).

At the same time that new technologies are increasing in power and flexibility, they are also becoming less expensive—and therefore more accessible to districts, schools, and classrooms. The thoughtful integration of these rapidly expanding new technologies into curriculum and instruction, framed by empirically based instructional decision making, is essential if their full potential is to be realized. These technologies must be used in new, creative ways in combination with proven instructional approaches and practices and not simply to mimic or emulate existing, more traditional approaches to instruction. Clearly, for good or bad, technology is changing the world we live in—and reading instruction.

Questions for Reflection

1. How would you illustrate and expand the discussion of historical stages that describe the appearance and implementation of technology in schools and classrooms?

2. What are some advantages of using technology in conjunction with more traditional instructional approaches? What might be some disadvantages of replacing traditional, teacher-directed strategies with technology?

3. How might new technologies relate to existing, more traditional instructional approaches, teaching strategies, curriculum, and tools?

4. What are some examples of appropriate educational uses of technology not directly designed or intended for classroom use?

5. What is the nature of the interaction between technologies that are present outside of schools with those specifically designed for and used inside schools? How does the age of students using the technologies affect the nature of the interaction?

6. Education is more than knowledge acquisition; it is about children forming character, values, respect, and a love of learning. How can technology help or hinder?

7. Is the implementation of educational technology, in and of itself, going to improve reading achievement for the children we teach? What advantages and potential disadvantages can be cited?

8. How can technology be seen and applied not as an end in itself but as a vital resource for providing all children with the best possible reading instruction? How can it be used to encourage children to think critically and creatively about their world?

REFERENCES

Alexander, R. (Ed.). (2010). *Children, their world, their education: Final report and recommendations of the Cambridge Primary Review.* New York: Routledge.

Andrews, R., Burn, A., Leach, J., Locke, T., Low, G., & Torgerson, C. (2002). *A systematic review of the impact of networked ICT on 5–16 year olds' literacy in English.* London: EPPI Centre, Social Science Research Unit, Institute of Education, University of London.

Atkinson, R.C., & Hansen, D.N. (1966). Computer-assisted instruction in initial reading: The Stanford Project. *Reading Research Quarterly, 2*(1), 5–25.

Aufenanger, S., & Bauer, P. (Eds.). (2010). Interaktive whiteboards [Interactive whiteboards]. *Computer + Unterricht, 78.*

Birkerts, S. (2010, Spring). Reading in a digital age. *The American Scholar.* Retrieved November 18, 2010, from www

.theamericanscholar.org/reading-in-a-digital
-age/

Blanchard, J., Mason, G.E., & Daniel, D.B. (1987). *Computer applications in reading* (3rd ed.). Newark, DE: International Reading Association.

Blanchard, J., & Moore, T. (2010). *The digital world of young children: Impact on emergent literacy.* Washington, DC: Pearson Foundation.

Blok, H., Oostdam, R., Otter, M.E., & Overmaat, M. (2002). Computer-assisted instruction in support of beginning reading instruction: A review. *Review of Educational Research, 72*(1), 101–130. doi:10.3102/00346543072001101

Brown, J.S. (2002). Learning in the digital age. In M. Devlin, R. Larson, & J. Meyerson (Eds.), *The Internet and the university: 2001 forum* (pp. 65–91). Cambridge, MA: Forum for the Future of Higher Education; Washington, DC: EDUCAUSE. Retrieved November 18, 2010, from net.educause.edu/forum/ffpiu01w.asp?bhcp=1

Bunce, S. (2010). Can Nintendo DS consoles be used for collaboration and enquiry-based learning in schools? *Journal of the Research Center for Educational Technology, 6*(1), 172–184.

Bundsgaard, J. (2006, September). *Searching the Internet is reading: Investigation of an unnoticed aspect of information literacy.* Paper presented at the annual meeting of the European Conference on Educational Research, Geneva.

Burke, A., & Hammett, R.F. (Eds.). (2009). *Assessing new literacies: Perspectives from the classroom.* New York: Peter Lang.

Burn, A., & Leach, J. (2004). *A systematic review of the impact of ICT on the learning of literacies associated with moving image texts in English, 5–16.* London: EPPI-Centre, Social Science Research Unit, Institute of Education, University of London.

Burnett, C. (2009). Research into literacy and technology in primary classrooms: An exploration of understandings generated by recent studies. *Journal of Research in Reading, 32*(1), 22–37. doi:10.1111/j.1467-9817.2008.01379.x

Burns, T., & Ungerleider, C. (2003). Information and communication technologies in elementary and secondary education: State of the art review. *International Journal of Educational Policy, Research, & Practice, 3*(4), 27–54.

Bus, A.G., & Neuman, S.B. (Eds.). (2009). *Multimedia and literacy development:* *Improving achievement for young learners.* New York: Routledge.

Byron, T. (2008). *Safer children in a digital world: The report of the Byron Review.* Annesley, Nottingham, United Kingdom: DCSF Publications.

Calvert, S.L., & Wilson, B.J. (Eds.). (2008). *The handbook of children, media, and development.* Malden, MA: Blackwell.

Campuzano, L., Dynarski, M., Agodini, R., & Rall, K. (2009). *Effectiveness of reading and mathematics software products: Findings from two student cohorts* (NCEE 2009-4041). Washington, DC: National Center for Education Evaluation and Regional Assistance, Institute of Education Sciences, U.S. Department of Education.

Carr, N. (2010, May 24). The Web shatters focus, rewires brains. *Wired Magazine.* Retrieved November 18, 2010, from www.wired.com/magazine/2010/05/ff_nicholas_carr/all/1

Carrington, V., & Robinson, M. (Eds.). (2009). *Digital literacies: Social learning and classroom practices.* Thousand Oaks, CA: Sage.

Cavanaugh, C., Gillan, K., Kromrey, J., Hess, M., & Blomeyer, R. (2004). *The effects of distance education on K–12 student outcomes: A meta-analysis.* Naperville, IL: Learning Point.

Chlong, C., & Shuler, C. (2010, November). *Learning: Is there an app for that? Investigations of young children's usage and learning with mobile devices and apps.* New York: The Joan Ganz Cooney Center at Sesame Workshop. Retrieved January 11, 2011, from www.joanganzcooneycenter.org/Reports-27.html

Clotfelter, C.T., Ladd, H.F., & Vigdor, J.L. (2008, December). *Scaling the digital divide: Home computer technology and student achievement.* Paper presented for the Program on Education Policy and Governance Education Policy Colloquia Series, Cambridge, MA. Retrieved November 18, 2010, from www.hks.harvard.edu/pepg/colloquia.htm

Coiro, J. (2009). Promising practices for supporting adolescents' online literacy development. In K.D. Wood & W.E. Blanton (Eds.), *Literacy instruction for adolescents: Research-based practice* (pp. 442–471). New York: Guilford.

Coiro, J., Knobel, M., Lankshear, C., & Leu, D.J. (Eds.). (2008). *Handbook of research on new literacies.* New York: Erlbaum.

Computers for Youth. (2010). *Impact: Impact on families.* New York: Author. Retrieved

November 19, 2010, from www.cfy.org/impact-on-families.php

Corn, J., & Osborne, J. (2009). *Mid-year evaluation report on the progress of the North Carolina 1:1 Learning Technology Initiative (fall semester, year 2)*. Raleigh, NC: Friday Institute for Educational Innovation, North Carolina State University.

Crook, C., & Joiner, R. (2010). "CAL"—past, present and beyond. *Journal of Computer Assisted Learning, 26*(1), 1–3. doi:10.1111/j.1365-2729.2009.00343.x

Cuban, L. (2001). *Oversold and underused: Computers in the classroom*. Cambridge, MA: Harvard University Press.

Cuban, L. (2010, November 16). A puzzling fact about high-tech use in classrooms. In *Larry Cuban on school reform* [Web log]. Retrieved January 19, 2011, from wp.me/pBm7c-vA

Drotner, K., & Livingstone, S. (Eds.). (2008). *The international handbook of children, media and culture*. Thousand Oaks, CA: Sage.

Druin, A. (Ed.). (2009). *Mobile technology for children: Designing for interaction and learning*. Burlington, MA: Morgan Kaufmann.

Dynarski, M., Agodini, R., Heaviside, S., Novak, T., Carey, N., Campuzano, L., et al. (2007). *Effectiveness of reading and mathematics software products: Findings from the first student cohort* (NCEE 2007-4005). Washington, DC: National Center for Education Evaluation and Regional Assistance, Institute of Education Sciences, U.S. Department of Education.

Edutopia Staff. (2008, March 17). Why integrate technology into the curriculum? The reasons are many. *Edutopia*. San Rafael, CA: George Lucas Educational Foundation. Retrieved November 19, 2010, from www.edutopia.org/technology-integration-introduction

Ennemoser, M., & Schneider, W. (2007). Relations of television viewing and reading: Findings from a 4-year longitudinal study. *Journal of Educational Psychology, 99*(2), 349–368. doi:10.1037/0022-0663.99.2.349

Ertmer, P.A., & Ottenbreit-Leftwich, A.T. (2010). Teacher technology change: How knowledge, confidence, beliefs, and culture intersect. *Journal of Research on Technology in Education, 42*(3), 255–284.

Fairlie, R.W., Beltran, D.O., & Das, K.K. (2010). Home computers and educational outcomes: Evidence from the NLSY97 and CPS. *Economic Inquiry, 48*(3), 771–792. doi:10.1111/j.1465-7295.2009.00218.x

Fuchs, T., & Woessmann, L. (2004). Computers and student learning: Bivariate and multivariate evidence on the availability and use of computers at home and at school. *Brussels Economic Review, 47*(3/4), 359–386.

Gainer, J.S., Valdez-Gainer, N., & Kinard, T. (2009). The Elementary Bubble Project: Exploring critical media literacy in a fourth-grade classroom. *The Reading Teacher, 62*(8), 674–683. doi:10.1598/RT.62.8.5

Gates, W. (2010, August 8). *In five years the best education will come from the Web*. Paper presented at the Techonomy Conference 2010, Lake Tahoe, CA. Retrieved January 11, 2011, from techonomy.com/videos

Gentzkow, M., & Shapiro, J.M. (2008). Preschool television viewing and adolescent test scores: Historical evidence from the Coleman Study. *The Quarterly Journal of Economics, 123*(1), 279–323. doi:10.1162/qjec.2008.123.1.279

Glaubke, C. (2007). *The effects of interactive media and preschoolers' learning: A review of the research and recommendations for the future*. Oakland, CA: Children Now.

Goswami, U. (2008). *Byron Review on the impact of new technologies on children [Annex H]: A research literature review: Child development*. London: Byron Review. Retrieved November 18, 2010, from www.dcsf.gov.uk/byronreview/actionplan/index.shtml

Gray, J., Bulat, J., Jaynes, C., & Cunningham, A. (2009). LeapFrog learning design: Playful approaches to literacy, from LeapPad to the Tag Reading System. In A. Druin (Ed.), *Mobile technology for children: Designing for interaction and learning* (pp. 171–194). Burlington, MA: Morgan Kaufmann.

Gray, L., & Lewis, L. (2009). *Educational technology in public school districts: Fall 2008* (NCES 2010-003). Washington, DC: National Center for Education Statistics, Institute of Education Sciences, U.S. Department of Education. Retrieved November 19, 2010, from nces.ed.gov/pubs2010/2010003.pdf

Gray, L., Thomas, N., & Lewis, L. (2010). *Teachers' use of educational technology in U.S. public schools: 2009* (NCES 2010-040). Washington, DC: National Center for Education Statistics, Institute of Education Sciences, U.S. Department of Education. Retrieved November 19, 2010, from nces.ed.gov/pubs2010/2010040.pdf

Hall, G.E. (2010). Technology's Achilles heel: Achieving high-quality implementation. *Journal of Research on Technology in Education, 42*(3), 231–253.

Harrison Group. (2010). *2010 kids and family reading report: Turning the page in the digital age.* New York: Scholastic. Retrieved November 19, 2010, from mediaroom .scholastic.com/kfrr

Hasebrink, U., Livingstone, S., Haddon, L., & Ólafsson, K. (2009). *Comparing children's online opportunities and risks across Europe: Cross-national comparisons for EU Kids Online* (2nd ed.). London: London School of Economics and Political Science & EU Kids Online.

Hisrich, K., & Blanchard, J. (2009). Digital media and emergent literacy. *Computers in the Schools, 26*(4), 240–255. doi:10.1080/07380560903360160

Hoffman, J. (2010, December 5). As bullies go digital, parents play catch-up. *New York Times,* p. A1.

International Reading Association. (2009). *New literacies and 21st-century technologies: A position statement of the International Reading Association.* Newark, DE: Author. Retrieved November 19, 2010, from www .reading.org/Libraries/Position_Statements _and_Resolutions/ps1067_NewLiteracies21st Century.sflb.ashx

International Reading Association & National Council of Teachers of English. (1996). *Standards for the English language arts.* Newark, DE; Urbana, IL: Authors. Retrieved November 19, 2010, from www.reading .org/General/CurrentResearch/Standards/ LanguageArtsStandards.aspx

Ito, M., Baumer, S., Bittanti, M., boyd, d., Cody, R., Herr-Stephenson, B., et al. (2010). *Hanging out, messing around, and geeking out: Kids living and learning with new media.* Cambridge, MA: MIT Press.

Jewitt, C. (Ed.). (2009). *The Routledge handbook of multimodal analysis.* New York: Routledge.

Kamil, M.L., & Intrator, S. (1998). Quantitative trends in publication of research on technology and reading, writing, and literacy. In T. Shanahan & F.V. Rodríguez-Brown (Eds.), *47th yearbook of the National Reading Conference* (pp. 385–396). Chicago: National Reading Conference.

Kamil, M.L., Intrator, S., & Kim, H.S. (2000). The effects of other technologies on literacy and literacy learning. In M.L. Kamil, P.B. Mosenthal, P.D. Pearson, & R. Barr (Eds.), *Handbook of reading research* (Vol. 3, pp. 773–788). Mahwah, NJ: Erlbaum.

Karemaker, A., Pitchford, N.J., & O'Malley, C. (2010). Enhanced recognition of written words and enjoyment of reading in struggling beginner readers through whole-word multimedia software. *Computers & Education, 54*(1), 199–208. doi:10.1016/j .compedu.2009.07.018

Kirkorian, H.L., Wartella, E.A., & Anderson, D.R. (2008). Media and young children's learning. *The Future of Children, 18*(1), 39–61. doi:10.1353/foc.0.0002

Kirshstein, R., Birman, B., Quinones, S., Levin, D., Stephens, M., & Loy, N. (2000). *The first-year implementation of the Technology Literacy Challenge Fund in five states.* Washington, DC: Office of Educational Research and Improvement, U.S. Department of Education. (ERIC Document Reproduction Service No. ED442474)

Krashen, S. (2005). Accelerated Reader: Evidence still lacking. *Knowledge Quest, 33*(3), 48–49.

Krashen, S., & Newman, M. (2004). A comment on the Accelerated Reader debate: The pot calls the kettle black. *Journal of Adolescent & Adult Literacy, 47*(6), 444–446.

Kulik, C.C., & Kulik, J.A. (1991). Effectiveness of computer-based instruction: An updated analysis. *Computers in Human Behavior, 7*(1/2), 75–94. doi:10.1016/0747 -5632(91)90030-5

Labbo, L.D., Kinzer, C.K., Leu, D.J., & Teale, W.H. (n.d.). *Technology: Connections that enhance children's literacy acquisition and reading achievement.* An IERI Research Grant, National Science Foundation. Retrieved November 19, 2010, from ctell .uconn.edu/about.htm

Lankshear, C., & Knobel, M. (2003). *New literacies: Changing knowledge and classroom learning.* Philadelphia: Open University Press.

Leu, D.J., Jr. (2002). The new literacies: Research on reading instruction with the Internet. In A.E. Farstrup & S.J. Samuels (Eds.), *What research has to say about reading instruction* (3rd ed., pp. 310–336). Newark, DE: International Reading Association.

Leu, D.J. (2006). New literacies, reading research, and the challenges of change: A deictic perspective. In J.V. Hoffman, D.L. Schallert, C.M. Fairbanks, J. Worthy, & B. Maloch (Eds.), *The 55th yearbook of the National Reading Conference* (pp. 1–20). Oak Creek, WI: National Reading Conference.

Leu, D.J., Castek, J., Hartman, D.K., Coiro, J., Henry, L.A., Kulikowich, J.M., et al. (2005). *Evaluating the development of scientific knowledge and new forms of reading* comprehension during online learning: Final report. Chicago: North Central Regional Educational Laboratory, Learning Point.

Leu, D.J., O'Byrne, W.I., Zawilinski, L., McVerry, J.G., & Everett-Cacopardo, H. (2009). Comments on Greenhow, Rebelia, and Hughes: Expanding the new literacies conversation. *Educational Researcher, 38*(4), 264–269. doi:10.3102/0013189X09336676

Linebarger, D.L., & Piotrowski, J.T. (2009). TV as storyteller: How exposure to television narratives impacts at-risk preschoolers' story knowledge and narrative skills. *British Journal of Developmental Psychology, 27*(1), 47–69. doi:10.1348/026151008X400445

Locke, T., & Andrews, R. (2004). *A systematic review of the impact of ICT on literature-related literacies in English, 5–16*. London: EPPI-Centre, Social Science Research Unit, Institute of Education, University of London.

Low, G., & Beverton, S. (2004). *A systematic review of the impact of ICT on literacy learning in English of learners between 5 and 16, for whom English is a second or additional language*. London: EPPI-Centre, Social Science Research Unit, Institute of Education, University of London.

MacArthur, C.A., Ferretti, R.P., Okolo, C.M., & Cavalier, A.R. (2001). Technology applications for students with literacy problems: A critical review. *The Elementary School Journal, 101*(3), 273–301.

Macaruso, P., & Walker, A. (2008). The efficacy of computer-assisted instruction for advancing literacy skills in kindergarten children. *Reading Psychology, 29*(3), 266–287. doi:10.1080/02702710801982019

Malamud, O., & Pop-Eleches, C. (2010). *Home computer use and the development of human capital* (NBER Working Paper No. 15814). Cambridge, MA: National Bureau of Economic Research.

Marsh, J., Brooks, G., Hughes, J., Ritchie, L., Roberts, S., & Wright, K. (2005). *Digital beginnings: Young children's use of popular culture, media and new technologies*. Sheffield, England: Literacy Research Centre, University of Sheffield.

Marsh, J., & Singleton, C. (2009a). Literacy and technology: Questions of relationship. *Journal of Research in Reading, 32*(1), 1–5. doi:10.1111/j.1467-9817.2008.01377.x

Marsh, J., & Singleton, C. (Eds.). (2009b). New developments in literacy and technology [Special issue]. *Journal of Research in Reading, 32*(1).

Mason, G.E., & Blanchard, J.S. (1979). *Computer applications in reading*. Newark, DE: International Reading Association.

Mason, G.E., Blanchard, J.S., & Daniel, D.B. (1983). *Computer applications in reading* (2nd ed.). Newark, DE: International Reading Association.

McHale, S.M., Dotterer, A., & Kim, J. (2009). An ecological perspective on the media and youth development. *American Behavioral Scientist, 52*(8), 1186–1203. doi:10.1177/0002764209331541

McKenna, M.C., Labbo, L.D., & Reinking, D. (2003). Effective use of technology in literacy instruction. In L.M. Morrow, L.B. Gambrell, & M. Pressley (Eds.), *Best practices in literacy instruction* (2nd ed., pp. 307–331). New York: Guilford.

McPake, J., Stephen, C., & Plowman, L. (2007). *Entering e-society: Young children's development of e-literacy*. City: Swindon, UK: Economic and Social Research Council; Stirling, UK University of Stirling.

Means, B. (2010). Technology and education change: Focus on student learning. *Journal of Research on Technology in Education, 42*(3), 285–307.

Means, B., Toyama, Y., Murphy, R., Bakia, M., & Jones, K. (2010). *Evaluation of evidence-based practices in online learning: A meta-analysis and review of online learning studies*. Washington, DC: Office of Planning, Evaluation, and Policy Development, Policy and Program Studies Service, U.S. Department of Education. Retrieved November 19, 2010, from www2.ed.gov/rschstat/eval/tech/evidence-based-practices/finalreport.doc

Merchant, G. (2009). Virtual worlds in real-life classrooms. In V. Carrington & M. Robinson (Eds.), *Digital literacies: Social learning and classroom practices* (pp. 95–110). Thousand Oaks, CA: Sage.

Mills, K.A. (2010). Shrek meets Vygotsky: Rethinking adolescents' multimodal literacy practices in schools. *Journal of Adolescent & Adult Literacy, 54*(1), 35–45. doi:10.1598/JAAL.54.1.4

Moos, D.C., & Azevedo, R. (2009). Learning with computer-based learning environments: A literature review of computer self-efficacy. *Review of Educational Research, 79*(2), 576–600. doi:10.3102/0034654308326083

Moran, J., Ferdig, R.E., Pearson, P.D., Wardrop, J.L., & Blomeyer, R.L., Jr. (2008). Technology and reading performance in the middle-school grades: A meta-analysis with recommendations for policy and practice. *Journal of Literacy Research, 40*(1), 6–58. doi:10.1080/10862960802070483

Moylan, M.S. (2010). Using digital video to enhance literacy. *Illinois Reading Council Journal, 38*(4), 26–32.

Murphy, R., Penuel, W., Means, B., Korbak, C., & Whaley, A. (2001). *E-DESK: A Review of recent evidence on the effectiveness of discrete educational software*. Menlo Park, CA: SRI International. Retrieved November 19, 2010, from ctl.sri.com/publications/display Publication.jsp?ID=204

National Institute of Child Health and Human Development. (2000). *Report of the National Reading Panel. Teaching children to read: An evidence-based assessment of the scientific research literature on reading and its implications for reading instruction* (NIH Publication No. 00-4769). Washington, DC: U.S. Government Printing Office.

The New London Group. (1996). A pedagogy of multiliteracies: Designing social futures. *Harvard Educational Review, 66*(1), 60–92.

Oakes, J.M. (2009). The effect of media on children: A methodological assessment from a social epidemiologist. *American Behavioral Scientist, 52*(8), 1136–1151. doi:10.1177/0002764209331538

Olson, D.R., & Bruner, J.S. (1974). Learning through experience and learning through media. In D.R. Olson & H.G. Richey (Eds.), *Media and symbols: The forms of expression, communication and education* (Vol. 73, No. 1, pp. 125–150). Chicago: National Society for the Study of Education.

Open Universiteit Nederland. (2009, September 8). Mobile cell phones: Key to learning of the future? *Science Daily*. Retrieved from science daily.com/releases/2009/09/090907142508 .htm

Papert, S. (1980). *Mindstorms: Children, computers, and powerful ideas*. New York: Basic Books.

Pasnik, S., Strother, S., Schindel, J., Penuel, W.R., & Llorente, C. (2007). *Report to the Ready to Learn Initiative: Review of research on media and young children's literacy*. Newton, MA: Education Development Center; Menlo Park, CA: SRI International.

Penuel, W.R., Kim, D.Y., Michalchik, V., Lewis, S., Means, B., Murphy, R., et al. (2002). *Using technology to enhance connections between home and school: A research synthesis*.

Washington, DC: Planning and Evaluation Service, U.S. Department of Education.

Penuel, W.R., Pasnik, S., Bates, L., Townsend, E., Gallagher, L.P., Llorente, C., & Hupert, N. (2009, October). *Summative evaluation of the Ready to Learn Initiative. Preschool teachers can use a media-rich curriculum to prepare low-income children for school success: Results of a randomized controlled trial*. Newton, MA: Education Development Center; Menlo Park, CA: SRI International.

Pilkington, R. (2008). Measuring the impact of information technology on students' learning. In J. Voogt & G. Knezek (Eds.), *International handbook of information technology in primary and secondary education* (pp. 1003–1018). New York: Springer.

Pinkley, D. (2010). *Computer technology in the primary classroom*. Washington, DC: Pearson Foundation.

Pipkin, G., Gadberry, E., Potter, M., & Morey, L. (2003). Librarians' and teachers' perspectives on accelerated reader. *Journal of Children's Literature, 29*(2), 46–49.

Plowman, L., Stephen, C., & McPake, J. (2010). *Growing up with technology: Young children learning in a digital world*. New York: Routledge.

Raffle, H., Ballagas, R., Revelle, G., Horii, H., Follmer, S., Go, J., et al. (2010, April). *Family story play: Reading with young children (and Elmo) over a distance*. Paper presented at the 28th ACM Conference on Human Factors in Computing Systems, Atlanta, GA.

Rideout, V.J., Foehr, U.G., & Roberts, D.F. (2010). *Generation M²: Media in the lives of 8- to 18-year olds*. Menlo Park, CA: Henry J. Kaiser Family Foundation. Retrieved November 19, 2010, from www.kff.org/entmedia/8010.cfm

Robb, M.B., Richert, R.A., & Wartella, E.A. (2009). Just a talking book? Word learning from watching baby videos. *British Journal of Developmental Psychology, 27*(1), 27–45. doi:10.1348/026151008X320156

Roberts, D.F., & Foehr, U.G. (2008). Trends in media use. *The Future of Children, 18*(1), 11–37.

Rogers, L. (2003). Computerized reading management software: An effective component of a successful reading program. *Journal of Children's Literature, 29*(2), 9–15.

Savage, R.S., Abrami, P., Hipps, G., & Deault, L. (2009). A randomized controlled trial study of the ABRACADABRA reading intervention program in grade 1. *Journal of Educational Psychology, 101*(3), 590–604.

Schmidt, M.E., & Vandewater, E.A. (2008). Media and attention, cognition, and school achievement. *The Future of Children, 18*(1), 63–85. doi:10.1353/foc.0.0004

Schmitt, J., & Wadsworth, J. (2006). Is there an impact of household computer ownership on children's educational attainment in Britain? *Economics of Education Review, 25*(6), 659–673. doi:10.1016/j.econedurev.2005.06.001

Shuler, C. (2009). *Pockets of potential: Using mobile technologies to promote children's learning.* New York: Joan Ganz Cooney Center. Retrieved November 19, 2010, from www.joanganzcooneycenter.org/Reports-23.htm

Smith, A. (2010). *Americans and their gadgets.* Washington, DC: Pew Internet & American Life Project.

Snow, C.E., Burns, M.S., & Griffin, P. (Eds.). (1998). *Preventing reading difficulties in young children.* Washington, DC: National Academy Press.

Stephen, C., McPake, J., Plowman, L., & Berch-Heyman, S. (2008). Learning from the children: Exploring preschool children's encounters with ICT at home. *Journal of Early Childhood Research, 6*(2), 99–117. doi:10.1177/1476718X08088673

Straub, E.T. (2009). Understanding technology adoption: Theory and future directions for informal learning. *Review of Educational Research, 79*(2), 625–649. doi:10.3102/0034654308325896

Striphas, T. (2010). The abuses of literacy: Amazon Kindle and the right to read. *Communication and Critical Cultural Studies, 7*(3), 297–317.

Teale, W.H., Leu, D.J., Jr., Labbo, L.D., & Kinzer, C. (2002). The CTELL Project: New ways technology can help educate tomorrow's reading teachers. *The Reading Teacher, 55*(7), 654–659.

Tondeur, J., van Braak, J., & Valcke, M. (2007). Towards a typology of computer use in primary education. *Journal of Computer Assisted Learning, 23*(3), 197–206. doi:10.1111/j.1365-2729.2006.00205.x

Torgerson, C., & Zhu, D. (2003). *A systematic review and meta-analysis of the effectiveness of ICT on literacy learning in English, 5–16.* London: EPPI-Centre, Social Science Research Unit, Institute of Education, University of London.

U.S. Department of Education. (2010a). *Overview budget history tables FY1980–FY2009. President's budget.* Washington, DC: Author.

Retrieved January 18, 2011, from www2.ed.gov/about/overview/budget/history/sthistbypr01to08.pdf

U.S. Department of Education, Office of Educational Technology. (2010b). *Transforming American education: Learning powered by technology: National educational technology plan 2010: Executive summary.* Washington, DC: Author. Retrieved November 19, 2010, from www.ed.gov/technology/netp-2010

van den Broek, P., Kendeou, P., & White, M.J. (2009). Cognitive processes during reading: Implications for the use of multimedia to foster reading comprehension. In A.G. Bus & S.B. Neuman (Eds.), *Multimedia and literacy development: Improving achievement for young learners* (pp. 57–73). New York: Routledge.

Vandewater, E.A., & Lee, S. (2009). Measuring children's media use in the digital age: Issues and challenges. *American Behavioral Scientist, 52*(8), 1152–1176. doi:10.1177/0002764209331539

van 't Hooft, M., Swan, K., Cook, D., & Lin, Y. (2007). What is ubiquitous computing? In M. van 't Hooft & K. Swan (Eds.), *Ubiquitous computing in education: Invisible technology, visible impact* (pp. 3–17). Mahwah, NJ: Erlbaum.

Verhallen, M.J.A.J., & Bus, A.G. (2010). Low-income immigrant pupils learning vocabulary through digital picture storybooks. *Journal of Educational Psychology, 102*(1), 54–61.

Voogt, J., & Knezek, G. (Eds.). (2008). *International handbook of information technology in primary and secondary education.* New York: Springer.

Waller, T. (2006). Literacy and ICT in the early years. In M. Hayes & D. Whitebread (Eds.), *ICT in the early years* (pp. 37–54). New York: Open University Press.

Wallis, C. (2010). *The impacts of media multitasking on children's learning and development.* New York: Joan Ganz Cooney Center.

Walters, J., Richards, J., & Dede, C. (2009). *Digital teaching platforms: A research review.* New York: Time To Know.

Warschauer, M. (2005). Going one-to-one. *Educational Leadership, 63*(4), 34–38.

Warschauer, M., & Matuchniak, T. (2010). New technology and digital worlds: Analyzing evidence of equity in access, use, and outcomes. *Review of Research in Education, 34*(1), 179–225. doi:10.3102/0091732X09349791

Weigel, M., James, C., & Gardner, H. (2009). Learning: Peering backward and looking forward in the digital era. *International Journal of Learning and Media, 1*(1), 1–18. doi:10.1162/ijlm.2009.0005

Wellings, J., & Levine, M. (2009). *The digital promise: Transforming learning with innovative uses of technology.* New York: Joan Ganz Cooney Center.

Willoughby, T., & Wood, E. (Eds.). (2008). *Children's learning in a digital world.* Malden, MA: Blackwell.

Wood, C., Pillinger, C., & Jackson, E. (2010). Understanding the nature and impact of young readers' literacy interactions with talking books and during adult reading support. Computers & Education, 54(1), 190–198. doi:10.1016/j.compedu.2009.08.003

Yelland, N., & Masters, J. (2007). Rethinking scaffolding in the information age. *Computers & Education, 48*(3), 362–382. doi:10.1016/j.compedu.2005.01.010

Yuill, N., Pearce, D., Kerawalla, L., Harris, A., & Luckin, R. (2009). How technology for comprehension training can support conversation towards the joint construction of meaning. *Journal of Research in Reading, 32*(1), 109–125. doi:10.1111/j.1467-9817.2008.01384.x

Zawilinski, L. (2009). HOT blogging: A framework for blogging to promote higher order thinking. *The Reading Teacher, 62*(8), 650–661. doi:10.1598/RT.62.8.3

Chapter 13

Teaching Reading in English as a Foreign Language to Young Learners: A Global Reflection

Annie Hughes

In this chapter, we consider the situation with regards to the teaching of reading in English as a foreign or second or additional language to young learners. On the whole, we focus on children learning English in a non-English setting, rather than children learning English in an English-speaking environment. However, many of the issues and principles raised for English as a foreign language (EFL) apply across the board to English as a second language (ESL) or English as an additional language (EAL). Throughout the chapter, we consider young learners learning English up to the age of around 11 or 12 years, or those in primary, or first, formal school of their educational careers.

Given that teaching English to young learners (TEYL) is delivered in varied forms by a variety of teachers in different teaching situations, we first take a look at the context of EYL teaching in some detail so that the rest of the discussion is set within this context. We briefly review what we believe the links are with children's development and learning and then discuss language learning for young learners before considering our understanding of the teaching of reading in TEYL and what different research tells us about aspects of it. Following on from this, we consider what the implications may be for the teaching of reading in TEYL, particularly the creation of an English literacy environment. We also review some practical strategies for the teaching of reading to young English language learners.

Sadly, there is a dearth of research in TEYL, and the teaching of reading in TEYL in particular, but we consider some of the research that has been carried out in this area. We also refer to research carried out by practitioners of TEYL and action research carried out by TEYL practitioner mature students of the MA in TEYL at the University of York.

What Research Has to Say About Reading Instruction (4th ed.) edited by S. Jay Samuels and Alan E. Farstrup. © 2011 by the International Reading Association.

As Shanahan (2002) outlines, not all researchers may be interested in whether findings make a difference in the classroom, when he states, "not all researchers are interested in whether their research is used by practitioners...Practitioners and researchers have different conceptions about what research is, how research should be read, and how it should be used" (p. 10). The TEYL practitioners carrying out action research in their own classrooms, and those researchers and reading specialists referred to later, do seem to be "interested in whether their research is used by practitioners" in classrooms.

The Context for TEYL

Reading, and the teaching of reading, is very complex in TEYL because of the varied settings in which we can find TEYL being carried out and the variables within TEYL classrooms. Sometimes children learning English as a second or foreign language are doing so after they have been taught to read in their first language, and sometimes not. Additionally, sometimes they have been, or are being, taught to read English as a totally different script from their first language. This script can be completely different from English, or just a little different, and often children learning to read in English are cognitively and chronologically more advanced than children would normally be when reading is introduced in their first language.

Importantly, we must also remember that, culturally, there may be huge differences between how reading is taught in the child's first language and how it is used in TEYL. This might depend on whether the first language is in an oral or text-driven culture, what local or cultural ideas of literacy are, what ideas on literacy children bring to the classroom, and how these might impact on the teaching of reading in TEYL (Au, 2002; Klippel, 2006). Additionally, materials available to children within the TEYL classroom may be linguistically suitable for their language level in the new language but totally unsuitable for, or even well below, their cognitive or interest level and vice versa.

Given the targets set for, and by, teachers, schools, and parents, in EFL, one can understand that teachers may be more concerned with teaching words and spellings in the new language but perhaps not even aware that initial reading in this target language should be built on a great deal of oral and repetitive input before the focus can shift to individual written words and letters (Ponterotto, 2001). As Au (2002) states,

A factor that handicaps the academic advancement of English language learners is teachers' tendency to be overly concerned about surface features of language, such as correct pronunciation of English, rather than the content of the ideas students are trying to communicate. (p. 403)

In many cases, TEYL teachers forget, or are just not pedagogically aware or trained to note, that the learners need to be highly supported when learning to read in the target language, in a very particular way, even though these learners may have had instruction in learning to read, or even be successful readers, in their first language. Problematically, these teachers might assume that the learners will be able to cope with reading in the target language by way of transferring skills from their first language, but this may just not be the case.

However, here we are, already thinking about issues and concerns about reading in TEYL when first, perhaps, we need to set the scene and describe the context for TEYL.

Why Are Young Learners Learning English as a Target Language?

How and why do children come to the TEYL classroom? There can be a number of routes into these classrooms for young learners. If we think globally about the TEYL, then we have to be aware that there is no typical classroom setting for this type of learning and no typical teacher providing the teaching and input. The child might be taught English at school as part of the regular curriculum. Although worldwide, until fairly recently, this was not so common, it is now becoming increasingly the case as more and more governments decide to take responsibility for teaching EFL (a) in formal state schooling and (b) to younger and younger age groups of learners (Rixon, 2000). Yet, the picture is so very different from country to country. For example, in some parts of Spain, it is quite normal for TEYL to be introduced to learners as young as 3 or 4 years of age, whilst in some parts of China, TEYL is introduced only at secondary school age. In Rixon's (2000) global survey of TEYL and its component parts, like the level and quality of teacher training, starting ages for the learners, and materials used, she found that of the 42 countries and regions surveyed, 32 had TEYL in state primary school, with more of the remaining 10 coming on-stream with some state teaching of English in the near future (Rixon, 2004).

Embarrassingly, in the United Kingdom, there is no formal introduction of foreign languages in the primary, or first, school in the National Curriculum. Although plans have been made for introducing language teaching at this level from 2012, we are still waiting to see much in the way of curriculum plans for this, and even if it does take place as forecast, there may be a great shortage of language teachers to carry out the teaching. However, just as in many other countries worldwide, in some state schools in the United Kingdom, foreign-language teaching is being carried out on an ad hoc basis, either within the school day, supported by the school head teachers and governors as part of their local curriculum, or as an after-school club activity.

In other European countries, however, there is more of a concerted effort at TEYL in the state primary or first school with many education ministries treating the teaching of English as a core aspect of their own curricula (Doye, 2001; Klippel, 2006). In other countries around the world, where provision of TEYL is not supported by the government, parents generally decide to send their children to private language schools. As with state provision, this teaching is extremely varied, both in level of knowledge and training of the teachers and in a suitable syllabus for language learning at different ages. As we cannot describe a typical view of the EFL class or teacher here, it may be valuable to see the many variables in TEYL as illustrated in Figure 13.1. To add to the already rather disparate view of TEYL, there is no typical age at which the teaching of English, and thus the teaching of reading in English, might start.

The teaching methodologies, syllabuses, and materials used in these different deliveries are not always standardised, may not even be evaluated, and therefore, the English language knowledge of the children locally, regionally, or nationally will be completely varied. This, in turn, leads to secondary schools inducting children into their English language lessons with wildly varied levels of knowledge, acquisition, and expertise. Sadly, what often happens, and what happened in the United Kingdom in the primary foreign languages teaching project of the 1970s, is that the secondary teachers will start at the beginning again, no matter what level individual learners may have reached. This, of course, can be extremely counterproductive for language learning, the individual's motivation, and the long-term language results.

Already you will be able to see the difficulties facing us when we try to get an overview of the TEYL situation, and so far we have only talked about the different age groups and delivery points! It seems that there are at least nine different but major variable issues in TEYL (see Figure

Figure 13.1. The Variables Involved in Teaching English to Young Learners (TEYL)

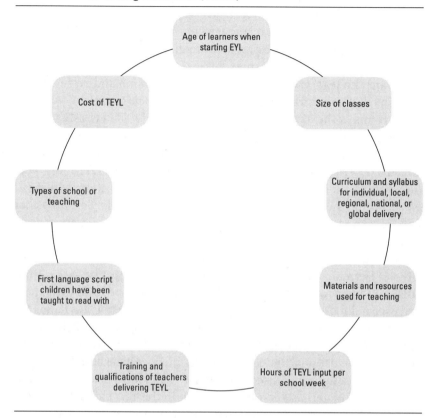

13.1). One of these is the huge variation in numbers of children in TEYL classes. Classes can range from one-to-one or small-group tuition in private teaching right through to class sizes of 60–70+ in some schools, with, of course, everything in between.

The background and training of the teachers who are involved in TEYL is also hugely varied, for a whole host of reasons. It is reassuring to find that in many countries where responsibility for teaching foreign languages in their primary schools is taking place, the training and development of TEYL professionals is now being taken seriously by the government. There are also many private language schools and chains of private language schools that are highly professional in their approach to teaching, and thus TEYL teacher training and development is a serious part of their work, too.

There are trained teachers specialising in TEYL (a wonderful but rare group), trained teachers who have been asked to get involved in TEYL with no training, and teachers with no qualifications in teaching but who might speak English as a first language from an English-speaking country but, again, are not necessarily trained; for example, in Argentina, around 40% of all TEYL teachers fall into this category (Rixon, 2000). There are also teachers with no teaching qualification and no fluency in English but who are told to do this teaching by their schools!

In terms of the local curriculum or syllabus for TEYL, as I am sure you will have guessed by now, the situation for TEYL teachers and learners is also as extremely varied as all other aspects of TEYL described already. (*Curriculum*, in this discussion, will be the overarching structure of any national, regional, or local provision of education, whilst *syllabus* will be the lesson-based and detailed planning for learning that will be carried out in the classroom). Sometimes, TEYL is set within a national curriculum, as is the case in 32 of the 42 countries and regions included in Rixon's (2000) survey. It is also presently the case in Norway, Greece, Germany, Mexico, Hong Kong, parts of Spain, and Japan from 2011, and many other countries. Whilst in others, the local providers, and especially the private language schools, will be using a syllabus for EYL provision based on their perceived understanding of the needs of local customers (in this case, of course, this is usually the parents). Given that the national and local teaching input may be based on different syllabus designs, because of the national and local demands for and of TEYL, the materials and resources used in the TEYL classrooms will also be extremely varied. Additionally, the approach to the syllabus and materials used in TEYL locally, regionally, or nationally will also have an impact on the formal or informal assessment of TEYL.

Linked to these differences in types of teaching is also the difference between hours of TEYL teaching. The range of input is from as little as 30 minutes per week to the staggering 50–100% of input per day in the target language, if the approach used is an immersion-type one (Rixon, 2000). So, the acquisition rates, amount of English being learned, and level of linguistic ability attained in the target language varies phenomenally from classroom to classroom, let alone region to region or country to country.

In addition, there has been a huge rise in the use of globally created and administered assessment tools in TEYL, particularly the use of such tests as Cambridge ESOL's TEYL exams, "Starters", "Movers", and "Flyers" and Trinity College's Graded Examinations in Spoken English, particularly the Initial Steps With Trinity. This enormous and continuously growing demand for language tests for young English language learners not only reflects the growth of TEYL around the world but also has a huge impact on syllabus design and the target-language learning outcomes established by schools and teachers, which have often become very assessment driven but which, sadly, does not always lead to successful language acquisition or use in the long run.

As Rixon (2004a) outlines:

> The most appropriate means of assessing language in children may also be somewhat unfamiliar to teachers, children [and parents!] used to the models of assessment that might exist in other curriculum areas. We may have to face the fact that in some contexts what seem to be the 'best' EYL assessment means may not yet be widely acceptable. (p. 36)

She further states,

> A very important issue is that exams have exam syllabuses and these can have very strong effects not only on the teaching of Young Learners but possibly on the contents of future publishing materials. We need to ask how the exam boards arrived at their syllabuses in the first place. A major source of a least one case was existing YL textbooks. There seems to be a danger of a 'closed and possibly vicious circle' here. (2004b, p. 4)

The Council of Europe has also designed a junior version of its language portfolio so that children and schools can keep a record of students' progress in the target language(s) (CILT, 2006). This particular approach to record keeping and language learning incentives is based on the children completing a portfolio, mainly with "I can..." statements completed about their learning, and keeping examples of their work in the portfolio. This is more of a child-centred approach to assessment, of course, but even so, some concerns and problems have arisen even with this. A few countries, including Eire and Norway, have had to adapt the portfolio to fit their own national needs more directly.

It also needs to be mentioned here that TEYL is expensive. Many parents have to pay a lot of money for the provision of this teaching if they use private schools, and even in countries where TEYL provision is made in state schools, there is often a feeling that the school is not teaching English as well as the private school, so parents will send their children for additional lessons in private schools or with a private tutor to speed up their acquisition of the target language. This creates an even wider ability range within state school classrooms delivering TEYL, and thus the problems outlined previously become further compounded.

How Do We Think Children Learn Language and Develop Cognitively, and How Does This Inform Our Understanding in TEYL?

If we want to look at how we can address the teaching of reading in TEYL, then we also need to be aware of how we think young learners learn foreign or other languages and link this understanding with what we know about how young learners learn in general. In this section, we briefly consider our understanding of first-language acquisition and cognitive development, then link this with our understanding of how young learners learn a foreign language.

We have no room here to consider all the studies that have been carried out into children's language learning and cognitive development in their first language or how these might inform our understanding in TEYL, but we mention some theories and ideas from first-language cognitive development and learning that seem to have particular relevance and interest for TEYL practitioners today. Given that we have illustrated the varied situation in the TEYL world, we here consider what might be seen as ideal or best practice rather than widespread practice in reality.

We understand that the child tries to work things out for himself as a lone scientist (Piaget, 1967), especially when this is particularly enhanced by the scaffolding of an adult or more able peer (Bruner, 1983, 1990; Bruner & Haste, 1987; Wood, Bruner, & Ross, 1976). Wood, Bruner, and Ross highlight features of scaffolding thinking for the child as keeping the child's interest in the task, encouraging the child to stay focused on the task, simplifying it for the child by splitting it into steps, showing the child a range of ways to carry it out, highlighting the important things which the child should or could do in the task, helping the child handle any confusion and/or frustration in the task, and modelling different ways to carry out the task. In addition, there need to be enough opportunities for plenty of zones of proximal development to take place in the child's learning, that is, opportunities for the adult or teacher to aid, enhance, or extend the child's understanding and thinking in a situation so that they can do it themselves in the future (Brewster, 1991; Brewster & Ellis, 2002; Cameron, 2001; Vygotsky, 1978). As Vygotsky says, "What a child can do with assistance today she will be able to do by herself tomorrow" (p. 87).

We also need to allow for the learner to assimilate and accommodate new knowledge and develop understanding (Piaget, 1967), although we would not now believe that the child could only develop when he or she had progressed chronologically through the stages Piaget said were necessary. Many of us will remember, perhaps with concern, the influence Piaget's work had on our understanding in the 1970s of reading readiness and how it was used, and critically, how some learners were stopped from moving on in their reading because teachers did not feel the learners were ready for the next stage. (Brewster, 1991; Cameron, 2001; Piaget, 1967).

However, being one of the first to identify that the child did try to make sense of the world for himself, and that learning and development was more of a bottom-up process than previously understood, Piaget has some relevance to us today. Much of his laboratory work and assumptions about children's development has been illustrated as flawed by the likes of Donaldson (1978), although she does agree with him that the child tries to make sense of the world for himself when she says the child "actively tries to make sense of the world from a very early part of his life: he asks questions, he wants to know" (Donaldson, 1978, p. 86). Linked with this, Donaldson believes that it is particularly through experiential learning, trying to make sense of their experiences, asking questions, and trying things out, or hypothesizing, that children are able to develop. One can infer, then, that if in any learning situation, including TEYL, children are highly scaffolded, given the support of innumerable zones of proximal development by adults/teachers, and are allowed to hypothesize as they make sense of the world around them, then they are likely to be in the most successful environment for cognitive development and learning.

In terms of new language acquisition, though, we should also link this understanding of child development with the more recent work of functionalists, who suggest that language develops within a functional context rather than, as the innatists believe, through a universal language acquisition device common to all (Chomsky, 1965, 1972; Halliday, 1975, 1993). Given a functional setting in the TEYL class, supported by routines, rituals, regular interaction with others, and exposure to functional language and, importantly, reasons for using it through everyday meaningful activities with the target language at the core, this should enable our young language learners to learn the target language. This understanding must guide our approach to teaching English as a foreign, second, or additional language (Halliday, 1993; Wells, 2009). As Wells describes, "Rather than operating with abstract rules derived from universal grammar, children form and modify hypotheses about regular linguistic patterns, based on their increasing experience of language in use" (p. 257).

This approach also echoes the suggestion by Bruner that there needs to be a language acquisition support system supplied by adults or carers that will help children develop their language (Bruner, 1983, 1990; Bruner & Haste, 1987). This understanding about language development is clearly evident in the research carried out by Wells (2009) in Bristol. He uses the term *meaning makers* to describe young children when describing their acquisition and use of language, and states,

> Children search for patterns based on their experience, both cognitive and linguistic, of the speech of the particular linguistic community in which they are growing up, where the distinction between what is lexical and what is grammaticized continues to change over generations. (p. 257)

This is further echoed in Donaldson's (1978) observations about the growth of linguistic skills in the child:

> The child acquires these skills before he becomes aware of them. The child's awareness of what he talks *about*—the things out there to which the language refers—normally take precedence over his awareness of what he talks *with*—the words that he uses. And he becomes aware of what he talks with—the actual words—before he is at all aware of the rules which determine their sequencing—the rules which control his own production of them (Indeed, a thoughtful adult has a very limited awareness of such processes in his own mind.) (pp. 87–88)

It would seem that this is likely to be the case with TEYL, too.

Thinking about the age of the learners, in terms of when might be a "best" or optimal time for children to learn a new language, it now seems as though there may not be such a thing (Aitchison, 2003). Lenneburg's critical period hypothesis suggests that there is a critical period, up to about 11 years of age, and this hypothesis has often been quoted as the reason for starting the teaching of languages to younger and younger children (Aitchison, 2003). However, this hypothesis has now been heavily criticised, and instead, it seems that if the learner is predisposed or motivated to learn language, whatever their age, child or adult, then he or she will be able to learn other languages (Aitchison, 2003). By deduction, then, it would seem that there is no "best" age at which children should start learning other languages. However, the movement for teaching languages to children has well and truly been established worldwide, and this is not likely to stop in the foreseeable future. Perhaps, though, there are other good reasons for introducing foreign languages to young learners, rather than because there is an organic cutoff point for language learning. We consider these later in this chapter.

Thinking back to individuals making sense of the world around them, we also need to consider here the theories that learners use preferred learning styles to learn, which are linked to the main sensory receivers (Revell & Norman, 1997). On the whole, this thinking tends to see learners as using their preferred visual, auditory, or kinaesthetic learning styles, although there is also a case for the use of olfactory and gustatory learning styles (Reid, 1995; Revell & Norman, 1997). This notion of each person learning in his own way has also become strongly linked, more recently, with the work of Gardner (1983, 1993), as he proposed that there are different types of *intelligences* that we all have at our disposal and which we individually use in different ways for different activities, and his work has been gaining huge popularity in educational communities around the world. Gardner set out to show that there was not just a psychometric view of intelligence and that the subsequent testing of intelligence in one particular form was not a sensible way to evaluate what learners were really able to do (Gardner, 1983, 1993). Initially, Gardner felt there were seven such multiple intelligences—logical-mathematical (the one usually tested in traditional examinations), linguistic, spatial, kinaesthetic, musical, interpersonal, and intrapersonal—but in his later work, it seems there may be even more than these, including naturalistic and, possibly, existential (Gardner, 1993).

So, How Do We Think Children Learn a Foreign Language?

Added to this, it is worth considering here the interesting suggestion by Cummins (1979a, 1979b) that there are two types of language that can be taught: basic interpersonal communicative skills (BICS) and cognitive academic language proficiency (CALP). Cummins tried to show how conversational fluency is often acquired by nonnative speakers in ESL classes, equivalent to their grade level, within around two years, whereas academic-type language, for talking about subjects at an academic level, often takes around five years by the same learners. His work is significant in showing us how a lack of understanding of the latter time scale issues has led to misjudged assessment of learners wrongly viewed as able to leave the language support classes when there was still a lot of language learning to be done. So, by way of a review, if our present understanding of how children learn is that they learn to think, understand, question, and try to make sense of the world (and for our case, language) around them best when they have the functionality, guidance, learning environment, and cognitive and social support of an adult who creates a scaffolded learning environment and takes part in zones of proximal development with the learners and inputs language at the BICS level before the CALP level and then combines them, this approach is likely to be the most applicable in a TEYL context.

In addition to this, we also need to help learners understand why they are learning, what they are learning, and how, as Cunningham and Cunningham (2002) rightly state, "children need cognitive clarity about what they are learning" (p. 88). So, we must remember that teaching is not a secretive activity, and the more we inform our learners about why they are involved in the activities we create for them, the more they will make sense of them, understand and enjoy them, and—when given the right scaffolding—will develop, grow, and learn more through this understanding. As Williams (2002) also states,

> General guidelines for teachers that derive from the research evidence... include the suggestions that teachers help students by explaining fully what it is they are teaching—what to do, why, how, and when; by modeling their own thinking processes; by encouraging students to ask questions and discuss possible answers among themselves; and by keeping students engaged in their reading by means of providing tasks that demand active involvement. (p. 256)

The TEYL teacher should also be able to model target-language learning and use and create interesting, meaningful, and purposeful situations in the target language, so that through this, the children will acquire the target language in a natural way (Bruner & Haste, 1987; Donaldson, 1978; Hughes, 2002, 2006a, 2006b, 2010; Vygotsky, 1978). Additionally, if we believe that we should support the child by appealing to their preferred learning styles and multiple intelligences, then this should also be reflected in our TEYL approach and methodology.

Why Teach a Foreign Language to Young Learners?

It is clear why we would teach English as a second or additional language in an English-speaking country, but why do we teach English, or any other language, as a foreign language to young children at primary school age? As outlined previously, we have heard the "youngest is best" mantra for some time now, but there is still little evidence to show that this is the real reason for TEYL. It has been found that young learners do not actually learn quicker or easier, and there does not now seem to be a critical period for learning a language (Aitchison, 2003; Cameron, 2001). Instead of thinking about an optimum age for learning here, when the evidence is too unclear at the moment to make any long-term decisions about early or later language learning, we should instead think about the environment for learning in the primary school and the reasons for teaching other subjects to young learners.

Language Learning as Another Subject in the Primary Curriculum

Why do we teach young learners anything? If we think now that first language is not quite totally acquired by around the age of 5, as Cameron (2001) and Aitchison (2003) both suggest, should we not wait until the learners are more mature, able to read and write in the first language, and have more cognitive agility before teaching them a new language? Perhaps, though, we ought to ask yet another question here, which is, why do we teach *anything* to such young learners? Why introduce them to science, maths, history, music, or any of the other subjects they are exposed to in primary school (Hughes, 2001)?

Traditionally, and this happens globally, we introduce a range of different subjects to young learners in their first school. Nobody thinks that they may be "too young" to start being introduced to these subjects or that these subjects should be introduced as pure or abstract subjects. Instead, these subjects are introduced to children in order for them to make sense of things that are part of the interesting world that surrounds them and that are to do with them and their lives. As educators, we believe that we are initially building the foundations of understanding in each subject in a very practical, hands-on way so that young children can interact with the "actual", "physical", and "here and now" of these subjects and may not even be aware that they are learning about maths, history, science, or music. They are learning about these subjects in concrete and practical ways that we believe link with their cognitive development at these ages. Ideally, we are supporting this by scaffolding their learning, creating a meaningful, dynamic, and functional learning environment, with the teacher as mentor and modeller of the thinking that is being introduced to the learners, and creating development of learners and their understanding of these subjects through zones of proximal development. For example, we teach the sort of maths that has a meaning to these learners but which deals with addition, subtraction, fractions, and multiplication of things that are important to them (e.g., addition of teddies and dolls together, what the taking away of building blocks leaves them with, how cutting a cake can be described in fractions, how they can work out how many pieces of cake they need for the class; Hughes, 2001).

This should also, then, be the case with language learning. As Rixon (1999) succinctly puts it, we are looking for optimal conditions for learning rather than optimal age. Teaching about language at this age will also enable us to scaffold young learners' thinking and understanding of language and communication in general and their own language and other languages through zones of proximal development in particular. Thus, we are laying the foundations for understanding of themselves, other peoples and cultures, and particularly, communication, which will be so very important for them in their futures.

The teaching of a foreign, or new, language should show children how this new language can have a link with their everyday lives, introduce them to the idea that it is positive to speak another language, and communicate more easily in a world in which they can interact with now and in which, in the future, they may travel and work. TEYL teachers, then, must act as language and thinking modellers of this other language, just as primary teachers need to act as modellers of all subjects and thinking that young learners are being introduced to in their primary education.

As Read (2003) echoes,

Primary schools generally provide an ideal context for a whole learning experience appropriately structured to meet children's needs. Through 'learning by doing', language competence can be built up gradually and naturally and provide the basis for more abstract, formal learning in secondary school. After all, no one ever suggests postponing the age of starting to learn maths because it will be easy to catch up later. (p. 6)

What of the Target-Language Learning Then?

First and foremost, the structure of the target language is not the first thing we want the young learners to focus on. Instead, we want it to be just a small part, initially, of what is being taught and introduced to them. We are introducing them to communication, sharing ideas and knowledge, working together, having fun with the sounds of the new language, and using this new language to interact with each other in a fun and motivating way.

At the same time, though, TEYL teachers have to make sure that there is a sound linguistic syllabus, as well as a syllabus focusing on the social, metalinguistic, and cognitive language learning that is going on. The child does not need to focus only on the language as a subject in the early stages of language teaching. Initially, we want them to just communicate and interact in and with the target language. We can also introduce them to enough simple metalanguage so that they can talk about the new language in easy ways, just as we would use simple mathematical metalanguage to help children talk about what they are doing in maths (e.g., *big, small, add, take away, split up*). So, some aspects of talking about the language should be introduced to younger learners for, as Cameron (2001) suggests, even very young learners are able to talk about some aspects of language (e.g., action words), As Garvie (1990) also recommends, "The handling of the tools must become second-nature to the handler" as they acquire more and more language (p. 56). Although, perhaps, we could also add here that the handling of all of the metalinguistic tools do not need to become second nature until we are sure that these learners are ready to use this level of CALP language in the target language.

It is only when children have the initial ability to communicate and use the target language as a tool (or science and maths as tools) that we can then expect them to start identifying and itemising parts of the language and its rules. It is fitting here to remind ourselves what Donaldson (1978) said about the child acquiring skills before he is aware of them. Activities in the young learner language class should be cognitively challenging and developmental for our learners, just as all teaching at this level should be. A language level just slightly beyond learners' present stage of understanding will encourage and interest them in the target activity more than if they are continually faced with activities that are too linguistically or cognitively easy for them (Krashen, 1981). It is really important that our young learners find a challenge in any learning activities in order that they may learn, gain a feeling of success, and perhaps more important, learn how to learn and think (Cameron, 2001; Hughes, 2010).

Therefore, we need to create a classroom in which the child is able to hypothesise about the language, consciously or subconsciously. In other words, as they are experiencing the new language (e.g., like the new maths, science, and music), they are constantly involved in a cycle of hypothesizing as they learn (see Figure 13.2).

Figure 13.2. The Language Learning Hypothesizing Cycle for Young Learners

4. The child uses the gathered feedback to establish his own rules about the target language, then internalises and remembers them for the next time he can use them.

1. The child creates a hypothesis about some aspect of the new language, then searches for meaning and patterns in the target language by using his existing experiential knowledge of language and communication.

3. The child tests the hypothesis by listening, questioning, or testing and adjusts the hypothesis according to the feedback received.

2. The child looks for clues for help and will use anything around them to support the child's hypothesis (e.g., realia, peers' reactions and language, teaching materials, teacher's gestures and intonation).

Note. Adapted from "Why Should We Make Activities for Young Language Learners Meaningful and Purposeful?" by A. Hughes, 2010, in F. Mishan & A. Chambers (Eds.), *Perspectives on Language Learning Materials Development* (p. 180), Bern, Switzerland: Peter Lang.

Teaching of Reading in TEYL

It is at this point, and given our understanding of the context described previously for TEYL and our pedagogic understanding of it, that we can now turn to discussing the teaching of reading within English language teaching for young learners. As Rixon (2007) rightly comments,

> Reading as a skill very often is *not* addressed in any depth, either in national syllabuses or in EYL teaching materials on which much of the onus of teacher support and development is placed in many parts of the world.... This lack of attention to how reading skills might best be launched with [young learners] contrasts greatly with the often furious debate about the most effective procedures for handling them with native speaking children. (p. 6)

Aitchison (2003) has described what she calls a *sensitive period* in which the children are naturally tuned in to acquiring language. Should we, in TEYL, try to link the teaching of reading in English to this sensitive period for our young language learners so that they can use, consciously or subconsciously, some of the strategies and cognitive skills they are using for first-language acquisition and reading? As Aitchison states, "Children acquire the main grammatical rules of their language between the ages of around two to five", with a "final phase of grammar" coming "between five and ten" (pp. 4–5).

Then, according to Aitchison (2003), at around 5, children have an active vocabulary of around 3,000 words with a passive vocabulary of around 10,000 words, after which there is a further huge leap in vocabulary acquisition at around age 13. However, Cameron (2001) states that young second-language learners add around 1,000 words in English a year to their vocabulary but that, in the first place, there is a gap of about 4,000–5,000 words between them and their native speaker peer group. Cameron also indicates that children in a foreign-language learning situation, rather than a second-language learning one, only acquire around 1,000–2,000 English words after five years of regular TEYL lessons.

This focus on vocabulary at this stage of our discussion about how reading is taught to young language learners is important, as it seems there is a strong link between the size of the lexicon and the link with the grammar of the language (Cameron, 2001). "Much important grammatical information is tied into words, and learning words can take students a long way into grammar" (Cameron, 2001, p. 72). And as Aitchison (2003) mentions, "word learning is interleaved with other dimensions of language learning, though continues long after other aspects of acquisition are complete" (p. 11). She additionally states that 20,000 words, usually acquired by native English speakers at around 13 years of age,

> seems to be a critical mass for being able to speak English fluently. Foreign learners who had reached this total could talk efficiently about any subject...and those with less than this number often struggled both to understand and to talk fluently. (p. 5)

Should TEYL be focusing more on vocabulary acquisition during the primary school age to try and give young learners this "critical mass" of 20,000 words over the long term in their EYL learning, which can then interleave so crucially with the grammar of English? If this is the case, this may be problematic, for we are aware that children are in TEYL classes for so little time, and it would be difficult to make up this time and amount of vocabulary. As we can see, the picture regarding hours of TEYL input is different all over the world, as information from Rixon's (2000) survey shows in Table 13.1.

Cameron (2001) relieves our worries about time and catch-up, however, when she describes what she believes is the optimum amount of words derived from the most frequently used vocabulary in written texts as 2,000 words. She suggests that vocabulary teaching in TEYL might be focused on these 2,000 words to give the learners a working lexicon in English. However, these are the words used most frequently in written texts, accounting for around 80% of the written texts in English according to Cameron, which raises concerns about focusing on the teaching of vocabulary linked only to a corpus created from the written word. Might it make fluency in the target language even more difficult to attain for our young learners, if there is a focus only on the most frequently used words in written texts? More research is needed here to clarify the situation.

Rixon (2007) raises other concerns for our young language learners in terms of the complexity of English words they may be coming into contact with and their understanding of them. She feels this is additionally compounded by the fact that many English learners, whilst possibly also learning to read in first language at the same time, are trying to apply some of the concepts they are using in first-language reading for reading in English, but if they are learning to read with totally different writing systems, this may be confusing for them. She also says that children "may need to make quite a conceptual leap when moving to an alphabetical system such as English" (p. 6). She further illustrates how the "multitudinous relationship between symbols and sounds that English permits" make it difficult to acquire English easily (p. 7).

Cameron (2001) also reminds us how it is not just knowing the word that is important to young English learners but also the knowing about it (i.e., word knowledge) in all senses that is crucial, including receptive, productive, phonological, decoding, orthographic, grammatical, pragmatic, style or register, collocation, and metalinguistic knowledges of the word. Cameron neatly shows these different aspects of word knowledge in Table 13.2. However, if we believe that vocabulary acquisition is so vital in TEYL learning to read, we may now be about to hit a brick wall. We want to support language learning and long-term fluency for our young learners, but we cannot rely on the written word to build their English vocabulary base, or teach them all aspects of every English word

Table 13.1. Information Regarding Timing of Teaching English to Young Learners in 42 Countries or Regions, 2005–2006

Country or region	Timing of instruction
Argentina	72 hours per year
Austria	1 hour per week
Bahrain	5 hours per week, 32 weeks per year
Bangladesh	*Years 1 and 2*; 44 hours per year
	Years 3 and 4; 82 hours per year
Brazil	2–5 hours per week
Colombia	45 minutes per day, 3 days per week
Croatia	*Years 1–4*; 70–170 hours per year
	Years 5–8; 105 hours per year
Cyprus	40 minutes per day, 3 days per week, 30–35 weeks per year
Czech Republic	40 minutes per day, 3 days per week, 33 weeks per year
Ecuador	No information
Ethiopia	45–55 minutes per day
France	15 minutes per day, 4 days per week
Greece	80 hours per year
Hong Kong	8–9 lessons per week, totalling about 180–210 hours per year
Hungary	1, 2, or 3 hours per week, 35 weeks per year, totalling 35–105 hours per year
Iceland	40 minutes per day, two days per week
India–Goa	35 minutes per day, 5 days per week
India–Gujarat	30 minutes per day, 4-6 days per week, 20 weeks per year, totalling about 40–60 hours per year
India–Maharashtra	30 minutes per week, 5 days per week, 32 weeks per year, totalling 80 hours per year
India–West Bengal	40 minutes per day, 5 days per week
Indonesia	90 minutes in one lesson per week
Israel	*Grade 3*; 2 hours per week
	Grade 4; 2–3 hours per week
	Grades 5 and 6; 3–4 hours per week
Korea	40 minutes per day, 2 days per week, 34 weeks per year
Latvia	40 minutes per day, 3 days per week
Malaysia	30 minutes per session, 8 sessions per week
Mexico	50 minutes per day, 3 days per week, 40 weeks per year
The Netherlands	100 hours during primary schooling, whenever school wants to deliver it
Pakistan	35 minutes per day, 6 days per week, 33 weeks per year
Poland	240 hours spread over grades 4–6
Romania	50 minutes per day, 2 days per week, 28 weeks per year
	50 minutes per day, 3 days per week, 28 weeks per year
Russia	*Grade 1*; 60 lessons per year
	Grades 2–4; 96 lessons per year
Slovenia	1–2 hours per week, totalling 30–70 lessons per year
South Africa	No information

(continued)

Table 13.1. Information Regarding Timing of Teaching English to Young Learners in 42 Countries or Regions, 2005–2006 (*continued*)

Country or region	Timing of instruction
Spain	*Ages 8–12*; 1 hour per day, 3 days per week, 30 weeks per year
Sri Lanka	*Grade 3*; 30 minutes per day, 5 days per week, totalling 80 hours per year
	Grade 4; 40 minutes per day, 5 days per week, totalling 140 hours per year
Sudan	*Forms 5 and 6*; 3 hours per week, 30 weeks per year
Taiwan	48 hours per year
Tunisia	No information
Turkey	*Grades 4 and 5*; 2 hours per week, 36 weeks per year
	Grades 6 and above; 3 hours per week, 36 weeks per year
Ukraine	*Years 1 and 2*; 3 hours per week, totalling 100 hours per year
	Years 3 and 4; 4 hours per week, totalling 130 hours per year
United Arab Emirates	40 minutes per day, 4 days per week
Venezuela	4 hours per week

Note. Adapted from *Worldwide Survey of Primary ELT* by S. Rixon, 2000b, London: British Council, retrieved December 15, 2010, from www.britishcouncil.org/worldwide_survey_of_primary_elt.pdf

they may be learning in the TEYL classroom for a number of reasons, which include the following:

1. The lack of understanding of these issues by TEYL teachers and a lack of specific TEYL training in the teaching of reading in particular

2. The overall approach taken locally in TEYL and the teaching of reading in the target language

3. The lack of extended time for the first school English lessons and the lack of opportunity to input the amount of TEYL acquisition that would equate to approximately five years of a child's native-language acquisition of language

4. The background writing system the child may be learning in the first language

5. Whether the child has been introduced to reading and writing in the first language at all before starting reading in the target language

6. The materials used to support TEYL locally and whether they support reading

7. The way literacy is viewed in the first-language culture

Table 13.2. Knowing About a Word

Type of knowledge	What is involved	Example
Receptive knowledge: Aural/decoding	To understand it when it is spoken/written	
Memory	To recall it when needed	
Conceptual knowledge	To use it with the correct meaning	Not confusing *protractor* with *compasses*
Knowledge of the spoken form: Phonological knowledge	To hear the word and to pronounce it acceptably, on its own, and in phrases and sentences	To hear and produce the endings of the verb forms, such as the /n/ sound at the end of *undertak<u>en</u>*
Grammatical knowledge	To use it in a grammatically accurate way; to know grammatical connections with other words	*She sang very well* not **she sang very good;* to know that *is* and *be* are parts of the same verb
Collocational knowledge	To know which other words can be used with it	*A beautiful view* not **a good-looking view*
Orthographic knowledge	To spell it correctly	*Protractor* not **protracter*
Pragmatic knowledge, knowledge of style and register	To use it in the right situation	*Would you like a drink?* is more appropriate in a formal or semi-formal situation than *what can I get you?*
Connotational knowledge	To know its positive and negative associations, to know its associations with related words	To know that *slim* has positive connotations, when used about a person, whereas *skinny* is negative
Metalinguistic knowledge	To know explicitly about the word, e.g., its grammatical properties	To know that *protractor* is a *noun;* to know that *pro* is a *prefix*

Note. Modified from *Teaching Languages to Young Learners* (p. 77), by L. Cameron, 2001, Cambridge, UK: Cambridge University Press.
*Indicates nongrammatically correct language

The first of these, the level of understanding, awareness, and training of TEYL teachers is, as discussed previously, one of the crucial variables. Center (2009) echoes these findings when she reports that during classroom observations or through conversations with teachers, they would tell her "that their preservice training has not equipped them to assist struggling readers satisfactorily" (p. 6). In Rixon's (2010) survey results, carried out amongst TEYL teachers from 2005 to 2006, she notes that some teachers of TEYL often had a negative experience when learning English as a target language themselves, and many of them had carried out little reading in English other than set texts or university handouts.

The majority of teachers in the survey reported they had had a "look and say" approach to reading themselves as learners, rather than a phonics or blended approach, and it seemed that a minority of these teachers focused on consonant cluster rather than syllable-initial consonants in reading development, which is particularly pertinent to teaching reading in English. In particular, her findings noted that 33% of the respondents who did not specialise in young learners had never heard of phonics, half of the nonspecialists had heard of phonics, and the rest were not sure what it was, although 90% of the young learner specialists had at least heard of it. However, when the young learner specialists were asked if they could explain it, this rate dropped dramatically.

What seems to be clear from Rixon's (2010) survey, like Center's (2009) findings, is that not many TEYL teachers seem to have had training in the teaching of reading in TEYL, and others are confused about what different aspects of teaching reading are and, perhaps, even what different aspects of TEYL are. Fox (2000) mentions his own concerns about this knowledge of TEYL when carrying out some action research in Hong Kong when he identified a

> dilemma between what I believe was the best way to help support my learners and the way most teachers and parents thought about ESL. Indeed, following a series of informal meetings and discussions, it appeared that there was little consensus amongst teachers, parents and, perhaps most importantly, the students as to what ESL was all about. (p. 36)

This lack of understanding on the part of some TEYL teachers is also mentioned by Olsen (2000) when she comments about the teaching of English in Norway:

> There are great regional differences...One of the reasons is the lack of qualified English teachers.... In some cases, the children learn more English outside the classroom than inside it, because they receive too little input in the language at school. (p. 45)

Olsen goes on to say that English is now being taught in Norwegian schools from the first day of their schooling, but due to the way teachers are trained to become English teachers, many of them do not seem to have knowledge of a sound TEYL methodology, and "teachers lack confidence to use the language themselves and rely in all their work on the textbook with the accompanying teachers' guide" (pp. 45–46).

Reading in First Versus Second or Foreign Language

What seems to be crucially important for learning to read in first language is the way language surrounds the learner and, importantly, that this is happening for a long time before the teaching of reading is started in a formalised way. The importance, then, of such approaches to literacy and literary activities in TEYL is made very clear and something we next consider in more detail (Au, 2002; Cameron, 2001).

There is a wealth of literacy surrounding native speaker children of any language as they grow up and before they even get into a formal classroom. There are labels and street signs, food packets, labelled boxes and storage, newspapers and magazines, letters and cards in post, writing on toys and children's books, shop signs and things in shop windows, as well as, of course, the computer screen, which their family may be interacting with and which they are certainly looking at over their family members' shoulders. For first-language users, there are many years of indirect input, creating a rich language literacy and many years of exposure before formal teaching of reading in first language, which impacts remarkably on their ability to recognise particular words, sounds, and symbols when they start the formal process of learning to read in first language (Rixon, 2010).

TEYL learners do not have such an extended time within a rich English literacy environment, so when they come to learning to read in English, there is a huge gap of knowledge which often the TEYL teacher is unaware of. TEYL practitioners, then, must try to create a rich TEYL literacy environment for their learners within the language classroom to try and fill some of this gap and make up for lost time. (We look at some practical ways of doing this later in the chapter.)

Yet, as Rixon (2007) found out, few TEYL teachers are trained to teach reading in the target language or are even aware of the need to create a rich English literacy in their language classrooms. If there is training and development for these teachers, it tends to focus on the development of their own confidence and abilities in English, which is similar to the situation Olsen (2000) described. Also, as Rixon mentions, often these teachers never experienced being taught another language as young learners themselves and so have no experiential memory of what it feels like to learn to read in a new language. Rixon reminds us that

Reading as a skill very often is <u>not</u> addressed in any depth, either in national syllabuses or in EYL teaching materials on which much of the onus of teacher support and development is placed in many parts of the world. The need to recruit or prepare new teachers of EYL often outstrips the capacity to give them a full orientation to the professional skills they will need...Issues such as the development of initial reading do not usually form part of this basis training. (p. 6)

Many of these EFL teachers are also not involved in the teaching of reading in their language learners' first language, so it could be that they are unaware of how to deal with reading in the first language, let alone the target language. However, as we are aware, the use of the written script in the target language is generally highly obvious in the materials teachers use, either formal materials created by publishers and often including children's workbooks, activity books, writing books, readers, ancillary materials, and so on, as well as teacher- and school-made materials.

As Cameron (2001) notes, "It is important to begin with, and to keep returning to the idea of reading and writing as language use for expressing and sharing meanings between people" (p. 123). She particularly emphasises the fact that literacy is both social and cognitive. "Socially, literacy provides people with opportunities to share meanings across space and time. Cognitively, literacy requires that individuals use specific skills and knowledge about how the written language operates by processing text" (p. 123).

If we expect our young language learners to be able to address both social and cognitive literacy in the target language without any protracted length of English literacy input, without a rich English literacy environment in the language classroom, and without them being made aware of or adept in their first-language skills of reading and writing and how their first language literacy skills may be different from or similar to the target language literacy, then we are doing our language learners a great injustice. Too often, this is exactly what is happening in the TEYL classrooms. Instead, teachers need to create a rich English literacy environment in the TEYL classroom by giving much rich, intensive exposure to the target language, which learners can interact with as much as possible during their language classes.

What is also important is that these learners are also scaffolded through their reading in the target language, baby step by baby step, when very young (up to around age 7 or 8 months) and small step by small step at a time when they are slightly older (until around age 10 or

11) to have a chance of mastering abilities and skills of reading in English. To do this, teachers have to create the right environment in the language class so that a great many English words and text types around them are available for the young learners to experience. Learners may be having to learn a whole host of new skills and strategies, in terms of reading in English, compared with those that they may be using in their first-language reading, depending on the literacy culture, script, and approach to reading in their first language.

Learners will be consciously or subconsciously trying to apply and hypothesise whatever they have learnt in first-language reading skills to the English words or texts they are being introduced to. Teachers need to be aware, though, that these may not be so appropriate, depending on the script of their first language and the graphophonemic relationships they encounter in their first-language script.

> Like the grammar issues in language teaching we feel that if we could just explain the rules, learning could be made much more efficient but, on the other hand, explaining the rules gets so technical that most children cannot understand the explanations...What we can say is that English is a complicated alphabetic written language, and almost always requires learners of it as a foreign language to develop new skills and knowledge, in addition to what can be transferred. (Cameron, 2001, p. 133)

As Rixon (2007) reports,

> Children coming from contexts in which their L1 uses a very different writing system, particularly a logographic system (such as Chinese) or a syllabic system (e.g. Sinhala) may need to make quite a conceptual leap when moving to an alphabetical system such as English. Children whose languages are written alphabetically like English but which do not use the Roman alphabet (e.g. Greek, Russian, Arabic) will also have adjustments to make. Less obviously, children whose languages share an alphabet with English (e.g. Spanish, Italian, German) may find the different sound values given to seemingly familiar letters frustrating. (pp. 6–7)

What the language teacher has to do is create as many opportunities as possible to support the learners' emerging and growing literacy in English in order to scaffold their learning of reading in English. The teacher needs to create plenty of opportunities for their young learners to interact with and use this new target language in the TEYL classroom in an informal, fun way and use it for the learners to carry out meaningful and purposeful social activities, for example, getting information on something they are keen to find out about, such as an event in the area; sharing their likes and dislikes in a survey; and seeing what the local or premier football results are (some practical examples are provided later in the chapter).

By interacting through and with English in such an environment, it is likely that the learners will come to feel comfortable and confident using the target language. Hopefully, they will then be motivated to use it, rather than demotivated or frustrated and confused, and will thus be more likely to acquire and recall it more readily. If learners are exposed to a great variety of examples of English in the language class environment, and if this is rich and varied, it should engender a more stress-free learning environment and long-term, meaningful acquisition of literacy and language in English for them (Hughes, 2010, 2011). As Rixon (2007) points out,

> if [young learners] can within a few years become confident and happy readers of real texts in English, the road to autonomy and enjoyment of the language is made that much clearer for them....this will not happen automatically; teachers need to know how to give [young learners] a happy and well staged start on that road, beginning with the very first steps. (p. 6)

Meaning or Word Level of Reading

When considering the mechanics of teaching reading, Center (2009) suggests that pupils need to be taught skills at both the "meaning...and word level", and further states, "put simply, reading is the product of decoding (word recognition) and comprehension (both listening and reading)" (p. 6). She then lists the U.S. National Reading Panel's five essential components of beginning reading instruction as "phonological/phonemic awareness, phonics, and fluency—which can all be classified as word-level skills—and vocabulary and comprehension—which come under the rubric of meaning-level skills" (p. 6). Martin, Lovat, and Purnell (2004, p. 17) illustrate the process of reading being overarched by the learner's need to link all these skills when trying to make meaning when reading, as illustrated in Figure 13.3. The reader approaches reading using all of the skills at the same time to make sense of the words they are reading.

Added to these views, of course, is the continuously raging debate of the phonics versus whole-word approach in reading in first language, let alone in a target language. Rixon (2007) points out the difficulty young

Figure 13.3. Making Meaning

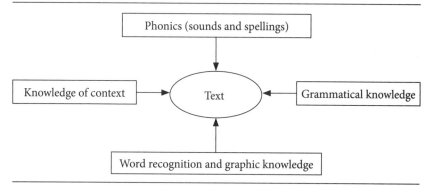

learners have with the transparency of English and its spelling and linked sounds when she notes,

> It is this mix of transparent versus variously tricky written forms in the English language that contributes to the debates amongst L1 reading experts concerning the effectiveness of phonics-based learning versus whole-word learning. In other words, English is a language in which it is not easy or straightforward to gain mastery in processing and understanding the written words, even for native speaker beginners. To this, we need to add the fundamental disadvantage at which Young Learners find themselves. Native speaker children have a large orally-learned data bank of language upon which they can draw when trying to match not-very-transparent symbols with meaningful language, but Young [language] Learners do not have this. (pp. 7–8)

Thus, Rixon highlights, once again, the need to create an English-literacy environment for our young language learners, which will go some way to helping them create their own data bank of the language to draw on when trying to make meaning as they read in English. (We discuss this further in the next section.)

Thinking about the specifics of the teaching of reading in TEYL for learners who can read in first language, though, it would seem that Calderón (2009) also thinks a focus on vocabulary growth is important for these learners. She described the work carried out in the School 319 project in New York, where the "extensive explicit vocabulary instruction became the basis of EAL success in these schools" (p. 14), which was not just in language lessons, as she further mentions, "There were also non-EAL pupils who were struggling readers because their word knowledge was limited. Teachers reported that teaching rich vocabulary and reading integrated into maths, science and social studies helped all pupils perform better" (p. 14). She particularly notes,

> a recent report from the US National Literacy Panel on Language Minority Children and Youth found that the components necessary for successful reading comprehension for mainstream pupils also become the building blocks for EAL language and literacy development: phonemic awareness, decoding, fluency, vocabulary, background knowledge and comprehension. However, the panel found the EAL pupils, need more explicit instruction and more time for comprehension. (p. 14)

It would seem valuable to list here some adapted instruction approaches used in this project, as outlined by Calderón (2009), as these may be useful for TEYL teachers to reflect on:

- Teach important words before reading, not after;
- Teach as many words as possible before, during and after reading;
- Teach simple everyday words [BICS]...along with information processing words,...and content specific/academic words [CALP];
- New words must be used within the context of reading, talking and writing within the same class period...;
- Lexical items (e.g., tense, root, affixes, phrasal and idiomatic uses) should be emphasized and used as strategic learning tools;
- Teach...pupils keywords for a reading assignment...;
- Avoid sending...pupils to look up words in the dictionary. This doesn't help; and
- Avoid having a peer translate for...pupils—this doesn't help either.
  With explicit vocabulary instructions for...pupils became a seven-step process:
  1. Teacher says and shows the word and asks pupils to repeat three times;
  2. Teacher reads and shows the word in a sentence (context) from the text;
  3. Teacher provides definition(s);
  4. Teacher explains meaning with pupil-friendly definitions or gives an example that pupils can relate to;

5. Teacher engages 100% of the pupils in ways to orally use the word and concept (e.g., turn to your partner and share how...; Which do you prefer...? Answer in a complete sentence..). Writing the word, drawing, or other word activities should come after reading. Before reading, pupils need to use the work orally several times in a variety of ways;

6. Teacher ends by highlighting an aspect of the word that might create difficulty: spelling, multiple meanings, cognates/false cognates, prefixes, suffixes, base words, synonyms, antonyms, homophones, grammatical variations etc.... Steps 1–6 move quickly, with no more than 10–15 minutes spent in pre-teaching key vocabulary; and

7. Teacher assigns peer reading with oral and written summarization activities, and further word study where...pupils can practise applying the new words. (adapted slightly from Calderon, 2009, p. 15)

Given the discussion so far, it would seem that a balanced approach to teaching of reading is necessary for our young language learners, which specifically includes support for making meaning in their reading, a balanced approach to both phonics and whole-word approaches, and a need to create a rich target-language literacy environment, or data bank, for them in the language classroom.

How Can We Create the Right English Literacy Environment?

How, then, in practical terms, can we create an English-literacy environment in the classroom? We can do several things, such as making the classroom represent a micro-English environment in which English language, in many different forms, in many different presentations, and for a variety of uses, is employed in the language classroom and with which the learners interact (Hughes, 2011). These forms should include the following:

- Labelling everything in the classroom in English

- Creating interactive English posters that will encourage learners to read and use them (e.g., a daily weather chart, an updated football poster with information about results of football matches)

- Having interactive games and quizzes in English in the classroom for learners to play or take part in when there are a few minutes spare either before, during, or after a lesson

- An English book/reading/story corner or an area in the classroom that includes a wide variety of reading material in a wide variety of different genres that is freely available for the learners to interact with
- Written instructions in English for using items in the classroom created both by the teacher and the learners (e.g., for filling in or interacting with the interactive posters, completing quizzes, how to use English games, how to use new software, how to borrow books from the English book library/corner)
- An English "sound" corner (If the learners have particular difficulties with any aspect of English pronunciation, such as between *v* and *b*, or *th* and *ph*, then an area with labelled pictures or real examples of things starting with these sounds will give practical, meaningful opportunities for practise and repetition.)
- English-language posters that show a range of things that would be helpful for everyday English use, such as useful phrases or words in English, lists of words (e.g., days of the week, months of the year, descriptive words, action words, colours), and examples of poems or chants containing alliterative language
- Posting news announcements about children in the class on the walls
- Hanging "Class rules for..." posters in English, in which you and the class have negotiated rules for behaviour in the class and during lessons, such as "Class rules for speaking and listening" (e.g., "When someone is speaking, listen and do not interrupt")
- A listening corner where students can listen to English audio or video recordings (e.g., stories, jokes, songs, adverts from British television, films, cartoons, instructions)
- A writing corner where students can create English stories, books, quizzes, and posters by themselves
- A survey corner/area where the teacher or students create surveys and ask students to complete them on a regular basis, then the findings are discussed with the whole class

Above all, the quality of the language environment lies in the small changes and additions made regularly and the inclusion of new materials that change on a rolling and regular basis, so that learners are motivated to read and interact with these new things they see every time they come into the language classroom (Hughes, 2011). As Wells (2009) notes, there is a "strong relationship between knowledge of literacy at age 5 and all later assessments of school achievements" (p. 166), and this must also be the case in target-language acquisition and reading. In particular, teachers should make sure that there is plenty of real interaction with English for the learners in order to support and scaffold their emergent literacy in English. Teachers can do this by creating opportunities in the classroom, like those outlined previously, and also by using a wealth of stories books, and real books with young language learners. The term *real books* here includes any books, comics, reference books, and literature that have been specially written for young readers, though not necessarily young language learners. However, there will also be space for books and materials that have been published for young language learners (i.e., created language materials), such as the sort of readers published by ELT (English language teaching) publishers (Hughes & Williams, 2000). Yet again, a balanced approach here with real and created books in TEYL will enhance the literacy environment for our language learners.

By using this wide range of reading materials in the classroom, learners will come to feel comfortable with the written word in English, will start to see patterns emerging in this written form, will start to link oral language with written language, and will see, through the use of language around the classroom and in stories and books, that reading English can be enjoyable, fun, fascinating, and good to do and thus will be motivated to try to read. Figure 13.4 gives an overview of what has been discussed so far on this.

The Importance of Story in TEYL

Once we have created a rich English literacy environment in the TEYL classroom and are using real and created literacy, we must also think seriously about the importance and use of story in TEYL. Just take a moment to think about the conversations you have had today. What did they consist of? Reflect on them carefully, and I think you will find that they are all based on story (e.g., "I just got stuck in a terrible traffic jam coming today"; "We went to the new store at the weekend, and it was a disappointment"; "We went camping in the woods for our last holiday"; "I had a terrible dream last night about...").

Because we are sophisticated adults, we tend to forget that, actually, a huge amount of what we talk about is really story based, as are the television programmes we watch and even the news stories we read. Story is

Figure 13.4. Children Engaged Actively in Meaningful and Purposeful Activities in English

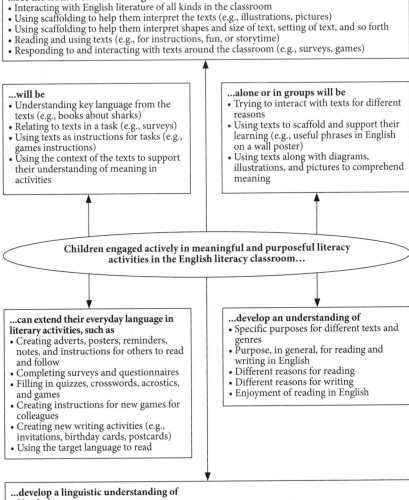

...see the teacher or their colleagues
- Interacting with English literature of all kinds in the classroom
- Using scaffolding to help them interpret the texts (e.g., illustrations, pictures)
- Using scaffolding to help them interpret shapes and size of text, setting of text, and so forth
- Reading and using texts (e.g., for instructions, fun, or storytime)
- Responding to and interacting with texts around the classroom (e.g., surveys, games)

...will be
- Understanding key language from the texts (e.g., books about sharks)
- Relating to texts in a task (e.g., surveys)
- Using texts as instructions for tasks (e.g., games instructions)
- Using the context of the texts to support their understanding of meaning in activities

...alone or in groups will be
- Trying to interact with texts for different reasons
- Using texts to scaffold and support their learning (e.g., useful phrases in English on a wall poster)
- Using texts along with diagrams, illustrations, and pictures to comprehend meaning

Children engaged actively in meaningful and purposeful literacy activities in the English literacy classroom...

...can extend their everyday language in literary activities, such as
- Creating adverts, posters, reminders, notes, and instructions for others to read and follow
- Completing surveys and questionnaires
- Filling in quizzes, crosswords, acrostics, and games
- Creating instructions for new games for colleagues
- Creating new writing activities (e.g., invitations, birthday cards, postcards)
- Using the target language to read

...develop an understanding of
- Specific purposes for different texts and genres
- Purpose, in general, for reading and writing in English
- Different reasons for reading
- Different reasons for writing
- Enjoyment of reading in English

...develop a linguistic understanding of
- Vocabulary
- Reading and writing
- Language chunks
- Aspects of language for different tasks (e.g., keywords, headlines, capital letters, punctuation)
- Text layouts for different things (e.g., surveys, books, film reviews, games, quizzes)
- Text structures from simple to more complex
- Grapheme–phoneme relationships (e.g., chants, rhymes, poems)
- Social literacy (e.g., surveys)
- Cognitive literacy (e.g., informational and reference materials and books)
- Looking for markers such as the beginning of text, end of text
- Looking for key language and vocabulary in the text

central to communication and language. If this is so central to language use, we must teach our young language learners about story. This means helping them listen to story, understand stories, tell stories, and raise their awareness and interaction with stories and the beginning, middle, and end of stories (Hughes, 2006b, 2010). Klippel (2006) also believes in the centrality of story, as she states,

> stories...are the bread and butter of our modern media, of TV and the popular press, of conversations between friends and strangers. We all tell stories all the time, in the shape of accounts of what happened to us or of what we think might happen, little narratives taken from the constantly flowing river of our lives. (p. 86)

She also suggests that there are three things that are necessary to reap the harvest of an encompassing literacy education through books:

1. Excellent picture books which are linguistically accessible to the learners and make it easy for them to start creating new worlds in the foreign language.
2. Enthusiastic and competent teachers who can bring the books alive and create a memorable experience of listening, understanding and talking about books.
3. School curricula which reflect a less technical attitude to language learning while at the same time providing enough freedom for each teacher to take her class on storytelling adventure trips to the English language. (p. 89)

In addition, two particularly powerful aspects of story in TEYL are that it contextualises new target language, leading to more understanding and meaningful acquisition of the new language for the young language learner, plus it encourages the listener/reader to predict what is going to happen next in the story. This prediction process can help our learners focus on their own English lexicon and language corpus to predict what is going to happen next, process the language in each next part, and try to make sense of the story as they listen or read (Hughes, 2006a, 2006b, 2010, 2011).

Garvie (1990), too, is convinced of the value of story in TEYL:

> I see story as being helpful in all varieties of the EFL situation. It helps to contextualise the items of the syllabus/course, offering a field of learning which is meaningful, interesting and motivating, while at the same time it covers the English work that has to be done. It can also give cohesion

to the work. Above all it brings a more informal, lively and communicative component to what at times can be a highly structured and often tedious programme. The structure would still be there but so would the other side of the language equation, giving the balance of the eclectic approach. (p. 12)

As Brewster and Ellis (2002) also highlight, "EFL Teachers of young learners are now more familiar with an acquistion-based methodology, and recognize the true value of using storybooks and the technique of storytelling as a way to create an acquistion-rich environment and ideal learning conditions" (p. 1).

Additionally, our pedagogical responsibilty as TEYL teachers should be such that we are aware that we need to be teaching our young learners about things in general through the target language, and the use of stories in TEYL is one excellent way of doing this. As Garvie (1990) additionally points out,

Story in its widest sense is also the carrier of life's messages and has, I believe, a vital part to play in the education of the young child, particularly in the development of language. I suppose that the teacher, working from a story 'bank' rich in all manner of literary genres and crossing a variety of cultures, can produce the kind of learning environment which not only stimulates and carries the children along on the crest of their interest and enjoyment, but offers meaning potential without which the learning of the language is rigid. (p. 56)

We must not forget here, though, that stories can have a magical quality for the listener/reader in the lesson and, as such, are a very powerful resource for our language classrooms. As Martin, Lovat, and Purnell (2004) illustrate when they describe reading a story to children,

At the really dramatic moments children's concentration can almost be felt in the room as their eyes stare at us and their breath is held... The appeal is basic...How do we ensure that all children experience the power of story? How do we then best utilise this power as a way into children learning? (p. 49)

Yet, what are children doing when they are processing stories, as they listen to teachers telling them, showing pictures that support the stories, or watching the teacher telling a story? Basically, a lot! As a quick overview shows, they are

- Listening to, following, and making sense of the story or book
- Understanding the key language being used
- Linking the language to the pictures, illustrations, and gestures they can see
- Linking the language with the actions in the story or book
- Using the pictures and gestures as support for language and language comprehension
- Following the story's or book's structure and stages
- Listening to and looking for story and book markers
- Listening out for the story's stages (Garvie, 1990)
- Visualising the situation in the story or book
- Making sense of the new things in the story or book as they are contextualised
- Making associations

How, then, can language teachers scaffold and support the language learners as they interact with stories? They must do the following:

- Allow the learners plenty of *thinking time* (Hughes, 2006a, 2006b, 2010)
- Create space gaps when reading or telling to allow for this thinking time before moving on
- Use a variety of approaches to cater for the range of intelligences and learner types
- Give learners lots of examples of books and stories to physically interact with
- Support all aspects of each book or story to allow for greater comprehension
- Scaffold learning constantly throughout the interaction with the story or book
- Encourage the learners to tell what is in the story or book by telling it back
- Extend the learners' interaction with the story or book by using meaningful and purposeful follow-up activities
- Use realia and props to make the reading or listening memorable

Young learners are using the same cognitive tools to process the story or book in the target language as they would in first language, so they are using and extending their cognitive skills in a variety of ways to support their language learning as well as their understanding of things in general. This is also described by Latham (2002) when she suggests,

> The ability to listen to and comprehend stories, and to reproduce or produce them, does have a facilitative effect on cognitive processes, and upon personal development, too....understanding of narrative involves very complex mental activity, and children who engage in listening to or reading stories on a wide scale are greatly enlarging their strategies for grasping meaning, their knowledge and understanding of the world around them and their imaginations. (p. 152)

We must not only encourage our language learners to listen to stories but also to try and tell stories and take part in tell-back (Bruner, 1986) activities with stories and books in order for them to use the target language we are introducing, consolidating, or practising in each particular story. Children can tell back by

- Retelling the story
- Retelling the story using pictures, puppets, or props
- Drawing a picture to capture the story or information
- Drawing a storyboard for the book or story
- Dramatising the story or information
- Dramatising key characters from the story or book
- Dramatising the beginning, middle, or end of a story in groups and putting the three together
- Working in groups with one narrator using story markers and others acting as characters or manipulating puppets, using dialogue from the story
- Creating and using story markers and keywords to create a story (Hughes, 2006b, 2010)

It is through story listening, telling, and reading that young language learners can develop an amazing understanding of many aspects of the target language and thus be further motivated to try to read these stories, in all their forms, in English for themselves. This will further enhance their reading skills and give them more reasons to make meaning through reading. It will also enhance their understanding of different aspects of reading and, eventually, writing in English, including the following:

- Sentence structure
- Story structure
- Organisation of texts
- Language used in different situations
- Language used with different audiences
- Use of vocabulary in a variety of contexts
- Use of language chunks
- Where to use story markers and signposts
- Keyword use
- The value of repetition to create drama
- Linking of illustration with context
- Dialogues, narrative, and onomatopoeic words
- Process writing (e.g., tell-back, their own story creation)
- Focused language use on particular aspects of language, such as nouns, pronouns, verbs, adjectives, connectors, and contractions (Hughes, 2006b, 2010)

When it comes to thinking about the right linguistic level for the language learners, there are several different ways of addressing this. A balanced use of well adapted and written ELT books for young learners (i.e., created materials) can be used (e.g., Penguin Young Readers series, Mary Glasgow Magazine's Popcorn readers series, Usborne Publishing's ELT readers for young learners) as well as real books and materials. Stories can be adapted when the teacher tells or reads them to the class in order for the learners to be able to access the meaning and see the use of illustrations, intonation, repetition, realia, and gestures by the teacher, which will, in turn, help learners comprehend, repeat, or tell back the story.

However, it is interesting to note the findings of research carried out on the use of story in Spain by Cabrera and Martinez (2001). When they made interactional adjustments (e.g., repetition, gestures, comprehension checks) to stories they told, the young learners were able to follow and understand. However, when only linguistic adjustments to the story were made, they found that the young learners could not follow the story. So, it seems it is important to make sure that all the interaction aspects of storytelling, such as repetition, use of gestures, and comprehension checks, are present when telling stories. Similarly, in an action research carried out by Hatta (2005) in Japan, as he looked at whether nonlinguistic support and the limited use of the mother tongue could facilitate comprehension of a story in EFL for 10-year-old Japanese learners of English, he found that the learners

> could possibly make intelligent guesses as to what the story is all about and what will happen next, if they are supported by visual aids like illustrations, the storyteller's skills of telling stories, or by a limited and controlled use of the mother tongue. (p. 48)

Angelil (2000) carried out action research into the TEYL teacher's reading of stories and the use of multimedia in storytelling for 6-year-olds in Switzerland and found that children who heard the teacher reading the story seemed to be emotionally involved with the story and able to reproduce clusters of words and to use more expression in tell-back. However, when another group of learners only listened to the same story from an audio recording, they did not show any emotional involvement with the story and had more difficulty reproducing key phrases from it. Angelil's findings also link to the point made by Martin, Lovat, and Purnell (2004):

> Children...need to see...short stories from which they may derive ideas and models. In fact, explicit teaching needs to be centred on this type of very short story, since this is the sort of story children are often encouraged to write...If we take the reading–writing connections seriously, we know that children will need to explore how authors achieve effects in very short stories if they are encouraged to generalise from these reading experiences! (p. 208)

Interestingly, in a rather dramatic piece of research by Olsen (2000) in Norway, all the TEYL textbooks of 9–10-year-olds were replaced by children's books—rather similar to an approach to reading and literacy strategies of the "Book Floods" used in New Zealand, Fiji, England, and Finland for native speaker children (p. 47). Her results after using the real books rather than textbooks showed that

> learners have increased their vocabulary, and that they have become readers of English, some even quite fluent readers. The most obvious result, which cannot be measured in an ordinary test, is that of increased

motivation. This is clear from talking to children, teachers and parents. (p. 52)

All of these real books tend to have in common the most wonderful use of illustration and design, which can particularly aid and support the child's comprehension of the story as well as appeal to those visual learners in our classes. Additionally, our young learners can hold and touch the books. Children's books are so often good enough to "eat", as publisher Peter Usborne put it during a presentation at the Realbooks Seminar at the University of York in 2006, and this great attractiveness can really motivate our learners to turn the page and want to read the text.

Arizpe (2006), also highlights the importance of visuals in books for deep understanding for young learners, when she discusses results from the Reading Pictures project at the University of Cambridge, which set out to explore how visual texts were read by children. She concluded, "it was the children who had had the most access to picture books and other visual media rather than the best textual 'decoders' who were able to reach deeper levels of meaning" (p. 46). This further shows us the importance of a rich English literacy in the classroom rather than a focus only on the form of the language in TEYL. Additionally, we know that native speaker children love revisiting the same stories and books again and again, which aids their development in language use and reading. This is also the case with young language learners, and we are very much aware that repetition supports and scaffolds learning in the target language.

Ponterotto (2001) seems quite adamant about the use of story in TEYL when she says,

> A psycholinguistic stance in primary L2 points to the validity of an organically constructed narrative mode as a facilitator of language development.... Most significantly, it permits the maximal use of repetition which is constitutive of the structure of language and the nature of its acquisition. In its combination with rhyme and metrical patterns, repetition is particularly suitable to children of primary school age, especially in the context of second language learning. (p. 71)

We must support the understanding of the story and the key language, vocabulary, and phrases in each story, and we must do this in a number of ways so that we reach all sorts of learner and intelligence types within the class. We can do this by using techniques such as emphasizing intonation, mime, gestures, props, dramatic voices, and emphasis of keywords and story markers, visuals, and texts to present the story and make it as comprehensible and engaging as possible for each young language learner.

To this end, we must also give lots of examples of different types of stories in different forms in the language class, real books, created books, picture stories, magazines, comics, props for a story, and big class books. Our objective should be that after much input, in terms of stories and activities linked to stories, we can encourage the learners to tell and write their own stories using the techniques we have modelled, such as use of intonation, story markers, and keywords (Hughes, 2006a, 2006b, 2010). As Garvie (1990) states, "Good stories can engage children's imagination by their rich, authentic, meaningful uses of the foreign language" (p. 159). Figure 13.5 shows an overview of what is happening in TEYL learners' heads when they are engaged in listening to stories, reading stories, storytelling, creating story, or telling story through drama.

In conclusion, this chapter has tried to show what is happening in the field of TEYL for our younger and younger language learners. As first outlined, it is rather complex and not easy for TEYL teachers, with little or no training in the teaching of reading, to create the most supportive classroom environment for the teaching of reading in the target language. If we are to be successful in teaching young language learners to read in the target language, we need to think about how best to support them, scaffold them, and create opportunities for plenty of zones of proximal development to take place within the rich English literacy environment of the language classroom, which will help young language learners comprehend and enjoy interacting in and with English texts and, ultimately, reading in English.

We should be aware that not all cultural literacies are the same and make sure that we support English literacy and the teaching of English words, sounds, letters, and spelling in the TEYL class in a balanced way to scaffold our learners' development in the target-language reading. With the addition of plenty of interactive reading opportunities, catering for different learner types and interests in our classes, plus the central use of many different reading materials, stories, and books, we will go a long way to creating a successful, motivating, and enriching experience for these language learners. As mentioned, there is very little research in the teaching of reading with young English language learners as foreign language learners, and as concerned professionals, we must address this huge gap in our knowledge and understanding of what is really going on in English language classes around the world in the very near future.

Figure 13.5. What Is Going On in Children's Heads When Using Story in Teaching English to Young Learners

...see the teacher or storyteller
- Dramatise stories with gestures and intonation
- Read out slowly and dramatically
- Tell the story using a book (big or small)
- Tell the story using step-by-step pictures
- Tell the story by reading from and showing the pages of the book
- Tell the story using puppets
- Deliver the story through a video or audio recording or via software

...will be
- Listening to, following, and enjoying the story
- Understanding key language being used
- Linking the language to pictures and gestures of the storyteller
- Linking the language to the actions in the story
- Using the pictures and gestures of the storyteller as support for new language within the story
- Following the story structure (i.e. beginning, middle, and end)
- Listening and looking for story markers (e.g., so, then, but)
- Listening and looking for stages of the story dialogue
- Visualizing the action in the story
- Making sense of new things and keywords not heard or seen before
- Using the context of the story to understand the new language

...alone or in groups will be
- Dramatising the story as the teacher told it
- Dramatising key characters' parts
- Miming the story
- Retelling the story in tell-back
- Telling the story with staged pictures
- Drawing pictures of each stage of the story
- Dramatising the beginning, middle, and end
- Using a narrator to tell story with children, as characters, adding to the story
- Using story markers and keywords to write a story

Children engaged in listening to stories, reading stories, storytelling, creating story, or telling story through drama...

...develop a linguistic understanding of
- Vocabulary
- Language chunks
- Aspects of language (e.g., story markers, keywords)
- Parts of language (e.g., adjectives, verbs, connectors)
- Sounds and letters
- A visual presentation of stories
- Use of repetition
- Dialogue and narrative
- Importance of prediction for storytelling and listening
- Different emotions and how to describe them
- When and how to use contractions
- The use and value of onomatopoeic words

...develop an understanding of
- Reading and writing
- Creating stories with a beginning, middle, and end
- Writing dialogues and narrative
- Frameworks for writing a story
- Process writing
- Strategies for reading and writing
- How books are written and made
- Using particular language to enhance a story
- The importance of using illustrations
- The speed of reading for an audience
- Drama in reading and writing stories

...can extend their everyday language in story activities, such as
- Telling the story as today's television news or writing a newspaper headline
- Playing a "who am I?" game by describing a character from the story
- Writing a sentence from a story and having a partner, the class, or a group guess the story (useful with well-known stories like fairy tales)
- Turning a story into a play for parents or other classes
- Dramatising the story in small groups in class
- Changing the ending of well-known stories and writing the new story
- Imagining what might happen next to a character from the story
- Creating a picture gallery of popular characters from stories

Note. Adapted from "The all-round use of real stories and authentic books in teaching English to young learners," by A. Hughes, (2006a), in L. Farago & G. Ambrus (Eds.), *Reading is for everyone: Publication of IATEFL-Hungary young learners special interest group* (pp. 5–9).

Questions for Reflection

1. Is reading instruction in TEYL different from reading instruction in the first language? If so, why? Can you highlight what would be the most important points to remember when either (a) teaching young language learners how to read in the target language or (b) training teachers to teach reading in TEYL classrooms?

2. What are the challenges facing TEYL teachers when it comes to reading, and how can these be addressed, physically and practically, in the language classroom? What strategies can those involved in TEYL use to overcome these challenges?

3. In what ways can a teacher involved in TEYL create a rich literacy environment for their classroom, and what lesson activities could be linked to the English literacy provided in the TEYL environment?

REFERENCES

Aitchison, J. (2003). Trickles, bangs, spurts, or whimpers? Profiling the development of the lexicon. In J. Begley & A. Hughes (Eds.), *Teaching English to young learners: Second international TEYL research seminar* (pp. 4–11). York, UK: University of York.

Angelil, P. (2000). Multimedia and storytelling with 6–11 year olds. In In M. Crook & A. Hughes (Eds.), *Teaching English to young learners: First international TEYL research seminar* (pp. 4–9). York, UK: University of York.

Arizpe, E. (2006). Young interpreters: Affective dimensions of bilingual children's response to pictures. In J. Enever & G. Schmid-Schonbein (Eds.), *MAAF picture books and young learners of English* (pp. 35–48). Munich, Germany: Langenscheidt.

Au, K.H. (2002). Multicultural factors and the effective instruction of students of diverse backgrounds. In A.E. Farstrup & S.J. Samuels (Eds.), *What research has to say about reading instruction* (3rd ed., pp. 392–413). Newark, DE: International Reading Association.

Brewster, J. (1991). What is good primary practice? In C. Brumfit, J. Moon, & R. Tongue (Eds.), *Teaching English to children: From practice to principle* (pp. 1–17). London: Collins ELT.

Brewster, J., & Ellis, G. (with Girard, D.). (2002). *The primary English teacher's guide* (2nd ed.). Harlow, Essex, UK: Penguin.

Bruner, J. (1983). *Child's talk: Learning to use language.* Oxford, UK: Oxford University Press.

Bruner, J. (1986). *Actual minds, possible worlds.* Cambridge, MA: Harvard University Press.

Bruner, J. (1990). *Acts of meaning.* Cambridge, MA: Harvard University Press.

Bruner, J., & Haste, H. (Eds.). (1987). *Making sense: The child's construction of the world.* London: Methuen.

Cabrera, M.P. & Martinez, P.B. (2001). The effects of repetition, comprehension checks and gestures on primary school chidren in an EGL situation. *ELT Journal, (55)*3 281–288.

Calderón, M. (2009). Language, literacy and knowledge for EAL pupils. *Better: Evidence-based Education, 1*(1), 14–15.

Cameron, L. (2001). *Teaching languages to young learners.* Cambridge, UK: Cambridge University Press. doi:10.1017/CBO9780511733109

Center, Y. (2009). Beginning reading. *Better: Evidence-based Education, 1*(1), 6–7.

Chomsky, N. (1965). *Aspects of the theory of syntax.* Cambridge, MA: MIT Press.

Chomsky, N. (1972). *Language and mind* (Rev. ed.). New York: Harcourt Brace Jovanovich.

CILT, The National Centre for Languages. (2006). *European language portfolio—junior version* (Rev. ed.). London: Author. Available: www.primarylanguages.org.

uk/resources/assessment_and_recording/european_languages_portfolio.aspx

Cummins, J. (1979a) Cognitive/academic language proficiency, linguistic interdependence, the optimum age question and some other matters. *Working Papers on Bilingualism, 19,* 121–129.

Cummins, J. (1979b). Linguistic interdependence and the educational development of bilingual children. *Review of Educational Research, 49*(2), 225–251.

Cunningham, P.M., & Cunningham, J.W. (2002). What we know about how to teach phonics. In A.E. Farstrup & S.J. Samuels (Eds.), *What research has to say about reading instruction* (3rd ed., pp. 87–109). Newark, DE: International Reading Association.

Donaldson, M. (1978). *Children's minds.* London: Fontana.

Doye, P. (2001). The intercultural dimensions of foreign language education in the primary school. In M.J. Raya, P. Faber, W. Gewehr, & A.J. Peck (Eds.), *Effective foreign language teaching at the primary level.* Frankfurt am Main: Peter Lang.

Fox, C. (2000). Thinking time: An effective metacognitive strategy for young learners? A classroom investigation into reflective writing with ESL students aged 9 and 10. In M. Crook & A. Hughes (Eds.), *Teaching English to young learners: First international TEYL research seminar 2000 papers* (pp. 34–44). York, UK: University of York.

Gardner, H. (1983). *Frames of mind: The theory of multiple intelligences.* New York: Basic Books.

Gardner, H. (1993). *Multiple intelligences: The theory in practice.* New York: Basic Books.

Garvie, E. (1990). *Story as vehicle: Teaching English to young children.* Clevedon, UK: Multilingual Matters.

Halliday, M.A.K. (1975). *Learning how to mean: Explorations in the development of language.* London: Edward Arnold.

Halliday, M.A.K. (1993). Toward a language-based theory of learning. *Linguistics and Education, 5*(2), 93–116.

Hatta, G. (2005). Storytelling at a primary school in Japan. In *Teaching English to young learners: Third international TEYL research seminar* (pp. 42–49). York, UK: University of York.

Hughes, A (2001). The teaching of language to young learners: Linking understanding and principles with practice. In M.J. Raya, P. Faber, W. Gewehr, & A.J. Peck (Eds.), *Effective*

foreign language teaching at the primary level (pp. 17–24). Frankfurt am Main: Peter Lang.

Hughes, A (2002). Supporting independence: Teaching English to young learners within a three-stage journey. *CATS IATEFL YL SIG Newsletter, 1,* 2.

Hughes, A. (2006a). The all-round use of real stories and authentic books in teaching English to young learners. In L. Farago & G. Ambrus (Eds.), *Reading is for everyone: Publication of IATEFL-Hungary young learners special interest group* (pp. 5–9).

Hughes, A. (2006b). The 'why,' 'what' and 'how' of using authentic picture books and stories in the EYL classroom: Some practical considerations. In J. Enever & G. Schmid-Schönbein (Eds.), *Picture books and young learners of English* (pp. 151–163). Munich, Germany: Langenscheidt.

Hughes, A. (2010). Why should we make activities for young language learners meaningful and purposeful? In F. Mishan & A. Chambers (Eds.), *Perspectives on language learning materials development* (pp. 175–200). Bern, Switzerland: Peter Lang.

Hughes, A. (2011). The literate classroom: How to support literacy classroom. *Grundschule Englisch. (35),* 4–5.

Hughes, A., & Williams, M. (2000). *Using Penguin Young Readers: A teacher's guide.* London: Penguin Longman.

Klippel, F. (2006). Literacy through picture books. In J. Enever & G. Schmid-Schönbein (Eds.), *Picture books and young learners of English* (pp. 81–90). Munich, Germany: Langenscheidt.

Krashen, S.D. (1981). *Second language acquisition and second language learning.* Oxford, UK: Pergamon Press.

Latham, D. (2002). *How children learn to write: Supporting and developing children's writing in school.* London: Paul Chapman.

Martin, T., Lovat, C., & Purnell, G. (2004). *The really useful literacy book: Being creative with literacy in the primary classroom.* London: RoutledgeFalmer.

Olsen, S. (2000). Winnie the Witch and international solidarity: The role of children's books as tools for learning. In M. Crook & A. Hughes (Eds.), *Teaching English to young learners: First international TEYL research seminar 2000 papers* (pp. 45–54). York, UK: University of York.

Piaget, J. (1967). *Six psychological studies* (A. Tenzer, Trans.). London: University of London Press.

Ponterotto, D. (2001). A story in rhyme, rhythm and repetition. In M.J. Raya, P. Faber, W. Gewehr, & A.J. Peck (Eds.), *Effective foreign language teaching at the primary level* (pp. 51–72). Frankfurt am Main, Germany: Peter Lang.

Read, C. (2003). Is younger better? *English Teaching Professional, 28,* 5–7.

Reid, J.M. (Ed.). (1995). *Learning styles in the ESL/EFL classroom.* Boston: Heinle & Heinle.

Revell, J., & Norman, S. (1997). *In your hands: NLP in ELT.* London: Saffire Press.

Rixon, S. (1999). *Young learners of English: Some research perspectives.* Harlow, Essex, UK: Longman.

Rixon, S. (2000). *Worldwide survey of primary ELT.* London: British Council. Retrieved December 15, 2010, from www.britishcouncil.org/worldwide_survey_of_primary_elt.pdf

Rixon, S. (2004a). *Assessment of young learners of English: Keeping track without turning them off.* Paper presented at the Amazing Young Minds conference, Cambridge, England. Retrieved December 15, 2010, from www.eltforum.com/forum/pdfs/aym04_papers.pdf

Rixon, S. (2004b). *Assessment of young learners of English: Does it cater for amazing young minds or are too many tired old minds working on it?* Paper presented at the Amazing Young Minds conference, Cambridge, England. Retrieved November 1, 2010, from www.pdfebooks downloads.com/Shelagh-Rixon.html

Rixon, S. (2007). EYL teachers: Background, beliefs and practices in the teaching of initial reading. In A. Hughes & N. Taylor (Eds.), *Teaching English to young learners: Fourth international TEYL research seminar 2007 papers* (pp. 6–14). York, UK: University of York.

Shanahan, T. (2002). What reading research says: The promises and limitations of applying research to reading education. In A.E. Farstrup & S.J. Samuels (Eds.), *What research has to say about reading instruction* (3rd ed., pp. 8–24). Newark, DE: International Reading Association.

Vygotsky, L.S. (1978). *Mind in society: The development of higher psychological processes* (M. Cole, V. John-Steiner, S. Scribner, & E. Souberman, Eds.). Cambridge, MA: Harvard University Press.

Wells, G. (2009). *The meaning makers: Learning to talk and talking to learn* (2nd ed.). Bristol, UK: Multilingual Matters.

Williams, J.P. (2002). Reading comprehension strategies and teacher preparation. In A.E. Farstrup & S.J. Samuels (Eds.), *What research has to say about reading instruction* (3rd ed., pp. 243–260). Newark, DE: International Reading Association.

Wood, D., Bruner, J.S., & Ross, G. (1976). The role of tutoring in problem solving. *Journal of Child Psychology and Psychiatry, 17*(2), 89–100.

Chapter 14

What the Research Says About Intentional Instruction

Douglas Fisher, Nancy Frey, and Diane Lapp

Intentional instruction is systematic and focused. It identifies a framework rather than offering a script. Highly scripted reading programs have not resulted in the uniform success that the public hoped. In some cases, highly scripted programs either deskilled teachers or had no effect (Demko, 2010; MacGillivray, Ardell, Curwen, & Palma, 2004; Moustafa & Land, 2002). In other cases, scripted programs provided teachers with a framework for instruction that improved student achievement (Foorman, Francis, Fletcher, Schatschneider, & Mehta, 1998; Shanahan, 2006). Although the issue of scripted reading programs is controversial and has even been "hot" (Cassidy & Cassidy, 2004), there is likely more to the issue than the dichotomy often presented between reading, or not reading, from a script. In fact, there is evidence that highly scripted reading programs are not better, and no worse, than other literacy instruction models (e.g., Tivnan & Hemphill, 2005).

Valencia, Place, Martin, and Grossman (2006) have found that "curriculum materials interacted with teachers' knowledge of reading and reading instruction, and with the contexts in which they worked" (p. 93), thus serving to facilitate learning in some classrooms and hinder it in others. Commeyras (2007) notes, "Perhaps like talented actors who bring to life the script of a play, there are talented teachers who can breathe life into a teaching script" (p. 405). In both of these cases, it was the teacher who mattered. Fairly consistently, researchers studying the outcomes of scripted and/or commercial reading programs identify teacher quality as the critical factor in successful reading instruction rather than the program (e.g., Pressley et al., 2001). Further, despite the focus on fidelity and external controls, teachers will modify the program (Datnow & Castellano, 2000) and thus need to understand how to increase their effectiveness.

Rather than attempt to script every lesson and demand teachers use those lessons, our research and that of many others suggest that focusing

What Research Has to Say About Reading Instruction (4th ed.) edited by S. Jay Samuels and Alan E. Farstrup. © 2011 by the International Reading Association.

on intentional instruction creates lasting changes, both in terms of teachers' repertoire and student achievement (Fisher & Frey, 2007; Frey, Lapp, & Fisher, 2009; Taylor, Pearson, Peterson, & Rodriguez, 2003). As Fullan, Hill, and Crévola (2006) have noted, the alternative to highly prescriptive (i.e., scripted) instruction is precision instruction, which requires teachers to internalize an instructional framework that gradually and intentionally transfers responsibility from the teacher to the student.

A Framework for Intentional Instruction

The five-part framework for intentional instruction requires that teachers (1) establish purpose, (2) model their thinking, (3) guide students' thinking through the strategic use of questions, prompts, and cues, (4) provide students with productive group tasks that are meaningful and allow students to practice language and consolidate understanding, and (5) assign independent tasks that require students to apply what they have learned.

Establish Purpose

There is a wealth of data suggesting that a clearly established purpose improves student learning (Fraser, Walberg, Welch, & Hattie, 1987). In fact, establishing the purpose of the lesson, often through a written objective, is a widely accepted educational practice (Marzano, Pickering, & Pollock, 2001). The established purpose has two components: content and language. The content component relates to the standard but is not simply a restatement of it. Rather, it is today's work toward the standard. The language component, based on an analysis of the linguistic demands of the content, builds students' skill in reading, writing, speaking, and listening.

In their study of teachers' language purpose, Fisher and Frey (2010) have identified three categories of language purpose statements: vocabulary, structure, and function. Some content purposes require attention to vocabulary, whereas others require focus on the ways in which language is structured, including grammar, syntax, and signal words. Still other content purposes require a careful analysis of language purposes, such as informing, describing, justifying, persuading, and summarizing. For example, a teacher might set this content purpose on a given day: to identify the life cycle of a frog. The language purpose could be: to use signal words when explaining the life cycle of a frog to another person. An established purpose is critical for intentional instruction to be effective, as the purpose drives teacher modeling and how the valuable instructional minutes are used to deepen student understanding.

Model Thinking

Modeling provides students with access to expert thinking, which they can use as they become increasingly skilled readers, writers, and thinkers. Modeling is intentional, as teachers must identify cognitive moves that are helpful in completing the task at hand. As teachers think aloud, they do not simply explain or demonstrate what they did, but rather they highlight the process they used to reach understanding. As Duffy (2003) has noted, "The only way to model thinking is to talk about how to do it. That is, we provide a verbal description of the thinking one does or, more accurately, an *approximation* of the thinking involved" (p. 11).

In the area of reading, Fisher, Frey, and Lapp (2008) have identified four areas in which modeling can occur: comprehension, word solving, text structure, and text features. More important, they noted that expert modeling provides students with the thinking behind the cognitive strategy. Rather than say, "I can predict...," teachers who are expert modelers say, "I can predict..., because the author told me...," or "I can see this in my mind, because I can visualize these three words:...." For example, while modeling her thinking from the book *The Life Cycle of a Frog* by Bobbie Kalman, the teacher paused on the heading "Double Life" and said, "I'm thinking about this phrase, 'double life,' and I'm thinking about my background knowledge. People say that cats have nine lives, so I wonder if frogs have two lives." After reading the page, the teacher modeled her thinking again,

> Oh, so now I understand the heading 'Double Life,' because the author told me that frogs live part of their life on land and part in the water. That's some good information to have, so I'm going to add that to my note page here, because it might have something to do with frogs' life cycle, which is our purpose today. I'm thinking that it must be important, because the author spends a whole page telling me about the double life of frogs, so it's part of their life. I hope the author tells me more about their life cycle soon.

Guide Students' Thinking Through Questions, Prompts, and Cues

Although purpose and modeling are critical aspects of intentional instruction, this phase of guiding students' thinking is where teachers truly differentiate their instruction. Rather than simply telling students information that they have missed or misunderstood, the use of questions, prompts, and cues allows teachers to address the errors and misconceptions their students have. Guided instruction, as we explore in greater detail later in this chapter, is not simply cataloging errors while listening to students read or watching them write. Rather, it is intentional, systematic, and direct instruction that results in greater student learning. The following classroom example illustrates this phase of the framework for intentional instruction.

As she surveys the room, the teacher notices that one of the groups has stopped working. The group members are not facing each other and are not displaying any of the nonverbal behaviors expected during productive group work. The joint attention to the task and materials clearly displayed by the other groups is absent in this one group. Walking over, she notices that the group members are not talking with each other. They are all looking at their own papers; some of them are writing. They have either decided to divide and conquer the task, or they have become confused and do not know how to resolve their misunderstanding. The teacher knows it is time for additional guided instruction.

Sitting down with the group, she asks, "What's up?" None of the students responds. The teacher continues,

> Remember that we're learning about the life cycle of frogs. To do that, we're working together to learn vocabulary and sequence the steps using signal words. I can see that you've sorted all of the words. Let me take a look at the categories and see what you've done.

There is a pause as she reviews their work "This is looking really good. I hope you're all pleased with your work. You must be trying to illustrate the frog life cycle then, right?" The students nod in agreement. "What's the first step? Can each of you write that on your dry-erase boards?" The students grab their boards and markers and start writing. Two of them write "eggs," while Mario looks at his board. Their conversation continues:

Teacher: Ana, tell me how you knew that. How did you know to write "eggs"?

Ana: Because of the picture.

Jacob: This one [points to an illustration of the life cycle].

Ana: See the egg? Tadpoles are inside.

Teacher: Mario, you didn't write "eggs." Do you have another idea?

Mario: Because where do they come from?

Teacher: The eggs? Where do the eggs come from?

Mario: Yeah, where do they get them eggs?

Teacher: The adult frog lays the eggs. It's kinda like a chicken. Remember at the zoo when we saw the chick sitting on her egg?

Mario: Yeah, the chicken made the egg.

Ana: The chicken is a bird not a frog.

Teacher: True, but they both lay eggs. Is that where you were stuck? Did your group not agree to start with the egg?

Jacob: Yeah, we got stuck.

Teacher: Let's agree to start with the egg. What comes next?

Jacob: A frog!

Teacher: Remember the book we read. What happened to the eggs?

Ana: Tadpoles came out.

Mario: Like little fishes.

Jacob: I saw a tadpole one time. I tried to catch it.

Teacher: Let's review. We agreed to start with the egg. And then, what comes next in the life cycle?

All: Tadpoles!

Teacher: Yes! Can you sketch a quick picture of a tadpole to help you remember? [She pauses while students sketch.] And then, what happens after the tadpole?

Jacob: A frog!

Teacher: Let's think back to the book we read. [The students look puzzled.] If we put the frog in the last box, what would go in this middle box? [The students look puzzled.] Take a look at our resources.

Mario: This one right here? With the legs and tail?

Jacob: Where?

Ana: Froglet!!!

Teacher: Yes! Look, you did it! Now can you illustrate all of the steps and talk with each other about the steps? Remember to use your signal words: first, next, then, finally.

Provide Productive, Meaningful Group Tasks and Allow Students to Practice Language and Consolidate Understanding

In most instructional models, this phase of learning, in which students collaborate with one another in the absence of their teacher, is neglected (Pearson & Gallagher, 1983). Too often, advice for teachers focuses on what the teacher is doing and not what the students are doing when the teacher is working with others (Burkins & Croft, 2010). During productive group work, students use academic language and validate and extend their knowledge. It is through these peer interactions that students consolidate their understanding. The key to productive group work lies in the individual accountability and the meaningful task (Frey & Fisher, 2010b). In other words, students must each produce something and interact while they are producing that product.

For example, while studying the life cycle of a frog, groups of students matched pictures with words, sorted words into categories, and then individually sketched the life cycle As part of the exploration, groups of students completed a webquest (Dodge, 1995), in which they used the Internet to learn more about frog and toad life cycles. As part of their conversation, one of the groups got a little confused. As they negotiated meaning, they each clarified their own understanding:

Amal: But you have five boxes. That's too many 'cuz it's just four.

Justin: Where you find it at?

Claudio: We was on this page [points to the laptop screen]. See right here.

Justin: But my picture has five. See, (1) eggs, (2) legless tadpole, (3) hind legs develop, (4) front legs develop, (5) adult frog.

Amal: You forgot froglet. See right here. It's the one with some tail, but it got feet, too.

Claudio: We should look more.

Justin: Hey, this one says three. See, egg, tadpole, adult. That can't be right.

Amal: You forgot froglet. See right here [holds the word sort card]. We gotta have this one, too. It's the one with some tail and some feet, too.

Claudio: I got another one [points to the webpage].

Amal: Does it got froglet?

Claudio: Yeah, it has it.

Amal: See, we gotta have froglet.

Justin: Where is it again? [He erases one of the boxes.]

Amal: Before adult.

Justin: Got it. So, we agree on four?

Assign Independent Tasks That Require Students to Apply What They Have Learned

The goal of an intentional instructional framework is not increased reliance on the teacher but, rather, the release of responsibility to students. At multiple points in every lesson, students have to complete independent tasks. Many of these tasks should be completed in the classroom while the teacher and peers are present to notice mistakes. Examples of in-class independent tasks include wide reading, journal writing, formative assessments, and individual projects. While studying the life cycle of the frog, for example, students were provided additional readings that they could read independently, such as *From Tadpole to Frog: Following the Life Cycle* by Suzanne Slade and *The Trouble With Tadpoles: A First Look at the Life Cycle of a Frog* by Sam Godwin. In addition, students wrote summaries of the life cycle and participated in formative assessments. The teacher uses the formative assessments to check for understanding and determine which students require additional instruction to learn the content.

Out-of-class independent work (i.e., homework) is given when students have demonstrated a level of understanding in the classroom with peers and alone. Homework is not given when students have just been introduced to the content. Rather, homework serves a spiral review, application, fluency-building, and extension function (Fisher & Frey, 2008).

This intentional instructional framework is based on decades of research on each of the components as well as the continued development of lesson design, starting with the lesson planning ideas of Hunter (1976/1995), through Tomlinson's (1999) research on differentiating instruction, and extending through the *Understanding by Design* work of Wiggins and McTighe (2005). Before we explore intentional guided instruction in greater detail, we delve deeper into the research roots of intentional instruction.

Roots of Intentional Instruction

Intentional instruction is borne out of three major theories: gradual release of responsibility in reading (Pearson & Fielding, 1991; Pearson & Gallagher, 1983), direct explanation (Duffy et al., 1987), and literacy as a social practice (Barton, Hamilton, & Ivanič, 2000). Together, these theories inform an instructional framework that provides students with expert modeling, procedural and conditional knowledge, and contexts for applying skills and concepts in the company of peers and the teacher.

Gradual Release of Responsibility in Reading

The work of Pearson and Gallagher (1983) has influenced reading instruction for almost three decades. This model of instruction presents a dual view of teacher instruction and student learning behaviors through a series of experiences that begin with teacher modeling and end with student practice and application. This model was further refined as a model of reading comprehension instruction to include teaching practices such as read-alouds and shared reading, guided reading, and independent reading (Pearson & Fielding, 1991). This systematic release of cognitive responsibility occurs through a series of scaffolded instructional experiences that encourage students to increasingly assume more independent use of the strategies being learned. Over time, learners become more adept and therefore more skilled, using strategies only when they need to resolve a comprehension problem (Afflerbach, Pearson, & Paris, 2008).

These influences can be seen in an intentional instruction framework that includes modeling during the focus lesson, as well as in the guided instruction and independent learning phases. More so, an intentional instruction framework owes a conceptual debt to the original work on gradual release as a model for purposefully building student competence through a series of instructional approaches designed and delivered by the teacher.

Direct Explanation

A second influence on intentional instruction is direct explanation (Duffy et al., 1987). This is especially apparent during purpose setting, modeling, and guided instruction, especially as a means for exposing not only the cognitive and metacognitive thinking of the teacher but also in clearly establishing the purpose for using a skill or strategy. The intent with direct explanation is to build the learner's declarative, procedural, and conditional knowledge. Direct explanation requires that the teacher be explicit in drawing the learner's attention to the strategy about to be taught, modeling its use and thinking aloud while doing so to expose decision making, and then monitoring the student's application as he or she tries it (Duffy, 2009). The power in this approach lies in not only providing the information but also in giving one's reasoning for using the information in that way at that time.

Literacy as a Social Practice

A third influence on an intentional instruction framework is the vital provision that learning is developed through the application of skills and concepts in the company of others. The combination of doing and talking about what is being done is thought to produce higher levels of learning, although it rarely occurs in most classrooms (Nystrand & Gamoran, 1997). In this perspective, learning is viewed as a sociocultural phenomenon and is achieved though interaction with others. Labeled the zone of proximal development, Vygotsky (1978) described a theoretical level of achievement that a novice could attain when supported by a more knowledgeable other.

Mehan (1979), Cazden (1986), and others have studied the occurrence and effects of student and teacher talk on learning, and expressed reservations about the limited opportunities to talk, think, and do in the company of others. Much of this can occur in discussion-based teaching practices at the large- and small-group levels to encourage rich opportunities for dialogic learning (see Nystrand, 2006, for an excellent review on the research of dialogic learning in the classroom). These opportunities exist in an intentional instructional framework during the guided instruction and productive group work phases of instruction. Perhaps the area in which teachers are most intentional, and the area that is the least understood, is guided instruction in which responsibility is shared between the student and the teacher. We next explore this area in greater depth.

Guided Instruction in Focus

Guided instruction has been viewed as an essential vehicle for providing scaffolded instruction. Wood, Bruner, and Ross used scaffolding as a metaphor for the acts of "holding in place" a child's nascent understandings until such time that he could see how the immediate event connected to a more generalized understanding (as cited in Wood, 1999, p. 260). This was observed and cataloged in a series of studies of children ages 3–5 and their mothers, as they jointly approached tasks such as making a pyramid of blocks. At the first level, the mother would ask questions to encourage thought and action, such as, "What are you going to do now?" When the child demonstrated some difficulty in proceeding, the mother would follow by prompting the child to locate what he or she needed (level 2; e.g., "I think you need the very big blocks"). Wood (1999) noted "the defining characteristic of this level was that the mother identified the critical features of material but took no part in the search for material" (p. 264).

If the child still could not successfully perform the task, "the mother actually intervened in the selection process itself by indicating materials to be used" by pointing and saying, "You need that little one, there" (level 3). If these scaffolds proved to be insufficient, the mother took back the task (level 4), leaving "the child with only one degree of freedom—to perform or not to perform the act" (p. 264). At times, this might involve a full demonstration of the task.

Wood (1999) also noted that when the child made an error or could not perform the task, the mother would move to the next level of increased adult control, then once again decrease support to allow the child the opportunity to resume the task. Although not labeled as such, this is analogous to the gradual release of responsibility described by Pearson and Gallagher (1983). Within guided instruction, a similar flow of increasingly more concrete scaffolds exists when learners have difficulty engaging correctly in recently introduced knowledge. We label these four types of scaffolds as (1) questions to check for understanding, (2) prompts for cognitive and metacognitive thinking, (3) cues to shift attention, and (4) direct explanation and modeling to demonstrate again. You can view a diagram of the use of these scaffolds in Figure 14.1.

Questions to Check for Understanding

These are the initial queries that open the dialogue of guided instruction. The purpose of the question is crucial, as it is not to test but to check for understanding. With crafting the question comes the purpose, What are you listening for? In this case, the teacher is listening for errors, misconceptions, and partial understandings. These questions can and should derive from a variety of types of knowledge to unearth possible confusions. The following are the types of questions that teachers should proffer to check for understanding:

- Elicitation questions focus on factual knowledge (e.g., "What characters did the musical instruments represent in Peter and the Wolf?").

Figure 14.1. Flowchart for Guided Instruction

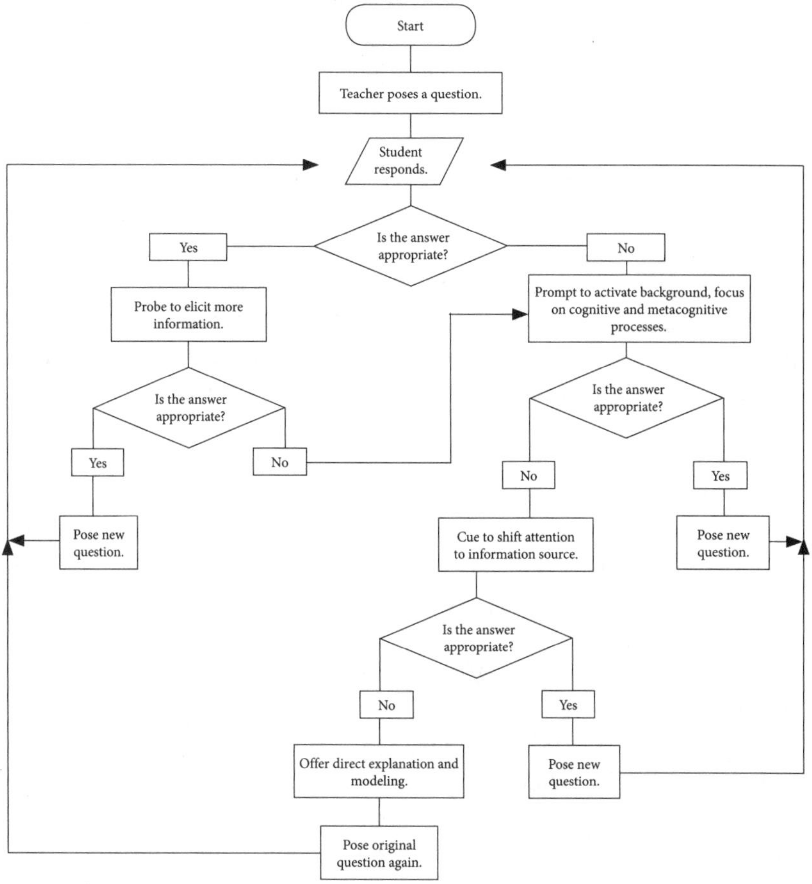

Note. From "Identifying Instructional Moves During Guided Learning," by N. Frey & D. Fisher, 2010, *The Reading Teacher,* 64(2), 87.

- Elaboration questions follow elicitation questions by asking for more information (e.g., "Say some more about that").
- Clarification questions also follow initial questions and are used to draw out a reason or justification (e.g., "Why do you think so?").
- Divergent questions challenge students to synthesize two or more knowledge bases (e.g., "How are a conductor and a storyteller alike?").

- Inventive questions require students to speculate and offer opinions (e.g., "Who was your favorite character in the story and why?").
- Heuristic questions invite students to use informal problem-solving skills (e.g., "How do you know that you've given the correct answer?").

The goal of guided instruction is to determine what parts of the lesson have stuck and what needs further teaching. Therefore, it is to be expected that students will not always be able to answer questions like these fully and accurately. Often, students will demonstrate a partial understanding or even a misconception. Therefore, cognitive and metacognitive prompts provide a means for the teacher to define critical features of needed knowledge, without engaging in the student's search for that information.

Cognitive and Metacognitive Prompts

Like the mothers in the studies using level 2 scaffolds (Wood, 1999), the purpose of prompting is to activate the requisite background knowledge needed to complete the task. These prompts may be cognitive in nature, meaning that they refer to processes and procedures the student needs to use to complete the task. When a first-grade teacher asks a student, "What should come first in the paragraph you're writing about bats?" she is attempting to activate both the student's knowledge of how paragraphs work and his or her background knowledge about bats. Prompts can also be metacognitive, in that they spur the learner to engage in reflective or heuristic thinking (i.e., problem solving). The same first-grade teacher might also prompt the young writer by delivering a metacognitive prompt: "What's the most important thing you want your readers to know about bats?" The samples of prompting scaffolds we observed occurred across four broad categories of knowledge: (1) background, (2) process or procedural, (3) heuristic, and (4) reflective.

Background Knowledge Prompts

This cognitive prompt encourages learners to use what they have previously learned to assist them in completing a newer skill or task. A feature of learning is that a novice is often unable to marshal what is known to solve the unknown. Therefore, it is important to activate useful background knowledge when figuring out how to do something less familiar. Background knowledge prompts cause a learner to use factual information. A kindergarten teacher prompts for background knowledge during this exchange with a student who is having difficulty decoding CVC (consonant-vowel-consonant) words:

Teacher: What's this word say? [She holds up a card with the word *flat*.]

Student: F-f-f...fot.

Teacher: You've got some of the sounds in there. Let's take the word apart like we've done before. [She covers "fl."] You've seen this before. Make that sound. [background knowledge prompt]

Student: /at/. That sound is /at/.

Teacher: There you go! Now look at this part. [She covers "at."] You know this one, too. [background knowledge prompt]

Student: F-f-f. No, fl-, fl-.

Teacher: That's it! Now put those sounds together. [procedural prompt]

Student: Fl-fl-flat!

As with any scaffold, background prompts are most effective when well timed. In the previous scenario, the teacher provided these background prompts at the same time that she used cues (discussed later) to cover parts of the word to shift the student's attention. In many cases, scaffolds are paired to magnify the effect.

Process or Procedural Prompts

Another type of cognitive prompt is one that involves reminding the student about a sequence of steps they will use. These may be as simple as, "Now what comes next?" or more specific, such as prompting a student who is editing his or her writing by saying, "How do you tell your reader you're asking a question? Be sure to check for this as you edit." Although they are often part of students' background knowledge, these prompts evoke specific information about how something is done. These processes and procedures are widely agreed upon, and include such things as lining up a math problem so the columns do not get mixed up, making an early prediction about a book using its cover and title, or following the procedures established by the teacher for partner talk in the classroom.

Cognitive prompts can also feature frames, templates, and models. It is common in classrooms to use language frames as a way to scaffold use of more formal academic language. Fourth-grade students studying the history of their state might be using the following frame in their writing (the length of the line is not indicative of the length of the response):

> We became a state on _____, but our history began before then. The first people who lived here were _____, and they _____. A little known fact about these people is that _____. If you lived during that time in our state's history, you would probably _____. When _____ arrived, the native population _____. A challenge in our state's history was in finding a way for the native population and the new arrivals to live together in peace.

Other examples of this include providing a student with a list of terms to use within a discussion with the teacher and using a mentor text as a model for writing an original work.

Heuristic Prompts

These are a type of metacognitive prompt that encourages students to use critical thinking skills to resolve a problem. Unlike process or procedural prompts, which are widely agreed upon, heuristic prompts are reserved for problems in which there is more than one correct approach. Heuristic prompts foster a use of common sense and creativity, and cause the learner to notice what seems to work. We use heuristic knowledge each time we look for a parking space in a crowded parking lot (e.g., drive up close to get a spot near the door, or park toward the back to avoid a door ding from other cars?). Likewise, students are encouraged to identify what works well for them. Taking notes is a good classroom example of a heuristic. There are a number of legitimate ways to take notes (e.g., Cornell, split-page, mind mapping), but once the techniques of each are learned, the student needs to be able to make conscious choices about which techniques work best in different circumstances. Therefore, when the teacher says, "Which note-taking system are you going to use for this reading?" he or she is delivering a heuristic prompt.

Reflective Prompts

Another type of metacognitive prompt is one that causes reflective thinking. These prompts include asking an older student (e.g., "How do you think you're doing so far in understanding the author's main points?") or a younger one (e.g., "Does that make sense?") after reading aloud a page from a guided reading book. Although students do not typically independently engage in metacognition (i.e., thinking about one's thinking) until the intermediate grades, it is important to foster this type of thought well before then.

Cues to Shift Attention

Prompts are often effective at moving students closer to a fuller understanding of a concept, but at times they are not enough. This is to be expected in guided instruction, as learners in this phase are still grappling with newer information. The purpose of a cue, much like Wood's (1999) level 3 scaffold, is to shift the learner's attention by directing them to notice. In our lives, we witness this anytime we watch a sporting event. The expert commentator slows down the action for us, so we can see what he or she sees. For example, in a figure skating competition, a triple axel is identified and replayed in slow motion, and quality indicators are discussed by the commentators. In similar fashion, teachers cue students to notice what is important, as when the first-grade teacher covered a portion of the word *flat* to focus attention on a portion of it.

There are a variety of cues that are used, and many are paired to increase the power of the cue. Some are nonverbal in nature, whereas others involve spoken language. In all cases, the use of cues should be precise and well timed to enhance their effectiveness. Types of cues include the following:

- Visual cues (e.g., highlighting or underlining text, furnishing a model of a molecule) provide visual stimulation.

- Verbal cues alert students to important information (e.g., "Listen to how the author describes the old house") and may include pauses, changes in intonation, and rate of speech.

- Gestural cues provide students with nonverbal information about the location of an object (e.g., by pointing) or a vital characteristic (e.g., spreading arms wide while using the word *enormous*).

- Physical cues rely on human touch (e.g., placing one's hand over a child's as he or she writes, touching the arm of a student to shift attention to the left side of the page).

- Positional cues rely on movement in space to change the focus (e.g., rearranging magnetic alphabet letters so that the learner can more clearly see the correct orientation of them to formulate a word).

- Environmental cues are those that rely on manipulatives and objects in the environment (e.g., previously constructed language charts, word walls, alphabet strips).

As noted earlier, these are often combined and frequently gathered ahead of time in case they will be needed. For instance, a fifth-grade teacher locates the language chart on verb tenses written earlier in the day near the table she will be using to meet with small groups during guided instruction. She has a student dictionary available in case it will be needed during the lesson and has flagged the page in the language arts textbook that features a diagram of how verb tenses change depending on the auxiliaries present. During guided instruction, she combines these environmental and visual cues with verbal cues (e.g., "Take a look at this example of the present perfect tense to see how that can help you") with gestural ones (e.g., pointing to the diagram in the book). By planning for possible cues in advance, she is able to time their use to scaffold the learners' understanding.

Direct Explanation and Modeling

Wood's (1999) observations of mothers of young children noted that there were times when the child was unable to perform the task despite increasingly specific scaffolds. In those instances, the mother reassumed control of the task and explained and demonstrated how to successfully do it (level 4), then turned it back to the child. This happens in classrooms as well. Despite the use of questions, prompts, and cues, the learner is sometimes not able to answer correctly. In those cases, the teacher reassumes cognitive responsibility through direct explanation and modeling.

As discussed earlier, direct explanation involves (a) identifying the skill, concept, or procedure to be demonstrated, (b) explaining how it is used, (c) thinking aloud to expose expert decision making, and (d) making a plan for the student to do so, then monitoring its application (Alfassi, 2004). This last step is vital in guided instruction, as the goal is to release cognitive responsibility back to the student as quickly as possible. Therefore, when a teacher says,

> I'm going to read these three sentences back to you, using the punctuation as a clue for what to do with my voice. I can see there's an exclamation mark there, so I know I should make my voice go up, but I have to read the sentences to know whether I should be excited, surprised, or afraid.

After reading the sentences back to the student, she says,

> I was paying attention to what the words meant, too, not just the punctuation mark. When the boy said, "Help! This is too hot!" I knew that instead of being excited, he was hurting! So, I made my voice sound like that, too. Now I want you to try it, and I'll listen as you read.

In this case, the teacher has identified what she will do, provided an explanation accompanied by a think-aloud about her decisions, made a plan for the student to try it, and then monitored its use. Once the learner has successfully accomplished this, the cycle begins again, with a new question posed to check for understanding.

Conclusion

As illustrated through the examples we have shared, successful implementation of intentional instruction is dependent on continuously observing the performance of the students both individually and as a class. If it appears that students are acquiring the knowledge needed to accomplish the targeted language and content tasks, the teacher can continue identifying and implementing subsequent instructional content, purpose(s), and ways of sharing by scaffolding on what has been learned. If instead some, or all, of the students are unable to move to independence, the teacher is able to reexamine the purpose, the ways in which the information was shared, and the tasks to determine what is interfering with the students' ability to transfer this information to the independent completion of novel tasks. Using this instructional framework allows for a continuous assessment of the entire instructional process, including the purposes, tasks, grouping arrangements, teacher performance, and student acquisition and transfer to independence.

Although the focus of intentional instruction is on the students, the onus for either learning or not learning identified content does not rest with them. This framework allows for a teacher to continually analyze the whys and hows of the instructional process. When the performance of the students indicates that they are not becoming skilled at the task, the teacher has the opportunity to again provide experiences that avail them of the missing links. There is no need for a student to fail at the end of the lesson or course, because the teacher has been able to continually assess, through multiple measures of the student's performance, his or her acquisition of knowledge from the onset of instruction.

These authentic indicators provide the teacher with a mental, if not tangible, portfolio of a student's performance over time that indicates his or her acquisition of knowledge, depth of understanding, and range of informational transfer (Flood, Lapp, & Monken, 1992). As a voyeur, the teacher can use the information being acquired from observing students' attempts to approach, process, monitor personal performance, and complete a task as a way to influence future instruction with the goal always being to improve and support student learning. These detailed insights allow the teacher to become more connected with the growth of each individual in the class, thus resulting in a Catch 22 situation of success for both the students and the teacher.

Questions for Reflection

1. What are the similarities and differences between scripted and intentional instruction?

2. In designing the initial segment of a lesson that illustrates your understanding of content and language purpose setting, why is purpose setting important in lesson planning, implementation, and assessment?

3. After clarifying the language and content purposes for the lesson, how might you model your thinking about the lesson content or vocabulary to your students? What is the intent of this modeling?

4. After adding tasks for guided instruction and productive group work to your lesson, illustrate through your example of guided instruction how you are differentiating instruction. Also, when adding the collaborative group work section, how will you be able to assess both individual and group engagement and production?

REFERENCES

Afflerbach, P., Pearson, P.D., & Paris, S.G. (2008). Clarifying differences between reading skills and reading strategies. *The Reading Teacher*, 61(5), 364–373. doi:10.1598/RT.61.5.1

Alfassi, M. (2004). Reading to learn: Effects of combined strategy instruction on high school students. *The Journal of Educational Research*, 97(4), 171–185. doi:10.3200/JOER.97.4.171-185

Barton, D., Hamilton, M., & Ivanič, R. (2000). *Situated literacies: Reading and writing in context*. New York: Routledge.

Burkins, J.M., & Croft, M.M. (2010). *Preventing misguided reading: New strategies for guided reading teachers*. Newark, DE: International Reading Association; Thousand Oaks, CA: Corwin.

Cassidy, J., & Cassidy, D. (2004). What's hot, what's not for 2005: Scientific evidence-based reading research and instruction tops list. *Reading Today*, 22(3), 1, 8–9.

Cazden, C.B. (1986). Language in the classroom. *Annual Review of Applied Linguistics*, 7, 18–33. doi:10.1017/S0267190500001628

Commeyras, M. (2007). Scripted reading instruction? What's a teacher educator to do? *Phi Delta Kappan, 88*(5), 404–407.

Datnow, A., & Castellano, M. (2000). Teachers' responses to Success for All: How beliefs, experiences, and adaptations shape implementation. *American Educational Research Journal, 37*(3), 775–799.

Demko, M. (with Hedrick, W.). (2010). Teachers become zombies: The ugly side of scripted reading curriculum. *Voices From the Middle, 17*(3), 62–64.

Dodge, B. (1995). WebQuests: A technique for Internet-based learning. *Distance Educator, 1*(2), 10–13.

Duffy, G.G. (2003). *Explaining reading: A resource for teaching concepts, skills, and strategies.* New York: Guilford.

Duffy, G.G. (2009). *Explaining reading: A resource for teaching concepts, skills, and strategies* (2nd ed.). New York: Guilford.

Duffy, G.G., Roehler, L.R., Sivan, E., Rackliffe, G., Book, C., Meloth, M.S., et al. (1987). Effects of explaining the reasoning associated with using reading strategies. *Reading Research Quarterly, 22*(3), 347–368.

Fisher, D., & Frey, N. (2007). Implementing a schoolwide literacy framework: Improving achievement in an urban elementary school. *The Reading Teacher, 61*(1), 32–43. doi:10.1598/RT.61.1.4

Fisher, D., & Frey, N. (2008). Homework and the gradual release of responsibility: Making "responsibility" possible. *English Journal, 98*(2), 40–45.

Fisher, D., & Frey, N. (2010). Unpacking the language purpose: Vocabulary, structure, and function. *TESOL Journal, 1*(3), 315–337.

Fisher, D., Frey, N., & Lapp, D. (2008). Shared readings: Modeling comprehension, vocabulary, text structures, and text features for older readers. *The Reading Teacher, 61*(7), 548–557.

Flood, J., Lapp, D., & Monken, S. (1992). Portfolio assessment: Teachers' beliefs and practices. In C. Kinzer & D. Leu (Eds.), *Literacy research, theory, and practice: Views from many perspectives* (41st yearbook of the National Reading Conference, pp. 119–128). Chicago: National Reading Conference.

Foorman, B.R., Francis, D.J., Fletcher, J.M., Schatschneider, C., & Mehta, P. (1998). The role of instruction in learning to read: Preventing reading failure in at-risk children. *Journal of Educational Psychology, 90*(1), 37–55. doi:10.1037/0022-0663.90.1.37

Fraser, B.J., Walberg, H.J., Welch, W.W., & Hattie, J.A. (1987). Synthesis of educational productivity research. *International Journal of Educational Research* [Special issue], *11*(2).

Frey, N., & Fisher, D. (2010a). Identifying instructional moves during guided learning. *The Reading Teacher, 64*(2), 84–95.

Frey, N., & Fisher, D. (2010b). Motivation requires a meaningful task. *English Journal, 100*(1), 30–36.

Frey, N., Lapp, D., & Fisher, D. (2009). The academic booster shot: In-school tutoring to prevent grade-level retention. In J.C. Richards & C.A. Lassonde (Eds.), *Literacy tutoring that works: A look at successful in-school, after-school, and summer programs* (pp. 34–45). Newark, DE: International Reading Association.

Fullan, M., Hill, P., & Crévola, C. (2006). *Breakthrough.* Thousand Oaks, CA: Sage; Melbourne, VIC, Australia: National Staff Development Council; Toronto, ON, Canada: Ontario Principals' Council.

Hunter, M. (1995). *Improved instruction.* Thousand Oaks, CA: Corwin Press. (Original work published 1976)

MacGillivray, L., Ardell, A.L., Curwen, M.S., & Palma, J. (2004). Colonized teachers: Examining the implementation of a scripted reading program. *Teaching Education, 15*(2), 131–144. doi:10.1080/1047621042000213575

Marzano, R.J., Pickering, D.J., & Pollock, J.E. (2001). *Classroom instruction that works: Research-based strategies for increasing student achievement.* Alexandria, VA: Association for Supervision and Curriculum Development.

Mehan, H. (1979). *Learning lessons: Social organization in the classroom.* Cambridge, MA: Harvard University Press.

Moustafa, M., & Land, R. E. (2002). The reading achievement of economically-disadvantaged children in urban schools using *Open Court* vs. comparably disadvantaged children in urban schools using non-scripted reading programs. *American Educational Research Association Yearbook,* 44–53.

Nystrand, M. (2006). Research on the role of classroom discourse as it affects reading comprehension. *Research in the Teaching of English, 40*(4), 392–412.

Nystrand, M., & Gamoran, A. (1997). The big picture: Language and learning in hundreds of English lessons. In M. Nystrand (with A. Gamoran, R. Kachur, & C. Prendergast, Eds.), *Opening dialogue: Understanding the dynamics of language and learning in the English classroom* (pp. 30–74). New York: Teachers College Press.

Pearson, P.D., & Fielding, L. (1991). Comprehension instruction. In R. Barr, M.L. Kamil, P. Mosenthal, & P.D. Pearson (Eds.), *Handbook of reading research* (Vol. 2, pp. 815–860). Mahwah, NJ: Erlbaum.

Pearson, P.D., & Gallagher, M.C. (1983). The instruction of reading comprehension. *Contemporary Educational Psychology, 8*(3), 317–344. doi:10.1016/0361-476X(83)90019-X

Pressley, M., Wharton-McDonald, R., Allington, R.L., Block, C.C., Morrow, L.M., Tracey, D., et al. (2001). A study of effective first-grade literacy instruction. *Scientific Studies of Reading, 5*(1), 35–58.

Shanahan, T. (2006). The worst confession: Using a scripted text. *Reading Today, 24*(1), 14.

Taylor, B.M., Pearson, P.D., Peterson, D.S., & Rodriguez, M.C. (2003). Reading growth in high-poverty classrooms: The influence of teacher practices that encourage cognitive engagement in literacy learning. *The Elementary School Journal, 104*(1), 3–28. doi: 10.1086/499740

Tivnan, T., & Hemphill, L. (2005). Comparing four literacy reform models in high-poverty schools: Patterns of first-grade achievement. *The Elementary School Journal, 105*(5), 419–441. doi:10.1086/431885

Tomlinson, C.A. (1999). *The differentiated classroom: Responding to the needs of all learners.* Alexandria, VA: Association for Supervision and Curriculum Development.

Valencia, S.W., Place, N.A., Martin, S.D., & Grossman, P.L. (2006). Curriculum materials for elementary reading: Shackles and scaffolds for four beginning teachers. *The Elementary School Journal, 107*(1), 93–120. doi:10.1086/509528

Vygotsky, L.S. (1978). *Mind in society: The development of higher psychological processes* (M. Cole, Trans. & Ed., V. John-Steiner, S Scribner, & E. Souberman, Eds.). Cambridge, MA: Harvard University Press.

Wiggins, G., & McTighe, J. (2005). *Understanding by design* (2nd ed.). Alexandria, VA: Association for Supervision and Curriculum Development.

Wood, D.J. (1999). Teaching the young child: Some relationships between social interaction, language, and thought. In P. Lloyd & C. Fernyhough (Eds.), *Lev Vygotsky: Critical assessments. Vol. 3: The zone of proximal development* (pp. 259–275). New York: Routledge.

Chapter 15

Using Assessment to Improve Teaching and Learning

Sheila W. Valencia

Assessment is part and parcel of everything we do in schools and in classrooms. As many have argued, assessment should be an integral part of instruction, growing out of what is important for students to know and be able to do, and it should inform both instruction and student learning. Clearly, there are multiple purposes for assessment and numerous forms and kinds of data that can be used for making decisions. The challenge is to assure that the right forms of data are linked to appropriate uses and purposes for assessment, assuring what Messick (1989) termed consequential validity. An impressive body of research conducted over more than 30 years has documented that assessments, by themselves, do not improve student achievement (see Valencia & Wixson, 2000, for a review). Rather, it is how assessment is used to inform teaching and learning that connects assessment and achievement, which is the focus of this chapter.

Now, in 2011, perhaps more than any previous time, the federal government and school systems are demanding more testing and assessment of students. Data-driven decision making is the new mantra, yet some have suggested that the result has been to leave educators data rich and information poor (Stringfield, Wayman, & Yakimowski-Srebnick, 2005); in other words, educators may be swimming in data, but the data may not be providing the sorts of information needed to improve teaching and learning. Equally worrisome is that some data may be misinterpreted or misused, leading to inappropriate teaching, learning, or inferences about schooling.

This chapter examines the literature and research on types of assessments that have surfaced since No Child Left Behind (NCLB) and Race to the Top entered the educational scene in 2001 and 2010, respectively. By all accounts, these types of assessments will be with us for some time to come, as federal funds have been allocated to state coalitions and

What Research Has to Say About Reading Instruction (4th ed.) edited by S. Jay Samuels and Alan E. Farstrup.
© 2011 by the International Reading Association.

independent testing groups to develop new assessment systems to align with the new Common Core State Standards. The goal of this chapter is to synthesize the research and theory behind this new thinking about assessment with the ultimate aim of understanding how assessment might be appropriately used to enhance teaching and learning, not simply measure it.

The New Assessment Triad

A bit of history is helpful in understanding the current assessment context. Prior to NCLB, states were required to administer assessments once each at the elementary, middle, and high school levels. States typically tested reading achievement of children in 4th, 7th, and 10th grades, which roughly paralleled the age bands used by the National Assessment of Educational Progress (NAEP). As part of the standards-based reform movement and efforts to have reading assessments reflect advances in reading research, theory, and practice, reading assessment in the 1990s looked considerably different than in the decades before. It was not unusual, for example, to find reading tests that included fairly long selections drawn from published reading material, open-ended questions requiring both extended and shorter written responses, and cross-text questions. The thinking was that to overcome some of the negative effects of high-stakes, end-of-year assessments that had been documented in the 1980s (e.g., narrowing of the curriculum, focus on low-level skills, inflated test scores, test preparation instruction), these assessments would be worth teaching to. The hope was that if teachers kept new assessment models in mind, they would be engaging in high-quality teaching, and students would be supported to achieve higher levels of literacy learning, even if the tests were high stakes.

At the same time as these "authentic" end-of-year assessments were gaining momentum, there was a concerted effort on the part of many school districts, and even some states, to implement classroom assessment. Recognizing that different types of assessments served different purposes and different audiences, classroom assessments such as portfolios, work samples, and informal teacher-designed assessments were acknowledged to be part of a complete assessment system. Unfortunately, they never gained the status or funding needed to become a full component of the system.

With the passage of NCLB in 2001 came additional testing requirements. All children in grades 3–8 were tested every year and once in high school. In addition, schools were held accountable for making adequate yearly progress or risk sanctions and possibly takeover by the state or private educational agencies. With so much testing on the scene, new possibilities emerged for accountability. For example, because scores were available for individual students at more grades every year, some schools and districts began using value-added and growth models to examine the effects of teachers and schools on student learning. In addition, since 2001, there has been a dramatic decrease in the use of performance assessments and open-ended responses, and a corresponding increase in multiple-choice tests, because more students must be tested and the cost of testing has skyrocketed (U.S. Government Accounting Office, 2009). Marion (2009) has suggested that in an era of limited funding, policymakers are likely to conclude that open-ended items and innovative approaches are not worth the additional cost, but he cautions that they may not fully understand the effects of such decisions on teaching and learning.

As in the 1990s, educators, policymakers, and measurement experts once again find themselves considering how to meet the multiple purposes of assessment: accountability, monitoring, and informing classroom teaching and learning. Years of experience have clearly documented that when one type of assessment is used to serve multiple purposes and audiences, it serves none very well (Herman, 2010). To address this concern, Perie, Marion, and Gong (2009) reconceptualized and labeled these three types or purposes of assessment as summative, interim, and formative, according to the frequency of administration, duration of testing cycle, and specificity of content, as illustrated in Figure 15.1. The triangle is framed by the x-axis showing increasing frequency of assessment and the y-axis indicating increasing scope and duration of cycle. Summative assessments are administered least frequently, have the longest time between administrations, and test content at a broader scope than either interim or formative assessment. For example, summative tests may include items that assess literal and inferential comprehension but are unlikely to include assessment of self-monitoring, questioning, or author's craft. These tests are usually associated with typical end-of-year standardized or state tests that are administered to large groups of students and used for accountability purposes.

At the other end of the continuum, formative assessment happens most frequently, which allows for a very short cycle between assessments and a finer grained analysis of reading skills and strategies. Formative assessment taps what students are learning in the classroom as part of

Figure 15.1. The New Assessment Triad

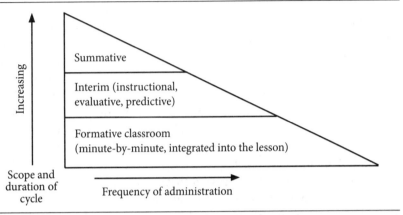

Note. From "Moving Toward a Comprehensive Assessment System: A Framework for Considering Interim Assessments," by M. Perie, S. Marion, & B. Gong, 2009, *Educational Measurement: Issues and Practice, 28*(3), p. 7. Used with permission.

instruction—what has sometimes been called classroom assessment. Yet, as elaborated in the *formative assessment* section of this chapter, new definitions include more than the typical classroom tasks, documentation, or even portfolios of student learning.

Between summative and formative assessment in Figure 15.1 is interim, or benchmark, assessment. This type of medium-scale, medium-cycle assessment is usually administered 3–5 times a year and is typically designed to measure the same broad goals as summative assessment and/ or predict performance on high-stakes summative assessments given at the end of the school year.

With this conceptual framework as background for the three types of assessment, I now turn to the research on each with an eye toward the constraints and affordances to inform classroom instruction. Because this chapter is focused on using assessments to inform classroom teaching and learning, I also focus on the concept of consequential validity (Messick, 1989; Moss, 1998)—that is, the consequences, social or educational, intended or unintended, of using assessment data to inform particular classroom actions or make particular classroom decisions. I begin with the work on summative assessment and then move to formative assessment. I leave interim assessments until the last, because there is a good deal of debate about new interim assessments, the research that undergirds them, and calls for their widespread use.

Summative Assessment

Summative assessments are most commonly associated with end-of-year, norm-referenced, and standards-based assessments. Although they do not have to be associated with high stakes, multiple-choice formats or large-group administration, they typically are because of the purposes they serve: accountability, comparisons across groups, and performance on state or district content standards. As a result, summative assessments must be efficient and economical to administer and score, designed to cover a wide range of content appropriate for students in a wide range of schools, and administered as late in the school year as possible under standardized conditions. Consequently, summative test results have assumed a major role in policy decisions and, unfortunately, in many curricular and classroom decisions.

The negative consequences of high-stakes summative assessments on curriculum and instruction have been well documented: narrowing of the curriculum, overemphasis on basic skills, inflated test scores, excessive time spent on test preparation, exclusion of low-achieving or special education students from testing, focus on the "bubble" kids (i.e., those who are close to passing), and negative impact on student motivation (Allington & McGill-Franzen, 1992; Koretz, 2008; Linn, 2000; Nolen, Haladyna, & Haas, 1992; Shepard, 2008). Many of these negative consequences are associated with the pressure that comes from the high stakes and the sanctions associated with them. However, other negative consequences have been less well articulated and understood by administrators, teachers, and parents and are equally, if not more, problematic than others, because they translate into more specific classroom practices.

Cautions

There are three cautions for using summative test results that merit further exploration at this time: sampling the learning, reader profiles, and floor and ceiling effects.

Sampling the Learning. Several research-based examples highlight the limitations of using the results of summative tests to inform classroom instruction. First, by their very purpose and requirements, the tests are designed to assess a broad range of content. Norm-referenced tests, for example, are designed to be used across many different states, each with its own unique set of content standards. Consequently, summative assessments can only sample the standards in a very general and superficial way, making the tests fairly insensitive to curriculum and instruction

(Linn, 1986, 2000; Popham, 2001). As a result, items that spread student scores in a normative way, as is required on norm-referenced tests, tend to be those most closely aligned with socioeconomic status instead of classroom instruction (Popham, 2008). The same problem exists with state standards-based assessments. Here, too, it is impossible to adequately assess all the reading content standards at each grade level. The coverage of content is limited, and the "grain size" or scope of what is tested by particular items is too broad to be useful (Valencia & Wixson, 2001). Without such information, teachers lack specific information to inform their instruction.

Even if summative tests, whether norm-referenced or standards-based, were to be augmented with some items that covered more of the standards, the information would not be useful. From a measurement perspective, results that are based on a few test items, even those clustered in a subscore, generally cannot provide reliable, trustworthy information to inform instruction (Linn, 1986). So, practices such as charting specific items on which students did poorly and then targeting instruction narrowly to these items or their corresponding standards is not a reliable way to identify students' needs. This is particularly true when analyzing reading comprehension results, because empirical research suggests that comprehension subareas such as sequencing, summarizing, cause and effect, literal comprehension, and inferential comprehension are not independent from one another (Bruce, Osborn, & Commeyras, 1994; Davis, 1944).

Reader Profiles. A second concern related to using summative test results for classroom decision making relates to the multidimensionality of reading and the particular array of strengths and weaknesses that contribute to a student's overall reading performance. This is sometimes referred to as a reader profile—the variability in reading skills and strategies within an individual student that characterizes his or her specific reading abilities (e.g., Aaron, Joshi, & Williams, 1999; Alexander, 2003; Carr, Brown, Vavrus, & Evans, 1990; Leach, Scarborough, & Rescorla, 2003; Spear-Swerling, 2004). Evidence suggests that there is substantial variability within groups of good readers as well as poor. All good readers do not exhibit the same strengths and weaknesses, nor do all poor readers.

Three findings from the reader profile literature raise concerns about using summative test data to make instructional decisions. First, diagnostic profiles of students who score similarly on summative tests indicate that they may have widely different sets of skills and strategies and even different instructional reading levels (Buly & Valencia, 2002; Rupp & Lesaux, 2006). For example, Buly and Valencia found that fourth-grade students who had similar failing scores on a state reading test had a range of abilities in the areas of decoding, fluency, comprehension, and vocabulary. Some of the fourth-grade students had beginning-level decoding skills, while others had word skills typical of ninth-grade readers; some had difficulty with vocabulary, while others did not; and some read very slowly with excellent decoding and comprehension, while other slow readers demonstrated difficulty with decoding and comprehension. Considering this variability, it is easy to understand why assigning all poor readers or all good readers to the same intervention program based solely on summative test scores is likely to produce mixed results, and individual students' reading needs would not be met. For example, a child with poor reading comprehension related to word identification difficulties requires a different instructional approach than a child who has low performance in both word recognition and overall language skills. Likewise, a student who is in the early stages of learning English requires different instruction than one who has strong English skills and limited decoding.

Overall, these researchers and others concluded that scores on norm-referenced or standards-based tests do not adequately reflect the diagnostic profiles of students that are needed to provide appropriate instruction (Leach et al., 2003; Shepard, 2009; Spear-Swerling, 2004). Information from multiple measures, classroom assessments, and measures of other reading components must be considered as instructional interventions are planned. In fact, studies of student–instruction interactions suggest that instruction targeted to a student's specific areas of need produces gains in that area. However, when instructional time is spent on skills and abilities in which a student is strong, no additional growth is detected. So, although instruction that targets a student's specific needs may increase learning, misdirected instruction may actually waste valuable instructional time (Connor, Morrison, & Katch, 2004; Connor, Morrison, & Petrella, 2004).

Research on reader profiles also suggests that readers' profiles, and consequently their instructional needs, change over time and across developmental levels (Alexander, 2003; Paris, Carpenter, Paris, & Hamilton, 2005; Spear-Swerling, 2004), which suggests that inferences drawn from summative tests are likely to be different depending on a student's age, grade level, and reading development. Research also reaffirms the problem of depending on annual assessment results to make timely and appropriate instructional decisions. For example, Leach and colleagues (2003) examined the reading profiles of fourth- and fifth-grade students, some of whom had been identified in third grade as reading disabled (early identified) and others who had not been identified as reading disabled until fourth or fifth grade (late identified). Surprisingly, the late-identified students did not simply demonstrate more severe forms of the difficulties experienced by children in early grades, nor were they inadvertently overlooked in earlier grades. These students displayed profiles of reading difficulty that were not present for them in earlier grades; their difficulties were not only late identified but were also late emerging. Thus, it is not enough to identify students in the primary grades who may need early intervention; students' reading profiles need to be reexamined at later grades using measures that align with increasing comprehension demands so that newly emerging reading difficulties can be identified.

Finally, in addition to illuminating individual and developmental differences represented by similar summative test scores, the research on reader profiles also reveals the limited scope of summative assessments. Readers' motivation, background knowledge, and strategy use are rarely assessed on summative reading assessments, yet they have been shown to contribute significantly to reading performance and may even maximize students' ability to comprehend more effectively (Alexander, 2003; Guthrie, 2008; Taboada, Tonks, Wigfield, & Guthrie, 2009). In sum, research on reader profiles highlights the need for a great deal of caution in interpreting and using results of summative assessment to determine the specific reading needs of individuals or even groups of students.

Floor and Ceiling Effects. A third related concern of using summative test scores to make classroom decisions is that these types of assessments are less reliable and less precise indicators of the reading ability of very low-performing and high-performing students. Two pieces of research make this point. The first comes from the results of the 2005 NAEP in reading. An analysis of the score spread for students between the 10th and 90th percentiles on the NAEP revealed an enormous range of reading abilities at each grade level (Bracey, 2009). Fourth-grade students who scored at the 10th percentile in reading were as much as 7–8 years behind those who scored at the 90th percentile. At eighth grade, there was a 5–6 year difference, and at 12th grade, a 7–8 year difference. These are huge differences in reading abilities—ones that are unlikely to be captured by a single grade-level summative test administered over 45–90 minutes.

This point about test insensitivity and unreliability is made even more strongly when test construction principles and score interpretation are considered (Baumann & Stevenson, 1982; Hopkins, 1997). Because summative tests are designed for students at a specific grade and reading level, and because they must be efficient and economical (i.e., not take too long to administer and score), the tests contain reading material that targets that grade level. So, for example, a summative reading test designed for fourth grade will likely include mostly fourth-grade reading material as well as some third- and fifth-grade material. However, it cannot include passages appropriate for students reading at all grade levels. As a result, students who are reading at a second-grade level or below and those reading above the sixth-grade level have few opportunities to demonstrate their reading abilities using appropriate material. This is what test makers call floors and ceilings. The point is that students can obtain scores that suggest they are reading below or above the target range of the test, even though they have never read such material on the test. All this is done by a mathematical extrapolation procedure that permits scores to be calculated based on predictions and estimations rather than the actual performance of students reading specific passages and answering specific questions. Therefore, inferring instructional needs of students who score near the floor or ceiling of a summative test, whether norm-referenced or standards-based, is tenuous at best.

Formative Assessment

Formative assessment is conducted in classrooms by teachers and students as part of the instructional process. This assessment has the shortest cycle, being implemented on a day-by-day and even minute-by-minute basis, and it is the most fine grained with respect to specific learning targets (see Figure 15.1; Wiliam & Thompson, 2008). Interest in formative assessment gained enormous momentum in 1998 with the publication of several papers in the United States and England by Black and Wiliam (1998a, 1998b). Although the idea that assessment should support learning rather than simply measure it dates back at least 30 years before then (e.g., Bloom, Hastings, & Madaus, 1971; Scriven, 1967) and had somewhat of a resurgence with the portfolio assessment movement of the early 1990s (Tierney, Carter, & Desai, 1991; Valencia, 1998; Wolf, 1989), the value of formative assessment seemed to take hold once again in 1998.

Shortly after the Black and Wiliam publications, other researchers began to pick up the call by distinguishing assessment *of* learning from assessment *for* learning (Popham, 2001; Shepard, 2000; Stiggins, 2002).

The formative assessment model that has advanced from this work was framed as a "new theory of formative assessment" (Wiliam, 2010, p. 18), because it brought together research from a range of fields, including sociocultural theories of learning and teaching, cognitive theories of teaching and learning, metacognition, motivation, and measurement, rather than drawing only on the work in measurement. Building on earlier reviews by Crooks (1988) and Natriello (1987), Black and Wiliam's (1998a) review of 250 studies found significant improvement in students' test scores (i.e., effect sizes between 0.4 and 0.7) when various aspects of formative assessment were implemented in classrooms. As the authors explain, an effect size of 0.4 would mean that the average student participating in a classroom using formative assessment would end up with the same achievement as a student in the top 35% of those who did not participate in such; an effect size of 0.7 would place the average student close to the top 10% of those who did not have a formative assessment intervention. Equally important, Black and Wiliam also found that improved formative assessment produced larger gains for low-achieving students than for other students; that is, the use of formative assessment appeared to close the achievement gap while raising achievement overall.

Definitions and Characteristics

It is not surprising that results such as these would lead to a rush for more formative assessment. However, as many have now cautioned, definitions of *formative assessment* vary widely, so it is essential to understand the conceptualization and particular characteristics of this assessment that were specified in Black and Wiliam's (1998a) review and more recent reviews spanning several countries (Brookhart, 2007; Educational Testing Service, 2009; Heritage, 2010).

Black and Wiliam (1998a) began with the premise that teaching and learning must be interactive. In this model, assessment refers to all activities used by teachers and those used by students that provide information to be used as feedback to adjust teaching and learning activities. More specifically, to be labeled *formative*, the evidence from the assessment must actually be used to modify teaching to meet students' needs. Thus, it is not the frequency of the assessment, speed of receiving results, location of implementation, specific assessment strategies, or even the purpose that make an assessment formative; it is the use of the information.

Action must be taken to close the gap between a student's current learning and the desired instructional goals for that student. The assessment forms the direction of the new learning (Shepard, 2008; Wiliam & Thompson, 2008). Consequently, formative assessment is a process rather than a measurement instrument or tool (Heritage, 2010).

Providing Specific Feedback. Nested within this conceptualization of formative assessment are specific features that derive from the research. First, the information teachers get from formative assessments must not only be used to make changes in teaching but also must be used to help students understand how they can improve their own learning. To that end, feedback must be focused on the specific task the student was asked to do and provide specific suggestions or cues about how to improve (Black & Wiliam, 1998b; Hattie & Timperley, 2007). General statements about performance or praise are not considered feedback. For example, if a student is told his score on a test or told that he needs to work harder and, as a result, does work harder and then improves his performance, this would not be considered formative assessment. Although the feedback may have precipitated the change, the feedback did not help the student learn how to work harder or what to work harder on. Similarly, although a diagnostic assessment may provide specific information about a student's strengths and needs, it would not be considered formative unless the information is fed back to the teacher and the student, so they both specifically know what it will take to improve learning.

Engaging Students in Self-Assessment. A second, related feature of formative assessment is a focus on teaching and engaging students in self-assessment. The aim is for students to gain a clear understanding of the standards for good performance similar to that of their teachers. Consequently, students should be able to monitor their own work, set appropriate goals, develop needed skills and strategies, and improve learning (Andrade, 2010; Black, Harrison, Lee, Marshall, & Wiliam, 2004). From a motivational perspective, students' self-assessment helps them take a specific proactive stance toward learning and develop a sense of self-efficacy. They become learning-oriented rather than performance-oriented; they are engaged in and employ self-regulation, as compared with students who work to get good grades, compete with others, or obtain extrinsic rewards. A learning community and a learning culture (Shepard, 2000) exist in these classrooms instead of an atmosphere of competition. Consequently, students are actively engaged in supporting one another's work and providing feedback to peers.

Responsive Instruction and Assessment. A third critical attribute of formative assessment grows out of its situated nature within instruction. Because the purpose of this assessment is to determine a student's learning in light of instructional goals that are specifically appropriate for him or her, formative assessment is associated with "the pedagogy of contingency" (Wiliam, 2006, p. 6). Simply put, this means that teaching should be contingent on, or responsive to, a student's responses during instruction. This deceptively simply statement is actually quite complex and leads to several of the key attributes of formative assessment. For example, teachers must know how to elicit learning from students using a variety of questioning strategies, tasks, observations, and interactions. These assessments take place both on-the-fly during instruction as well as more systematically as part of the curriculum; they can take a few minutes or an entire class period. Because formative assessment must be appropriate for a student and responsive to his or her needs, not all students will experience the same assessment or the same feedback, and as a consequence, the teacher will need to differentiate instruction (Black & Wiliam, 2010; Wiliam, 2010).

Professional Development. The critical features of formative assessment described previously require teachers to have deep pedagogical content knowledge as well as knowledge of the subject matter they are assessing (Shulman, 1987). They must know what and how to assess, interpret student performance, and identify and implement instructional steps to move learning forward. Therefore, scholars who advocate and study formative assessment view long-term, site-based professional development as a necessary part of its successful implementation (Heritage, 2010; Popham, 2008; Shepard, 2000; Wiliam, 2007).

Ongoing Research

The concept of formative assessment has gained widespread acceptance in the past 10 years, most especially internationally. At least three policy groups have advanced the purpose and characteristics of formative assessment, including the Formative Assessment for Students and Teachers State Collaboratives on Assessment and Student Standards, the Third International Conference on Assessment for Learning, and the Assessment Reform Group. Entire books, edited volumes, and numerous articles have explored the issue. Despite these endorsements and the great number of studies that were part of the research synthesis, there have been very few comprehensive studies of the effects of formative assessment on student learning. This is probably because the concept and implementation are complex, encompassing assessment, instruction, and professional development, and because the goal aims to improve teaching and student learning, both of which are long-term projects. Several initial studies are informative in thinking about the potential of formative assessment, and several others are informative in highlighting how formative assessment has been misunderstood.

A series of studies by Black, Wiliam, and colleagues (Black et al., 2004; Wiliam, Lee, Harrison, & Black, 2004) analyzed the effects of implementing the kind of formative assessment that is aligned with the research base summarized previously. They studied 24 teachers working with students, ages 11–18, in six schools located in England. Although the results of this study are reported for science and math teachers, the work has since been extended to English teachers and elementary schools. The teachers in the study were provided with professional development opportunities for approximately six months before they began implementing formative assessment in their classrooms. Then, they were provided with additional professional development support off-site and in their schools while they implemented it during the following school year. The focus of the intervention was to help teachers improve their teaching by implementing their own formative assessments designed to align with their individual classroom curriculum and instructional practice. Teachers worked to change the "learning contract" in their classrooms to assure their students were partners in learning and assessment. After a year, the mean effect size was 0.32, producing an additional half year of growth for students in the formative assessment classes over those in control classrooms. In addition, the results indicated that implementing formative assessment altered teachers' views of themselves as professionals and produced substantive changes in their questions (e.g., higher level questions, longer wait time, more active student participation, more classroom dialogue), feedback to students (e.g., providing comments without grades, giving specific comments), and strategies for engaging students in peer and self-assessment (e.g., student goal setting, more peer dialogue, small-group work).

More specific to the field of reading, Ross (2004) investigated whether third-grade students whose teachers were supported to implement running records in line with the concept of formative assessment would have higher overall reading achievement than a control group. Like many classroom teachers, Ross conceptualized running records as a formative assessment—an intervention—in which assessment was integrated with teaching and actively used by teachers to make instructional decisions. Teachers participated in professional development sessions in their schools that focused on how to administer, interpret, and use running record information. Professional development was also provided for principals, so they could serve as instructional leaders to support the schools' professional learning communities that developed around the intervention. Teachers administered different levels of running records to children as needed and differentiated instruction based on the results. The findings indicated that the children in the running record formative assessment intervention improved their reading and writing scores and significantly outperformed students in schools that did not implement the intervention. Because Ross randomly assigned schools to running record or nonrunning record interventions, this is one of the few studies that can point to a causal relationship between implementing formative assessment and improved reading achievement.

Other studies of formative assessment are just beginning to emerge in other content areas and grades. Some early findings suggest that other efforts may not be as promising as those of Wiliam et al. (2004) or Ross (2004; see Bell, Steinberg, Wiliam, & Wylie, 2008; Shavelson et al., 2008). Formative classroom assessment is complex and multifaceted, requiring a shift in classroom interactions, deep understanding of teaching and learning, and ongoing professional development. When these aspects of formative assessment are not sufficiently addressed and nurtured, there is a great deal of variability in how teachers interactively use formative assessment with students to inform their teaching and their students' learning. In turn, student achievement is less likely to improve.

Misunderstandings

The enthusiasm for formative assessment and hope for its potential to improve teaching and learning has led to the overuse and, perhaps, misuse of the term in both research and classroom practice. Some studies, for example, use the term *formative assessment* to refer to a range of tests administered by teachers, including commercially developed tests drawn from item banks, adaptive computerized assessments, teacher-made tests, and curriculum-provided tests designed to be given at regular intervals (e.g., Militello, Schweid, & Sireci, 2010; Sharkey & Murnane, 2006). Other studies and curricular materials use *formative* to refer to tests such as oral-reading fluency measures (e.g., Dynamic Indicators of Basic Early Literacy Skills [DIBELS], AIMSweb, curriculum-based measurements [CBMs]), maze completion tests, and written retellings that are used to predict students' later performance on a summative test; they are labeled *formative* because they inform teachers which students may be at risk of later failure (Marcotte & Hintze, 2009). In some cases, people other than the classroom teacher administer and score the assessment, entering students' results on a database or spreadsheet for teachers to see.

The emphasis in these "formative" assessment approaches is on providing information to teachers in a timely manner, so they have the possibility of using it to shape instruction, not the requirement or expectation to use it to inform their teaching. As Militello and colleagues (2010) note, "These systems offer the potential to close the 'virtuous circle' of curriculum, instruction, and assessment by providing 'just-in-time' feedback for teachers and administrators" (p. 30). In comparison with the characteristics of formative assessment derived from the research, these assessments are missing many of the essential components: integration of instruction and assessment, responsiveness of assessment and instruction to individual needs at the moment of instruction, specificity and immediacy of feedback, student as active participant in assessment and learning, and professional development support for assessment and instruction. As I next describe, these so-called formative assessments are closer to what is now called interim or benchmark assessments. Shepard (2009) warns, "Just because it's labeled formative assessment doesn't make it so" (p. 33).

Interim Assessment

I turn now to the last and newest of the three layers of the assessment system: interim, or benchmark, assessment. As Figure 15.1 indicates, this type of assessment is situated between summative and formative assessment with respect to frequency of administration, duration of testing cycle, and specificity of content. In general, these assessments are designed to measure the same broad curricular goals that are measured on summative, high-stakes tests but are given more frequently (i.e., 3–5 times a year), and the schedule of test administration is often determined by district or school administrators. The format and content of these tests often mimic the summative test used in a state or school district. They are usually group administered and can be given and scored by classroom teachers or others, but unlike formative assessments, the results of interim assessments can be aggregated and reported to a broader audience.

Researchers and practitioners have suggested that interim assessments might serve three purposes at the school level and beyond: instruction, prediction, and evaluation. For example, many are hopeful that these assessments will provide teachers with data to guide instructional decisions, while others hope the data can provide an early warning sign to identify students who may be at risk or likely to fail the end-of-year summative test. In addition, some school and district administrators want to use results to evaluate particular programs or instructional approaches and monitor for accountability (Perie et al., 2009). Ultimately, the expectation is that using interim assessments will lead to improved student achievement.

Interim Reading Assessments

In reading, interim assessments have taken a number of different forms. At early reading levels, these assessments represent a slightly different model than the one described previously, because there is rarely an end-of-year summative test given to students below third grade and because the focus is on more discrete skills associated with early reading and decoding. As a result, interim measures at K–2 typically focus on specific skills in phonemic awareness, decoding, and early text reading, and the tests are often individually administered. At third grade and above, the most common interim assessments are commercially or district-developed multiple-choice comprehension tests that are modeled after state assessments, running records, and oral reading fluency measures. Although running records are often used in ways consistent with formative assessment, some schools use them more as interim assessments, especially at the intermediate grades, to document student progress according to overall reading level. Oral reading fluency measures such as DIBELS and AIMSweb are also frequently used as interim assessments. Students read aloud for one minute (three different passages are usually administered, each for one minute), while teachers record errors and calculate scores as words correct per minute (WCPM). Although in special education settings oral-reading fluency assessments can be administered at various time intervals (i.e., from several times a week to every six weeks), in regular education settings, they are most often administered 3–5 times per year as interim assessments.

Oral reading fluency assessment was built on early work in CBM, the goal of which was to help teachers use technically sound, but simple, data to monitor student progress, modify instruction, and predict performance on an end-of-year summative test (Deno, 1985, 2003; Fuchs & Deno, 1994). It is important to understand that these oral reading assessments were originally designed to "produce reliable and valid indicators of student growth in reading proficiency broadly defined" (Deno & Marston, 2006, p. 180). Because WCPM scores are correlated with scores on summative assessments of comprehension, the rationale is that oral reading fluency measures could help identify students who might be at risk for failing the summative test or were not making progress across the school year. These oral reading CBMs were never intended to be direct measures of comprehension or align with instruction; they simply correlated with comprehension. In addition, oral reading CBMs were not intended to measure fluency, nor were they originally labeled "oral reading fluency"; they were simply called "general outcome measurement" to indicate they were measuring overall reading ability. Thus, measures of oral reading fluency most closely fit the predictive purpose of interim assessments rather than instructional or evaluative purposes.

Prevalence of Interim Assessments

There has been a dramatic increase in the use of interim reading assessments over the past 10 years (Olson, 2005; Perie et al., 2009). In 2005, just four years after NCLB was adopted, 70% of superintendents reported that they periodically gave districtwide tests (usually 3–5 times per year), and another 10% said they were planning to give them the next academic year (Olson, 2005). One popular interim test provider documented a 950% increase between 2001 and 2009 in the number of districts using its assessment system, and another provider reported a 45% increase in the use of computer-based multiple-choice comprehension test (Marion, 2009). According to Sharp (2004), this emphasis on interim assessments has led to more teachers using the same assessments in their classrooms than ever before. She reported that of the 45 Reading First plans available online, 39 include DIBELS, 11 include the Texas Primary Reading Inventory, and 5 include the Phonological Awareness Literacy Survey either as a requirement or as one of several options to be given several times a year in Reading First schools.

In part, this burgeoning use of interim assessments reflects a growing understanding that summative assessments cannot provide the detailed information needed to improve classroom teaching and learning, and in part, it is a response to the high stakes associated with NCLB and Race to the Top. School districts want to be able to monitor student progress along the way instead of waiting for the results of the summative assessment and accompanying sanctions. Most important, they want to be able to intervene with students who are at risk before they fail. Despite the striking speed with which interim assessment has been implemented and widespread belief about its potential, this type of assessment is perhaps the most confusing, controversial, and untested component of the new assessment triad.

Confusions and Controversies

Definitions and Research Base. One of the most confusing aspects of interim assessment is distinguishing it from formative assessment, not because the two have the same purposes, characteristics, or processes— they do not. Many researchers and practitioners have argued that the confusion stems from the misappropriation of the term *formative* by test publishers and others in an effort to convince educators that interim assessments can contribute to improved student achievement (Bulkley, Oláh, & Blanc, 2010; Goertz, Oláh, & Riggan, 2009; Perie et al., 2009; Popham, 2008; Shepard, 2010). What makes this point most clearly is that measurement scholars uniformly agree that there is a strong research base for formative assessment, but the "formative assessments" that are being marketed commercially or developed by districts do not satisfy the research-based criteria; therefore, they cannot claim to improve student achievement based on that research.

A close examination of many of the interim assessments given 3–5 times a year in reading would reveal a host of inconsistencies with the research base. Most do not integrate assessment during daily instructional interactions, provide immediate and specific feedback to learners and teachers, involve students in self-assessment, or provide information at the moment of instruction and learning. Thus, the use of the label *formative* assessment is inconsistent with the research base on which it rests. The other problem is that, to date, there has been very little research on the use of interim assessment to improve student learning. So, claims that these "formative assessments" (i.e., actually interim assessments) can contribute to student learning still remain to be tested.

Emerging Research. A few recent studies have begun to examine interim assessments and their impact on instruction and student learning. Several researchers studied a reform project in Philadelphia schools that centered on administering interim assessments every six weeks in math and reading at grades 3–8, using a data management and reporting system, and adopting a core curriculum. Results from a series of studies on this large-scale project found that although teachers reported using the data from the assessments to inform their instruction, they required support to use the data in meaningful ways. For example, teachers tended to use the information more procedurally than conceptually, reviewing the tests item by item to target reteaching rather than analyzing the concepts that were confusing for students or trying to understand students' thinking (Oláh, Lawrence, & Riggan, 2010). Although the information was useful in helping teachers identify students who needed additional instruction, it did not help them identify what or how to teach. In part, this is because interim assessments are not designed to provide that level of specificity.

Overall, evidence from the Philadelphia project and other studies suggest that teachers have difficulty moving from interpreting interim assessment data to developing and implementing appropriate instruction (Goertz et al., 2009; Heritage, Kim, Vendlinski, & Herman, 2009; Sharkey & Murnane, 2003). This finding is also consistent with a review of oral reading fluency CBMs showing that teachers needed support when they tried to use results of oral reading fluency measures to modify instruction (Stecker, Fuchs, & Fuchs, 2005).

The results of these studies may help explain the findings of two additional studies that found no statistical difference in achievement scores between schools that implemented interim assessments and those that did not (Henderson, Petrosino, Guckenburg, & Hamilton, 2008; Quint, Sepanik, & Smith, 2008). Taken together, the research to date suggests that student learning will not improve simply from the use of interim tests; if interim assessments are to be used to inform instruction, teachers must have the support of strong school leaders who help them focus on data-driven decisions in a "culture focused on strengthening instruction, professional learning, and collective responsibility for student success" (Blanc, Christman, Liu, Mitchell, Travers, & Bulkley, 2010, p. 206). Without this support, interim assessment seems to have limited influence on teacher practice and student learning, but with this support, interim assessment may be a good addition to a teacher's assessment toolkit.

Concerns and Possibilities

Format and Data. The research conducted on interim assessment foreshadows concerns that have been raised by researchers and educators. One concern widely discussed in the literature targets the format of these assessments and how the data are used. With increasing demand for interim tests, the concern is that cost and efficiency will lead to an overreliance on multiple-choice formats and assessments that can be quickly administered, scored, entered into databases, and returned to teachers (Perie et al., 2009). The risk in such a scenario is that there will be a tendency of interim test developers to focus on easily tested skills and lower level learning (Olson, 2005).

A related concern is that interim assessments, by their very nature and purpose, are too broad in scope, not timely with respect to what has been most recently taught, and unable to provide useful data about specific student needs. Just as with summative assessments, these assessments do not provide the level of specificity or support needed by teachers to move from results to instruction. These concerns about the instructional utility of interim assessment data resonate with the research findings on teachers' inability to use the results to modify instruction. Some experts have questioned whether the vast amounts of money being spent on interim assessments are worth it and others have suggested that resources might be better spent helping teachers learn formative assessment techniques, including using the information to intervene with students (Perie et al., 2009; Shepard, 2009).

Two suggestions have been proposed to address concerns about using data from interim tests to inform instruction. The first is that results should be supplemented with formative classroom assessment data and, if needed, more diagnostic data when making instructional decisions about individual students. Results of a study of an oral reading fluency assessment used with second-, fourth-, and sixth-grade students highlighted how this might work (Valencia, Smith, et al., 2010). The researchers found that 50% of the students who fell below the WCPM benchmark did not need additional instruction in either rate or accuracy, which are the two variables included in WCPM oral reading scores; rather, these students needed comprehension instruction. The researchers were able to discover this only through additional assessment and working directly with the students. In another study, researchers used think-aloud interviews with English learners to supplement information from an interim assessment (Valencia, Westover, Lucero, & Alvarez, 2010). During a rereading of the interim assessment passage, students talked with the researchers while they were processing the text, and afterward they responded to questions such as,

- What parts of this were easy for you?
- What parts were difficult?

- I noticed that you...[e.g., stopped and reread this line, skipped over]. Tell me more about what you did here?
- How is the way you read on this test similar or different from the way you read during silent reading?

The result of these interviews was a finer grained analysis of the students' strengths and needs, which led to more targeted instruction. Using supplemental data and engaging students in collaborative assessment mitigates the limitations of interim assessment to provide instructionally relevant, actionable data and allows teachers to use the interim assessment to target specific children for additional data gathering.

The second suggestion offered in the literature is that data from interim assessments should be used primarily for predictive and evaluative purposes. The thinking here is that interim assessments may help teachers and administrators identify students who may be at risk, and may help them identify general areas of strengths and weaknesses in school or district programs (Halverson, 2010; Shepard, 2009). That information is then used as the basis for grade-level, school, or district self-study. To ensure that data are used in productive, meaningful, and valid ways, teachers and administrators need to engage in regular opportunities to discuss data, ask questions, follow up on hunches, gather more data, and follow up on actions taken, all of which are essential to a cycle of improving instruction and student achievement (Boudett, City, & Murnane, 2005; Halverson, 2007, 2010; Valencia, 2007).

Impact on Teaching and Learning. A second concern about interim assessment is its potential to negatively impact both teaching and learning—the exact opposite of its intended purposes. The problem seems to be that because interim assessments are often mandated and used to monitor student progress and classroom instruction, they may exacerbate the well-documented problems associated with teaching to high-stakes tests (i.e., narrowly focusing instruction on just what is tested, practicing test formats, focusing on lower level skills; Shepard, 2008, Valencia, 2007). Instead of having a once-a-year summative test drive instruction, some worry that we will now have three or five of these mini–summative assessments driving it. If interim assessments are excellent models of the kind of rigorous and in-depth reading and thinking students should be doing throughout the year, then this concern is minimized. However, if assessments do not reflect higher level outcomes, then negative consequences are likely to result. A good example of this in reading is the dominance of oral reading fluency interim assessments. By some accounts, in 2007, more than two million students in 49 states had been given oral-reading tests, causing scholars to caution against growing classroom practices that target speed and accuracy at the possible cost of comprehension (Pearson, 2006; Pressley, Hilden, & Shankland, 2006; Samuels, 2007).

Low-Achieving Students. If interim assessments drive instruction, then another concern is how lower achieving students will fare. The problem is not about students' performance on the assessments; clearly, if students are reading substantially below grade level, then they would not be expected to score well on grade-level interim assessments. The problem results if teachers feel the need to instruct, drill, or have students practice with material that is not instructionally appropriate in an effort to try to improve their interim test scores. Running records provide a good example of how this concern might be mitigated or aggravated. In the best case, running records, used as interim assessments, would be administered to students at their appropriate instructional level. In addition, instead of simply recording a score or reading level, as might be required of an interim assessment, teachers would be supported to analyze the data more diagnostically, perhaps for a subgroup of students in their class, and use those data together with other formative assessment information to plan instruction. In the worst case, districts would mandate that running records be administered only at the grade level, resulting in little useful information, frustration, and wasted resources.

Conclusion

As the new assessment triad takes hold, and educators are inundated with more and more assessments, it will be important to keep in mind the different purposes and audiences for assessment. Perie and colleagues' (2009) visual (Figure 15.1) is a good reminder of how summative, interim, and formative assessment can contribute to an expanded understanding of our students and our own teaching. At the bottom of Figure 15.1, with the largest area, is formative assessment, which is the minute-to-minute, day-to-day work of contingency teaching, collaborative learning, and shared assessment with students. At the top, in the smallest area, is summative assessment, which is the annual assessment that shapes curriculum and communicates with external audiences but has relatively little to contribute to the detailed decision making and expert instruction necessary to move student learning forward. In the middle is the new, and unexplored, territory of interim assessments. Only time will tell if we can navigate this territory to make productive use of these assessments while holding firm to the power of formative classroom assessment. The best path seems to commit ourselves to assessment *for* learning and to a deeper understanding of the affordances and limitations of each type of assessment. Only then can we use assessment strategically to improve teaching and learning for all students.

Questions for Reflection

1. After reviewing the research-based features of formative assessment, identify two or three strategies that you might integrate into your classroom assessment and instruction routines.

2. With a colleague, make a list of the summative, interim, and formative assessments that you use or are used in your district or school. What are the purposes of each assessment, and how might you make the best use of each to enhance teaching and learning in your district, school, or classroom?

3. Sometimes students surprise us and perform better or worse on an assessment than we expected. If that were to happen to one of your students, how might you go about figuring out what contributed to the student's performance? In other words, what kinds of assessments and assessment strategies would you use to dig beneath a score to determine the student's strengths and needs?

4. The research has shown that although most teachers do not have difficulty interpreting the results of assessments, they sometimes have difficulty going to the next step of planning and implementing specific instructional strategies. Why do you think that happens? What might be most helpful to you as you think about this step?

5. If you could ask anyone a question about assessment and the link between it and instruction, who and what would you ask?

REFERENCES

Aaron, P.G., Joshi, M., & Williams, K.A. (1999). Not all reading disabilities are alike. *Journal of Learning Disabilities, 32*(2), 120–137. doi:10.1177/002221949903200203

Alexander, P.A. (2003). Profiling the developing reader: The interplay of knowledge, interest, and strategic processing. In C.M. Fairbanks, J. Worthy, B. Maloch, J.V. Hoffman, & D.L. Schallert (Eds.), *52nd yearbook of the National Reading Conference* (pp. 47–65). Oak Creek, WI: National Reading Conference.

Allington, R.L., & McGill-Franzen, A. (1992). Unintended effects of educational reform in New York. *Educational Policy, 6*(4), 397–414. doi:10.1177/0895904892006004003

Andrade, H.L. (2010). Students as the definitive source of formative assessment: Academic self-assessment and the self-regulation of learning. In H.L. Andrade & G.J. Cizek (Eds.), *Handbook of formative assessment* (pp. 90–105). New York: Routledge.

Baumann, J.F., & Stevenson, J.A. (1982). Understanding standardized reading achievement test scores. *The Reading Teacher, 35*(6), 648–654.

Bell, C., Steinberg, J., Wiliam, D., & Wylie, C. (2008, March). *Formative assessment and student achievement: Two years of implementation of the* Keeping Learning on Track program. Paper presented at the annual meeting of the National Council on Measurement in Education, New York.

Black, P., Harrison, C., Lee, C., Marshall, B., & Wiliam, D. (2004). Working inside the black box: Assessment for learning in the classroom. *Phi Delta Kappan, 86*(1), 8–21.

Black, P., & Wiliam, D. (1998a). Assessment and classroom learning. *Assessment in Education: Principles, Policy & Practice, 5*(1), 7–74.

Black, P., & Wiliam, D. (1998b). Inside the black box: Raising standards through classroom assessment. *Phi Delta Kappan, 80*(2), 139–148.

Black, P., & Wiliam, D. (2010). Kappan classic: A pleasant surprise. *Phi Delta Kappan, 92*(1), 47–48.

Blanc, S., Christman, J.B., Liu, R., Mitchell, C., Travers, E., & Bulkley, K.E. (2010). Learning to learn from data: Benchmarks and instructional communities. *Peabody Journal of Education, 85*(2), 202–225.

Bloom, B.S., Hastings, J.T., & Madaus, G.F. (Eds.). (1971). *Handbook on formative and summative evaluation of student learning.* New York: McGraw-Hill.

Boudett, K.P., City, E.A., & Murnane, R.J. (Eds.). (2005). *Data wise: A step-by-step guide to using assessment results to improve teaching and learning.* Cambridge, MA: Harvard Education Press.

Bracey, G.W. (2009). Our eternal (and futile?) quest for high standards. *Phi Delta Kappan, 91*(4), 75–76.

Brookhart, S.M. (2007). Expanding views about formative classroom assessment: A review of the literature. In J.H. McMillan (Ed.), *Formative classroom assessment: Theory into practice* (pp. 43–62). New York: Teachers College Press.

Bruce, B.C., Osborn, J., & Commeyras, M. (1994). The content and curricular validity of the 1992 NAEP reading framework. In R. Glaser, R. Linn, & G. Bohrnstedt (Eds.), *The trial state assessment: Prospects and realities: Background studies* (pp. 187–216). Stanford, CA: National Academy of Education.

Bulkley, K.E., Oláh, L.N., & Blanc, S. (2010). Introduction to the special issue on benchmarks for success? Interim assessments as a strategy for educational improvement. *Peabody Journal of Education, 85*(2), 115–124. doi:10.1080/01619561003673920

Buly, M.R., & Valencia, S.W. (2002). Below the bar: Profiles of students who fail state reading assessments. *Educational Evaluation and Policy Analysis, 24*(3), 219–239.

Carr, T.H., Brown, T.L., Vavrus, L.G., & Evans, M.A. (1990). Cognitive skill maps and cognitive skill profiles: Componential analysis of individual differences in children's reading efficiency. In T.H. Carr & B.A. Levy (Eds.), *Reading and its development: Component skills approaches* (pp. 1–55). San Diego, CA: Academic.

Connor, C.M., Morrison, F.J., & Katch, L.E. (2004). Beyond the reading wars: Exploring the effect of child–instruction interactions on growth in early reading. *Scientific Studies of Reading, 8*(4), 305–336. doi:10.1207/s1532799xssr0804_1

Connor, C.M., Morrison, F.J., & Petrella, J.N. (2004). Effective reading comprehension instruction: Examining child x instruction interactions. *Journal of Educational Psychology, 96*(4), 682–698. doi:10.1037/0022-0663.96.4.682

Crooks, T.J. (1988). The impact of classroom evaluation practices on students. *Review of Educational Research, 58*(4), 438–481.

Davis, F.B. (1944). Fundamental factors of comprehension in reading. *Psychometrika, 9*(3), 185–197. doi:10.1007/BF02288722

Deno, S.L. (1985). Curriculum-based measurement: The emerging alternative. *Exceptional Children, 52*(3), 219–232.

Deno, S.L. (2003). Developments in curriculum-based measurement. *The Journal of Special Education, 37*(3), 184–192. doi:10.1177/00224669030370030801

Deno, S.L., & Marston, D. (2006). Curriculum-based measurement of oral reading: An indicator of growth in fluency. In S.J. Samuels & A.E. Farstrup (Eds.), *What research has* to say about fluency instruction (pp. 179–203). Newark, DE: International Reading Association.

Educational Testing Service. (2009). *Research rationale for the Keeping Learning on Track' program*. Princeton, NJ: Author.

Fuchs, L.S., & Deno, S.L. (1994). Must instructionally useful performance assessment be based in the curriculum? *Exceptional Children, 16*(1), 15–24.

Goertz, M.E., Oláh, L.N., & Riggan, M. (2009, December). *Can interim assessments be used for instructional change?* (CPRE Policy Brief No. RB-51). Philadelphia: Consortium for Policy Research in Education.

Guthrie, J.T. (Ed.). (2008). *Engaging adolescents in reading*. Thousand Oaks, CA: Corwin.

Halverson, R. (2007). Distributed leadership perspective on how leaders use artifacts to create professional community in schools. In L. Stoll & K.S. Louis (Eds.), *Professional learning communities: Divergence, detail, and difficulties* (pp. 93–105). Maidenhead, UK: Open University Press.

Halverson, R. (2010). School formative feedback systems. *Peabody Journal of Education, 85*(2), 130–146. doi:10.1080/01619561003685270

Hattie, J., & Timperley, H. (2007). The power of feedback. *Review of Educational Research, 77*(1), 81–112. doi:10.3102/003465430298487

Henderson, S., Petrosino, A., Guckenburg, S., & Hamilton, S. (2008). *A second follow-up year for "Measuring how benchmark assessments affect student achievement"* (REL Technical Brief No. 002). Washington, DC: National Center for Education Evaluation and Regional Assistance, Institute of Education Sciences, U.S. Department of Education.

Heritage, M. (2010). *Formative assessment and next-generation assessment systems: Are we losing an opportunity?* Washington, DC: Council of Chief State School Officers.

Heritage, M., Kim, J., Vendlinski, T., & Herman, J. (2009). From evidence to action: A seamless process in formative assessment? *Educational Measurement: Issues and Practice, 28*(3), 24–31. doi:10.1111/j.1745-3992.2009.00151.x

Herman, J.L. (2010, April). *Next generation assessment systems: Toward coherence and utility*. Paper presented at the National Research Council's "Best practices for state assessment systems: Improving assessment while revisiting standards" workshop 1, Washington, DC. Retrieved January 24, 2011, from www7.nationalacademies.org/

bota/Best_Practices_for_State_Assessment _presentation_Herman.pdf

Hopkins, K.D. (1997). *Educational and psychological measurement and evaluation* (8th ed.). Boston: Allyn & Bacon.

Koretz, D. (2008). *Measuring up: What educational testing really tells us*. Cambridge, MA: Harvard University Press.

Leach, J.M., Scarborough, H.S., & Rescorla, L. (2003). Late-emerging reading disabilities. *Journal of Educational Psychology, 95*(2), 211–224. doi:10.1037/0022-0663.95.2.211

Linn, R.L. (1986). Educational testing and assessment: Research needs and policy issues. *American Psychologist, 41*(10), 1153–1160. doi:10.1037/0003-066X.41.10.1153

Linn, R.L. (2000). Assessments and accountability. *Educational Researcher, 29*(2), 4–16.

Marcotte, A.M., & Hintze, J.M. (2009). Incremental and predictive utility of formative assessment methods of reading comprehension. *Journal of School Psychology, 47*(5), 315–335. doi:10.1016/j.jsp.2009.04.003

Marion, S.F. (2009, December). *Changes in assessments and assessment systems since 2002*. Paper presented at the National Research Council's "Best practices for state assessment systems: Improving assessment while revisiting standards" workshop 1, Washington, DC. Retrieved September 20, 2010, from www7.nationalacademies.org/ bota/Scott%20Marion.pdf

Messick, S. (1989). Validity. In R.L. Linn (Ed.), *Educational measurement* (3rd ed., pp. 13–103). New York: Macmillan.

Militello, M., Schweid, J., & Sireci, S.G. (2010). Formative assessment systems: Evaluating the fit between school districts' needs and assessment systems' characteristics. *Educational Assessment, Evaluation and Accountability, 22*(1), 29–52. doi:10.1007/ s11092-010-9090-2

Moss, P.A. (1998). The role of consequences in validity theory. *Educational Measurement: Issues and Practice, 17*(2), 6–12. doi:10.1111/ j.1745-3992.1998.tb00826.x

Natriello, G. (1987). The impact of evaluation processes on students. *Educational Psychologist, 22*(2), 155–175. doi:10.1207/ s15326985ep2202_4

Nolen, S.B., Haladyna, T.M., & Haas, N.S. (1992). Uses and abuses of achievement test scores. *Educational Measurement: Issues and Practice, 11*(2), 9–15.

Oláh, L.N., Lawrence, N.R., & Riggan, M. (2010). Learning to learn from benchmark assessment data: How teachers analyze results. *Peabody Journal of Education, 85*(2), 226–245. doi:10.1080/01619561003688688

Olson, L. (2005). Benchmark assessments offer regular checkups on student achievement. *Education Week, 25*(13), 13–14.

Paris, S.G., Carpenter, R.D., Paris, A.H., & Hamilton, E.E. (2005). Spurious and genuine correlates of children's reading comprehension. In S.G. Paris & S.A. Stahl (Eds.), *Children's reading comprehension and assessment* (pp. 131–160). Mahwah, NJ: Erlbaum.

Pearson, P.D. (2006). Foreword. In K.S. Goodman (Ed.), *The truth about DIBELS: What it is, what it does* (pp. v–xix). Portsmouth, NH: Heinemann.

Perie, M., Marion, S., & Gong, B. (2009). Moving toward a comprehension assessment system: A framework for considering interim assessments. *Educational Measurement: Issues and Practice, 28*(3), 5–13. doi:10.1111/j.1745-3992.2009.00149.x

Popham, W.J. (2001). *The truth about testing: An educator's call to action.* Alexandria, VA: Association for Supervision and Curriculum Development.

Popham, W.J. (2008). Classroom assessment: Staying instructionally afloat in an ocean of accountability. In C.A. Dwyer (Ed.), *The future of assessment: Shaping, teaching, and learning* (pp. 263–278). Mahwah, NJ: Erlbaum.

Pressley, M., Hilden, K.R., & Shankland, R.K. (2006). *An evaluation of end-grade-3 Dynamic Indicators of Basic Early Literacy Skills (DIBELS): Speed reading without comprehension, predicting little.* East Lansing: Literacy Achievement Research Center, Michigan State University.

Quint, J.C., Sepanik, S., & Smith, J.K. (2008). *Using student data to improve teaching and learning: Findings from an evaluation of the Formative Assessments of Student Thinking in Reading (FAST-R) program in Boston elementary schools.* New York: MDRC.

Ross, J.A. (2004). Effects of running records assessment on early literacy achievement. *The Journal of Educational Research, 97*(4), 186–195. doi:10.3200/JOER.97.4.186-195

Rupp, A.A., & Lesaux, N.K. (2006). Meeting expectations? An empirical investigation of a standards-based assessment of reading comprehension. *Educational Evaluation and Policy Analysis, 28*(4), 315–333. doi:10.3102/01623737028004315

Samuels, S.J. (2007). The DIBELS tests: Is speed of barking at print what we mean by reading fluency? *Reading Research Quarterly, 42*(4), 563–566.

Scriven, M. (1967). The methodology of evaluation. In R.W. Tyler, R.M. Gagné, & M. Scriven (Eds.), *Perspectives of curriculum evaluation* (pp. 39–83). Chicago: Rand McNally.

Sharkey, N.S., & Murnane, R.J. (2003). Learning from student assessment results. *Educational Leadership, 61*(3), 77–81.

Sharkey, N.S., & Murnane, R.J. (2006). Tough choices in designing a formative assessment system. *American Journal of Education, 112*(4), 572–588.

Sharp, D. (2004). *Supporting teachers' data-driven instructional conversations: An environmental scan of Reading First and STEP literacy assessments, data visualizations, and assumptions about conversations that matter: Report to the Information Infrastructure System Project.* Chicago: John D. and Catherine T. MacArthur Foundation; Menlo Park, CA: William and Flora Hewlett Foundation.

Shavelson, R.J., Young, D.B., Ayala, C.C., Brandon, P.R., Furtak, E.M., Ruiz-Primo, M.A., et al. (2008). On the impact of curriculum-embedded formative assessment on learning: A collaboration between curriculum and assessment developers. *Applied Measurement in Education, 21*(4), 295–314. doi:10.1080/08957340802347647

Shepard, L.A. (2000). The role of assessment in a learning culture. *Educational Researcher, 29*(7), 4–14.

Shepard, L.A. (2008). Formative assessment: Caveat emptor. In C.A. Dwyer (Ed.), *The future of assessment: Shaping, teaching, and learning* (pp. 279–303). Mahwah, NJ: Erlbaum.

Shepard, L.A. (2009). Commentary: Evaluating the validity of formative and interim assessment. *Educational Measurement: Issues and Practice, 28*(3), 32–37. doi:10.1111/j.1745-3992.2009.00152.x

Shepard, L.A. (2010). What the marketplace has brought us: Item-by-item teaching with little instructional insight. *Peabody Journal of Education, 85*(2), 246–257. doi:10.1080/01619561003708445

Shulman, L.S. (1987). Knowledge and teaching: Foundations of the new reform. *Harvard Educational Review, 57*(1), 1–22.

Spear-Swerling, L. (2004). A road map for understanding reading disability and other reading problems: Origins, prevention, and intervention. In R.B. Ruddell & N.J. Unrau (Eds.), *Theoretical models and processes of reading* (5th ed., pp. 517–573). Newark, DE: International Reading Association.

Stecker, P.M., Fuchs, L.S., & Fuchs, D. (2005). Using curriculum-based measurement to improve student achievement: Review of research. *Psychology in the Schools, 42*(8), 795–819. doi:10.1002/pits.20113

Stiggins, R.J. (2002). Assessment crisis: The absence of assessment FOR learning. *Phi Delta Kappan, 83*(10), 758–765.

Stringfield, S., Wayman, J.C., & Yakimowski-Srebnick, M.E. (2005). Scaling up data use in classrooms, schools, and districts. In C. Dede, J.P. Honan, & L.C. Peters (Eds.), *Scaling up success: Lessons learned from technology-based educational improvement* (pp. 133–152). San Francisco: Jossey-Bass.

Taboada, A., Tonks, S.M., Wigfield, A., & Guthrie, J.T. (2009). Effects of motivational and cognitive variables on reading comprehension. *Reading and Writing, 22*(1), 85–106.

Tierney, R.J., Carter, M.A., & Desai, L.E. (1991). *Portfolio assessment in the reading-writing classroom.* Norwood, MA: Christopher-Gordon.

U.S. Government Accounting Office. (2009). *No Child Left Behind Act: Enhancements in the Department of Education's review process could improve state academic assessments* (GAO-09-911). Washington, DC: Author. Retrieved January 24, 2011, from www.gao.gov/new.items/d09911.pdf

Valencia, S.W. (1998). *Literacy portfolios in action.* Fort Worth, TX: Harcourt Brace.

Valencia, S.W. (2007). Inquiry-oriented assessment. In J.R. Paratore & R.L. McCormack (Eds.), *Classroom literacy assessment: Making sense of what students know and do* (pp. 3–20). New York: Guilford.

Valencia, S.W., Smith, A.T., Reece, A.M., Li, M., Wixson, K.K., & Newman, H. (2010). Oral reading fluency assessment: Issues of construct, criterion, and consequential validity.

Reading Research Quarterly, 45(3), 270–291. doi:10.1598/RRQ.45.3.1

Valencia, S.W., Westover, A., Lucero, A., & Alvarez, L. (2010, May). *Reading comprehension challenges of English-language learners.* Paper presented at the annual conference of the American Educational Research Association, Denver, CO.

Valencia, S.W., & Wixson, K.K. (2000). Policy-oriented research on literacy standards and assessment. In M.L. Kamil, P.B. Mosenthal, P.D. Pearson, & R. Barr (Eds.), *Handbook of reading research* (Vol. 3, pp. 909–935). Mahwah, NJ: Erlbaum.

Valencia, S.W., & Wixson, K.K. (2001). Inside English/language arts standards: What's in a grade? *Reading Research Quarterly, 36*(2), 202–217. doi:10.1598/RRQ.36.2.5

Wiliam, D. (2006, September). *Assessment for learning: Why, what and how.* Paper presented at the Cambridge Assessment Network conference, Cambridge, England. Retrieved November 22, 2010, from web.me.com/dylanwiliam/Dylan_Wiliams_website/Papers_04-10.html

Wiliam, D. (2007). Changing classroom practice. *Educational Leadership, 65*(4), 36–42.

Wiliam, D. (2010). An integrative summary of the research literature and implications for a new theory of formative assessment. In H.L. Andrade & G.J. Cizek (Eds.), *Handbook of formative assessment* (pp. 18–40). New York: Routledge.

Wiliam, D., Lee, C., Harrison, C., & Black, P. (2004). Teachers developing assessment for learning: Impact on student achievement. *Assessment in Education: Principals. Assessment in Education: Principles, Policy & Practice, 11*(1), 49–65.

Wiliam, D., & Thompson, M. (2008). Integrating assessment and learning: What will it take to make it work? In C.A. Dwyer (Ed.), *The future of assessment: Shaping, teaching, and learning* (pp. 53–82). Mahwah, NJ: Erlbaum.

Wolf, D.P. (1989). Portfolio assessment: Sampling student work. *Educational Leadership, 46*(7), 35–39.

Chapter 16

Parents and Reading: What Teachers Should Know About Ways to Support Productive Home–School Environments

Jeanne R. Paratore

Engaging parents in their children's learning is widely considered to be an important strategy in improving children's achievement. Studies indicate that children whose parents are involved in their learning have higher rates of attendance, higher levels of academic achievement on both teacher-made measures and large-scale assessments, lower rates of retention, and higher rates of postsecondary education (e.g., Baker & Soden, 1997; Dearing, Kreider, Simpkins, & Weiss, 2006; Fan, 2001; Fan & Chen, 2001; Henderson & Berla, 1994; Henderson & Mapp, 2002). Moreover, although parent involvement is thought to be helpful for all students, studies indicate that, for parents with less education, involvement in their children's learning is of even greater importance for later academic achievement (Dearing, McCartney, Weiss, Kreider, & Simpkins, 2004; Domina, 2005; Lopez, Barrueco, Feinauer, & Miles, 2007).

However, recent studies have underscored the complexity of getting parent involvement programs "right." In a review of 41 studies, Mattingly, Prislan, McKenzie, Rodriguez, and Kayzar (2002) found that when the content of such programs is broadly defined, the results are mixed; they concluded that there is little empirical support for the claim that parent involvement programs are an important instructional intervention. White, Taylor, and Moss (1992) reviewed evidence used to support a conclusion that parent involvement is important in early intervention programs. Based on a series of analyses of different types of studies, they found that "the benefits of involving parents in early intervention programs, at least in the way parents have been involved heretofore, are nonexistent or very small" (p. 118). White et al. acknowledged, however, that because of the methodological flaws in the studies reviewed, their finding was primarily

What Research Has to Say About Reading Instruction (4th ed.) edited by S. Jay Samuels and Alan E. Farstrup.
© 2011 by the International Reading Association.

a characterization of the state of rigorous studies, rather than a conclusion about the effectiveness of parent involvement. In another example, St. Pierre, Ricciuti, and Rimdzius (2005) found little empirical support favoring families who participated in Even Start programs, the United States' largest, federally funded, family literacy initiative. Their findings led to the defunding of Even Start in the 2009 U.S. Department of Education budget. Other studies, though, dispute this evidence and suggest that the issue isn't *whether* parents are involved, but *how* (e.g., Paratore & Yaden, 2011; Sénéchal & Young, 2008; Sheldon & Epstein, 2005).

The purpose of this chapter is to review and summarize studies that help us understand the effects of parent involvement in children's literacy development and the types of programs that are likely to yield positive literacy outcomes. The evidence can then be used to guide teachers, administrators, and policymakers in the design and implementation of parent involvement initiatives that have a high likelihood of improving and increasing students' opportunities to learn and, in turn, their literacy achievement.

Is There Support for the Claim That Parent Involvement Matters?

To understand the effects of parent involvement on children's school achievement, in preparing this chapter I turned first to a meta-analysis of studies in this area. Fan and Chen (2001) identified 25 investigations (with a total sample size of about 133,500) that fit study criteria—that is, they included Pearson correlations between any parent involvement indicator and any achievement outcome variable. From these, they collected 92 correlation coefficients. The researchers coded each study for type of parent involvement (e.g., parent–child involvement, home supervision, educational aspiration for children, school contact and participation), achievement outcome variables (e.g., overall grades, test scores, grade promotion or retention), and study features (e.g., sample size, age, participant ethnicity, areas of academic achievement, measure of academic achievement). Results indicated a small to moderate relationship between parent involvement and student achievement, with an overall effect size of about 0.25.

However, Fan and Chen's (2001) findings also suggested the complexity of the issue. They found a strong relationship with parents' aspiration and expectation for children's academic achievement, but a weak relationship with parents' supervision of children at home (defined as rules for TV viewing, doing school work, etc.). They also found a stronger relationship when the area of academic achievement was broadly defined (e.g., grades in several academic areas) than specifically focused (e.g., math, science), and they found that ethnicity and age had very small effects on the interaction between the variables.

To present the findings in "practical terms" (p. 16), Fan and Chen (2001) explained that "a correlation coefficient of .30 between the two variables [i.e., parental involvement and student achievement] translates into increasing the success rate of academic achievement by 30%.... Put in this perspective, the findings of this meta-analysis make a good case for the positive influence of parental involvement on students' academic achievement" (pp. 16–17).

I next turned to studies that examined the effects of parent involvement on populations that often experience low rates of academic success. Jeynes (2003) identified 26 studies that examined effects of parent involvement on minority children's academic achievement, 20 of which (representing a total of 12,000 students) had sufficient quantitative data to include in his meta-analysis. Studies were coded according to the particular type of parent involvement (i.e., communication with children about school, checking homework, having high expectations for children's school success, encouraging children to read outside of school, attending school meetings, having household rules about school vs. leisure activities, having a warm and supportive parenting style), by racial group (African American, Asian American, Latino), and by outcome measure (academic achievement, grades, standardized tests, and such things as teacher rating scales and behavior or attitude indexes).

Analyses yielded an overall finding that parental involvement had a positive effect on the academic achievement of the minority groups studied. Effect sizes for each of the ethnic groups varied only slightly, ranging between 0.43 and 0.48. The relationship between parent involvement and the "Other Measures" outcome (consisting primarily of teacher ratings and available only for studies with mostly African American students) yielded the largest effect size (0.62), but all measures yielded statistically significant correlation coefficients. Jeynes (2003) speculated that teacher ratings are likely influenced by perceptions of the child's (and, by extension, the child's family's) overall cooperation and are therefore highly susceptible to change based on teacher perceptions of the level of family involvement.

Further evidence of a relationship between parent involvement and the achievement of minority students can be drawn from the work of

Dearing et al. (2004). They examined the relationship between family involvement during kindergarten and children's attitudes toward literacy and literacy achievement in kindergarten through fifth grade. With a sample of 167 children from low-income families selected for ethnic (African American, Latino, Caucasian) and geographic (urban and rural) diversity, they found that family involvement during the children's kindergarten years had "stable, promotive effects" (p. 457) on the literacy performance for all children throughout the elementary years, with the strongest effects noted for children of less educated mothers. Moreover, high levels of family involvement correlated with more positive feelings about literacy—which, in turn, correlated with higher literacy achievement. Motivational effects were again greatest for children of less educated mothers. This is especially noteworthy because in kindergarten, the children of low-education mothers had the least positive feelings about literacy, suggesting that parent involvement worked in both a compensatory and facilitative fashion.

A review by Gonzalez-DeHass, Willems, and Doan Holbein (2005) provides additional insight into the relationship between parent involvement and students' attitudes and motivation. They reviewed 13 studies that varied widely in sample size (from 10 to 6,400), student grade level (kindergarten to 12th), definitions of parent involvement (e.g., parenting style, knowledge of classroom procedures and practices, homework help, parent–teacher communication), and outcome measures (e.g., child self-report, teacher report, observations of reading behaviors). They found a consistently positive relationship between parent involvement and outcome variables and concluded that parent involvement correlates with greater interest in learning, greater self-efficacy, greater persistence in challenging situations, and greater satisfaction with school work.

Yet other studies have specified the relationship between parent involvement and the particular targeted academic area. In response to the finding of Mattingly et al. (2002) that parent involvement has little or no effect on student achievement, Sheldon and Epstein (2005) returned to the universe of 41 studies examined in the earlier study. They identified those with a sample size of more than two students that focused on parent involvement in reading and language arts activities. Of the 16 studies that fit those criteria, 15 indicated that significant gains in students' reading or language achievement test scores had been noted. Sheldon and Epstein argued that the negative findings reported by Mattingly et al. were the result of an analysis that was overly broad in its definition of parent involvement. They concluded that "if parent involvement programs were designed to involve families with reading or language arts skills, then students' achievement would improve in those subjects" (p. 109).

So, is there support for a claim that parent involvement matters? The combined results of these meta-analytic studies and critical literature reviews indicate that the answer is yes. There is a clear relationship between parent involvement programs and children's school success, and this has been noted specifically in targeted academic area is reading and language arts. Moreover, this relationship holds across different ethnic and income groups, different grades and ages, and among parents of differing levels of education.

These positive results notwithstanding, the failure to document positive outcomes of large-scale programs such as Even Start indicates that although such programs have the potential to succeed, many do fail. So the next question that must be answered relates to the particular features of effective programs.

What Are the Characteristics of Effective Parent Involvement Programs?

Effective parent involvement initiatives grow out of three fundamental elements: a sound process, important content, and an appropriate context. In this section, I will address research related to each.

The Process of Parent Involvement

More than 15 years ago, Hoover-Dempsey and Sandler (1995) argued that promoting and supporting parent involvement requires understanding the process. Over the years, they have refined the model, and the current iteration (Hoover-Dempsey & Whitaker, 2010) describes the parent involvement process as one in which parents move through five levels. The first three are grounded in an understanding of parents' motivation to become involved, an awareness of the forms for involvement (e.g., conveying values and aspirations, supporting children's schoolwork at home, communication with teachers or school, involvement at school), and knowing the mechanisms of involvement (e.g., encouragement, modeling, reinforcement, instruction). The last two levels are focused on student outcomes: academic self-efficacy, motivation to learn, self-regulation, ways to relate to teachers, and overall student achievement.

The first level, motivation, is, of course, fundamental to each subsequent stage. It has been widely studied and the resulting evidence is especially instructive. Hoover-Dempsey et al., (2005) described motivation as having two parts: role construction (i.e., parents' beliefs about what they *should do* to support their children's learning) and self-efficacy (i.e., parents' beliefs about what they *are capable of doing*). There is sound evidence that parents' personal experiences with schooling and aspirations for themselves and for their children shape their beliefs about the ways they should support their children's learning (e.g., Chrispeels & Rivero, 2001; DeGaetano, 2007; Smrekar & Cohen-Vogel, 2001; Souto-Manning & Swick, 2006). But of critical importance is evidence that beliefs are also socially constructed, and as such they are potentially influenced by input from various social groups—other parents, community leaders, and perhaps most important, teachers.

Sheldon's (2003) work is especially persuasive in relation to the role that the school and teacher play in parent involvement. In a study of parent involvement in a large, high-poverty, urban school system, regression analyses controlling for other school-related factors indicated a clear relationship between the schools' outreach efforts and children's achievement on the state test: Students attending schools with excellent outreach outperformed their peers in schools with less outreach. Sheldon explained,

> This aspect of partnership program development is not easy to achieve. Schools need to go beyond establishing the "basics" of a partnership program to recognize and address obstacles to family and community involvement to improve students' learning and academic achievement. Some of the challenges schools face in trying to increase involvement include providing information about the school and students' progress to family members who do not speak or read English well and finding ways for parents who cannot visit the school to help their children at home. (p. 161)

Conceiving and implementing the outreach strategies that will effectively overcome the challenges Sheldon (2003) outlines is not part of the standard repertoire of many teachers. Epstein (2001) reported that, although advances have been made in recent years, in general, teacher education programs pay scant attention to issues of parent involvement. In a survey of first-year teachers (National Comprehensive Center for Teacher Quality & Public Agenda, 2007), just over half (51%) of respondents reported that their teacher education program prepared them to work with families and communities. The lack of understanding about parents and strategies for parent involvement is evident in teacher practices. A stereotype of low-income and minority parents as disengaged and disinterested in their children's education persists despite evidence to the contrary (e.g., Allen, 2007; Compton-Lilly, 2003, 2007; DeGaetano, 2007; Edwards, 1999).

Related to improving teacher understanding is development of awareness of the forms of parent involvement that are especially consequential, and perhaps a rethinking and reshaping of our understanding of the types of parent involvement that make a difference. Epstein (2001) described parent involvement as including six types: parenting, communicating, volunteering, learning at home, decision making, and collaborating with the community. She explained that each type is associated with different practices, presents different challenges, and is likely to lead to different results. Effective parent involvement requires a clear understanding of the purpose and the desired outcome. However, parents may be predisposed to some forms of involvement. For example, many Latino parents perceive their roles and responsibilities related to children's education to center around fulfilling children's basic needs (e.g., Delgado-Gaitan, 1996; Valdés, 1996; Vasquez, Pease-Alvarez, & Shannon, 1994). They explain that their responsibility is to make sure children are well nourished, clean, and rested, and that they act respectfully toward teachers. These actions fit the category of Parenting, Type 1, in Epstein's (2001) typology.

In another example, Lapp, Fisher, Flood, and Moore (2002) studied the perceptions and understandings of parents in a high-poverty, ethnically diverse school system who were described by teachers as being uninvolved. In results similar to those in studies of Latino parents, these parents perceived their responsibilities as those primarily related to what Epstein (2001) defined as Parenting. In addition, they drew a sharp difference between their responsibilities and those of the teachers. They emphatically believed that they should not "teach" their children about reading and writing. In the words of one parent, "I don't want to teach him wrong. I know the teacher can do it right" (Lapp et al., p. 280). Some parents noted their discomfort with requests to help children with homework: "I'm not sure I get it all right in English" (p. 280). Yet another challenge was lack of resources: Some noted lack of space where children could quietly complete homework; others commented on lack of books for shared reading. And, as the work of Neuman and Celano (2001) demonstrates, we cannot assume that a paucity of books at home can be resolved through a visit to a local library. As they reported, libraries in "low-income communities had smaller overall collections, fewer books per child, and more limited nighttime hours than those in the middle-income communities" (p. 22).

In their study of successful urban schools in which parents were perceived to be highly involved, Ingram, Wolfe, and Lieberman (2007) found the most common practices were those that fit Epstein's (2001) Parenting or Learning at Home categories. The researchers speculated that the high emphasis placed on parenting and learning at home could be attributed to parents' familiarity and comfort with these types of activities and, that in contexts in which parents are less involved, these might represent appropriate starting points for parent involvement. They also found types of involvement that parents rarely engaged in: communicating with teachers; volunteering in their children's school or classroom; participating in school decision making; and collaborating with community members as a strategy for supporting their children's education. Ingram et al. noted that although these are commonly considered important indicators of family involvement, they may not be appropriate in all contexts. Families in which parents work for long hours or have substantial childcare responsibilities are unlikely candidates for school volunteering or even attendance at routine school or community meetings and events.

The second part of motivation is self-efficacy—essentially a belief that actions taken will lead to desired outcomes (Bandura, 1997; Hoover-Dempsey et al., 2005)—and this likely interacts with the third level specified by Hoover-Dempsey and Whitaker (2010): learning mechanisms engaged by parents (e.g., encouragement, modeling, reinforcement instruction). Here again, teachers have tremendous power in helping parents develop self-efficacy. Chrispeels and Rivero (2001) found that in high-quality parent involvement programs in which parents were explicitly taught how to undertake activities that supported their children's learning, parents gained new information, and they used what they learned both at home (e.g., monitoring homework, limiting television viewing, praising their children for academic accomplishments) and at school (e.g., initiating more teacher contacts, asking specific questions, advocating for their children).

The Content of Parent Involvement

As previously noted, parent involvement activities that are subject specific typically result in greater academic learning outcomes for children (Henderson & Mapp, 2002; Sheldon & Epstein, 2005). Moreover, in the case of literacy, a recent meta-analysis by Sénéchal and Young (2008) indicated that particular types of home literacy interventions benefit children differentially. Sénéchal and Young identified 16 studies (representing

1,340 families) that tested effects of parent involvement on children's literacy learning (and also met other inclusion criteria). Using meta-analytic techniques, they calculated a mean weighted effect size of 0.65, which they explained "would correspond to a 10-point gain on a standardized test (with a standard deviation of 15) for the intervention children as compared to the control children" (p. 889). However, Sénéchal and Young also noted the large variability in the effect sizes across studies (0.07 to 2.02), and they speculated that particular types of interventions might explain the differences. To test this hypothesis, they classified interventions into three categories: parents read to child, parents listen to child read books, and parents tutor specific literacy skills (e.g., activities for alphabet naming, letter–sound association, word or sentence reading). Tutoring children in specific literacy activities (seven studies) resulted in the most positive outcomes, yielding an effect size of 1.15. Listening to children read books (six studies) yielded an effect size of 0.52, a significant outcome, but also significantly less effective than tutoring. Reading to children (three studies) yielded an effect size of 0.18, indicating small or no effect. Further analyses indicated that effect sizes did not vary according to length of intervention or inclusion of supportive feedback, nor did effects vary according to age of children (kindergarten or grades 1–3), children's reading facility (above or below grade level), or family background (working, middle, or high economic class).

Sénéchal and Young's (2008) outcomes related to the positive effects of parents' direct teaching of emergent and early literacy skills are largely consistent with other studies (Baker, Fernandez-Fein, Scher, & Williams, 1998; Sénéchal, 1997; Sénéchal & LeFevre, 2002; Sénéchal, LeFevre, Thomas, & Daley, 1998); their finding of positive effects of parents' listening to children read is also validated by previous work (e.g., Hindin & Paratore, 2007; Toomey, 1993). However, the finding that parents reading to children has little or no effect on children's reading achievement differed from the findings of two previous meta-analyses (Bus, van IJzendoorn, & Pellegrini, 1995; Scarborough & Dobrich, 1994), both of which yielded evidence of positive, significant effects of storybook reading on children's language and reading achievement. Although these analyses yielded effect sizes that differed in strength (for further discussion, see Bus et al., 1995; Dunning, Mason, & Stewart, 1994; Paratore, Cassano, & Schickedanz, 2011; van Kleeck, Stahl, & Bauer, 2003), for the most part, there is convergence around a conclusion that parents reading to children positively affects preschool literacy and language development—but to a smaller degree than previously thought, partially because the process of shared book reading is more complex than generally assumed (van Kleeck et al.; Yaden, 2003).

The complexity of parent–child book reading resides in interactions and relationships among an array of factors. For example, children's interest and engagement in book reading relates to the degree of mother–child bonding and social-emotional qualities of the parent–child interaction (Bus, 2003). Children's engagement and subsequent learning also relates to the ways parents read. For example, dialogic reading (i.e., engaging children in questioning and conversation about illustrations, events, and interesting words) has positive effects on preschool children's language and emergent literacy development (Zevenbergen & Whitehurst, 2003), and these effects are evident in both typically developing and language-delayed preschoolers (Crain-Thoreson & Dale, 1999; Dale, Crain-Thoreson, Notari-Syverson, & Cole, 1996). Further, not only does parent–child dialogue matter, but the type or style of dialogue (i.e., parent acting as describer or as comprehender) also has differential effects, and these effects vary in relation to children's levels of vocabulary knowledge (Reese, Cox, Harte, & McAnally, 2003). In addition, what children take away from the read-aloud varies in relation to the overall responsiveness of parent to child and the extent to which the parent successfully follows the child's lead to facilitate her or his meaning construction (Yaden, 2003). Quality and quantity of parent talk during book reading also relates to children's performance on measures of vocabulary, comprehension, and emergent literacy (e.g., DeTemple & Snow, 2003), and, in turn, the types of books parents read (i.e., ABC, concept books, narrative, or exposition) influence acquisition of letter name, letter sound, and word knowledge (Baker et al., 1998; Stahl, 2003), as well as the nature of parent talk (e.g., vocabulary sophistication, syntactical complexity, and amount; see Price, van Kleeck, & Huberty, 2009; Tabors, Beals, & Weizman, 2001).

The task of determining which types of activities are more or less beneficial to children's literacy learning is further complicated by the developmental nature of literacy acquisition. That is, literacy achievement in the early years is primarily dependent on what Paris (2005) has called "constrained skills" (p. 184)—skills such as phonemic awareness and phonics that are well defined and limited in scope and, as such, can be taught and learned in a relatively brief time. In contrast, reading development in the later years is largely dependent on vocabulary knowledge and comprehension abilities, referred to by Paris as "unconstrained skills" (p. 184) because they are both broader in nature and also never completely mastered. Vocabulary knowledge continues to grow throughout the school years and beyond, and comprehension skills and strategies are refined as texts become linguistically and conceptually more complex. Moreover, the acquisition of these different types of skill knowledge is not linear—that is, students do not first acquire skills necessary to decode and subsequently acquire skills and concepts necessary to comprehend. Rather, studies indicate that the vocabulary, conceptual, and narrative knowledge that children acquire in prekindergarten and kindergarten accounts for a substantial amount (88%) of the variance in such knowledge in grades 1 and 2 (Whitehurst & Lonigan, 2002). So, although phonemic awareness has been widely documented as the strongest predictor of first-grade reading achievement (National Institute of Child Health and Human Development, 2000) and as a result has become a dominant part of the curriculum in many early childhood interventions for both home and school activities, Whitehurst and Lonigan cautioned that "interventions that hope to impact outside-in skills such as vocabulary and knowledge of narrative structure need to occur early in the preschool period if they are to have later effects" (p. 22) on children's reading achievement.

The Context of Parent Involvement

In their analysis of effective parent involvement programs, Paratore and Yaden (2011) noted that such programs shared not only a common focus on important literacy content but also allotted time to explain, model, and guide parents in implementation of the types of literacy events and interactions that prepare children for success in school. By so doing these programs support the development of parents' self-efficacy that Hoover-Dempsey et al. (2005) described as a critical component of effective home–school partnerships. (For detailed descriptions of effective programs, see, e.g., Jordan, Snow, & Porche, 2000; Lapp, 2010; Paratore, Krol-Sinclair, David, & Schick, 2010; Rodriguez-Brown, 2010; Yaden, Madrigal, & Tam, 2003.) Moreover, Paratore and Yaden reported that in effective programs, literacy events were embedded in engaging, high-quality texts and in motivating, interesting, and playful games and activities, often within contexts that were of social importance for family members. This, too, is consistent with the emphasis that Hoover-Dempsey and Whitaker (2010) placed on attention to "life context variables" as part of parental motivation. Further, it is consistent with research on the importance of having books and texts that are worthy of parents' and children's time and that are likely to prompt meaningful and important conversations over books (Roser, 2010). Finally, Paratore and Yaden noted that effective programs commonly grounded the work in parents' existing knowledge and skills, establishing a pathway to new knowledge by building on familiar routines and events. This, too, is consistent with Hoover-Dempsey and Whitaker's process of supporting and developing parental self-efficacy and parental knowledge and skills.

To summarize, effective parent involvement initiatives share three important characteristics:

- First, they consider and respond to parents' motivation for involvement and parents' knowledge of how to be effectively involved. In so doing, they emphasize outreach efforts that will help parents to overcome the particular challenges that stand in the way of involvement, and they emphasize the types of involvement that are known to be consequential in children's academic learning.

- Second, they establish a clear relationship between focal content and desired outcomes.

- Third, they situate parent–child interactions within rich literature and socially important, practical, and meaningful reading and writing contexts.

What Are the Implications for Teachers, Administrators, and Policymakers?

There is ample evidence that parent involvement initiatives that build on the components of effective programs meet with noteworthy success, and positive effects include both higher levels of student achievement and greater motivation and interest in learning. Further, the effectiveness of such programs is not related to race, ethnicity, income, English language proficiency, or parent education. In fact, when effectively designed and implemented, children of low-education mothers achieve the greatest benefits. Moreover, effective parent involvement initiatives in children's early school years show sustained effects into later elementary grades.

Those familiar with Even Start programs may question these findings, arguing that Even Start met requisite characteristics and yet failed to show effectiveness. However, a close examination of the specific activities described as part of Even Start programs provides an explanation. According to St. Pierre et al. (2003), among the projects studied in the third national Even Start evaluation, parent–child activities varied widely. They included arts and crafts, making toys or books, making food or play materials, playing active games, story reading, group singing, and at times volunteering in their child's classroom. In some projects, parents were taught how to use a toy or game at home, how to support children's language development, and how to read to their children. Although the amount of time spent on particular literacy activities was undocumented, the range in types of activities suggests a lack of intensive focus on parent–child literacy interactions. In instances when projects described weekly routines, only one to two of the five days of the week focused on parent–child literacy interactions.

The subsequent failure and defunding of Even Start may be useful as a cautionary tale: The task of developing and implementing productive parent involvement programs is complex and multifaceted. Implementations that sample many different activities without sufficient intensity on those that support the desired outcomes invite failure. Such implementations are unacceptable not because they risk squandering educational resources (although they do), but rather because they risk failure to deliver on a promise to parents and children that as educators, we can be depended on to act in their best interests.

Based on evidence of effective home–school partnerships, the development and implementation of parent involvement initiatives that can be predicted to make a difference should be guided by the following:

- Effective programs show evidence of an understanding of a theoretically and empirically grounded parent involvement process (Hoover-Dempsey & Sandler, 1995; Hoover-Dempsey et al., 2005; Hoover-Dempsey & Whitaker, 2010). This process includes an understanding of parents' motivation to become involved, an awareness of the forms for involvement (e.g., conveying values and aspirations, supporting children's schoolwork at home, communication with teachers or school, involvement at school), and knowing the mechanisms of involvement (e.g., encouragement, modeling, reinforcement, instruction). It also addresses student outcomes, including academic self-efficacy, motivation to learn, self-regulation, ways to relate to teachers, and overall student achievement.

- Effective programs include exemplary outreach efforts that help parents overcome the challenges that often work against their participation. These efforts may include, in part, a rethinking of such things as school-based meetings and workshops, volunteer activities, and other traditional forms of parent involvement.

- Effective programs are based on an understanding of the short- and long-term effects of focal activities; in turn, focal activities are thoroughly aligned with this understanding. In the early grades, a focus on specific code-related skills will support early literacy achievement, but by itself, this may have little influence on achievement after first grade. Across grade levels, a focus on listening to children read will support children's development of word-reading accuracy and fluency but may have little influence on development of vocabulary and concept knowledge. A focus on reading aloud to children beginning in early childhood will support acquisition of vocabulary, language, and concept knowledge that will, in turn, support children's comprehension in grade 2 and beyond.

- Initiatives that are designed to support parent–child book reading require attention to the multiple facets of productive reading interactions, including parents' read-aloud and interaction styles, and an understanding of the types and quantity of interactions that different book genres and topics are likely to prompt.

- Effective programs not only focus on important literacy content, but they also support parents' self-efficacy by allocating time to explain, model, and guide parents in implementation of the types of literacy events and interactions that prepare children for success in school.

- Effective parent involvement programs embed literacy events in engaging, high-quality texts and in motivating, interesting, and playful games and activities, within contexts that are of social importance for family members.

- Effective programs embed their work within parents' existing knowledge and skills, establishing a pathway to new knowledge by building on familiar routines and events.

- Many teacher education programs provide inadequate preparation related to parent involvement. Professional development through which teachers can develop the requisite understandings may be required to ensure effective home–school partnerships.

In closing, the words of Joyce Epstein (2001) effectively and eloquently capture the ever-present role that parents have in their children's learning lives, and the undeniable need that we, as teachers, have to build effective home-school partnerships:

However configured, however constrained, families come with their children to school. Even when they do not come in person, families come in children's minds and hearts and in their hopes and dreams. They come with the children's problems and promise. Without exception, teachers and administrators have explicit or implicit contact with their students' families every day. (p. 4)

I hope that in this chapter, I have provided a clear pathway toward developing understandings such that parents will "come to school" in ways that are productive and supportive as they strive to help their children become successful readers and writers.

Questions for Reflection

1. Consider the parents of children in your classroom or school district and the challenges that might work against their participation in their children's school learning. What types of outreach efforts might you implement to help parents overcome these obstacles?

2. Describe a literacy event or activity that you would like parents and their children to engage in together at home. What procedures will you use to coach parents toward effective implementation?

3. Interview a principal and two or three teachers from the same school about their home–school partnership initiatives. In what ways are these practices aligned with the evidence about effective partnerships? Based on your understanding of the evidence, are there refinements you would recommend to increase the likelihood that these activities and interactions will contribute to children's reading and writing success?

4. Conduct one or two home visits for the purpose of finding out what the families know about literacy, what they do, and how they do it. Consider what you learn in light of the classroom literacy curriculum and related instruction. How might you use the information collected during the home visit as a pathway to introducing parents and children to new knowledge or new literacy routines?

REFERENCES

Allen, J. (2007). *Creating welcoming schools: A practical guide to home-school partnerships with diverse families.* New York: Teachers College Press; Newark, DE: International Reading Association.

Baker, A.J.L., & Soden, L.M. (1997). *Parent involvement in children's education: A critical assessment of the knowledge base.* Paper presented at the annual meeting of the American Educational Research Association, Chicago.

Baker, L., Fernandez-Fein, S., Scher, D., & Williams, H. (1998). Home experiences related to the development of word recognition. In J.L. Metsala & L.C. Ehri (Eds.), *Word recognition in beginning literacy* (pp. 263–288). Mahwah, NJ: Erlbaum.

Bandura, A. (1997). *Self-efficacy: The exercise of control.* New York: W.H. Freeman.

Bus, A.G. (2003). Social-emotional requisites for learning to read. In A. van Kleeck, S.A.

Stahl, & E.B. Bauer (Eds.), *On reading books to children: Parents and teachers* (pp. 3–15). Mahwah, NJ: Erlbaum.

Bus, A.G., van IJzendoorn, M.H., & Pellegrini, A.D. (1995). Joint book reading makes for success in learning to read: A meta-analysis on intergenerational transmission of literacy. *Review of Educational Research, 65*(1), 1–21. doi:10.3102/00346543065001001

Chrispeels, J.H., & Rivero, E. (2001). Engaging Latino families for student success: How parent education can reshape parents' sense of place in the education of their children. *Peabody Journal of Education, 76*(2), 119–169. doi:10.1207/S15327930pje7602_7

Compton-Lilly, C. (2003). *Reading families: The literate lives of urban children.* New York: Teachers College Press.

Compton-Lilly, C. (2007). The complexities of reading capital in two Puerto Rican families. *Reading Research Quarterly, 42*(1), 72–98.

Crain-Thoreson, C., & Dale, P.S. (1999). Enhancing linguistic performance: Parents and teachers as book reading partners for children with language delays. *Topics in Early Childhood Special Education, 19*(1), 28–39. doi:10.1177/027112149901900103

Dale, P.S., Crain-Thoreson, C., Notari-Syverson, A., & Cole, K. (1996). Parent–child book reading as an intervention technique for young children with language delays. *Topics in Early Childhood Special Education, 16*(2), 213–235. doi:10.1177/027112149601600206

Dearing, E., Kreider, H., Simpkins, S., & Weiss, H.B. (2006). Family involvement in school and low-income children's literacy: Longitudinal associations between and within families. *Journal of Educational Psychology, 98*(4), 653–664. doi:10.1037/0022 -0663.98.4.653

Dearing, E., McCartney, K., Weiss, H.B., Kreider, H., & Simpkins, S. (2004). The promotive effects of family educational involvement for low-income children's literacy. *Journal of School Psychology, 42*(6), 445–460. doi:10.1016/j.jsp.2004.07.002

De Gaetano, Y. (2007). The role of culture in engaging Latino parents' involvement in school. *Urban Education, 42*(2), 145–162. doi:10.1177/0042085906296536

Delgado-Gaitan, C. (1996). *Protean literacy: Extending the discourse on empowerment.* Washington, DC: Falmer.

De Temple, J., & Snow, C.E. (2003). Learning words from books. In A. van Kleeck, S.A. Stahl, & E.B. Bauer (Eds.), *On reading books*

to children: Parents and teachers (pp. 16–36). Mahwah, NJ: Erlbaum.

Domina, T. (2005). Leveling the home advantage: Assessing the effectiveness of parental involvement in elementary school. *Sociology of Education, 78*, 233–249.

Dunning, D.B., Mason, J.M., & Stewart, J.P. (1994). Reading to preschoolers: A response to Scarborough and Dobrich (1994) and recommendations for future research. *Developmental Review, 14*(3), 324–339. doi:10.1006/drev.1994.1012

Edwards, P.A. (with Pleasants, H.M., & Franklin, S.H.). (1999). *A path to follow: Learning to listen to parents.* Portsmouth, NH: Heinemann.

Epstein, J.L. (2001). *School, family, and community partnerships: Preparing educators and improving schools.* Boulder, CO: Westview.

Fan, X. (2001). Parental involvement and students' academic achievement: A growth modeling analysis. *Journal of Experimental Education, 70*(1), 27–61. doi:10.1080/002 20970109599497

Fan, X., & Chen, M. (2001). Parental involvement and students' academic achievement: A meta-analysis. *Educational Psychology Review, 13*(1), 1–22. doi:10.1023/A:1009048817385

Gonzalez-DeHass, A.R., Willems, P.P., & Doan Holbein, M.F. (2005). Examining the relationship between parental involvement and student motivation. *Educational Psychology Review, 17*(2), 99–123. doi:10.1007/ s10648-005-3949-7

Henderson, A.T., & Berla, N. (Eds.). (1994). *A new generation of evidence: The family is critical to student achievement.* Washington, DC: Center for Law and Education.

Henderson, A.T., & Mapp, K.L. (2002). *A new wave of evidence: The impact of school, family, and community connections on student achievement.* Austin, TX: National Center for Family and Community Connections with Schools.

Hindin, A., & Paratore, J.R. (2007). Supporting young children's literacy learning through home-school partnerships: The effectiveness of a home repeated-reading intervention. *Journal of Literacy Research, 39*(3), 307–333.

Hoover-Dempsey, K.V., & Sandler, H.M. (1995). Parental involvement in children's education: Why does it make a difference? *Teachers College Record, 97*(2), 310–331.

Hoover-Dempsey, K.V., Walker, J.M.T., Sandler, H.M., Whetsel, D., Green, C.L., Wilkins, A.S., et al. (2005). Why do parents become involved? Research findings and implications. *The Elementary School Journal, 106*(2), 105–130. doi:10.1086/499194

Hoover-Dempsey, K.V., & Whitaker, M.C. (2010). The parental involvement process: Implications for literacy development. In K. Dunsmore & D. Fisher (Eds.), *Bringing literacy home* (pp. 53–82). Newark, DE: International Reading Association.

Ingram, M., Wolfe, R.B., & Lieberman, J.M. (2007). The role of parents in high-achieving schools serving low-income, at-risk populations. *Education and Urban Society, 39*(4), 479–497. doi:10.1177/0013124507302120

Jeynes, W.H. (2003). A meta-analysis: The effects of parental involvement on minority children's academic involvement. *Education and Urban Society, 35*(2), 202–218. doi:10.1177/0013124502239392

Jordan, G.E., Snow, C.E., & Porche, M.V. (2000). Project EASE: The effect of a family literacy project on kindergarten students' early literacy skills. *Reading Research Quarterly, 35*(4), 524–546. doi:10.1598/RRQ.35.4.5

Lapp, D. (2010). Stories, facts, and possibilities: Bridging the home and school worlds for students acquiring a school discourse. In K. Dunsmore & D. Fisher (Eds.), *Bringing literacy home* (pp. 136–158). Newark, DE: International Reading Association.

Lapp, D., Fisher, D., Flood, J., & Moore, K. (2002). "I don't want to teach it wrong": An investigation of the role families believe they should play in the early literacy development of their children. In D.L. Schallert, C.M. Fairbanks, J. Worthy, B. Maloch, & J.V. Hoffman (Eds.), *51st yearbook of the National Reading Conference* (pp. 276–287). Oak Creek, WI: National Reading Conference.

Lopez, M.L., Barrueco, S., Feinauer, E., & Miles, J.C. (2007). *Young Latino infants and families: Parental involvement implications from a recent national study.* Cambridge, MA: Harvard Family Research Project.

Mattingly, D.J., Prislin, R., McKenzie, T.L., Rodriguez, J.L., & Kayzar, B. (2002). Evaluating evaluations: The case of parent involvement programs. *Review of Educational Research, 72*(4), 549–576. doi:10.3102/00346543072004549

National Comprehensive Center for Teacher Quality & Public Agenda. (2007). *Lessons learned: New teachers talk about their jobs, challenges, and long-range plans. Issue 3: Teaching in changing times.* Chicago & New York: Authors.

National Institute of Child Health and Human Development. (2000). *Report of the National Reading Panel. Teaching children to read: An evidence-based assessment of the scientific research literature on reading and its implications for reading instruction* (NIH Publication No. 00-4769). Washington, DC: U.S. Government Printing Office.

Neuman, S.B., & Celano, D. (2001). Access to print in low-income and middle-income communities: An ecological study of four neighborhoods. *Reading Research Quarterly, 36*(1), 8–26. doi:10.1598/RRQ.36.1.1

Paratore, J.R., Cassano, C., & Schickedanz, J.A. (2011). Supporting early (and later) literacy development at home and at school: The long view. In M.L. Kamil, P.D. Pearson, E.B. Moje, & P.P. Afflerbach (Eds.), *Handbook of reading research* (Vol. 4, pp. 107–135). New York: Routledge.

Paratore, J.R., Krol-Sinclair, B., David, B., & Schick, A. (2010). Writing the next chapter in family literacy: Clues to long-term effects. In K. Dunsmore & D. Fisher (Eds.), *Bringing literacy home* (pp. 265–288). Newark, DE: International Reading Association.

Paratore, J.R., & Yaden, D.B., Jr. (2011). Family literacy on the defensive: The defunding of Even Start—Omen or opportunity? In D. Lapp & D. Fisher (Eds.), *Handbook of research on teaching the English language arts* (3rd ed., pp. 90–96). New York: Routledge.

Paris, S.G. (2005). Reinterpreting the development of reading skills. *Reading Research Quarterly, 40*(2), 184–202. doi:10.1598/RRQ.40.2.3

Price, L.H., van Kleeck, A., & Huberty, C.J. (2009). Talk during book sharing between parents and preschool children: A comparison between storybook and expository book conditions. *Reading Research Quarterly, 44*(2), 171–194. doi:10.1598/RRQ.44.2.4

Reese, E., Cox, A., Harte, D., & McAnally, H. (2003). Diversity in adults' styles of reading books to children. In A. van Kleeck, S.A. Stahl, & E.B. Bauer (Eds.), *On reading books to children: Parents and teachers* (pp. 37–57). Mahwah, NJ: Erlbaum.

Rodríguez-Brown, F.V. (2010). Latino culture and schooling: Reflections on family literacy with a culturally and linguistically different community. In K. Dunsmore & D. Fisher (Eds.), *Bringing literacy home* (pp. 203–225). Newark, DE: International Reading Association.

Roser, N. (2010). Talking over books at home and in school. In K. Dunsmore & D. Fisher (Eds.), *Bringing literacy home* (pp. 104–135). Newark, DE: International Reading Association.

Scarborough, H.S., & Dobrich, W. (1994). On the efficacy of reading to preschoolers. *Developmental Review, 14*(3), 245–302. doi:10.1006/drev.1994.1010

Sénéchal, M. (1997). The differential effect of storybook reading on preschoolers' acquisition of expressive and receptive vocabulary. *Journal of Child Language, 24*(1), 123–138. doi:10.1017/S0305000996003005

Sénéchal, M., & LeFevre, J. (2002). Parental involvement in the development of children's reading skill: A five-year longitudinal study. *Child Development, 73*(2), 445–460.

Sénéchal, M., LeFevre, J., Thomas, E.M., & Daley, K.E. (1998). Differential effects of home literacy experiences on the development of oral and written language. *Reading Research Quarterly, 33*(1), 96–116. doi:10.1598/RRQ.33.1.5

Sénéchal, M., & Young, L. (2008). The effect of family literacy interventions on children's acquisition of reading from kindergarten to grade 3: A meta-analytic review. *Review of Educational Research, 78*(4), 880–907. doi:10.3102/0034654308320319

Sheldon, S.B. (2003). Linking school–family–community partnerships in urban elementary schools to student achievement on state tests. *The Urban Review, 35*(2), 149–165. doi:10.1023/A:1023713829693

Sheldon, S.B., & Epstein, J.L. (2005). School programs of family and community involvement to support children's reading and literacy development across the grades. In J. Flood & P.L. Anders (Eds.), *Literacy development of students in urban schools: Research and policy* (pp. 107–138). Newark, DE: International Reading Association.

Smrekar, C., & Cohen-Vogel, L. (2001). The voices of parents: Rethinking the intersection of family and school. *Peabody Journal of Education, 76*(2), 75–100. doi:10.1207/S15327930pje7602_5

Souto-Manning, M., & Swick, K.J. (2006). Teachers' beliefs about parent and family involvement: Rethinking our family involvement paradigm. *Early Childhood Education Journal, 34*(2), 187–193. doi:10.1007/s10643-006-0063-5

St. Pierre, R.G., Ricciuti, A.E., & Rimdzius, T.A. (2005). Effects of a family literacy program on low-literate children and their parents: Findings from an evaluation of the Even Start family literacy program. *Developmental Psychology, 41*(6), 953–970. doi:10.1037/0012-1649.41.6.953

St. Pierre, R., Ricciuti, A., Tao, F., Creps, C., Swartz, J., Lee, W., Parsad, A., & Rimdzius, T. (2003). *Third national Even Start evaluation: Program impacts and implications for improvement.* Washington, DC: Planning and Evaluation Service, U.S. Department of Education.

Stahl, S.A. (2003). What do we expect storybook reading to do? How storybook reading impacts word recognition. In A. van Kleeck, S.A. Stahl, & E.B. Bauer (Eds.), *On reading books to children: Parents and teachers* (pp. 363–383). Mahwah, NJ: Erlbaum.

Tabors, P.O., Beals, D.E., & Weizman, Z.O. (2001). "You know what oxygen is?" Learning new words at home. In D.K. Dickinson & P.O. Tabors (Eds.), *Beginning literacy with language: Young children learning at home and school* (pp. 93–110). Baltimore: Paul H. Brookes.

Toomey, D. (1993). Parents hearing their children read: A review: Rethinking the lessons of the Haringey Project. *Educational Research, 35*(3), 223–236.

Valdés, G. (1996). Con respeto [With respect]: *Bridging the differences between culturally diverse families and schools: An ethnographic portrait.* New York: Teachers College Press.

van Kleeck, A., Stahl, S.A., & Bauer, E.B. (Eds.). (2003). *On reading books to children: Parents and teachers.* Mahwah, NJ: Erlbaum.

Vasquez, O., Pease-Alvarez, L., & Shannon, S.M. (1994). *Pushing boundaries: Language and culture in a Mexicano community.* New York: Cambridge University Press.

White, K.R., Taylor, M.J., & Moss, V.D. (1992). Does research support claims about the benefits of involving parents in early intervention programs? *Review of Educational Research, 62*(1), 91–125.

Whitehurst, G.J., & Lonigan, C.J. (2002). Emergent literacy: Development from prereaders to readers. In S.B. Neuman & D.K. Dickinson (Eds.), *Handbook of early literacy research* (pp. 11–29). New York: Guilford.

Yaden, D.B., Jr. (2003). Parent–child storybook reading as a complex adaptive system: Or "an igloo is a house for bears." In A. van Kleeck, S.A. Stahl, & E.B. Bauer (Eds.), *On reading books to children: Parents and teachers* (pp. 336–362). Mahwah, NJ: Erlbaum.

Yaden, D.B., Jr., Madrigal, P., & Tam, A. (2003). Access to books and beyond: Creating and learning from a book lending program for Latino families in the inner city. In G. Garcia (Ed.), *English learners: Reaching the highest level of English literacy.* (pp. 357–386). Newark, DE: International Reading Association.

Zevenbergen, A.A., & Whitehurst, G.J. (2003). Dialogic reading: A shared picture book reading intervention for preschoolers. In A. van Kleeck, S.A. Stahl, & E.B. Bauer (Eds.), *On reading books to children: Parents and teachers* (pp. 177–200). Mahwah, NJ: Erlbaum.

Chapter 17

Diversity and Literacy

Alfred W. Tatum

D*iversity* is a sociologically influenced term that does not fit neatly into literacy research. It's messy. It is dynamic and fluid. Diversity is everywhere. The interdisciplinary scope of diversity and the entanglements of multiple diversities warrant the need to embrace its complexity and to avoid shallow theorizing.

It is clear from the literature that diversity defies generalizations; it is made up of tangled spaces, is comprised of myriad factors, and is full of ambiguities and merging components (Ayers, Quinn, & Stovall, 2009; Lynch, 2000; Troia, 2009). One student, for example, can enter a learning environment embodying several elements of diversity—ethnic, gender, linguistic, and religious. What does the research suggest about advancing the literacy development of

- Mamir, a 15-year-old male from a middle-income Kurdish family who has functional conversational English and is entering a 10th-grade history classroom in a high-performing school in a rural community

- Phuong Lee, a 5-year-old new to the United States, entering kindergarten as an emergent reader with limited English skills

- Jackson, a socially conscious, high-achieving African American eighth-grade queer male in a suburban school who rejects the curriculum because of its lack of consanguinity to his social, sexual, and familial realities

- Sara, a white female 10-year-old with a learning disability entering a public school that fails to honor the religious sensitivities of her parents, who recently became underemployed and can no longer afford to send her to the parochial school of their choice

- Peter, an average-achieving 11-year-old native of a small Midwestern town in the United States, who feels overwhelmed by the number of

What Research Has to Say About Reading Instruction (4th ed.) edited by S. Jay Samuels and Alan E. Farstrup.
© 2011 by the International Reading Association.

social and academic activities he is required to engage in because of his parents' desire to have him accepted into a top university

- Nicole, a 17-year-old ward of the state, who was initiated into a gang at 11, sexually assaulted at 13, and now receives her reading instruction as she moves between a juvenile detention facility and an alternative high school
- Andrew, an academically gifted 8-year-old who loves reading, science, and art and whose worst nightmare is missing a day of school

Mathematically speaking, a classroom teacher can encounter almost unlimited diversity(ies) among students, particularly in a school where multiple languages are spoken. Place that school in a community experiencing high mobility because of community gentrification or urban dislocation, and the diversity(ies) increase. Honoring students' diversities can be viewed as an overwhelming task because there is no clear cutoff point to diversity. Additionally, the growth of cultural, linguistic, and other diverse demographies has outpaced the research, and policy decisions have not delineated a clear path for practitioners. Conversations about literacy and diversity often teeter on the fence between possibility and praxis (Ayers et al., 2009).

In this chapter, I provide a cross-disciplinary view of the research that has examined the roles of diversity(ies) and their impact or potential impact on students' literacy development across grade levels and school settings. This view is rather limited in scope because of the sheer volume of the literature that exists. I examined both the literacy research and research from other disciplines (e.g., curriculum studies, gender studies, law, psychology, and sociology) to uncover what they offered. I give attention to the challenges and tensions identified in the research and discuss the implications for teachers, teacher educators, administrators, and researchers. I focus on students in the United States, with full acknowledgment that providing a limited discussion of research and literature that fails to span international communities is egregiously shortsighted.

A two-step process was used for writing this chapter. First, I identified the salient categories of diversity, nine of which appeared repeatedly throughout the literatures and standards documents—namely, ethnicity, socioeconomic status, gender, language, race, geographical area, religion, exceptionalities, and sexual orientation. I show these in Figure 17.1 but, as I constructed the graphic representation, diversity refused to behave itself or to become contoured in a definitive way. It is not clear from the

Figure 17.1. Nine Categories of Diversity Salient for Literacy Educators

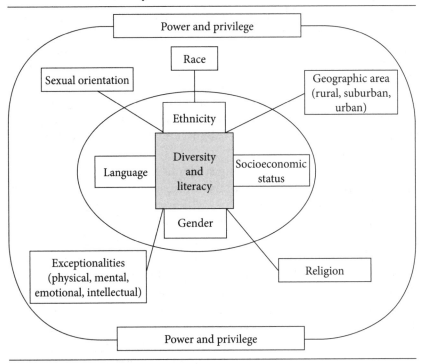

research which form of diversity takes precedence over the others for advancing students' literacy development. There are too many interactions that can exist within and across each of the categories, and each is affected by dynamics of power and privilege (Purcell-Gates, 2007). For example, in the United States, the dynamics of privilege are observed in and outside schools in the forms of heterosexuality over homosexuality, male over female, and English over Spanish and other languages. Therefore, the salient categories in Figure 17.1 are encircled within power and privilege.

Second, I reviewed journal articles, handbooks of research, books, position statements from professional organizations, policy documents from philanthropic and governmental organizations and agencies, and standards documents of professional and accreditation agencies published between 2000 and 2010 that related to the salient categories. I examined each for current findings and implications for research. I paid particular attention to the conceptual and theoretical frames used by researchers who investigated categories of diversity and relationships to reading, writing, and language development. Although the chapters in this book and its previous editions focus on what the research says, I decided to examine theoretical and conceptual pieces as well, in hopes of identifying appropriate research orientations—because the research on literacy and diversity is too incomplete and, at best, ambiguous. I framed the review of the research and other literatures with an eye toward what it might tell four primary beneficiaries—teachers, teacher educators, administrators, and researchers—about how they can protect the rights of all students.

Conversations about honoring students' diversity(ies) are generally tied to struggling readers and writers (International Reading Association, 2007; Morrow, Rueda, & Lapp, 2009; Wilkinson, Morrow, & Chou, 2008). This is not without good reason, but we must expand the lens to other students who are not struggling. The "othering" of students, or continuing the ongoing academic comparisons of students across ethnicities and income levels based on reading and writing outcomes, is very limited and static in scope. Therefore, I intentionally avoided comparing students' reading and writing outcomes on the National Assessment of Educational Progress (NAEP) or other formal reports of students' reading performances as a rationale for honoring students' diversity(ies). It is common knowledge that many students are grossly underprepared in schools and as a result are unable to gain entry into postsecondary institutions or secure professional opportunities that grant them full participation in society. Instead, I opted for a more productive stance to advocate for *all* students across ethnicities, income levels, languages, academic abilities, and developmental pathways who may be underserved or overlooked or who fail to encounter literacy experiences in and outside of school that they consider meaningful and worthwhile.

Certain stances toward diversity—namely, focusing on particular groups of students—can create more tension and antidiversity postures among teachers, teacher educators, administrators, and researchers, some of whom readily balk when asked to address the needs of *all* students (the Mamirs, Phuong Lees, Jacksons, Saras, Peters, and Andrews included) because of the overwhelming nature of their professional realities, the uncritical acceptance of scientifically based reading research, the favored theoretical orientations and research methodologies, or a blatant disregard for students' out-of-school contexts (e.g., familial, community) and discourses. Certain stances contribute to deracialized, delanguaged, deethnicized, degenderized, desexualized and delegitimate educational experiences for students who enter "traditional" schools with their multiple diversities (Tatum, in press).

I also approached this chapter with cautious optimism in light of tensions evolving from federally sanctioned research syntheses on what works (e.g., from the National Reading Panel), policy statements (e.g., National Center on Education and the Economy, 2006; National Governors Association Center for Best Practices, 2005), political posturing, cultures of accountability, restructuring of schools in large urban areas, and a limited vision for reconciling the multiple, often competing, definitions and associated roles of literacy instruction. Each of these variables can run counter to honoring students' multilayered diversities, ultimately affecting students' life outcomes.

Challenges and Tensions to Honoring Students' Diversities

Diversity is as central to the United States as the preamble to its Constitution, which begins, "We, the People of the United States, in Order to form a more Perfect Union...." Increasingly, the lines across international borders are being blurred. There are now more than 29 million foreign-born residents of the United States (U.S. Census Bureau, 2007). In 2006, 12.5% of the U.S. population was foreign born, compared with 6.2% in 1980. The populations of 18 states include more than 10% foreign-born residents, compared with five states in 1990. California, the state with the largest foreign-born population, includes 27% foreign-born residents amounting to more than 9.9 million people. As I have offered elsewhere,

> With more than 55 million students enrolled in public and private schools in the United States and 3.3 million teachers, it is inconceivable that any approach to education that fails to account for cultural, historical, linguistic, sociological, and psychological factors of the students will be effective. A failure to become astute about these factors and how they impact educational outcomes not only becomes inimical to students of color, but to the nation and our national imagination as a whole. (Tatum, in press)

Changes in the linguistic landscape are presenting innumerable challenges for a nation whose schools employ a large number of English monolingual teachers informed by their own national traditions, but who are now responsible for teaching students from a wide array of traditions and national backgrounds. This is occurring on the heels of the No Child Left Behind Act of 2001 (NCLB), legislation that intended to address the needs of students in chronically underperforming schools by placing highly qualified teachers in classrooms. Still a relatively small percentage of 4th-, 8th-, and 12th-grade students exceed national norms on the NAEP (Perie, Grigg, & Donahue, 2005) reading and writing assessments. Large numbers of adolescents drop out of high schools daily (National Governors Association Center for Best Practices, 2005). These factors, coupled with a widening gulf and associated disparities between rich and poor, increases in violence and bullying among children and youth, environmental disasters, the downturn in the U.S. national economy, and the prevalence of teen parents, have altered in-school and out-of-school contexts. They affect, either directly or indirectly, students, teachers, teacher educators, administrators, policymakers, and researchers.

It became clear in my review of the various literatures that the current literacy landscape has also been affected by at least three major issues that may serve to disrupt optimal conditions for honoring students' diversity(ies) in the context of literacy instruction and its delivery (Apple, Kenway, & Singh, 2005; Ayers et al., 2009; Morrow et al., 2009):

1. The demonization of certain students

2. Debates in the legal and political spheres

3. Teachers' beliefs and dispositions

Since September 11, 2001, there has been a demonization of certain students (Ayers et al., 2009), particularly those who exercise religious diversity and associate with Islam. The demonization and separatist ethos are also evident with some forms of linguistic imperialism such as the legislation against bilingualism (August & Shanahan, 2006, 2008; Bailey, 2007). Federal funds are no longer administered via competitive grants designed to ensure equity and promote quality programs for English learners as a result of Title III of NCLB. Cultural and linguistic tensions continue to grow as national disputes take place over immigration policies.

Debates in the legal and political spheres anchored by neoliberalism and conservatism have led for calls to standardize and inculcate monoculturalism (Apple et al., 2005). This fuels conservative and neoliberal approaches to raising test scores based on the premise that standards and standardized testing are the only way to ensure that all students have an opportunity to learn. A move to establish Common Core State Standards is placed in the altruistic context that students will no longer be permitted to fail because we have reached the end of industrialization and globalization is the new world order. These barriers can lead to charged debates about honoring students' diversity(ies) during literacy instruction.

Although the field of literacy research has moved away from conceptualizing diversity as a deficit to considering diversity as a resource paradigm (Nocon & Cole, 2009), there are some who still believe, because of their expectations or dispositions, that students' home or other experiences are irrelevant to learning to read and write. This conceptual frame may lead to the deliberate exclusion of children's and youth's out-of-school experiences by well-intentioned teachers because these experiences are devalued, stigmatized, or even pathologized (Morrow et al., 2009). This is more widespread if these out-of-school contexts deviate from the "norm" or "mainstream."

The beliefs of teachers can be influenced by misinformation spread in teacher education programs or the neglect of some programs to adequately prepare teachers to advance the literacy development of diverse students (Murray, 1996; Salili & Hoosain, 2007). They can also be influenced by the political landscape, national mood, or a range of other factors that shape teachers' own diversity(ies). For example, my upbringing as an African American male in a culture of compulsory heterosexuality in an urban community may have contributed to the fact that I never considered using queer texts in my teaching, opting instead for other forms of texts that I assessed as culturally compatible. This well-intentioned stance could have contributed to the silencing of my students in a homophobic society. A lack of knowledge about the associations among sexual orientations, race, and gender could have quite possibly rendered my literacy instruction and classroom context "unsafe" for some students. Did my own undergraduate and graduate school education victimize me, whether intentionally or unintentionally? Or was I a victim of the research grounded in frames unaware of racialized, gendered, sexualized, or languaged shortcomings?

Although the challenges and tensions are numerous, researchers have contributed a body of literature with implications for honoring students' diversity(ies) in reading and writing classrooms (see, e.g., C.A.M. Banks, 2005; J.A. Banks, 2009; Biancarosa & Snow, 2004; Blackburn, Clark, Kenney, & Smith, 2010; Brayboy, 2005; Bursztyn, 2007; Graham & Harris, 2005; Guzzetti, Young, Gritsavage, Fyfe, & Hardenbrook, 2002; Israel & Duffy, 2009; Lee, 2007; Morrell & Duncan-Andrade, 2002; Pfeiffer, 2008; Sleeter, 2006; Tatum, 2008; Tsui & Tollefson, 2007). This research is framed by several theoretical orientations—cognitive, socio-cultural, critical race, feminist, and cultural-ecological among them. The researchers have employed methodologies including experimental, quasi-experimental, correlational, descriptive, microethnographical, case study, interview, and survey to investigate the relationships among literacy and the aforementioned salient characteristics of diversity. Research efforts have focused on

- Identifying research-based literacy practices
- Protecting the democratic goal of education
- Creating possibilities for subjugated populations
- Ensuring linguistic human rights
- Advancing a social justice ethos and teacher activism
- Examining the effects of legal frameworks on educational outcomes
- Advancing knowledge to better serve students across a wider spectrum

I now discuss the outcomes of some of this research as it relates to four beneficiaries.

Honoring Diversity(ies) to Advance Students' Literacy Development

It became clear from my review of the research and other literature that the ways in which reading, writing, and language instruction are conceptualized and theorized can serve as conduits or barriers to students' full participation in the world and their capacity to fully express their humanity. Poorly conceptualized practices can lead some students to become an "accomplice to [their] own erasure" (Blackburn et al., 2010, p. 58; see also Koschoreck & Tooms, 2009; Rymes, 2001).

I identified 29 findings from the research and literature that demonstrated empirical support ranging from strong to weak. As can be seen in Table 17.1, where these 29 findings are listed, the lion's share of honoring students' diversity(ies) relies on teachers—their competencies, conceptualizations of the roles of reading and their roles as educators, and their dispositions, freedoms, and constraints. Teacher educators, administrators, policymakers, and researchers affect each of these. There is a strong interdependence among several key players inside and outside of classrooms that exists for honoring students' diversity(ies) without constraints and apology.

Table 17.1. What the Research Says Literacy Educators Can Do to Honor Students' Diversity(ies)

Research Finding	Beneficiaries			
	Teachers	Teacher educators	Administrators	Researchers
Value diversity.	✓	✓	✓	✓
Examine ideologies that inform pedagogical, curricular, policy, and research orientations.	✓	✓	✓	✓
Avoid essentializing students.	✓	✓	✓	✓
Take proactive stances around issues of diversity.	✓	✓	✓	✓
View classrooms as spaces in which identities are not settled.	✓	✓	✓	✓
Expand notions of what counts as reading.	✓	✓	✓	✓
Develop a greater understanding of language complexity and use in academic settings.	✓	✓	✓	✓
Link schools to the communities they serve.	✓	✓	✓	
Establish a school vision.			✓	
Assess curricular decisions.	✓	✓	✓	
Use data inquiry as a starting point to lead to various kinds of change.			✓	
Make connections between instruction and children's and youth's experiences.	✓	✓	✓	
Nurture respectful collaboration with families and communities.	✓		✓	
Diversify texts.	✓		✓	
Link disciplinary and everyday knowledge.	✓	✓		
Address the moral and educational dilemmas created by the competing pressures of school finance, corporate relations, and education.			✓	
Model transformative and intellectual leadership.			✓	

(continued)

Table 17.1. What the Research Says Literacy Educators Can Do to Honor Students' Diversity(ies) *(continued)*

Research Finding	Beneficiaries			
	Teachers	Teacher educators	Administrators	Researchers
Understand diagnostic tools to interpret data in order to offer appropriate differentiated instruction.	✓		✓	
Provide intensive first-language instruction when necessary.	✓			
Provide research-based cognitive strategy instruction.	✓			
Develop content area knowledge, academic proficiency, and English language proficiency simultaneously.	✓			
Create opportunities for student autonomy, and group students strategically.	✓			
Assign teacher candidates in field placements that serve diverse populations.		✓		
Provide better quality formal training around teaching in diverse settings.		✓		
Provide opportunities for teacher candidates to tutor struggling readers as a way to learn to differentiate instruction.		✓		
Connect course content to real experiences in schools.		✓		
Diversify faculty.		✓	✓	
Examine intersections of diversity in substantive ways.				✓
Develop improved language assessments.				✓
Draw heavily on theoretical orientations and methodologies that have deep respect for students' diversity(ies).				✓

(continued)

Table 17.1. What the Research Says Literacy Educators Can Do to Honor Students' Diversity(ies) *(continued)*

Research Finding	Beneficiaries			
	Teachers	Teacher educators	Administrators	Researchers
Investigate the dual obligations of teaching English learners—to help them meet grade-level standards in the content areas and develop English-language proficiency.				✓
Generate a greater understanding of the nature of language complexity and its use in academic settings.				✓

Six converging guideposts for teachers, teacher educators, administrators, and researchers emerged from the literature; these can be seen as paramount for honoring students' diversity(ies):

1. Value diversity.

2. Examine ideologies that inform pedagogical, curricular, policy, and research orientations.

3. Avoid essentializing students.

4. Take proactive stances on issues of diversity.

5. View classrooms as spaces in which identities are not settled.

6. Expand notions of what counts as reading and writing.

Recommendations for Teachers

There are by far more findings and recommendations in the research literature for teachers than for any of the other beneficiaries (Au, 2009; August & Shanahan, 2008; Deshler, Palincsar, Biancarosa, & Nair, 2007; Gambrell, Morrow, & Pressley, 2007; Gay, 2000; Morrow et al., 2009; Richardson, 2001; Troia, 2009). I identified 18, including the 6 noted in the preceding list. As a former eighth-grade teacher who needed a nap at the end of each school day because of the energy I expended to provide responsive reading instruction to my urban school's lowest performing adolescents, I pause to appreciate the enormous task faced by teachers in classrooms more diverse than was my own. During my tenure as an eighth-grade teacher, I had two students with religious orientations that stood in stark contrast to those of other students, one student who was openly lesbian and another who was secretly gay, and several with identified disabilities. All of the students spoke English.

A list of 18 findings and recommendations for teachers seems a bit overwhelming, but it serves as a useful litmus test for honoring students' diversity(ies). I will not list them all (they are indicated in Table 17.1 by the checkmarks in the "Teachers" column), but I note the six that were most prominent throughout the literature.

1. Make connections between instruction and children's and youth's experiences.
2. Provide research-based cognitive strategy instruction.
3. Link disciplinary and everyday knowledge.
4. Create opportunities for student autonomy, and group students strategically.
5. Diversify texts.
6. Understand diagnostic tools to interpret data in order to offer appropriate differentiated instruction.

Other findings and recommendations were more specific to diverse populations (e.g., providing intensive first-language instruction). I also identified instructional activities with strong to moderate empirical support that honor students' diversity(ies), such as having students read and write texts to challenge a status quo that oppresses or erases people who deviate from the norm (Kenney, 2009). Space does not permit me to describe each activity here.

Recommendations for Teacher Educators

Framing their work in the achievement gap narrative and focusing on literacy achievement in urban schools, Wilkinson et al. (2008) made it clear that the best ways to prepare teachers for diverse school setting are not clearly defined and that the quality of teacher preparation in the United States is inconsistent. In an attempt to remedy this, efforts by the federal government, accreditation bodies such as the National Council for the Accreditation of Teacher Education and the Teacher Education Accreditation Council, and other entities such as the Alliance for Excellent Education and the Carnegie Foundation have made inroads to bolster or highlight the quality of teacher education programs. As part of this effort, the International Reading Association (IRA) established a Quality Undergraduate Elementary and Secondary Teacher Education in Reading task force and a certificate of distinction to recognize undergraduate teacher education programs that, among other things, honor differences among people based on ethnicity, race, socioeconomic status, gender, exceptionalities, language, religion, sexual orientation, geographical area, and the ever-expanding lens of diversity. IRA's (2010) *Standards for Reading Professionals—Revised 2010* has a new diversity standard. This is a timely development. Before this change, diversity was loosely attached to the other stand-alone standards. The following statement describes the thinking behind the standard:

> The Diversity Standard focuses on the need to prepare teachers to build and engage their students in a curriculum that places value on the diversity that exists in our society, as featured in elements such as race, ethnicity, class, gender, religion, and language. This standard is grounded in a set of principles and understandings that reflect a vision for a democratic and just society and inform the effective preparation of reading professionals. (p. 12)

In its development, the diversity standard offered several rationales, considerations, and guideposts for honoring students' diversity(ies). Included among them were

- A curriculum that ignores or treats diversity superficially is doomed to fail.
- A curriculum that values diversity requires that teacher educators and teachers step outside their personal experience within a particular linguistic, ethnic, and cultural group to experience others.
- The elements of diversity (ethnicity, gender, religion, language) interact in the form of multiple identities that may move from the background into the foreground (or in the other direction) as a function of the context and the moment.
- A commitment to social justice guides the development of a curriculum that values diversity. It is the responsibility of teachers and schools to prepare learners not only in ways that value their diversity but to engage in active citizenship to redress areas of inequity and privilege.

It is clear that honoring students' diversity(ies) is garnering greater attention in the assessment of teacher preparation programs. In addition to the findings to guide all beneficiaries, the research and literature offered the following recommendation for efforts specific to teacher education:

- Assign teacher candidates in field placements that serve diverse populations.
- Provide better quality formal training around teaching in diverse settings.
- Provide opportunities for teacher candidates to tutor struggling readers as a way to learn to differentiate instruction.
- Connect course content to real experiences in schools.
- Diversify faculty.

The research and literature also suggest postcertification opportunities such as mentoring to support teachers as they enter the profession and to improve teacher retention rates in diverse settings that may prove challenging for those who come to them without full knowledge and capacity to teach effectively in those settings.

Recommendations for Administrators

Too often teachers have expressed that they cannot honor students' diversity(ies) because of administrative pressures or constraints. "I have to follow the mandates," I often hear teachers say. Administrators, who may find themselves acquiescing to external pressures, are implicated in this statement. This presents a dilemma that is not easily resolved without bold, prudent, and unapologetic leadership. Administrators must find the capacity and the acuity as leaders to promote positive relations among diverse people and groups. This may require that they honestly confront their own biases and shortcomings by looking within.

Henze, Katz, Norte, Sather, and Walker (2002, p. 3) offer three reasons for administrators to address issues of diversity:

1. Students are unlikely to focus on academic learning if they feel unsafe or threatened in schools. They must be free from physical violence and from slurs and harassment based on ethnicity language, religion, and other aspects of identity.

2. Students and adults in multicultural schools and work environments need to get along and work productively with those who are different from themselves.

3. Schools should become laboratories for a more just society.

Assessing school contexts is one of the initial steps administrators should take to promote positive relations among diverse groups. As Henze et al. (2002) put it,

> Before school leaders can develop a plan for the improvement of race or ethnic relations, they need to consider their particular school's context and the way it affects human relations in general and, specifically, race or ethnic relations. There are many areas of context that are beyond the immediate control of school leadership. These include, for example, the demographics of the school, the economic disparities of the surrounding community, the physical structure and condition of the school, the district's policies and practices, and the legacy left at the school by previous leaders. All these contextual features can have an impact, positive or negative, on interethnic relations ad group relations more generally. (p. 25)

The research and literature offered the following recommendations for administrators to honor students', staff's, and the community's diversity(ies):

- Link schools to the communities they serve.
- Establish a school vision.
- Assess curricular decisions.
- Use data inquiry as a starting point to lead to various kinds of change.
- Nurture respectful collaboration with families and communities.
- Address the moral and educational dilemmas created by the competing pressures of school finance, corporate relations, and education.
- Model transformative and intellectual leadership.
- Diversify faculty.
- Diversify texts.

Recommendations for Researchers

I examined several theoretical and methodological orientations in writing this chapter. There were cognitive orientations as well as sociocultural and critical race theory orientations. Some researchers focused on a combination of risk factors and the growing need to pay attention to diverse texts, contexts, forms, spaces of literacy learning, and approaches to literacy teachers as they attempted to use research to deconstruct social inequalities and power structures. Others conducted research sanctioned by the Institute of Educational Sciences of the U.S. Department of Education, using research criteria similar to what is privileged by the What Works Clearinghouse—research that is viewed cautiously by some as being undertheorized or oversimplified. For example, Lewis, O'Connor, and Mueller (2009) put forward that there is an underconceptualization of race in educational research. While conducting their study, Daiute and Jones (2003) questioned whether there is a lack of theory and methodology to recognize unfamiliar social understandings and realize what is unknown about familiar ones.

It is clear that researchers have embedded ideologies that shape their research questions, methodologies, conceptual and theoretical frames, and interpretations. These ideologies, rooted in their own diversity(ies), can affect the ways they negotiate or ignore diversity in classroom research, their evaluation designs of what works, how they share research in teacher education programs, and how they conduct research that will inform policy.

It became obvious while writing this chapter that a culture of impatient research exists, impatient in the sense that short-term studies are attempting to address diversity issues that are deeply rooted in century-old dilemmas and tensions. At the same time, our rapidly changing society and students' livelihoods demand immediate answers to guarantee certain educational rights and to restore students' confidence in reading, writing, and language as legitimate tools of human development.

The research and literature offered the following recommendations for researchers to honor students' diversity(ies):

- Examine intersections of diversity in substantive ways.

- Develop improved language assessments.

- Draw heavily on theoretical orientations and methodologies that have deep respect for students' diversity(ies).

- Investigate the dual obligations of teaching English learners—to help them meet grade-level standards in the content areas and develop English language proficiency.

- Generate a greater understanding of the nature of language complexity its use in academic settings.

Creating Safe Spaces and Pathways

I opened this chapter with seven profiles of the sorts of diverse students for whom I hoped my review of the research and literature would yield some clear directions for simultaneously honoring diversity(ies) and advancing literacy development. Ultimately, I wanted to uncover ways we can create safe spaces and pathways for them. In writing this chapter, I continued to reflect on my own experiences as a student, teacher, teacher educator, and researcher, and how I have felt isolated at times and comfortable at others. I resented being the only African American male in my undergraduate elementary education courses for more than two years, having to respond to insidious comments about "the underperforming at-risk black male student" that resided in my classmates' and instructors' imaginations. Their descriptions seemed too limited. Then, I reflected on my years spent teaching adolescents and the power they began to feel after reading the texts I had the autonomy to select in a building with supportive administrators.

I continue to reflect on the language I use as a poet to help students who live in communities of turmoil develop a consciousness about U.S. political discourse, the role of texts in their lives, and how the United States, in all its glory and gloom, rightfully belongs to them. I shared the following poem with a group of young writers in August 2009 in response to the clarion call of some in the political sphere and national media to "give us our America back."

Against America's Concrete

The grand experiment was to destroy my consciousness
Bury my thoughts beneath the ocean and dry out my memory in the
Southern heat
I resisted and I still resist
To be caricatured although I am still on display
To those who want their America back
I'll give it freely if you can give me back what I offered in return
You were my first kiss
My huffy bicycle
My corner store
My red ten-speed
My embarrassment and my shame
You continue to be my auction block
Looking on to see what I will do next
I see you looking over my shoulder

Wondering what I will say
Wondering...
I will not crack
Still intact
I am home.

I use poetry as a tool of activism as I continue to work with adolescents from urban areas littered with violence and nihilistic tendencies. Writing is one way I carry the social justice mantle, the same call for social justice that now appears in diversity standards offered by professional organizations and accreditation bodies. It gives me comfort and allows me to feel safe as I attempt to create safe spaces for students.

Honoring students' diversity(ies) ultimately depends on the ability to create safe spaces and pathways for them inside and outside of schools. Consider the following examples that have emerged from my research and teaching on selecting and mediating texts with students (Tatum, 2009). I use the following questions as a litmus test to ensure that my curricular decisions serve the best interests of *all* students:

- Will students be underserved by this text?
- What makes this text essential or useful?
- Out of all of the texts in the world, why this one for these students in this time and space?
- Will I love to rush in to teach this text?
- Will this text allow me to find out more about me as I find out more about my students? Will it help me reconcile differences?
- How can this text be appropriately paced to engage students?
- What is the appropriate starting point for this text?
- Is this a considerate and challenging text?
- Does this text lend itself to academic excellence (i.e., kids becoming smarter) and identity development?
- Will this text restore confidence in literacy instruction?
- Does this text serve as a writing and language coach?

Responding to these questions allows me to examine if I am creating legitimate instructional engagement for students, engagement that can lead them to assess the instruction as meaningful and worthwhile.

Using this litmus test led me to use an excerpt from Naomi Klein's *The Shock Doctrine* in a demonstration lesson to a group of high school students in New Orleans' Ninth Ward following Hurricane Katrina. The text was presented this way:

> The news racing around **the shelter** that day was that…a **prominent** [very important] Republican congressman from this city, had told a group of lobbyists, **"We finally cleaned up public housing in New Orleans. We couldn't do it, but God did** [referring to Hurricane Katrina]".… **"I think we have a clean sheet to start again.** And with that clean sheet we have some very big opportunities"….lower taxes, fewer **regulations** [controls or laws], cheaper workers and a "smaller, safer city"—which in practice meant plans to level the public housing projects and replace them with condos. Hearing all the talk of "fresh starts" and "clean sheets," you could almost forget the **toxic** [deadly or poisonous] stew of rubble, chemical outflows and human remains just a few miles down the highway. (p. 4)
>
> I call these **orchestrated** [planned] raids on the public sphere in the wake of catastrophic events, combined with the treatment of disasters as exciting **market** [money-making] opportunities, "**disaster capitalism**." (p. 6)

My goal was to support students in multiple ways during this lesson and with the selection of the text. I provided built-in supports such as a knowledge-focused statement, spacing, embedded definitions and questions, and boldface type. To honor students' diversity(ies), I decided to pay attention to their community contexts (i.e., New Orleans, one of America's most storied cities, and the disaster capitalism taking place there) instead of their ethnicity. In this case, all of the students were African American, but this was less important for mediating the selected texts. It is the combination of powerful instruction and powerful texts that benefit students.

The approach used for selecting the text for this lesson was similar to the approach I use for selecting and mediating texts for all students to ensure they have an opportunity to engage using the identity(ies) they prefer. For each text I teach, I identify a text starter to engage the students and construct questions that allow multiple diverse pathways for responding (see Table 17.2). For example, the question that aligns with the text starter for Walter Dean Myers' *Handbook for Boys*—What does it take to escape vulnerable-producing conditions unscathed?—can be answered using an ethnic, gender, religious, personal, or community lens. The students have the agency to choose.

Table 17.2. Sample Texts, Text Starters, and Essential Questions

Text	Text Starters	Essential Questions
47 by Walter Mosley	And every night they chained your feet to an eyebolt in the floor. The men out there were mostly angry and so they were always fighting or crying of just plain sad. (p. 12)	• What are the alternatives when someone tries to stamp out the existence of others? • Are there appropriate responses? Inappropriate responses?
Bang by Sharon Flake	A black boy don't get a hundred chances to get it right. Sometimes he just gets one. That's it.... You blow your chance, you blow your life. (pp. 124–125)	• Is the United States a redemptive society? • Is the society constructed to save some and sacrifice others?
Handbook for Boys by Walter Dean Myers	The problem with so many young men…is that when they're young, they really don't know how to get their lives together.... After a while they just give up and start talking about how they really don't care. (p. 135)	• How does one recover a part of one's soul? • What does it take to escape vulnerable-producing conditions unscathed?
Narrative of the Life of Frederick Douglass by Frederick Douglass	I often found myself regretting my own existence.... (p. 55)	• What does it mean to exist? • What are the factors that contribute to one's existence?

Note. From *Reading for Their Life: (Re)building the Textual Lineages of African American Adolescent Males* by A.W. Tatum, 2009, Portsmouth, NH: Heinemann.

Navigating schools for some students is akin to traveling the Wadi Kelt, a treacherous path along the Judean wilderness where the landscape is bleak, barren, and dangerously steep. This wilderness likely inspired the biblical scripture, "Yea, though I walk through the valley of the shadow of the death, I will fear no evil." Evil is an ever-present reality for some students.

The research is clear that these safe spaces must be created in our classrooms, schools, and universities. More important, safe spaces must be created in our hearts and national imagination. This offers the best hope for bridging the gaps among research, theory, practice, teacher preparation, and policy and finding the tangible intersections to support students in their multiple diverse cloths.

Questions for Reflection

1. How can students, teachers, administrators, teacher educators, and researchers align their efforts to offer literacy instruction that students consider meaningful and worthwhile?

2. What are the productive intersections among instructional practices, texts, assessments, and contexts for advancing the literacy development of all students and honoring their diversity(ies)?

3. How should literacy instruction be reconceptualized so that it is broad enough and deep enough for today's diverse landscape?

REFERENCES

Apple, M.W., Kenway, J., & Singh, M. (Eds.). (2005). *Globalizing education: Policies, pedagogies, and politics.* New York: Peter Lang.

Au, W. (Ed.). (2009). *Rethinking multicultural education: Teaching for racial and cultural justice.* Milwaukee, WI: Rethinking Schools.

August, D., & Shanahan, T. (Eds.). (2006). *Developing literacy in second-language learners: Report of the National Literacy Panel on Language-Minority Children and Youth.* Mahwah, NJ: Erlbaum; Washington, DC: Center for Applied Linguistics.

August, D., & Shanahan, T. (Eds.). (2008). *Developing reading and writing in second-language learners: Lessons from the report of the National Literacy Panel on Language-Minority Children and Youth.* New York: Routledge.

Ayers, W., Quinn, T., & Stovall, D. (Eds.). (2009). *Handbook of social justice in education.* New York: Routledge.

Bailey, A.L. (2007). *The language demands of school: Putting academic English to the test.* New Haven, CT: Yale University Press.

Banks, C.A.M. (2005). *Improving multicultural education: Lessons from the intergroup education movement.* New York: Teachers College Press.

Banks, J.A. (Ed.). (2009). *The Routledge international companion to multicultural education.* New York: Routledge.

Biancarosa, G., & Snow, C.E. (2004). *Reading next—A vision for action and research in middle and high school literacy: A report to Carnegie Corporation of New York.* Washington, DC: Alliance for Excellent Education.

Blackburn, M.V., Clark, C.T., Kenney, L.M., & Smith, J.M. (Eds.). (2010). *Acting out! Combating homophobia through teacher activism.* New York: Teachers College Press.

Brayboy, B.M.J. (2005). Toward a tribal critical race theory in education. *The Urban Review, 37*(5), 425–446. doi:10.1007/s11256-005-0018-y

Bursztyn, A.M. (Ed.). (2007). *The Praeger handbook of special education.* Westport, CT: Praeger.

Daiute, C., & Jones, H. (2003). Diversity discourses: Reading race and ethnicity in and around children's writing. In S. Greene & D. Abt-Perkins (Eds.), *Making race visible: Literacy research for cultural understanding* (pp. 178–200). New York: Teachers College Press.

Deshler, D.D., Palincsar, A.S., Biancarosa, G., & Nair, M. (2007). *Informed choices for struggling adolescent readers: A research-based guide to instructional programs and practices.* Newark, DE: International Reading Association.

Gambrell, L.B., Morrow, L.M., & Pressley, M. (Eds.). (2007). *Best practices in literacy instruction* (3rd ed.). New York: Guilford.

Gay, G. (2000). *Culturally responsive teaching: Theory, research, and practice.* New York: Teachers College Press.

Graham, S., & Harris, K.R. (2005). Self-regulated strategy development: Helping students with learning problems develop as writers. *The Elementary School Journal, 94*(2), 169–181.

Guzzetti, B.J., Young, J.P., Gritsavage, M.M., Fyfe, L.M., & Hardenbrook, M. (2002). *Reading, writing, and talking gender in literacy learning.* Newark, DE: International Reading Association; Chicago: National Reading Conference.

Henze, R., Katz, A., Norte, E., Sather, S.E., & Walker, E. (2002). *Leading for diversity: How school leaders promote positive interethnic relations.* Thousand Oaks, CA: Corwin.

International Reading Association. (2007). *Teaching reading well: A synthesis of the International Reading Association's research on teacher preparation for reading instruction.* Newark, DE: Author.

International Reading Association. (2010). *Standards for reading professionals—Revised 2010.* Newark, DE: Author.

Israel, S.E., & Duffy, G.G. (Eds.). (2009). *Handbook of research on reading comprehension.* New York: Routledge.

Kenney, L.M. (2010). Being out and reading queer-inclusive texts in a high school English classroom. In M.V. Blackburn, C.T. Clark, L.M. Kenney, & J.M. Smith (Eds.), *Acting out! Combating homophobia through teacher activism* (pp. 56–73). New York: Teachers College Press.

Koschoreck, J.W., & Tooms, A.K. (Eds.). (2009). *Sexuality matters: Paradigms and policies for educational leaders.* Lanham, MD: Rowman & Littlefield.

Lee, C.D. (2007). *Culture, literacy, and learning: Taking bloom in the midst of the whirlwind.* New York: Teachers College Press.

Lewis, A., O'Connor, C., & Mueller, J. (2009). Discrimination, culture, or capital? The challenges of underconceptualizing race in educational research. In W. Ayers, T. Quinn, & D. Stovall (Eds.), *Handbook of social justice in education* (pp. 249–276). New York: Routledge.

Lynch, S.J. (2000). *Equity and science education reform.* Mahwah, NJ: Erlbaum.

Morrell, E., & Duncan-Andrade, J.M.R. (2002). Promoting academic literacy with urban youth through engaging hip-hop culture. *English Journal, 91*(6), 88–92.

Morrow, L.M., Rueda, R., & Lapp D. (Eds.). (2009). *Handbook of research on literacy and diversity.* New York: Guilford.

Murray, F.B. (Ed.). (1996). *The teacher educator's handbook: Building a knowledge base for the preparation of teachers.* San Francisco: Jossey-Bass.

National Center on Education and the Economy. (2006). *Tough choices or tough times: The report of the New Commission on the Skills of the American Workforce.* San Francisco: Jossey-Bass.

National Governors Association Center for Best Practices. (2005). *Reading to achieve: A governor's guide to adolescent literacy.* Washington, DC: Author.

Nocon, H., & Cole, M. (2009). Relating diversity and literacy theory. In L.M. Morrow, R. Rueda, & D. Lapp (Eds.), *Handbook of research on literacy and diversity* (pp. 13–31). New York: Guilford.

Perie, M., Grigg, W., & Donahue, P. (2005). *The Nation's Report Card: Reading 2005* (NCES 2006-451). Washington, DC: U.S. Department of Education, National Center for Education Statistics.

Pfeiffer, S.I. (Ed.). (2008). *Handbook of giftedness in children: Psycho-educational theory, research, and best practices.* New York: Springer.

Purcell-Gates, V. (Ed.). (2007). *Cultural practices of literacy: Case studies of language, literacy, social practice, and power.* Mahwah, NJ: Erlbaum.

Richardson, V. (Ed.). (2001). *Handbook of research on teaching* (4th ed.). Washington, DC: American Educational Research Association.

Rymes, B. (2001). *Conversational borderlands: Language and identity in an alternative urban high school.* New York: Teachers College Press.

Salili, F., & Hoosain, R. (Eds.). (2007). *Culture, motivation, and learning: A multicultural perspective.* Charlotte, NC: Information Age.

Sleeter, C.E. (2006). *Un-standardizing curriculum: Multicultural teaching in the standards-based classroom.* New York: Teachers College Press.

Tatum, A.W. (2008). Toward a more anatomically complete model of literacy instruction: A focus on African American male adolescents and texts. *Harvard Educational Review, 78*(1), 155–180.

Tatum, A.W. (2009). *Reading for their life: (Re)building the textual lineages of African American adolescent males.* Portsmouth, NH: Heinemann.

Tatum, A.W. (in press). The legitimacy of culturally relevant pedagogy: Resolved or unresolved. In L. Scherff & K. Spector (Eds.), *Culturally relevant pedagogy: Clashes and confrontations.* Lanham, MD: Rowman & Littlefield.

Troia, G.A. (2009). *Instruction and assessment for struggling writers: Evidence-based practices.* New York: Guilford.

Tsui, A.B.M., & Tollefson, J.W. (Eds.). (2007). *Language policy, culture, and identity in Asian contexts.* Mahwah, NJ: Erlbaum.

U.S. Census Bureau. (2007). *American community survey.*

Wilkinson, L.C., Morrow, L.M., & Chou, V. (Eds.). (2008). *Improving literacy achievement in urban schools: Critical elements in teacher preparation.* Newark, DE: International Reading Association.

LITERATURE CITED

Douglass, F. (2006). *Narrative of the life of Frederick Douglass.* Hollywood, FL: Simon & Brown.

Flake, S.G. (2007). *Bang.* New York: Hyperion.

Klein, N. (2008). *The shock doctrine: The rise of disaster capitalism.* New York: Metropolitan.

Mosley, W. (2006). *47.* Boston: Little, Brown.

Myers, W.D. (2002). *Handbook for boys: A novel.* New York: HarperTrophy.

Chapter 18

How Reading Research and Federal Policy on Reading Instruction Have Interrelated Over the Past 35 Years

Richard M. Long and Ramsay Selden

Twenty years ago, if one asked whether policymakers use research to inform the education laws, the answer would have been yes. Today, the answer is resoundingly yes. Taking a snapshot of each of the last four decades provides us with the ability to see several key trends in the increasingly greater use of selective research in the making of policy. Yet, it also tells us that while research may be looking to inform instruction, policymakers can and do make decisions that have consequences far beyond the simple hope of trying to ensure that more children learn how to read and are reading to learn.

Before the 1950s, research, policy, and practice had a relatively limited and linear relationship. Mainly, developments in understanding learning were used to make changes—gradually—in materials or instruction. This relationship was very different from the one we have now, which is much more dynamic. In the 1970s and 1980s, Guthrie regularly described developments in research on reading and addressed how they related to policy and practice to the extent that he could at that time. Those relationships were more complex and dynamic, but they still were far less complex and rich than they are now.

Research is now a major cornerstone of virtually all reading policy in the United States. It is almost impossible to have a discussion about improving literacy without a Congressional staff member, legislator, or member of the executive branch asking about the research. Part of this concern is the desire to make good policy, but another part is the policymaker's concern of trying to figure out what will be acceptable to political allies and opponents. For good or evil, that concern has as a central feature the fear of being caught up in the "reading wars" (Vacca, 1996).

What Research Has to Say About Reading Instruction (4th ed.) edited by S. Jay Samuels and Alan E. Farstrup.
© 2011 by the International Reading Association.

So, what is policy? Basically, it is the decision to allocate resources under a specific set of purposes. Establishing the federally funded interstate highway system was a policy decision that the federal government made to increase the nation's ability to move goods from one place to another. However, it had a profound impact on towns, cities, and communities, as well as other forms of transportation. Policy related to reading has ranged from simply declaring that reading achievement needed to be improved and providing resources, to declaring how reading achievement will be measured and thus deciding what elements are more important than others. At some state capitals, decisions are made as to what materials will be used, how teachers will be certified, and how students will be measured—all with an impact on how resources will be allocated.

Since the massive expansion of the federal role in education with the passage of the Elementary and Secondary Act of 1965, one of the major justifications for the federal role in education has been the belief that all children in the United States should have access to a basic education (Johnson, 1965), and reading and mathematics have always been at the core of that belief. Before 1965, the source of funding for elementary and secondary education was limited for most schools to the local property tax and differing kinds of state funding (Griffith, 2004), which meant that a child's educational opportunity was impacted by the wealth of the area he or she was born in. Because disadvantaged children were heavily concentrated in poor communities, the result was unequal access to a basic education. This inequality of resources translated to a push to create educational opportunity that was seen as critical to creating the education system that would enhance equality and be a part of the remedy implied in *Brown v. Board of Education* in 1954.

Simply providing more money to school districts with large numbers of low-income families was found not to work. To build an effective set of school systems across the United States, the federal government needed to move into supporting teacher training, developing national assessments to measure educational progress, and monitoring states and districts to see if money was being appropriately spent. Thus, the National Assessment of Educational Progress (NAEP) was created in 1964 (U.S. Department of Education, 2010). The federal government also had to develop concepts of supplement, rather than supplanting and providing funds, to ensure that handicapped children were not ignored, and students whose home language was different from the language of instruction were not overlooked. Following the court case *Lau v. Nichols* of 1974, which changed how the education of non–English-speaking children would be seen, these elements were included in the Education of All Handicapped Children Act of 1975. Each of these decisions added to the body of law that the federal government was specifically protecting two key groups of learners: handicapped students and English language learners. This protection pushed the federal government not only to make specific rules around who was in each group but also to demand that teachers be specifically trained to work with the specific needs of these learners, assessments be crafted to measure these learners, and funds be spent on providing services. The NAEP's assessments as the national report card became the measure and set of definitions for what had previously constituted an academic area of study. Now, the discipline was no longer defined by academic scholars but by the government.

In the initial rewriting of the Elementary and Secondary Education Act in 1974 and 1978, reading and literacy practice were cornerstones. In 1970, the Nixon Administration pushed for and supported the creation of the Right to Read program. This program convened experts, provided demonstration grants, and disseminated examples of good practice in reading. With the change in administrations in 1976, the Carter Administration changed the name of the program to Office of Basic Skills and slightly expanded the program's mission to include the need to teach reading as part of the nation's continued push to improve its economic standing. By the end of the 1970s, all of these elements were in place, and still progress was deemed unsatisfactory by the government and U.S. citizens. The political debate continued with the core question for the federal policy community, Is this working?

Reading Research: 1970–1990

Federal education policy is constantly evolving, sometimes in major ways. What started in 1964 as ensuring equity and access became something more—equity, access, and quality—during the 1980s, with the publication of *A Nation at Risk: The Imperative for Educational Reform* (The National Commission on Excellence in Education, 1983). For the first time, quality was sought beyond basic skills, because reading achievement was seen as in need of improvement. Measures of children in the high-poverty program Title I found that there was little sustained progress being achieved (Kaskowitz & Klibanoff, 1982). Reading specialists were being hired by schools, programs were being purchased, and other programs were being added. Still, achievement stagnated. At the same time, *A Nation at Risk* noted that America's education system lagged behind those of other countries, and said very explicitly that specific, substantive standards needed to be sought. The National Commission on Excellence in Education included a list of courses that students must take in high school, and suggested that standards in the states and localities needed to be raised. The commission also said that teacher training, assessment, and many other areas needed to be reformed.

In 1976, Marshall Smith, then in the Office of Education's policy office, convened a series of 10 panels to make recommendations on different aspects of reading and reading instruction. These panels represented many significant backgrounds and points of view on the issue of reading. Each of the panels submitted a report that was compiled by Smith and integrated into an overall report. This work encompassed many different areas of the status of research on reading, especially comprehension, language, and literacy issues for young children.

A key part of the issue that Smith was looking at was that a simple way of understanding America's educational system is to consider that the only achievement problem is with disadvantaged students. This is because differences in achievement scores are associated almost entirely with disadvantage. Differences among schools, districts, or states are due almost entirely to the numbers of poor and minority students they serve. Our elementary/secondary school system still has not discovered how to bring about high achievement among poor and minority students. The system is set to enable advantaged students to do well, and that's what it does. Instead of being an equalizer that enables poor and minority children to leap forward, the system perpetuates inequities.

Poor and minority students have ended up in mainly urban and poor school systems. This concentration reveals and confirms the powerlessness of the school system to do well with disadvantaged children, and our system still has not developed ways to serve them. Efforts to close the gap have only recently been effective, and then only minimally. The hard truth is that the elementary/secondary school system has not really begun to provide the instructional approaches and quality that are needed.

From this information base, a series of actions were taken. One was to bring together various federal research initiatives and house them in one unit, which became the Center for the Study of Reading at the University of Illinois at Urbana-Champaign, under the direction of Richard Anderson. The work of the center was too expansive, but one of its landmark accomplishments was understanding reading as a cognitive function. Anderson's team produced research on reading comprehension and metacognition that is considered by many as critical to the overall understanding of the teaching of reading. As Lyon (personal interview, 2010) points out, "the Center's work produced findings that supported what became the research based push for change in how reading is taught." In particular, it provided a basis for better instruction of reading comprehension.

Another trend needs to be understood: the role of research in changing practice. Pearson (2007) identified three trends in the use of research and its impact policy. Key to this timeline is that most believed at this time that if the results of good research were widely and effectively disseminated, then practice would naturally change. The questions are, of course, How quickly, and how much? The rub is understanding that the rate of dissemination that translates to widespread utilization is full of guesswork in every profession. For education, it is even that much harder. Classrooms are isolated and face many factors, including the fact that they cannot stop to change. In *The New Meaning of Educational Change*, Fullan and Stiegelbauer (1994) point out that most kindergarten teachers have over 100,000 interactions a year, and to ask that person to change at the same time is essentially impossible. In testimony to Congress in 1998, education demographer Harold Hodgkinson, the former dean of the Simmons College School of Education and the former director of the National Institute of Education, said that given the geography, the vastly different classrooms, and the isolation of educators across the country, it is highly unlikely that any research that uses classrooms as its base should have its findings generalized ("A Conversation About Demography," 1999).

With the creation of the Center for the Study of Reading, or partly because of it, the drive for the nation to agree on how best to teach reading was strong. As early as 1980, the impact of Toffler's (1970) *Future Shock* and the beginning of the personal computer revolution was creating a demand for students to graduate with a greater ability to work and learn in a knowledge-based society. To address what seemed to be a permanent rift between those who saw reading as more skill based and those who saw it as more holistic, the new U.S. Department of Education commissioned a panel to produce a report, which became *Becoming a Nation of Readers: The Report of the Commission on Reading* (Anderson, Hiebert, Scott, & Wilkinson, 1985). This report recommended the following:

- Parents should read to preschool children and informally teach them about reading and writing....
- Parents should support school-aged children's continued growth as readers....

- Preschool and kindergarten reading readiness programs should focus on reading, writing, and oral language....
- Teachers should maintain classrooms that are both stimulating and disciplined....
- Teachers of beginning reading should present well-designed phonics instruction....
- Reading primers should be interesting, comprehensible, and give children opportunities to apply phonics....
- Teachers should devote more time to comprehension instruction....
- Children should spend less time completing workbooks and skill sheets....
- Children should spend more time in independent reading....
- Children should spend more time writing....
- Textbooks should contain adequate explanations of important concepts....
- Schools should cultivate an ethos that supports reading....
- Schools should maintain well-stocked and managed libraries....
- Schools should introduce more comprehensive assessments of reading and writing....
- Schools should attract and hold more able teachers....
- Teacher education programs should be lengthened and improved in quality....
- Schools should provide for the continuing professional development of teachers. (pp. 117–120)

Did these actions significantly impact reading achievement that the Congressional leaders were looking for? The short answer is no. By the late 1980s, the states' governors began to rally around the idea that education reform needed to be driven by the states, which led to the 1989 Education Summit and the set of national education goals (Vinovskis, 1999). The concept that good ideas would push out bad practices was taking too long, and the arguments that schools and states lacked the resources to enact the improvements needed for better educational outcomes was beginning to wear thin. Some advocated the need for assessment programs that actually would highlight poor outcomes and thus force changes. Many saw the production of the national standards for mathematics instruction by the National Council of Teachers of Mathematics (1989) as the direction for all content areas.

Reading Research: 1990–2000

Internationally, the world was coming together in the Education for All movement that changed the relationship between education and decision making in some fundamental ways. It was not just the education ministries that were being brought together to reflect on good practice. The movement brought the heads of government, heads of finance, and representatives of nongovernment organizations together with education ministers to make education a central part of government. In the United States, the states' governors began to set the agenda and demanded that federal resources be spent on specific targets, and the federal government demanded state accountability.

Yet, another important shift occurred. When the National Council of Teachers of Mathematics (1989) issued its set of standards, it chose to define how research would be applied to instruction in the classroom. This was seen as a model that could be done in other subjects. In adopting the standards movement in the early 1990s as the method of policy, both the state and federal governments were launched on a path to define issues that moved from the schoolhouse door to inside the classroom.

By the mid-1990s, it was clear that the standards movement in and of itself was not going to make the big impact that many had hoped. By 1997, with G. Reid Lyon as the director of the Child Development and Behavior Branch, the National Institute for Child Health and Human Development had launched a set of studies looking at beginning reading instruction. Lyon believed that if good research could be brought forward, then the argument over beginning reading could be answered, and more attention and resources would flow. By 1994, his branch was reporting what he thought were conclusive studies. In a series of meetings and Congressional testimony, he was able to communicate the branch's work to the policy community. In doing so, the reading wars became somewhat personalized (Lyon, 1997). Leaders in the field took positions not only on the work but also on the proponents. It was not simply the work that legislators were hearing about but also the personalities of the various advocates.

During this time, one Senate staffer sought to put into legislation the requirement that specific features from the findings of the National Institute of Child Health and Human Development be implemented. This was attempted not only in education legislation but also legislation to direct the U.S. Department of Defense. In a separate set of events, the House of Representatives Committee on Appropriations wrote the Comprehensive School Reform Demonstration Act (see U.S. Department of Education, 2004a) into its annual spending bill to reform schools by requiring the use of criteria to select programs of instruction that reflected some very specific criteria. Although the legislation did not require the use of any one specific program, it listed as examples several programs that met the nine criteria required. A very important change in federal education policy and how it relates to practice had occurred. (Created in 1998 and authorized under the No Child Left Behind Act of 2001, the Comprehensive School Reform Program provides financial assistance to help schools develop and implement systematic approaches to schoolwide improvement that are grounded in scientifically based research and effective practices. The goal of the program is to enable all children to meet challenging state academic content and achievement standards. The annual grants of at least $50,000 per school support the initial implementation costs of adopting a research-based reform strategy over a three-year period. Since the program's inception in 1998, federal appropriations totaling nearly $1.4 billion have supported grants to more than 5,000 recipients.)

Meanwhile, Congressional attention on reading was the repeated subject of hearings and discussion. (Lyon testified several times during this decade.) The nation was talking more about the "information age," and frustration with the rate of change was building. By 1990, President George Bush had signed into law the creation of the National Institute for Literacy as a centralizing agency for labor, welfare, and education to promote effective adult basic education (the mission of this agency would again change with the passage of No Child Left Behind).

In addition, the National Academy of Sciences was empowered in 1997 to empanel a group of experts to determine what was known about reading instruction. This panel, supported by Lyon, was to bring to clarity what he and others had been advocating, that reading instruction should be designed based on what was scientifically based. Lyon had supported the development of a research base supported by the National Institute of Child Health and Human Development to study beginning reading instruction. The findings of these studies convinced him that there were several critical elements that needed to be central in all beginning reading programs. A key element was "specific and direction instruction in phonemic awareness and phonics" (personal communication, 2010). Lyon later testified before Congress that the research was also supporting the finding that many of the children who needed "direct and systematic instruction in phonemic awareness and phonics also needed direct instruction in comprehension" (personal communication, 2010).

These events came together as Congress wrote the Reading Excellence Act of 1998, which amended the Elementary and Secondary Education Act of 1965. As a side note, it is rare for a measure such as this to be enacted by Congress. Usually, programs like this one are passed as part of the rewriting of the Elementary and Secondary Education Act every 5–6 years, yet the Reading Excellence Act passed on its own. William Goodling (R-PA), the chair of the House Committee on Education, had been a longtime advocate of literacy, and he frequently cited his wife, a former teacher, as having a significant impact on his thinking. She had motivated him to enact this legislation, which provided a federal definition of *reading* for the first time. The Act was designed to provide resources to selected school districts to fund professional development activities for classroom teachers to teach reading. The purpose, as outlined in the bill, was to support three key elements: professional development, out-of-school tutoring, and family literacy. The plan was to provide children with the readiness skills and support they need in early childhood to learn to read once they enter school, to teach every child to read by the end of the third grade, and to improve the instructional practices of teachers and other instructional staff in elementary schools.

Reading Research: 2000–2010

According to some advocates, the Reading Excellence Act did not go far enough (personal communication, 2010). Although professional development was being supported in schools that had low achievement in reading, some observers thought that the Act was not specific enough. The National Reading Panel had been commissioned, and it looked at research studies of early reading. The panel stated that reading consisted of five critical elements: phonemic awareness, phonics, vocabulary development, fluency, and comprehension. These elements became the most specific set of recommendations to be published by a federally supported panel and was used to retool Reading Excellence into Reading First with the concept of scientifically based reading research.

According to the No Child Left Behind Act (U.S. Department of Education, 2004b), the term *reading* is defined as

> a complex system of deriving meaning from print that requires all of the following:

(A) The skills and knowledge to understand how phonemes, or speech sounds, are connected to print.

(B) The ability to decode unfamiliar words.

(C) The ability to read fluently.

(D) Sufficient background information and vocabulary to foster reading comprehension.

(E) The development of appropriate active strategies to construct meaning from print.

(F) The development and maintenance of a motivation to read. (sec. 1208)

The Act then defines *scientifically based reading research* as research that

(A) applies rigorous, systematic, and objective procedures to obtain valid knowledge relevant to reading development, reading instruction, and reading difficulties; and

(B) includes research that—

    (i) employs systematic, empirical methods that draw on observation or experiment;

    (ii) involves rigorous data analyses that are adequate to test the stated hypotheses and justify the general conclusions drawn;

    (iii) relies on measurements or observational methods that provide valid data across evaluators and observers and across multiple measurements and observations; and

    (iv) has been accepted by a peer-reviewed journal or approved by a panel of independent experts through a comparably rigorous, objective, and scientific review. (sec. 1208)

Of note were not the specifics but rather the question of whether all of these criteria were to be met, or did each point pass muster to make something scientifically based. The reality was that the U.S. Department of Education chose to interpret the criteria as all having to be met. In addition, the Department chose not to allow "home-grown" programs that embodied all of these elements to meet this criteria either.

Now, reading research was being used to decide what type of reading instruction would be supported. The impact of the findings of the National Reading Panel was much wider than Reading First and No Child Left Behind. Several states developed legislation that looked at the syllabuses being used in teacher education programs in public universities, and others crafted their state requirements to reflect the findings of the National Reading Panel. In short, specific research was influencing policy and practice in several different areas.

Although many see Reading First with scientifically based reading research as the most significant example of a specific set of research impacting instruction, this is not the only major initiative. In 2006, the Individuals with Disabilities Education Act was rewritten with the inclusion of many of the concepts that revolve around Response to Intervention (RTI; for more information, visit the RTI Action Network website at www.rtinetwork.org). *RTI* is a general term used to describe a set of educational changes designed to intervene with a struggling learner before an Individualized Education Plan is created. The thinking is that if classroom teachers are able to change how they teach, then some students who were previously thought to be learning disabled would not need to be so identified. However, if this first change is unsuccessful, the student is then placed with a professional who will best be able to meet the child's education needs. Although many view RTI and its multitiered intervention process as a special education process being used in regular education, it is a bit more. The ideas behind RTI are based in scientifically based reading research. Since most students who are thought to be learning disabled are struggling to learn how to read, most advocates are pushing for the use of scientifically based reading research to design instructional programs for these students.

In contrast to the highly specific research being quoted in developing these policies and procedures, there are two other areas that have been touched by reading research and are impacting policy. First is the revision of the NAEP reading framework (U.S. Department of Education, 2008), which brings in a comprehensive view of reading, including a full set of cognitive dimension, early skills, vocabulary, and personal aspects. Second, the Common Core State Standards for English language arts (Council of Chief State School Officers & National Governors Association, 2010) reflect an interpretation of the research that is much more cognitive than the interpretations that have driven Reading First and RTI. In these standards, *reading* is defined as part of a complex constellation that includes oral language and writing as integrated, not separate, skills. Even one of the most difficult parts of the core standards, the interpretation of text complexity, is in a totally different range of concept from the five areas as defined in Reading First. How this is implemented will take the discussion of how reading research impacts policy and practice into an entirely new arena.

Summary

The use of reading research to impact policy has taken many specific forms since the passage of the Elementary and Secondary Education Act in 1964. From the simple belief in the 1960s that having reading programs supported by the federal government, with the hiring of reading specialists who practice the diagnostic prescriptive model, would make *the* difference, the country moved to the next step of developing an agenda in the 1970s to impact the development of reading research to inform instruction. This became the impetus to create the Center for the Study of Reading in 1976, which created a significant basis of understanding comprehension (Center for the Study of Reading, n.d.). The center was established with funding from the U.S. Department of Education to address the unacceptably high number of American schoolchildren who were failing to learn to read. The center's main priorities continue to guide its work:

- Reading research and development must be to discover and put into practice the means for reaching children who are failing to read.
- Reading research and development must be to discover how to help all children acquire knowledge from and reason about the written word.
- Reading research and development must be to improve the education of reading teachers. (para. 1)

However, as these processes unfolded, the public increasingly demanded a program that would increase the number of students who were reading well. New measurements of what that meant began to take hold. The previous proxy of the school system's effectiveness (i.e., SAT scores) was replaced by the NAEP's reading framework at state and national levels, and the adequate yearly progress measurement for local schools. Unfortunately, about every four years, the NAEP consistently reports only minor improvements in scores. It also reports that states vary widely in the quality of their standards, and that states are below the rigorous, objective standards of the NAEP, especially for disadvantaged kids.

The pressure for faster results changed the focus from looking at developing comprehension and vocabulary to developing a stronger understanding of the relationship of several key areas of beginning reading instruction. Yet, what also changed was the model of change itself. No longer was it acceptable to conduct research, disseminate it, and watch change slowly take place. With the passage of the Reading Excellence

Act and Reading First, along with the introduction of RTI, change was to take place now. In reality, as the nation's report card, the NAEP has continued to show modest changes in reading scores.

So, where does research and policy go next? The Common Core State Standards seem to be the next stage in the intertwining of research and policy. Will the idea of more complex relationships between cognition and language lead to success? This is an open question. The answer will most likely be a factor of how universally the notions are quickly accepted and how long they are given to take hold.

Questions for Reflection

1. One of the key issues that this chapter touches on but never defines is the issue of how much time it takes for a researched concept to come into practice. How would you quantify the cycle from research to practice?

2. The chapter ends with the Common Core State Standards being cited as a researched-based document. How would you evaluate the research that supported these standards? Is it current? Is it on the cutting edge?

3. One of the statements in the chapter relates to the fact that America's challenge to closing the achievement gap is mostly a function of the level of poverty found in our nation's schools. Yet, the Program for International Student Assessment (2009, p. 3) data indicate that socioeconomic status only explains 6% of the variable in academic achievement. How do you reconcile these two statements?

REFERENCES

Anderson, R.C., Hiebert, E.H., Scott, J.A., & Wilkinson, I.A.G. (1985). *Becoming a nation of readers: The report of the Commission on Reading.* Washington, DC: National Institute of Education, U.S. Department of Education. (ERIC Document Reproduction Service No. ED253865)

Center for the Study of Reading. (n.d.). *History.* Urbana-Champaign: College of Education, University of Illinois. Retrieved January 7, 2011, from csr.ed.uiuc.edu/about.html

A conversation about demography with Harold Hodgkinson. (1999). *New England Journal of Higher Education, Summer.* Retrieved January 7, 2011, from findarticles.com/p/articles/mi_qa3895/is_199907/ai_n8870361

Council of Chief State School Officers & National Governors Association. (2010). *Common core state standards for English language arts and literacy in history/social studies, science, and technical subjects.* Retrieved January 7, 2011, from www.corestandards.org/the-standards

Fullan, M. & Stiegelbauer, S.M. (1991). The new meaning of educational change (2nd ed.). New York: Teachers College Press.

Griffith, M. (2004, June). Taxation and spending policies. *ECS StateNotes.* Retrieved

January 7, 2011, from www.ecs.org/clearing house/52/94/5294.htm

Johnson, L.B. (1965, April 11). *Remarks in Johnson City, Texas, upon signing the Elementary and Secondary Education Bill, April 11, 1965* [Speech]. Retrieved January 7, 2011, from www.lbjlibrary.org/collections/selected-speeches/1965/04-11-1965.html

Kaskowitz, D.H., & Klibanoff, L.S. (1982, March). *Results from the analyses of Title I project vector data.* Paper presented at the 66th annual meeting of the American Educational Research Association, New York. (ERIC Document Reproduction Service No. ED218326)

Lyon, G.R. (1997, July 10). *Testimony of G. Reid Lyon, Ph.D. on children's literacy.* Washington, DC: Committee on Education and the Workforce, U.S. House of Representatives.

The National Commission on Excellence in Education. (1983). *A nation at risk: The imperative for educational reform.* Washington, DC: U.S. Government Printing Office.

National Council of Teachers of Mathematics, Commission on Standards for School Mathematics. (1989). *Curriculum and evaluation standards for school mathematics.* Reston, VA: Author.

OECD (2010). PISA 2009 results: Overcoming social background: Equity in learning opportunities and outcomes (Volume II). Paris: OECD. Retrieved from http://dx.doi.org/10.1787/9789264091504-en

Pearson, P.D. (2007). An endangered species act for literacy education. *Journal of Literacy Research, 34*(2), 145–162.

Toffler, A. (1970). *Future shock.* New York: Bantam.

U.S. Department of Education. (2004a). *Comprehensive School Reform Program.* Washington, DC: Author. Retrieved January 7, 2011, from www2.ed.gov/programs/comprefrom/2pager.html

U.S. Department of Education. (2004b). *Elementary and secondary education: Part B—Student reading skills improvement grants: Subpart 1—Reading First.* Washington, DC: Author. Retrieved January 7, 2011, from www2.ed.gov/policy/elsec/leg/esea02/pg4.html

U.S. Department of Education, National Assessment Governing Board. (2008). *Reading framework for the National Assessment of Educational Progress.* Washington, DC: Author.

U.S. Department of Education, Institute of Education Sciences, National Center for Education Statistics. (2010). *NAEP: Measuring student progress since 1964.* Washington, DC: Author. Retrieved January 7, 2011, from nces.ed.gov/nationsreportcard/about/naephistory.asp

Vacca, R.T. (1996). The reading wars: Who will be the winners, who will be the losers? *Reading Today, 14*(October/November), 3.

Vinovskis, M.A. (1999). *The road to Charlottesville: The 1989 Education Summit.* Washington, DC: National Education Goals Panel. Retrieved January 7, 2011, from govinfo.library.unt.edu/negp/reports/negp30.pdf

Author Index

A

Aaron , P.G., 187, 192, 197, 384
Abbeduto, L., 227, 228
Abbott, R.D., 75, 76
Abbott, S.P., 76
Aber, J.L., 118
Abrami, P., 300
Abrams, S.G., 36, 37
Achilles, C.M., 248, 253
Achugar, M., 173
Adams, B.C., 200
Adams, E., 247
Adams, M.J., 5, 8,15, 19, 219
Adlof, S.M., 187, 188, 192, 196, 197, 202, 203
Afflerbach, P., 153, 366
Agodini, R., 298
Ahlgrim-Delzell, L., 217
Ainley, M., 60
Aitchison, J., 324, 327, 331
Al Otaiba, S., 225
Alao, S., 57
Alborz, A., 227
Alexander, J.F., 71
Alexander, K.L., 238
Alexander, P.A., 169–170, 174, 249, 384, 385, 386
Alexander, R., 290
Alfassi, M., 374
Algozzine, B., 217, 244
Allen, J., 412
Allen, N.L., 58
Allington, R.L., 59, 60, 94, 143, 146–147, 150, 151, 153, 154, 155, 239, 242, 243, 244, 245–246, 247, 249, 250, 251, 252, 255, 256, 257–258, 383
Allor, J.H., 217, 226, 228, 229–230, 230–232
Alloway, T.P., 223, 227
Allsop, D., 242
Almasi, J.F., 153
Alvarez, L., 398
Amanti, C., 181
American Association on Intellectual and Developmental Disabilities, 216–217
American Literacy Council, 13
American Psychiatric Association (APA), 216
Ames, C., 154
Anders, P.L., 57
Anderson, V., 168
Anderson, D.R., 290
Anderson, E., 57
Anderson, M., 251
Anderson, R.C., 53, 57, 72, 144, 155, 452

Anderson, R.H., 81
Andrade, H.L., 389
Andrews, R., 297
Angelil, P., 352
Anthony, J.L., 16, 203, 219
Apple, M.W., 430, 431
Applebee, A.N., 72
Apthorp, H.S., 74–75
Ardell, A.L., 359
Arguelles, M.E., 64
Arizpe, E., 353
Aro, M., 13
Atkinson, R.C., 294
Atwell, J.A., 223–224
Au, K.H., 66, 250, 316–317, 337
Au, W., 435
Aufenanger, S., 288
August, D., 430, 435
Ausubel, D.P., 164
Ausubel, P., 164, 165
Ayers, W., 425, 426, 430
Azevedo, R., 289
Azuma, T., 9

B

Badian, N.A., 195
Bailey, A.L., 430
Baker, A.J.L., 406
Baker, J.M., 244, 254
Baker, L., 414, 415
Bakia, M., 290
Baldwin, L.E., 201
Bandura, A., 413
Banks, C.A.M., 431
Banks, J.A., 431
Barber, J., 57
Barbosa, P., 63
Barksdale-Ladd, M.A., 76
Barnes, A.C., 266
Barnes, W.S., 51
Barnett, W.S., 246
Barr, R., 252
Barron, R.F., 172
Barrueco, S., 406
Barth, A.E., 202
Barton, D., 366
Batsche, G., 283
Bauer, E.B., 82, 414
Bauer, P., 288
Bauerlein, M., 148
Baumann, J.F., 64, 74, 387
Beals, D.E., 415
Bean, T.W., 135

Beatty, A.S., 96
Becerra, A.M., 229
Beck, I.L., 67, 72, 74, 160, 163, 167, 168, 169, 174, 175
Beers, A., 200
Bell, C., 392
Bell, L.C., 6, 200
Belsky, J., 251–252
Beltran, D.O., 300
Bembry, K.L., 251
Berch-Heyman, S., 287
Bereiter, C., 77
Beretvas, S.N., 59
Bergeron, B.S., 64
Berla, N., 406
Berliner, D.C., 153
Berninger, V.W., 75, 76
Berrueta-Clement, J.R., 246
Bertelson, P., 232
Best, R., 57
Betjemann, R.S., 190
Betts, J., 80
Beverton, S., 297
Biancarosa, G., 162, 163, 171, 431, 435
Bianco, M., 207
Biemiller, A., 74–75
Biggs, M., 106
Biklen, D., 217
Billman, A.K., 57, 60, 80
Binder, J.R., 7
Birkerts, S., 295
Birlem, E.D., 145
Birman, B., 303
Bishop, D.V.M., 204
Bitter, C., 72
Black, L., 266
Black, P., 387, 388, 389, 390, 391, 392
Blackburn, M.V., 431, 432
Blake, R.G.K., 67, 160
Blanc, S., 396, 397
Blanchard, J., 287, 289, 290, 292, 294–295
Block, C.C., 60, 64
Blok, H., 296
Blomeyer, R.L., Jr., 288, 297
Bloom, B.S., 387
Blumenfield, P.C., 119
Bolt, S., 80
Bond, G.L., 2
Boote, C., 74–75
Booth, J.R., 18
Borman, G.D., 240
Borstrøm, I., 203
Bos, C.S., 57
Boudett, K.P., 399
Boulay, B., 250
Bowen, C.T., 103
Bowen, N.K., 122

Bowyer-Crane, C., 207
Boyd-Zacharias, J., 253
Brabham, E.G., 74–75
Bracey, G.W., 386
Brandeis, D., 7
Brantlinger, E., 279
Bravo, M.A., 57
Brayboy, B.M.J., 431
Braze, D., 187, 200
Brem, S., 7, 19
Brenner, D., 152, 153
Brewster, J., 322, 323, 348
Bridges, M.S., 204
Brock, C.H., 250
Broerse, A.C., 41
Brookhart, S.M., 388
Brooks, G., 247
Brophy, J., 60
Browder, D.M., 217, 218, 219, 226
Brown, A.L., 63, 162, 165, 166, 167, 172
Brown, J.S., 291
Brown, T.L., 384
Brownell, M., 206
Bruce, B.C., 384
Bruner, J.S., 291, 322, 324, 326, 350, 367
Bruno, J.L., 7, 18
Brunstein, J.C., 63
Bryant, B.R., 5, 198
Bryk, A.S., 252
Brysbaert, M., 41
Buchanan, L., 7
Bucher, K., 7
Buckley, S., 228
Bulat, J., 301
Bulgren, J., 175, 178, 179
Bulkley, K.E., 396, 397
Buly, M.R., 79, 385
Bunce, S., 301
Bundsgaard, J., 288
Burgess, S.R., 203, 282
Burkam, D.T., 201
Burke, A., 290
Burkins, J.M., 364
Burn, A., 297
Burnett, C., 296, 298–299, 299
Burns, M.K., 283
Burns, M.S., 15, 75, 206, 272, 295
Burns, T., 297
Bursztyn, A.M., 431
Bus, A.G., 249, 290, 301, 414, 415
Byrne, A., 228
Byrne, B., 15
Byron, T., 291

C
Cabrera, M.P., 351
Cairns, H.S., 75

Calderón, M., 341, 342, 343
Calfee, R.C., 168
Calvert, S.L., 290
Cambria, J., 123
Cameron, L., 322, 323, 327, 329, 331, 332, 337, 338, 339
Camine, D.W., 5
Campbell, J.R., 58, 96
Campione, J.C., 165
Campuzano, L., 298
Carbo, M., 103
Carnegie Council on Advancing Adolescent Literacy, 172
Carpenter, D.M., II, 122, 123
Carpenter, R.D., 385
Carr, N., 295
Carr, T.H., 384
Carrington, V., 290
Carroll, J.H., 250
Carson, B, 127
Carter, M.A., 387
Cartwright, K.B., 80
Cassano, C., 414
Cassidy, D., 96, 111, 359
Cassidy, J., 96, 111, 205, 359
Castellano, M., 359
Castillo, J.G., 8
Cattell, J.M., 33, 34
Catto, S.L., 252
Catts, H.W., 187, 188, 190, 193, 195, 196, 202, 204
Caughlan, S., 59
Cavalier, A.R., 296
Cavanaugh, C., 297
Cazden, C.B., 249, 367
Celano, D., 155, 256, 412
Center for the Study of Reading, 459
Center, Y., 336, 340
Cervetti, G.N., 57, 76
Chalfant, J.C., 241
Chall, J.S., 5, 98, 191, 201
Chambliss, M.J., 168
Champlin, T.M., 217, 226, 228
Chandler, J., 51
Chapman, R.S., 227, 229
Chard, D.J., 94–95, 95, 278
Cheatham, J.P., 217, 228
Cheek, E.H., 172
Chen, M., 406, 407, 408
Chen, R.S., 187
Chiang, B., 99
Chiesim, H.L., 200
Chinn, C.A., 72
Chlong, C., 290
Chomsky, C., 103
Chomsky, N., 323
Chou, V., 428

Chrispeels, J.H., 411, 413
Christman, J.B., 397
CILT, 321
City, E.A., 399
Clancy-Menchetti, J., 222
Clark, C.T., 431
Clark, K., 58, 251, 272
Clarke, P., 196
Clausen-Grace, N., 134, 151–152
Clay, M.M. 249
Clotfelter, C.T., 300
Cocksey, J., 199, 204
Coddington, C.S., 118
Cohen, L., 6
Cohen-Vogel, L., 411
Coiro, J., 82, 290, 300
Cokley, K.O., 121
Cole, C.A.S., 201
Cole, K., 415
Cole, M., 431
Coles, G., 248, 258
Collins, J.L., 77, 78
Collins, P., 150
Colt, J.M., 252
Commeyras, M., 359, 384
Compton, D.L., 195, 198, 200, 202, 275
Compton-Lilly, C., 412
Connell, J.P., 118, 120
Conners, F.A., 223–224, 227
Connor, C.M., 81, 207, 385
Conway, T., 249
Cook, D., 286
Cooke, C.L., 166
Cooper, M, 138–139
Corn, J., 303
Cortiella, C., 239
Cossu,G., 220
Council of Chief State School Officers (CCSSO), 54–55, 60, 172, 458
Courtade, G., 217
Cowles, L., 135
Cox, A., 415
Coyne, M.D., 74–75
Craig, S.A., 76
Crain-Thoreson, C., 415
Crévola, C., 360
Croft, M.M., 364
Crook, C., 289
Crooks, T.J., 388
Crosson, A.C., 72
Cuban, L., 287, 293–294, 295
Cummins, J., 325
Cunningham, A., 301
Cunningham, A.E., 57, 59, 144, 155, 200, 246, 250, 326
Cunningham, J.W., 146
Cunningham, P.M., 248, 256

Cupples, L., 223–224
Curtis, M.E., 5
Curwen, M.S., 359
Cutting, L.E., 190, 201
Cziko, C., 173

D

Da Fonte, M.A., 228
Daane, M.C., 96, 98, 99
D'Agostino, J.V., 240
Dahl, K.L., 247
Daiute, C., 440
Dale, P.S., 415
Daley, K.E., 414
Dalton, B., 172, 173
Daniel, D.B., 289, 292
Darling-Hammond, L., 256, 258
Darvin, J., 135
Das, K.K., 300
Datnow, A., 359
David, B., 416
Davis, F.B., 384
Davis, M.H., 9
Day, J.D., 165
De La Paz, S., 77
de Moor, J., 221
Dean, V.J., 75
Dearing, E., 406, 409
Deault, L., 300
De Cara, B., 200
Deci, E.L., 154
Dede, C., 289
Dedrick, R., 106
Deford, D.E., 252
DeGaetano, Y., 411, 412
Dehaene, S., 6–8
Delgado-Gaitan, C., 412
Demko, M., 359
Dennis, D.V., 247
Deno, S.L., 41, 99, 271, 395
Denton, C.A., 198, 199, 244, 272, 274–275, 282
Desai, L.E., 387
Deshler, D.D., 175, 179, 435
DeTemple, J., 415
DeVoogd, G., 146–147, 149
Devlin, J.T., 9
Dewitz, P., 82
The Diagram Group, 191
Dickinson, D.K., 246
Doan Holbein, M.F., 409
Dobler, E., 82
Dobrich, W., 198, 414
Dodge, R., 27, 364
Dolan, L.J., 250
Dole, J.A., 67
Domina, T., 406

Donahue, P.L., 58, 430
Donaldson, M., 323, 324, 326, 329
Dong, T., 72
Donnellan, A.M., 218, 231
Dorph, R., 58
Dotterer, A., 291
Doye, P., 318
Drake, D.A., 13
Dreyer, L.G., 187. 205
Droter, K., 290
Druin, A., 287, 290
Dubburi, R., 191
Duffy, G.G., 67, 251, 256, 258, 361, 366–367, 431
Duffy, G.R., 59
Duffy-Hester, A.M., 250, 251, 253
Duke, N.K., 59, 60–61, 63, 64, 71, 79, 80, 82, 137, 206
Duncan, L.G., 5, 17
Duncan-Andrade, J.M.R., 431
Dunn, D.M., 204
Dunn, L.M., 204
Dunning, D.B., 414
Durand, M., 196
Dykstra, R., 2
Dynarski, M., 298

E

Early Child Care Research Network, 251–252
Ediger, K., 229
Edmonds, M.S., 174, 198
Educational Testing Service, 388
Edutopia, 289
Edutopia Staff, 301–302
Edwards, P.A., 412
Ehri, L.C., 11, 12–13, 15, 75, 272
Elbaum, B., 275
Elbro, C., 203
Elkins, J., 241, 243
Elleman, A.M., 195, 200
Ellis, D., 135–136
Ellis, G., 322, 348
Ellis Weismer, S., 196
Englert, C.S., 76
Ennemoser, M., 276, 299
Entwisle, D.R., 238
Epstein, A.S., 246
Epstein, J.L., 407, 409, 411, 412, 413, 419
Epstein, T., 181
Erskine, J.M., 13
Ertmer, P.A., 301
Espin, C., 271
Ettenberger, S., 251
Evans, M.A., 384
Evertt-Cacopardo, H., 290

F

Fairlie, R.W., 300
Fan, X., 406, 407, 408
Fanuele, D.P., 247
Fautsch-Partridge, T., 220, 229
Fawson, P.C., 63, 99, 149
Fayol, M., 76
Feinauer, E., 406
Feinberg, R., 31, 40, 42, 45
Felton, R.H., 199
Ferdig, R.E., 288
Fernandez-Fein, S., 414
Ferretti, R.P., 296
Fey, M.E., 187, 193, 204
Fielding, L.G., 67–68, 144, 366
Fielding-Barnesley, R., 15
Fink, R.P., 60
Finn, C.E., 161
Finn, J.D., 119
Finnegan, R.J., 58
Fisher, C.W., 153
Fisher, D., 360, 361, 364, 365, 412
Fishman, B.J., 207
Fitzgerald, J., 76
Fletcher, J.M., 190, 202, 244, 248, 252, 266, 272, 282, 359
Flood, J., 376, 412
Flowerday, T., 60
Flowers, C., 217
Flowers, D.L., 187
Floyd, R.G., 57
Foehr, U.G., 287, 290
Foley, S., 75
Foorman, B.R., 248, 272, 359
FORI, 149
Fountas, 80
Fox, C., 336
Fox, J., 77
Francis, D.J., 80, 190, 248, 272, 282, 359
Frank Porter Graham Child Development Center, 246
Fraser, B.J., 360
Fredricks, J.A., 119
Freire, P., 180
Freppon, P.A., 247
Frey, N., 360, 361, 364, 365
Friedauer, J.A., 98
Fries, C.C., 39
Frith, U., 10, 203
Frost, S.J., 12, 18
Fry, E., 107
Frye, B., 251
Fuchs, D., 195, 220, 225–226, 268, 271, 275, 397
Fuchs, L.S., 195, 268, 271, 275, 395, 397
Fuchs, T., 300
Fullan, M., 360, 452

Furrer, C.J., 119
Fyfe, L.M., 431

G

Gadberry, E., 296
Gainer, J.S., 301
Galileo, 26
Gallagher, A., 5, 18, 203
Gallagher, M.C., 64, 364, 366, 368
Gambrell, L.B., 103, 143, 153, 154, 435
Gamoran, A., 72, 367
Gamse, B.C., 250
Gantt, W.N., 153
Garan, E.M., 146–147, 149
García, G.E., 82
Gardner, H., 305, 325
Garlock, V.M., 199
Garvie, E., 329, 347, 348, 349, 354
Gaskins, I.W., 248
Gates, W., 293–294
Gathercole, S.E., 223, 227
Gaur, A., 43
Gay, G., 435
Gelzheiser, L.M., 251
Gentzkow, M., 299
George Lucas Educational Foundation, 301–302
Germane, C.E., 40
Germane, E.G., 40
Gersten, R., 271, 272, 274, 276
Geudens, A., 18
Gibbs, S.L., 217
Gilbert, J.K., 195
Gilbert, L.C., 39, 41
Gillan, K., 297
Gillon, G.T., 222
Glaubke, C., 290
Glover, T.A., 266
Goatley, V.J., 239, 250
Godwin, S., 365
Goertz, M.E., 396, 397
Goetz, E.T., 60
Goetz, K., 225
Goldinger, S.D., 9
Goldman, J.G., 7
Goldschmidt, P., 57
Golinkoff, R.M., 165
Golos, D., 206
Gomez, E., 251
Gong, B., 381
Gonnerman, L.M., 9
Gonzalez, N., 181
Gonzalez-DeHass, A.R., 409
Good, R.H., 198, 204, 278
Goodman, I.F., 51
Goodman, K., 41–42
Goodman, M.J., 96

Goswami, U., 13, 200, 290
Gough, P.B., 33–34, 96, 187, 190, 193, 249
Gough, W.E., 186
Graden, J., 244
Graetz, J.E., 174
Graham, S., 76, 431
Graves, M.F., 166
Gray, D.B., 242
Gray, E.S., 138
Gray, J., 301
Gray, L., 287
Greenleaf, C., 58
Greenleaf, C.L., 173
Griffin, P., 15, 206, 272, 295
Griffith, L.W., 106
Griffith, M., 449
Griffiths, A., 283
Grigg, W.S., 96, 430
Gritsavage, M.M., 431
Grogan, P.R., 247
Gromoll, E.W., 72
Grossman, P.L., 359
Gubbins, P., 72
Guckenburg, S., 397
Gury, E.C., 252
Guthrie, J.T., 57, 60, 62, 63, 81, 117, 118, 134,
    152, 153, 154, 175, 250, 386
Guthrie, L.F., 253
Guzzetti, B.J., 431

H
Haas, N.S., 383
Haddon, L., 288
Haladyna, T.M., 383
Hall, D.P., 250
Hall, G.E., 301
Hall, V.C., 121, 137
Halladay, J.L., 60
Halliday, M.A.K., 323
Halverson, R., 399
Hamilton, E.E., 385
Hamilton, M., 366
Hamilton, R.L., 74
Hamilton, S., 397
Hamman, P., 97
Hammett, R.F., 290
Hammill, D.D., 6
Hampston, J.M., 76
Hansen, D.N., 294–295
Hansen, L.E., 150
Hapgood, S., 82
Hardenbrook, M., 431
Harlacher, J.E., 266
Harper, B., 118
Harper, H.J., 135
Harris, A., 301
Harris, A.J., 240, 243

Harris, K.R., 431
Harrison, C., 389, 391
Harrison Group, 286, 300, 306
Hart, L., 10, 199
Harte, D., 415
Hartt, J., 205
Hasbrouch, J., 269
Hasebrink, U., 288
Haste, H., 322, 324, 326
Hastings, J.T., 387
Hatta, G., 352
Hattie, J.A., 360, 389
Hauser, R.M., 239
Heathington, B.S., 143
Heaviside, S., 298
Hebb, D., 9, 10
Hebert, M., 76
Hedges, L.V., 240, 248, 251
Heim, P, 98
Hemphill, L., 51, 359
Henderson, A.T., 406, 413
Henderson, S., 397
Hennessey, M.N., 71
Henze, R., 438–439
Herber, H.L., 163, 164, 172
Heritage, M., 388, 389, 390, 397
Herman, J., 57
Herman, J.L., 381, 397
Herrmann, B.A., 253
Hertweck, A., 242
Hesketh, L.J., 227
Hess, M., 297
Heubach, K.M., 149, 250
Heubert, J.P., 239
Hickman, P., 244, 277
Hiebert, E.H., 74, 99, 151, 152, 153, 154, 155,
    252, 254, 452
Hilden, K.R., 60, 79, 80, 81, 82
Hilden, K.D., 400
Hill, D.F., 187
Hill, P., 360
Hill, S., 17
Hindin, A., 414
Hines, S., 74–75
Hintze, J.M., 393
Hipps, G., 300
Hirsch, E.D., Jr., 201, 161–162
Hisrich, K., 292
Ho, A., 123
Hoff, D.J., 239
Hoffman, J., 306
Hoffman, J.V., 59, 258
Hogan, T.P., 187, 193, 195, 200
Holcomb, A., 250
Holloway, K, 127
Homan, S., 106
Hoosain, R., 431

Hoover, W.A., 186, 187
Hoover-Dempsey, K.V., 410–411, 413, 416, 418
Hopkins, K.D., 387
Horsley, T.M., 205
Horst, M., 250
Hoskyn, M., 253–254
Hosp, M.K., 225, 271
Houts, R., 251–252
Howard, T.C., 119
Howe, A., 121
Huberty, C.J., 415
Hudley, C., 116
Hudson, R.F., 153
Hughes, A., 326, 327–328, 340, 343, 345, 347, 349, 350, 351, 354
Hughes, K.E., 205
Hughes, J.N., 120, 128
Hughes, M.T., 64, 275
Huhn, 164
Hulme, C., 187
Humenick, N.M., 152
Hunt, L.C., Jr., 143, 145
Hunter, M., 365

I
Iacono, T., 223–224
Idol, L., 64
Ikeda, M., 40
Individuals with Disabilities Education Act (IDEA), 216, 217, 221
Ingram, M., 413
Institute of Education Sciences, 217, 296; computers/Internet in schools, 287
International Reading Association (IRA), 249, 302, 428, 437; purpose of, 266
Intrator, S., 292, 294–295
Invernizzi, M., 204, 253
Israel, S.E., 431
Ito, M., 300
Ivanic, R., 366
Ivens, S.H., 191
Ivey, G., 153

J
Jackson, E., 301
Jacob, R.T., 250
Jacobs, V.A., 201
James, C., 305
James, K.H., 19
Jamison, H.L., 9
Javal, L.E., 26–27, 40
Jaynes, C., 301
Jencks, C., 123
Jenkins, J.R., 244, 271
Jenkins, S., 61
Jensema, C.J., 103
Jetton, T.L., 169

Jewitt, C., 290
Jeynes, W.H., 408
Jiménez, L., 60–61
Jiménez, R., 279
John, A.E., 229
Johnson, A.S., 135
Johnson, E., 266
Johnson, L.B., 449
Johnson, M., 273
Johnsrude, I.S., 9
Johnston, F.R., 253
Johnston, P.H., 243, 251, 257
Johnston, S., 96, 198
Joiner, R., 289
Jonides, J., 36
Jones, C.D., 99
Jones, C.J., 145
Jones, F.G., 217, 226
Jones, H., 440
Jones, J., 82
Jones, K., 290
Jordan, G.E., 416
Jordan, H.R., 251
Jordan, L., 242
Jorgenson, G.W., 153
Joseph, L.M., 219
Joshi, M., 192, 384
Juel, C., 204, 253
Justice, L.M., 204
Juzwik, M.M., 59

K
Kaleba, D., 257
Kalman, B., 190, 361
Kame'enui, E.J., 5, 278
Kamhi, A., 193
Kamil, M.L., 74, 292, 294–295
Kaminski, R.A., 198, 204
Kane, K.W., 103
Kapp, S., 74–75
Karemaker, A., 300
Kasa-Henrickson, C., 217
Kaskowitz, D.H., 450
Kasten, W.C., 143
Katch, L.E., 385
Katims, D.S., 217, 222
Katz, A., 438
Katz, L., 12, 187
Kavanagh, J.F., 242
Kayzar, B., 406
Kearns, G., 5
Keenan, J.M., 190
Kelley, M.J., 134, 151–152
Kemmerer, D., 8
Kendeou, P., 57, 187, 192, 197, 291
Kenney, L.M., 431, 436
Kenway, J., 430

Kerawalla, L., 301
Kerr, 42
Kieschke, U., 63
Kilgore, K.L., 240
Kim, H., 180
Kim, H.S., 292
Kim, I., 72
Kim, J., 291, 397
Kim, J.S., 59
Kim, K., 180
Kinard, T., 301
Kindermann, T.A., 119
Kintsch, W., 53, 56–57, 58, 77, 200
Kinzer, C.K., 287, 295
Kirk, S.A., 241, 243
Kirkorian, H.L., 290
Kirschenbaum, M., 148
Kirschner, B.W., 76
Kirshstein, R., 303
Kiser, T., 223–224
Klein, N., 153, 443
Klibanoff, L.S., 450
Kliewer, C., 217
Klingner, J.K., 64, 206, 279
Klippel, F., 316, 318, 347
Knapp, M.S., 76, 247
Knezek, G., 288
Knight, S., 251
Knobel, M., 290, 297
Knoblauch, D., 118
Konopak, B.C., 76
Konstantopoulos, S., 248, 251
Korbak, C., 292
Koretz, D., 383
Koschoreck, J.W., 432
Koskinen, P.S., 103
Kovaleski, J.F., 266
Krashen, S.D., 146–147, 296, 329
Krasnegor, N.A., 242
Kreider, H., 406
Kristmundsson, G., 288
Krol-Sinclair, B., 250, 416
Kromrey, J., 297
Kronbichler, M., 7
Kucan, L., 72, 74, 82, 160, 163, 168, 169
Kuhn, M.R., 95, 149
Kulich, L.S., 109
Kulik, C.C., 292, 294–295
Kulik, J.A., 292, 294–295
Kulikowich, J.M., 169
Kumar, V.K., 153
Kumin, L., 229
Kwok, O., 120

L
Labbo, L.D., 287, 289, 295
LaBerge, D., 36, 46, 95, 166, 197

Ladd, H.F., 300
Lagemann, E.C., 163
Lambert, D., 191
Land, R.E., 359
Landi, N., 187, 192
Lanford, C., 246, 247
Langer, J.A., 71, 72, 172
Lankshear, C., 290, 297
Lapp, D., 360, 361, 376, 412, 416, 428
Latham, D., 350
Latour, P.L., 27
Lawrence, N.R., 397
Lawson, L.L., 247
Laxon, V., 5, 18
Leach, J., 297
Leach, J.M., 195, 384, 385, 386
Leahy, S., 82
Lederer, J.M., 64
Lederman, N., 121
Lee, C., 389, 391
Lee, C.C., 116
Lee, C.D., 431
Lee, J., 77, 122, 187
Lee, P.J., 181
Lee, S., 287
Lee, V.E., 201
LeFevre, J., 414
Leftwich, S.A., 64
Legge, G.E., 31, 45
Lehman, S., 60
Lemons, C.J., 220, 225–226
Lenz, B.K., 175
Lesaux, N.K., 195, 385
Leslie, 80
LeTendre, M.J., 240
Leu, D.J., 82, 287, 288, 290, 295, 304, 305
Levin, D., 303
Levin, I., 76
Levine, M., 288
Levine, T.M., 201
Levorato, M.C., 230
Lewis, A., 440
Lewis, L., 287
Lewis, M., 143
Lewkowicz, N.K., 15
Li, Y., 72
Liberman, A.M., 16
Liebenthal, E., 7
Lieberman, J.M., 413
Lin, Y., 286
Linan-Thompson, S., 95, 244, 254, 277
Lindo, E.J., 200
Linebarger, D.L., 299
Linek, W., 108
Linn, R.L., 383, 384
Lipka, O., 195
Lipson, M.Y., 66

Little, T.D., 187
Liu, R., 397
Livingstone, S., 288, 290
Llorente, C., 298
Locke, T., 297
Logan, G.D., 95
Lomax, R.G., 76
Long, J.F., 118, 130
Lonigan, C.J., 16, 199, 203, 219, 221, 222, 246, 256, 416
Lopez, M.L., 406
Louwerse, M., 57
Lovat, C., 340, 348, 352
Lovett, M.W., 248
Low, G., 297
Loxterman, J.A., 167
Loy, N., 303
Loyd, L.K., 120
Lu, Z., 7
Lucero, A., 398
Luckin, R., 301
Luo, W., 120
Lutkus, A.D., 58, 154
Lynch, J.S., 187
Lynch, S.J., 425
Lynch-Brown, C., 74–75
Lynn, R., 121
Lyon, G.R., 238, 239, 242, 245, 452, 454, 455
Lyons, C.A., 252

M
MacArthur, C.A., 296
Macaruso, P., 306
MacDonald, J., 228
Macedo, D., 180
MacGillivray, L., 359
MacGinitie, W.H., 205
MacLatchy-Gaudet, H., 64
MacWhinney, B., 18
Madaus, G.F., 387
Madden, N.A., 250
Madigan, T.P., 77
Madrigal, P., 416
Magnusson, S.J., 57
Mahone, E.M., 201
Malamud, O., 300
Malatesha Joshi, R., 187
Malkin, C., 227
Malone, P.S., 122
Mandel, B.J., 161
Manis, F.R., 7
Manning, G.L., 154
Manning, M., 143, 145, 148, 154
Mapp, K.L., 406, 413
Marcotte, A.M., 393
Maria, K., 205

Marion, S.F., 381, 395
Marsh, J., 290
Marshall, B., 389
Marshall, C.M., 196
Marshall, J.C., 220
Marston, D., 395
Martin, A., 8
Martin, M.A., 76
Martin, N., 59
Martin, S, 359
Martin, S.H., 76
Martin, T., 340, 348, 352
Martineau, J.A., 60
Martinez, P.B., 351
Martinez, M., 106
Marzano, R.J., 360
Mason, 66
Mason, G.E., 289, 292, 294–295
Mason, J.M., 414
Masters, J., 290
Masterson, J., 5, 18
Mastropieri, M.A., 174
Materick, A., 201
Mather, N., 5
Mathes, P.G., 217, 226, 228, 238, 254, 258, 275
Matthews, P.M., 9
Mattingly, D.J., 406, 409
Mattingly, I.G., 16
Matuchniak, T., 287
Mau,W., 121
Maurer, U., 7, 17–18
Maxwell, L., 271
Mayer, R.E., 173
McAnally, H., 415
McCandliss, B.D., 6, 18
McCann, A.D., 81
McCartney, K., 406
McClelland, J.L., 6, 8, 15
McCoach, D.B., 74–75
McConkie, G, 31, 40, 42
McCullough, C., 1
McGill-Franzen, A., 155, 238, 239, 242, 243, 244, 245, 246, 247, 249, 255, 256, 383
McGrew, K.S., 5
McHale, S.M., 291
McIntyre, E., 247
McKenna, M.C., 289
McKenzie, T.L., 406
McKeon, C.A., 98
McKeown, M.G., 67, 72, 74, 160, 161, 167, 175
Mcmaster, K., 197
McMaster, K.L., 275
McMurrer, J., 58
McNamara, D.S., 57
McPake, J., 286–287, 291

McRae, A., 154
McTighe, J., 365
McVerry, J.G., 290
The Meadows Center for Preventing
    Educational Risk, 278
Means, B., 288, 290, 292
Medler, D.A., 7
Mehan, H., 242, 367
Mehta, P., 272, 359
Meihls, J.L., 242
Meisinger, E.B., 95
Mellard, D.F., 266
Melzi, G., 250
Mencl, W.E., 18, 187
Mendro, R.L., 251
Menon, S., 206
Mercer, A.R., 242
Mercer, C.D., 242
Merchant, G., 300
Mergendollar, J.R., 247
Merkel, S., 121
Mervis, C.B., 229
Messick, S., 379, 382
Metsala, J.L., 199
Meyer, M.S., 187, 198
Mickelson, R.A., 119
Midgley, C., 143
Miles, J.C., 406
Militello, M., 392, 393
Millard, R.T., 191
Miller, A., 139
Miller, D.C., 145
Miller, J., 198
Miller, P.D., 247
Mills, K.A., 290, 291
Minick, V., 106
Mirkin, P.K., 99
Mistretta, J., 76, 251
Mitchell, C., 397
Mizelle, N.B., 143
Moats, L.C., 238, 239, 245
Moje, E.B., 58, 174, 175, 176–178, 180, 181
Molfese, P.J., 202
Moll, L.C., 181
Monken, S., 376
Monoi, S., 118
Moody, S.W., 275
Moore, J.C., 145
Moore, K., 412
Moore, T., 287, 290
Moos, D.C., 289
Moran, C., 222
Moran, J., 288, 298
Morais, J., 11, 15
Moran, R., 154
Morey, L., 296
Morphy, P., 200

Morrell, E., 431
Morris, D., 253
Morris, R., 220
Morrison, F., 251–252
Morrison, F.J., 82, 207, 385
Morrow, L.M., 60, 76, 247, 428, 430, 431,
    435
Mosborg, S., 181
Moss, P.A., 382
Moss, V.D., 406
Moustafa, M., 248, 359
Moylan, M.S., 301
Mueller, F.L., 173
Mueller, J., 440
Murdock, T.B., 139
Murnane, R.J., 392, 397, 399
Murphy, P.K., 71, 118, 169–170
Murphy, R., 290, 292, 294–295
Murray, B.A., 15, 16
Murray, D.W., 122
Murray, F.B., 431
Muter, V., 187
Myers, 165
Myers, W.D., 443

N
Naceur, A., 60
Nagy, W.E., 74, 75, 200
Nair, M., 435
Nation, K., 190, 196, 199, 204
National Assessment of Educational
    Progress (NAEP), 380
National Association for the Education of
    Young Children, 302
National Center for Education Statistics
    (NCES), 236
National Comprehensive Center for
    Teacher Quality & Public Agenda, 411
National Council of Teachers of English
    (NCTE), 302
National Council of Teachers of
    Mathematics (NCTM), 453, 454
National Endowment for the Arts (NEA),
    147–148
National Governors Association Center for
    Best Practices, 429, 430
National Governors Association (NGA),
    54–55, 60, 458
National Institute of Child Health and
    Human Development (NICHD), 14,
    64, 74, 94, 146, 149, 162, 172, 197, 206,
    215, 216, 218, 222–223, 228, 229, 230,
    251–252, 258, 295, 416
National Reading Panel (NRP), 2, 14–15,
    74, 94, 110, 146–148, 149, 215, 216, 218–
    219, 222, 228, 229, 230, 295, 340, 429
Natriello, G., 388

Necoechea, D.M., 6
Neff, D., 181
Nelson, J.R., 75
Neuman, M., 296
Neuman, S.B., 59, 155, 201, 206, 247, 256, 290, 412
New London Group, 290
Nicolich, M., 172
Nobre, A.C., 9
No Child Left Behind Act, 217
Nocon, H., 431
Nolen, S.B., 60, 383
Norman, S., 325
Norte, E., 438
Notari-Syverson, A., 415
Nunes, S., 272
Nye, B., 248, 251
Nystrand, M., 72, 367

O
Oakes, J.M., 287
Oakhill, J., 205
O'Byrne, W.I., 290
O'Connor, C., 440
O'Connor, E.M., 247
O'Connor, R.E., 199
O'Day, J., 72
Odden, A., 255
Office of Educational Technology, 290, 301
Ogbu, J.U., 116
Okolo, C.M., 296
Ólafsson, K., 288
Oláh, L.N., 396, 397
Olivetti Belardinelli, M., 8
Olsen, S., 336, 337, 352–353
Olson, D.R., 9, 16, 291
Olson, L.S., 238, 395, 398
Olson, R.K., 5, 190, 249, 273
O'Malley, C., 300
Oostdam, R., 296
Open Universiteit Nederland, 287
Oranje, A., 96
Osborn, J., 384
Osborne, J., 303
Osborne, J.W., 119
Oteíza, T., 173
Ottenbreit-Leftwich, A.T., 301
Otter, M.E., 296
Ouellette, G., 199, 200
Overmaat, M., 296

P
Padak, N.D., 98, 108, 110
Palincsar, A.S., 57, 63, 82, 159, 162, 165, 166, 167, 172, 435
Palma, J., 359
Palmiero, M., 8
Papert, S., 291

Paratore, J.R., 250, 407, 414, 416
Paris, A.H., 119, 385
Paris, S.G., 61, 165, 167, 366, 385, 415
Parish, H., 75
Parodi, G., 76
Parris, S.R., 64
Parson, L.B., 283
Pasnik, S., 298
Pate-Bain, H., 253
Patterson, S., 8
Paul, R., 57
Paul, T., 150
Paulson, E., 41–42
Pay, J., 18
Payne, R.L., 247
Pearce, D., 301
Pearson, P.D., 51, 53, 57, 58, 63, 64, 67–68, 71, 82, 251, 272, 288, 360, 364, 366, 368, 400, 452
Pease-Alvarez, L., 412
Peeters, M., 221
Pellegrini, A.D., 414
Penuel, W.R., 292, 298, 299–300
Perencevich, K.C., 62, 175
Perfetti, C.A., 6, 10, 15, 18, 186, 196, 196–197, 199, 200
Perie, M., 154, 381, 394, 395, 396, 398, 400, 430
Peters, C.W., 161, 162
Peterson, D.K., 203
Peterson, D.L., 244
Peterson, D.S., 51, 82, 187, 360
Peterson, L., 39
Peterson, M.J., 39
Petrella, J.N., 82, 385
Petrosino, A., 397
Pfeiffer, S.I., 431
Phillips, B.M., 222
Phillips, G., 238, 254
Phillips, M., 123
Piaget, J., 164, 322, 323
Pianta, R.C., 251
Pickering, D.J., 360
Pikulski, J.J., 94–95, 96, 254
Pilkington, R., 288
Pillinger, C., 301
Pinkley, D., 306
Pinnell, G.S., 80, 96, 98, 99, 252, 254
Piotrowski, J.T., 299
Pious, C.G., 244
Pipkin, G., 296
Pitchford, N.J., 300
Place, N.A., 359
Plowman, L., 286–287, 291
Pluck, M., 103
Pollatsek, A., 6, 40, 46
Pollock, J.E., 360

Pond, R.E., 204
Ponterotto, D., 316, 353
Pop-Eleches, C., 300
Popham, W.J., 384, 388, 390, 396
Porche, M.V., 416
Potter, M., 296
Pressley, M., 5, 15, 60, 61, 76, 79, 82, 249, 251, 256, 359, 400, 435
Price, C.J., 9
Price, J., 227
Price, L.H., 415
Prislan, R., 406
Proctor, C.P., 172
Pufpaff, L.A., 228
Pugach, M., 279
Pugh, K.R., 18
Puma, M.J., 244, 254
Purcell-Gates, V., 60, 62, 137, 247, 427
Purnell, G., 340, 348, 352

Q
Quinn, T., 425
Quinones, S., 303
Quint, J.C., 397

R
Rabiner, D.L., 122
Rack, J.P., 5
Raffle, H., 301
Rall, K., 298
Ramirez, ., 122, 123
Rankin, J., 76
Ranking, J., 251
Raphael, T.E., 76, 250
Rapp, D., 197
Rashotte, C.A., 5, 198, 249
Rasinski, T., 95, 96, 97, 98, 99, 102, 105, 106, 107, 109, 108, 110, 198, 227
Ravitch, D., 161, 237
Rayner, K., 6, 30–31, 31, 40, 42, 45–46
Read, C., 95, 328
Reddex, 42
Reese, E., 415
Reid, J.M., 325
Reijntjes, A., 205
Reinking, D., 289
Rescorla, L., 195, 384
Resnick, L.B., 72
Reutzel, D.R., 63, 95, 99, 149, 151, 154, 155
Revell, J., 325
Reynolds, P.L., 64
Ricciuti, A., 407
Rice, M.L., 204
Richards, J., 289
Richards, T., 76
Richardson, V., 279, 435
Richert, R.A., 300
Rideout, V.J., 287, 290

Riggan, M., 396, 397
Rikli, A., 96, 198
Rimdzius, T.A., 407
Rinehart, J., 57
Ring, J., 273
Rivero, E., 411, 413
Rixon, S., 317, 321, 328, 330, 332, 335–336, 337, 339, 340, 340–341
Robb, M.B., 300
Roberts, D.F., 287, 290
Roberts, G., 198
Roberts, J.E., 227, 229
Roberts, J.K., 226
Roberts, K.L., 59, 82, 199
Robinson, A.H., 40
Robinson, H.M., 243
Robinson, M., 290
Roch, M., 230
Rock, D.A., 119
Rodd, J.M., 9
Rodriguez, J.L., 406
Rodriguez, M.C., 51, 60, 82, 272, 360
Rodriguez-Brown, F.V., 416
Roehler, L.R., 67
Rogers, L., 296
Rogers-Sirin, L., 120
Roit, M., 168
Romance, N.R., 57, 64
Rosenquist, C.J., 223–224
Rosenthal, J., 11–12
Roser, N., 106, 416
Ross, G., 322, 367
Ross, J.A., 391–392
Rossini, F., 220
Roswell, F.G., 5
Roth, E., 276
Rothstein, R., 258
Rowan, B., 253
Rueda, R., 428
Rupp, A.A., 385
Ryan, R.M., 154
Rymes, B., 432
Rynders, J., 227

S
Sacks, C.H., 247
Sadoski, M.C., 11, 60, 145
Saida, S., 40
Sailors, M., 59
Salili, F., 431
Samols, D., 205
Samuels, J., 150
Samuels, S.J., 36, 46, 95, 97, 104–105, 146, 149, 151, 197, 198, 205, 229, 400
Sandak, R., 18
Sanders, P.L., 164
Sandler, H.M., 410, 418

Sandora, C., 72, 160
Santa, C.M., 139
Sather, S.E., 438
Saunders, K.J., 219, 220
Savage, R., 192
Savage, R.S., 300
Scanlon, D.M., 247, 249, 251, 252, 254, 256
Scarborough, H.S., 187, 190, 195, 198, 203, 384, 414
Scardamalia, M., 77
Schafer, W., 153
Scharer, P.L., 247
Schatschneider, C., 207, 251, 272, 359
Schaudt, B.A., 144
Scher, D., 414
Schick, A., 416
Schickedanz, J.A., 414
Schiefele, U., 60
Schindel, J., 298
Schlaggar, B.L., 18
Schleppegrell, M.J., 173
Schmid, L., 122
Schmidt, M.E., 290
Schmitt, J., 300
Schneider, W., 276, 299
Schoenbach, R., 173
Schorzman, E.M., 172
Schraw, G., 60, 79
Schreiber, P.A., 95, 99
Schumaker, J.B., 179
Schutz, 159, 165, 167
Schwanenflugel, P.J., 95, 149, 198, 199
Schweid, J., 392
Schweinhart, L.J., 246, 247
Scott, J.A., 200, 452
Scott, S.E., 160
Scriven, M., 387
Scruggs, T.E., 174
Secord, W.A., 204
Seery, M.E., 219
Seidenberg, M.S., 6, 15
Seltzer, M., 252
Semel, E., 204
Sénéchal, M., 407, 413–414
Sepanik, S., 397
Sereno, S.C., 31
Seymour, P.H.K., 5, 13, 17
Shanahan, C., 174
Shanahan, T., 76, 174, 221, 252, 316, 359, 430, 435
Shankland, R.K., 400
Shankweiler, D.P., 6, 187
Shannon, S.M., 412
Shapiro, J.M., 299
Share, D.L., 15, 76, 218–219
Sharkey, N.S., 392, 397
Sharp, D., 395

Shatil, E., 76
Shavelson, R.J., 392
Shaywitz, B.A., 18, 19, 220, 248, 282
Shaywitz, S.E., 220, 248, 255, 282
Shearer, B., 251
Sheldon, S.B., 407, 409, 411, 413
Shepard, L.A., 383, 385, 388, 389, 390, 393, 396, 398, 399
Short, R., 251
Shuell, T.J., 163
Shuler, C., 287, 290
Shulman, L.S., 390
Siegel, L.S., 195, 240
Silbert, J., 5
Silverman, R., 74–75
Silverman, W., 220, 222, 227
Simmons, D.S., 278
Simpkins, S., 406
Sinatra, G.M., 167
Sindelar, P.T., 240
Singh, M., 430
Singleton, C., 290
Sipay, E.R., 240, 243
Sireci, S.G., 392
Sirin, S.R., 120
Skinner, E.A., 119, 128
Skjelfjord, V.J., 15
Slade, Suzanne, 365
Slavin, R.E., 250, 252, 253
Sleeter, C.E., 242, 431
Sligh, A.C., 223–224
Small, S.G., 247
Smith, A., 286
Smith, A.T., 398
Smith, J.A., 63, 99, 149
Smith, J.K., 247, 397
Smith, J.M., 431
Smith, M.W., 246
Smith, P., 238, 254
Smrekar, C., 411
Snow, C.E., 15, 51, 162, 163, 171, 206, 258, 272, 295, 415, 416, 431
Snowling, M.J., 5, 187, 190, 203, 252
Socias, M., 72
Soden, L.M., 406
Solan, H., 47
Son, E.H., 67
Soter, A.O., 71
Souto-Manning, M., 411
Spear-Swerling, L., 243, 384, 385
Spencer, M.B., 118
Speyer, J., 175, 176-178, 182
Spilich, G.J., 200
Spooner, F., 217
Spörer, N., 63
Spycher, P., 74–75
St. Pierre, R.G., 407, 417

Stage, S.A., 75
Stahl, K.A.D., 82, 253
Stahl, S.A., 74, 149, 247, 250, 253, 272, 414, 415
Stallings, J., 251
Stanovich, K.E., 57, 59, 144, 155, 193, 200, 240
Stauffer, R.G., 172
Stecker, P.M., 397
Steinberg, J., 392
Steiner, V.G., 204
Stephen, C., 286, 291
Stephens, M., 303
Sternberg, R.J., 243
Stevens, R.J., 172
Stevenson, B., 106, 110
Stevenson, J., 187
Stevenson, J.A., 387
Stewart, J.P., 414
Stiegelbauer, S.M., 452
Stiggins, R.J., 388
Stockdill, D., 180
Stoel-Gammon, C., 227
Stone, T.D., 64
Storch, S.A., 187
Stovall, D., 425
Strambler, M.J., 130
Strangman, N., 173
Straub, E.T., 288
Strecker, S., 106
Stringfield, S., 379
Striphas, T., 295
Strother, S., 298
Stuebing, K.K., 202, 282
Sturtevant, E., 108
Su, Y.F., 34
Swan, K., 286
Swank, L., 204
Swanson, H.L., 6, 199, 253–254
Sweeney, J.M., 247, 251
Sweet, R.W., Jr., 237
Swick, K.J., 411
Symons, S., 64

T
Taber-Doughty, T., 228
Taberski, S., 81
Taboada, A., 386
Tabor, W., 187
Tabors, P.O., 415
Tavage, T., 8
Tam, A., 82, 416
Tarver, S.G., 5
Tatum, A.W., 429, 431, 442
Taylor, B., 251
Taylor, B.M., 51, 58, 72, 82, 251, 272, 360
Taylor, D., 242

Taylor, E., 47
Taylor, J.S.H., 204
Taylor, M.J., 406
Taylor, S.E., 37, 40, 42, 43, 44
Teale, W.H., 287, 295
Temple, E., 19
Thomas, E.M., 414
Thomas, K.F., 76
Thomas, N., 287
Thompson, M., 387, 389
Thurlow, M.L., 244
Tierney, R.J., 76, 387
Tilly, W.D., 283
Tilstra, J., 197
Timperley, H., 389
Tindal, G.A., 269
Tinker, M.A., 47
Tivnan, T., 51, 359
Toffler, A., 452
Tollefson, J.F., 431
Tomblin, J.B., 187, 190, 204
Tomlinson, C.A., 365
Tompkins, R., 153
Tondeur, J., 289
Tonks, S.M., 175, 386
Toomey, D., 414
Tooms, A.K., 432
Topping, K.J., 102, 103, 150–151, 152
Torgeson, C., 297
Torgeson, J.K., 5, 153, 198, 204, 206, 219, 249, 272, 273, 282
Tower, C., 137
Toyama, Y., 290
Tracey, D.H., 76
Trainin, G., 6
Trathen, W., 79
Travers, E., 397
Treiman, R., 5, 15, 16, 17
Troia, G.A., 248, 425, 435
Tsui, A.B.M., 431
Tunmer, W.E., 186
Turner, J., 61
Turner, S., 227

U
Underwood, P., 207
Ungerleider, C., 297
Unlu, F., 250
Urbach, J., 206
U.S. Census Bureau, 429
U.S. Department of Education, 217, 288, 289, 290, 296, 301, 455, 456–457
U.S. National Assessment of Educational Progress (NAEP), 236–237

V
Vacca, R.T., 448
Valcke, M., 289

Valdés, G., 412
Valdez-Gainer, N., 301
Valencia, S.W., 79, 359, 379, 384, 385, 387, 398, 399
van Balkom, H., 221
van Braak, J., 289
van Bysterveldt, A.K., 222
van den Bos, K.P., 18
Van den Branden, K., 72
Van den Broeck, W., 18
van den Broek, P., 57, 187, 192, 197, 271, 291
van der Schoot, M., 205
van IJzendoorn, M.H., 249, 414
van Kleeck, A., 414, 415
van Leeuwe, J., 200
van Lieshout, E.C.D.M., 205
Vandenberghe, R., 9
VanDerHeyden, A., 283
Vandewater, E.A., 287, 290
van 't Hooft, M., 286
Vasbinder, A.L., 205
Vasquez, O., 412
Vaughn, S., 64, 198, 199, 244, 254, 266, 272, 274–275, 276, 277, 278, 279, 282
Vaughn Gross Center for Reading and Language Arts, 276
Vavrus, L.G., 384
Vellutino, F.R., 187, 206, 238, 244, 247, 249, 250, 251, 252, 254, 255
Vendlinski, T., 397
Venezky, R.L., 243, 250
Verhallen, M.J.A.J., 301
Verhoeven, L., 200, 221
Vesonder, G.T., 200
Vigdor, J.L., 300
Vinovskis, M.A., 453
Vitale, M.R., 57, 64
Vitu, F., 41
Voelkl, K.E., 117–118
Voogt, J., 288
Voss, J.F., 200
Vygotsky, L.S., 322, 326, 367

W
Wade, S.E., 79
Wadsworth, J., 300
Waggoner, M.A., 72
Wagner, M., 238
Wagner, R.K., 5, 198, 219, 249
Wakeman, S.Y., 217
Walberg, H.J., 360
Walker, A., 306
Walker, E., 438
Waller, T., 298, 306
Walley, A.C., 199
Wallis, C., 287, 301
Walmsley, S.A., 246

Walp, T., 251
Walpole, S., 58, 251, 272
Walters, J., 289
Wang, J., 57
Wang, Y.Y., 153
Wanzek, J., 275, 276, 278
Wardrop, J.L., 288
Warren, S.F., 227, 229
Warschauer, M., 150, 287, 294–295
Wartella, E.A., 290, 300
Wasik, B.A., 250, 252, 253
Wayman, J.C., 379
Wechsler, D., 5
Weigel, M., 305
Weikart, D.P., 246, 247
Weinstein, R.S., 130
Weiss, B., 202
Weiss, H.B., 406
Weizman, Z.O., 415
Welch, W.W., 360
Well, A.D., 40
Wellings, J., 288
Wells, G., 323, 324, 345
Westbury, C.F., 7
Westover, A., 398
Wexler, J., 198, 199
Wexler, K., 204
Whaley, A., 292
Wharton-McDonald, R., 60, 76, **251**
What Works Clearinghouse, 252
Whitaker, M.C., 410, 413, 416, 418
White, A., 199
White, K.R., 406
White, M.J., 187, 291
White, T.G., 59
Whitehurst, G.J., 187, 246, 256, **415**, 416
Whiteley, C.S., 64
Wiederholt, J.L., 5, 198
Wiesel, E., 136
Wiesendanger, K.D., 145
Wigfield, A., 62, 63, 117, 118, 123, **127**, 175, 176, 386
Wiggins, G., 365
Wiig, W.H., 204
Wilce, L.S., 11,12–13
Wiley, C., 8
Wilfong, L.G., 98, 143
Wiliam, D., 387, 388, 389, 390, **391**, 392
Wilkinson, I.A.G., 67, 71, 452
Wilkinson, L.C., 428, 436
Willems, P.P., 409
Williams, H., 414
Williams, J.P., 326
Williams, K.A., 192, 384
Williams, K.T., 204, 205
Williams, M., 345
Willoughby, T., 290

Willows, D.M., 272
Wilson, B.J., 290
Wilson, P.T., 144
Wilson, R.M., 153
Wilson, W.J., 115–116
Winfield, L., 240
Wise, B.W., 249, 273
Wishart, J., 227
Wixson, K.K., 66, 96, 161, 162, 165, 167, 379, 384
Woessmann, L., 300
Wolf, D.P., 387
Wolf, M.K., 72
Wolfe, R.B., 413
Wong, K.K., 240
Woo, D.G., 76
Wood, C., 301
Wood, D., 322
Wood, D.J., 367–369, 370, 373, 374
Wood, E., 290
Wood, F.B., 187, 204
Woodcock, R.W., 5, 198, 204
Worthy, J., 72, 160
Wright, R, 127
Wu, Y., 146, 149, 151
Wundt, W., 33
Wylie, C., 392

Y
Yaden, D.B., Jr., 407, 414, 415, 416
Yakimowski-Strebnick, M.E., 379
Yelland, N., 290
Yoki, L., 76
Yokoi, L., 247, 251
Yoon, J., 145
You, W., 117
Young, C., 106
Young, J.P., 431
Young, L., 407, 413–414
Ysseldyke, J.E., 244
Yuill, N., 75, 301

Z
Zawilinski, L., 290, 301
Zeno, S.M., 191
Zevenbergen, A.A., 415
Zhang, X, 187, 204
Zhu, D., 297
Ziegler, J.C., 13
Zigmond, N., 244, 254
Zimmerman, I.L., 204
Zipke, M., 75
Zola, 42
Zuber, B.L., 36
Zumberge, A., 7
Zwaan, E.J., 41

Subject Index

Note. Page numbers followed by *f* or *t* indicate figures or tables, respectively.

A

Abecedarian Project study, 246
academic-type language, 325
accelerated reader, 150, 296
accelerated schools, 251
acceleration design, classroom corrective reading as, 250–252
accountability, as assessment purpose, 381
accuracy: as measure of fluency, 198; speed and, 197
achievement: of African American student, 118–120; behavioral engagement and, 129–130; dedication and, 124–125, 125*f*, 127–129; of European American student, 119–120; homework and, time spent on, 121; outreach and, 411; parental involvement and, 407–410; parental involvement in, 406; reading, time spent on, 144–145; Student Team Reading and Writing, 172; teaching English to young learners (TEYL) and, 345; vocabulary building and, 342
achievement gap, 122–123; closing of, 128–129; cultural knowledge and, 161; dedication and, 128; reading and, 125–126
acoustical information, in short-term memory, 39
action, 121
active learning, reading achievement and, 121–122
active vocabulary, 331
add-on instructional program, 252–254
administrators: diversity recommendations for, 437; parental involvement and, 417
adolescent literacy instruction, reading strategies/knowledge building in, 159–179
Adolescent Literacy Toolkit, 172
adolescent students, reading topics for, 135–139
African American student, 127, 133*t*; achievement gap in, 122–123; achievement of, 118–120; behavioral engagement qualities and, 120–121; dedication and achievement in, 124–125, 125*f*, 127–129; dedication growth in, 132–133, 134; dedication levels, interpretation of, 126; engagement in reading, 117; homework versus reading

achievement, 121; motivation factors, controlling for, 126–127; motivation of, 118–119; social influences of, 115–117
after-school program, 257
AIMSweb, as oral-reading fluency measure, 394
alphabetic principle, 219
analytic phonics instruction, 223
Application-based learning (ABL), 289
assessment: engaging students in, 389; frequency and scope of, 381, 382*f*; history of, 380; for learning, 388; learning and teaching, to improve, 379; misdirected instruction and, 385; negative consequences of, 386; purpose of, 381; requirements for, 380–381; *See also* interim assessment
Assessment Reform Group, 390–391
assisted reading, 102–103
attention, 10–11
attitude, reading and, 145–146
attuned practice, 152
audio-assisted reading, 103
autism, intellectual disabilities and, 228
automaticity theory, 35, 95–96; comprehension and, 97
automatic word recognition, 206, 229

B

background knowledge, 176, 370–371; reading/language comprehension and, 200
backward eye movement, 28
backward saccade, 27
basic interpersonal communicative skills (BICS), 325–326
behavioral engagement, 117; achievement and, 129–130; action in, 121; definition of, 119; grades reflecting, 120; in primary grades, 120; qualities in, 120–121
Benchmark assessment. *See* interim assessment
Benchmark Assessment System, 80
Berch-Heyman, S., 286–287
bidirectionality, brain and, 9
binocular coordination, 47
biography, 135–136
blending, 249
book: children interest/engagement in, 415; literacy education through, 347;

479

for TEYL, 353; See *also* story; young language learners and, 345
Book Club, 250
Book Floods, 352
brain: as bidirectional, 9; reading, role in, 8–9; saccadic movements and, 43; See *also* visual word form area
The Breadwinner, 136
bridging knowledge, 174
Britain, 167–168
British Ability Scales II, 225
Bubble kid, 383

C
Cambridge ESOL's TEYL exam, 320–321
cell phone, 287
census-based approach, 257
child-care centers, text variety and volume in, 59
China, teaching English to young learners in, 317
Chinese orthography, 34–35
choice, for dedication growth, 132–133, 133*t*
choral reading, 102
class size: benefits of, 256; reduction of, 248; for TEYL, 319, 319*f*
classroom corrective reading, 250–252
coaching, during real-time reading, 66
code-based skills, for word recognition, 206
cognition, attention, role in, 10–11
cognitive ability: nonverbal, 201–202; reading and, 144
cognitive academic language proficiency (CALP), 325–326, 329
cognitive development: first-language acquisition and, 322; learning and, 323
cognitive function, 164
cognitive prompt, 165; background knowledge as, 370–371; features of, 371; process/procedural prompt as, 371–372; types of, 370
cognitive psychology, 163
cognitive structure, 164
collaboration, for dedication growth, 132, 133*t*
collaborative reading strategy, 60
Common Core State Standards, 54–55, 60; assessments and, 380; establishment of, 430–431
comprehension assessment, 191
comprehension. *See* language comprehension; reading comprehension
comprehension-oriented instruction, efficacy of, 207
comprehensive literacy instructional plan, crafting, 256–258
comprehensive reading intervention, phonics and PA, 224–225

computer access, 287; in schools, 292–293
Computer for Youth, 300
computer-assisted instruction (CAI), 289–290; effect of, 296–297; as Web-based, 297
computer-assisted learning (CAL), 289
computer-based application technology, 297
computer-based learning (CBL), 289
computer-based learning environment, 289
Concept-Oriented Reading Instruction (CORI), 58, 250; idea circles and, 81; intrinsic motivation growth and, 176; reading comprehension and, 62; reading dedication and, 130–131; structure of, 63*t*
Concepts of Comprehension Assessment, 80
conceptualization, 173
concrete operations, 164
cone cell, 30
conjunction, 106
connected teaching, 302
connectivity, 293
consequential validity, 382
consonant-vowel-consonant spelling, 11
consonant-vowel-consonant word, 224, 271
constrained skill, 415
construction, 53
construction-integration model, 53, 77
content enhancement routine (CER), 178–179
content immersion, 162
content process framework, 164
content purpose, 360
content-focused reading instruction, 160
conversational fluency, 325
core knowledge, 161–162
CORI. *See* Concept-Oriented Reading Instruction (CORI)
cornea, 28*f*, 29
Cowles, L., 134–135
criterion-referenced test, 271
cue, 361–363; purpose/types of, 373–374
cultural diversity, 426
cultural knowledge, achievement gap and, 161
culture: dedication qualities and, 127–128; parent involvement by, 409; teaching English to young learners and, 316–317; See *also* African American student; European American student
Current Population Survey Computer and Internet Use Supplements, 300
curriculum: independent reading and, 146–150, 155; language learning as, 327; for TEYL, 320
curriculum-based measure, 271

curriculum-based measurement (CBM), as oral-reading fluency measure, 393, 394–395

D

data-based decision making: progress monitoring and, 270–271; Response to Intervention (RTI) and, 268; in Tier 1 prevention, 274; for Tier 2 intervention, 277*f*; universal screening and, 269–270

data-driven decision making, 379

decoding: assessment of skills in, 204; automacity in, 38, 95; of content words, 191; importance of, 4; language comprehension and, 186–187; in nonfluent reader, 37; onset-rime approach and, 248; process of, 36; spelling and, 11, 16

decoding deficit, 194; as late-emerging, 195

"decoding difficulties" group, 193–194, 193*f*

decontextualized preparatory subskill-based training, 217

dedication: achievement and, 124–125, 125*f*, 127–129; achievement gap and, 128–129; culture and socioeconomic status, 127–128; growth in, 131–133, 133*t*; indicators of, 123–124; levels of, 126; motivation and, 129; reading, effective practice for, 130–131; real-world materials and, 134–135; *See also* African American students; behavioral engagement; European American students

deep reading, 104

demonization, 430

Diagnostic and Statistical Manual of Mental Disorders, 216

Diagnostic Assessment of Reading Comprehension, 80

dialogic reading, 256; effects of, 415

DIBELS. *See* Dynamic Indicators of Basic Early Literacy Skills (DIBELS)

differentiated instructional delivery, 274

digital literacy, 172, 291

digital media: definition of, 289; technology, reading instruction and, 286–304

direct explanation: intentional instruction and, 366–367; modeling and, 374–375

direct reading instruction, 273

directed reading-thinking activity, 172

disability, reading difficulties as, 238

disciplinary knowledge, 174

discursive knowledge, 177

discussion: asking questions to elicit, 168; for attuned reading practice, 152;

metacognitive awareness through, 162–163; Questioning the Author (QtA), 73*t*; for reading comprehension, 71–72, 78

diversity: administrators, recommendations for, 438–439; categories of, 426–427, 427*f*; challenges/tensions in honoring, 429–432; guideposts for honoring, 437; issues disrupting, 430–431; literacy and, 425; literacy development and, 432, 435; recommendations for teachers, 436–438; research on, 426, 432; researcher, recommendations for, 439–440; safe spaces/pathways for, 442; teacher beliefs and, 431; teacher educators, recommendations for, 436–438; teacher guidelines for, 435; teacher honoring, 432, 433*t*–434*t*; in traditional schools, 429

diversity standards, 437

domain knowledge, 169–170

double image, 47

Down syndrome, 222; intellectual disabilities and, 220–221; intelligence quotient of, 223; multicomponent studies for, 224–225; reading comprehension and, 230–231; strengths and weaknesses with, 227–228

drop out rate, 122–123

Dynamic Indicators of Basic Early Literacy Skills (DIBELS), 4–5, 395; as oral-reading fluency measure, 394

dyslexia: incidence of, 13; onset-rime approach and, 248; phonological awareness and, 220; profile of, 193, 193*f*; visual word form area and, 18

E

early literacy intervention, 251

early school years, reading assessment in, 204–205

"early-emerging" reading difficulty, 196

Education for All Handicapped Children Act, 238

education level, of mother, 203–204

educational research, cognitive psychology in, 163

educational spending, 287–288

Educator's Word Frequency Guide database, 191

effective practice, engaged reading and, 152–153

effectiveness of Educational Technology Intervention, 298

electronic augmentative communication device, 228

The Elementary and Secondary Education Act, 288

embedded instruction, 273

end-of-year assessment, 380; summative test as, 381

engaged reading, 151–152; effective practice and, 152–153

engagement, evidence-based model of, 117–118

English as a foreign language (EFL), 315; cultural context for teaching, 316–317; functional setting for learning, 323–324; purpose for teaching, 326–327; reading instruction as, 337–340

English as a second language (ESL), 315; cultural context for teaching, 316–317; functional setting for learning, 323–324; purpose for teaching, 326–327; reading instruction as, 337–340

English as an additional language (EAL), 315; cultural context for teaching, 316–317; functional setting for learning, 323–324; purpose for teaching, 326–327; reading comprehension and, 342; reading instruction as, 337–340; success of, 341–342

English language development, 4; as an alphabetic language, 249; Information and communication technology (ICT) and, 297

English-language learner, 321; teacher experience as, 335–336

English-language teaching, 345; environment for, 343–344; purposeful activities for, 346f; reading instruction with, 354

English-literacy environment, 343–345

environmental cue, 374

ERIC database, 148

e-society, 291

European American student, 118–119, 133t; achievement gap in, 122–123; achievement of, 119–120; dedication and achievement in, 124–125, 125f; dedication growth in, 132–133; dedication levels, interpretation of, 126; engagement in reading, 117; homework versus reading achievement, 121; motivation factors, controlling for, 126–127

Even Start, 256, 417; defunding of, 407, 418; results documentation for, 410

Evidence for Policy and Practice Information and Co-ordinating Centre (eppi-Centre), 297

evidence-based model of engagement, 117–118

evidence-based practice in reading, 206; intellectual disabilities and, 215

experiential deficits, 252

experiential learning, 323

explicit instruction, 272–274; examples of, 273t

expository text, 190–191

expressive language, 228

extrinsic motivation, 121

eye: anatomy of, 28, 28f; instructional implications of, 32; reading difficulties and, 46–48; shortcoming with reading, 29, 31–32; stabilization of, 36

eye fixation. See fixation

eye movement: categories of, 27; discovery of, 26; instructional implications of, 28; rapid eye motion as, 30; reading and, 25–47; saccade and, 27; stabilization from, 36

eye physiology: discovery of, 26; reading instruction and, 38

F

family preventive intervention program, 250

Fast Start, 110

feedback, 9, 11

feedback loop, 9

The Field Guide to Geology, 191–192

First-grade reading study, purpose of, 2

first-language acquisition, cognitive development and, 322

fixation, 27; activities during, 35f, counting number of, 38; focused letters on, 31–32; importance of, 39; oral versus silent reading and, 41; on partial word, 41–42; preferred location for, 42; role of, 42; time sequence for, 35–36

fixation pause, 33–38; purpose of, 39

fluency: accuracy as measure of, 198; assessment of, 229–230; beyond primary grades, 98; characteristics of, 37; components of, 95–96; conversational, 325; definition of, 33, 38, 94–95, 198, 229; fast reading and, 97; intervention for, 199; MAPPS and, 100–110; modeling for, 100–101; in oral reading, 99; from phonic to comprehension, 95f; practice reading for, 103–106; reading aloud and, 229; as reading instruction component, 94; reading rate and, 97, 105; repeated reading for, 104, 106; teaching of, 97, 100; in word reading, 197–199

fluency deficit, 198

Fluency Development Lesson: development/steps of, 108–109; effectiveness of, 109–110

Fluency-Oriented Reading Instruction, 250

fluent reader: fixation, activities during, 36f; nonfluent reader versus, 35–36; span

of apprehension, 40; strategies of, 165; text comprehension/processing by, 165
foreign language teaching, 317–318, 325
foreign population, 429
FORI treatment condition, 149
formative assessment, 381–382, 382*f*; cycle/purpose of, 387; definition/ characteristics of, 388–389; interim assessment versus, 396; "just in time" feedback, 393; misunderstandings with, 392–393; professional development and, 390; research on, 390–391; responsive instruction, 390; running records as, 392; student learning and, 396; tests as, 392–393
Formative Assessment for Students, 390–391
forward saccade, 27; characteristics of, 45; disadvantage of, 45–46
foundational knowledge, 178
Four Blocks, 250
fovea, 28*f*; cone cells in, 32; function of, 30; letter identification and, 31–32
fragile X syndrome, 229
French/Indian War, 167–168, 174
From Tadpole to Frog: Following the Life Cycle, 365
functional genre, 59
functional linguistic analysis, 174

G

gaze duration, 39
general outcome measure, 271
generation M² survey, 287
genre: comprehension strategies for, 64; of grade books, 135; knowledge building and, 173; text variety and volume in, 59
geographical knowledge, 177
gestural cue, 373
Gettin' Through Thursday, 138–139
good reader: Iowa longitudinal database classification of, 203; *See also* fluent reader; skilled reader
"good reader" group, 192–193, 193*f*
grade level: definition of, 236; retaining at, 240–241
grade point average: behavioral engagement and, 120; dedication and, 123–124; motivation and, 121; on standardized comprehension test, 123
Graded Examinations in Spoken English, 320–321
grade-level book genres, 135
grade-level proficiency standards, state, 242
gradual release of responsibility model, 64–67, 65*f*; in reading, 366; as strategy instruction, 64–67, 65*f*

grammar deficit, 228–229
grammar learning, 331
grammatical knowledge, 204
graphic organizer, 172; use of, 178–179
group reading, 102
group work, productive, 364–365
grouping of words, 106–107
guided instruction, 367–369, 368*f*; goal of, 370; methods for, 361–363; using cues in, 373–374
guided repeated oral reading, Scaffolded Silent Reading (ScSR) versus, 149

H

Handbook for Boys, 443
Handbook of African American Psychology, 116
Hawthorne effect, 75
Head Start, 221, 256
heuristic prompt, 372
hidden deficits, 196
High Scope study, 246
high-frequency word, adult-like responses to, 18
Hispanic student, homework versus reading achievement, 121
historical fiction, 139
historical knowledge, 177
home literacy intervention, 413
home–school partnership, 416; effectiveness of, 418–419; professional development and, 419
homework: intentional instruction and, 365; reading achievement and, 121
homogeneous small group, 275–276
Hudson, R.F., 153
hybrid genre, 59

I

idea circle, 81
illiteracy, school attendance and, 242
illusory recovery, 198
immigration quota, 177–178
implicit instruction, 273
importance, for dedication growth, 132–133, 133*t*
in-between genre, 59
in-class support service, 240
independent reading: in classroom, 151; comprehension and, 63–64; curriculum goal of, 155; definition/ goal of, 143; importance of, 143–155; literacy curriculum, role in, 146–150; misconceptions about, 146–147; R⁵ as, 151; reading tests and, 147; research supporting, 145–151; in school, time for, 153; social interaction during, 153, 154; successful, characteristics of, 151;

teacher monitoring during, 150–151; text difficult level for, 153; time devoted to, 144–145

Individualized Education Plans, dedication growth and, 133

inferences, reading comprehension and, 53–54

information and communication technology (ICT), 297

informational genre, 59

Informational Strategic Cloze Assessments, 80

instruction: exemplary from teachers, 251; quality, factors influencing, 2; *See also* adolescent literacy instruction; literacy instruction

instructional aid: types of, 165; *See also* reading aid

instructional deficits, 252

instructional strategy teaching, 254

integration, 53; of technology, 304

intellectual disability (ID): analytic/synthetic approaches with, 223–224; cautions about, 227; definition of, 216; Down syndrome and, 220–221; intelligence quotient (IQ) and, 216; phonological awareness and, 219; reading comprehension and, 230–231, 231; research on, 215, 217; speech/language needs with, 228–229; spoken-language abilities and, 221; teaching students with, 217; vocabulary and, 228–229

intelligence, types of, 325

intelligence quotient (IQ): Down syndrome and, 223; intellectual disabilities and, 216

intentional instruction: direct explanation for, 366–367; framework for, 360–365; gradual release of responsibility in reading, 366; guided instruction for, 367–369, 368f, 370; guiding student thinking in, 361–363; independent tasks for, 365; modeling for, 361; productive group work for, 364–365; purpose of, 360; research on, 359–360; theories for, 366–367

interest, knowledge and, 169–170

interim assessment, 382, 382f; concerns for, 397–400; confusions and controversies for, 396; formative assessments versus, 396; low-achieving students and, 400; prevalence of, 395–396; purpose of, 393–394; in reading, 394–395; read-alouds supplementing, 398–399; research on, 396–397; running record as, 400; types/intervals for, 394

Internet access, 287; in schools, 293

intervention: categories of, 414; home literacy, 413

intrinsic motivation, 117, 118, 126–127; growth in, 176; social interaction fostering, 154

Iowa longitudinal database: kindergarten reading assessment and, 203; nonverbal IQ deficits and, 202

Iowa Test of Basic Skills, 243

iris, 28f, 29

J

Journal of Learning Disabilities, 238

K

Kamehameha Early Education Program, 250

kindergarten: phonological awareness and, 221; phonological awareness intervention for, 276; as preventive literacy intervention design, 246–247; reading assessment in, 203–204; skills versus meaning instructional focus in, 247

knowledge: bridging and necessary, 174; comprehension and, 53, 55; interest and, 169–170; process-oriented reading perspectives and, 161; reading comprehension and, 161; strategy and, integration of, 170–171, 175–179; types of, 177, 180, 370–373

knowledge building: in adolescent literacy instruction, 159–179; organizers for, 166; questioning the author (QtA) for, 161; reading apprenticeship and, 173; in reading comprehension, 165; social interaction/thinking aloud for, 169; strategy use and, 170–171, 175; text written for, 168; through questioning/dialogue, 168

knowledge model, 162

L

language: BICS and CALP, 325; diversity in, 429; in European countries, 13; hypothesizing cycle for, 329–330, 330f; knowledge building and, 173; permissible syllables in, 13; reading comprehension and, 74–75; Student Team Reading and Writing, 172; in text versus talking, 190; word translation to, 8

language comprehension: background knowledge and, 200; follow-up assessment in, 205; measurement of, 186; reading and, 186–187; reading

comprehension and, 188–189; in skilled reader, 192; vocabulary and, 199
language comprehension deficit, 196
language learner: linguistic level for, 351; story interacting and, 349–350; tell-back activities for, 350
language purpose statement, 360
language teaching, 317–318; as primary curriculum, 327
language-based performing arts, 106
late-emerging poor reader, 195–196; nonverbal cognitive abilities and, 202
Latino parents, 412
learning: assessment for, 379, 388; attention, role in, 10–11; cognitive development and, 323; establishing purpose for, 360; formative assessment and, 396; Hebbian explanation of, 10; misdirected instruction and, 385; motivation and, 60–62; from negative example, 101; optimal conditions for, 328; parental involvement in, 406; preferred styles of, 325; reading achievement and, 121–122; technology effect on, 296–297, 300–301, 305–306
learning contract, 391
learning disability: identification of, 241–242, 244; indication of, 240; labeling children with, 239; onset-rime approach and, 248; reading difficulties as, 239; reconceptualizing, 254–255; as socially constructed, 242; teacher disability versus, 252
learning disability intervention. See reading/learning disability intervention
Learning Initiative Pilot program, 303
learning at home, 413
least dangerous assumption, 218; application of, 219
legal/political spheres, debates in, 430–431
lens, 28f, 29
letter–sound correspondence, 219; instruction for, 204; synthetic phonics instruction and, 223–224
lexical restructuring model, 199
library, in low-income communities, 412–413
The Life Cycle of a Frog, 361
linguistic analysis, functional, 174
linguistic knowledge, 174
linguistic syllabus, 329
listening comprehension, 230
listening comprehension assessment, 201
literacy: advancing development of, 425–426; diversity and, 425, 432, 435; as social practice, 367
literacy achievement, 415

literacy educator. See teacher
literacy instruction: content-focused versus strategies-focused, 160; creation of, 256–258; intellectual disabilities and, 217; process-oriented approach to, 159; technology use in, 296; See also reading instruction
literacy instruction model, 359
literacy learning, 61–62; Information and communication technology (ICT) and, 297; parental involvement and, 413
literacy skill: acquisition of, 13; assessment of, 186; parents' direct teaching of, 414; word awareness and, 16
long /oo/ phoneme, 13
look–say method, 33
low achiever, 243; interim assessment and, 400
low background knowledge, 201
low income: libraries and, 412–413; parental involvement and, 411–412

M
macula, 28f
manipulatives, 249
mapping, 16, 40
MAPPS: assisted reading for support, 102–103; modeling for, 100–101; phrasing of words, 106–107; practice reading, wide and deep, 103–106; synergy and, 107–108
mathematical knowledge, 177
meaning maker, 324
memory: word spelling and, 11; See also word memory
mental retardation, 216
metacognitive awareness, 162–163
metacognitive prompt, 370; heuristic prompt as, 372; reflective prompt as, 372–373
micro-English environment, 343
middle school: reading assessment in, 205; strategy instruction in, 172
middle school strategy instruction, 172, 173
mini-summative assessment, 399
minority parent stereotype, 412
minority student, parental involvement and, 408–410, 412
mixed deficits, as late-emerging, 195–196
"mixed-difficulties" group, 193, 193f, 195
mobile technology, 287
model thinking, 361
modeling, 100–101; direct explanation and, 374–375
More Than Just Race: Being Black in the Inner City, 115
morphological analysis skills, 228–229
mother, education level of, 203–204

mother–child bonding, 415
motivation, 60–62; in African American students, 115–117, 118; dedication and, 129; as extrinsic, 121; factors, controlling for, 126–127; as intrinsic, 117, 118; parental involvement and, 410–411; self-assessment for, 389; self-efficacy and, 413; six Cs of, 61–62
multicomponent phonics-based study, 224–226
multimodal technology, 286–287
multiple-meaning words, 75

N
narrative genre, 59
narrative text, 190–191
National Assessment of Educational Progress (NAEP), 98, 428; achievement gap and, 122
National Early Literacy Report, 221
national educational technology plan (NETP), 288, 301
National Institute of Child Health and Human Development (NICHD), 238
National Longitudinal Survey of Youth, 300
nature walk, 176
necessary knowledge, 174
neoliberalism, 430–431
neuron, firing of, 10
Night, 136
No Child Left Behind Act, 217, 295–296; goals of, 2; passage of, 239; Reading First program in, 171, 250; Title III of, 430
nonfluent reader: decoding in, 37; fixation, activities during, 35*f*; fluent reader versus, 35–36; span of apprehension, 40; text comprehension/processing by, 165; word recognition process in, 37
nonsense word: use of, 5–6; visual word form area and, 6–7
nonspecified reading difficulties, 195
nonverbal cognitive ability, 201–202
nonverbal intelligence, 202, 204
norm-referenced test, 383, 384; reader profile and, 385
note-taking system, 372
noun marker, 106
novel, 135–136

O
oculomotor deficiency, in reading, 46–48
oculomotor eye movement. *See* eye movement
once-a-year summative test drive instruction, 399
One Second of Reading, 33

one-on-one tutoring, small, homogeneous intervention groups versus, 275–276
onset-rime approach, 248
optic nerve, 28*f*, 29
oral language weakness, 203
oral reading, 41; comprehension and, 198; fluency in, 99, 100; prosody/expressiveness in, 95, 99; Scaffolded Silent Reading (ScSR) versus, 149
oral-reading fluency: as general outcome measure, 271; as progress-monitoring tool, 269; scores for, 270*f*
oral-reading fluency measure, 400; curriculum-based measurement as, 394–395; DIBELS and AIMSweb as, 394; types of, 393; WCPM and, 398–399
orthography: in China, 34–35; in European countries, 13; phonology and, 12
out-of-class independent work, 365
outreach: achievement and, 411; parental involvement and, 418
outside-classroom technology, 290; effects of, 299–301
Oversold and Underused: Computers in the Classroom, 295

P
paired reading, 102–103
parafoveal region, 31; function of, 32; importance of, 42
paraprofessional training, 253
parent talk, 415
parental involvement: characteristics of, 417; content of, 413–416; context of, 416–417; elements of, 410; literacy learning and, 413; minority student and, 408–410, 412; outreach and, 418; process of, 410–413; reading instruction and, 406; student achievement and, 407–410
parent–child book reading, 415, 419
parent–child interaction, 415
parenting, 412, 413
partner reading, 60
passive vocabulary, 331
PBS series/website, 299
peer reading, 343
pen pal(s), 135
Penguins, 190–191
perceived difficulty, 126–127
peripheral vision, 31–32
phoneme, 219; word meaning and, 14
phoneme blending, 14
phoneme categorization, 14
phoneme deletion, 15
phoneme identity, 14
phoneme isolation, 14
phoneme segmentation, 15

phoneme segmentation skills, 226
phonemic awareness: definition/
  development of, 14–15; techniques for,
  250
phonemic segmentation, 249–250
phonemic sensitivity, 16
phonics: analytic/synthetic approaches to,
  223; benefits of, 17; cautions about, 227;
  comprehensive reading interventions
  and, 224–225; definition of, 219;
  definition/application of, 222
phonics/word study, as explicit instruction,
  273t
phonological awareness intervention,
  248–250; for kindergartners, 276
Phonological Awareness Literacy Survey,
  395
phonological awareness (PA), 199; cautions
  about, 227; comprehensive reading
  interventions and, 224–225; definition
  of, 219; Down syndrome and, 220,
  225; dyslexia and, 220; instruction for,
  204; intellectual disabilities and, 219;
  intervention for, 221; word reading
  instruction and, 206
phonological awareness plus letter-sound
  correspondence intervention, 276
phonological core deficit, 248
phonological skills-emphasis intervention,
  247–248
phonology, orthography and, 12
phrasing of words, 106; instruction for, 107
physical cue, 373
pleasure reading. *See* independent reading
poignant text, 135–136
policymakers, parental involvement and,
  417
poor comprehender, 196
poor reader: definition of, 193; Iowa
  longitudinal database classification of,
  203; language comprehension deficits
  in, 206–207; late-emerging, 195–196;
  low background knowledge and,
  201; subgroups of, 194, 194t; See *also*
  nonfluent reader
population, 429
positional cue, 373
practice reading, 103–106
pragmatic knowledge, 177
preposition, 106
prereading plan, 172
preschool: comprehension-oriented
  instruction, efficacy of, 207;
  phonological awareness in, 221; as
  preventive literacy intervention design,
  246–247; reading assessment in, 203

*Preventing Reading Difficulties in Young
  Children*, 295
preventive literacy intervention design,
  246; class-size reduction as, 248;
  family programs as, 250; phonological
  awareness intervention as, 248–250;
  preschool and kindergarten as, 246–248
preview guide, 166
primary grades: behavioral engagement
  in, 120; fluency beyond, 98; reading
  assessment in, 204–205
printed word: memory and, 11; in short-
  term memory, 39
problem space model of writing, 77
procedural prompt, 371–372
process model, 162
process prompt, 371–372
process-oriented reading perspective,
  161–163
productive group work, 364–365
professional development, 303–304;
  formative assessment and, 390; home-
  school partnership and, 419; for running
  record information, 392
progress monitoring: assessment feasibility
  for, 281–282; indications for, 270–271;
  tools for, 269–270
prompt, 361–363; cognitive and
  metacognitive, 370
pronounceable nonwords, 5
pronunciation, word memory and, 12
prosodic reading, 95–96; in oral versus
  silent reading, 99
pseudoword, 5; recognition of, 18
public health model of intervention,
  Response to Intervention (RTI), 266–267
pupil, 28, 28f
purpose, establishing, 360

Q
Qualitative Reading Inventory, 80
quality, in reading, 150
Quality Undergraduate Elementary
  and Secondary Teacher Education in
  Reading task force, 437
question of the week (day), 132
questioning: asking to elicit discussion,
  168; guiding student thinking through,
  361–363; for understanding, 369–370
Questioning the Author (QtA),
  72–73; efficacy of, 73–74; questions
  for discussion in, 73t; as strategy
  instruction, 175; for strategy use and
  knowledge building, 161

R
R⁵, 151–152
rapid automatic naming (RAN), 203

rapid eye motion, 30
reader profile, 384
reading, 26, 59; achievement gap and, 125–126; African American student, engagement of, 117; attitude and, 145–146; attuned practice in, 152; behavioral engagement in, 117–118; below basic grade level, 237; binocular coordination in, 47; brain role in, 8–9; in child-care centers, 59; children's approach to, 15–16; components of, 216; consonant-vowel-consonant spellings and, 11; dedication and achievement in, 128–129; effective practice for, 130–131; in European countries, 13; eye movements and, 25, 26; eye shortcoming and, 29; fluency versus nonfluency in, 35; gradual release of responsibility model as, 366; importance of, 215; intellectual disabilities and, 215; interim assessment in, 394–395; language comprehension and, 186–187; learning assessment in, 5; as mapping problem, 40; meaning versus word level of, 340; motivation for, 118–119; nonsense words and, 5–6; oculomotor deficiencies in, 46; "One Second of Reading", 33; oral versus silent, 41; parent talk during, 415; poignant topics for, 135–136; prosody in, 95–96; quality instruction in, 2–3; rereading and regression in, 28; research on, 163; software programs for, 150; span of apprehension, 40; speed, importance of, 44–45; strategies used in, 166–167; summer reading program, 59; teaching beginning, 2; time devoted to, 144–145; will and thrill of, 60–61; writing and, 76–79; See also skilled reader; text
reading achievement: homework and, time spent on, 121; tutoring programs for, 253; with within-classroom technology, 294–295
reading aid: preview guide as, 166; See also instructional aid
reading aloud, 74–75; benefits of, 246; fluency and, 229; words correct per minute and, 394–395
reading apprenticeship, 173–174
reading assessment: in early school years, 204–205; indications for, 202; in middle school, 205; in preschool and kindergarten, 203–204
reading comprehension: assessment of, 201; automaticity theory and, 97; background knowledge and, 200; building disciplinary/world knowledge for, 56; of challenging texts, 60; changes over time, 188–192; coaching for, 66; cognitive ability and, 201–202; construction and integration, 53; CORI as, 62; developmental changes in, 186–208; discussions for, 71–72, 78; elements of, 52; English as an additional language (EAL) and, 342; fluency intervention for, 199; fostering and teaching, 51–85, 83f–84f; in good/poor reader, 165; gradual release of responsibility model for, 64–67, 65f; inferences and, 53–54; intellectual disabilities and, 230–231; intellectual disability (ID) and, 231; knowledge and, 53, 55, 161; language, vocabulary and, 74–75; levels of, 53; motivating texts/contexts for, 60–62; oral reading and, 198; prior knowledge for, 168–169; purpose of, 62; questions/ assessment of, 191; research and development in, 82; schools/districts, coordinating instruction in, 84–85; of short stories, 166; simple view of, 196–197; six Cs of motivating texts for, 61–62; skills measurement for, 187–188; strategies for, 63–64, 162, 174–175, 230; strategy use and knowledge building in, 165; strengths and weaknesses in, 79–81; Student Team Reading and Writing, 172; teacher role in, 51–52; text, role of, 167; text structure influencing, 68–69, 69t, 70t, 71; variance in, 188–189, 188f, 189, 196–197; will and thrill for, 60–61; word reading and, 188–190
reading comprehension deficit, as late-emerging, 195–196
reading comprehension strategy instruction, 58
Reading Counts!, 150
reading curriculum, goal of, 155
reading difficulty, 187–188; cause of, 254; as disability, 238; early grade assessment of, 204; early-emerging, 196; indication of, 240; phonological core deficit and, 248; preschool/kindergarten assessment of, 202; prevention intervention for, 266–267; redefining, 237–238
reading disability: definition of, 241; identification of, 244; reconceptualizing, 254–255; in SFA schools, 243; as socially constructed, 242
reading elements: criterion-referenced test for, 271; measurement of, 270
Reading First program, 171, 250
reading fluency: definition of, 229; See also fluency
reading forecaster technique, 66

reading instruction: components of, 218, 340; with English-language teaching, 354; evidence-based practice in, 206; in first versus second/foreign language, 337; focus/goal of, 206; parental involvement in, 406; technology, digital media and, 286–304; technology use in, 292, 296, 301–302; types of, 273–274; *See also* adolescent literacy instruction; literacy instruction

reading intervention, phonics and PA, 224–225

reading level, 61

reading material. *See* Text

Reading Next—A Vision for Action and Research in Middle and High School Literacy, 171–172, 174

reading quality, 150

reading rate, 97; fluency and, 105

Reading Recovery, 252

reading research. *See* research

reading speed, 96, 198

reading strategy: in adolescent literacy instruction, 159–179; application of, 159; in middle school, 172; *See also* strategy; strategy instruction

reading subgroup, 192–195, 193*f*

The Reading Teacher, 238

reading test, independent reading and, 147

reading/learning disability intervention: preventive designs for, 246; research on, 236–258, 245–246; school attendance and, 242; types of, 240

real books. *See* book

real-time reading, coaching during, 66

real-world material, for dedication growth, 134–135

reciprocal teaching: comprehension and, 63–64; focus/goal of, 166–167

reflective prompt, 372–373

regression, 28; cause of, 43–45; decrease in, 45

relevance: for adolescent students, 135–139; for dedication growth, 131–132, 133, 133*t*, 134–135; process of, 138; teacher creation of, 136–137; in teacher-student relationship, 139; text and, 138–139

remedial reading program, 238

remedial support service, 241

repeated reading, 104; as fluency intervention, 199; in language-based performance arts, 106; as valid, authentic, effective, 105

rereading, 28, 43–45

research: assessments, negative consequences of, 386; on diversity, 426, 432; diversity and, 432, 433*t*–434*t*;

for independent reading, 145–151; on interim assessment, 396–397; on reading/learning disability intervention, 236–258, 245–246; strategy and knowledge in, 163–170; for strategy instruction, 171–175; for Sustained Silent Reading (SSR), 145–146

researcher, diversity recommendations for, 439–440

Response to Intervention (RTI), 257; data-based decision making and, 268–271; decision-making process for, 266–267, 267*f*; implementation benefits, 279–280; implementation difficulties, 280–281

responsive instruction, 390

retention rate, 406

retina, 28*f*, 29; cells in, 30; function of, 38

retinal cell: function of, 29; types of, 29–30

rod cell, function of, 30, 38

round-robin reading system, 41

running record, as interim assessment, 400

running records, as formative assessment, 392

S

saccade, 27, 37; brain planning, 43

Scaffolded Silent Reading (ScSR), 99–100; guided repeated oral reading versus, 149

scaffolding, 151–152, 179; "holding in place", 367; language learning and, 328; language learning and story interacting, 349; types of, 369; using cues in, 374

schema theory model, 53

school attendance, illiteracy and, 242

school literacy program, 254

science, concept development in, 58

science inquiry strategy, 58

science-literacy instruction, 57

scripted reading program, 359

secondary school, teacher credentials in, 3

Seeds of Science/Roots of Reading, 57

self-assessment, engaging students in, 389

self-determination, 127

self-efficacy, 126–127; motivation and, 413; parental involvement and, 410–411; of parents, 416, 419; self-assessment for, 389

self-esteem, 119; reading and, 149

self-regulation, 389; parental involvement and, 410

self-teaching, 218–219

semantics, 177

The Shock Doctrine, 443

short story comprehension, 166

short-term memory: decoded/partial words in, 44; information stored in, 39

sight word, 103

sight-based instruction, 217

sight-word reading, 271
silent reading, 41; comprehension in, 96; fluency in, 100; prosody in, 99
situation model, 53; development standards for, 54–55
skilled reader: advantages of, 55; decoding in, 37; effective practices of, 56t; fixation in, 43; nonwords and, 6; span of apprehension, 40; strategies of, 165; visual word form area in, 9–10; word reading/language comprehension in, 192; word recognition in, 7, 35; See also fluent reader; nonfluent reader; reading
small-group intervention, 254, 275–276
Snellen eye chart, 46
social interaction: for effective reading practice, 152; during independent reading, 153, 154; intrinsic motivation and, 154; for knowledge building, 169; metacognitive awareness through, 162–163; See also discussion
social practice, literacy as, 367
social studies, integration strategies in, 77
sociocognitive problem-space, structure of, 78
socioeconomic status, dedication qualities and, 127–128
software program, 150; in schools, 293
sound blending, 224
sound box, 249
sound matching, 224
sound stretching, 249
sounding-out, 224
space, as critical reading cue, 32, 37
special education: entitlement for, 239; for reading difficulties, 238; Title I remediation program, 240
special education law, 216
specific comprehension difficulties group, 193–194, 193f
specific reading comprehension deficit: as late-emerging, 195–196; nonverbal cognitive abilities and, 201
speech/language disability, 228–229; intellectual disabilities, halting tone in, 229–230
speed, 44–45
speed, accuracy and, 197
speed-reader, 198
spelling: decoding and, 11, 16; visual word form area and, 8; word memory and, 11
spelling–sound correspondence, 12; decoding and, 17
spoken-language ability, intellectual disability (ID) and, 221
standardized reading and listening comprehension assessment, 201

Standards for Reading Professionals— Revised 2010, 437
standards-based assessment, 384; reader profile and, 385
standards-based reform movement, 380
state grade-level proficiency standards, 242
state standards-based assessment, 384
story, 345; children processing, 348–349; target-language learning and, 350–351; teaching English to young learners (TEYL) and, 345, 353, 355; tell-back activities for, 350; types and forms of, 354; See also book
story hour, 256
strategies-focused reading instruction, 160
strategy instruction: in adolescent literacy, 172; criticism of, 163; for digital literacy, 172; effectiveness of, 67; genre and, 64; goal of, 159–160; gradual release of responsibility model as, 64–67, 65f; knowledge and, integration of, 170–171, 175–179; lessons about, 68; in middle school, 172; questioning the author (QtA) for, 161, 175; reading aloud as, 74–75; for reading comprehension, 63–64, 174–175; research/policy relating to, 171–175; See also reading strategy; strategy
strategy use: knowledge building and, 170–171, 175; in reading comprehension, 165; research on, 175; in secondary reading situations, 173
Student Team Reading and Writing, 172
student–teacher conference, 152, 154
student–teacher relationship, 137–138; reading relevance in, 139
Success for All (SFA) program, 243, 250
summative assessment, 381, 382, 382f; floor/ceiling effects of, 386–387; insensitivity/unreliability of, 387; negative consequences of, 383; purpose of, 383; reader profile and, 384
summer reading program, 59
summer school program, 257
Sustained Silent Reading (SSR), 100, 143; reading practice and, 154; research supporting, 145–146; value of, 148
syllable, in English, 13
syllabus design, for TEYL, 321, 329
synergistic instruction, 107–108
synthetic phonics instruction, 223–224
systematic instruction, 272–274

T
target-language learning, 321; guidelines for teachers, 326; stories and, 350–351

teacher: coursework for, 25; credentials of, 2–3; diversity, recommendations for, 436–438; diversity and beliefs of, 431; exemplary instruction from, 251; faulty eye movements, awareness of, 28; goal of, 143; learning English, experience of, 335–336; monitoring independent reading, 150–151; parental involvement and, 417; reading comprehension, role in, 51–52; relevance creation by, 136–137; student diversity, guidelines for, 435; student diversity, honoring, 432, 433t–434t; target-language learning guidelines for, 326; technology, role in, 298; as tutor, 253; visual problems, awareness of, 47–48

teacher disability, 252

teacher educator, diversity, recommendations for, 436–438

teacher referral, 240

teacher scaffolding, 151–152

Teachers State Collaboratives on Assessment, 390–391

teacher–student conference, 152, 154

teacher–student relationship, 137–138; reading relevance in, 139

Teaching Children to Read, 146

teaching English to young learners (TEYL), 315; age for, 324–325; approaches to, 342–343; assessment tools for, 320–321; cultural context for, 316–317; curriculum for, 320; first-language acquisition and, 322, 337–340, 341–342; future achievements and, 345; global setting for, 317–318; guidelines for, 326; hypothesizing cycle for, 329–330, 330f; importance of story in, 345, 347; linguistic syllabus for, 329; mother tongue enhancing, 352; purpose of, 326–327; scaffolding in, 323; stories and, 345, 353–354, 355; syllabus design for, 321; teaching reading in, 330; textbooks for, 352; time devoted to, 320, 332–334, 333t–334t; variables involved in, 318–320, 319f; vocabulary acquisition in, 331; word knowledge and, 335t

technology: adaptation of, 292–293; for class management/monitoring, 304–305; connectivity of, 293–294; curiosity, discovery, experimentation with, 292; definition of, 289; digital media, reading instruction and, 286–304; impact of, 291, 295; infrastructure and, 302–303; integration/coordination of, 294, 304; learning, effect on, 296–297, 300–301, 305–306; outside-classroom, effects of, 299–301; professional development and, 303–304; in reading instruction, 292, 296, 301–302; teacher role in, 298; time-use study of, 287; See *also* outside-classroom technology; within-classroom technology

Technology Literacy Challenge Fund, technology and, 303

tell-back activity, 350

Tennessee Student Teacher Achievement Ratio (STAR), 248

test insensitivity/unreliability, 387

Test of Word Reading Efficiency, 5, 198

Texas Primary Reading Inventory, 395

text: cognitive prompts for, 165; comprehension, role in, 167; deliberate intensive interaction with, 174; difficulty level of, 60, 153; language in versus talking, 190; as motivating, 60; relevance and teacher-student relationship, 139; variety and volume of, 58–59; writing for knowledge building, 168

text base, 53

text knowledge, 174

text structure: elements in narrative text, 69t; importance of, 71; influencing reading comprehension, 68–69; for informational text, 70t; knowledge building and, 173; tools for, 71

textbook. *See* book

text-emphasis intervention, 247–248

The Trouble With Tadpoles: A First Look at the Life Cycle of a Frog, 365

thematic unit, for dedication growth, 132–133, 133t

theme-driven instruction, 251

think sheet, 77

think-alouds, 162; for knowledge building, 169

Third International Conference on Assessment for Learning, 390–391

Tier 1 prevention: criterion-referenced test for, 271; data-based decision making in, 274; differentiated instructional delivery, 274; importance of, 271; instructional elements of, 272; Response to Intervention (RTI) and, 267–268, 267f; systematic/explicit instruction, 272–274; universal screening for, 269–270

Tier 2 prevention: considerations for, 274; criterion-referenced test for, 271; data-based decision making in, 277f; duration of, 276; instructional elements of, 275; Response to Intervention (RTI) and, 267–268, 267f; small, homogeneous intervention groups, 275–276; universal screening for, 269–270

Tier 3 intervention: criterion-referenced test for, 271; instructional elements of, 278; Response to Intervention (RTI) and, 267–269, 267f

time: for independent reading in school, 153; reading, devoting to, 144–145; reading comprehension changing over, 188–192; TEYL, devoting to, 320, 332–334, 333t–334t

Title I remediation program, 240

To Read or Not to Read, 146

Trinity College, 320–321

Turtletalk, 249

tutoring program, 253

U

unconstrained skill, 415

understanding, questions to check for, 369–370

Understanding by Design, 365

Uninterrupted Sustained Silent Reading (USSR), 143

United Kingdom, teaching English to young learners in, 318

universal screening: assessment feasibility for, 281–282; for Tier 1/Tier 2 instruction, 269–270

"untrained" word, 217

U.S. Common Core State Standards, 302

U.S. Government Accounting Office, 381

U.S. National Literacy Panel on Language Minority Children and Youth, 342

U.S. Ready to Learn Initiative, 298

V

verbal cue, 373

verbal-efficiency theory, 197

vis-à-vis comprehension instruction, 57

vision. *See* eye movement; eye physiology

visual acuity, lack of, 46

visual cue, 373

visual image, in short-term memory, 39

visual processing, Downs syndrome and, 227

visual word form area: development of, 17–19; dyslexia and, 18; location of, 17; nonsense words and, 6; role of, 7; in skilled reader, 9–10; spelling recognition in, 8

vitreous gel, 28f

vocabulary: for English as an additional language (EAL), 341–342; as explicit instruction, 273t; intellectual disabilities and, 228–229; knowledge building and, 173; language comprehension and, 199; reading comprehension and, 74–75; Student Team Reading and Writing, 172; words known by age, 331

vocabulary building, 228–229; achievement and, 342; throughout school years, 415

volunteer training, 253

vowel-consonant word, 224

W

Web-based learning (WBL), 289

What Works Clearinghouse, 289, 296, 298–299, 440

whole-school model, 240

whole-word instruction, 217

wide reading, 104; as fluency intervention, 199

will and thrill reading, 60–61

Williams syndrome, 220

within-classroom technology: history of, 292; reading achievement with, 294–295

Woodcock Reading Mastery Test–Revised, 198

Woodcock-Johnson, 5

word attack subtest, 5

word caller, 79

word construction, knowledge building and, 173

word identification, 32

word knowledge, 335t

word length, 32, 38; elimination of, 43

word mapping, 16

word meaning, 340, 341f; comprehension and, 37; phonemes and, 14

word memory: pronunciation and, 12; in second/fifth graders, 11; See *also* memory

word reading: deficits in, 204; fluency in, 197–199; follow-up assessment in, 205; as good versus poor, 194; measurement of, 187; phonological awareness and, 206, 219; reading comprehension and, 188–190, 188f, 189f; in skilled reader, 192; vocabulary and, 199; vocabulary size influencing, 199; See *also* reading

word recognition, 30–31; automacity in, 95, 97, 229; code-based skills for, 206; in nonfluent reader, 37; process of, 33–34; study for, 33–34

word shape: elimination of, 43; importance of, 42

word-by-word process, 165

word-level fluency, 229

word(s): gaining awareness of, 16; phrasing of words, 106; sounding out, 17; See *also* high-frequency word

words correct per minute (WCPM), 394–395, 398

World Wide Web. *See* Internet access

writing: problem-space model of, 77; reading and, 76–79

writing strategy, application of, 159